SPRINGER PUBLISHING

MW00448094

GET THE MOST FROM YOUR BOOK

SPRINGER PUBLISHING
C⊖NNECT™

VOUCHER CODE:

SDS166S8

Online Access

Your print purchase of *The Couple, Marriage, and Family Practitioner* includes **online access via Springer Publishing Connect**™ to increase accessibility, portability, and searchability.

Insert the code at https://connect.springerpub.com/content/book/978-0-8261-8775-8 today!

Having trouble? Contact our customer service department at cs@springerpub.com

Instructor Resource Access for Adopters

Let us do some of the heavy lifting to create an engaging classroom experience with a variety of instructor resources included in most textbooks SUCH AS:

INSTRUCTOR MANUAL

POWERPOINTS

TEST BANK

Visit **https://connect.springerpub.com/** and look for the **"Show Supplementary"** button on your **book homepage** to see what is available to instructors! First time using Springer Publishing Connect?

Email **textbook@springerpub.com** to create an account and start unlocking valuable resources.

THE COUPLE, MARRIAGE, AND FAMILY PRACTITIONER

Stephen V. Flynn, PhD, LPC, LMFT-S, NCC, ACS, earned his MA degree from Rowan University and his PhD from the University of Northern Colorado. Dr. Flynn is a professor of counselor education, a research fellow, the founding director of the Marriage and Family Therapy program, and the Play Therapy program coordinator at Plymouth State University, Plymouth, New Hampshire. He teaches couple, marriage, and family; child and adolescent; and research and writing courses for the Counselor Education, Marriage and Family Therapy, and Educational Leadership graduate programs at Plymouth State University. He is a licensed professional counselor (Colorado), a licensed marriage and family therapist (Colorado, New Hampshire), a national certified counselor, an approved clinical supervisor, an American Association for Marriage and Family Therapy (AAMFT) Clinical Fellow, and an AAMFT Approved Supervisor. Dr. Flynn has diverse clinical experiences in a wide range of applied settings, including inpatient psychiatric care; ED multidisciplinary teams; agencies; residential treatment programs serving youth and families; wrap-around services for youth and families; chemical dependency intensive outpatient programs; university counseling centers; as a private practice provider of individual, couple, and family counseling; and as the founding director of a university-based counseling and school psychological service center.

THE COUPLE, MARRIAGE, AND FAMILY PRACTITIONER

Contemporary Issues, Interventions, and Skills

Stephen V. Flynn, PhD, LPC, LMFT-S, NCC, ACS

SPRINGER PUBLISHING

Springer Publishing Company, LLC
11 West 42nd Street, New York, NY 10036
www.springerpub.com
connect.springerpub.com/

Acquisitions Editor: Rhonda Dearborn
Compositor: S4Carlisle Publishing Services

ISBN: 978-0-8261-8774-1
ebook ISBN: 978-0-8261-8775-8
DOI: 10.1891/9780826187758

SUPPLEMENTS:

 A robust set of instructor resources designed to supplement this text is located at http://connect.springerpub.com/content/book/978-0-8261-8775-8. Qualifying instructors may request access by emailing textbook@springerpub.com.

Instructor Manual: 978-0-8261-8951-6
Instructor Test Bank: 978-0-8261-8953-0
Instructor Chapter PowerPoints: 978-0-8261-8952-3

23 24 25 26 27 / 5 4 3 2 1

Library of Congress Cataloging-in-Publication Data

Names: Flynn, Stephen V., author.
Title: The couple, marriage, and family practitioner : contemporary issues, interventions, and skills / Stephen V. Flynn, PhD, LPC, LMFT-S, NCC, ACS.
Identifiers: LCCN 2022050686 (print) | LCCN 2022050687 (ebook) | ISBN 9780826187741 (paperback) | ISBN 9780826187758 (ebook)
Subjects: LCSH: Marriage—Philosophy. | Family psychotherapy. | Couples—Philosophy.
Classification: LCC HQ734 .F6145 2024 (print) | LCC HQ734 (ebook) | DDC 306.8—dc23/eng/20221102
LC record available at https://lccn.loc.gov/2022050686
LC ebook record available at https://lccn.loc.gov/2022050687

Contact sales@springerpub.com to receive discount rates on bulk purchases.

Printed in the United States of America by Gasch Printing.

To my spouse, Meredith, and my children, Corrina, Anelie, and Eliza, whose love inspires an endless amount of passion and creativity.

CONTENTS

Foreword Tracy Baldo Senstock, PhD, LPC, NCC *xi*
Preface xiii
Acknowledgments xix
Instructor Resources xxi

SECTION I: INTRODUCTION AND PROFESSIONAL ORIENTATION

1 **The Professional Identity of Couple, Marriage, and Family Practitioners 3**
   Learning Objectives 3
   Introduction to the Systems Approach 3
   Working With Families, Couples, Networks, and Groups 6
   Professional Roots, Identity, and Training 10
   Contemporary Specialization 18
   Current Scholarly Trends 21
   Summary 25
   Student Activities 26
   Additional Resources 27
   References 28

2 **Introduction to the Theory and Practice of Couple, Marriage, and Family Therapy 33**
   Learning Objectives 33
   Introduction to Professional Issues in Couple, Marriage, and Family Therapy 33
   Understanding and Differentiating the Systemic Paradigm 35
   Overview of Psychoanalytic and Psychodynamic Therapy 36
   Overview of Behavioral Therapy 41
   Overview of Humanistic Therapy 50
   Overview of Cognitive Therapy 57
   Unique Ethical Issues Relevant to Systemic Work 62
   Ethical Issues Unique to Working With Children 63
   Ethical Issues Unique to Working With Couples and Families 66
   Ethically Incorporating Technology and Telebehavioral Health 69
   Diversity and Intersectionality in Systemic Work 71
   The Role of the Couple, Marriage, and Family Practitioner 73
   Summary 77
   Student Activities 78
   Additional Resources 79
   References 80

SECTION II: UNDERSTANDING AND INTEGRATING SKILLS

3 **The Theories That Influence Systemic Practice 87**
   Learning Objectives 87
   Introduction to the Theoretical Underpinnings of Systemic Work 87
   Unitary Theory, Integration, Eclecticism, and Pluralism 88

Feminism, Minority Stress Model, and Racial Battle Fatigue   90
First-Order Cybernetics   93
Second-Order Cybernetics   96
Constructionism and Constructivism   97
Postmodernism   98
Gestalt Theory and Therapy   100
Gestalt Techniques   102
Attachment Theory   104
Summary   107
Student Activities   108
Additional Resources   109
References   111

4   The Integration of Foundational Counseling and Systemic Skills   115
Learning Objectives   115
Introduction to Systemic and Counseling Skills and Interventions   115
Session Management   117
Foundational Systemic Skills   121
Invitational Skills in Systemic Practice   128
Attending Skills in Systemic Practice   130
Influencing Skills in Systemic Practice   134
Marriage and Family Therapy Model-Based Techniques   138
Transgenerational Family Therapy Techniques   142
Structural Family Therapy Techniques   146
Strategic Family Therapy Techniques   150
Communication and Validation Family Therapy Techniques   157
Solution-Focused Therapy Techniques   160
Narrative Therapy Techniques   163
Cognitive Behavioral Family Therapy Techniques   169
Emotionally Focused Therapy Techniques   172
Summary   176
Student Activities   177
Additional Resources   182
References   184

SECTION III: CONTEMPORARY ISSUES AND INTERVENTIONS

5   Racism, Discrimination, and Underrepresented Families   189
Learning Objectives   189
Introduction to Contemporary Racism and Discrimination   189
Racism, Discrimination, and Underrepresented Families   193
Understanding the Effects Racism Has on Families and Couples   196
The Impact of Racial and Ethnic Socialization   203
Understanding Intersectionality in Relationships   206
Working With Underrepresented Families   207
Interracial Couples and Families   209
Summary   210
Student Activities   211
Additional Resources   212
References   214

6   Contemporary Issues in Couple and Marriage Therapy   217
Learning Objectives   217
Introduction to Contemporary Issues That Affect Couples and Marriages   217
The Changing Interest in Marriage   218
Increased Rates of Infertility   220
Delayed Motherhood   221
Adult Attachment   223
Premarital Issues and Warning Signs   224
Marital and Relationship Distress   226
Effects of Crisis and Disaster on Relationships   228
Substance Abuse   231
Financial Stress   232
Infidelity   233
Intimate Partner Violence   234
Reducing Divorce Conflict   236
The Internet   237
Sex Addiction and Compulsivity   241
Summary   242
Student Activities   243
Additional Resources   245
References   247

7   Couple and Marriage Therapy Skills and Interventions   259
Learning Objectives   259
Introduction to Couple and Marriage Interventions and Skills   259
Helping Couples Struggling With Infertility   262
Helping Couples Heal From Attachment Injuries   265
Helping Couples Through Premarital Therapy   267
Helping Couples Experiencing Marital and Relationship Distress   270
Helping Couples Experiencing Crisis and Disaster   274
Helping Couples Experiencing Substance Abuse   277
Helping Couples Experiencing Financial Stress   280
Helping Couples Recover From Infidelity   282
Helping Couples Who Have Experienced Intimate Partner Violence   286
Helping Couples Minimize Divorce/Separation Conflict   290
Helping Couples Who Are Struggling With Internet Addiction   293
Helping Couples With Sexual Addiction and Compulsivity   296
Assessing Contemporary Couple Therapy Issues   298
Summary   301
Student Activities   302
Additional Resources   304
References   305

8   Contemporary Issues in Family Therapy   315
Learning Objectives   315
Introduction to Contemporary Issues in Family Practice   315
Understanding How Racism and Intersectionality
  Affect Families   317
Family Cohesion and Flexibility   320
Blended and Stepfamilies   322
Multiracial Families   325

Contemporary Parenting   327
Obesity   333
Family Issues Related to Internet Use   335
Child Abuse and Neglect   341
Grandparents Raising Grandchildren   345
Parental Grief After the Death of a Child   348
Summary   350
Student Activities   351
Additional Resources   353
References   354

9   **Family Therapy Skills and Interventions**   **367**
Learning Objectives   367
Introduction to Family Therapy Interventions and Skills   367
Influencing Family Cohesion and Adaptability   371
Helping Blended and Stepfamilies   373
Helping Multiracial Families   375
Helping Parents   381
Helping Families With Obesity   385
Helping Families Experiencing Issues With the Internet   387
The Mandatory Reporting of Child Abuse and Neglect   389
Helping Grandparents Raise Grandchildren   392
Helping Parents Grieve the Death of a Child   395
Assessing Contemporary Family Therapy Issues   397
Summary   399
Student Activities   400
Additional Resources   402
References   404

10   **Contemporary Issues and Skills in Youth-Based Therapy**   **409**
Learning Objectives   409
Introduction to Working With Children and Adolescents   409
Child and Adolescent Resistance to Treatment   412
Childhood Attachment Issues   416
Sibling Abuse and Violence   424
Bullying   428
Learning Disabilities   434
Play Therapy   437
Filial Therapy   440
Theraplay   442
Sandtray and Sandplay Therapy   443
Assessing Contemporary Child and Adolescent Therapy Issues   444
Summary   446
Student Activities   447
Additional Resources   448
References   450

Index   457

FOREWORD

While this text was unwritten and still just a prospectus, I was selected by the publisher to review the proposal for possible publication. I began my review as usual, expecting to find the traditional content and format. I began reading and was quickly convinced this text was different and an important and critically needed resource.

I supported the prospectus for two key reasons. First, the author offered a unique approach that would bring systems models into the present in a practical way with techniques linked to current and relevant family issues. Second, the author courageously proposed to cross a boundary that is often taboo to cross—to bond and align professional identities by providing content relevant to the Council for the Accreditation of Counseling and Related Educational Programs (CACREP) standards and the Commission on Accreditation for Marriage and Family Therapy Education (COAMFTE) key elements. Given my own career spent navigating the politics of professional identities, I was pleased and intrigued! I confidently sent my strong support to move this prospective text forward for publication.

The author's desire to address both CACREP and COAMFTE "philosophies" resonated with my career-long professional identity development and struggles that have seemed to parallel those within our profession, or should I say professions? I was trained and educated as a counselor in the 1980s. In 1990 I received my doctoral degree in professional counseling, a program that included aspects of counselor education, counseling psychology, and family systems, and I found myself often explaining or even defending my identity. Was I a counseling psychologist, a counselor, a family therapist, or a counselor educator? Counseling as a profession was growing and separating from psychology, systems theory was gaining greater awareness, and people had some idea what a counselor was (i.e., did guidance work in schools, led kids at summer camp, right?), but when introducing myself as a counselor to new friends and acquaintances, especially in the early 1990s, I often received blank or confused stares. I found saying "I am in the psychology field" brought a sigh of relief and "understanding."

One of my early faculty positions exemplified further the identity and political challenges I, and I am confident others, experienced. I was hired as an assistant professor of counseling psychology, where 2 years into my role I was told I needed to be licensed as a professional counselor, not a psychologist, because I was going to be working with the CACREP-accredited degrees and not the American Psychological Association degrees within our department. Additionally, I was to publish in "counseling" journals and present at "counseling" conferences.

Then our department decided to add marriage, couple, and family counseling/therapy. Yes, the "counseling/therapy" was truly in the title, creating more confusion with identities. I became well-versed in both CACREP and COAMFTE. I endured more professional identity and political confusion as I went on to hold leadership positions with both CACREP and COAMFTE aligned and accredited master's and doctoral programs.

As a counselor educator (yes, that is who I am!), I have watched the careers of hundreds of counseling (MS and EdD/PhD) and marriage and family therapy (MFT/DMFT) alumni for whom I have had the honor to have been part of their educational and professional journeys. I have kept in touch with many, and I feel like a very proud mama many days. One of these individuals is Dr. Stephen Flynn, the author of this textbook. I am very proud of his accomplishment in this text and what he offers to the readers. He, too, understands the identity challenges within and between American

Counseling Association/CACREP and AAMFT/COAMFTE and has very successfully and impressively created a resource that should leave both bodies proud.

This textbook purposefully, professionally, and politically correctly covers CACREP standards and COAMFTE key elements and brings awareness to the application of systemic models and techniques in today's world. Current-day concerns such as COVID-19, relevant social justice issues, and telebehavioral health are discussed along with ethical implications to help develop appropriate and timely systemic skills. Educators who are seeking a resource that provides an excellent and objective presentation of systemic history, ethics, skills, current issues, and even current topics more specifically related to youth will find this the ideal resource.

The first section of this text offers an excellent overview of family systems, including a history of antecedents in the field; accrediting bodies; licensure; ethics; and racism, culture, and oppression. The second section highlights theoretical movements and skills associated with prominent models. The final section pulls readers to the next phase of bringing the past forward by looking at contemporary issues and interventions to consider for families today. The textbook has a naturally and effectively scaffolded flow.

Readers of this resource will increase their clinical self-efficacy and therapeutic effectiveness with their clients. The text is a resource that has obtained a prominent location on my office shelves, and I anticipate many clinicians will also keep this book easily accessible. I sincerely hope you find the same value I found in this text and enjoy your journey through the chapters.

Tracy Baldo Senstock, PhD, LPC, NCC
Associate Dean, School of Counseling
Walden University

PREFACE

"In all cultures, the family imprints its members with selfhood. Human experience of identity has two elements: a sense of belonging and a sense of being separate. The laboratory in which these ingredients are mixed and dispensed is the family, the matrix of identity."

—Salvador Minuchin

The first edition of *The Couple, Marriage, and Family Practitioner: Contemporary Issues, Interventions, and Skills* symbolizes a comprehensive clinical journey emphasizing the philosophy, science, and practice of couple, marriage, and family therapy. Understanding the complexities of contemporary families; the multiple contextual levels of diversity and intersectionality that families, couples, and individuals embody; and the skills and interventions necessary to produce positive outcomes is paramount to the success and rigor of our profession. The unique histories, cultural events, societal changes, politics, societal norms, and mores create a constant need to reexamine how we are therapeutically treating individuals, couples, families, networks, and groups. These unique and ever-changing aspects of the human experience captivate our imagination, create a sense of curiosity, and serve as a motivator to take action in discovering what helps a particular individual, couple, or family who is experiencing a specific contemporary issue (e.g., racism, infidelity, infertility, crisis, divorce, intimate partner violence, addiction). *The Couple, Marriage, and Family Practitioner: Contemporary Issues, Interventions, and Skills* provides clinicians with the information needed to fully understand their role and the contemporary issues, theories, professional orientation, skills, and interventions that will allow them to provide high-quality service to their future clients.

GOALS OF THIS TEXTBOOK

The overall goal of this textbook is centered on informing students enrolled in master's and advanced doctoral degree programs about (a) the professional identity of couple, marriage, and family practitioners; (b) family systems and the systems approach to family therapy; (c) contemporary issues affecting today's families, couples, and youth; (d) how to apply skills, interventions, and assessments to contemporary issues in marriage, couple, and family therapy; (e) the major techniques related to popular theories of marriage and family therapy; (f) the integration of foundational counseling skills and systemic interventions; (g) common skill-based and conceptualization issues related to working with families affected by racism, discrimination, hatred, and inequity; (h) the integration of multicultural and social justice principles into clinical work; (i) the relevance to Council for the Accreditation of Counseling and Related Educational Programs (CACREP) standards and Commission on Accreditation for Marriage and Family Therapy Education (COAMFTE) key elements; (j) issues affecting today's youth and relevant youth-based skills, interventions, and assessments; and (k) contemporary issues related to crisis, disaster, mental health, technology, and telebehavioral health. Each chapter concludes with student activities centered on understanding contemporary issues and skills.

By providing clear and in-depth information on contemporary issues, therapeutic skills, and interventions, *The Couple, Marriage, and Family Practitioner: Contemporary Issues, Interventions, and Skills* provides both an in-depth and pragmatic understanding of the practice, professional identity, philosophies, and conceptualization skills associated with systemic therapy. After reading this textbook, students will increase their clinical self-efficacy; enhance their ability to accurately match a skill and/or intervention with the relevant contemporary issue; understand core couple, marriage, and family theories and general theories of psychotherapy; and build a foundation for an emerging professional identity.

This textbook has chapters dedicated to topics and traditions that are often not included in books related to marriage and family therapy theories, skills, interventions, and contemporary issues. There are entire chapters that are dedicated to (a) the professional identity of couple, marriage, and family practitioners; (b) professional issues in couple, marriage, and family therapy; (c) the integration of core counseling microskills, systemic therapy interventions, and model-based interventions; (d) racism, discrimination, and understanding underrepresented families; (e) contemporary issues in couple, marriage, and family therapy; (f) couple, marriage, and family skills and interventions; and (g) a specific chapter that assists emerging systemic practitioners in understanding credible youth-based modalities, assessments, and how to clinically help children and adolescents around key contemporary issues.

The chapters of this textbook are as follows:

- Chapter 1: The Professional Identity of Couple, Marriage, and Family Practitioners
- Chapter 2: Introduction to the Theory and Practice of Couple, Marriage, and Family Therapy
- Chapter 3: The Theories That Influence Systemic Practice
- Chapter 4: The Integration of Foundational Counseling and Systemic Skills
- Chapter 5: Racism, Discrimination, and Underrepresented Families
- Chapter 6: Contemporary Issues in Couple and Marriage Therapy
- Chapter 7: Couple and Marriage Therapy Skills and Interventions
- Chapter 8: Contemporary Issues in Family Therapy
- Chapter 9: Family Therapy Skills and Interventions
- Chapter 10: Contemporary Issues and Skills in Youth-Based Therapy

INSTRUCTOR RESOURCES

The Couple, Marriage, and Family Practitioner: Contemporary Issues, Interventions, and Skills is accompanied by an Instructor Manual and comprehensive instructor resources, which include PowerPoint slides, classroom exercises, and a test bank. Structurally, all chapters have learning objectives, a summary, student exercises, helpful books, website links, video links, and a reference section.

This textbook has an easily accessible chapter flow that lends itself nicely to graduate school courses. Educators can direct students' attention to the chapter-based learning exercises and skill examples, and encourage further student learning with the suggested web links and readings. Four of the skill-based chapters have sections entitled Voices From the Field. These sections include direct quotes from practitioners who represent a wide range of diversity and intersectionality. Educators can weave these meaningful quotes into a variety of lessons and student exercises to enhance student understanding of social justice, diversity, and multicultural issues. Lastly, throughout the textbook, readers are provided clear, detailed, and contextually accurate examples of a variety of couple, family, and youth-based issues, interventions, skills, and assessments. Incorporating these examples into student learning can greatly enhance and contextualize students' understanding of the material.

INTENDED AUDIENCE

The intended audiences of this textbook are doctoral and advanced master's degree programs in behavioral sciences. While the target audiences of this book are master's- and doctoral-level counselor education and marriage and family therapy programs, it has a secondary audience of master's- and doctoral-level social work, psychology, and addictions programs. The following are five potential courses in which this textbook could be adopted:

- Family Counseling
- Contemporary Issues in Marriage and Family Therapy
- Working With Children and Families
- Foundational Methods in Marriage and Family Therapy
- Couple and Family Counseling Skills and Interventions

Mid- and late-career professionals who have some experience with couple, marriage, and family work will also find this book useful for understanding various contemporary issues, theories, skills, and interventions. Professors and seasoned practitioners will hopefully see this textbook as including state-of-the-art skills, techniques, contemporary issues, and clinical conceptualization, and as a resource created to provide a foundational level of training.

ORGANIZATION OF THE CONTENT

The Couple, Marriage, and Family Practitioner: Contemporary Issues, Interventions, and Skills is an introduction as well as an in-depth, detailed synopsis of the practice of couple, marriage, and family therapy. This 10-chapter textbook includes information on professional identity, the connection between contemporary issues and systemic theory, professional organizations, accreditation, unique history, specialty areas, and relevant systemic practice-based information (Chapter 1); overview of the systemic paradigm, cybernetics, theoretical movements in applied psychology, ethics, diversity and intersectionality in systemic work, the role of the couple, marriage, and family practitioner, and communication and neurolinguistic clinical information (Chapter 2); eclecticism, integration, pluralism, and the use of a sole theory of practice, the theoretical relevance of feminism, the minority stress model, racial battle fatigue, #*MeToo*, and cancel culture to clinical practice, and theoretical movements that have heavily influenced systemic therapy (Chapter 3); understanding the practice of couple, marriage, and family therapy, the integration of core microcounseling skills with systemic interventions, and a breakdown of the salient schools of marriage and family therapy and their core interventions (Chapter 4); and a review of the important contemporary issues and interventions centered on working with diverse, intersectional, and underrepresented families affected by hatred, racism, discrimination, bias, ethnic microaggressions and macroaggressions, racial and ethnic socialization, homophobia, issues relevant to LGBTQIA+ couples, and key factors related to working with interracial families (Chapter 5). The remainder of the textbook (Chapters 6–10) explores contemporary couple, family, and youth-based issues; the appropriate skills and/or interventions aimed at supporting positive clinical outcomes with couples, families, and youth; and pertinent assessment measures and clinical considerations.

Throughout the textbook, readers are provided direct quotes from practitioners who represent a wide range of diversity and intersectionality and have experiences in applied settings within the field. These sections are entitled Voices From the Field. Eleven clinicians representing various contextual backgrounds and intersectional identities have shared their perspectives and experiences on how best to help marginalized communities who have experienced various barriers, including, but not limited to, hatred, inequity, bias, discrimination, racism, microaggressions, and macroaggressions, and their unique experiences relate to a variety of contemporary issues. The participants fold into their discussions many examples of foundational and advanced skills, pertinent readings, conceptualization, and theory.

To help organize the distinct yet interrelated sections of this textbook, the chapters are organized into three sections: Section I: Introduction and Professional Orientation; Section II: Understanding and Integrating Skills; and Section III: Contemporary Issues and Interventions.

Section I: Introduction and Professional Orientation

The first two chapters of this textbook thoroughly prepare emerging clinicians with relevant information on (a) the professional identity of couple, marriage, and family practitioners; (b) the historical antecedents to the emergence of the field; (c) the influence of context, diversity, multiculturalism, and intersectionality on clients and clinicians; (d) the major accreditation and professional organizations in the field; (e) licensure and certification information; (f) the relevant technological and telebehavioral health standards; (g) unique systemic therapy specialty areas; (h) the nature of the systemic therapeutic paradigm; (i) the main applied psychological movements that have impacted the therapeutic world; (j) a review of practice-based ethical issues; (k) systemic racism, cultural responsiveness, and oppression; (l) the nuances of working with someone in a systemic manner; and (m) understanding verbal and nonverbal communication. In short, this section sets the stage for the remainder of the textbook by providing emerging practitioners with relevant multicultural/social justice issues; ethical considerations; detailed nuances of couple, marriage, and family therapy professional identity; and foundational theoretical and skill-based information.

Section II: Understanding and Integrating Skills

Chapter 3 investigates the additional theoretical movements that are influential to systemic practice, and Chapter 4 provides a detailed review of systemic techniques and counseling microskills and their relevance to systemic practice. Chapter 4 also reviews the skills that are associated with prominent models of marriage and family therapy. In short, these chapters provide synopsis of the philosophy and theory associated with couple, marriage, and family therapy, and the pertinent foundational and intermediate skills and interventions. Additional areas covered within Chapters 3 and 4 include, but are not limited to, (a) the way theories are connected during clinical practice (e.g., sole theory, integration, eclecticism, pluralism), (b) an overview of feminism's relationship to systemic practice, (c) the minority stress model, (d) racial battle fatigue as it relates to systemic practice and contemporary issues, (e) the nuances of session management, (f) the essence of cotherapy, and (g) the context for using reflection teams.

Section III: Contemporary Issues and Interventions

The overarching emphasis of Chapters 5 through 10 is to explore couple, family, and youth-based contemporary issues and helpful skills, interventions, and assessment measures. In addition, the skills-oriented chapters (i.e., Chapters 5, 7, 9, and 10) within this section will review segments entitled Voices From the Field. These segments include quotes from 11 helping professionals representing a wide range of contextual, cultural, and professional backgrounds. The information provided will actualize the multicultural, intersectionality, and sociopolitical information detailed in the chapters.

Chapter 5 reviews important contemporary issues, theories, and skills centered on working with underrepresented couples and families, including discrimination and racism, ethnic microaggression, racial and ethnic socialization, homophobia, issues relevant to LGBTQIA+ couples, and key factors related to working with interracial families.

Chapter 6 explores the contemporary issues that affect people's lives and motivate them to seek couple and marriage therapy. Chapter 7 provides conceptualization, skill-based descriptions, relevant assessment measures, and examples aimed at empowering clinicians to assist couples suffering from the contemporary issues explored in Chapter 6. The contemporary issues and interventions explored within these two chapters include the changing views of marriage, rising rates of infertility, delayed motherhood, adult attachment, premarital issues and warning signs, marital and relational distress, effects of crisis and disaster on relationships, substance abuse, financial stress, infidelity, intimate partner violence, conflict during divorce, online issues that affect relationships, and sex addiction and compulsivity.

Chapter 8 explores the contemporary issues that affect people's lives and motivate them to seek family therapy. Chapter 9 provides conceptualization, skill-based descriptions, relevant assessment measures, and examples aimed at empowering clinicians to assist families suffering from the contemporary issues explored in Chapter 8. The contemporary issues and interventions explored within these two chapters include racism and intersectionality, family cohesion and flexibility, blended and stepfamilies, multi-racial families, contemporary parenting practice and issues, obesity, various issues regarding the internet, child abuse and neglect, grandparents raising grandchildren, and parental grief after the death of a child.

The Couple, Marriage, and Family Practitioner: Contemporary Issues, Interventions, and Skills ends with Chapter 10, which provides theoretical conceptualization, concise skill-based descriptions, and examples to provide readers with pertinent information related to treating a variety of child and adolescent contemporary issues. The contemporary issues that are reviewed in this chapter include child and adolescent resistance, issues related to resistance to therapy, childhood attachment, sibling abuse, bullying, and learning disabilities. This chapter provides readers with a comprehensive review of play therapy, filial therapy, theraplay, and sandtray and sandplay models of treatment. The chapter ends with a review of key assessment measures centered on helping youth.

CACREP STANDARDS AND COAMFTE FOUNDATIONAL AND ADVANCED CURRICULUM

Graduate programs that adopt this textbook may be accredited or seeking accreditation. The Instructor Manual provides tables with a breakdown of CACREP standards and relevant textbook chapters, as well as a breakdown of the COAMFTE foundational and advanced curriculum and the applicable textbook chapters. CACREP-accredited counseling programs are the premier training programs for emerging counselors, while COAMFTE-accredited programs are the leading training program for emerging marriage and family therapists. CACREP accreditation is the training standard for counselors that has been recognized by the National Academy of Medicine, the Veterans Administration, and the Council for Higher Education Accreditation (CHEA). In most states, a CACREP-approved education meets the curriculum required for educational training for counseling licensure and its specialties, one of which is marriage, couple, and family counseling. Counselor education programs with a specialty area in marriage, couple, and family counseling must document how students meet a wide variety of standards in the areas of (a) marriage, couple, and family counseling foundations; (b) contextual dimensions; and (c) practice.

COAMFTE is the accrediting agency for marriage and family therapy education and training. It is recognized by the U.S. Office of Education, the Association of Specialized and Professional Accreditors, and CHEA as the only accrediting agency for a graduate degree in clinical training programs in marriage and family therapy in the United States and Canada. Regarding COAMFTE accreditation, there are nine foundational curriculum areas that programs must have. These areas all require a certain amount of college credits (i.e., courses). The foundational curriculum for COAMFTE includes (a) the foundations of relational and systemic practice theories and models; (b) clinical treatment with individuals, couples, and families; (c) diverse multicultural and/or underserved communities; (d) research and evaluation; (e) professional identity, law, ethics, and social responsibility; (f) biopsychosocial health and development across the life span; (g) systemic relational assessment and mental health diagnosis and treatment; (h) contemporary issues; (i) community intersections and collaboration; and (j) preparation for teletherapy practice.

Stephen V. Flynn

ACKNOWLEDGMENTS

This textbook and my process have benefited tremendously from many individuals and their contributions. I begin by thanking Springer acquisitions editor Rhonda Dearborn for her coordination, encouragement, and support throughout the project. In addition, I would like to thank Springer assistant editor Kirsten Elmer for all of her help throughout the writing and editing process. I would also like to thank the entire Springer staff for their encouragement of the field of couple, marriage, and family therapy.

I wish to acknowledge the following reviewers for their helpful feedback: Tracy Senstock, Walden University; Sherritta Hughes, Georgian Court University; Kent Becker, Saybrook University; Katherine Murphy, The University of South Dakota; Jonathan Naveen, Chapman University; Dodie Limberg, The University of South Carolina; Joshua Castleberry, Kent State University; and Michelle Hinkle, William Paterson University.

I would like to extend my deepest gratitude to the following 11 individuals who graciously provided their thoughts and experiences within the textbook's sections entitled Voices From the Field: Sherritta Hughes, Alexandra Manigault, Tahira Matthews, Yu-Wei Wang, Danny J. Shearer, Harvey Peters, Jennifer Kassing, Jyotsana Sharma, James Thomas, Long Hin Siu, and Michael Lopez-Jensen.

I would like to acknowledge a number of family members who were important in helping me with the writing of this textbook. None of this would have been possible without my supportive spouse, Meredith Flynn.

I am eternally grateful to my bright, energetic, and delightful children, Corrina Flynn, Anelie Flynn, and Eliza Flynn, for providing a tremendous amount of inspiration and motivation to complete the first edition of this textbook.

I would like to thank my mother, Joyce Flynn, for her unconditional support during this project and in all aspects of my life. And a very special thanks to my sisters, Suzy Ueberroth and Janet Flatley, for their unconditional love and support.

I would like to thank Plymouth State University Marriage and Family Therapy Program Graduate Assistant Samantha Waterhouse for all of her support and contributions to this project.

INSTRUCTOR RESOURCES

 A robust set of instructor resources designed to supplement this text is located at http://connect.springerpub.com/content/book/978-0-8261-8775-8. Qualifying instructors may request access by emailing textbook@springerpub.com.

- **Instructor Manual** containing lists of the Council for the Accreditation of Counseling and Related Educational Programs (CACREP) standards and the Commission on Accreditation for Marriage and Family Therapy Education (COAMFTE) foundational and advanced curriculum covered in each chapter, as well as an overview, learning objectives, true/false questions, and class activities for each chapter.

- **Test Bank** with 100 multiple-choice and true/false questions. All questions include answers with full rationales and are available on Respondus.

- **Instructor Chapter PowerPoints**

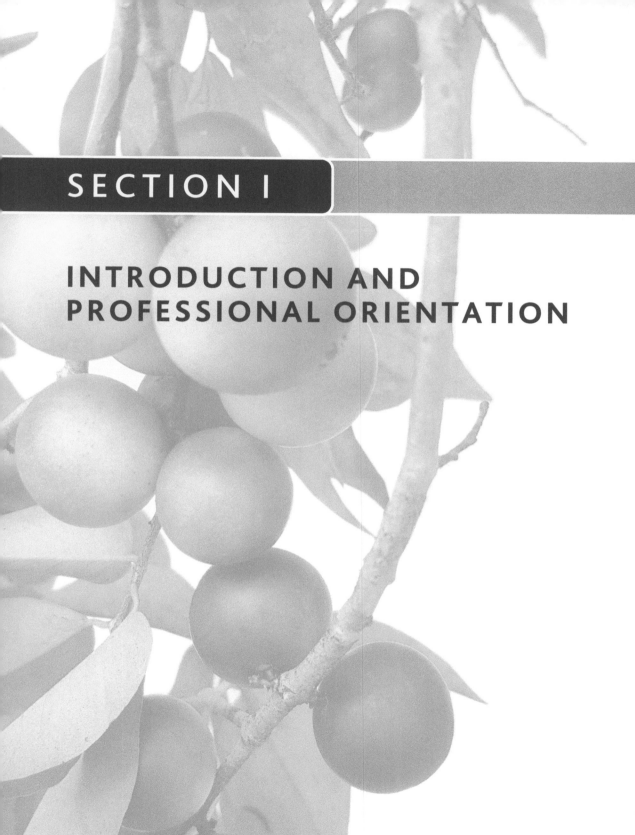

SECTION I

INTRODUCTION AND PROFESSIONAL ORIENTATION

THE PROFESSIONAL IDENTITY OF COUPLE, MARRIAGE, AND FAMILY PRACTITIONERS

LEARNING OBJECTIVES

After reading this chapter, you will be able to:

- Describe the professional identity of couple, marriage, and family practitioners.

- Recognize the nuances of relevant couple, marriage, and family associations.

- Provide details regarding accreditation of professionals in this field.

- Recognize the specific licensure and professional certifications associated with systemic practice.

- Describe the basic elements of professional practice.

- Explain trends in telebehavioral health and other therapeutic technology.

- Identify the basic contextual, diversity, multicultural, and intersectional factors of professional practice.

INTRODUCTION TO THE SYSTEMS APPROACH

Couple, marriage, and family practitioners treat a wide range of clinical issues, including, but not limited to, depression, anxiety, trauma, child and adolescent behavioral issues, child and parent relational matters, marital problems, and parenting concerns. This textbook explores current issues that affect families and describes appropriate interventions and/or skills. Each chapter provides enough information to enable readers to thoroughly understand a plethora of professional factors, contemporary issues, and the associated interventions in the context of couple, marriage, and family counseling. From a theoretical standpoint, this textbook will provide early-, mid-, and late-career professionals with an in-depth exploration of systemic, cybernetics, social constructivist, experiential, attachment, behavioral, and postmodern theories and therapies and their relation to the practice of couple, marriage, and family counseling. The overall goal of this textbook is to help emerging couple, marriage, and family practitioners understand the connection between a specific couple and family issue and systemic practice. Throughout the text, the terms *clinician*, *helping professional*, and *practitioner* are frequently used to describe all professional helpers, to be inclusive, and to aid in the readability of the text. This textbook uses *therapy* and *counseling* interchangeably to describe the act of professional therapeutic service. Lastly, when general references to gender are suggested, I deliberately apply the term *they* and avoid the binary terms *he* and *she*.

Chapter 1 introduces the practice and identity of practitioners who assist couples and families. Most professional counselors, marriage and family therapists (MFTs), psychologists, and social workers entering graduate school or the workforce acknowledge that change often takes place at a systemic level. While most individuals can relate to the idea that a single person has deeply touched or affected them at some point, most would agree that positive structural or rule adjustment can create long-term sustainable change more effectively than an individual person could. A common phrase that promotes this notion and is often expressed in the workplace or sporting events is "There is no *I* in *team*." Within the helping professions, this idea is typically reinforced by experiences in the field. For example, most early-career practitioners quickly notice that it is much easier to increase a child's self-esteem if there is a healthy sense of cohesion, flexibility, and support within the caregiver dyad, so they consider overall family functioning rather than focusing solely on helping the child adjust their habits, cognitions, emotions, and/ or behaviors. This notion of optimal systemic functioning can also be seen in the morale of any agency, hospital, or group private practice. Using an agency setting as a common reference point, most practitioners can compare their experience working in an agency that promoted a positive sense of support and collaboration among staff members with one in which staff members were treated poorly and/or unfairly. While an agency that treats employees negatively may have had very positive individual staff members, the overall dismal systemic experience is often far more powerful and influential in an employee's experience of the organization.

A contemporary issue that carried immense systemic significance was the videotaped murder of George Floyd in May 2020. Floyd, a 46-year-old Black man, was murdered by Derek Chauvin, a White police officer with the Minneapolis Police Department. The graphic video of former Officer Chauvin kneeling on Floyd's neck for nearly 9 minutes went viral and ultimately ignited global outrage and protests. Within the United States, George Floyd's murder served as an antecedent to the most significant racial justice protests since the civil rights movement. Those who subscribe to a more individualistic perspective may frame the problem as discerning the motives for one individual's actions. This perspective emphasizes factors like Derek Chauvin's actions and his beliefs, and it seeks to understand Chauvin's brutal and terrifying behavior in the context of his life. In contrast, those who view events more systemically tend to look for a deeper understanding within the oppressive systems at work. These individuals might view George Floyd's murder at the hands of former Officer Chauvin as stemming from oppressive systems, including institutionalized racism, a culture grounded in White supremacy, inequity, classism, and normalizing of police brutality in America. While this example appears to pit individual- and systems-level awareness/change against each other, the two often work together. For example, from an individual perspective, Derek Chauvin was tried and found guilty of second-degree unintentional murder, third-degree murder, and second-degree manslaughter and was sentenced to 22.5 years in prison. Systemically, the influence of Floyd's murder is apparent in the passage of the George Floyd Justice in Policing Act, efforts to repeal qualified immunity, and the approximately 30 states that have made changes to police tactics regarding duty to intervene and changes in neck restraint protocols.

Over the past 70 years, the systemic approach to therapeutic practice has been described as a paradigm, theory, epistemology, worldview, or model. All of these descriptors promote a therapeutic method that simultaneously views and serves clients from an individual and relational perspective. This holistic philosophy of human interaction has been described as a circular and reciprocal cause-and-effect relationship. Part of the reason the systems perspective is viewed as a paradigm rather than a theory is that it represents a complete shift from the intrapsychic paradigm that served as the main therapeutic framework for theories in applied psychology during the formative years of the discipline (e.g., psychoanalysis, behaviorism, humanism). Intrapsychic models are often considered more objective than other models, and they tend to emphasize linear cause-and-effect relationships. Linear cause-and-effect relationships can be helpful in understanding simple experiences. For example, due to **(A)** a genetic predisposition (i.e., cause), the client met the criteria of **(B)** major depressive disorder (i.e., effect). In addition, intrapsychic models often focus on individual characteristics and traits (e.g., cognition, behavior, unconscious drive). In contrast, systemic models (e.g., structural family therapy, Bowenian therapy, the Milan model of family therapy, general systems theory) emphasize the importance of circularity, subjective interactions, relationships, and patterns. A circular interaction for the same problem could be the following: The client has **(A)** a genetic predisposition to depression and typically qualifies for major depressive disorder, **(B)** is presently jobless and does not have a home, and **(C)** cannot afford medication or therapy. Then **(A)** more intensive depressive symptomology ensues, and **(B)** the client has increasing difficulty attaining work and adequate housing (Table 1.1).

TABLE 1.1 KEY CONSIDERATIONS FOR DIFFERENTIATING INTRAPSYCHIC AND SYSTEMIC THEORIES

Construct	Intrapsychic Theoretical Tenets	Systemic Theoretical Tenets
View of presenting problems and issues	Either/or dichotomies	Dialectical
Orientation to client care	Individual orientation (e.g., behaviors)	Systems orientation (e.g., relational patterns)
Overarching goal of therapy	Understanding the internal thoughts and experiences of the individual	Understanding the thoughts and experiences of the individual to better understand their relationships with others
Essence of change	Therapeutic refuge with counselor creates change	Interacting physically or symbolically with other(s) creates change
Cause and effect	Linear causality	Circular causality
The knower and what is known	Subject/object dualism	Holistic
Understanding the presenting problem	The presenting problem is divided, with one person's behavior being labeled as the cause of the other	The presenting problem is the behavior of a person relative to what preceded it and what followed it
Conceptualization	Focus is on the individual and their subjective experience	Focus is on the client and client system
Approach to analyzing client factors	Reductionism (i.e., breaking down the whole into smaller and less complicated parts)	Nonsummativity (i.e., the whole is greater than the sum of its parts)

Sources: Data from Becvar, D., & Becvar, R. (2013). *Family therapy: A systemic integration.* Pearson Education; Walsh, W. M., & McGraw, J. A. (2002). *Essentials of family therapy: A structured summary of nine approaches.* Love Publishing Company.

From a systems perspective, individuals who come into therapy are viewed in relation to their context. In other words, clients are not viewed as having a stable collection of traits that appear in the same manner across variations in time and place. Instead, clients' traits reflect the situation and context. Certain traits may appear when interacting with one person and have a particular degree of intensity and seemingly disappear with a different person or have an entirely different degree of power. Understanding clients through reciprocal, interdependent, and relativistic relationships is a change from linear, black-and-white, and/or cause-and-effect thinking. Systemic practitioners understand that all issues are relationally bound, and all roles mutually reinforce each other. For example, a helping professional cannot maintain their role as a family counselor without a family taking the role of clients. Within the family counselor and client reciprocal relationship, both parties share a sense of responsibility and dependency with the other. The family counselor can maintain their role because the client system responds to their influence and enacts the role of a client. Context affects both parties in the sense that the aforementioned roles are meaningful only because the family chose to reach out for therapeutic service and the family counselor agreed to work with them.

WORKING WITH FAMILIES, COUPLES, NETWORKS, AND GROUPS

Whether systemic practitioners are working with a family, couple, network (e.g., friends, roommates), or a group, they are vacillating between a client's internal experience and their interconnectedness and interdependence with other relevant people. Systemic counseling is a style of therapy that encourages physical and symbolic interactions between people. These interactions create a sense of awareness and action around the issue(s) that brought the client into therapy. Although it is typically a systemic practitioner's goal to include all relevant people in a session simultaneously, if a client comes into a session alone, their issues are not viewed in isolation. Practitioners will use skills (e.g., circular questioning, reframing, open-ended questioning, reflection of feeling) and interventions (e.g., role-play, genogram, empty chair, hot seat) to symbolically understand the deeply entrenched relational patterns within a client's life. Whether these interventions involve in-session physical interaction or symbolic contact, they create a context in which individuals can express and explore difficult issues in a safe environment. Ultimately, these interactions between individuals, and the accompanying awareness and understanding, build on family strengths and create helpful change.

Families and Parents

The family is a complex human social system. Systemically speaking, the family is a whole that is based on the interactions among its members within the context of the broader societal system. Family members are interconnected, interdependent, and influential with each other. These interactions create phenomena like boundaries, subsystems, coalitions, hierarchies, communication patterns, and roles that ultimately establish a whole that is greater than the sum of its parts. The frequent and consistent interactions that take place within the family create the stable rules that govern the system and make it resistant to change. In this sense, the family system strives to maintain homeostasis (i.e., equilibrium). This homeostasis provides a predictable process that helps members feel secure. Furthermore, equilibrium creates a family identity. While the drive toward homeostasis is ever-present, family systems are not rigid. Using rule-based inclusion and exclusion criteria, families are constantly integrating information from their surroundings to promote growth.

According to Becvar and Becvar (2018), "[w]hile the traditional idea of family refers to father, mother, and children, we believe that a family can also be more broadly construed as being whatever one experiences it as being" (p. 58). The modern family is complex, diverse, and less rigid than previously conceptualized notions of a family. Family units constitute an ever-changing, culturally diverse group of people. Contextually speaking, families can vary in many ways, including size, composition, cultural beliefs and values, acculturation, membership criteria, sex, gender, ethnicity, race, sexuality, expression of gender, ability, religious affiliation, and intersections among these factors. When one or more contextual factors change, there is also a simultaneous change in the familial relationship(s). This reflects a sense of logic within a given context (Becvar & Becvar, 2018). While there is clearly a connection and interdependence in most families, individual family members can and often do think, behave, emote, and communicate in very different ways. For example, most parents can attest to the notion that while their children may be coming from the same place biologically, they often differ greatly in temperament, emotional expression, behavior, and cognition, among other variables.

According to Kreider and Ellis (2011), fewer children in the current generation have two married biological parents, and there has been a significant increase in the following relationship structures: unmarried parents, two cohabiting biological and/or stepparents, single parents, and children residing in stepfamilies. Modern parents are a contextually and behaviorally diverse group with a seemingly endless range of resources. Long gone are the days of relying on Dr. Benjamin Spock's (1946) book *The Common Sense Book of Baby and Child Care* and being completely dependent on one's pediatrician for advice on how to be an effective parent. With the internet at parents' disposal, there is no monolithic leading expert in childcare. Parents can watch a YouTube video from an anonymous source or text a friend with a similar-age child for quick advice. While many of Dr. Spock's words may still ring true today, modern parents face challenges that differ from those of their counterparts in the 1940s. Changes in parenting can become obvious when noticing factors like the spread of information on pedophilia (e.g., proliferation of Catholic Church sexual abuse cases) and the location of sexual predators (e.g., criminalwatchdog.com); the rise of information on helicopter and hovering parenting styles, the barrier-removing bulldozer or snowplow parenting style, and the overly ambitious and goal-oriented parenting style (i.e., tiger parenting); the fact that many parents are juggling more responsibilities (i.e., supermom/dad) than ever before; and the accelerating pace of technological advances and the accompanying social and family challenges (e.g., adolescent screen time issues and the accompanying lack of physical/social experiences).

Couples

Couples are as contextually diverse as modern families, encompassing married, unmarried, same-sex, opposite-sex, interracial relationships, religious differences, age differences, differences in ability, and the intersection of these factors. Further, people sexually relate to one another in various ways (e.g., monogamous, polyamorous, open relationship, swinging), attachment styles (e.g., secure, anxious/preoccupied, avoidant/dismissive, disorganized/fearful, reactive), and patterns related to one's own family of origin. Combinations of these factors can create a sense of compatibility or incompatibility. According to Becvar and Becvar (2018), "[o]ne hypothesis about marital dyad, which may also apply to unmarried couples, is that its members are attracted to each other on the basis of the perceived compatibility of the rules each brings from their family of origin" (p. 58).

Significant evidence has been generated indicating the effects of transgenerational and family-of-origin early interactions on an individual's future relational patterns. Scholars have long been interested in the development of intimate relationships across the life cycle (Barnhill & Longo, 1978; Carter & McGoldrick, 1980), transmission of attachment styles from one generation to the next (Bowlby, 1940), relational conflict management skills learned from the family of origin (O'Leary, 1988), and relationship-promoting behaviors experienced during early family interactions and repeated in later intimate relationships (Bryant & Conger, 2002).

John Gottman and his colleagues (Busby et al., 2009; Carstensen et al., 1995; Gottman, 1993; Gottman & Levenson, 2000; Holman & Jarvis, 2003) have been at the forefront of relational compatibility research. Gottman and his associates discovered that there are at least three styles of couple conflict that can lead to successful relational outcomes: avoidant (i.e., minimizing conflict with others), validating (i.e., understanding and appreciating others), and volatile (i.e., expressing intense emotions and engaging in debates with others). While additional styles likely exist and much more research is needed in this area, these initial scholarly explorations shed light on the positive effects of sharing similar communication and relational values and the negative effects of mismatches.

From a developmental perspective, once partners have engaged in the initial attraction phase of a relationship, which usually occurs during the early stages of courtship, each partner attempts to harmonize the relationship rules, patterns, and rituals learned within their family of origin. When partners engage in a marriage or a similar long-term/permanent commitment to a relationship, there is an adjustment when creating the long-term relational system. If the couple fully adapts to one another (e.g., friendships, lifestyle choices, habits) and integrates or compromises on differences between their respective families of origin (e.g., generational rules, family legacies, expectations of relatives), there should be a subsequent promotion and maintenance of relational intimacy. Although relational stability is often attained, it should be noted that issues related to separation, divorce, and death can affect or end a relationship during any stage of its development.

If the relational partners choose to become parents through procreation or adoption, there are constant adjustments and changes to the couple system. Child-rearing adjustments include taking on the parenting role; compromising and accepting the values (e.g., education, nurturing) of each partner; making psychological, physical, and financial room for the child; accepting the influence of each member's family of origin; making room for the couple (e.g., attention, affection, discussion); and maintaining one's own sense of self in the relationship (e.g., personal wellness, reflection, career interest). Each stage of child-rearing brings its own challenges to couples, including preschool-age children (e.g., coping with lack of privacy, energy depletion), school-age children (e.g., increased socialization with other couples and families), adolescent children (e.g., refocusing on midlife career and relationship issues), and launching young adults (e.g., parental acceptance of frequent family exits and entrances, weaning parents from children; Becvar & Becvar, 2018; Sperry et al., 2006).

Middle relationship/marriage issues emerge after partners have been together for a long period of time. Couples are challenged by midlife relational issues that consist of maintaining connection and intimacy after years of being together (e.g., sexual desire discrepancy), rebuilding the couple's relationship after children leave home, midlife career adjustments (e.g., going back to school, embarking on a second career), and taking care of the aging older generation.

During the final stage of development, the couple encounters issues associated with aging and retirement. This phase could include adjusting to no longer working full time, coping with chronic illness, maintaining the couple relationship and one's sense of self, accepting support from children, and dealing with the death of one's partner (Becvar & Becvar, 2018; Barnhill & Longo, 1978; Carter & McGoldrick, 1980; Sperry et al., 2006).

Groups and Networks

Group work is a form of helping in which systemic practitioners treat a group of clients together. Whether a practitioner is facilitating a task group, psychoeducational group, couples group, counseling group, or psychotherapy group, they are working with an interconnected and interdependent system. Group leaders strive to be inclusive, socially just, and intersectional. Furthermore, group leaders are intentional about aligning their skills and interventions with the nature of the group and the stage of the group process. According to the Association for Specialists in Group Work (ASGW; 2021),

> [g]roup specialists are familiar with and able to effectively implement group work theories, techniques, and skills appropriate to the type, modality, and developmental level and goals of the group. They consider the purpose and membership of the group and select activities and interventions that are culturally informed. When selecting interventions for online groups, group facilitators consider the benefits and limits of technology whenever making decisions and adaptations (p. 9).

While group work is clearly systemic and has been a well-researched standard treatment for decades, organizations and practitioners have not always been forthright in acknowledging the systemic nature of group work. In fact, the practice of group psychotherapy has consistently been omitted from the Commission on Accreditation for Marriage and Family Therapy Education (COAMFTE) accreditation standards, and group therapy hours currently do not qualify for direct systemic contact hours for MFT graduate students. One notable exception to this perspective is expressed in *Group Work: Cybernetic, Constructivist, and Social Constructionist Perspectives* (Becvar et al., 1997). This book is a must-read for systemic practitioners who frequently engage in group work.

Chapter 4 explores in depth the basic microskills of the helping relationship (e.g., invitational, attending, and influencing skills). These skills are frequently used in group counseling. In addition to these foundational skills, group therapists use a variety of unique skills and interventions. The four foundational skills unique to the practice of group therapy are linking, holding the focus, cutting off, and drawing out members (Corey et al., 2021). In the following, these four skills are defined and then illustrated with concise examples.

Linking

When group leaders engage in the linking process, they focus on uncovering the common themes in the group and making them over to the group members. This can create a positive sense of interconnectedness and increase member interactions and cohesion.

> *Clinician:* John, both you and Nancy have been exploring how family and friends are so important to you.

> *Clinician:* Juanita, you're echoing the feelings of many of the group members.

Group members feel a sense of safety when they are not beholden to an intimate relationship.

Holding the Focus

It is extremely common for therapeutic groups to get off topic. In fact, most groups frequently have trouble sticking to the group's focus (e.g., substance use, trauma, psychoeducation). While it might not always be apparent, most group members want and expect the group leader to keep them focused. Holding the focus is a skill that the group leader uses to bring the group back to the topic of conversation.

Clinician: That sounds very interesting, I wonder how it relates to finding meaning in your job.

Clinician: I wonder what caused the group to talk about online shopping when we were just talking about overdosing.

Cutting Off

A variety of issues may come up in group experiences that may make it difficult to keep the group on topic or to ensure that everyone can share. For example, a client could be monopolizing a group experience with their own stories and needs. To keep the group equitable and fair, group leaders will occasionally need to cut off certain members or topics.

Clinician: Sharon, I need to stop you there. What do other people think about this?

Clinician: Felipe, we are running out of time, so let's put a bookmark on this and open up to it next time.

Drawing Out Members

A key factor in group therapy is having balance in participation. The group leader will occasionally bring forth quiet members of a group and ask them to participate.

Clinician: Kris, I noticed that you were nodding your head when Tasha made that comment.

Clinician: Felicia, you have been quiet all group. I wonder what is going on.

While not always promoted as a systemic method of therapy, working with a client and their social network certainly constitutes a systemic therapeutic effort. Social networks are systems that represent relational ties between a finite number of entities and/or people (Mason et al., 2017). A client's social networks could include one or more of the following: friendship groups, coworkers, roommates, peer networks, teammates, and acquaintances. While the same skills and interventions could be used within a network therapy context, network-based relationships often do not have the same level of history and/or intimacy that occurs in family or couple and marriage work. Further, given the nature of network-based relationships, therapy may be brief. Recent research has supported the clinical effectiveness of targeting adolescent peer groups with network-based interventions (Chung et al., 2015; Mason et al., 2017). While much more research needs to be done, networks are an important population for systemic practitioners to understand, receive training in, and include within the scope of their practice.

PROFESSIONAL ROOTS, IDENTITY, AND TRAINING

A common question from students who are interested in this field is "Who can become a couple, marriage, and family practitioner?" While MFTs have extremely high standards regarding systemic training and practice (including, but not limited to, many key elements required for accreditation, profession-based research, and professional identity), any helping professional (e.g., counseling professional, social worker, psychologist) can practice from a systemic perspective. In fact, from a systemic vantage point, the collaboration, interdependence, and complementarity that emerge from like-minded professionals who have diverse educational and clinical backgrounds could create an optimal state of therapeutic effectiveness. Key considerations for adopting any niche form of therapeutic practice (e.g., systems-oriented practitioner) include attaining foundational training and professional development, supervised professional practice, abidance to the appropriate ethics and standards, and continuing education.

The following are brief descriptions of the key factors that encompass the roots, identity, training, accreditation, and practice of marriage and family therapy and couple, marriage, and family counseling. Since there are numerous professional and personal ways to define oneself, these descriptions are meant to describe two nationally recognized groups of professionals that follow unique national accreditation standards and have distinctive licensure and national certifications aimed at treating couples and families. Please note that the notion of identity presented within this chapter is meant to provide a brief description of how a particular group of professionals have been identified within the literature and on profession-based websites. These descriptions are not meant to be comprehensive, nor are they meant to limit the number of identities a professional can have. For example, I am a licensed professional counselor, an approved clinical supervisor, a nationally certified counselor, a licensed MFT, and an American Association for Marriage and Family Therapy (AAMFT) Clinical Fellow and Approved Supervisor. I have found the integration of various forms of counseling and therapy-based training extremely helpful to my professional growth, development, and identity as a clinician, supervisor, and educator.

The Roots of Marriage and Family Therapy

While the formal beginning of MFT took place during the decade following World War II (1946–1956), the roots of MFT can be traced to the late 1800s and early 1900s. The earliest efforts can be categorized into the following groups: early psychological theory and conceptualization (e.g., Sigmund Freud's attempt to help individuals work through childhood conflicts from past family interactions, Alfred Adler's family constellations); marriage and family life education initiated by the U.S. Hatch Act of 1887; social work (e.g., in 1898 Columbia University offered a social work class); marriage counseling (e.g., in 1929 Abraham and Hannah Stone opened the Marriage Consultation Center); child psychoanalyst Nathan Ackerman's 1937 article entitled "The Family as a Social and Emotional Unit"; cybernetics conferences organized by the Josiah Macy Jr. Foundation (e.g., Kubie's [1950] "The Relationship of Symbolic Function in Language Formation and in Neurosis"); and family research in the area of schizophrenia (e.g., Gregory Bateson, Theodore Lidz, and Murray Bowen). While it is very difficult to pinpoint the exact time a professional service truly began, World War II is often considered the formal beginning of MFT due to the wide array of family, relationship, interpersonal, cultural, gender-based, and situational issues that emerged during this time frame. In short, conflicts arose due to mental health issues affecting soldiers, challenges associated with reuniting families, and difficulty returning to the prewar culture after the war had ended.

During the 1950s, Palo Alto, California, served as a hub for MFT pioneers (e.g., Gregory Bateson, Don Jackson, Jay Haley, and Virginia Satir). During this time, anthropologist Gregory Bateson and psychiatrist Don Jackson led two key efforts that would help legitimize the practice of marriage and family therapy. Bateson and his student Jay Haley applied cybernetics to patterns of communication in living organisms, with an emphasis on paradoxes. Concurrently, Don Jackson and Virginia Satir founded the Mental Research Institute (MRI) and focused primarily on family therapy (Wetchler & Hecker, 2003).

The field of MFT further demonstrated its legitimacy through the founding of professional organizations such as the National Council on Family Relations (NCFR) in 1938 and the American Association of Marriage Counselors (AAMC) in 1945. The AAMC renamed itself to AAMFT during the 1970s (Flynn & Sangganjanavanich, 2014; Goldenberg & Goldenberg, 2004).

The Professional Identity of Marriage and Family Therapists

Marriage and family therapists (also known as MFTs, systemic practitioners, and family therapists) are relationship experts. Whether MFTs work with individuals, families, or couples, they assist clients by communicating, adjusting, understanding, and interacting with the relationships of their clients. A relationship in this sense can be a conjoint session that is observed within the counseling office or the symbolic nature of relationships within someone's mind (e.g., genogram work, empty chair, hot seat, role-play). Factors at the forefront of relationship work include communication, homeostasis, hierarchy, boundaries, feedback loops, attachment, flexibility, cohesion, behaviors, and compatibility. MFTs understand that many mental health issues are rooted in relationships rather than intrapsychic distress (Kaslow, 1993). In short, throughout treatment, MFTs consider the relationships that continually affect the client. The Ohio Counselor, Social Worker, and Marriage and Family Therapist Board (CSWMFT) provided a concise definition of the MFT process. According to Ohio licensure law as drafted by the CSWMFT, the essence of MFT is "the diagnosis, evaluation, assessment, counseling, management and treatment of mental and emotional disorders, whether cognitive, affective, or behavioral, within the context of marriage and family systems, through the professional application of marriage and family therapies and techniques" (Ohio CSWMFT, 2014, p. 2). Similarly, the AAMFT defines *MFTs* as "mental health professionals trained in psychotherapy and family systems and licensed to diagnose and treat mental and emotional disorders within the context of marriage, couples and family systems" (AAMFT, 2021a, para. 4).

Training of Marriage and Family Therapists

MFTs have diverse educational backgrounds, including education, counseling, nursing, psychology, psychiatry, and social work. In addition to fulfilling the requirements for licensing, many therapists complete accredited graduate and postgraduate marriage and family therapy programs (AAMFT, 2021b). Typically, master's-level MFT programs last 2 to 3 years, and most MFT doctoral programs last 4 to 5 years. During graduate school, students have to meet certain curriculum standards and engage in a rigorous field experience (i.e., practicum, internship). COAMFTE-accredited MFT programs provide students with a foundational-level series of courses (e.g., marriage and family theories, marriage and family therapy techniques), and the master's-level field experience (practicum and internship) must include a minimum of 500 direct service hours, with at least 250 of these hours being relational (i.e., couple and/or family therapy) direct service.

The COAMFTE is an accrediting agency for marriage and family therapy education and training. It is recognized by the Council for Higher Education Accreditation (CHEA) as the only accrediting agency for graduate-degree clinical training programs in marriage and family therapy in the United States and Canada. To receive COAMFTE accreditation, programs must include nine foundational curriculum areas. These areas all require a certain amount of graduate college credits (i.e., courses). Currently, the foundational curriculum for the COAMFTE includes the following areas of study: (a) foundations of relational and systemic practice theories and models; (b) clinical treatment with individuals, couples, and families; (c) diverse multicultural and/or underserved communities; (d) research and evaluation; (e) professional identity, law, ethics, and social responsibility; (f) biopsychosocial health and development across the life span; (g) systemic relational assessment and mental health diagnosis and treatment; (h) contemporary issues; and (i) community intersections and collaboration (COAMFTE, 2021).

After graduating from a training program, MFT practitioners must take a national/statewide exam, engage in clinical practice, and participate in clinical supervision with an approved MFT supervisor. In the United States, all 50 states honor the MFT license and have the infrastructure to support the regulation of professional practice. Furthermore, Canada has two provinces that regulate and support the professional practice of MFT. While all states require specific and rigorous clinical and educational experiences, there are some variations in the required professional postgraduate exam. A first step may be to develop a plan of supervision with the state regulatory board. Most states require either the Association of Marriage and Family Therapy Regulatory Board's (AMFTRB's) national exam or a unique statewide exam (e.g., the California MFT Clinical Exam). Regarding supervised practice, in the United States most states and jurisdictions require either 2,000 or 3,000 hours of direct professional practice with individuals, couples, and families. During postgraduate professional practice, most states require 200 to 300 hours of supervision over a specified period (e.g., a minimum of 2 years). Supervisors must be approved by the state, and many states require supervisors to have the AAMFT Approved Supervisor designation (AAMFT, 2021b). The AAMFT Approved Supervisor designation is a rigorous credential managed by the AAMFT. The minimum requirements for this designation include (a) completion of a 30-hour AAMFT-provided or preapproved course on fundamentals of MFT supervision, (b) 180 hours of MFT supervision experience, and (c) a minimum of 36 hours of supervised supervision.

During or following the postgraduate supervised professional practice, practitioners can earn the AAMFT Clinical Fellow membership credential. Clinical Fellow is the credentialed level of membership in the AAMFT. Specific educational, supervisory, and clinical experience criteria must be met before achieving this credential. Many of the Clinical Fellow requirements fall in line with state licensure criteria, and a few states and provinces rely on the AAMFT Clinical Fellow to identify MFTs (AAMFT, 2021c).

The Roots of Professional Counseling

According to Hackney and Cormier (2009), the practice of counseling goes as far back as the incantations offered by Enlightenment Era priests from Egypt, Persia, and Mesopotamia. Contemporary counseling emerged in the late 1800s. These early practitioners were primary and secondary teachers who provided counseling to students with academic or personal issues (Beesley, 2004; Flynn & Sangganjanavanich, 2014). Notable early efforts within the counseling profession can be categorized in the following ways: (a) the emergence of the Child Guidance Movement in 1906; (b) Frank Parsons's (1854–1908) 1909 book *Choosing a Vocation* and his work establishing the Boston Vocation Bureau in 1908; (c) Jesse B. Davis becoming the first school counselor in 1907; (d) the counseling practice, publications, theory, and research of American psychologist Carl Rogers (1902–1987); and (e) the Union of Soviet Socialist Republics' (USSR's) 1957 launch of the Sputnik satellite and the United States's subsequent passing of the National Defense Education Act of 1958 (NDEA; Flynn & Sangganjanavanich, 2014; Limberg et al., 2021).

The foundation of professional counseling practice can be traced to the writing, research, and enterprising efforts of Frank Parsons, who is often referenced as the "Father of Vocational Guidance" (Blocher, 2000; Limberg et al., 2021). Parsons authored 14 books; developed and validated the first self-inventory for interests, aptitudes, personality traits, and work settings; and pioneered the first counseling agency that sparked the development of vocational guidance in American schools (Limberg et al., 2021). While Parsons's impact was massive, Carl Rogers's theory and practice of counseling created the foundation of counseling clinical practice. Rogers's research-based skills, "core conditions," and overarching theory of person-centered counseling continue to influence the field today.

In 1952, four organizations merged to form the American Personnel and Guidance Association (APGA): the National Vocational Guidance Association (NVGA), the National Association of Guidance and Counselor Trainers (NAGCT), the Student Personnel Association for Teacher Education (SPATE), and the American College Personnel Association (ACPA). More than 30 years later, the APGA changed its name to the American Association for Counseling and Development (AACD). In 1992, the AACD became the current American Counseling Association (ACA; Flynn & Sangganjanavanich, 2014; Limberg et al., 2021). The division within the ACA that supports marriage, couple, and family counseling is the International Association of Marriage and Family Counselors (IAMFC). This division was chartered in 1989 and supports marriage, couple, and family counseling through its rigorous training standards, national/international family counseling and therapy certification, conferences and other professional development opportunities, and an international journal (International Association of Marriage and Family Counselors, 2021).

The Professional Identity of Counselors

Professional counselors (also known as counselors; clinical mental health counselors; school counselors; marriage, couple, and family counselors; group counselors; and addictions counselors) apply affective, psychological, cognitive, behavioral, humanistic, and systemic interventions to address a variety of interpersonal and intrapersonal concerns. According to the ACA 2014 Code of Ethics (ACA, 2014),

> [t]he mission of the American Counseling Association is to enhance the quality of life in society by promoting the development of professional counselors, advancing the counseling profession, and using the profession and practice of counseling to promote respect for human dignity and diversity (p. 2).

According to Emerson's (2010) analysis of the literature, the professional identity of counselors encompasses human development, wellness, prevention, and empowerment. Furthermore, on October 28, 2010, the ACA Governing Council approved the following definition of counseling: "Counseling is a professional relationship that empowers diverse individuals, families, and groups to accomplish mental health, wellness, education, and career goals" (ACA, 2021, para. 2). The professional identity of counseling can be further understood by reviewing the 18 chartered ACA divisions. For example, an important aspect of counselor identity is the provision of group counseling. This identity factor is represented by one of ACA's chartered divisions, the ASGW.

Training of Professional Counselors

Training programs in the counseling profession prepare students to have a unified professional identity and provide opportunities for specialized training. As previously mentioned, one specialty area is marriage, couple, and family counseling. Counseling master's degree programs typically last 2 to 3 years, and counselor education doctoral programs often last 4 to 5 years. Graduate students in the counseling profession master a content-based curriculum and complete a rigorous field experience.

The Council for the Accreditation of Counseling and Related Educational Programs (CACREP), established in 1981, is a CHEA-recognized accreditation organization that provides standards related to the education and training of professional counselors. CACREP-accredited programs operating under the 2016 standards, regardless of specialty area, must have a minimum of 60 semester hours or 90 quarter credit hours. CACREP-accredited counseling programs provide students with a foundational-level series of courses (e.g., group counseling, counseling theories), and the master's-level field experience (practicum and internship) must equate to a total of 600 hours, with 240 of these hours being direct service (CACREP, 2021a). In many states, CACREP-accredited clinical mental health counseling programs meet the educational and foundational training curriculum requirements for counseling licensure. Furthermore, pursuing a specialized track in marriage, couple, and family counseling typically involves completing approximately 15 to 21 additional college credits in courses focusing on marriage, couple, and family counseling. Graduate students who enroll in this specialization are expected to possess the knowledge and skills necessary to address a wide variety of issues in the context of relationships and families. Counselor education programs specializing in marriage, couple, and family counseling must document how students meet a wide variety of standards in the following three core areas: (a) marriage, couple, and family counseling foundations; (b) contextual dimensions; and (c) practice (CACREP, 2021b).

In the United States, every state has some form of counseling licensure and an infrastructure to support the regulation of professional practice. While some states informally use CACREP educational standards as a blueprint for foundational training expectations, many states require coursework beyond CACREP standards. Furthermore, there are state-by-state structural differences in counseling licensure tier systems (e.g., provisional licensure, single-tiered licensure, two-tiered licensure), national exam expectations (e.g., National Counselor Examination [NCE], National Clinical Mental Health Counseling Examination [NCMHCE]), and what a license professional counselor is called (e.g., licensed professional counselor, licensed clinical professional counselor, licensed professional clinical counselor, licensed mental health counselor, licensed professional clinical mental health counselor, licensed clinical mental health counselor, licensed professional counselor—mental health; Olson et al., 2018). While this may sound confusing, an easy first step is to communicate with the statewide licensure regulatory board and review the statewide licensure standards.

After graduating from a training program, counseling practitioners will need to take a national/statewide exam, engage in clinical practice, and participate in clinical supervision with an approved counseling supervisor. A first step may be to develop a plan of supervision with the state regulatory board. This often includes documenting who the practitioner plans to engage in supervision with and creating a tentative plan for completing the required hours. Regarding supervised practice, in the United States most states and jurisdictions require either 2,000 or 3,000 hours of direct professional practice over a minimum of 2 years. During the postgraduate professional practice, most states require 200 to 300 hours of supervision over the specified period. Supervisors must be approved by the state, and states may require supervisors to have the Center for Credentialing and Education (CCE) Approved Clinical Supervisor (ACS) designation (CCE, 2021a). To attain the ACS credential, a clinician must (a) possess a master's degree in a mental health field, (b) receive professional licensure or board certification in counseling, (c) attain 5 years of post-master's degree experience in mental health services that includes at least 4,000 hours of direct service with clients, (d) submit a professional disclosure statement, and (e) acquire experience as a clinical supervisor (CCE, 2021b; Table 1.2).

TABLE 1.2   COMPARISON OF PIONEERS, ORGANIZATIONS, EXAM, LICENSURE, CERTIFICATION, AND SUPERVISION

Element	Marriage and Family Therapy	Professional Counseling
Influential pioneers	Gregory Bateson, Theodore Lidz, Murray Bowen, Nathan Ackerman, Don Jackson, Jay Haley, Virginia Satir	Frank Parsons, Carl Rogers, Jesse B. Davis
Accreditation agency	Commission on Accreditation for Marriage and Family Therapy Education (COAMFTE)	Council for the Accreditation of Counseling and Related Educational Programs (CACREP)
Leading organizations	American Association for Marriage and Family Therapy (AAMFT)	American Counseling Association (ACA), International Association of Marriage and Family Counselors (IAMFC)
National exam	Association of Marriage and Family Therapy Regulatory Boards (AMFTRB)	National Counselor Examination (NCE), National Clinical Mental Health Counseling Examination (NCMHCE)
Licensure	Licensed marriage and family therapists (including other title variations)	Licensed professional counselor (including other title variations)
Certification and supervision credential	AAMFT Clinical Fellow AAMFT Approved Supervisor	National Certified Counselor Approved Clinical Supervisor (ACS)
Statewide direct contact licensure hours	2,000–3,000 hours in most states	2,000–3,000 hours in most states
Statewide supervision hours	200–300 hours in most states	200–300 hours in most states

AAMFT, American Association for Marriage and Family Therapy.

While any mental health practitioner can work from a systemic perspective and treat families, couples, networks, and groups, those who specialize in marriage and family therapy and professional counseling demonstrate excellence in professional preparation (e.g., professional identity, training standards, accreditation, organization-based representation). While individuals who are deeply engaged in one or both of these professional preparation programs (MFT and professional counseling) see many differences in accreditation standards, pioneers, education, and fieldwork, others may not. In fact, these two professions are so similar that the Bureau of Labor Statistics groups them together. One obvious similarity is that both MFT and professional counseling produce master's-level mental health professionals qualified to diagnose and treat mental conditions. Additional similarities include the typical duration of a degree program (2–3 years), the number of postdegree direct contact hours (2,000–3,000 in most states), the number of postdegree supervision hours (200–300 in most states), and completion of a postdegree profession-based national exam. While MFTs and professional counselors strive to distinguish themselves, the reality is that "[w]e are more alike, my friends, than we are unalike" (paraphrasing Angelou, 1994, p. 224).

Additional Organizations That Support Couple, Marriage, and Family Practitioners

Four additional organizations that support couple, marriage, and family work are the American Family Therapy Academy (AFTA; www.afta.org), the American Psychological Association (Division 43: Society for Couple and Family Psychology; www.apa .org/about/division/div43), the International Family Therapy Association (IFTA; www .ifta-familytherapy.org), and the NCFR (www.ncfr.org). Becoming familiar with these organizations, engaging in opportunities for professional development, and reviewing literature produced by their members are excellent ways to develop a meaningful connection with the couple, marriage, and family therapy community; develop one's professional identity in the field; and stay current with the research, news, and science of systemic practice.

The AFTA was founded in 1977 with an emphasis on promoting the importance of systemic theory and practice among experts and diverse professionals. The AFTA has a core commitment to equality, social responsibility, and justice, and welcomes family therapists and allied clinicians, academics, researchers, and policy makers. The AFTA synergistically discusses various systemic phenomena, including models, investigations, and trainings. The organization's website describes AFTA as "a professional community that studies the interaction of biological, psychological, relational, and socio-cultural dimensions contributing to mental health and wellbeing" (AFTA, 2021a, para. 2). The AFTA produces a publication entitled *AFTA Springer Briefs in Family Therapy*. This journal provides brief articles on systemic practices and family therapy in a format that is reader-friendly, practical, and conversational (AFTA, 2021b).

Division 43 of the American Psychological Association, previously called Family Psychology, has been a recognized specialty area of the American Psychological Association since 1990. In 2008, the name of the organization was changed to the Society for Couple and Family Psychology. Similar to previously described organizations, this organization focuses on ". . . the emotions, thoughts, and behavior of individuals, couples, and families in relationships and in the broader environment in which they function" (American Psychological Association, 2021a, para. 1). According to the Society for Couple and Family Psychology's website, practitioners within this specialty area focus on helping individuals, couples, families, work groups, community groups of all kinds, and organized systems. Division 43 produces two publications related to the practice, research, and science of family psychology: a peer-reviewed journal entitled *Couple and Family Psychology: Research and Practice* and the vibrant Division 43 Discussion Blog (American Psychological Association, 2021b).

The IFTA was founded in 1987 with the mission of collaboratively promoting, improving, and strengthening family therapy practice; offering continuing education; encouraging peace within the world; and enhancing the quality of interpersonal relationships. The IFTA provides members with a scholarly journal and an electronic newsletter. The journal is entitled the *Journal of Family Psychotherapy*, and according to the IFTA website it "is an important forum for initial clinical observations, exciting therapeutic discoveries, and novel approaches in family psychotherapy" (IFTA, 2021a, para. 3). Published semiannually, IFTA's e-newsletter provides current information regarding research in the IFTA community (IFTA, 2021b).

Founded in 1938, the NCFR is the oldest nonprofit, nonpartisan, multidisciplinary organization focused on family therapy research, practice, and education. The NCFR supports scholars and professionals in many countries who work to better understand, strengthen, and empower families. The NCFR publishes three scholarly journals—the

Journal of Marriage and Family, Family Relations: Interdisciplinary Journal of Applied Family Science, and the *Journal of Family Theory & Review*—and hosts an annual international conference aimed at disseminating cutting-edge research and practice. Lastly, the NCFR established and coordinates the nationally recognized Certified Family Life Educator (CFLE) credential (NCFR, 2021).

CONTEMPORARY SPECIALIZATION

For some clinicians, there is nothing more important than being part of a clinical team. This team could be a group of diverse professionals who are part of a multidisciplinary treatment team or perhaps an integrated primary and behavioral health team. According to Epstein (2014), the use of multidisciplinary teams is a best-practice method that improves client outcomes and reduces unhelpful, negative events. In short, well-organized teams of profession-based experts can provide a thorough and comprehensive level of client care. These teams are found in agencies, hospitals, and clinics around the world.

While a team-based atmosphere may be ideal for some, other clinicians prefer to start a private practice or join a group private practice. Private and group practitioners are essentially business owners. Owning a business requires a set of additional skills, including, but not limited to, business management, picking an ideal office location, working with insurance companies (e.g., obtaining reimbursement, placement on insurance panels), establishing a cash fee structure (e.g., sliding scale), charging rent for office space, choosing a Health Insurance Portability and Accountability Act (HIPAA)-compliant note/file structure, and networking with various community entities to obtain referrals. Whether one is working in a private practice, group practice, agency, or hospital, there are countless ways couple, marriage, and family practitioners can specialize, including, but not limited to, theoretical model-based specialization, multisystemic therapy, parent management training, group therapy, play therapy, filial therapy, family planning counseling, discernment counseling, divorce therapy, sandtray therapy, sandplay therapy, applied behavioral analysis, functional family therapy, certified family-life educator, adventure-based therapy, medical family therapy (MedFT), premarital therapy, mediation, and sex therapy. The following are descriptions of the unique elements of four common specialty areas.

Medical Family Therapy

According to Tyndall (2010), MedFT aims to be

> [a]n approach to healthcare sourced from a BPS-S (i.e., biopsychosocial-spiritual) perspective and marriage and family therapy, but also informed by systems theory. The practice of MedFT spans a variety of clinical settings with a strong focus on the relationship of the patient and the collaboration between and among the healthcare providers and the patient. MedFTs are endorsers of patient and family agency and facilitators of healthy workplace dynamics (pp. 68–69).

MedFT works hard to ensure multiple systemic healthcare relationships are understood and addressed by all team members. According to McDaniel et al. (1992), a key component of MedFT is the interconnected nature of biomedical and psychological problems. Linville et al. (2007) expanded this description of MedFT by emphasizing that it is "an approach to healthcare from a biopsychosocial-spiritual perspective, informed by systems theory" (p. 86). The interconnected nature of MedFT was further theorized by Doherty et al.'s (2014) description of five unhelpful ecosystemic splits that MedFT works hard to integrate: (a) mindbody dualism (i.e., the inappropriate separation of physical and mental health); (b) individual versus the family (i.e., downplaying the importance of the family); (c) individual, family versus institutional settings (i.e., the disconnection between family members and the healthcare team); (d) clinical, operational, and financial (i.e., disconnection of operational and financial administrators from healthcare providers); and (e) separation of community from clinical healthcare (i.e., lack of understanding that neighborhoods, culture, and larger institutions directly impact the health of individuals).

MedFT was officially started in the late 1970s. Today, MedFT is an independent field with clinicians practicing at all levels of healthcare. On a day-to-day basis, MedFT enables agency, communion, communication, and collaboration between staff in healthcare settings, between healthcare organizations and families, and between mental health and physical health professionals. Additionally, MedFT promotes health parity and equity, and aims to reduce health inequalities based on age, race, class, gender, and sexual and gender identity (Hodgson et al., 2012).

Given the prominence and importance of medical family therapy, MedFT training programs and accreditations have expanded over the past 25 years. In 2005, the first accredited MedFT doctoral program was created at East Carolina University. Currently, there are two accredited MedFT doctoral programs and 17 MedFT professional programs in the United States (Medical Family Therapy, n.d.).

Sex Therapy

Sex therapy is a common specialization among couple, marriage, and family practitioners. Sex therapists help couples and individuals who are experiencing sexual difficulties or issues with general intimacy. Sex therapists help people make sense of their sexual lives, find solutions to relevant problems, and improve communication and understanding of intimacy and sex-related issues. While a well-trained sex therapist could assist couples or individuals with a plethora of issues, most sexual dysfunction falls into three categories: (a) disorders of desire (ranging from low sex drive to complete aversion to sex), (b) arousal disorders (e.g., erectile dysfunction, lubrication issues), and (c) orgasm disorders (e.g., problems with orgasm timing, quality, and requirements). Additional commonly treated issues include difficulty having orgasms, sexual arousal disorder, premature ejaculation, sex and disability-related conditions, sex and chronic illness, abuse and neglect, cultural differences, reproductive anatomy, transgender and LGBTQ education, and religious or faith-based issues.

In a wide range of forms (e.g., manuals, spells and incantations, aphrodisiacs, tantric yoga, counseling), sex therapy has existed since the beginning of written history. Much of contemporary Western 20th-century sex therapy began in the 1950s with the control of sexual expression. The next 40 years focused on emotional and intrapsychic issues underlying sexual dysfunction (e.g., psychoanalysis), behavioral techniques designed to resolve sexual issues (e.g., Masters and Johnson's Sensate Focus), and medication to enhance sexual performance (e.g., Viagra, penile injections). According to Weir (2019), the current generation of sex therapists emphasizes the use of empirically validated therapeutic modalities (emotion-focused therapy, cognitive behavioral therapy) and mindfulness-based interventions, combining psychological interventions and medications, recognizing the full span of human sexuality and gender identity, and using telehealth and web-based interventions.

Sex therapy is a highly credentialed specialization. The American Association of Sexuality Educators, Counselors, and Therapists (AASECT) is a not-for-profit, interdisciplinary professional organization that was founded in 1967. The AASECT offers training, credentialing, professional development, and impeccable standards to safeguard sexual health. Most certification programs require a graduate degree or a minimum of bachelor's degree, supervised experience, and, in some states, continuing education hours. Standards vary, depending on one's country of practice. The AASECT offers three levels of credentialing: AASECT Certified Sexuality Counselor, AASECT Certified Sex Therapist, and AASECT Certified Sexuality Educator. Each level of credentialing has a different scope of practice, and the requirements vary (see www.aasect.org).

Premarital Counseling

Most people who have pondered the seemingly endless issues that arise in marriages and long-term relationships have asked themselves, "Shouldn't there be some kind of education or test for getting married?" While premarital counseling is not a requirement for marriage, it helps couples prepare for the ups and downs of married life. For clients interested in ensuring that their marriage will have the best possible chances of survival, stability, and satisfaction, premarital counseling is one path they can take. While MFTs are uniquely qualified for this work, premarital counseling can be offered by any helping professional who has completed the required training. There is no certification or credentialing requirement for premarital counselors beyond having the relevant educational degree, appropriate supervision, and continuing education coursework.

Premarital counselors help improve the success rates of marriages and support couples so they can avoid the serious consequences (e.g., physical, mental, emotional, and financial distress) that can come with divorce. According to the AAMFT (2021d, para. 13),

> [p]remarital counseling usually involves spending 5 to 7 sessions with a family therapist interpreting test results, setting goals for improvement, and discussing other important topics related to marriage, such as finances, roles in marriage, and having children. Premarital counseling also helps the couple improve their communication skills.

According to Sweatt-Eldredge (2017), premarital counselors help couples improve their communication and conflict management skills, understand their similarities and differences in their core values, recognize their communication styles and needs, experience working together as a team, and achieve a deeper sense of shared meaning.

Mediation

Whether a helping professional describes their services as therapeutic mediation, family mediation, or therapeutic family mediation, the goal is to create a sense of emotional relief and establish a set of boundaries when a couple goes through a divorce. A mediation meeting is a process in which two potentially hostile parties meet with a trained mediator to work through and potentially resolve disputes or other issues. If a resolution is agreed upon, the plan of action should be acceptable to both parties. MFTs who become therapeutic and/or family mediators often work with divorcing partners. Although the marriage may end, the job of parenting is likely to continue. Mediators can assist with the divided interests of the marriage and facilitate communication about parenting the children.

Therapeutic family mediation is time-limited, and the length of individual sessions varies (i.e., could range anywhere from 1 to 10 hours), and the ethos of mediation is to move past an impasse through decision-making. According to Irving and Benjamin (2002), the process of therapeutic family mediation includes (a) establishing a structure for mediation, (b) being an advisor, and (c) monitoring the affective states and patterned behavior of each spouse. There is also considerable variability in the structure of a mediation session. The structure can range from very strict rules about the questions asked, who speaks, and the allowance of any processing of emotions to a more open and

TABLE 1.3 DISTINGUISHING MODALITY AND CLINICAL SPECIALIZATION

Type of Modality	Clinical Specializations
Family-oriented modalities	Theoretical model-based specialization, family planning counseling, multisystemic therapy, family planning counseling, functional family therapy, certified family-life educator, adventure-based therapy, medical family therapy
Couple/marriage-oriented modalities	Theoretical model-based specialization, discernment counseling, divorce therapy, adventure-based therapy, premarital therapy, mediation, sex therapy
Child-oriented modalities	Theoretical model-based specialization, play therapy, filial therapy, theraplay, sandtray therapy, sandplay therapy, applied behavioral analysis, adventure-based therapy
Parent-oriented modalities	Parent management training, filial therapy, applied behavioral analysis, premarital therapy

Note: This overview does not constitute a comprehensive reflection of all specializations within a modality. Certain specializations are duplicated across multiple modalities.

process-oriented structure. For some couples, it is a major achievement just to stay in the same room in a civil manner, while others are seeking a sense of forgiveness within themselves and the other. Given this degree of inconsistency, all mediation sessions must have goals that are uniquely tailored to the couple's issues.

During the early years in the field of mediation, several professional organizations approached conflict resolution from a similar perspective. These organizations included the Family Mediation Association (founded in 1975), the Academy of Professional Family Mediators, the Society of Professionals in Dispute Resolution, the Conflict Resolution in Education Network, the National Association for Family and Community Education, and the National Association for Mediation in Education. In 2000, several of the organizations merged to create the Association for Conflict Resolution (ACR). Following this merger, a new organization focusing on family mediation was created in 2011: the Academy of Professional Family Mediators (APFM). Among many initiatives and changes, this organization has developed a system of credentialing family mediators. APFM-certified professionals are APFM members who have met the criteria for advanced practitioner and practitioner membership levels (Table 1.3).

CURRENT SCHOLARLY TRENDS

There are many scholarly trends in the therapeutic world. This book is primarily centered on exploring trends that are specifically related to couple, marriage, and family practitioners. While many unique areas of systemic therapy have been receiving scholarly attention, there are four contemporary areas of professional practice that have received a tremendous amount of scholarly attention across all helping professions and specializations: (a) multiculturalism, intersectionality, and social justice; (b) crisis, trauma, and disaster (CTD); (c) telebehavioral health and other digital therapeutic technology; and (d) wellness. The following sections provide an orientation to these trends. They will also be explored repeatedly in subsequent chapters.

Orientation to Multiculturalism, Intersectionality, and Social Justice

Pioneering cultural theorist Stuart Hall (1932–2014), widely considered the "Godfather of Multiculturalism," coined the term *multiculturalism*. At its heart, multiculturalism is the coexistence of diverse cultures encompassing differences in race, ethnicity, gender, gender identity, religion, sexuality, social capital, socioeconomic status, age, and disability (Ratts et al., 2016). Contextual factors play a part in everyone's lives and contribute to mental illness, power, oppression, discrimination, marginalization, social status, and differing access of individuals, couples, families, and groups to material and nonmaterial possessions. Couple, marriage, and family practitioners consider the attainment of multicultural competence to be a never-ending journey. Similarly, multicultural counseling offers accessible and effective interventions to culturally diverse clients. According to the ACA Code of Ethics (2014), multicultural counseling aims to encourage counselors to gain knowledge, skills, sensitivity, dispositions, and personal awareness for working with diverse clientele. These new levels of awareness create a deep level of respect for others, which ultimately enhances therapeutic effectiveness (Lee, 2019; Ratts & Pedersen, 2014).

While it is important for couple, marriage, and family practitioners to understand that contextual categories exist, it is important not to address them in isolation. In 1989, Kimberlé Crenshaw coined the term *intersectionality* to describe the overlapping identities that individuals possess. Intersectionality also describes the overlapping contextual issues that affect people's daily lives. These interwoven factors affect every couple, family, group, network, and individual. Cultural constructs such as equity, privilege, and equality are deeply affected by the overlapping identities one represents. Consequently, practitioners must use an intersectional framework to tailor their conceptualization and treatment of client issues (Lee, 2019; Ratts & Pedersen, 2014).

Adopting a social justice perspective is a key component of couple, marriage, and family therapeutic practice. This perspective adds a sense of action to multiculturalism and intersectionality, and it has been a burgeoning contemporary issue for at least 30 years in the helping professions. According to the homepage of ACA's Counselors for Social Justice Division,

> [s]ocial justice in counseling represents a multifaceted approach in which counselors strive to simultaneously promote human development and the common good through addressing challenges related to both individual and distributive justice. This approach includes empowerment of individuals and groups as well as active confrontation of injustice and inequality in society, both as they impact clientele and in their systemic contexts . . . (Crethar & Ratts, 2008, p. 82).

Couple, marriage, and family practitioners have an ethical responsibility to adopt a social justice framework to recognize how context, relationships, and history drive systemic power imbalances and create widespread injustice. From a macro perspective, practitioners must understand and challenge the institutions and social structures that perpetuate injustice and encourage them to extend access to resources to include underprivileged individuals and groups (Seedall et al., 2013). This ethics toward public participation (e.g., policy advocacy and political participation) enhances the lives of oppressed groups and creates a better society.

While political activism is a key social justice factor related to systemic change, practitioners working with families, couples, groups, networks, and individuals must analyze the intersection of critical contextual factors and the constructs of power, oppression, and privilege. These contextual factors include, but are not limited to, ability, culture, race and ethnicity, socioeconomic status, social class, gender, sexuality, and religious affiliation (Garcia & McDowell, 2010). Throughout this textbook, contemporary issues affecting couples, families, and children are analyzed with these pertinent intersections in mind.

Orientation to Crisis, Trauma, and Disaster Work

Events involving CTD have been pervasive since the dawn of time. The unique and intersecting elements of CTD have been at the forefront of therapeutic work across all helping professions. At the time this chapter was written, May 28, 2022, 6,310,095 people had died from the coronavirus (COVID-19) outbreak. The COVID-19 outbreak and the subsequent quarantine is a nature-based disaster that has risen to the level of a global health emergency. In addition to the death and sickness caused by COVID-19, the nation/state-based stay-at-home orders caused many businesses to close their doors. The subsequent layoffs, furloughs, and workforce reductions created an additional large-scale societal crisis.

During the summer of 2020, at the height of the COVID-19 pandemic, undue and inhumane police violence against Black people led to widespread public demonstrations, political unrest, and protests. Specifically, the police killings of George Floyd, Breonna Taylor, and countless other Black individuals sparked the resurgence of the Black Lives Matter (BLM) movement. These events and the accompanying awareness of the ever-present, deep-rooted systemic racism in the United States constitute a significant humanitarian crisis.

The effects of crises, traumas, and disasters include personal hardship (e.g., a family member's death from COVID-19), communal distress (e.g., widespread joblessness due to local layoffs), and societal turmoil (e.g., resurgence of the BLM movement in response to undue police violence). While crisis and disaster mental health interventions are short-term, coping skills-oriented, and centered on mitigating the stressful situation, trauma-based therapies are often deep, multifaceted, and long-term (Black & Flynn, 2020). Crisis counseling often includes interventions aligned with triage, psychological first aid, a specific model of crisis interventions (e.g., the developmental–ecological model of crisis counseling; Collins & Collins, 2005), and community care coordination. According to Halpern and Tramontin (2007), "[a] disaster could qualify as a crisis, but not all crises are disasters" (p. 2). Disaster events (e.g., floods, hurricanes, pandemics, earthquakes) are condensed, collectively experienced, and broad in scope/scale, with a clear start and finish. Disaster mental health interventions often involve the same skills as crisis interventions; however, the scale is much different, and it usually involves receiving outside aid, intensive community stabilization, and collective meaning-making. The treatment of trauma-based disorders (e.g., posttraumatic stress disorder, acute stress disorder, multiple traumas, complex trauma) is typically long-term, is done in a professional setting (e.g., therapist's office), and should involve an empirically based treatment modality, including, but not limited to, prolonged exposure therapy, cognitive processing therapy, cognitive behavioral therapy, eye movement desensitization and reprocessing, trauma-focused cognitive behavioral therapy, and/or brainspotting.

Orientation to Telebehavioral Health

While innovation and technology have been steadily influencing the therapeutic world, the 2020 global pandemic (COVID-19) created a sense of urgency toward increasing the use of digital technology to continue working with clients during quarantine. Telebehavioral health is the use of a secure (i.e., encrypted) digital platform to communicate with clients in a synchronous format. This includes a wide array of technology, vendors, and clinical services. The technology includes, but is not limited to, telephone, video conferencing, smartphone, tablet, PC desktop system, or other electronic means.

Vendors such as SimplePractice provide a comprehensive digital practice package that helps clinicians in a variety of ways, including, but not limited to, confidential sessions, billing, scheduling, and insurance (see www.simplepractice.com/acaaffinity/). Lastly, contemporary HIPAA- and Health Information Technology for Economic and Clinical Health (HITECH) Act-compliant video conferencing software options include Zoom for Healthcare, Healthie, Doxy.me, Webex for Healthcare, and GoToMeeting (Healthie, n.d.). Encryption and compliance with the HIPAA and the HITECH Act are crucial to ethical telebehavioral health practice. The delivery method must be protected by two-way encryption to be considered secure. To use telebehavioral health services effectively, clients and clinicians will need access to, and familiarity with, the appropriate technology.

While there are many benefits of using telebehavioral platforms to conduct therapy (e.g., convenience, flexibility), there are limitations and disadvantages to their effectiveness. There may be a disruption to the service (e.g., phone gets cut off, video drops). These interruptions can be frustrating for both clinicians and clients because they interrupt the normal flow of personal communication. Specifically, there is a risk of misunderstanding one another when communication lacks visual or auditory cues (e.g., facial expression, tone of voice). While clinicians are responsible for ensuring that all sessions are conducted in a technologically secure and environmentally private context, both clinicians and clients are responsible for finding a private, quiet location where sessions can take place without interruption. This can be difficult for clients who are engaging in therapeutic services at their home where interruptions are ever-present (e.g., children, noise) or there is limited private space. Telebehavioral health can also create situations in which the boundaries of normal sessions are challenged (e.g., casually drinking alcohol, others being allowed to secretly listen in on conversations). These issues require both the clinician and the client to regularly assess the appropriateness of continuing to engage in treatment with technologies and to modify as needed.

Orientation to Wellness

Whether clinicians are facing burnout (i.e., mental and physical fatigue), impairment (i.e., decrease in competence and ability to provide effective and ethical care), compassion fatigue (i.e., intense sadness over someone's suffering), or vicarious trauma (i.e., psychological anguish due to frequently witnessing a client reexperience trauma), the outcome will differ depending on many factors, including one's level of personal wellness and resilience (Black & Flynn, 2020; Figley, 1995). The notion that helping professionals need to maintain a sense of health and wellness to best serve their clients has been evident for decades. In fact, 40 years ago, Farber and Heifetz (1982) indicated concern over the noticeable paucity in research on impairment and burnout. They further indicated that concerns over the lack of wellness within the helping professions have been evident since Freud's fear over the dangers of psychoanalysis on the analyst. While a tremendous amount of attention and research has been spent analyzing the constructs of wellness and burnout, we still do not seem to have a strong ability to indicate which clinicians will succumb to burnout and how to intervene.

To further complicate matters, there has also been quite a lot of attention given to the notion of resilience. Resilience can be measured when individuals are confronted with serious trauma and/or stress. According to Buckwalter (2011), *resilience* is the process of adapting during times of tragedy, threat, trauma, and significant stress. Resilience seems to emerge when a person faces a potentially traumatic situation, and it is measured by the speed in which the traumatized person can return their body and mind to a steady state. What can be done to engage the world in a resilient manner? How do we know which people will respond resiliently? These questions remain largely unanswered.

In addition to the ethical imperative to sustain a sense of wellness, actively engaging in wellness activities is a good first step for clinicians who are looking for positive lifework balance, providing excellent client care, and protection from burnout and impairment (Black & Flynn, 2020). Activities like maintaining clear professional boundaries, spending time with family, engaging in personal therapy, eating a healthy diet, attaining proper sleep, mindfulness activities, yoga, meditation, physical fitness, and engaging in a spiritual and/or religious practice can be very helpful in preserving optimal wellness (Dass-Brailsford, 2010).

An important wellness-based model that can help emerging clinicians is called the indivisible self: an evidence-based model of wellness (IS-WEL model; Myers & Sweeney, 2004). This evidence-based wellness is a holistic approach to wellness that is partly based on individual psychology (Sweeney, 1998). Throughout this textbook, considerable attention will be given to contemporary issues that, if taken on in an extreme manner (i.e., unreasonably large caseloads, only taking on acute clientele), could compromise a clinician's wellness and create a sense of burnout and/or impairment. While all of us have our own degree of resilience, it is important to remember that in order to do our best work we need to make space for our own needs and engage in helpful wellness-oriented activities.

SUMMARY

In this chapter, you were introduced to the identity of couple, marriage, and family practitioners; couple, marriage, and family professional associations; relevant accreditation organizations; pertinent specializations; the nuances of professional practice; scholarly trends; the use of telebehavioral health and therapeutic technology; applications involving crisis, trauma, and disaster; professional wellness; and aspects of context, diversity, multiculturalism, and intersectionality. As you continue your journey through the remainder of this textbook, relevant topics will be scaffolded onto this initial foundation of knowledge. Specifically, additional theoretical traditions, skill-based information, and contemporary issues and associated interventions will be integrated into your understanding of what it means to be a couple, marriage, and family practitioner. I wish you well in your future work as a systemic practitioner, and I hope you will contribute, in your own way, to the world around you.

END-OF-CHAPTER RESOURCES

STUDENT ACTIVITIES

Exercise 1: Understanding the Differences and Similarities Between Modern and Traditional Families

Directions: Review the following information and answer the questions:

Families are becoming increasingly diverse in a number of ways, including, but not limited to, families living in poverty, increases in multiracial families, increases in households headed by members of the LGBTQIA+ population, longer life expectancy, postponed marriage, delay in childbearing, increases in cohabitation, and increases in having children outside of marriage, remarriage, stepfamilies, and single parenthood. Contemporary families and traditional families have many differences, but there are also similarities between their dynamics. This chapter introduces these family dynamics, and a great deal of current research has been conducted on this topic. While it may be helpful to consider the differences between modern and traditional families, it may be equally helpful to consider ways in which they are connected and similar.

- Describe how contemporary families and traditional nuclear families are similar.
- Name a few shared aspects of contemporary and traditional nuclear families that could help with the overall family dynamic, satisfaction, and resilience.
- Consider the intricacies of working with a contemporary family and working with a traditional nuclear family. What are some ways you would strive as a therapist to highlight the positive aspects of each family dynamic?

Exercise 2: Article Review

Directions: Go to your university's online EBSCO Database and find Academic Search Premier. Search and find an article focused on multiculturalism or intersectionality work within couple, marriage, and family therapy. Review the article in its entirety and answer the following questions:

- How is the theory behind multiculturalism/intersectionality utilized throughout this article?
- What specific multicultural/intersectionality behaviors or skills can you identify?
- How do the multicultural/intersectional theoretical tenets, skills, and behaviors relate to your future work as a couple, marriage, and family practitioner?

Exercise 3: Working With Families of Origin

Directions: Review the following information and respond to the follow-up questions:

When working with couples, their respective families of origin can affect the work that is done in ways couples do not fully understand. It can be important for couples to identify the way these familial influences have shaped their communication style and relationship.

- How do you think families of origin directly impact individuals in a relationship?
- How would you directly address family-of-origin impact during a therapy session with a couple?
- When you are working with a couple, how would you address negative family-of-origin involvement? How would you address positive family-of-origin involvement?

Exercise 4: Understanding Group Work Within Couple, Marriage, and Family Therapy

Directions: Review the following information and answer the questions that follow:

Group work can be both similar to and different from work with individuals, couples, or families. This chapter introduces group work within this field. While it may be helpful to consider the differences between group work and individual work, it may be equally helpful to consider how they are connected and similar.

- Describe the ways in which group work is similar to work with individuals, families, and couples.
- Consider the dynamics of individual and group therapy. How are they relatable to each other? In what ways could individual therapy techniques be used within group therapy?
- What are some techniques that are best utilized within group therapy?

Exercise 5: Understanding Specializations

Directions: Go to your university's online EBSCO Database and find Academic Search Premier. Search and find an article focused on one of the specializations within couple, marriage, and family therapy discussed in this chapter, whether it is medical family therapy, sex therapy, premarital counseling, or mediation. Review the article in its entirety and answer the following questions involving the specialization and how it fits within the marriage and family field:

- How does the article showcase the specialization within the couple, marriage, and family field?
- Within this specialization, what specific techniques would work best?
- What aspects of this specialization do you identify with?

ADDITIONAL RESOURCES

HELPFUL LINKS

- "The Surprising History of Marriage Counseling": https://www.pbs.org/wgbh/americanexperience/features/eugenics-surprising-history-of-marriage-counseling/
- "Family Therapy": https://www.newworldencyclopedia.org/entry/Family_therapy
- International Association of Marriage and Family Counselors (IAMFC): https://www.iamfconline.org/public/main.cfm
- American Association for Marriage and Family Therapy (AAMFT): https://www.aamft.org/
- "The History of Mental Health Counseling: 1800s–Present Day": https://www.newyorkbehavioralhealth.com/history-of-mental-health-counseling-part-i/

- ■ "Medical Family Therapy": https://www.medicalfamilytherapy.org/
- ■ American Association of Sexuality Educators, Counselors, and Therapists (AASECT): https://www.aasect.org/
- ■ Academy of Professional Family Mediators: https://apfmnet.org/
- ■ National Association of Certified Mediators (NACM): https://www.mediatorcertification.org/
- ■ National Council on Family Relations (NCFR): https://www.ncfr.org
- ■ "Family Therapy": https://www.mayoclinic.org/tests-procedures/family-therapy/about/pac-20385237
- ■ American Psychological Association: Society for Couple and Family Psychology: https://www.apa.org/about/division/div43
- ■ American Family Therapy Academy (AFTA): https://www.afta.org/
- ■ International Family Therapy Association (IFTA): https://www.ifta-familytherapy.org/

HELPFUL BOOKS

- ■ Becvar, D., & Becvar, R. (2013). *Family therapy: A systemic integration*. Pearson Education.
- ■ Black, L. L., & Flynn, S. V. (2020). *Crisis, trauma, and disaster: A clinician's guide*. Sage.
- ■ Blocher, D. H. (2000). *The evolution of counseling psychology*. Springer Publishing Company.
- ■ Collins, B. G., & Collins, T. M. (2005). *Crisis and trauma: Developmental-ecological intervention*. Lahaska Press.
- ■ Sperry, L., Carlson, J., & Peluso, P. R. (2006). *Couples therapy: Integrating theory and technique*. Love Publishing Company.

HELPFUL VIDEOS

- ■ Family Therapy: https://www.youtube.com/watch?v=mPW0UZd9gQ4
- ■ Bowen Family Systems Theory: https://www.youtube.com/watch?v=-GK7LaT5rxY
- ■ Systemic Family Therapy: https://www.youtube.com/watch?v=5VVI4_1ZbVU
- ■ What Does a Sex Therapist Do?: https://www.youtube.com/watch?v=jy9Tgt0XWu8
- ■ Premarital Counseling: What Can I Expect?: https://www.youtube.com/watch?v=G08DJX64PZU
- ■ Family Mediation Demo: https://www.youtube.com/watch?v=BeMNWrjyxw0
- ■ How to Become a Marriage and Family Therapist: https://www.youtube.com/watch?v=O-6fB0IWXEU
- ■ Medical Family Therapy: What to Expect: https://www.youtube.com/watch?v=v4_cET5KevQ

REFERENCES

American Association of Marriage and Family Therapists. (2021a). *About marriage and family therapists.* https://www.aamft.org/About_AAMFT/About_Marriage_and_Family_Therapists.aspx

American Association of Marriage and Family Therapists. (2021b). *MFT licensing boards.* https://www.aamft.org/Directories/MFT_Licensing_Boards.aspx

American Association of Marriage and Family Therapists. (2021c). *AAMFT designations*. https://www.aamft.org/Shared_Content/Membership/Designations.aspx

American Association of Marriage and Family Therapists. (2021d). *Marriage preparation: Should we marry or not?* https://aamft.org/Consumer_Updates/Marriage_Preparation.aspx

American Counseling Association. (2014). *2014 ACA Code of Ethics*. https://www.counseling.org/resources/aca-code-of-ethics.pdf

American Counseling Association. (2021). *20/20: Consensus definition of counseling*. https://www.counseling.org/about-us/about-aca/20-20-a-vision-for-the-future-of-counseling/consensus-definition-of-counseling

American Family Therapy Academy. (2021a). *About AFTA*. https://www.afta.org/about-afta/

American Family Therapy Academy. (2021b). *AFTA publications*. https://www.afta.org/publications/

American Psychological Association. (2021a). *Society for Couple and Family Psychology homepage*. https://www.apadivisions.org/division-43/

American Psychological Association. (2021b). *About the Society for Couple and Family Psychology*. https://www.apadivisions.org/division-43/about

Angelou, M. (1994). *The complete collected poems of Maya Angelou*. Random House.

Association for Specialists in Group Work. (2021, May). *ASGW guiding principles for group work*. https://asgw.org/wp-content/uploads/2021/07/ASGW-Guiding-Principles-May-2021.pdf

Barnhill, L. R., & Longo, D. (1978). Fixation and regression in the family life cycle. *Family Process, 17*(4), 469–478. https://doi.org/10.1111/j.1545-5300.1978.00469.x

Becvar, R. J., & Becvar, D. S. (2018). *Systems theory and family therapy: A Primer*. Hamilton Books.

Becvar, D., & Becvar, R. (2013). *Family therapy: A systemic integration*. Pearson Education.

Becvar, R. J., Canfield, B. S., & Becvar, D. S. (1997). *Group work: Cybernetic, constructivist, and social constructionist perspectives*. Love Publishing Company.

Beesley, D. (2004). Teachers' perceptions of school counselor effectiveness: Collaborating for student success. *Education, 125*(2), 259–270.

Black, L. L., & Flynn, S.V. (2020). *Crisis, trauma, and disaster: A clinician's guide*. Sage.

Blocher, D. H. (2000). *The evolution of counseling psychology*. Springer Publishing Company.

Bowlby, J. (1940). The influence of early environment in the development of neurosis and neurotic character. *The International Journal of Psychoanalysis, 21*, 154–178.

Bryant, C. M., & Conger, R. D. (2002). An intergenerational model of romantic relationship development. In A. Vangelisti, H. Reis, & M. Fitzpatrick (Eds.), *Stability and change in relationships* (pp. 57–82). Cambridge University Press. https://doi.org/10.1017/cbo9780511499876.005

Buckwalter, G. (2011). *My definition of resilience*. Retrieved June 1, 2022, from https://www.headington-institute.org/resource/my-definition-of-resilience/

Busby, D. M., Holman, T. B., & Niehuis, S. (2009). The association between partner enhancement and self-enhancement and relationship quality outcomes. *Journal of Marriage and Family, 71*(3), 449–464. https://doi.org/10.1111/j.1741-3737.2009.00612.x

Carstensen, L. L., Gottman, J. M., & Levenson, R. W. (1995). Emotional behavior in long-term marriage. *Psychology and Aging, 10*(1), 140–149. https://doi.org/10.1037/0882-7974.10.1.140

Carter, E. A., & McGoldrick, M. M. (1980). *The family life cycle: A framework for family therapy*. Gardner Press.

Center for Credentialing and Education. (2021a). *CCE Approved Clinical Supervisor (ACS) Program*. https://www.cce-global.org/credentialing/acs

Center for Credentialing and Education. (2021b). *Requirements: Approved Clinical Supervisor (ACS)*. https://www.cce-global.org/credentialing/acs/requirements

Chung, T., Sealy, L., Abraham, M., Ruglovsky, C., Schall, J., & Maisto, S. A. (2015). Personal network characteristics of youth in substance use treatment: Motivation for and perceived difficulty of positive network change. *Substance Abuse, 36*(3), 380–388. https://doi.org/10.1080/08897077.2014.932319

Collins, B. G., & Collins, T. M. (2005). *Crisis and trauma: Developmental-ecological intervention*. Lahaska Press.

Commission on Accreditation for Marriage and Family Therapy Education. (2021). *Commission on Accreditation for Marriage and Family Therapy Education homepage*. https://www.coamfte.org/

Corey, M. S., Corey, G., & Corey, C. (2021). *Groups: Process and practice*. Cengage Learning.

Council for the Accreditation of Counseling and Related Educational Programs. (2021a). *Section 3: Professional practice*. https://www.cacrep.org/section-3-professional-practice/

Council for the Accreditation of Counseling and Related Educational Programs. (2021b). *Section 5: Marriage, couple, and family counseling*. https://www.cacrep.org/section-5-entry-level-specialty-areas-marriage-couple-and-family-counseling/

Crethar, H., & Ratts, M. (2008). Why social justice is a counseling concern. *Counseling Today, 50*(2), 82–87.

Dass-Brailsford, P. (2010). Secondary trauma among disaster responders: The need for self-care. In P. Dass-Brailsford (Ed.), *Crisis and disaster counseling: Lessons learned from Hurricane Katrina and other disasters* (pp. 213–228). Sage.

Doherty, W. J., McDaniel, S. H., & Hepworth, J. (2014). Contributions of medical family therapy to the changing health care system. *Family Process, 53*(3), 529–543. https://doi.org/10.1111/famp.12092

Emerson, C. H. (2010). *Counselor professional identity: Construction and validation of the counselor professional identity measure* [Doctoral dissertation, The University of North Carolina at Greensboro]. NC Digital Online Collection of Knowledge and Scholarship. http://libres.uncg.edu/ir/uncg/f/emerson_uncg_0154d_10396.pdf

Epstein, N. E. (2014). Multidisciplinary in-hospital teams improve patient outcomes: A review. *Surgical Neurology International, 5*(7), S295–S303. https://doi.org/10.4103/2152-7806.139612

Farber, B. A., & Heifetz, L. J. (1982). The process and dimensions of burnout in psychotherapists. *Professional Psychology, 13*(2), 293–301. https://doi.org/10.1037/0735-7028.13.2.293

Figley, C. R. (1995). Compassion fatigue as a secondary traumatic stress disorder: An overview. In C. R. Figley (Ed.), *Compassion fatigue: Coping with secondary traumatic stress disorder in those who treat the traumatized* (pp. 1–20). Brunner/Mazel.

Flynn, S. V., & Sangganjanavanich, V. F. (2014). Professional roles, functions, and consultation with other professionals. In V. F. Sangganjanavanich & C. A. Reynolds (Eds.), *Introduction to professional counseling* (pp. 47–71). Sage.

Garcia, M., & McDowell, T. (2010). Mapping social capital: A critical contextual approach for working with low-status families. *Journal of Marital and Family Therapy, 36*(1), 96–107. https://doi.org/10.1111/j.1752-0606.2009.00186.x

Goldenberg, I., & Goldenberg, H. (2004). *Family therapy: An overview (Vol. 6)*. Wadsworth Publishing.

Gottman, J. M. (1993). The roles of conflict engagement, escalation, and avoidance in marital interaction: A longitudinal view of five types of couples. *Journal of Consulting and Clinical Psychology, 61*(1), 6–15. https://doi.org/10.1037/0022-006x.61.1.6

Gottman, J. M., & Levenson, R. W. (2000). The timing of divorce: Predicting when a couple will divorce over a 14-year period. *Journal of Marriage and Family, 62*(3), 737–745. https://doi.org/10.1111/j.1741-3737.2000.00737.x

Hackney, H. L., & Cormier, S. (2009). *The professional counselor: A process guide to helping* (6th ed.). Pearson Publishing.

Halpern, J., & Tramontin, M. (2007). *Disaster mental health: Theory and practice*. Thomson Brooks/Cole.

Healthie. (n.d.). *The 5 best HIPAA compliant telehealth tools*. https://www.gethealthie.com/blog/the-5-best-hipaa-compliant-telehealth-tools

Hodgson, J., Lamson, A., Mendenhall, T., & Crane, R. (2012). Medical family therapy: Opportunity for workforce development in healthcare. *Contemporary Family Therapy, 34*(2), 143–146. https://doi.org/10.1007/s10591-012-9199-1

Holman, T. B., & Jarvis, M. O. (2003). Hostile, volatile, avoiding, and validating couple-conflict types: An investigation of Gottman's couple-conflict types. *Personal Relationships, 10*(2), 267–282. https://doi.org/10.1111/1475-6811.00049

International Association of Marriage and Family Counselors. (2021). *About IAMFC*. https://www.iamfconline.org/public/-3.cfm

International Family Therapy Association. (2021a). *Journal*. https://www.ifta-familytherapy.org/publicationsjournal.php

International Family Therapy Association. (2021b). *Publications*. https://www.ifta-familytherapy.org/publications.php

Irving, H. H., & Benjamin, M. (2002). *Therapeutic family mediation: Helping families resolve conflict*. Sage.

Kaslow, F. W. (1993). The military family in peace and war. *Journal of Marriage and the Family, 56*(4), 1053. https://doi.org/10.2307/353622

Kreider, R. M., & Ellis, R. (2011). *Living arrangements of children: 2009*. Household Economic Studies.

Lee, C. C. (2019). *Multicultural issues in counseling: New approaches to diversity* (5th ed.). American Counseling Association.

Limberg, D., Guest, J. D., & Gonzales, S. K. (2021). History of research in the social sciences. In S. Flynn (Ed.), *Research design for the behavioral sciences: An applied approach* (pp. 43–70). Springer Publishing Company.

Linville, D., Hertlein, K. M., & Lyness, A. M. (2007). Medical family therapy: Reflecting on the necessity of collaborative healthcare research. *Families, Systems, & Health, 25*(1), 85–97. https://doi.org/10.1037/1091-7527.25.1.85

Mason, M. J., Sabo, R., & Zaharakis, N. M. (2017). Peer network counseling as brief treatment for urban adolescent heavy cannabis users. *Journal of Studies on Alcohol and Drugs, 78*(1), 152–157. https://doi.org/10.15288/jsad.2017.78.152

McDaniel, S. H., Hepworth, J., & Doherty, W. J. (1992). *Medical family therapy: A biopsychosocial approach to families with health problems*. Basic Books.

Medical Family Therapy. (n.d.). *Master's programs*. https://www.medicalfamilytherapy.org/masters-programs

Myers, J. E., & Sweeney, T. J. (2004). The indivisible self: An evidence-based model of wellness. *Journal of Individual Psychology, 60*(3), 234–245.

National Council on Family Relations. (2021). *Strengthening families*. https://www.ncfr.org/

Ohio Counselor, Social Worker, and Marriage and Family Therapist Board. (2014). *Section 4757.01: Counselor, social worker, and marriage and family therapist definitions*. Ohio Laws & Administrative Rules: Legislative Service Commission. http://codes.ohio.gov/orc/4757.01

O'Leary, K. D. (1988). Physical aggression between spouses. In V. B. Van Hasselt, R. L. Morrison, A. S. Bellack, & M. Hersen (Eds.), *Handbook of family violence* (pp. 31–55). https://doi.org/10.1007/978-1-4757-5360-8_3

Olson, S., Brown-Rice, K., & Gerodias, A. (2018). Professional counselor licensure portability: An examination of state license applications. *The Professional Counselor, 8*(1), 88–103. https://doi.org/10.15241/so.8.1.88

Parsons, F. (1909). *Choosing a vocation*. Houghton Mifflin Co.

Ratts, M. J., Singh, A. A., Nassar-McMillan, S., Butler, S. K., & McCullough, J. R. (2016). Multicultural and social justice counseling competencies: Guidelines for the counseling profession. *Journal of Multicultural Counseling and Development, 44*(1), 28–48. https://doi.org/10.1002/jmcd.12035

Ratts, M. J., & Pedersen, P. B. (2014). *Counseling for multiculturalism and social justice: Integration, theory, and application* (4th ed.). American Counseling Association.

Seedall, R. B., Holtrop, K., & Parra-Cardona, J. R. (2013). Diversity, social justice, and intersectionality trends in C/MFT: A content analysis of three family therapy journals, 2004–2011. *Journal of Marital and Family Therapy, 40*(2), 139–151. https://doi.org/10.1111/jmft.12015

Sperry, L., Carlson, J., & Peluso, P. R. (2006). *Couples therapy: Integrating theory and technique*. Love Publishing Company.

Spock, B. (1946). *The common sense book of baby and child care: With illustration by Dorothea Fox*. Duell, Sloan and Pearce.

Sweatt-Eldredge, C. (2017). *Do you really need premarital counseling?* Psychology Today. https://www.psychologytoday.com/us/blog/the-connected-life/201706/do-you-really-need-premarital-counseling

Sweeney, T. J. (1998). *Adlerian counseling: A practitioner's approach* (4th ed.). Taylor & Francis.

Tyndall, L. E. (2010, January). *Medical family therapy: Conceptual clarification and consensus for an emerging profession* [Doctoral dissertation, East Carolina University]. The ScholarShip. http://hdl.handle.net/10342/2794

Weir, K. (2019, February). *CE Corner: Sex therapy for the 21st century: Five emerging directions*. American Psychological Association. https://www.apa.org/monitor/2019/02/cover-ce-corner#

Wetchler, J. L., & Hecker, L. L. (2003). *An introduction to marriage and family therapy*. Routledge.

CHAPTER 2

INTRODUCTION TO THE THEORY AND PRACTICE OF COUPLE, MARRIAGE, AND FAMILY THERAPY

LEARNING OBJECTIVES

After reading this chapter, you will be able to:

- ■ Identify the systemic approach to therapy.
- ■ Recognize the nuances of major theoretical movements in clinical practice.
- ■ Identify unique ethical issues in marriage and family work.
- ■ Recognize diversity and intersectionality in systemic work.
- ■ Describe the basic elements of professional practice.
- ■ Distinguish verbal and nonverbal behaviors in systemic practice.

INTRODUCTION TO PROFESSIONAL ISSUES IN COUPLE, MARRIAGE, AND FAMILY THERAPY

This chapter provides a foundation for the remainder of the textbook. Specifically, it prepares graduate students to understand cutting-edge professional interventions, skills, contemporary issues, and theories aimed at attaining excellence in conducting therapy with couples and families. In addition to discussing the importance of systemic therapy and theory in relation to other major theoretical movements, this chapter helps emerging clinicians understand key ethical issues relevant to systemic practice; decipher verbal and nonverbal messages in couple, marriage, and family work; and embrace the diversity and intersectionality that permeate systemic work.

The Systemic Paradigm

The systemic paradigm differs significantly from other major forces in applied psychology. According to Smith-Acuña (2011), ". . . *systems theory* can be defined as a set of unifying principles about the organization and functioning of systems. Systems are defined as meaningful wholes that are maintained by the interaction of their parts" (p. 6). While systems can include a variety of entities, the goal of the present description is to help readers understand systems in the context of families (e.g., couple/marriage therapy, family therapy, child and adolescent counseling) and other relevant human social systems (e.g., group counseling, network therapy).

You may be asking yourself, "What are the unifying principles that encompass systems thinking?" The concept of systems has evolved through the years. General systems theory was at least partly founded by Austrian biologist Karl Ludwig von Bertalanffy (1901–1972) and American mathematician Norbert Wiener (1894–1964). von Bertalanffy set the stage for a modern systems paradigm by trying to examine biological specimens in a holistic and orderly manner. von Bertalanffy's general systems theory shifted the more mechanistic and linear approaches of the time to a model that defined organisms as organized, interactive, and interdependent (i.e., holistic). Wiener also explored systemic notions and, through his mathematical work, set the stage for understanding artificial intelligence and cybernetics (Smith-Acuña, 2011). Metaphorically, a way to understand the interaction, interdependence, and holistic nature of family systems is to consider the movement of a mobile (Satir, 1967). If one aspect of the mobile is touched, the rest of the mobile also moves. Within families, there is a deep sense of interconnectedness at both conscious and unconscious levels. In this sense, family members are constantly interacting or communicating with one another. Virginia Satir adds: ". . . if the wires on one of the pieces of the mobile are twisted, the mobile would spin improperly. . . . each piece would get entangled and out of balance at the slightest breeze" (Renaissance Ranch Treatment Centers, 2021, para. 1). Couple, marriage, and family practitioners use their skills and knowledge to help untangle families, couples, networks, groups, and individuals.

In addition to general systems theory, first- and second-order cybernetics help describe the essence of the systemic paradigm. While it is difficult to determine an official start date, cybernetics and cybernetic thinking are generally thought to have emerged in the late 1940s (e.g., Wiener, 1948). Although cybernetics will be covered in more depth later in this textbook, it is important for readers to understand that first-order cybernetics inspired couple, marriage, and family practitioners to suspend their judgment, ideas about truth, and the use of dichotomies for a thorough exploration of context, interdependence, and relativism. This emphasis on context encouraged clinicians to stop separating individuals from their families and instead urged them to analyze individuals relative to their relationships. Consequently, instead of continuing the tradition of dissecting the psyches of individual clients, practitioners began to embed clients in their intimate, familial, and social networks to determine the context of the issue(s) or presenting problem(s) (Amatea & Sherrard, 1994; Becvar & Becvar, 2013). Second-order cybernetics took this process a step further by suggesting that the observer (i.e., clinician) is also part of the system they are attempting to observe (i.e., participant-observer). Thus, the systemic paradigm was further enhanced through reminding practitioners that ". . . the real nature of someone or something can be defined only in relationship to oneself as observer, and through this relationship, a new and different real nature evolves" (Becvar et al., 1997, p. 15).

The Systemic Paradigm and the Clinical World

It is important to balance the inspiring nature of the systemic paradigm with the reality of clinical practice in most statewide organizations and hospitals. First, most agencies and hospitals in America still rely on traditional models of individual psychiatric assessment and diagnosis. These models are somewhat deficit-based, pathology-focused, and are often referred to as the "disease model." Consequently, despite the importance of understanding the nuances of relational work, emerging practitioners will be expected to have a solid working knowledge of individual psychopathology and of the individual diagnostic clusters. This information allows for a shared understanding between healthcare providers; enables clinicians to comprehend individual treatment planning and case conceptualization; delivers evidence required for reimbursement of services from managed care and insurance companies; provides a platform for practitioners to competently use the *Diagnostic and Statistical Manual of Mental Disorders*, Fifth Edition, Text Revision (*DSM-5-TR*; American Psychiatric Association, 2022), to diagnose client symptomology; and helps to ensure that systemic practitioners are regarded as credible by the greater medical community. While there is ample contemporary evidence indicating that there may be superiority with systemic/relational assessment and diagnosis (e.g., Turri et al., 2020), systemic practitioners must understand the current clinical reality and move to a more individualistic psychology worldview when appropriate.

Currently, mental health practitioners are not licensed on a national level, and no state-by-state licensure reciprocity arrangements exist in the United States. Because each state has its own licensing laws, regulations, and case law, clinicians must make sure that they are working within their scope of practice. While accreditation organizations (Council for the Accreditation of Counseling and Related Educational Programs, Commission on Accreditation for Marriage and Family Therapy Education) direct couple, marriage, and family graduate programs and specialty areas to provide students with coursework in the areas of psychopathology, assessment, and diagnosis, controversy has recently surfaced regarding the scope of practice for licensed marriage and family therapists (LMFTs). Specifically, the right for marriage and family therapists (MFTs) to independently diagnose came under scrutiny in the state of Texas (see Caldwell, 2016; Kocian, 2017). While those who engage in relational therapy have often taken issue with the medical profession's focus on individual diagnosis, having their diagnosis rights temporarily removed in a prominent state sent a powerful ripple through the marriage and family therapy profession. Texas, like many other states, has historically allowed MFTs to independently diagnose mental health conditions, despite the omission of the word *diagnosis* in the state mental health statutes. In 2016, the Texas Medical Association sued the Texas State Board of Examiners of Marriage and Family Therapists when the board sought to add the term *diagnosis* to the statewide description of the scope of practice for MFTs. Ultimately, MFTs' right to diagnose was preserved in Texas, and while many states need to add the word *diagnosis* to the MFT scope of practice all states grant MFTs the right to engage in the diagnosis and treatment of mental health disorders (Caldwell, 2016; Kocian, 2017).

The fact that a clinician must, at times, vacillate between the intrapsychic (e.g., individual assessment and diagnosis) and systemic clinical world (e.g., systemic therapy and relational case conceptualization) seems to be in line with systemic and cybernetic theoretical leanings. After all, the notion that some persons or groups of people could control a session, a clinical process, or the direction of the therapeutic world so that it is in line with only one paradigm or theory is inconsistent with being a systemically oriented clinician. The systemic paradigm promotes the notion of a shared process in which reality is perceptually created (Becvar & Becvar, 2013) and is heavily based on context. Contextual factors that appear relevant to the aforementioned example include a systemic clinician's interactions with the medical community, managed care system, statewide licensure laws, insurance companies, and the federal government. To more fully convey the various nuances of being a couple, marriage, and family practitioner, the next section briefly reviews the relevance of various psychological movements to the work of couple, marriage, and family therapy, including psychodynamic, behavioral, humanistic, and cognitive theoretical tenets and interventions.

UNDERSTANDING AND DIFFERENTIATING THE SYSTEMIC PARADIGM

This section explores four waves of psychotherapy (Henriques & Glover, 2012). Retracing the four major movements in the psychotherapy world will provide a foundation for understanding contemporary issues and associated skills. The waves of psychotherapy that will be explored within this chapter are (a) psychoanalytic and psychodynamic therapy, (b) behavior therapy, (c) humanistic therapy, and (d) cognitive therapy. The chapter will also explore pertinent topics related to practice, including theory-based techniques, ethical issues, working with individual clients in a systemic manner, diversity and intersectionality in systemic work, and verbal and nonverbal messages. Please note that the forthcoming sections represent a brief summary of an important therapeutic movement, not a comprehensive review of the various waves of psychotherapy.

OVERVIEW OF PSYCHOANALYTIC AND PSYCHODYNAMIC THERAPY

Psychoanalysis started in Vienna during the last two decades of the 19th century. The impact that Sigmund Freud (1856–1939) and his psychoanalytic approach had on understanding the human mind and how to conduct therapy is unrivaled. He is considered to be the founder of psychoanalysis and of modern psychotherapy. Symbolically, everyone in the therapeutic world stands on the shoulders of Sigmund Freud. Freud's scholarly contributions were vast, including an awesome 23 volumes of his collective work published as the definitive *Standard Edition* (Wolitzky, 2003). In addition to Freud, other important figures who shaped the psychoanalytic/psychodynamic movement include, but are not limited to, Josef Breuer (1842–1925), Alfred Adler (1870–1937), Erik Erikson (1902–1994), Wilhelm Stekel (1868–1940), Sándor Ferenczi (1873–1933), Carl Gustav Jung (1875–1961), Karen Horney (1885–1952), Frieda Fromm-Reichmann (1889–1957), Clara Thompson (1893–1958), Melanie Klein (1882–1960), Otto Rank (1884–1939), Alfred Ernest Jones (1879–1958), Max Eitingon (1881–1943), A. A. Brill (1874–1948), Michael Balint (1896–1970), Wilhelm Reich (1897–1957), Heinz Kohut (1913–1981), and Anna Freud (1895–1982). Each of these individuals made a unique contribution to psychoanalytic/psychodynamic therapy and depth psychology, often departing from Freud's original work. See Table 2.1 for a concise breakdown of the major contributors and the nature of their contributions. Some of these individuals have been identified as neo-Freudians (e.g., Alfred Adler, Erik Erikson, Karen Horney, Carl Gustav Jung), while others have been associated with specific theoretical movements (e.g., Freud's drive psychology, ego psychology, object relations theory, self-psychology, American relational theory; Wolitzky, 2003). Please note that a comprehensive analysis and review of every major psychoanalytic/psychodynamic contributor is beyond the scope of this textbook. For a thorough overview of key figures and principles, please consider reading the *Handbook of Psychodynamic Approaches to Psychopathology* (Luyten et al., 2017) and/or *Psychodynamic Theory for Therapeutic Practice* (Higdon & Higdon, 2011).

Early family therapy pioneers such as Don Jackson (1920–1968), Salvador Minuchin (1921–2017), and Carl Whitaker (1912–1995) dropped their psychoanalytic training and embraced systems theory and case conceptualization. This new version of therapy included a *here and now* focus in which families would outwardly express the relevant nuances of their inner life and past experiences during a given session. This therapeutic trust in the here and now was a massive change from classic psychoanalysis. Namely, a clinician could promote healing without needing to deeply explore a client's personal conflicts and fixations that had occurred earlier in life. From this vantage point, past issues were not buried deep within the unconscious mind but were always at play in the present. While these early systemic revelations were and still are important to the family systems movement, the 1980s saw a surprising shift within the family therapy world as clinicians began to demonstrate a revived interest in depth psychology (psychodynamic, psychoanalytic approaches; Davis & Nichols, 2020). This revival happened for two main reasons: (a) systemic clinicians recognized the importance of personal introspection into

TABLE 2.1 PSYCHOANALYTIC PIONEER, LIFE SPAN, CONTRIBUTION, AND SALIENT PUBLICATION

Contributor	Life Span	Contribution	Salient Publication
Sigmund Freud	1856–1939	Founded the field of psycho-analysis and paved the way for modern psychotherapy	Freud, S. (2010). *The interpretation of dreams: The complete and definitive text* (J. Strachey, Ed. & Trans.). Basic Books (original work published 1900).
Josef Breuer	1842–1925	Developed the *talking cure* and laid the foundation for psychoanalysis	Breuer, J., & Freud, S. (1895). *Studies on hysteria.* Basic Books.
Alfred Adler	1870–1937	Founded the field of individual psychology	Adler, A. (1924). *The practice and theory of individual psychology.* Harcourt Brace.
Erik Erikson	1902–1994	Coined the phrase *identity crisis,* created the *stages of psychoso-cial development*	Erikson, E. H. (1959). *Identity and the life cycle.* Norton.
Wilhelm Stekel	1868–1940	Cofounded the first psycho-analytic society with Freud, contributed significantly to psy-choanalytic theory	Stekel, W. (1950). *Auto-erotism: A psychiatric study of onanism and neu-rosis.* Liveright.
Sándor Ferenczi	1873–1933	Contributed to Freud's psycho-analytic theory	Ferenczi, S., Newton, C., & Rank, O. (1925). *The development of psy-choanalysis.* Nervous and Mental Disease Publishing Company.
Carl Gustav Jung	1875–1961	Founded analytic psychology, developed the theory of the col-lective unconscious	Jung, C. (1921). *Psychological types.* Rascher Verlag.
Karen Horney	1885–1952	Founded feminist psychology and pioneered feminist psychiatry	Horney, K. (1967). *Feminine psychol-ogy.* Norton.
Frieda Fromm-Reichmann	1889–1957	Coined the term *schizophrenic mother,* paved the way for women in psychology and treat-ment of schizophrenia	Fromm-Reichmann, F. (1950). *Prin-ciples of intensive psychotherapy.* University of Chicago Press.
Clara Thompson	1893–1958	Cofounded the William Alanson White Institute, influenced the psychoanalytic practice	Thompson, C. (1950). *Psychoanal-ysis: Evolution and development.* Routledge.
Melanie Klein	1882–1960	Developed object relations the-ory, shaped the psychoanalysis of children	Klein, M. (1932). *The psycho-analysis of children.* Norton.
Otto Rank	1884–1939	Extended Freud's psychoanalytic theory	Rank, O. (1936). *Will therapy: An analysis of the therapeutic process in terms of relationship.* Knopf.
Alfred Ernest Jones	1879–1958	Established both the British Psychoanalytical Society and the American Psychoanalytic Association	Jones, E. (1913). *Papers on psycho-analysis.* Williams & Wilkins.
Max Eitingon	1881–1943	Instrumental in establishing the institutional parameters of psychoanalytic education and training	Eitingon, M. (1912). Genie, talent und psychoanalyse. *Zentralblatt für Psychoanalyse, 2,* 539–540.
A. A. Brill	1874–1948	Initiated the practice of psycho-analysis in the United States	Brill, A. A. (1921). *Fundamental con-ceptions of psychoanalysis.* Green-wood Press.

(continued)

TABLE 2.1 PSYCHOANALYTIC PIONEER, LIFE SPAN, CONTRIBUTION, AND SALIENT PUBLICATION (CONTINUED)

Contributor	Life Span	Contribution	Salient Publication
Michael Balint	1896–1970	Influenced the development of object relations theory, was a leading exponent of the independent group	Balint, M. (1968). *The basic fault: Therapeutic aspects of regression.* Tavistock Publications.
Wilhelm Reich	1897–1957	Played a central role in the development of body psychotherapy, coined the phrase *sexual revolution*	Reich, W. (1933). *Character analysis.* Farrar, Straus and Giroux.
Heinz Kohut	1913–1981	Developed the school of self-psychology	Kohut, H. (1971). *The analysis of the self: A systematic approach to the psychoanalytic treatment of narcissistic personality disorders.* International Universities Press.
Anna Freud	1895–1982	Founded psychoanalytic child psychology, worked significantly within ego psychology	Freud, A. (1937). *The ego and the mechanisms of defense.* Hogarth Press.

Note: This table is not meant to be comprehensive.

the past, and (b) theoretical movements such as object relations embraced family and relationships while also valuing introspection into the past (Davis & Nichols, 2020).

Paradigmatically, psychoanalytic and psychodynamic approaches represent a deterministic (all events are determined by previous ones) and naturalistic (themes are true during a particular time and place) framework. The basic model of psychoanalytic theory is vast, complex, and evolving, and includes multiple theoretical systems that operate together within the human mind. These systems include, but are not limited to, (a) *Eros* (life instinct that motivates pleasure-seeking tendencies) and *Thanatos* (death instinct that motivates the use of aggression); (b) the *topographic theory* (unconscious, preconscious, and conscious levels of the human mind); (c) the *structural theory of personality* (the conflict between ego [reality principle], id [pleasure principle], and superego [perfection principle]); (d) *the dynamic model* (the dynamic interaction between the id, ego, and superego to contend for libidinal energy); and (e) *psychosexual stages of development* (Freud's five stages of sexual drive: oral, anal, phallic, latency, and genital; Prochaska & Norcross, 2018).

Controversial Aspects of Psychoanalysis

The concept of psychosexual stages of development was created and popularized by Sigmund Freud in 1905 in his publication *Three Essays on the Theory of Sexuality*. While this work is important, it has generated controversy in recent decades. Much of the controversy stems from Freud's sexualized view of childhood exploratory behavior, the level of specificity in his notions of certain psychological phenomena (i.e., the Oedipus and Electra complexes), and his bias against girls and women.

The first controversy involves Freud's likening of childhood experiences, fixations, and stages with human sexuality. While oral, anal, and genital exploration and fixation may be natural parts of childhood, Freud took things a step further and viewed these activities as gratifying childhood sexual experiences. For example, during the oral stage of development (birth to 18 months), Freud considered the child's mouth to be their erogenous zone and their sexual gratification to be generated through behaviors like eating, mouth movement, sucking, gumming, and biting. The infant/child must overcome the conflict between their sex drive and the rules of society. Failure to resolve the conflict would result in a fixation later in life (e.g., smoking, nail biting, overeating, sarcasm, verbal hostility; Prochaska & Norcross, 2018).

A second major controversy regarding Freud's psychosexual stages of development involves the gratifying event and fixation that occurs during the phallic stage of development (4–5 years of age). While activities like masturbation and genital fondling are the outward expression of the gratifying activity, Freud postulated that the key event at this stage of development was attraction to the parent of the opposite sex and feelings of anxiety/fear regarding the same-sex parent. Freud's Oedipus complex was centered on boys fearing their father due to their attraction to their mother and an intense *castration anxiety* regarding what the father might do to them if he learned of their desire. Freud simultaneously postulated that girls developed an Electra complex during the phallic stage of development which involved *penis envy*. According to Freud, a girl believes that she once had a penis but that it was removed. To compensate for her loss, the girl wants to have a child with her father. This desire and the girl's fear of her mother's discovery of the desire are at the core of Freud's notion of child development. The concept of penis envy has garnered considerable debate. In short, feminists consider this aspect of his theory to be both distorted and condescending to women and girls (Kelman, 1967).

A third major controversy regarding Freud's theory is his postulation that women never fully progress past the phallic stage of development and always maintain a sense of envy and inferiority. While additional controversies exist within the traditional psychoanalytic model, let's turn our attention to the therapeutic process and techniques.

Psychoanalytic Family Therapy

Psychoanalytic and psychodynamic approaches generally nurture insight by exploring beyond the behavioral level to the unconscious, preconscious, and otherwise unknown motives that individuals have hidden in their minds. While Freud set the stage for psychoanalytic work with notions related to instincts, unconscious, preconscious, and conscious thought, bidding for libidinal energy, and the effects of psychosexual stages of development, object relations theorists and practitioners view infants as needing to be in a relationship with a nurturing and engaging primary caregiver. Impulses, drives, and other intrapsychic phenomena are now viewed as desperate attempts to relate with others (especially a primary caregiver) or the product of past relationship difficulties (Scharff & Scharff, 1991). General psychoanalytic/psychodynamic theory views the family as an interlocking, intrapsychic system. Psychoanalytic treatment involves uncovering and interpreting unconscious impulses and defenses. Family interactions are analyzed so the clinician can identify basic desires, needs, and fears that keep individuals from interacting in an effective way. Families often demonstrate a great deal of defensiveness when in therapy, so it can be a tall order to expect them to explore old wounds, longings, fears, and hidden drives within a family therapy context. To increase trust and safety, therapists establish a trusting and open environment by creating a slow-paced and safe atmosphere that occupies a predictable time and space (Davis & Nichols, 2020).

General psychoanalytic techniques include, but are not limited to, analytic neutrality, free association, interpretation and analysis of dreams, working with resistance, and working with transference (Elzer & Gerlach, 2014; Kernberg, 2004, 2008). Analytic neutrality is both a technique and an attitude toward therapy. Clinicians using the psychoanalytic approach must attempt to be neutral in regard to topics such as religion, ethics, and personal interest. The clinician is nondirective and utilizes an evenly suspended listening style that encourages deeper levels of free association (Gay, 1989). Free association occurs when a practitioner taps into the client's unconscious by exploring spontaneous word association that eventually forms patterns. For example:

> *Therapist:* I'm going to say a string of words, and I want you to say the first thing that comes up for you after each one.

> *Therapist:* Marriage.

> *Client:* Forever.

> *Therapist:* Wife.

> *Client:* Mine.

> *Therapist*: Husband.

> *Client:* Power.

The technique of interpreting and analyzing dreams has been a cornerstone of the psychoanalytic approach since Freud's 1899 book *The Interpretation of Dreams*. This technique is centered on the investigation of repressed thoughts and feelings that are expressed symbolically in a client's dreams. This technique is somewhat related to free association in that the clients are asked to free-associate to content from a dream in order to arrive at its latent content (Kernberg, 2004, 2008). For example:

> *Client:* I keep having this recurring dream that I'm burying a big box. I don't know what's inside it, but every time I try to cover it, it pokes back up.

> *Therapist:* It sounds like you were trying to get rid of something but that it's not ready to be put to rest yet. Let's do some free association around this and see what comes up.

Resistance can be conceptualized as a conscious or unconscious process that hinders the positive process of psychoanalysis. Resistance is anything within the client's mind that opposes the progress of the analysis (Elzer & Gerlach, 2014). Client resistance is common, and there is always a reason for the manner in which the client is responding. Couple, marriage, and family practitioners focus on the client and the client's world to better understand their resistance to counseling (Shallcross, 2010). The forthcoming example demonstrates how a clinician might respond to resistance:

> *Therapist:* Last session, we talked about your relationship with your mother.

> *Client:* I got a dog; did I tell you?

> *Therapist:* Your mother seems to be a difficult subject.

> *Client:* His name is Hank. I love labs. I've always loved dogs. I grew up with dogs. They're really good at picking up on emotions and stuff. Man's best friend, right?

The notion of client transference was initially conceived in psychoanalysis; however, it has since become a cross-theoretical phenomenon that most clinicians acknowledge. Transference has to do with transferring personal unconscious feelings and thoughts onto a new object. The unconscious material used in transference is often retained from childhood (Howes, 2012). In other words, this phenomenon is the transference of feelings from the past to someone in the present, or "the unconscious repetition in the 'here and now' of unconscious, conflicting pathogenic relationships from the past" (Kernberg, 2008, p. 13). This phenomenon is often demonstrated by the client transferring feelings and thoughts onto the therapist. The therapist uses this information to reach deeper into the client's past to create new levels of awareness. For example:

Client: Doug hasn't been coming home on time. I think he's cheating on me. That unfaithful bastard! Men always cheat.

Therapist: Agnes, I recall you mentioning earlier that your ex-husband cheated on you, and that's the reason your marriage ended. Do you think you could be afraid of getting into another serious relationship because of your fear of being cheated on again?

Applying Psychoanalytic and Psychodynamic Theory to Systemic Work

While all the previously covered material is important to consider as one thinks about the relationship between systems theory, practice, and psychoanalysis, object relations theory is a natural bridge between the psychoanalytic and systemic approaches. According to Nichols (2011),

> [a]lthough the details of object relations theory can be quite complicated, its essence is simple: We relate to others on the basis of expectations formed by early experience. The residue of these early relationships leaves internal objects—mental images of self and others built up from experience and expectation (p. 166).

Those who would like to explore the theoretical connection between object relations and family therapy are encouraged to read the following textbooks: *Object Relations Family Therapy* (Scharff & Scharff, 1987) and *Object Relations: A Dynamic Bridge Between Individual and Family Treatment* (Slipp, 1993).

While family systems advocates initially resisted the psychoanalytic approach, there are a few key areas that both schools of thought agree on. First, Solomon's (1973) family-oriented revision to Erikson's (1950) psychoanalytic model of individual development is helpful in conceptualizing the development of the family. Second, it is well-established that Anna O (Josef Breuer's patient who suffered from hysteria) described psychoanalysis as the talking cure (Breuer & Freud, 1957). One of the most important analytic skills used in the process of the talking cure (i.e., psychoanalysis) and family systems work is silence. While the trained analyst may use silence to elicit communication or to observe transference or projection, most practitioners use periods of silence to reduce the therapist's level of activity, provide clients time to think, and return responsibility to the client (Flynn & Hays, 2015). Regardless of the reason for using silence, from both a family systems and psychoanalytic framework it is a very useful technique.

Lastly, most therapeutic schools of thought, including psychoanalysis, acknowledge the power of empathy. The trained psychoanalyst is attempting to connect and empathize with the client's conscious feelings to help them open up and to clarify latent aspects of the family experience. Similarly, most couple, marriage, and family therapy training programs teach emerging practitioners how to use empathy-oriented skills such as reflection of feelings (i.e., the clinician's accurate statement of the feeling initially expressed by the client). Skills such as reflection of feelings and paraphrasing can be viewed as microskills (Ivey et al., 2018) that are key to basic therapeutic competency.

OVERVIEW OF BEHAVIORAL THERAPY

Behaviorism is a powerful form of therapy and intervention. While no single figure is conceptualized as the founder of behavioral therapy, the field has been cocreated by many influential individuals, including, but not limited to, John B. Watson (1878–1958), Rosalie Rayner (1898–1935), Ivan Pavlov (1849–1936), B. F. Skinner (1904–1990), Joseph Wolpe (1915–1997), Edward L. Thorndike (1874–1949), Mary Cover Jones (1897–1987),

Albert Bandura (1925–2021), Edna Foa (b. 1937), Thomas G. Stampfl (1923–2005), John W. Thibaut (1917–1986), and Harold H. Kelley (1921–2003). (Please note that analysis and review of every major contributor to the field of behavioral therapy are beyond the scope of this textbook. For a thorough overview of applied principles, please consider reading *Applied Behavior Analysis, Third Edition* [Cooper et al., 2020] and/or *Behavior Principles in Everyday Life, Fourth Edition* [Baldwin & Baldwin, 2000].) During the 1970s and 1980s, behavioral therapy's cocreated strategies and theoretical tenets were absorbed into various models and integrative approaches (e.g., cognitive behavioral therapy, dialectical behavioral therapy, parent management training). This integration is ongoing, and as a result there is no single theory or unitary group of techniques representing behavioral therapy.

It is hard to imagine where the mental health world would be without behavioral theory and interventions. For example, behaviorism is the backbone of many complex interventions, including, but not limited to, systematic desensitization, sensate focus and other sex therapy interventions, assertiveness training, token economies, biofeedback, bell and pad conditioning (i.e., enuresis treatment), and behavioral contracts. In 1985, Bellack and Hersen listed more than 150 different behavioral strategies for treating various mental health issues (Bellack & Hersen, 1985). One can only imagine how many strategies there are today.

Paradigmatically, behavioral approaches represent a positivistic and postpositivistic epistemologic framework. Behavioral practitioners often consider themselves to be scientists, and they test and study human and animal behaviors (e.g., touch, taste, sight, smell, hearing) to create legitimate data for treatment of mental health concerns. Consequently, behavioral treatment strives to change the factors that are thought to predispose, strengthen, maintain, and/or trigger problematic behaviors. Whether it involves encouraging clients to decrease avoidance of feared situations, eliminating compulsive rituals, improving social skills, changing unhealthy eating patterns, improving a couple's sex life, or enhancing a child's ability to respond to authority, a behavioral therapist works directly with antecedents, behaviors, and consequences of any issue (Antony & Roemer, 2003). Table 2.2 highlights a selection of the most influential behaviorists and identifies the key contributions and a salient publication for each.

TABLE 2.2 BEHAVIORIST, LIFE SPAN, CONTRIBUTION, AND SALIENT PUBLICATION

Contributor	Life Span	Contribution	Salient Publication
John B. Watson	1878–1958	Created the theory of behaviorism/applied behavioral psychology	Watson, J. B. (1913). Psychology as the behaviorist views it. *Psychological Review, 20*(2), 158–177. https://doi.org/10.1037/h0074428.
Rosalie Rayner	1898–1935	Assisted Watson in developing applied behavioral psychology	Watson, J. B., & Rayner, R. (1920). Conditioned emotional reactions. *Journal of Experimental Psychology, 3*(1), 1–14. https://doi.org/10.1037/h0069608.
Ivan Pavlov	1849–1936	Created the Pavlovian/classical conditioning	Pavlov, I. (1926). *Conditioned reflexes.* Read Books Ltd.
B. F. Skinner	1904–1990	Founded the experimental analysis of behavior and operant conditioning	Skinner, B. F. (1938). *The behavior of organisms: An experimental analysis.* Copley.

(continued)

TABLE 2.2 BEHAVIORIST, LIFE SPAN, CONTRIBUTION, AND SALIENT PUBLICATION (*CONTINUED*)

Contributor	Life Span	Contribution	Salient Publication
Joseph Wolpe	1915–1997	Developed the concept of reciprocal inhibition, created the technique of systematic desensitization	Wolpe, J. (1954). Reciprocal inhibition as the main basis of psychotherapeutic effects. *Archives of Neurology and Psychiatry, 72*(2), 205. https://doi.org/10.1001/archneurpsyc.1954.02330020073007.
Edward L. Thorndike	1874–1949	Created the theory of connectionism, helped lay the foundation for educational psychology	Thorndike, E. L. (1898). Animal intelligence: An experimental study of the associative processes in animals. *The Psychological Review: Monograph Supplements, 2*(4), 1–109. https://doi.org/10.1037/h0092987.
Mary Cover Jones	1897–1987	Pioneer of behavior therapy, specialist in child and adolescent development	Jones, M. C. (1924). A laboratory study of fear: The case of Peter. *The Pedagogical Seminary and Journal of Genetic Psychology, 31*(4), 308–315. https://doi.org/10.1080/08856559.1924.9944851.
Albert Bandura	1925–2021	Creator of social learning theory (renamed social cognitive theory) and the theoretical construct of self-efficacy	Bandura, A. (1962). Social learning through imitation. In M. R. Jones (Ed.), *Nebraska symposium on motivation, 1962* (pp. 211–274). University of Nebraska Press.
Edna Foa	b. 1937	Renowned authority within the field of psychopathology and treatment of anxiety	Foa, E. B., & Kozak, M. J. (1986). Emotional processing of fear: Exposure to corrective information. *Psychological Bulletin, 99*(1), 20–35. https://doi.org/10.1037/0033-2909.99.1.20.
Thomas G. Stampfl	1923–2005	Creator of implosive therapy	Stampfl, T. G., & Levis, D. J. (1967). Essentials of implosive therapy: A learning-theory-based psychodynamic behavioral therapy. *Journal of Abnormal Psychology, 72*(6), 496–503. https://doi.org/10.1037/h0025238.
John W. Thibaut	1917–1986	Codeveloped the social exchange theory	Thibaut, J. W., & Kelley, H. H. (1959). *The social psychology of groups*. Wiley.
Harold H. Kelley	1921–2003	Codeveloped the social exchange theory	Thibaut, J. W., & Kelley, H. H. (1959). *The social psychology of groups*. Wiley.

Note: This table is not meant to be comprehensive.

Classical Conditioning

Ivan Pavlov was a Nobel Prize-winning Russian physician/neurophysiologist who famously studied digestive secretions in dogs. His contributions set the stage for what would later be known as Pavlovian or classical conditioning. Andrew Salter's 1949 book *Conditioned Reflex Therapy* is an excellent example of a practitioner actively using the Pavlovian conditioning principles in therapeutic practice. According to Pavlov (1927), Pavlovian conditioning creates physiologic and behavioral change by establishing a predictive relationship between a neutral stimulus and a biologically significant consequence. Pavlov conceptualized that individuals could be conditioned and unconditioned through the interaction of four phenomena: (a) *conditioned stimulus* (CS; learning is needed for this stimulus to elicit a reflexive response), (b) *unconditioned stimulus* (US; no learning is needed for this stimulus to elicit a reflexive response), (c) *conditioned response* (CR; conditioning is necessary for response to occur), and (d) *unconditioned response* (UR; no learning is necessary for this response to occur; Baldwin & Baldwin, 2000). While most are familiar with the experiment involving Pavlov's dogs, classical conditioning can be used in a variety of ways to enhance couple, marriage, and family life. For instance, some couples use classical conditioning to enhance their relational intimacy. For example, partner A pairs the nonsexual comment "I think we should turn off the technology" (CS) and reaches over and gives partner B a foot massage (US). The foot massage (US) creates a sense of relaxation and sexual arousal (UR) within partner B. After enough pairings, whenever partner A states "I think we should turn off the technology" (CS) partner B immediately starts to feel relaxed and sexually aroused (CR). In other words, this arousal does not require the initial unconditioned stimulus (i.e., foot massage).

Counterconditioning

Joseph Wolpe developed procedures centered on the principles of classical conditioning to treat a variety of mental health disorders. Specifically, Wolpe developed *counterconditioning* procedures. Counterconditioning is the weakening and/or eliminating of an undesired response by introducing and strengthening a second response that is incompatible with it. This process reverses the original conditioning by combining extinction (CS is no longer linked with the stimuli from which it was originally conditioned) and new conditioning (CS is associated with a new US or CS that elicits a new response incompatible with the former one). In short, if a response-inhibiting emotion can be made to occur in the presence of anxiety-evoking stimuli, it will weaken the bond between the stimuli and anxiety (Baldwin & Baldwin, 2000; Wolpe, 1958). Wolpe's landmark 1958 book entitled *Reciprocal Inhibition* provides an arsenal of counterconditioning behavioral therapeutic techniques. While Wolpe's work is vast, he is best known for a few key counterconditioning techniques. Examples include systematic desensitization (inhibiting anxiety by combining it with deep muscle relaxation), assertiveness training (inhibiting social anxiety through engaging in assertiveness responses), and sex therapy (inhibiting anxiety by progressing through phases of sexual arousal). Similar to classical conditioning, counterconditioning can be used to help individuals, couples, and families. For example, systematic desensitization could be used to help a man who is having issues with sexual arousal. This would occur by initially asking the client to identify when they first feel intimacy/sex-based anxiety. The clinician would connect gradual desensitization (muscle relaxation, breathing) to the client's visual imagery of anxiety-provoking activities (e.g., impotence just prior to penetration). The relaxation techniques are used progressively as the client works up their identified hierarchy (i.e., progressing from least to most intense) of anxiety-provoking activities (Anderson et al., 1981). When the client imagines an experience that causes considerable anxiety, they are encouraged to go down a level and then move back up when they are better prepared and in a more relaxed state.

Operant Conditioning

Influential American psychologist Burrhus Frederic (B. F.) Skinner made an enormous impact on the psychological world. Skinner's scholarly work ranged from his evolutionary, biologically oriented, language-based 1957 book *Verbal Behavior* to his 1948 quasiscience fiction book *Walden Two*. Using Edward L. Thorndike's Law of Effect as part of his foundation, Skinner created a psychological theory called operant conditioning. Like other behaviorists, Skinner used animal experiments to study his theory. The Skinner Box attempted to objectively record an animal's behavior (e.g., lever pressing, key pecking) in a strict time frame. Skinner identified three main responses that follow a behavior: reinforcement (positive or negative response that increases the probability of a behavior), neutral operant (response that neither increases nor decreases the probability of a behavior being repeated), and punishment (positive or negative response that decreases the likelihood that a behavior will be repeated). Table 2.3 provides a closer look at how operant reinforcement and punishment should be conceptualized. An important caveat to operant conditioning is understanding that reinforcement and punishment are in the eyes of the beholder. An example that demonstrates this notion could be adolescent substance use. From a positive reinforcement perspective (adding something that is desirable), an adolescent may choose to abuse substances to attain approval from peers, increase the courage to engage in intimacy, or get attention from adults. Negative reinforcement (removing something that is undesirable) may come into play because the adolescent is potentially getting out of homework or temporarily escaping a stressful situation with their parents. From a positive punishment perspective (adding something that is undesirable), abusing substances is illegal and could lead to getting arrested and having a police record. Lastly, negative punishment (removing something that is desirable) would become apparent when the adolescent is arrested and loses their freedom and ability to spend time with friends.

It is difficult to discuss the profound influence of B. F. Skinner without mentioning contingency management training. You have probably heard the phrase *contingent relationship* at some point in your education or life. This term refers to the notion that one event is the consequence of another event. Contingencies have natural occurring reinforcers and punishers. For example, a natural contingency that might relate to sleeping late could be the punishments of rushing to work and skipping breakfast (B1→Cp). A natural contingency associated with waking up early could be the positive reinforcer of having the time to go for a jog and enjoy a leisurely breakfast (B2→Cr). Skinner (1953) popularized the three-term contingency, which included antecedents, behaviors, and consequences (A: B→C). Antecedent stimulus occurs first in any contingency and signals that reinforcement or punishment is available on the contingency of a specific behavior. Antecedents do not cause certain behaviors; however, they do set the stage for certain consequences. **B**ehavior is any observable and measurable action. Behavior is also known as an *operant* because it changes the environment in some way. **C**onsequence of the behavior is an experience that follows the behavior and is either reinforcing or punishing in nature. The consequence of a behavior can be a positive/negative reinforcer or a positive/negative punisher. The reinforcing consequences increase the likelihood of behavior reoccurrence, while punishment decreases the likelihood of a behavior. For example, the positive reinforcer of waking up early (behavior) was jogging and enjoying

TABLE 2.3   THE NATURE OF OPERANT REINFORCEMENT AND PUNISHMENT

Add or Subtract	Increase the Likelihood	Decrease the Likelihood
Add (provide)	Positive reinforcement (+)	Positive punishment (+)
	Adding something that is desirable	Adding something undesirable
Subtract (remove)	Negative reinforcement (−)	Negative punishment (−)
	Removing something undesirable	Removing something that is desirable

Note: The words *provide* and *remove* serve as synonyms for add (+) and subtract (−).

TABLE 2.4 BEHAVIORAL SYMBOL, LETTER, AND MEANING KEY

Symbol/Letter	Meaning
A	Antecedent
B	Behavior
C	Consequence
A: B→C	Antecedent sets the stage for behavior and the contingency between the consequence.
B1→Cp	Behavior 1 is contingent upon a consequence that is punishing in nature.
B2→Cr	Behavior 2 is contingent upon a consequence that is reinforcing in nature.

Note: The colon (:) stands for the antecedent. The antecedent sets the stage for the behavior; it does not cause the behavior. The arrow (→) indicates a contingent relationship.

a leisurely breakfast. An antecedent of this contingency could be going to bed early the night before. A key factor is ensuring that the individual understands the relationship (i.e., contingency) between going to bed early **(A)**, waking up early **(B)**, and jogging/ eating a leisurely breakfast **(C)**. There are many different elements to think about when considering increasing or decreasing the power of the reinforcer or the punisher. Two important considerations are timing and repetition. In general, the shorter the delay between the behavior and the consequence, the more impactful the learning will be. For example, while it is easy for most to see the relationship between going to bed early and waking up early with energy, it can be difficult for some high school freshmen to see the connection between studying for a test and getting into a preferable college 4 years in the future. Lastly, the more repetitions people have of the behavior being followed (i.e., paired) with the consequence, the stronger, faster, and longer lasting the learning will be. Behavioral symbols, letters, and meanings are summarized in Table 2.4.

Token economies are an example of a popular contingency management system that relies heavily on operant conditioning (i.e., tokens are turned in for a reinforcer at a later time). Token economies are frequently used to help children at homes and in schools or to help youth within agencies and residential treatment centers. They are also some- times used in psychiatric inpatient hospitals. All clinicians, regardless of theoretical leaning(s) and specialization(s), should understand the nuances of an effective token economy. A token economy is a complicated, highly organized, and detailed exchange system that uses tokens (symbolic reinforcers) that can be exchanged for an item (direct reinforcement). Effective economies clearly describe the target behaviors that people must do to earn tokens and the rate of responding that is required to earn a certain num- ber of tokens. Token economies can be highly detailed and tailored to a single person or segment of a group, or used in a more general way with a large group of individuals. The number of tokens that must be submitted to attain a particular item depends on the value of the item. In this sense, the value of the item is in the eye(s) of the behold- er(s). For example, when used with children, many items have high symbolic value and low monetary value (e.g., lunch with the teacher, more recess time, conducting the morning announcements). While a basketball may cost the most money on a particular token economy, it may require fewer tokens than conducting the morning announce- ments (Ayllon & Azrin, 1968; Prochaska & Norcross, 2018). Token economies are geared toward achieving the targeted baseline behavior. As behaviors improve and rules are consistently followed, the economy will be faded. The use of social reinforcers, token reinforcers, and the gradual spacing of positive reinforcers all play into effective fading. Table 2.5 outlines nine considerations to contemplate when creating a token economy.

TABLE 2.5 TOKEN ECONOMY CONSIDERATIONS AND RELEVANCE

Consideration	*Relevance*
Select the token.	Choose something safe and durable that will be turned in later for the reinforcement. The token should have no intrinsic value (e.g., poker chip, hole punch, sticker, stamp, mark on a board). Establish a policy regarding lost tokens; for example, "Lost tokens will not be replaced." There are problems with physical tokens (e.g., they get lost, tend to be stolen, are sometimes counterfeited, students will play with them or count them in class). Make rules about trading tokens (e.g., "There will be no trading of tokens").
Select behaviors to change.	The behavior should be observable and measurable. The token economy will be more powerful if the behavior is individualized to the participant. Be careful to avoid externally rewarding participants for things they are already internally motivated to do.
Select backup reinforcers.	This is what participants turn in their tokens for. Be creative, have a wide variety, and use both tangibles and intangibles. Include items that have different values. Some should be small and inexpensive, while others require participants to save up for something that has a higher value and is more expensive. Start with a richer schedule of reinforcement that you can always thin out later.
Select the frequency of reinforcers.	Participants do not have to be able to buy something every day; however, it should not take a long time to save up enough tokens to redeem. Every participant should be able to earn at least one token every day; if they cannot, your schedule is too lean. Even participants who are struggling should be able to buy something. Put something expensive on the menu that someone can get if they really save up (e.g., 225 tokens for a basketball). Do not rely on a *raincheck* system—participants need to redeem the tokens at store time.
Decide how tokens will be dispensed.	Token dispensing should be a consistent and predictable occurrence. It might be too disruptive to pass out tokens throughout the day, so perhaps you make a mark on the dry-erase board and distribute the tokens later in the day. Physical tokens should be kept away from participants until shopping time. For example, you could use an easel and have an envelope for each participant.
Decide how the store works.	You must consider an appropriate shopping time that minimizes disruption (e.g., once a week, every day). You could use a motivator to determine order (e.g., "The row that is the quietest will go first"). Post a menu early to expedite the buying process.
Decide how to turn in tokens.	This will depend on whether you are using physical tokens or a chart. If possible, you should be the one taking the tokens out of each participant's envelope.
Decide whether you want to use response cost.	A response cost is charged when somebody loses a token that has already been earned. Response cost is a punishment, and it is optional. The advantages are that it changes behavior quickly and allows the staff member/teacher to avoid direct confrontation with the participant. The disadvantages are that it can increase aggressiveness and losing points/tokens can negatively impact other behaviors.
Decide how to handle hoarding.	Participants cannot hoard their tokens. This only pertains to those who have more tokens than the highest priced item. Potential solutions include taxing your tokens a certain percent, creating an expiration date if tokens are not used, or scheduling a sale to motivate shopping (e.g., 25% off, 2 for the price of 1 sale).

Source: Data from Baldwin, J. D., & Baldwin, J. I. (2000). *Behavior principles in everyday life*. Prentice Hall.

Self-Efficacy and Modeling

Psychologist Albert Bandura's research (e.g., Bobo doll; Bandura et al., 1961) and theories (e.g., social learning theory [later renamed social cognitive theory] and self-efficacy) made a large and lasting impact on psychology and helped shift the direction of behaviorism to a more cognitive–behavioral integration. While often associated with behaviorism, Bandura does not appear to truly fit in the behavioral camp. Throughout his career, Bandura theorized that operant and classical conditioning phenomena have associated cognitive processes. Bandura's scholarship has emphasized cognition, social influences, and personal control. First, Bandura's social cognitive theory postulated that learning is observational, and it often involves modeling and imitation. Bandura's famous Bobo doll study made a significant impact within the behavioral and psychological world because children were observing and imitating others without reinforcers, punishments, or conditioned stimuli. According to Bandura and Walters (1977), when children watched adults beating up a Bobo doll, they were much more likely to do it as well. While there is much more to this landmark research, the general findings were centered on learning through imitation and social modeling. The process of observational learning encompassed attention, retention, reciprocation, and motivation. Regarding modeling, Bandura described two major types: live (i.e., someone you come into contact with) and symbolic (e.g., someone you encounter online, see on television, read about in books, or observe in sports events). Modeling-based learning could include things like observing motor behaviors (e.g., tying shoes, driving a car), interpersonal behaviors (e.g., dating, gaining social acceptance), cognitive behaviors (e.g., problem-solving strategies, understanding regional accents), and emotional behaviors (e.g., becoming afraid when you notice that someone else is afraid; when one baby starts crying, other babies start crying).

Understanding modeling is particularly important for couple, marriage, and family practitioners who work with children and parents. This theory reminds families that children are always watching and learning. Let's take a closer look at a few of the major outcomes associated with Bandura's modeling theory. Many of these outcomes are somewhat related to operant and classical conditioning and involve learning new operant behavior. Two potential outcomes of modeling include the inhibition or disinhibition of previously learned operant behavior. This includes previously acquired behaviors that someone uses now or does not use in a new situation because of modeling. From an inhibition and punishment perspective, this could include refraining from behaviors after witnessing others being punished for doing them (i.e., vicarious punishment). An example of this might be witnessing someone being rejected by their peer group after making an insensitive joke. Disinhibition (vicarious reinforcement) occurs when someone knows they are doing something that is socially incorrect but still gets away with it. This will increase the likelihood that they will engage in the observed behavior. For example, a driver might break the speed limit after watching someone who was speeding drive by a police officer and not get pulled over. While Bandura postulated many more, two additional examples of consequences of modeling are response facilitation of the operant behavior and the vicarious respondent reflexive behavior. With response facilitation, learners are looking to see if the behaviors of someone they are observing are reinforced positively. For example, a student might watch someone stand up in class and walk out halfway through without getting criticized by the teacher. One final potential outcome of modeling is vicarious respondent reflexive behavior. This occurs when someone produces a reflexive response because of something that happens to someone else. For example, when you see someone else yawn, you might yawn. This is associated with classical conditioning because it is a reflexive response.

The cognitive leanings of Albert Bandura came into full bloom with his work on self-efficacy. Supporting the development of self-efficacy greatly enhances people's lives and can be salient to being a high-impact, influential, and inspirational therapist. Working with couples, families, children, parents, and individuals to facilitate a sense of self-efficacy and resilience in the face of all of their doubts will help them reach their goals and perform at an optimal level. According to Bandura (1995), "[t]he striving for control over life circumstances permeates almost everything people do because it can secure them innumerable personal and social benefits. . . . Inability to exert influence over things that adversely affect one's life breeds apprehension, apathy, or despair" (p. 1). The construct of self-efficacy refers to one's active capabilities to produce a specific result in life. This cognitive process is centered on beliefs about one's ability to achieve designated levels of performance that create some control over the elements in one's life. In contrast, people who question and fail to trust their capabilities avoid difficult challenges and responsibilities, which they often view in a fearful manner. You may be asking yourself, "How can I create more self-efficacy in my clients' lives?" Bandura theorized four main sources of efficacy beliefs: (a) mastery experiences (successful experiences), (b) vicarious experiences provided by social models (seeing people similar to you succeed increases your ability to achieve success), (c) social persuasion (being persuaded by others that you can do something), and (d) stress reaction reduction (reducing your stress and viewing arousal as a motivating factor; Bandura, 1995). An example of self-efficacy in an institutional context would be a student with a learning disability involving mathematics considering whether they should take a high-level mathematical elective that would likely help them fulfill their future career aspirations. Despite their issue with having a learning disability, they have enrolled in relevant courses that were outside of their comfort zone in the past and have been successful (i.e., mastery experience). In speaking with their advisor, the student is encouraged to go for it. The advisor mentions that the instructor is supportive, kind, has high standards, and will make accommodations for students with documented learning disabilities (i.e., social persuasion). Despite the potential difficulties, the student chooses to enroll in the course. After passing the course with a solid grade, the student's sense of academic and mathematical self-efficacy has been boosted to a higher level.

Applying Behaviorism to Systemic Work

When systemically oriented clinicians implement a behavioral contract, contingency management system, problem-solving technique, communication training, or homework assignment, they are augmenting their systemic therapeutic modality with a behavioral technique. According to Lester et al. (1980), "techniques are needed to interrupt coercive relationships and reciprocal exchanges of negative behavior as well as to foster reciprocal exchanges of positive behavior" (p. 189). While there may be few couple, marriage, and family practitioners who identify as pure behaviorists, most clinicians, agencies, and hospitals freely and frequently use behavioral techniques to augment their theoretical leanings. Behavioral techniques in these contexts might include (a) teaching individuals to solve problems using specific words, (b) teaching couples effective communication skills, or (c) contracting.

Teaching individuals to solve problems using specific words is an important behavioral intervention that typically consists of three parts: (a) deciding and stating the problem, (b) writing a list of potential solutions, and (c) reaching consensus on a final solution. This intervention is often implemented because the couple/family members are using hurtful, vague, emotional words that do not lend themselves to workable solutions, or because the couple/family members use very general terms that make an issue seem unsolvable (e.g., "We just don't get along"). Behaviorists may teach the couple/family how to use specific, descriptive, and behavioral terms when discussing the issue (e.g., "I feel we don't get along because he constantly interrupts me when I'm talking and never asks me how I'm doing"; Crisp & Knox, 2008; Lester et al., 1980).

Behavioral communication coaching is a second behavioral technique commonly employed by couple, marriage, and family practitioners regardless of theoretical orientation. Throughout therapeutic contact, the couple's problematic communication is monitored, and when the therapist notices a problematic interaction they will stop the couple and instruct them on how to communicate in a more effective manner. This typically involves labeling the problematic interaction, providing a rationale for why this form of communication is problematic, and working with the couple to implement a more effective form of communication. In addition to pointing out problematic communication patterns and teaching clients how to communicate in a more effective manner, the therapist also notices and encourages the good communication that the individuals are making. This typically involves labeling a positive communication pattern and explaining why it is positive (Crisp & Knox, 2008; Lester et al., 1980).

Whether a contract is made in a *quid pro quo* format (the reward for one partner's change is the other partner's change in behavior) or a *good faith* format (change in one partner is not contingent on the change in the other), the goal is making changes and increasing positive reinforcement between the individuals involved (Crisp & Knox, 2008; Lester et al., 1980). Often, behavioral contracts are written and signed with the counselor present. Good-faith contracts are set up with a problem-solving reinforcement format. After the partner changes a behavior, the other partner reinforces the person who changed. The reinforcement the other partner provides must not be aversive in nature. For example, one partner has agreed to wake up early and get a child ready for school and the other partner reinforces this commitment by taking a 15-minute walk with the partner at the end of the day. While the good-faith contract is easy, it may be limited by the number of reinforcers available to be linked to behavioral change. The quid pro quo contract is more complicated because the behavior change stops after one partner ignores or fails to perform their part of the contractual arrangement. This form of contract is augmented with the stipulation that there is a cycle that goes into effect on a regular basis. In other words, if one side of the contract is left unfulfilled, the other aspect is also stopped for one day. The new cycle will begin the next day.

OVERVIEW OF HUMANISTIC THERAPY

While the 1970s were the heyday of humanistic psychology, today humanism is a well-established wave of psychology that encompasses a large number of theories, models, techniques, and approaches. Overall, these approaches emphasize the holistic nature of the human condition, show respect for the entirety of each individual (i.e., antireductionistic and antimechanistic view), place a high value on a client's emotional world, acknowledge the client and the counselor as persons of worth, and of course the clinical hallmark of the humanistic wave was and still is the cocreation of a meaningful and empathic therapeutic relationship. The way the humanistic wave typically enters a practitioner's theoretical and skill-based position is through foundational counseling microskills training (e.g., invitational skills, attending skills, certain influencing skills; Flynn & Hays, 2015), person-centered therapy and theory, and other closely related experiential and existential psychotherapies (e.g., gestalt therapy, emotionally focused therapy, Satir's growth model, the symbolic-experiential approach to therapy, American and European existentialism). Person-centered therapy and theory and the additional aforementioned experiential and existential approaches are examples of humanistic psychotherapies. As is true for behaviorism, there is no single figure that is conceptualized as the founder of humanistic therapy. It has been cocreated by many influential individuals, including, but not limited to, Carl Rogers (1902–1987), Abraham Maslow (1908–1970), Otto Rank (1884–1939), Fritz Perls (1893–1970), Virginia Satir (1916–1988),

TABLE 2.6 HUMANIST, LIFE SPAN, CONTRIBUTION, AND SALIENT PUBLICATION

Contributor	Life Span	Contribution	Salient Publication
Abraham Maslow	1908–1970	Created the theory of pre-potent needs (i.e., Maslow's hierarchy of needs)	Maslow, A. H. (1943). A theory of human motivation. *Psychological Review, 50*(4), 370–396. https://doi.org/10.1037/h0054346.
Carl Rogers	1902–1987	Founder of client-centered theory and therapy, and considered one of the founding fathers of psychotherapy research	Rogers, C. R., & Koch, S. (1959). *A theory of therapy, personality, and interpersonal relationships, as developed in the client-centered framework.* McGraw Hill.
Otto Rank	1884–1939	A pioneer in the areas of existential, transpersonal, psychoanalytic, and gestalt psychology	Rank, O. (1936). *Will therapy: An analysis of the therapeutic process in terms of relationship.* Knopf.
Fritz Perls	1893–1970	Cofounder of gestalt therapy	Perls, F., Hefferline, R. E., & Goodman, P. (1951). *Gestalt therapy: Excitement and growth in the human personality.* Dell.
Virginia Satir	1916–1988	Considered the "Mother of Family Therapy," created the Virginia Satir change process model	Satir, V. M. (1964). *Conjoint family therapy: A guide to theory and technique.* Science and Behavior Books.
Carl Whitaker	1912–1995	Founder of symbolic experiential family therapy	Whitaker, C. A., & Bumberry, W. M. (1988). *Dancing with the family: A symbolic-experiential approach.* Routledge.

Note: This table is not meant to be comprehensive.

and Carl Whitaker (1912–1995). Table 2.6 highlights some of the most influential humanists, their key contributions, and salient publications.

Paradigmatically, humanistic-oriented theories and therapies are influenced by subjectivity, constructionism, and social constructivism. While there are many nuances, variations, and deviations, humanism is considered a subjectivism-based paradigm. Furthermore, theoretically most humanistic approaches have been heavily influenced by phenomenology. Humanistic practitioners often value phenomena such as free will, agency, personhood, self-actualization, context, the client's worldview, and the notion that truth resides in one's own subjective vantage point (Scholl et al., 2012). Additionally, Scholl et al. (2013) have described humanism as entailing four growth-oriented principles: (a) antireductionism and viewing others as whole beings, (b) individualism, (c) valuing subjective experiences, and (d) respecting the dignity of the individual. The paradigmatic philosophy and the key theoretical principles underscore everything that emerges within the humanistic world.

Humanistic psychology is far from outdated. While humanism is a psychological perspective that emerged around the mid-20th century, it continues to be reflected in important contemporary trends, including, but not limited to, humanistic-oriented journals celebrating new contemporary scholarship and societies, clinical information, tools, and models. Important scholarly journals that promote the humanistic movement include *The Journal of Humanistic Counseling, Journal of Humanistic Psychology, The Humanistic Psychologist, The Person-Centered Journal, Person-Centered and Experiential Psychotherapies,* and the *Journal of Creativity in Mental Health.* Within the American Psychological Association and the American Counseling Association (ACA), contemporary humanistic events, training, scholarship, and information are disseminated through the Society for Humanistic Psychology (American Psychological Association Division 32) and the Association for Humanistic Counseling (ACA Division).

Client-Centered Therapy

Carl Rogers was an American psychologist who is considered the founder of client-centered approach, one of the founders of the humanistic movement, and a pioneer of psychotherapy research (Bohart, 2003). As an author, Rogers is known for two highly influential books: *On Becoming a Person: A Therapist's View of Psychotherapy* (1961) and *A Way of Being* (1980). Rogers was also one of the first helping professionals to apply positive psychology to his theory and practice (e.g., recognizing the fully functioning person). While entire books have been written on Carl Rogers and the client-centered approach, this section will focus on some of his basic theoretical ideas and core skills.

It is extremely difficult to imagine the therapeutic world without the influence of Carl Rogers. As one considers his influence, the notions of the therapeutic relationship/alliance, empathy, awareness, congruence, genuineness, unconditional positive regard, conditions of worth, and nondirective therapy all come to mind. Heavily influenced by his childhood experiences, his own interactions with clients, and Rankian ideas emphasizing creativity, human potential, acceptance of self, and the notion that the client is the center of the treatment process and that the client is their own counselor (Raskin & Rogers, 1989), Rogers made an enormous mark on the therapeutic world. According to Bohart (2003), the person-centered approach was "characterized by a fundamental emphasis on non-directiveness: The goal was to create a permissive, non-interventive atmosphere. The major therapeutic 'interventions' were acceptance and clarification. In the 1950s, empathic understanding of the client increasingly came to be emphasized" (p. 108). Lastly, the client-centered approach emphasizes self-actualization. According to Rogers (1963), every person strives to be a creative and *fully functioning being* who endeavors to reach their potential. This effort to actualize is ongoing, motivational, and innate.

Client-centered theory and skills have truly stood the test of time. While it is unclear how many counselors consider themselves to be purely person-centered, the core counseling skills that are often required in training programs are person-centered in nature. A few of these skills include nonverbal communication, silence, reflection of feeling, reflection of meaning, paraphrasing, open-ended questioning, immediacy, confrontation, clarification, self-disclosure, and summarization (Flynn & Hays, 2015). Individuals practicing counseling from a client-centered theoretical perspective encourage clients to take the lead during sessions (i.e., nondirective therapy), with the counselor serving as a traveling partner and mirror reflecting what the client has stated. Prolific author and humanist Robert R. Carkhuff was a student of Rogers who helped organize and disseminate some of his most salient therapeutic skills and dispositions while developing his own model, the Carkhuff method. Carkhuff believed it was essential for any helping professional to use the following skills: accurate empathy, genuine respect, concreteness, self-disclosure, confrontation, and immediacy (Carkhuff & Benoit, 2019). The following are definitions and examples of core client-centered skills (Carkhuff & Benoit, 2019; Flynn & Hays, 2015; Rogers, 1970). All of these skills are used by the clinician to create a strong therapeutic alliance with the client.

Nonverbal Communication

The therapist flexibly uses variations in nonverbal communication given the client's cultural background; is culturally and contextually appropriate with eye contact, facial expression, posture, and spatial distance; maintains open and relaxed posture; and conveys professionalism in appearance and attire.

Silence

The therapist uses unfilled pauses or periods of silence to serve various functions in the therapy sessions (e.g., reducing own level of activity, slowing down session pace, giving the client time to think, and returning responsibility to the client). For example:

Client: I don't know . . . I'm just not sure what to do about it (tearful about recent breakup). I just just . . .

Clinician: (attentive nonverbals and giving client space to figure out the issue).

Clarification

The therapist asks the client to elaborate on vague, ambiguous, or implied statements, with the request for clarification usually expressed as a question beginning with phrases such as "Are you saying this?" or "Could you try to describe that?" or "Can you clarify that?" For example:

Client: They always put me down and never give me a chance.

Clinician: When you say *they*, who do you mean?

Client: My friends John and Pete.

Reflection of Feelings

The therapist states succinctly the feeling and the content of the problem expressed by the client on the implied and stated level, adding to a paraphrase an emotional tone and/or feeling word (e.g., hurt, mad, sad, jealous, confused, terrified, scared). For example:

Client: I'm so tired of everything. I'm working so hard. My kids need me to be a dad. My graduate program is so much work that I feel like I'm going to have a heart attack.

Clinician: John, you're feeling torn. Part of you really wants to be close to your family and take care of those closest to you. The other part is trying to survive your graduate program.

Immediacy

The therapist recognizes here and now feelings, expressing verbally something occurring at a particular moment within the session, and makes note of patterns, themes, client/counselor relationship issues, and discussion of currently experienced emotions. For example:

Client: I guess so . . . I'm not really sure. I like the idea of happiness, yet . . . I don't really see things the way you do.

Clinician: You find yourself having mixed reactions to what I say. One side wants to agree, the other to disagree.

Confrontation and Pointing Out Discrepancies

The therapist describes discrepancies, conflicts, and mixed messages apparent in the client's feelings, thoughts, and action. For example:

Client: I'm actually very invested in getting my assignments in on time.

Clinician: You say your work is in on time, yet you have three assignments overdue.

Self-Disclosure

The therapist provides both direct and indirect self-disclosures appropriately in a manner that fosters rapport-building, feelings of universality, therapeutic trust, and hope. Self-disclosure is not used for the counselor's personal gain. For example:

> *Client:* I tried so hard to do the right thing, but I just couldn't seem to keep her happy.
>
> *Clinician:* Fawn, I have been in a similar situation, and it took me a long time to realize that it wasn't my fault, that no matter what or how much I did, my partner still would have left.

Concreteness

The therapist moves from abstract to specific information, attempting to be concrete to connect directly with the client's experience. This fosters a sense of understanding in the relationship. For example:

> *Client:* I am completely overwhelmed. My job is giving me extra work, I didn't sleep well, and I am so lonely! It seems like the whole world is out to get me.
>
> *Clinician:* I can tell that you are very stressed. Let's organize the issues you presented and focus on one at a time.

Genuineness

The therapist engages in authentic contact with the client, providing genuine and congruent communication.

The Growth Model

The late Virginia Satir has been honored with the title "Mother of Family Therapy." Satir was an author, family therapist, and pioneer of the family therapy and humanistic movement. As a scholar, she is best known for her books *Conjoint Family Therapy* (1964), *Peoplemaking* (1972), and *The New Peoplemaking* (1988). Her experiential, humanistic family systems approach is growth-oriented and transformative. Similar to Carl Rogers, Virginia Satir believed that change is possible for all human beings. In contrast with behaviorists, Satir believed that events are interconnected rather than linear in cause and effect. All human beings come into the world with intrinsic value, yet family rules, incongruent or dysfunctional communication, and repression of feelings and emotions block the freedom to grow and change. Satir described the hierarchical *threat and reward model* and contrasted it with her growth model or the *seed model*. In the threat and reward model, people take on dominant and submissive roles, and these roles shape their identities as they fulfill expectations. People conform to expectations and obey rules to maintain the status quo. Since there is only one defined right way in this model, events have a linear cause and effect. Unlike the hierarchy of the threat and reward model, Satir's growth model posits that all human beings are equal and have the potential to be whole. Rather than conforming to a mold, people are unique, yet "we are all manifestations of the same life force" (Satir et al., 1991, p. 17).

Satir portrayed the interplay of mind and body using the personal mandala as a symbol, with an individual, the I, at the center of eight universal human resources: the body, physical; the left brain, intellectual; the right brain, emotional; the five senses, sensual; communication with self and others, interactional; food and drink, nutritional; the immediate environment, contextual; and connection to life force and energy, spiritual. Stress occurs when any of these aspects of self are denied or dismissed—a truly systemic model. Since these universal human resources are interwoven, there are "no simple cause-and-effect answers, only a process for discovery" (Satir et al., 1991, p. 279).

Satir postulated that positive self-worth is the foundation of mental health for individuals and families. A high level of self-esteem is essential for a good life and healthy functioning. Healthy individuals and families are in touch with their feelings and needs and act and speak with a sense of congruence and connection with their feelings and needs. Satir outlined five freedoms: "[t]he freedom to see and hear what is here, instead of what should be, was, or will be; the freedom to say what you feel and think, instead of what you should; the freedom to feel what you feel, instead of what you ought; the freedom to ask for what you want, instead of always waiting for permission; the freedom to take risks on your own behalf, instead of choosing to be only secure and not rocking the boat" (Satir, 1995, p. 62). Closed systems, which reflect the threat and reward model, do not recognize or allow these freedoms to thrive, preventing growth and change. Consistent with the five freedoms, open systems, which reflect the seed model or the growth model, allow for open, clear communication, flexible, up-to-date rules, and constructive choices and change. The skills described in the following are based on the Satir model of family therapy (i.e., the seed model; Satir, 1972; Walsh & McGraw, 2002). All of these skills are used by the experiential family therapist to create awareness and build a strong therapeutic alliance with the family.

Active Engagement by Therapist

The therapist uses directives to help family members engage with each other, express their feelings, and interact in a way that may include compassionate touch. For example:

> *Clinician:* I noticed when Gunther talks about your relationship with your son, you sigh and look away. Can you tell me what you're thinking?

> *Client:* I'm thinking that he is so critical of my parenting, and I'm wondering why he doesn't support me when Xavier acts out. I worry so much about him and I hardly know if I'm doing the right thing. I feel so alone.

> *Clinician:* Okay, now I want you to look at Gunther and repeat what you just said.

Ropes

The therapist uses metaphors to communicate the connections and dynamics between family members. The use of a physical rope with family members demonstrates relational interconnections, dependency, and responsibility. Each family member holds the rope, and the therapist can manipulate the scenario to demonstrate familial phenomena (e.g., boundaries, hierarchy, and communication patterns). The use of a rope also breaks down defenses and stagnation, and increases a sense of creativity in exploring novel ways of thinking. For example:

> *Clinician:* Let's use the ropes to better understand the issue. As a reminder, these ropes should be used in a variety of ways to demonstrate what's going on in your relationship.

> *Client A:* Okay, I remember this from a few sessions ago.

> *Client B:* Let's give it a shot.

> *Clinician:* Stephen, I would like you to hold one end of the rope, and Esther, I would like you to hold the other. Please hold the rope in a way that symbolically demonstrates your relationship.

Client A: Okay, I think I understand…

Clinician: I notice that the two of you are standing somewhat apart from each other. The rope is slumped in the middle, and you are each holding the rope casually with one hand.

Client B: What does all this mean for us?

Clinician: It could mean many things. For example, the slump in the middle and casually holding the rope with one hand symbolizes a distant and loose relationship. In addition, the slump in the middle indicates that there is enough slack in the relationship and each of you can move about independently.

Reframing

The therapist offers a new way of looking at a situation to potentially change the perceptions of family members. By promoting the notion that there are good intentions behind certain behaviors, the therapist decreases blame and scapegoating. For example:

Client: As you can see, Jason is just getting in trouble everywhere with everyone.

Clinician: I hear that you are upset by this. Jason, I am impressed with how you have selflessly been the focus of the family so that no one will notice your parents' arguments.

Humor

Humor can be used to promote connection between the individuals engaging in therapy, to lessen intensity, to clarify or amplify a dynamic, and to encourage therapeutic contact in a way that reduces defensiveness. For example:

Client A: I want to be able to both watch TV and talk with Janet, but I can't seem to do it.

Client B: You don't even try. You know how important it is for me that you listen to what I'm saying.

Clinician: Brian, I can imagine that when you are watching TV and Janet has said something important to you but you didn't absorb the info, there is a reaction.

Client A: Oh yeah! She'll ask me a question and I won't know what to say.

Clinician: I imagine you're kind of like a duck. Above the water you look calm and cool, but below the surface your legs are moving wildly (couple laughs).

Family Rules

The therapist raises awareness and understanding of problematic or outdated family rules so members can modify them. The therapist indicates that rules are spoken or unspoken expectations for how to behave, communicate, and cohabitate. The therapist also communicates to families the evolving nature of rules and how they change during developmental stages. Lastly, parents are encouraged to communicate rules clearly and in a manner that fosters understanding among children.

Clinician: Greg and Martha appear to think the rule around an 8:00pm curfew is outdated. Joyce, what do you think about this concern?

Client A: I think that there can be some flexibility on weekend nights. Maybe 10:00pm.

Clinician: Your mom is interested in maintaining an 8:00pm curfew on school nights and possibly extending your curfew to 10:00pm during the weekend.

Client B: That's an improvement.

OVERVIEW OF COGNITIVE THERAPY

Cognitive psychotherapy is a form of counseling that is based on the notion that psychological problems can be partly explained by faulty ways of thinking and distorted cognitions about self, others, and the world. The cognitive therapy approach is relevant to contemporary systemic practice. Cognitive and cognitive behavioral family therapists can use any of the aforementioned behavioral interventions within the context of a multiperson session. Cognitive family therapy is conducted in tandem with systemic therapy and simultaneously focuses on systemic interaction and the cognitions of individual family members. The goal of treatment is to replace faulty and dysfunctional cognitions with adaptive and healthy ones (i.e., cognitive restructuring; American Psychological Association, 2020). This form of therapy has attracted a tremendous amount of attention over the past 45 years. This shift in focus is often described as the *cognitive revolution* due to the 1956 Massachusetts Institute of Technology (MIT) symposium on information processing and the tremendous number of scholarly contributions from early cognitive theorists and researchers (Reinecke et al., 2003). Like the previously reviewed theory-based sections, the cognitive branch of psychotherapy has successfully been applied to a variety of therapeutic models and psychopathology. Further, it is clear in today's contemporary light that one of the contributions for which cognitive psychotherapies will be most remembered is their influence on various integrative approaches to treatment, especially cognitive behavioral therapy. A few of the influential individuals who helped create cognitive therapy include, but are not limited to, George Kelly (1905–1967), Albert Bandura (1925–2021), Albert Ellis (1913–2007), Aaron T. Beck (b. 1921), Donald Meichenbaum (b. 1940), Arnold Lazarus (1932–2013), and Martin Seligman (b. 1942). Table 2.7 lists these individuals, describes their impact, and mentions a salient publication written by each therapist.

Cognitive Distortions and Irrational Beliefs

One area that cuts across most cognitive camps is the notion of cognitive distortions and/or irrational beliefs. In addition, graduate students in the helping professions and clients almost always find that descriptions of these various distortions/irrational beliefs are extremely helpful and interesting when they are introduced in class or in session. You may be wondering, "Why do people find these maladaptive cognitions interesting?" First, all of our experiences in life are influenced by prior events, our current emotional state, and our current attentional capacities (i.e., some experiences are attended to, while others are overlooked). As such, it is not uncommon for an individual's thoughts to become irrational and/or distorted. While Ellis considered his irrational beliefs to come from early childhood experiences (Ellis et al., 2010), Beck conceptualizes cognitive distortions as an unhelpful way to cope with adverse life events (Beck, 1967). Some of these thoughts may become adaptive, while others turn out to be maladaptive. Maladaptive cognitions often become a focal point in treatment and are also sprinkled through many of the criteria for emotional disorders within the *Diagnostic and Statistical Manual of Mental Disorders (DSM) I–5-TR* and the *International Statistical Classification of Diseases and Related Health Problems (ICD)*. The cognitive-oriented practitioner will work with clients to create awareness around these cognitions and to recognize how they

TABLE 2.7 COGNITIVE THERAPIST, LIFE SPAN, CONTRIBUTION, AND SALIENT PUBLICATION

Contributor	Life Span	Contribution	Salient Publication
George Kelly	1905–1967	"Father of Cognitive Clinical Psychology," best known for his theory of personal construct psychology	Kelly, G. (1963). *Theory of personality: The psychology of personal constructs*. Norton.
Albert Bandura	1925–2021	Creator of social learning theory (renamed social cognitive theory) and the theoretical construct of self-efficacy	Bandura, A. (1962). Social learning through imitation. In M. R. Jones (Ed.), *Nebraska symposium on motivation, 1962* (pp. 211–274). University of Nebraska Press.
Albert Ellis	1913–2007	Founded rational emotive behavioral therapy	Ellis, A., & Greiger, R. (1977). *Handbook of rational-emotive therapy*. Springer Publishing Company.
Aaron T. Beck	b. 1921	"Father of Cognitive Therapy and Cognitive Behavioral Therapy," developed the Beck Depression Inventory	Beck, A. T., Rush, A. J., Shaw, B. F., & Emery, G. (1978). *Cognitive therapy of depression*. Guilford Press.
Donald Meichenbaum	b. 1941	Developed cognitive behavioral modification, helped Beck develop cognitive behavioral therapy	Meichenbaum, D. (1977). Cognitive behaviour modification. *Scandinavian Journal of Behaviour Therapy*, 6(4), 185–192. https://doi.org/10.1080/16506073.1977.9626708.
Arnold Lazarus	1932–2013	Developed multimodal therapy	Lazarus, A. A. (1981). *The practice of multimodal therapy: Systematic, comprehensive, and effective psychotherapy*. The Johns Hopkins University Press.
Martin Seligman	b. 1942	Developed the theory of learned helplessness, leader in the positive psychology movement	Seligman, M. (1992). *Helplessness: On depression, development, and death*. Freeman.

Note: This table is not meant to be comprehensive.

affect their day-to-day lives. As practitioners and clients carefully scrutinize particular thought patterns, distortions, and irrational beliefs, they will consider whether they want to work on changing to a more adaptive thought process. Table 2.8 breaks down common distortions and irrational beliefs.

Rational Emotive Behavior Therapy

Albert Ellis was an American psychologist and founder of rational emotive behavioral therapy (REBT) and the Albert Ellis Institute in New York City. Albert Ellis is often labeled the *"Grandfather of Cognitive Behavioral Therapy"* and is frequently cited as one the founders of the cognitive therapy movement, as his theories were first popularized in the 1950s. Albert Ellis's REBT set the stage for Aaron T. Beck's work in the area of cognitive therapy. Ellis was a prolific author and scholar. Two of his most notable works were *A Guide to Rational Living* (1961) and *How to Stubbornly Refuse to Make Yourself Miserable* (1988). A major element of Ellis's REBT approach is the notion that people hold irrational assumptions about themselves and the world. The REBT practitioner helps clients analyze these assumptions and develop a more rational way of thinking (Ellis, 1957, 1962).

TABLE 2.8 COGNITIVE DISTORTIONS AND IRRATIONAL BELIEFS

Ellis's 12 Irrational Beliefs

1. I need love and approval, and I must avoid disapproval from any source.
2. To be worthwhile, I must achieve, succeed at whatever I do, and make no mistakes.
3. People should always do the right thing, and when they don't they must be blamed and punished.
4. Things must be the way I want them to be; otherwise life will be intolerable.
5. My unhappiness is caused by things outside my control, so there is little I can do to feel better.
6. I must worry about things that could be unpleasant or frightening; otherwise they might happen.
7. Because they are too much to bear, I must avoid life's difficulties and responsibilities.
8. Everyone needs to depend on someone stronger than themselves.
9. Events in my past are the cause of my problems, and they continue to influence me now.
10. I should become upset when other people have problems and feel unhappy when they are sad.
11. I shouldn't have to feel discomfort and pain, I can't stand them and must avoid them at all costs.
12. Every problem should have an ideal solution, and it's intolerable when one cannot be found.

Beck's 15 Common Cognitive Distortions

1. *Filtering*: Magnify the negative details and filter out all positive aspects of a situation.
2. *Polarized thinking*: Things are either black or white. We have to be perfect, or we are a failure.
3. *Overgeneralization*: We come to a conclusion based on a single incident or piece of evidence.
4. *Jumping to conclusions*: Without actual knowledge, we know why others act the way they do.
5. *Catastrophizing*: We expect disaster to strike, no matter what.
6. *Personalization*: We think that everything people do or say is some kind of reaction to us.
7. *Control fallacies*: If we feel *externally controlled*, we see ourselves as a helpless victim of fate.
8. *Fallacy of fairness*: We feel resentful because we know what is fair, despite differing opinions.
9. *Blaming*: We hold other people responsible for our pain or blame ourselves for every problem.
10. *Shoulds*: We have a list of ironclad rules about how others and we should behave.
11. *Emotional reasoning*: We believe that what we feel must be true.
12. *Fallacy of change*: We expect that people will change to suit us if we just pressure them enough.
13. *Global labeling*: We generalize one or two qualities into a negative global judgment.
14. *Always being right*: We are continually on trial to prove that our opinions and actions are correct.
15. *Heaven's reward fallacy*: We expect our sacrifice and self-denial to pay off.

Sources: Data from Beck, A. T. (1967). *Depression: Clinical, experimental, and theoretical aspects.* Harper and Row; Ellis, A. (1957). Rational psychotherapy and individual psychology. *Journal of Individual Psychology, 13*, 38–44; Ellis, A., David, D., & Lynn, S. J. (2010). Rational and irrational beliefs: A historical and conceptual perspective. In D. David, S. J. Lynn, & A. Ellis (Eds.), *Rational and irrational beliefs: Research, theory, and clinical practice* (pp. 3–22). Oxford University Press.

Ellis's ABCDE model, also known as the ABC model, provides a consistent platform for REBT practitioners to practice from. Within the ABCDE model, **A** stands for activating event (i.e., life events); **B** stands for beliefs (e.g., irrational beliefs, adaptive beliefs); **C** stands for consequences (e.g., emotions, thoughts, behaviors); **D** stands for disputation (i.e., arguing), and this is put into play by the therapist if the client has an irrational belief; and **E** stands for new effect (i.e., change resulting from disputation of irrational belief). Within this framework, many REBT techniques are utilized, including, but not limited to, disputing irrational beliefs, cognitive homework, coping self-statements, and rational emotive imagery (Ellis, 1957, 1962).

Disputing Irrational Beliefs

The therapist disputes the client's irrational thoughts and explains how to check and modify their rigid beliefs about themselves, others, and their life conditions. For example:

Client: People must treat me fairly.

Clinician: Humans do not always treat others fairly.

Client: I guess you're right, but I can't stand to be without my friends.

Clinician: What is it about being alone that is so unbearable?

Cognitive Homework

The therapist helps the client apply the ABCDE model to many of the problems that occur in daily life outside of session time. For example:

Client: I must find love this year.

Clinician: I want you to document all the times this week that you use absolutes such as *must, should, need, ought, will.* Then replace those words with a word that is not an absolute.

Coping Self-Statements

Clients are taught how self-destructive beliefs can be countered by rational coping self-statements. For example:

Client: I must perform well. I simply can't stand it when I don't attain perfection.

Clinician: In order to fully accept yourself, understand that you may have some imperfections down the road.

Rational Emotive Imagery

Clients are asked to vividly imagine one of the worst things that might happen to them. Clients then train themselves to develop healthy emotions in place of disruptive ones. For example:

Client: I keep imagining myself as a mom and not doing the right things.

Clinician: Imagine that you just forgot about your daughter's school play, and you feel awful, but when you see your daughter later, she says that she still loves you.

Cognitive Therapy

Aaron T. Beck is an American psychiatrist who is regarded as the "Father of Cognitive Therapy and Cognitive Behavior Therapy" and cofounder of the Beck Institute for Cognitive Behavior Therapy. Beck's pioneering work produced a tremendous amount of scholarship, including *Cognitive Therapy and the Emotional Disorders* (1976) and *Cognitive Therapy of Depression* (1978). Cognitive theorists divide cognitions into automatic thoughts (immediate thoughts that pop up in the mind), assumptions (intermediate beliefs), and schemata (schemas, core beliefs). Within this framework, they seek to understand how intentions, expectations, cognitive distortions, and maladaptive belief systems influence the onset of mental health issues. The development of long-term negative schemata results from a persistent idiosyncratic belief system. The way someone believes or perceives themselves, their world, and their future (i.e., cognitive triad; Beck, 1967) is heavily influenced by memories. Because people create their own memories around particular events, they seek evidence that confirms their cognitions and they overlook information that is inconsistent with those cognitions. After determining the cognitive issue, a general goal of cognitive therapy is to understand the client's subjective thoughts about their experiences and to then assist them in creating more adaptive judgments. Specifically, a cognitive therapist helps clients determine how they are interpreting events and situations and how these interpretations influence their behavior (Beck, 1976; Reinecke et al., 2003).

According to Reinecke et al. (2003), "[a]n element common to the different cognitive-behavioral models is their emphasis on helping patients examine the manner in which they construe or understand themselves and the world (cognitions) and to experiment with new ways of responding (behavioral)" (p. 240). While a strong therapeutic alliance is not viewed as the primary intervention for creating change, cognitive therapists believe that the therapeutic relationship can serve as the vehicle that practitioners and clients use to achieve goals, understand the cognitive triad, and delve into preexisting schemata. The schemata affect an individual's assumptions, automatic thoughts, and emotions. Within a cognitive framework, to change an individual's emotions, their thoughts and schemata must be changed. Schemata are deeply entrenched beliefs that provide memories, meaning, encoding, retrieval, focus, and inference for incoming information (Beck, 1976). Maladaptive schemata often serve an adaptive function (e.g., childhood experience, parenting behavior) and can develop as a result of a single traumatization (Hembree et al., 2003; Reinecke et al., 2003). Examples of maladaptive schemata include internalized beliefs such as "I am a bad person," "I am inadequate," "I am unlovable," and "I am substandard" (Beck, 1976). Within this framework, many cognitive techniques are utilized, including, but not limited to, Socratic questioning, the downward arrow, cognitive restructuring, and thought recording.

Socratic Questioning

This technique involves asking questions that challenge the accuracy of the client's thoughts and then working with the client to cocreate a healthier way of thinking. For example:

Clinician: At the beginning of our session last week, you rated your mood as a 2. How would you rate your mood this week?

Client: I would rate it as a 5. I feel better after we worked through how to talk to my parents about my grades, and the conversation went well.

Clinician: What do you mean when you say the conversation went "well"?

Client: They didn't agree with me, but they also didn't ground me or take away my cell phone.

Clinician: Are you saying that avoiding punishment is the main criterion for a good conversation with your parents?

The Downward Arrow

In this technique, the therapist guides the client from automatic thought to schemata via relationship-building, assessing the presence of maladaptive beliefs, and questioning to elicit the meaning behind an automatic thought to determine what the schemata are. For example:

Clinician: What were you feeling when your father took your phone away?

Client: I felt like I really screwed up.

Clinician: What would it mean if that was true?

Client: That I am a failure and can't do anything right.

Cognitive Restructuring

This technique uses processes such as self-monitoring, questioning assumptions, gathering evidence, preparing a costbenefit analysis, and generating alternatives to stop negative thought patterns. For example:

Client: I got in a terrible fight with my spouse because I'm totally useless as a husband, father, and provider.

Clinician: This is another example of the negative pattern of self-talk we recently discussed. Let's change your thoughts about this latest argument to something more realistic. How about "That argument wasn't my best work as a husband, but I'm a valuable member of my family and I contribute in many ways"?

Client: Yes, that is more accurate and positive.

Thought Recording

This technique involves journaling automatic thoughts and assumptions that take place between sessions. The client lists negative thoughts and then creates an alternative positive thought to counteract the negative one. For example:

Client: My spouse would rather be at work than at home with me and the kids.

Clinician: What about that bothers you?

Client: I'm not really sure of the exact feeling, but overall, I feel like he doesn't love me.

Clinician: During the next week I would like you to journal a comprehensive list of negative thoughts that go in and out your mind. Please try very hard to journal when you're experiencing challenges with your husband. After writing down your negative thoughts, challenge yourself to write down an alternative positive thought to counteract each of the negative ones.

Cognitive Behavioral Modification

Donald Meichenbaum developed cognitive behavioral modification (CBM), cocreated cognitive behavioral therapy with Aaron T. Beck, and cofounded and directs The Melissa Institute. The Melissa Institute is a nonprofit organization designed to build safe communities and prevent violence through community outreach, research, and education. Two of Meichenbaum's most notable texts are *Cognitive-Behavior Modification: An Integrative Approach* (1977) and *The Evolution of Cognitive Behavior Therapy: A Personal and Professional Journey* (2017).

CBM centers on changing negative self-talk, rewriting negative life narratives, and forgiving oneself for past behavior. While there are behavioral elements, CBM is primarily a cognitive technique. The first phase of CBM involves self-observation. Specifically, clients are instructed to listen closely to their negative self-talk and to observe their behavior. Clients are then informed that their identified negative self-talk patterns greatly contribute to various mental health issues. During the second phase of the CBM process, clients are asked to begin utilizing new positive self-talk. Whether the new self-talk takes place in the client's mind or in a journal is idiosyncratic to the client a clinician is working with. The goal is for these new self-talk patterns to guide the client's behavior in a positive direction. In addition, the therapist helps the client develop better coping strategies. During the third phase of CBM, clients are identifying and restructuring their thought process with less guidance from the clinician. One additional hallmark of the third phase of CBM is an increase in the client's self-awareness and ability to recognize negative self-talk (Meichenbaum, 1977, 2017).

UNIQUE ETHICAL ISSUES RELEVANT TO SYSTEMIC WORK

Is there anything more salient to emerging practitioners than their profession's code of ethics? These standards unite practitioners and create a shared set of rules, standards, and values. The ethical codes of any organization define the structure and boundaries of the work. Couple, marriage, and family therapy requires clear standards and rules, and the vulnerable populations engaging in this work require a therapist who has a deep sense of integrity and aspirational guidelines for professional practice. This textbook focuses on the contemporary issues of the profession, and consequently this section will shed light on relevant contemporary issues requiring ethical clarification. Lastly, mental health laws vary considerably from state to state, and consequently clinicians must be cognizant of the laws in their jurisdiction.

Ethical codes provide practitioners with a foundational understanding on how to navigate professional situations appropriately; however, we live in a complex society where the experiences and circumstances of individuals may vary greatly. Consequently, whether something is ethical or unethical is not always clear, and situations can be open to interpretation. Consultation and ethical decision-making are key factors in navigating ethically questionable situations. A consultant can provide a different or confirming vantage point. Consultants can take many forms, including, but not limited to, supervisors, mentors, colleagues, experts, and legal consultants. Practitioners should also be comfortable consulting the professional literature for specific information. In addition to seeking a consultant, it is important to follow an ethical decision-making model that exemplifies the five ethical principles identified as most critical for members of the helping professions, namely autonomy (allowing others freedom of choice), nonmaleficence (not causing harm to others), beneficence (contributing to the welfare of clients), fidelity (trust in the therapeutic relationship), and justice (treating individuals fairly; Beauchamp & Childress, 2001). In addition, practitioners should consider the notion of universalizability (i.e., implied universal judgment) in their decision-making process. For example, it is important to be honest with clients about the limits of confidentiality (i.e., informed consent) at the start of treatment because in an identical situation most clinicians would do the same.

ETHICAL ISSUES UNIQUE TO WORKING WITH CHILDREN

There are numerous important ethical issues related to working with children. This section will highlight three contemporary ethical concerns related to treating children: the child's right to confidentiality, children and divorce, and the use of therapeutic touch. In the United States, any human under the age of 18 is considered a child. The *age of majority* is the law governing when a person ceases to be a child and officially enters adulthood.

Children's Rights to Confidentiality

Children generally have fewer rights than adults and are normally unable to make unilateral legal decisions outside of adult supervision and permission. Confidentiality during the therapeutic process is typically no exception to these decision-making processes and authority. While parents provide approval during the informed consent process, minors typically participate in the assent process. Depending on the child's/adolescent's age and developmental level, they should be participating in the informed consent process via client *assent*. Assent is typically in the form of information sharing (e.g., nature of treatment, role of therapist, expectations for treatment, agreement to participate; McCabe, 2006). As the child's age and developmental level increase, they should be expected to participate more fully in the assent and treatment planning process. This participation can increase youth interest and openness in the therapeutic process (Chenneville et al., 2010).

You may be asking yourself, "What about the parent's right to determine the parameters of child treatment?" First, as a clinician, it is imperative that you know the laws in your jurisdiction regarding the age requirement for what constitutes a minor, the rights for guardian participation in the treatment, the legal age of consent, as well as any exceptions when minors have the legal right to consent to their own treatment and/or protect clinical information from parents. This information should be communicated to the guardians during the informed consent process (e.g., in writing and verbally). A somewhat related exception to parental access to information is the Federal Education Rights and Privacy Act of 1994 stipulation that professional school counselors can refrain from disclosing information to parents. In many situations, helping professionals can limit what is disclosed to the caregiver(s) if sharing the information would be harmful to the child (Roberts & Dyer, 2004). At times, a child under the age of 18 (but above 14) may petition the court for emancipation. If the court grants emancipation, the child will have the same legal rights as an adult (e.g., confidentiality, privilege). This includes the right to receive and refuse therapy. Any practitioner who works with youth who claim legal emancipation must obtain a copy of the legal decree for confirmation and record-keeping purposes (McNary, 2014). Legally speaking, caregivers or parents typically have the right to access all information from their child's/adolescent's treatment, the legal right to consent to their minor's participation in counseling, and the right to influence the goals of treatment. While these parental rights exist, clinicians often negotiate with parents regarding their impact and influence on treatment. For example, if a 14-year-old comes to counseling for help with feeling a sense of mistrust with their romantic partner, it is quite probable that heavy caregiver involvement will create immense resistance or result in the client discontinuing treatment altogether. In this and other situations, helping professionals will try to collaborate with the caregivers and the minor on determining the appropriate course of treatment and the extent of parental involvement (Coffman & Barnett, 2015).

Children and Divorce

Couple, marriage, and family practitioners working with children whose parents are in the throes of a divorce are often vulnerable to legal charges of ethical misconduct (Murphy & Hecker, 2017). Children whose parents are going through a divorce are in situations that are often emotionally charged with destructive loyalty conflicts (i.e., parentification, triangulation, cross-generational coalitions). Further, the toxicity of separations and divorces can be a breeding ground for intensive scapegoating, collusion, and side-taking. While children can experience initial positive reinforcement when boosted up into the family executive subsystem (e.g., acting as mom's informant or dad's confidant), ultimately they are deeply hurt and forever affected by their parental collusion, scapegoating, and attempts to create coalitions against the other parent. From a legal perspective, parents are often wrapped up in a variety of battles, including, but not limited to, issues around child custody, decision-making authority, visitation, and child support payments. These legal battles can include a divide regarding the custody of the child and issues around participation in individual and/or family therapy (Murphy & Hecker, 2017).

Given the potential legal action that surrounds custody litigation, practitioners are advised to clarify at the start of treatment who the client is and what the therapist's role will be. In most situations, the client will be the child, the parent(s), and/or the family as a whole. Similarly, regarding roles, the helping professional often plays one of two main professional roles: (a) the therapist helping the child, family, and/or parents; or (b) the mediator assisting the couple in achieving a civil separation (Woody, 2000). Sori and Hecker (2015) advise that practitioners should clearly state to the clients at the start of treatment that they are not siding with a particular parent in custody disputes because children are often harmed when caught in the grips of parental conflict. In addition, Sori and Hecker (2015) suggest that practitioners create a waiver that clients sign indicating that if the parents decide to divorce at a later date they will not subpoena the clinician's records. While this waiver will not hold up in court, it could persuade the parents to respect the child's confidentiality.

You may be asking, "What should I do if I receive a subpoena?" If clinicians receive a subpoena, their initial action should be to read the entire document. Clinicians should not release confidential information to an attorney simply because the attorney requested the information. Here are a few key steps to take in responding to a subpoena: (a) determine what the attorney is requesting; (b) discuss the situation with the client and determine whether or not they are willing to share the information; (c) if the client does not wish to share the information, inform the attorney that they will need a signed court order; (d) determine whether the child and the parents are interested in sharing the confidential information if a court order is sent; (e) if everyone agrees, have the legal guardian(s) sign the release of information; (f) if any additional people were involved in the treatment, their permission and signatures are also required prior to revealing any information; (g) do not take case files to the court unless you are sent a subpoena; and (h) throughout the process, inform clients as to why confidentiality is being broken, provide them with opportunities to discuss any concerns about what will be revealed, and allow clients some participation in the process (Bartlett, 1996; Mappes et al., 1985; Sori & Hecker, 2015). If the client and the parents want the clinician to deny the court order, ask to speak to the judge privately about the client's desire for privacy. Despite the clinician's rationale and advocacy, the judge may order the information to be turned over to the court or shared with the judge privately (Sori & Hecker, 2015).

The Use of Therapeutic Touch

What should you do if a child wants to hug you at the end of a session? How should you respond if a child is acting out during a session in a destructive manner? These questions and others are important for all child and family practitioners to consider. Nonerotic therapeutic touch is a controversial topic. A few years ago, a student in one of my courses asked me the following question: "If there is any possibility that therapeutic touch could be misconstrued by the client or do more harm than good, why should we even consider it?" At the time I was caught off guard because I was so accustomed to fielding questions related to the opposite side of the debate (e.g., touch is natural and healing, children developmentally need touch). I acknowledged that the student had asked a very good question, and I opened up the topic for further discussion.

Given our litigious culture and the fact that children represent a vulnerable population, it is surprising to find so little information in the professional literature regarding the ethics of therapeutic touch. Touch is a very natural and developmentally appropriate way for children to play, explore the world, and communicate. Depending on a number of factors, therapeutic touch can be either appropriate or inappropriate. When young children reach for a hug, it is normal for adults to want to reciprocate; in fact, in many cultures it would seem taboo not to hug a child. If a child touches a practitioner or asks for a hug, it is a good opportunity to address therapeutic boundaries; however, it is essential that young children do not feel shamed or rejected when the therapist clarifies boundaries (McNeil-Haber, 2004).

During the first counseling session, the therapist should provide information regarding therapeutic touch as part of the informed consent process. This explanation should be communicated in two ways. First, it should be provided in the form of a written explanation with parental signature space. Second, it should be explained verbally to both the child and the parent(s). The explanation should review the context for the behavior. For example, "During our special time together I allow for a hug at the end of every session." The therapist should also acknowledge how they will handle in-session discipline issues (Sori & Hacker, 2015). For example, "At times children physically act out during session. To prevent them from hurting themselves, me, or my property, I may intervene and physically hold them until they calm down." Lastly, in considering the ethical issues related to nonerotic therapeutic touch, McNeil-Haber (2004, p. 128) suggests addressing the following questions and comments during the decision-making process:

- What are the possible benefits of touch? Touch can be reinforcing and calming.
- How might this child perceive the touch? It could enhance self-esteem or make the child feel powerless to comment on it.
- What considerations are related to the counselor? Whose needs are being met? Is touch genuine?
- What safety issues are related to the child? Is it harmful to the child? Does this child have a history of abuse? If so, touch could be alarming (abused children have trouble separating fact from fantasy).
- What in this child's family background might be an issue?
- What are some practical considerations? Culture should be considered, as people from different cultural backgrounds have different attitudes toward using touch in expressing emotion or in socializing children.

ETHICAL ISSUES UNIQUE TO WORKING WITH COUPLES AND FAMILIES

Important ethical issues are involved when a therapist works with couples and families. In fact, many practitioners are very supportive of the idea of systemic work yet choose not to engage in it due to litigious and ethically oriented factors. This section will closely review three contemporary ethical issues related to working with couples and families: defining the client in multiperson therapy, consent to treatment, and change of format and participation.

Defining the Client in Multiperson Therapy

Describing couple, family, network, and group therapy as "multiperson" may sound somewhat mechanistic. However, it does convey an important point—namely, that more than one client is present during the session. According to Gottlieb et al. (2008), for ethical reasons practitioners must determine who the client is and whom they are responsible for. Is the client an individual, the couple, the entire family, or a subsection of the family (e.g., mother and daughter, father and daughter, grandmother and son)? Furthermore, the notion of identifying one client and placing the toxicity of systemic issues onto one family member (e.g., symptom bearer, scapegoat) is an unfortunate yet common occurrence in systemic work. In this sense, the practitioner may disagree with the family's conceptualization of who the client is, and part of the treatment may involve broadening the family's opinion on the nature of the presenting problem.

The ethical concern with defining the client in a multiperson therapy centers on balancing competing interests and recognizing the ripple or reverberation effect that any individual member's change and/or empowerment can have on the entire system. Even if treatment is individual in nature, the objectives of treatment are at least partly defined by the client's view of the presenting problem and their goals. The family problems and treatment goals would consequently be grounded in the subjective view of the family member(s) seeking treatment and may not be aligned or in the best interest of the other members of the family (Gottlieb et al., 2008). Many practitioners who have treated individual clients with intimate relationship concerns have undoubtedly asked themselves if they truly have a full picture of the relational difficulties and, because they are deeply aligned with one partner's view of the problem, whether they are empowering their clients out of a perfectly good or salvageable relationship.

Addressing and contending with concerns related to competing interests, scapegoating, and systemic change can sound like an incredibly difficult series of ethical concerns for a clinician to handle. While the process can be difficult, clinicians can successfully navigate these ethical issues with the frequent use of multidirectional partiality (i.e., clinical attitude that allows the practitioner to empathize with each family member; Boszormenyi-Nagy, 1966), a thorough intake assessment of the presenting concerns, clarifying who the client is and the practitioner's role in treating all of the individuals in the family during the informed consent process, and clearly detailing the course of treatment as early as possible (Gottlieb et al., 2008). Most of the aforementioned ethical strategies are completed very early in the treatment process. In most clinical situations, the practitioner should have completed the intake assessment, clarified their role with the family, and detailed the course of treatment by the third session. Multidirectional partiality, on the other hand, is something that should continue throughout treatment. Being able to simultaneously empathically hold all of the family members' perspectives and emotions is achievable and is considered a hallmark of systemic therapy.

Consent to Treatment

While it is always best practice for practitioners to attain consent from both parents prior to treating a child, parents who have divorced or separated may or may not share the ability to make decisions on behalf of their children (i.e., joint legal and physical custody). In arrangements involving joint custody, each parent can independently make decisions on behalf of their children. Whenever couple, marriage, and family practitioners work with a minor child of divorced, separated, or annulled parents, they must review the divorce decree to ensure they have full permission to treat the child. The family court may have awarded decision-making rights to one or both parents. Typically, courts award custody according to the "best interest of the child" standard (Gottlieb et al., 2008; Murphy & Hecker, 2017; Sori & Hecker, 2015). Please note, stepparents have no legal authority to consent to the treatment of minor stepchildren unless the stepparent has adopted the children.

Consent issues have to do with child custody. Child custody involves guardianship, which is a legal term that encompasses legal custody (i.e., the right to make decisions about the minor) and physical custody (i.e., the right to house, provide, and care for the minor). When considering the issues of child custody, it is important to distinguish between legal and physical custody. Specifically, therapists need to determine who has legal custody because that is who makes decisions about mental health treatment. Physical custody is somewhat irrelevant because the person the child lives with often shares decision-making authority with the other parent. While courts tend to grant joint legal custody more frequently, when a parent has sole legal custody, that parent has the sole right to make decisions for their child. When one parent loses legal custody of their child, they have likely done something egregious. A straightforward solution to determining consent authority is to require the parents to provide a copy of the custody order prior to engaging in treatment of the child. The language on the custody order will provide the practitioner with information on who has legal custody and whether both parents need to provide consent for the child to receive treatment (Gottlieb et al., 2008; Murphy & Hecker, 2017; Sori & Hecker, 2015).

Change of Format and Participation

An ethical dilemma can occur when practitioners change therapeutic format from individual to conjoint therapy or vice versa. When the format of counseling changes, so does the definition of the client and the responsibility of the practitioner (Gottlieb et al., 2008). To understand how this works, let's start with the notion of bringing another person or multiple people into an individual counseling experience. Can a practitioner be expected to maintain therapeutic neutrality and lack of bias when they have already developed a long-standing therapeutic alliance with one member of the couple/family? The practitioner would likely have a bias in favor of the individual they had spent time building a relationship with, since they would have had little to no information or relationship with the other client(s). Not only does the practitioner have a bias, but they have to simultaneously develop a new relationship with the incoming clients and maintain responsibility to everyone undergoing treatment. What if one member of a couple counseling experience leaves treatment for multiple sessions and then wants to come back to do more couples work? How should the practitioner use the information they learned during the previous individual sessions (Gottlieb et al., 2008)? A final issue that should also be considered is the possibility that the gains and improvements made by the individual initially participating in individual therapy may be jeopardizing the success of the joint therapy or, at a minimum, that the long-time client may become jealous or resentful of the therapist developing new relationship(s) with the incoming family member(s).

When practitioners change from a conjoint counseling format to an individual format, there are also ethical issues to consider. In couples counseling, one member may start to improve and feel empowered, while the other member deteriorates and disengages. The practitioner will also start to get very accustomed to understanding only one side of the couple's story. This could eventually lead to bias and alignment with the partner attending treatment more frequently. The negative outcome of empowering a partner out of a perfectly good relationship could eventually occur. Regarding a family therapy experience, it is normal to ask children to leave sessions while the therapist discusses issues with the parents. It is also quite common to have family therapy and parent education meetings simultaneously. An ethical issue to be aware of within a family context is scapegoating and colluding against the absent member. It is very easy to speak negatively about someone who is not present in the session because they are not there to defend themselves. When the absent member returns to treatment, they may feel that everyone is against them, including the therapist (Gottlieb et al., 2008).

Having a change of format and participation is a common phenomenon in systemic therapy. A key aspect of ethically navigating these situations is the informed consent process. This process should begin with a clear and detailed discussion of the risks and benefits of changing format and participation. During the informed consent process, the therapist needs to clarify their *no secrets* policy. The therapist should clearly state that they use their discretion as to what and how much they disclose during treatment.

In addition, if the format started individually and then moved to conjoint therapy, the therapist should check in with the original client to see how they are handling the change in format and participation. I also recommend that practitioners discuss the risks of working on relationship issues within an individual format (e.g., therapist only hearing one side of the story; empowering people out of a relationship). Lastly, it is advisable for the therapist to take some time to develop a solid therapeutic relationship with the incoming client(s) while not neglecting the original client.

ETHICALLY INCORPORATING TECHNOLOGY AND TELEBEHAVIORAL HEALTH

Therapy can be offered in a variety of formats, including online platforms such as Zoom for Healthcare, Healthie, Doxy.me, Webex for Healthcare, and GoToMeeting (Healthie, 2020). While the COVID-19 global pandemic may have increased the use of telebehavioral health platforms, the helping professions were already moving in that direction. When engaging in teletherapy, the clinician must engage in professional development and comply with profession-based ethical codes as well as with the stipulations of the Health Insurance Portability and Accountability Act (HIPAA) and the Health Information Technology for Economic and Clinical Health (HITECH) Act. Additionally, the delivery method must be protected by two-way encryption to be considered secure. To effectively and ethically use this technology, clinicians must thoroughly understand the ethics, technology, and security issues involved.

While reviewing all of the rules, standards, and expectations in HIPAA and HITECH is beyond the scope of this textbook, it is important to understand certain key factors. To fully understand all of the key standards, clinicians are encouraged to review Hecker and Edward's (2014) article entitled "The Impact of HIPAA and HITECH: New Standards for Confidentiality, Security, and Documentation for Marriage and Family Therapists." First, clients must be made aware of the risks and responsibilities associated with teletherapy. The clinician should advise clients in writing of these risks and of both the therapist's and clients' responsibilities for minimizing such risks. For example, when engaging in teletherapy, clinicians should consider the differences between face-to-face and electronic communication (e.g., nonverbal and verbal cues, internet glitches, authentication, privacy issues) and how these may affect the treatment process. To assist clients in making an informed choice, practitioners should educate them on how to prevent and address potential misunderstandings arising from the lack of visual cues, voice intonations, and unpredictable technological issues. After clients receive this information, they will be able to make an informed decision between teletherapy and in-person therapy (Caldwell, 2015; Hecker & Edwards, 2014; HITECH Act, 2009).

It is impossible for clinicians to conduct teletherapy without handling protected healthcare information. When personally identifiable information is used in conjunction with one's mental health condition, healthcare, or one's payment for that healthcare, it becomes protected health information (PHI). HIPAA and HITECH provide guidelines for handling PHI. Most information is in the form of online identifiers. The HIPAA provides 18 identifiers that must be protected or deidentified, including, but not limited to, name, address, telephone number, social security number, and medical record number (HIPAA of 1996, Pub. L. No. 104-191). When communicating with clients, it is essential that these 18 identifiers be removed (i.e., deidentified) from any data set. Please note that the HIPAA also protects the PHI of dead people for 50 years following the date of death. There are also ethical issues related to protecting PHI that are controlled directly by the practitioner and the client. For example, both clinicians and clients should conduct counseling in a private and nonpublic space. Lastly, the scope and practice of licensed practitioners are governed by the state where they are licensed. While COVID-19 waivers were made in certain states (see Zencare, 2021), this does not change the fact that state licenses are only valid in the state where they were attained. If a clinician is curious about the legality of professional practice in a state where they are not a resident and are not licensed, they should contact the appropriate licensing board within the state where their clients reside. Table 2.9 provides a breakdown of the American Association for Marriage and Family Therapy (AAMFT) Code of Ethics related to the practice of teletherapy, a description of each code, and examples of how the standard is actualized in practice.

TABLE 2.9   TECHNOLOGY-ASSISTED PROFESSIONAL SERVICES

Standard Name	Description	Examples
6.1: Technology-assisted services	Marriage and family therapists ensure that they are compliant with all relevant laws for the delivery of such services.	Determining whether technology-assisted work is appropriate for the client(s); informing clients of the potential risks and benefits; ensuring the security of client information; attaining the appropriate professional training prior to engaging in clinical work
6.2: Consent to treat or supervise	Marriage and family therapists must make clients and supervisees aware of the risks and responsibilities associated with technology-assisted services.	Advising clients and supervisees in writing of these risks; ensuring both the therapist's and the clients'/supervisees' responsibilities in minimizing such risks
6.3: Confidentiality and professional responsibilities	Marriage and family therapists are responsible for choosing technological platforms that adhere to standards of best practice.	Determining whether certain technological platforms adhere to standards of best practice related to confidentiality and quality of services and meet applicable laws; clients and supervisees are to be made aware in writing of the limitations and protections of the technology
6.4: Technology and documentation	Marriage and family therapists ensure all documentation is stored in a way that uses technology that adheres to the standards of best practice.	All documentation containing identifying information that is electronically stored and/or transferred is done so using technology that adheres to standards of best practice related to confidentiality and quality of services and meets applicable laws; clients and supervisees are to be made aware in writing of the limitations and protections of the technology
6.5: Location of services and practice	Marriage and family therapists follow all applicable laws regarding the location of practice and services.	Not using technologically assisted means for practicing outside of allowed jurisdiction; working with clients only within the jurisdiction allowed by licensure and appropriate laws
6.6: Training and use of current technology	Marriage and family therapists ensure they are well-trained and competent in the use of all chosen technology-assisted professional services.	Carefully choosing audio, video, and other options to optimize quality and security of services; adhering to standards of best practice for technology-assisted services; choosing technology that is suitably advanced and current to best serve the professional needs of clients and supervisees

Source: Information taken directly from American Association for Marriage and Family Therapy. (2015). *AAMFT Code of Ethics.* AAMFT. American Counseling Association.

DIVERSITY AND INTERSECTIONALITY IN SYSTEMIC WORK

It is important to understand the concepts of diversity and intersectionality before applying them to couple, marriage, and family work. *Diversity* is the practice of involving people from a range of different contextual backgrounds, including, but not limited to, ethnicity, race, sexual orientation, gender identity, age, socioeconomic status, and ability (Mercieca & Mercieca, 2018). *Intersectionality* is the recognition of various and related systems of discrimination, domination, and/or oppression that emerge from a position of power and privilege in society (Crenshaw, 1991). Davis (2008) expanded the definition of intersectionality by adding the following description: *Intersectionality* is "the interaction between gender, race, and other categories of difference in individual lives, social practices, institutional arrangements, and cultural ideologies and the outcomes of these interactions in terms of power" (p. 68). For example, someone who is experiencing oppression via racism may also be experiencing oppression through sexism. Multiple identities and life narratives provide a deeper description of what is taking place within an individual.

In couple, marriage, and family therapy, these issues compound and interact within the various relationships and contexts people engage in. For example, in a couple therapy situation, a Hispanic woman who is dating an Asian American woman would integrate her experiences of cultural oppression, sexism, and heterosexism, and these experiences would partly shape her interaction and relationship with her partner. When her Asian partner adds her experiences and specific contextual factors, which could include additional areas of oppression, the fluidity of intersectionality can be observed. It is important for therapists to understand the cultural influences, unique individual differences, and relational factors that can affect relationships. The following section outlines the impact of systemic racism and oppression, then underscores the importance of providing culturally responsive services.

Systemic Racism, Oppression, and Cultural Responsiveness

One only needs to observe the news to witness the racism, oppression, and marginalization taking place daily around the world. Before considering the notion of systemic racism, let's contemplate the nuances of a definition of racism. According to Gee and Ford (2011), structural racism is socially created racial hierarchies that create inequities that permeate societal norms, mores, politics, laws, and institutions. In the United States, the individuals most frequently negatively affected by these large-scale inequities are Black, Indigenous, and People of Color. To ensure clients feel a sense of acceptance, understanding, and safety, it is essential for practitioners to embrace an antiracist position and demonstrate cultural competency (Bean et al., 2001). According to Waites et al. (2004), culturally competent therapists engage clients from a variety of cultural contexts in a nonpathologizing, heritage-honoring, context-oriented, and strength-based stance.

While racism is centered on socially constructed hierarchies of power, inequity, and oppression, systemic racism (i.e., institutional racism) is embedded in the laws, mores, norms, and regulations of a culture. This form of discrimination emerges culturally in religion, criminal justice, politics, employment, housing, healthcare, and education (Lewis et al., 2017; Mosley et al., 2020). Common examples include, but are not limited to, voter suppression, racial profiling by police, biased and unfair treatment in the criminal justice system, favoritism in hiring for certain ethnic and racial groups, lower funding for schools that serve non-White ethnic/race populations, and the much higher dropout and expulsion rates in public schools.

An example of systemic racism that is currently taking place in U.S. schools centers on the information provided to students regarding racism. Specifically, as of October 2021, a number of states have passed or are considering passing into law bills that would disallow providing education on certain aspects of critical race theory. The areas of critical race theory that appear to be creating the most controversy have to do with America being founded on racism, racial oppression, and a concept suggesting that people are inherently racist. In addition to signing bills, there is evidence of strategic monopolization of school boards and school board meetings where these issues are being discussed, and financial support of candidates running on platforms against critical race theory (Anderson & Gatwiri, 2021). Among other negative consequences, removing the accurate portrayal of American history essentially silences the voice of people and groups who have been historically oppressed and marginalized.

As a couple, marriage, and family practitioner, you will need to understand oppression and the human motivation around maintaining political structures that favor certain groups at the expense of others. Hanna et al. (2000) define *oppression* as "an unjust, harsh, or cruel exercise of power over another or others. From a psychosocial perspective, the term can be viewed more specifically in the context of abuse or similar mistreatment that leads to psychological distress or emotional pain and suffering" (p. 431). Families are systems that are affected by a multitude of socio-psychological-political systems and structures (Hanna, 2018). Practitioners must work with families to help unpack and bring awareness to these forces that affect their daily lives. Some of the most noticeable areas of oppression can be the awareness of how some family members are benefiting more from the larger society. For example, men may be earning more money than the women in the family, and this could cause further oppression in the home, marital challenges, and/or sibling discord. Similarly, individuals who represent a sexual minority, including, but not limited to, lesbian, gay, bisexual, transgender, intersex, queer/questioning, asexual, and many other identifiers (e.g., nonbinary, pansexual; LGBTQIA+), may feel oppressed and marginalized within their home and community, while their heterosexual family members feel supported and comfortable (Crisp & Turner, 2014). The impact of these issues can vary in severity, with Black and Latinx transgender and gender nonconforming individuals often being at greatest risk of fatal violent attacks (e.g., hate crimes; Karimi, 2021).

Couple, marriage, and family practitioners work tirelessly to promote diversity, social justice, equity, and inclusion in everything they do. Specifically, practitioners are dedicated to ensuring that diverse groups of people receive equal access to decision-making power, tangible and intangible resources, and opportunity. Furthermore, they are firmly committed to cocreating and sustaining structural and systemic changes that will directly empower, include, and assist individuals and groups that have been subjected to historical and contemporary systemic racism, marginalization, discrimination, oppression, violence, and hatred. While this way of engaging in the world is ethically correct and deeply meaningful to most practitioners, therapeutic work is provided for all people, including those with differing political affiliations and belief systems (Seponski et al., 2012). For example, a couple, marriage, and family practitioner would not treat a conservative and racist couple presenting with communication issues with any less effectiveness than they would treat a liberal, nonracist couple.

Outside of therapy and client care, many helping professionals feel a moral and professional obligation to denounce and reform institutions that have historically created large-scale inequity for non-White citizens. Advocacy is a skill centered on turning the theory of social justice into something tangible and actionable (Flynn & Hays, 2015). Clinicians use this skill when they are advocating for the welfare of clients, groups, and the counseling profession within systems. Clinicians seek to eliminate obstacles that interfere with access, progress, and development. For example, a clinician might work to establish more after-school programming for diverse and low-income families within their community.

Recent examples of atrocities caused by systemic racism include domestic terrorist attacks conducted by White supremacists (American Oversight, 2022), brutalization and murder of countless African Americans by police (*BBC News*, 2021), a recent mass shooting that targeted Asian Americans (*The New York Times*, 2021), proposed legislation banning transgender girls and women from participating in interscholastic sports (Selbe, 2021), and the detention and separation of refugee families at the southern border of the United States (Domonoske & Gonzales, 2018). To address these issues and others, couple, marriage, and family practitioners advocate and collaborate with stakeholders, including politicians, policy makers, citizens, fellow professionals, students, and police to update policies, organize relevant taskforces and committees, gather data to support just action, publicly denounce egregious hate-based acts, model and empower groups to create a culturally responsive environment, and demonstrate the profession's solidarity with oppressed and marginalized populations.

THE ROLE OF THE COUPLE, MARRIAGE, AND FAMILY PRACTITIONER

According to Minuchin (1974), human life is influenced by social context, which we also influence. Couple, marriage, and family work is predicated on the theory that people are not isolated from each other. Individuals are acting and reacting members of social groups. Reality is dependent on internal and external components, and human interaction is dependent on environment. A family is a natural social group that governs its members' responses to inputs from within and without. In many cases, the family can be seen as the extracerebral part of the mind. Every theory of family therapy offers its own conceptualization of how members communicate and are regulated. For example, structural family therapy postulates that a family has six ways of regulating its members: methods of relating, rules, roles, boundaries, hierarchy, and power (Minuchin, 1974).

From the vantage point of couple, marriage, and family practitioners, problems are viewed as interactional in nature and the result of group dynamics. Instead of a reflection of the individual members, the family is a complex system where phenomena like boundaries, roles, and patterns are viewed as holistic and recursive. Each member of the family is responsible for and dependent on the others (i.e., interdependence). While different theories offer different objectives, a major goal of any family therapy work is to help family members become *systems experts* who can understand their family system so well that they can eventually change the rules and dynamics without the assistance of a helping professional (Kerr & Bowen, 1988). Systems are ruled by patterns of change and stability. Most of the time, families come to therapy because they need to find a new and meaningful way to change in order to properly stabilize (i.e., homeostasis). This *change of change* requires a deep level of understanding, humility, and skill on the part of the family and the practitioner (Keeney & Ross, 1983). Couples also come to therapy hoping for change. As each member works with their partner's pain and unmet needs from the past, they are working toward improved communication, relationship satisfaction, enduring compatibility, and partner self-soothing.

As humans, we are each unique. No two humans are exactly the same. We each have our own way of communicating and expressing ourselves verbally and nonverbally. As humans, we use our five senses to experience the world and communicate with others. Nobody understands our unique communication patterns as well as our families and intimate partners do. They are with us every day and witness our distinctive way of relating to others. Couple, marriage, and family practitioners specialize in communication and must be able to communicate effectively as well as understand the verbal and nonverbal messages their clients are sending. Therapy as an art and science is a deeply personal experience that depends on communication. The final section of this chapter explores verbal and nonverbal communication in systemic work.

Verbal Communication in Systemic Work

According to Merriam-Webster (n.d.), *communication* is the act or process of using words, sounds, signs, or behaviors to express or exchange information or to express ideas, thoughts, feelings, and so forth to someone else. When therapy is done effectively, clients are experiencing emotions, thoughts, and levels of awareness that are likely very new to them, and practitioners deeply listen and empathize with clients' verbal and nonverbal messages. Because many of these client-based levels of awareness, emotions, thoughts, and experiences are coming from an internal frame of reference, they may seem confusing to the listener. In a single sentence, a client may express two completely different messages. While any odd or confusing communication during therapy can reflect the notion that people have various thoughts and feelings about others, a situation, or a phenomenon, it may also reflect the unique context, behaviors, and communication style of the client(s).

Verbal communication confusion can reflect an individual's, couple's, and/or family's context and/or unique communication style. A few common verbal issues include culturally specific terms (e.g., *woke, bae, hella, spirit animal*), ambiguous phrases (e.g., *you know, cryptic*), inclusive terms (e.g., *guys, them, parents*), words that have double meaning (e.g., *break, gay, stoned, trip*), labile or slow and monotonous vocal pace and tone, and speaking without listening. Some clients have biological and/or psychological issues that affect their verbal communication (e.g., Tourette syndrome, stutter, speech impediment), while other differences reflect lifestyle choices (e.g., alcohol abuse, smoking; Cormier et al., 2017; Ivey et al., 2018; Young, 2016).

Mixed messages are another common issue that emerges during communication between clients and clinicians. Clients often smile, laugh, or joke when discussing serious, traumatic, and painful issues. This may reflect their culture, the unsettling nature of expressing certain information, their underlying anxiety, or the fact that their coping skills are the opposite of the emotion being expressed. Certain nonverbal messages (e.g., tearfulness, sudden body jerk, fast tapping of foot) can provide evidence of the severity of the issue being expressed (Cormier et al., 2017). Practitioners note all aspects of a client's speaking voice and they clarify confusing messages. Specifically, clinicians ask the client to elaborate on vague, ambiguous, or implied statements, with the request for clarification usually expressed as a question beginning with phrases such as "Are you saying this?" "Could you try to describe that?" or "Can you clarify that?" Clarifications can also be in the form of statements with a questioning connotation, with phrases such as "*They* are always talking about you?" (Cormier et al., 2017; Flynn & Hays, 2015).

Geldard (1989) described three important ways in which people communicate: kinesthetic/feeling mode, seeing/visual mode, and auditory/hearing mode. Couple, marriage, and family practitioners learn which senses the client uses to experience the world and employ those words to connect more deeply with the client. For example, some people use auditory-oriented phrases like "I hear what you say" or "That rings a bell for me" and "It sounds like you mean. . . ." Others may use a visual mode and say things like "I see what you mean," "It looks good," and "I've got a clear picture." Still others, using a kinesthetic mode, might say "It feels good," "You touched a raw nerve there," and "I sense your discomfort."

Visual (Seeing) Mode

According to Geldard (1989), clients who experience the world primarily through sight tend to use visual imagery in their communication. When practitioners use this mode to respond, they join at a much deeper level. For example:

Client: It seems to me that the *writing is on the wall*, there's nothing that I can do to save the situation, and I can *see* nothing but disaster from now on.

Clinician: The *outlook's* a really bad one.

Client: It's as though there is a brick wall around him. It has no door, and no way in or out. When I *look* over the wall, I *see* a very strange person.

Clinician: You *picture* him as a strange man surrounded by a brick wall.

Kinesthetic (Feeling) Mode

Clients who primarily use a feeling mode to experience their world tend to use kinesthetic terms in their communication (Geldard, 1989). For example:

Client: I went back there once more, but as before, the place gave me *bad vibes*. I had to leave because my *stomach was churning* and my *hands were sweating*.

Clinician: You *felt* so uncomfortable that you left.

Client: She gave me a bunch of flowers and I was really *touched* by that. In fact, I feel quite different about our relationship now because the *coldness* we experienced before has been replaced by *warmth*.

Clinician: Your *feelings* towards her have changed and are now very pleasant.

Auditory (Hearing) Mode

Clients who predominantly experience the world in an auditory manner tend to use terms related to hearing (Geldard, 1989). For example:

Client: In the past, my mother has *frequently criticized* my wife, and I have always *listened* to what she has said. Recently, though, I've started to *question* what she's told me, and I'm inclined to say that some of her *statements* about Monica may be wrong.

Clinician: It *sounds* as though you've got doubts about the accuracy of what your mother tells you.

Nonverbal Communication in Systemic Work

According to communication experts, 80% to 90% of communication between humans takes place nonverbally (Yaffe, 2011). According to Mehrabian (1971), all communication reflects the 7-38-55 rule. Specifically, communication is 7% words, 38% tone, and 55% facial expression. While this rule is referenced in many places, it is based on two classic research studies (e.g., Mehrabian & Ferris, 1967; Mehrabian & Wiener, 1967). Nonverbal communication includes eye contact, body position, silence, facial expressions and gestures, and physical distance. In the context of family and couple therapy, a very important nonverbal assessment involves where family members sit in relation to others. For example, two family members sitting close together could represent a subsystem or a coalition. Triangulation is often symbolized when two family members sit close together while a third sits far away. In a couple therapy situation, the couple, marriage, and family practitioner will consider a variety of aspects of nonverbal behavior, including, but not limited to, "How close are they sitting together?" "Are they touching one another?" "Are there changes in body positioning when certain topics are brought up?" and "Do they make occasional eye contact?" Understanding nonverbal systemic behavior is the first step in *family mapping* (Minuchin & Fishman, 1981).

In Western and Northern European culture, eye contact is often considered the most important indicator of listening. Lack of eye contact is associated with dishonesty, indifference, or shame. Those who sustain eye contact are seen as ambitious, confident, assertive, intelligent, independent, and decisive (Cormier et al., 2017; Ivey et al., 2018; Young, 2016).

Other cultural groups do not place the same value on eye contact. Some cultures may find direct eye contact to be a sign of defiance, a rude gesture, a sexual invitation, or a sign that you consider yourself superior. Some Asian cultures may be offended by direct eye contact, while some African Americans may have been taught to look away when listening.

As a clinician, you may choose to mirror your client's use of eye contact. Matching eye contact is part of the joining process and relates to the structural family therapy skill *mimesis*. Mimesis is a nonverbal/verbal technique popularized by Minuchin and Fishman (1981). When using this skill, the therapist adopts the family's communication style and conforms to its affective range. In addition, the practitioner adopts the family language, manners, style, affective range, and behaviors.

Body posture is essentially the way one holds their body. Helping professionals attempt to engage clients with an open and accepting body posture, and at times they mirror a client's posture to enhance and deepen the level of connection. Posture is the most frequently noticed aspect of body language. A relaxed alertness communicates "I am comfortable with myself, and I have time to listen to you." Lounging or sprawling out adds a level of informality and may communicate that the level of the clinician's involvement is minimal. While different styles exist, in general, clinicians ought to lean the torso slightly forward to engage clients and maintain an open posture (e.g., no crossed arms or legs in most situations; Cormier et al., 2017; Ivey et al., 2018; Young, 2016).

Unfilled pauses or periods of quiet can serve various functions in therapy sessions (e.g., reducing one's level of activity, slowing down session pace, giving client time to think, and returning responsibility to the client). While silence is a powerful tool in therapy, there is a social norm to fill awkward voids in conversation. From a different perspective, excessive talking can be perceived as attempts to sweep things under the rug and/or deny the validity of the other person's experiences. Moments of silence give the client time to reflect, ponder, and see things from different perspectives. While some silence is helpful, practitioners should be careful not to use too much silence in the initial stages because the client may feel unsupported or awkward. In general, clients feel better about sessions if the helper talks about one-third of the time or less (Cormier et al., 2017; Flynn & Hays, 2015; Ivey et al., 2018; Young, 2016).

Systemic practitioners work hard to convey specific facial expressions, gestures, and reactions to clients. Often the more favorable facial expression and gesture is moderately reactive. Sadness, joy, anger, contempt, surprise, disgust, and fear are expressed facially regardless of culture (Humintell Admin, 2010). Incongruities between facial expression and verbal messages are clues to deceit, lack of awareness, and conflict. Excessive movement may signal anxiety, whereas a motionless pose communicates aloofness. Fidgeting, playing with a pencil, drumming one's fingers, frequently shifting body position, and checking a watch can be viewed as nervousness, impatience, or lack of interest (Cormier et al., 2017; Ivey et al., 2018; Young, 2016).

SUMMARY

Within this chapter, the systemic paradigm; the four waves of psychotherapy (psycho-analytic/dynamic, behavioral, humanistic, and cognitive); the unique ethical issues related to couple, marriage, child, and family therapy; ethical issues involved in tele-therapy; the concerns involving diversity, intersectionality, systemic racism, and cultural responsiveness; and the role of the couple, marriage, and family practitioner in relation to verbal and nonverbal communication were reviewed. This chapter sets the framework and serves as the backbone for the remainder of the textbook. The themes of diversity and racism, telebehavioral health, theory, skills, ethics, and contemporary issues will be revisited throughout the remainder of the book. It is my hope that this theoretical and pragmatic experience will result in a deeply rooted enhancement of your understanding of skills and theory.

END-OF-CHAPTER RESOURCES

STUDENT ACTIVITIES

Exercise 1: Licensure

Directions: Review the following information and follow the instructions provided:

Licensure requirements and qualifications for treating couples, families, and children vary from state to state. Being aware of the licensure expectations of your state is very important. Find your state's mental health licensure regulatory board website and investigate the licensure standards and requirements for your desired mental health license. If you are planning on practicing in multiple states, it may also be helpful to consider the licensure requirements of additional states that you are interested in working in.

Exercise 2: Article Review

Directions: Review the following instructions and answer the questions:

Go to your university's online EBSCO Database and find Academic Search Premier. Search and find an article focused on one of the master therapists listed within this chapter (e.g., Virginia Satir, Carl Rogers). Review the article in its entirety and answer the following questions related to how that frontrunner made significant contributions to the field of psychology:

- What was your chosen practitioner's major contribution to their field?
- Are they known for carrying out any important research studies?
- Did this person create their own theory? If so, what are the background and influences of the theory?

Exercise 3: Therapeutic Techniques

Directions: Review the following instructions and create a mock plan for potential clients:

After reading through this chapter, you should have a basic understanding of some of the contributions to psychology by many major theorists. Using one of these theories, create a mock plan for a potential future client that you could use within the counseling sessions. How would your knowledge of these theories support your effectiveness in helping your clients? Did one theory stand out to you more than others? Research this theory in more depth and then explore how you could use this theory with future clients.

Exercise 4: Understanding the Ethics of Telehealth

Directions: Review the following information and answer the reflection questions:

Telehealth has become more commonplace within all helping professions, including systemically oriented therapy. It is important to understand the ethics involved in providing services via telehealth platforms.

- Describe the qualifications of any telehealth platform used for therapy.
- Consider how telehealth may change the therapeutic relationship with your client(s). What work can you do to maintain this relationship while not being in the room with them?
- When conducting telehealth, what are the necessary standards for maintaining protected health information?

Exercise 5: Informed Consent

Directions: Review the following instructions and create a mock informed consent form:

Ethics within the couple, marriage, and family therapy field can be a gray area, and the answers to our questions are not always clear. This is especially true when working with minors or with more than one client within a family system. Understanding the specific ethics involved in working with these types of clients is important, and informing your clients of their rights within a consent form is even more so. After reading this chapter and doing some research of your own, create a mock informed consent form that could be used when working with a minor, with a couple, or with a family system. Since informed consent differs for each category of client, it is important to be aware of what those differences are.

ADDITIONAL RESOURCES

HELPFUL LINKS

- "What Is Telemental Health?": https://www.nimh.nih.gov/health/publications/what-is-telemental-health
- "Introduction to Telehealth for Behavioral Health Care": https://telehealth.hhs.gov/providers/telehealth-for-behavioral-health/
- "The Fourth Wave of Psychotherapies": https://www.psychologytoday.com/us/blog/finding-new-home/201804/the-fourth-wave-psychotherapies
- "Different Approaches to Psychotherapy": https://www.apa.org/topics/psychotherapy/approaches
- "Understanding the Unsaid: Enhancing Multicultural Competence Through Nonverbal Awareness": https://www.counseling.org/docs/default-source/vistas/understanding-the-unsaid-enhancing-multicultural.pdf?sfvrsn=9
- "Nonverbal Communication Skills: 19 Theories and Findings": https://positivepsychology.com/nonverbal-communication/
- "Deadly Attacks on Black Trans Women Are Going Up. This Grieving Mom Is Fighting Back": https://www.cnn.com/2021/06/13/us/black-transgender-women-attacks-trnd/index.html
- "The January 6 Attack on the U.S. Capitol": https://www.americanoversight.org/investigation/the-january-6-attack-on-the-u-s-capitol
- "In Atlanta, Biden Condemns Attacks on Asian Americans": https://www.nytimes.com/live/2021/03/19/us/atlanta-shootings-massage-spa
- "George Floyd: Timeline of Black Deaths and Protests": https://www.bbc.com/news/world-us-canada-52905408

HELPFUL BOOKS

- Baldwin, J. D., & Baldwin, J. I. (2000). *Behavior principles in everyday life*. Prentice Hall.

- Bandura, A. (Ed.). (1995). *Self-efficacy in changing societies*. Cambridge University Press.

- Becvar, R. J., Canfield, B. S., & Becvar, D. S. (1997). *Group work: Cybernetic, constructivist, and social constructionist perspectives*. Love Publishing Company.

- Carkhuff, R. R., & Benoit, D. (2019). *The art of helping*. Human Resource Development Press.

- Caldwell, B. E. (2015). *User's guide to the 2015 AAMFT Code of Ethics*. American Association for Marriage and Family Therapy.

- Cooper, J. O., Heron, T. E., & Heward, W. L. (2020). *Applied behavior analysis* (3rd ed.). Pearson.

- Cormier, L. S., Nurius, P., & Osborn, C. J. (2017). *Interviewing and change strategies for helpers*. Cengage Learning.

- Elzer, M., & Gerlach, A. (2014). *Psychoanalytic psychotherapy: A handbook*. Routledge.

- Meichenbaum, D. (1977). *Cognitive-behavior modification: An integrative approach*. Plenum.

- Murphy, M. J., & Hecker, L. L. (2017). *Ethics and professional issues in couple and family therapy* (2nd ed.). Routledge/Taylor & Francis Group.

- Prochaska, J. O., & Norcross, J. C. (2018). *Systems of psychotherapy: A transtheoretical analysis*. Oxford University Press.

- Satir, V. M. (1972). *Peoplemaking, by Virginia Satir*. Science and Behavior Books.

HELPFUL VIDEOS

- Family Systems #1: Introduction: https://www.youtube.com/watch?v=32qux1OCYMw&t=7s

- Family Systems #2: Cybernetics: https://www.youtube.com/watch?v=Fh3gzICZ3KA

- Sigmund Freud's Psychoanalytic Theory Explained: https://www.youtube.com/watch?v=lT4wQ02sALE

- Psychotherapy—Sigmund Freud: https://www.youtube.com/watch?v=mQaqXK7z9LM

- What Is Behavior Therapy?: https://www.youtube.com/watch?v=soJMOj-7iNQ

- The Difference Between Classical and Operant Conditioning (Peggy Andover): https://www.youtube.com/watch?v=H6LEcM0E0io

- Approaches in Psychology: Humanistic: https://www.youtube.com/watch?v=dtiQV_mg2bg

- What Is Cognitive Therapy? (Beckian Therapy): https://www.youtube.com/watch?v=xYauAv4Gd68

- Defining Cognitive Therapy: https://www.youtube.com/watch?v=ZZt-Q1DR3Ds

REFERENCES

Amatea, E. S., & Sherrard, P. A. D. (1994). The ecosystemic view: A choice of lenses. *Journal of Mental Health Counseling, 16*(1), 6–21. https://psycnet.apa.org/record/1994-26501-001

American Association for Marriage and Family Therapy. (2015). *AAMFT Code of Ethics*. AAMFT. American Counseling Association.

American Oversight. (2022, May 2). *The January 6 attack on the U.S. capitol*. https://www.americanoversight.org/investigation/the-january-6-attack-on-the-u-s-capitol

American Psychiatric Association. (2022). *Diagnostic and statistical manual of mental disorders* (5th ed., Text Revision). https://doi.org/10.1176/appi.books.9780890425787

American Psychological Association. (2020). Cognitive therapy (CT). In *APA dictionary of psychology*. Retrieved October 19, 2021, from https://dictionary.apa.org/cognitive-therapy

Anderson, L., & Gatwiri, K. (2021, June 22). *The Senate has voted to reject critical race theory from the National Curriculum. What is it, and why does it matter?* The Conversation. https://theconversation.com/the-senate-has-voted-to-reject-critical-race-theory-from-the-national-curriculum-what-is-it-and-why-does-it-matter-163102

Anderson, N. B., Lawrence, P. S., & Olson, T. W. (1981). Within-subject analysis of autogenic training and cognitive coping training in the treatment of tension headache pain. *Journal of Behavior Therapy and Experimental Psychiatry, 12*(3), 219–223. https://doi.org/10.1016/0005-7916(81)90049-5

Antony, M. M., & Roemer, L. (2003). Behavior therapy. In A. S. Gurman & S. B. Messer (Eds.), *Essential psychotherapies: Theory and practice* (pp. 182–223). Guilford Press.

Ayllon, T., & Azrin, N. H. (1968). Reinforcer sampling: A technique for increasing the behavior of mental patients1. *Journal of Applied Behavior Analysis, 1*(1), 13–20. https://doi.org/10.1901/jaba.1968.1-13

Baldwin, J. D., & Baldwin, J. I. (2000). *Behavior principles in everyday life*. Prentice Hall.

Bandura, A. (Ed.). (1995). *Self-efficacy in changing societies*. Cambridge University Press. https://doi.org/10.1017/CBO9780511527692

Bandura, A., & Walters, R. H. (1977). *Social learning theory*. Prentice-Hall.

Bandura, A., Ross, D., & Ross, S. A. (1961). Transmission of aggression through imitation of aggressive models. *The Journal of Abnormal and Social Psychology, 63*(3), 575–582. https://doi.org/10.1037/h0045925

Bartlett, E. E. (1996). Protecting the confidentiality of children and adolescents. In *The Hatherleigh guide to child and adolescent therapy* (Vol. 5, pp. 275–290). The Hatherleigh Guides series. Hatherleigh Press.

BBC News. (2021, April 22). *George Floyd: Timeline of Black deaths and protests*. https://www.bbc.com/news/world-us-canada-52905408

Bean, R. A., Perry, B. J., & Bedell, T. M. (2001). Developing culturally competent marriage and family therapists: Guidelines for working with Hispanic families. *Journal of Marital and Family Therapy, 27*(1), 43–54. https://doi.org/10.1111/j.1752-0606.2001.tb01138.x

Beauchamp, T. L., & Childress, J. F. (2001). *Principles of biomedical ethics*. Oxford University Press.

Beck, A. T. (1967). *Depression: Clinical, experimental, and theoretical aspects*. Harper and Row.

Beck, A. T. (1976). *Cognitive therapy and the emotional disorders*. International Universities Press.

Becvar, D., & Becvar, R. (2013). *Family therapy: A systemic integration*. Pearson Education.

Becvar, R. J., Canfield, B. S., & Becvar, D. S. (1997). *Group work: Cybernetic, constructivist, and social constructionist perspectives*. Love Publishing Company.

Bellack, A. S., & Hersen, M. (1985). *Dictionary of behavior therapy techniques*. Pergamon Press.

Bohart, A. C. (2003). Person-centered psychotherapy and related experiential approaches. In A. S. Gurman & S. B. Messer (Eds.), *Essential psychotherapies: Theory and practice* (pp. 107–148). Guilford Press.

Boszormenyi-Nagy, I. (1966). From family relationships to a psychology of relationships: Fictions of the individual and fictions of the family. *Comprehensive Psychiatry, 7*(5), 408–423. https://doi.org/10.1016/S0010-440X(66)80070-6

Breuer, J., & Freud, S. (1957). *Studies on hysteria*. Basic Books.

Carkhuff, R. R., & Benoit, D. (2019). *The art of helping*. Human Resource Development Press.

Caldwell, B. E. (2015). *User's guide to the 2015 AAMFT Code of Ethics*. American Association for Marriage and Family Therapy.

Caldwell, B. (2016). *MFTs lose diagnosis fight at Texas Supreme Court*. Psychotherapy Notes. https://www.psychotherapynotes.com/mfts-lose-diagnosis-fight-texas-supreme-court/

Chenneville, T., Sibille, K., & Bendell-Estroff, D. (2010). Decisional capacity among minors with HIV: A model for balancing autonomy rights with the need for protection. *Ethics & Behavior, 20*(2), 83–94. https://doi.org/10.1080/10508421003595901

Coffman, C., & Barnett, J. E. (2015, October). *Informed consent with children and adolescents*. Society for the Advancement of Psychotherapy. https://societyforpsychotherapy.org/informed-consent-with-children-and-adolescents/

Cooper, J. O., Heron, T. E., & Heward, W. L. (2020). *Applied behavior analysis* (3rd ed.). Pearson.

Cormier, L. S., Nurius, P., & Osborn, C. J. (2017). *Interviewing and change strategies for helpers*. Cengage Learning.

Crenshaw, K. (1991). Mapping the margins: Intersectionality, identity politics, and violence against women of color. *Stanford Law Review, 43*(6), 1241. https://doi.org/10.2307/1229039

Crisp, B., & Knox, D. (2008). *Behavioral family therapy: An evidenced based approach*. Carolina Academic Press.

Crisp, R. J., & Turner, R. (2014). *Essential social psychology*. Sage.

Davis, K. (2008). Intersectionality as buzzword. *Feminist Theory, 9*(1), 67–85. https://doi.org/10.1177/1464700108086364

Davis, S. D., & Nichols, M. P. (2020). *The essentials of family therapy* (7th ed.). Pearson.

Domonoske, C., & Gonzales, R. (2018, June 19). *What we know: Family separation and 'zero tolerance' at the border*. NPR. https://www.npr.org/2018/06/19/621065383/what-we-know-family-separation-and-zero-tolerance-at-the-border

Ellis, A. (1957). Rational psychotherapy and individual psychology. *Journal of Individual Psychology, 13*, 38–44.

Ellis, A. (1962). *Reason and emotion in psychotherapy*. Lyle Stuart.

Ellis, A., David, D., & Lynn, S. J. (2010). Rational and irrational beliefs: A historical and conceptual perspective. In D. David, S. J. Lynn, & A. Ellis (Eds.), *Rational and irrational beliefs: Research, theory, and clinical practice* (pp. 3–22). Oxford University Press.

Elzer, M., & Gerlach, A. (2014). *Psychoanalytic psychotherapy: A handbook*. Routledge.

Erikson, E. H. (1950). *Childhood and society*. W. W. Norton.

Flynn, S. V., & Hays, D. G. (2015). The development and validation of the comprehensive counseling skills rubric. *Counseling Outcome Research and Evaluation*. https://doi.org/10.1177/2150137815592216

Gay, V. P. (1989). Philosophy, psychoanalysis, and the problem of change. *Psychoanalytic Inquiry, 9*(1), 26–44. https://doi.org/10.1080/07351698909533753

Gee, G. C., & Ford, C. L. (2011). Structural racism and health inequities: Old issues, new directions. *Du Bois Review: Social Science Research on Race, 8*(1), 115–132. https://doi.org/10.1017/S1742058X11000130

Geldard, D. (1989). *Basic personal counselling: A training manual for counsellors*. Cengage.

Gottlieb, M. C., Lasser, J., & Simpson, G. L. (2008). Legal and ethical issues in couple therapy. In A. S. Gurman (Ed.), *Clinical handbook of couple therapy* (pp. 698–717). Guilford Press.

Hanna, F. J., Talley, W. B., & Guindon, M. H. (2000). The power of perception: Toward a model of cultural oppression and liberation. *Journal of Counseling & Development, 78*(4), 430–441. https://doi.org/10.1002/j.1556-6676.2000.tb01926.x

Hanna, S. M. (2018). *The practice of family therapy: Key elements across models* (5th ed.). Routledge. https://doi.org/10.4324/9781351051460

Healthie. (2020). *The 5 best HIPAA compliant telehealth tools*. https://www.gethealthie.com/blog/the-5-best-hipaa-compliant-telehealth-tools

Health Information Technology for Economic and Clinical Health (HITECH) Act, Title XIII of Division A and Title IV of Division B of the American Recovery and Reinvestment Act of 2009 (ARRA), Pub. L. No. 111-5, 123 Stat. 226. (2009, February 17). Full-text, *codified at* 42 U.S.C. §§300jj *et seq.*; §§17901 *et seq.*

Health Insurance Portability and Accountability Act (HIPAA). Pub. L. No. 104-191, § 264, 110 Stat. 1936.

Hecker, L. L., & Edwards, A. B. (2014). The impact of HIPAA and HITECH: New standards for confidentiality, security, and documentation for marriage and family therapists. *The American Journal of Family Therapy, 42*(2), 95–113. https://doi.org/10.1080/01926187.2013.792711

Hembree, E. A., Rauch, S. A. M., & Foa, E. B. (2003). Beyond the manual: The insider's guide to prolonged exposure therapy for PTSD. *Cognitive and Behavioral Practice, 10*(1), 22–30. https://doi.org/10.1016/S1077-7229(03)80005-6

Henriques, G. R., & Glover, A. (2012). *A unified approach to conceptualizing people in psychotherapy*. PsycEXTRA Dataset. https://doi.org/10.1037/e699542011-001

Higdon, J., & Higdon, J. (2011). *Psychodynamic theory for therapeutic practice*. Palgrave Macmillan.

Howes, R. (2012). *A client's guide to transference*. Psychology Today. https://www.psychologytoday.com/us/blog/in-therapy/201206/clients-guide-transference

Humintell Admin. (2010, June 24). *The seven basic emotions: Do you know them?* Humintell.com. https://www.humintell.com/2010/06/the-seven-basic-emotions-do-you-know-them/

Ivey, A. E., Ivey, M. B., & Zalaquett, C. P. (2018). *Intentional interviewing and counseling: Facilitating client development in a multicultural society* (9th ed.). Cognella Academic Publishing.

Karimi, F. (2021, June 13). *Deadly attacks on Black trans women are going up. This grieving mom is fighting back*. CNN. https://www.cnn.com/2021/06/13/us/black-transgender-women-attacks-trnd/index.html

Keeney, B. P., & Ross, J. M. (1983). Cybernetics of brief family therapy. *Journal of Marital and Family Therapy, 9*(4), 375–382. https://doi.org/10.1111/j.1752-0606.1983.tb01525.x

Kelman, H. C. (1967). Human use of human subjects: The problem of deception in social psychological experiments. *Psychological Bulletin, 67*(1), 1–11. https://doi.org/10.1037/h0024072

Kernberg, O. F. (2004). Borderline personality disorder and borderline personality organization: Psychopathology and psychotherapy. In J. J. Magnavita (Ed.), *Handbook of personality disorders: Theory and practice* (pp. 92–119). John Wiley & Sons.

Kernberg, O. F. (2008). *Contemporary controversies in psychoanalytic theory, techniques, and their applications.* Yale University Press. https://doi.org/10.12987/9780300128369

Kerr, M. E., & Bowen, M. (1988). *Family evaluation: An approach based on Bowen theory.* W. W. Norton & Company.

Kocian, R. (2017, February). *Family therapists win in Texas Supreme Court.* Courthousenews.com. Retrieved October 19, 2021, from https://www.courthousenews.com/family-therapists-win -texas-supreme-court/

Lester, G. W., Beckham, E., & Baucom, D. H. (1980). Implementation of behavioral marital therapy. *Journal of Marital and Family Therapy, 6*(2), 189–199. https://doi.org/10.1111/j.1752-0606.1980 .tb01305.x

Lewis, J. A., Williams, M. G., Peppers, E. J., & Gadson, C. A. (2017). Applying intersectionality to explore the relations between gendered racism and health among Black women. *Journal of Counseling Psychology, 64*(5), 475–486. https://doi.org/10.1037/cou0000231

Luyten, P., Maynes, L., Fonagy, P., Target, M., & Blatt, S. (2017). *Handbook of psychodynamic approaches to psychopathology.* Guilford Press.

Mappes, D. C., Robb, G. P., & Engels, D. W. (1985). Conflicts between ethics and law in counseling and psychotherapy. *Journal of Counseling & Development, 64*(4), 246–252. https://doi .org/10.1002/j.1556-6676.1985.tb01094.x

McCabe, M. (2006). Involving children and adolescents in decisions about medical and mental health treatment. *The Register Report, 32,* 20–23.

McNary, A. (2014). Consent to treatment of minors. *Innovations in Clinical Neuroscience, 11*(3-4), 43–45. PMID: 24800133.

McNeil-Haber, F. M. (2004). Ethical considerations in the use of nonerotic touch in psychotherapy with children. *Ethics & Behavior, 14*(2), 123–140. https://doi.org/10.1207/s15327019eb1402_3

Mehrabian, A. (1971). *Silent messages.* Wadsworth Publishing Company.

Mehrabian, A., & Ferris, S. R. (1967). Inference of attitudes from nonverbal communication in two channels. *Journal of Consulting Psychology, 31*(3), 248–252. https://doi.org/10.1037/h0024648

Mehrabian, A., & Wiener, M. (1967). Decoding of inconsistent communications. *Journal of Personality and Social Psychology, 6*(1), 109–114. https://doi.org/10.1037/h0024532

Meichenbaum, D. (1977). *Cognitive-behavior modification: An integrative approach.* Plenum.

Meichenbaum, D. (2017). *The evolution of cognitive behavior therapy: A personal and professional journey with Don Meichenbaum.* Routledge/Taylor & Francis Group. https://doi.org/10.4324/9781315748931

Mercieca, D. P., & Mercieca, D. (2018). Judgements on young children by early years practitioners: Working with phronêsis. *International Journal of Inclusive Education, 24*(13), 1431–1443. https://doi.org/10.1080/13603116.2018.1532534

Merriam-Webster. (n.d.). Communication. In *Merriam-Webster.com dictionary.* Retrieved October 19, 2020, from https://www.merriam-webster.com/dictionary/communication

Minuchin, S. (1974). *Families & family therapy.* Harvard University Press.

Minuchin, S., & Fishman, H. C. (1981). *Family therapy techniques.* Harvard University Press.

Mosley, D. V., Hargons, C. N., Meiller, C., Angyal, B., Wheeler, P., Davis, C., & Stevens-Watkins, D. (2020, March 26). Critical consciousness of anti-Black racism: A practical model to prevent and resist racial trauma. *Journal of Counseling Psychology.* Advance online publication. https://doi.org/10.1037/cou0000430

Murphy, M. J., & Hecker, L. L. (2017). *Ethics and professional issues in couple and family therapy* (2nd ed.). Routledge/Taylor & Francis Group.

Nichols, M. P. (2011). *The essentials of family therapy.* Allyn & Bacon.

Pavlov, I. (1927). Conditioned reflexes: An investigation of the physiological activity of the cerebral cortex. *Archives of Neurology and Psychiatry, 23*(5), 1090. https://doi.org/10.1001/archneurpsyc.1930.02220110256018

Prochaska, J. O., & Norcross, J. C. (2018). *Systems of psychotherapy: A transtheoretical analysis.* Oxford University Press.

Raskin, N. J., & Rogers, C. R. (1989). Person-centered therapy. In R. J. Corsini & D. Wedding (Eds.), *Current psychotherapies* (pp. 155–194). F. E. Peacock Publishers.

Reinecke, M. A., Dattilio, F. M., & Freeman, A. (Eds.). (2003). *Cognitive therapy with children and adolescents: A casebook for clinical practice* (2nd ed.). Guilford Press.

Renaissance Ranch Treatment Centers. (2021, July 13). *Virginia Satir and her thoughts about family therapy*. Retrieved October 19, 2021, from https://renaissanceranch.net/virginia-satir/

Roberts, L. W., & Dyer, A. R. (2004). *Concise guide to ethics in mental health care*. American Psychiatric Publishing.

Rogers, C. R. (1970). Toward a theory of creativity. In P. Vernon (Ed.), *Creativity: Selected readings* (pp. 137–151). Penguin Books.

Rogers, C. R. (1963). The concept of the fully functioning person. *Psychotherapy: Theory, Research & Practice, 1*(1), 17–26. https://doi.org/10.1037/h0088567

Satir, V. M. (1967). *Conjoint family therapy: A guide to theory and technique by Virginia Satir*. Science and Behavior Books.

Satir, V. M. (1972). *Peoplemaking, by Virginia Satir*. Science and Behavior Books.

Satir, V. M. (1995). *Making contact*. Celestial Arts.

Satir, V. M., Banmen, J., Gerber, J., & Gomori, M., (1991). *The Satir model: Family therapy and beyond*. Science and Behavior Books.

Scharff, D. E., & Scharff, J. S. (1987). *Object relations family therapy*. Jason Aronson.

Scharff, D. E., & Scharff, J. S. (1991). *Object relations couple therapy*. Jason Aronson.

Scholl, M. B., McGowan, A. S., & Hansen, J. T. (2012). *Humanistic perspectives on contemporary counseling issues*. Routledge.

Scholl, M. B., Ray, D. C., & Brady-Amoon, P. (2013). Humanistic counseling process, outcomes, and research. *The Journal of Humanistic Counseling, 53*(3), 218–239. https://doi.org/10.1002/j.2161-1939.2014.00058.x

Selbe, N. (2021, March 26). Multiple governors sign bills banning transgender athletes from school sports. *Sports Illustrated*. https://www.si.com/high-school/2021/03/25/arkansas-governor-signs-bill-transgender-girls-ban-school-sports

Seponski, D. M., Bermudez, J. M., & Lewis, D. C. (2012). Creating culturally responsive family therapy models and research: Introducing the use of responsive evaluation as a method. *Journal of Marital and Family Therapy, 39*(1), 28–42. https://doi.org/10.1111/j.1752-0606.2011.00282.x

Shallcross, L. (2010, February 14). Managing resistant clients. *Counseling Today*. https://ct.counseling.org/2010/02/managing-resistant-clients/

Skinner, B. F. (1953). *Science and human behavior*. Macmillan.

Slipp, S. (1993). *Object relations: A dynamic bridge between individual and family treatment* (2nd ed.). Jason Aronson.

Smith-Acuña, S. (2011). *Systems theory in action: Applications to individual, couples, and family therapy*. John Wiley & Sons.

Solomon, M. A. (1973). A developmental, conceptual premise for family therapy. *Family Process, 12*(2), 179–188. https://doi.org/10.1111/j.1545-5300.1973.00179.x

Sori, C. F., & Hecker, L. L. (2015). Ethical and legal considerations when counselling children and families. *Australian and New Zealand Journal of Family Therapy, 36*(4), 450–464. https://doi.org/10.1002/anzf.1126

The New York Times. (2021, March 19). *In Atlanta, Biden condemns attacks on Asian Americans*. https://www.nytimes.com/live/2021/03/19/us/atlanta-shootings-massage-spa

Turri, M. G., Merson, S., McNab, S., & Cooper, R. E. (2020). The systemic assessment clinic, a novel method for assessing patients in general adult psychiatry: Presentation and preliminary service evaluation. *Community Mental Health Journal. Advance online publication*. https://doi.org/10.1007/s10597-020-00694-5

Waites, C., Macgowan, M. J., Pennell, J., Carlton-LaNey, I., & Weil, M. (2004). Increasing the cultural responsiveness of family group conferencing. *Social Work, 49*(2), 291–300. https://doi.org/10.1093/sw/49.2.291

Walsh, W. M., & McGraw, J. A. (2002). *Essentials of family therapy: A structured summary of nine approaches*. Love Publishing Company.

Wiener, N. (1948). *Cybernetics: Or control and communication in the animal and the machine*. John Wiley.

Wolitzky, D. L. (2003). The theory and practice of traditional psychoanalytic treatment. In A. S. Gurman & S. B. Messer (Eds.), *Essential psychotherapies: Theory and practice* (pp. 24–68). Guilford Press.

Wolpe, J. (1958). *Psychotherapy by reciprocal inhibition*. Stanford University Press.

Woody, R. H. (2000). Professional ethics, regulatory licensing, and malpractice complaints. In F. W. Kaslow (Ed.), *Handbook of couple and family forensics: A sourcebook for mental health and legal professionals* (pp. 461–474). John Wiley & Sons.

Yaffe, P. (2011). The 7% rule. *Ubiquity, 2011*(October), 1–5. https://doi.org/10.1145/2043155.2043156

Young, M. E. (2016). *Learning the art of helping: Building blocks and techniques* (6th ed.). Merrill.

Zencare. (2021, March 2). *Can I provide teletherapy across state lines during the pandemic?* https://blog.zencare.co/teletherapy-across-state-lines-coronavirus/

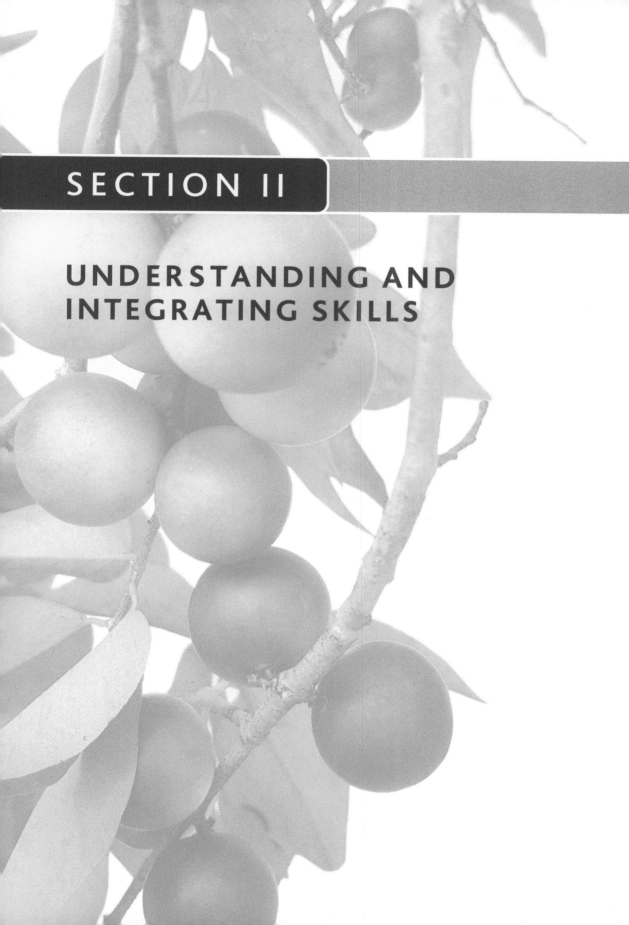

SECTION II

UNDERSTANDING AND INTEGRATING SKILLS

CHAPTER 3

THE THEORIES THAT INFLUENCE SYSTEMIC PRACTICE

LEARNING OBJECTIVES

After reading this chapter, you will be able to:

- ◼ Identify the methods for integrating theories.

- ◼ Recognize the issues related to feminism and feminist family therapy.

- ◼ Describe salient contemporary social justice issues.

- ◼ Identify the use of a sole, integrative, eclectic, and pluralistic theoretical practice.

- ◼ Distinguish the differences between first- and second-order cybernetics.

- ◼ Describe the constructionist, constructivist, postmodern, gestalt, and attachment theoretical frameworks.

- ◼ Distinguish the similarities and differences between social constructivism and constructionism.

INTRODUCTION TO THE THEORETICAL UNDERPINNINGS OF SYSTEMIC WORK

This chapter outlines the salient theoretical movements that couple, marriage, and family practitioners, and their relevant professional organizations, have attached themselves to over the years. There is no theory that encompasses the collective interest of all systemic practitioners; however, feminism, the minority stress model, racial battle fatigue (RBF), first- and second-order cybernetic concepts, constructionism and constructivism, postmodernism, gestalt theory and therapy, and attachment theory are so integral to the work of couple, marriage, and family therapy that they have stood the test of time, continue to influence the field, and/or should be explored. While this is not a theory textbook per se, it is important to investigate major theoretical movements prior to fully exploring various contemporary issues and their respective interventions. The importance of theory and experience were prophetically stated by Immanuel Kant in 1781 within the following quote: "Thoughts without content are void; intuitions without conceptions, blind" (Kant & Meiklejohn, 2009, p. 116).

The chapter begins with two key areas of professional orientation that cut across all theories and practice: (a) using eclecticism, integration, pluralism, and the use of a sole theory of practice; and (b) the theoretical relevance of feminism, the minority stress model, and RBF to clinical practice. Additional areas that are explored within each theoretical model are the legacies of each founding theory-based leader, definitions of the approaches, the core theoretical concepts, technique descriptions and examples, and the connection to contemporary systemic practice.

There is no best method or theory for enhancing someone's relationships, cognitions, behaviors, emotions, attachment security, and experiences. Each clinician's choice of a theoretical orientation, or integration of multiple theories, reflects their personal values, interests, and style. While personal choice exists, there have been various theoretical waves that have cut across the helping professions that support couple, marriage, and family counseling. Over the past two decades, the systemic approach to therapy has seen a lot of growth, including, but not limited to, the Gottman method (Gottman & Silver, 2015); behavioral couple therapy (e.g., integrative behavioral couple therapy; Christensen & Doss, 2017); attachment-oriented, emotionally focused couple and family therapy (Johnson, 2019); and multiculturalism, intersectional, and social justice-oriented approaches (Sue et al., 2019). While there always appears to be a new cutting-edge wave that slightly redefines the field of couple, marriage, and family therapy, there are certain elements that have remained relatively stable. Stable aspects of systemic theory and therapy include, but are not limited to, multiculturalism, diversity, and context; the nuances of cybernetic principles; attachment styles and enhancing attachment security; experiential methods; social constructivist and constructionist theoretical leanings; and postmodernism and the associated techniques. These long-standing systemic theoretical preferences will be reviewed in this chapter.

UNITARY THEORY, INTEGRATION, ECLECTICISM, AND PLURALISM

A unitary theoretical model is the classic method for developing a theoretical orientation. Practitioners often pledge a bold adherence to a particular theoretical school of therapy, including its own epistemology, process of counseling, maintenance of progress, role of the counselor and the client, nature of human development, assessment methods, techniques, multicultural and social justice standards, and empirical backing. Adherence to a particular approach provides an effective method for helping others and a blueprint for understanding the psychology of human behavior. Most individuals who deeply adhere to a singular approach to therapy will maintain that if they dig deeply enough into their theoretical framework they will find what they need to help their clients. While the most recent edition of the *SAGE Encyclopedia of Theory in Counseling and Psychotherapy* lists over 300 unique approaches to therapy, most theoretical schools trace back, at least partly, to one or more of six major theoretical categories: humanistic, cognitive, behavioral, psychoanalytic, constructionist, and systemic (Neukrug, 2015). Although sticking to a single unitary approach is not as popular as it once was, it is still a very viable option for practitioners to consider.

Integration

A survey of over 1,000 helping professionals concluded that only a small number of practitioners considered themselves to be reliant on a sole theory of therapy (Tasca et al., 2015). Most practitioners within the aforementioned study identified themselves as either integrative or eclectic. *Integration* can be defined as the theoretical combination of different psychotherapy approaches that enhance or complement each other. Integration entails a commitment to a conceptual synthesis beyond the technical blend of methods. The goal is to create a unified conceptual framework that synthesizes the best elements of two or more approaches of therapy into one (Benito, 2018; Lebow, 1997). Integration is the theoretical combination of different therapeutic schools, and entails theoretical, practical, and conceptual synthesis. This synthesis combines theory and techniques to create an optimal model that deeply helps clients. Models of integrative practice include common factors (i.e., therapeutic elements that collectively shape a theoretical model), technical eclecticism (i.e., systemic approach balancing theory and treatment), theoretical integration (i.e., combining concepts from different therapeutic approaches), and assimilative integration (i.e., a technique is incorporated into a preferred therapeutic approach; Benito, 2018).

Common factors are an important integrative approach to therapy. According to Wampold and Imel (2015), the various models and theories of therapy all produce similar positive outcomes. Given the consistent positive findings across theoretical approaches, this integrative approach seeks to identify what the successful approaches to therapy have in common. Common factors include phenomena such as therapeutic relationship, empathy, client expectations, being collaborative, and teaching the client skills with tangible examples (Wampold & Imel, 2015). Common factors models, such as the contextual model (Wampold & Imel, 2015), are meta-models because they are models that symbolize how all therapies produce benefits.

Technical eclecticism is centered on using an empirically driven technique or modality to help with a particular issue. In other words, a clinician would treat most clients from a core perspective and deviate if there are particular techniques and modalities empirically proven to be helpful with specific issues and disorders. For example, despite having a core humanistic theoretical perspective, a clinician may use dialectical behavior therapy (DBT) as an empirically validated technique for treating borderline personality disorder (BPD). If the humanistic-oriented clinician uses DBT only for clients diagnosed with BPD, they would be practicing technical eclecticism. To take this example a step further, this same humanistic clinician may use a more neurologic treatment for posttraumatic stress disorder (e.g., eye movement desensitization and reprocessing, brainspotting; Lazarus, 1967).

When clinicians discuss the construct of integration, they are typically referring to theoretical integration. The goal of theoretical integration is to produce a framework that synthesizes the best aspects of two or more theoretical traditions. The integration of various theoretical components is created with the assumption that the creation is better than either theory alone. While this synthesis could create an optimal integrative theory, the integration does not imply the elimination of the various theories. An example of a gold standard theoretical integration is cognitive behavioral therapy (CBT). CBT is an action-oriented integrative model that is centered on changing cognitions and behaviors.

Assimilative integration is an approach in which a thorough commitment to one theoretical orientation is complemented by an openness to incorporate techniques from other therapeutic approaches. For example, if a couple, marriage, and family practitioner practices emotionally focused family therapy, they would practice from that model most of the time. While maintaining the consistency of their primary theoretical orientation, they might occasionally incorporate a behavioral intervention, such as assertiveness training or systematic desensitization. This is done in a seamless manner, so it does not feel like a complete shift in the clinician's therapeutic style (Stricker & Gold, 1996).

Eclecticism

Clinicians are considered eclectic when they apply techniques from a variety of theories to best fit their clients' needs. They may use a range of empirically validated methods to determine the best combination of therapeutic interventions to help their clients. Essentially, an eclectic clinician customizes the therapeutic process by using whatever form of treatment, or integration of treatments, that has been shown to produce the most efficacy for treating a particular disorder or issue. While eclecticism can be extremely helpful and effective, the theories and techniques used should be based on empirical evidence (Benito, 2018).

While eclectic practice can and often is used effectively, when it is used improperly the clinician will choose a technique or modality without fully understanding the theory, rationale, effectiveness, and integrative compatibility. Syncretism is the label used to describe a technique choice without fully understanding the procedure, its underlying theory, effectiveness, and without a sound rationale. This haphazard method is generally avoided, is considered ineffective, and can reflect different and contradictory theoretical tenets (Benito, 2018).

Pluralism

The pluralistic approach to therapy emerged in 2006 and was partly a reaction to the inflexibility within the helping professions (Cooper & McLeod, 2006). The pluralistic approach suggests that there is no right or wrong way to conduct therapy. The basic principle of pluralistic therapy is that different people are helped by unique methods and skills at different times, and that the best way of determining how therapy should proceed is to engage the client in a process of mutual decision-making (Cooper & Dryden, 2016).

Cooper and Dryden (2016) provided a blueprint for understanding the nuances of pluralism. First, a pluralistic practitioner is open to a variety of ways in which clients experience emotional and psychological distress, and consequently a variety of methods for helping them heal. Second, given this level of diversity across clientele, practitioners customize their approach to therapy. Third, pluralism offers shared decision-making and feedback process between the client(s) and the clinician(s).

FEMINISM, MINORITY STRESS MODEL, AND RACIAL BATTLE FATIGUE

Working with marginalized populations is an important aspect of couple, marriage, and family therapy that will be revisited throughout this textbook. When working with oppressed groups that face frequent bouts of inequity, racism, discrimination, oppression, and hate, it is important for helping professionals to work to ensure marginalized clients feel understood, safe, and validated, and to have a supportive experience with the various clinical interventions being utilized. The next sections review feminism, the minority stress model, and RBF. These models provide a starting point for understanding many of the experiences marginalized populations endure daily.

Feminism

Modern feminism has been a prominent force in the United States since the 1850s (Luepnitz, 1989). The feminist theory is aligned with the practice of couple, marriage, and family therapy. In a general sense, feminism has to do with the socially constructed assignment of power assigned to men in society. According to Tong (2001), the foundation of feminist theory is based on three core beliefs: (a) traditionally, society is set up to prioritize men and is patriarchal; (b) historically, the subordination of women is supported; and (c) identifying ways to achieve equality for all should be the priority. Feminism has had a significant philosophical impact on couples, marriage, and family therapy for over 40 years.

According to Hill and Ballou (1998), feminist therapy is primarily "a lived experience of politics" (p. 14). This involves deconstructing cultural narratives and societal norms related to bias, stereotypes, oppression, sexism, inequality, inequity, and gender roles. Feminist therapy is based on valuing women's experience, recognizing the sociocultural causes of distress, giving attention to power in therapy, providing an integrated analysis of oppression, and incorporating the goal of social change (Hill & Ballou, 1998). This deep valuing, dissecting of cultural norms, and empowerment can create a sense of freedom, encouragement, and happiness within clients.

Feminist family therapy (FFT) originated in 1978. FFT is centered on the notion that therapeutic treatment should involve attention to the larger cultural and gender-based issues and their impact on women, couples, and families (Barrett et al., 1990). The feminist approach empowers women to advocate for social equality, engage in creative cooperation, promote peace, and reject the notion of patriarchy and linear thinking. FFT encourages relational cooperation, empowerment, individual identity and strengths, and a supportive environment in relationships, and urges couples and parents to refrain from a dominance and competition perspective. Isomorphically, as clients experience a sense of collaboration and empowerment with FFT, they can recreate this synergy in their future relationships. FFT and the feminist theory tend to work best when augmented with a psychological theory (e.g., CBT, DBT, emotionally focused therapy [EFT]) that has pragmatic clinical utility. For example, feminist theoretical tenets, including, but not limited to, deconstructing political structures, empowerment, and advocating for equality, could be augmented to core CBT theory and skills (e.g., Socratic questioning, downward arrow, homework) when supporting a female survivor of sexual assault (Barrett et al., 1990).

Classic scholarship pioneered by Lois Braverman (1988) describes the important complementarity and the inherent mutual benefit between family therapy and feminism. Braverman describes the skills and techniques embedded in the models of family therapy lend themselves nicely to feminist theory. Braverman (1988) encourages systemic practitioners to consider seven elements central to feminist sensitive models of therapy: (a) clinicians must comprehend the impact of patriarchy (e.g., politics, family life, social issues) on all people regardless of sex and gender; (b) clinicians must understand the limitations of most psychological theories as they are based on the male model of maturity; (c) clinicians must understand women's problem-solving process (e.g., relationships and connections); (d) clinicians should understand that areas like motherhood, marriage, and child-rearing are political institutions that symbolize a sociocultural legacy for women; (e) clinicians need to understand the biological effects of the female life cycle and their effects on relationships and symptom presentation; (f) clinicians need to recognize women's sexuality, intimacy, and sexual responsiveness to ensure accuracy and to demystify false information; and (g) clinicians must understand the importance of women supporting other women and how this is different from their relationships with men.

#MeToo and Cancel Culture

The #MeToo movement is a contemporary feminist effort centered on raising awareness, empowerment, and accountability to issues that surround sexual misconduct perpetrated against women. According to Meyers (2018), activist Tarana Burke first coined the phrase *Me Too* in 2006 to begin a dialogue and to raise awareness of women impacted by sexual harassment, violence, and abuse. In 2017, the phrase gained much more cultural prominence as women began coming forward through news and social media with stories about sexual assault and harassment. For many participants and observers of the movement, the countless stories have created a culture of empathy, safety, hope, and connection. By saying "me too," the survivor stands with a group and creates a sense of solidarity with others who have been harassed, assaulted, and raped. According to Levy and Mattsson (2019), the #*MeToo* movement increased reporting of sex crimes by 10% during its first 6 months. It also ushered in an increase in the number of arrests for sexual assaults. While the accountability regarding male sexual misconduct has been salient, it has also encouraged men to examine their role in relationships and how to treat women, and has provided men insight into what causes many women to feel offended (Meyers, 2018). These implications have created a significant impact in relationships and therapy sessions around the world.

In addition to the massive social media and media influence of #*MeToo*, a phenomenon known as *cancel culture* (i.e., call out culture) has created an enormous impact on people. Cancel culture emerged in 2014 and initially involved a sense of empowerment for victims of sexual assault, sexism, and other social maladies. Cancel culture has changed drastically from its initial purpose. Following the initial push to cancel perpetrators, the cancel culture movement increased to include more than the perpetrators of sexual assault and extreme sexism. When one is cancelled, their missteps or errors in judgment are essentially paraphrased and used against them. Cancelling moves beyond accountability and means the target is being mobbed, de-platformed, and/or excommunicated. This cancelling of people is taking place primarily on social media platforms (e.g., Twitter, Instagram) and most often involves corporate figures, celebrities, and corporations (Spelman, 2021).

Minority Stress Model

The minority stress model is a theory that provides a blueprint for understanding the lived experiences of people in oppressed communities in a larger sociological context (Meyer, 2007). The minority stress model supports the social structure (e.g., political inclusion, healthcare, education) of cultures that house oppressed groups (e.g., race, ethnicity, gender, sexuality, disability) who experience a greater degree of minority stress, prejudice, and inequity. For example, research has discovered that lower levels of well-being and higher degrees of mental illness generally exist in communities of color (e.g., Black, African American, Native American, Latinx, Asian; Eylem, 2020) and within the LGBTQIA+ community (Semlyen et al., 2016).

For example, Dentato (2012) poignantly described a minority stress perspective regarding the lived experiences of individuals in the LGBTQIA+ community and HIV/AIDS risk. Specifically, he detailed the sociocultural impact of and the role stigma, heteronormativity, internalized homophobia, and prejudice play with regard to the increase in HIV risk and substance abuse. Dentato pointed out the connection between sexual minority health risk and the minority stress model. According to Dentato (2012), the "[m]inority stress theory proposes that sexual minority health disparities can be explained in large part by stressors induced by a hostile, homophobic culture, which often results in a lifetime of harassment, maltreatment, discrimination and victimization. . . ." (para. 3). These factors ultimately affect mental (e.g., anxiety, depression, substance abuse) and physical (e.g., risky sexual encounters with multiple partners resulting in HIV/AIDS) health outcomes.

Racial Battle Fatigue

People of color (POC) experience frequent overt and covert social, political, and physical attacks, which can create a sense of stress, frustration, fear, and preoccupation with when the next incident will come. *Racial battle fatigue* (RBF) was first coined by critical race theorist William Smith in 2008. "Racial battle fatigue addresses the physiological, psychological, and behavioral strain exacted on racially marginalized and stigmatized groups and the amount of energy they expend coping with and fighting against racism" (Smith, 2008, p. 617). There are three major interconnected stress responses POC experience related to RBF: (a) physiologic (headaches, grinding teeth, clenching), (b) psychological (e.g., frustration, apathy, defensiveness), and (c) behavioral (e.g., loss of appetite, quickness to argue, isolation; Smith, 2008).

Microaggressions are an aspect of RBF, and these interactions are covert forms of racism that largely go unseen by onlookers and unacknowledged by offenders. *Racial microaggression* has been defined "as subtle snubs, slights, and insults directed toward minorities, as well as to women and other historically stigmatized groups, that implicitly communicate or engender hostility" (Lilienfeld, 2017, p. 139). Pierce (1974) was the first to describe racial microaggressions in the literature. He described them as put-downs, done in an instinctive, preconscious, or unconscious fashion. Smith (2008) adds that microaggressions are acts of racism that reinforce pathologic stereotypes and inequitable social norms. According to Williams's (2019) operationalized definition, racial microaggressions can be

> negative statements (e.g., "Asians are bad drivers") and seemingly positive statements (e.g., "Black people are good at basketball"), they can include actions (e.g., crossing the street to avoid walking past a Black man), inaction (e.g., failing to offer aid to a person of color in distress because "someone else will do it"), being unseen (e.g., everyone at a banquet getting served except the lone person of color; p. 6).

FIRST-ORDER CYBERNETICS

The following is a concise review of some of the most salient first- and second-order cybernetic tenets. Individuals who are interested in a more comprehensive review are encouraged to read Becvar and Becvar's 2018 book *Systems Theory and Family Therapy: A Primer*. During the 1940s and 1950s, cybernetic concepts served as a theoretical framework for the in-depth understanding of the complexities of family interaction and as an antecedent to modern systemic therapy. Cybernetics was influenced by a number of disciplines, including sociology, anthropology, mathematics, and biology, as well as a large array of great thinkers, including, but not limited to, Norbert Wiener (1894–1964), George Spencer Brown (1923–2016), Gregory Bateson (1904–1980), Margaret Mead (1901–1978), Heinz von Foerster (1911–2002), and Warren McCulloch (1898–1969).

Systems theory, at the first level of cybernetics, is centered on processes, patterns, and relationships. Cybernetically, everything in the world and the universe is connected and interdependent (i.e., responsible and dependent on others). It can be helpful, at times, to compare cybernetics perspectives with individual psychotherapy; however, since this was provided earlier in the textbook, the attention of this chapter will be centered on describing the details of first- and second-order cybernetics perspective. A major difference between first- and second-order cybernetics is that the systemic practitioner is viewing the system of feedback loops and homeostatic mechanisms from the outside. This is different from the second-order cybernetics perspective, which acknowledges that the clinician is influencing and is also part of the system being observed (Becvar & Becvar, 2018; Becvar et al., 1997).

Cybernetically speaking, the behavior people generate changes from one setting to another. Change is constantly present and is contextually bound. First-order cybernetics brought the possibility of understanding an individual outside of context to the forefront. Systemic practitioners became aware that behavior does not maintain itself on its own energy. Instead, behavior is constantly changing and is interdependent on contextual factors (e.g., the people present, the nature of the interaction). These ideas are central to *reciprocal causality*. Specifically, each member of a relationship is the cause and effect of the other. People can play a particular role as long as it is complemented by another person. Cybernetic role examples include, but are not limited to, client and counselor, teacher and student, parent and child, and police officer and criminal. These relationships are reciprocal and naturally complementary to each other (Becvar & Becvar, 2018; Becvar et al., 1997).

Recursion is the notion that meaningful experiences are created from the interaction between individuals as each defines and identifies with the other. At this more microlevel of cybernetic functioning, relationships are bilateral, mutually interactive, and require members to participate. For example, in the context of a couples therapy session, the therapist will look at the relationship and observe how each member of the system interacts and influences the other. The meaning the couple and the therapist derive from the interaction may symbolize a mutually agreed-upon goal of therapy that will later be placed on the couple's treatment plan. Because of the context of mutual influence and meaning-making, the treatment goals may be somewhat different depending on who is working with the couple (Becvar & Becvar, 2018; Becvar et al., 1997).

A powerful cybernetic philosophical tenet that has stood the test of time is the *feedback loop*. Communication feedback loops absorb information from past behavior, in a circular manner, to maintain a steady state and/or change course. This can include information on the performance of the system (e.g., parenting, coupling, sibling behavior, family as a whole). For example, when one partner of a married couple attempts to change the parenting style of another, they may start to nag or demand change. This nagging and demanding likely produces a sense of defensiveness within the other partner. Unfortunately, this nagging and defensiveness behavior combination is *complementary* and thus does not create any change in parenting behavior. In other words, the partner's attempts to change the other person and the resulting predictable defensiveness maintains the status quo. The type of feedback that maintains a system's steady state is known as negative feedback (i.e., no change, stability, continuing redundant pattern). Please note, the words *positive* and *negative* do not imply a sense of goodness or badness. They imply complementary or logical pattern (negative feedback) and noncomplementary or illogical pattern (positive feedback; Becvar & Becvar, 2018; Becvar et al., 1997).

Positive feedback has to do with illogical behavior that has the potential to produce something new and different. The illogical behavior is not complementary to the other behavior and thus has the potential to create change. Because this behavior is a new phenomenon (i.e., not a redundant pattern), it only retains the label of positive feedback during its initial use. For example, when one spouse begins to nag and demand that the other adjust their parenting style, the other partner could graciously thank them for their concern or present them with a gift. This would constitute a change in the rules of interaction and would not feed energy into the nagging defensive dynamic that constitutes the system's steady state (i.e., homeostasis; Becvar & Becvar, 2018; Becvar et al., 1997).

Family rules and boundaries are essential elements of the cybernetic model. Relational rules form the boundaries and govern the behaviors, emotional expression, and communication that take place in any given system. In a general sense, rules express the values embedded within the system, as well as the behaviors and the associated roles that create a logical steady state (i.e., homeostatic range). Negative feedback overtly and covertly functions as an enforcer (e.g., guilt, punishment, nonverbal rejection) of the established rules. Positive feedback takes place when the family is caught in a vicious cycle and needs to change. Cybernetic change takes place at two levels. First-order change takes place within the system and is in line with the previously established rules of engagement. Second-order change is more profound and is when the rules of the system change and consequently the entire system is changed. For example, if an adolescent stays out late, receives a punishment that involves an earlier curfew, and argues with their parents about this new punishment, increasing the amount of positive punishment, the family is likely engaging in first-order change due to the complementary nature of the engagement. Alternatively, if the adolescent were to thank their parents for caring and looking out for them, resulting in a lessening of the punishment, this would likely be a second-order change due to the illogical interaction and the subsequent changing of the rules. Lastly, relational rules and boundaries assume a systemic hierarchy. In this sense, any system exists as part of a larger system (i.e., suprasystem) and has smaller subsystems. For example, parents and siblings may make up a family system; however, the subsystems are hierarchical, typically with the parents on top (i.e., executive subsystem) and the siblings below (i.e., sibling subsystem; Becvar & Becvar, 2018; Becvar et al., 1997; Minuchin, 1974).

A few additional first-level cybernetic constructs include (a) openness and closedness, (b) entropy and negentropy, and (c) equifinality and equipotentiality. Openness and closedness are the extent that a system screens out and/or permits the inputs of new information. Cybernetically, it is helpful to have a healthy balance between these two levels of functioning. The level that a family takes in new information or screens it out has to do with context. For example, during the COVID-19 global pandemic, many family systems demonstrated a stronger degree of closedness (e.g., maintaining family traditions, screening out negative news) to maintain a good steady state. Entropy and negentropy are centered on systems allowing helpful information to influence and change the functioning, while screening out the negative information. When a system allows too much or not enough information in, it tends toward maximum disorder (i.e., entropy). When a system allows the right amount of influence in and out, it is tending toward maximum order (i.e., negentropy). Equifinality is the tendency toward a characteristic final state from a different initial state. For example, a wealthy person from a high socioeconomic status family acquires the same job as a poor person from a family with low socioeconomic status. Equipotentiality is the notion that different end states may be arrived at from the same initial conditions. Two individuals with similar upper class demographics start life and attend the same schools; however, one individual dies at a young age in extreme poverty, while the other attains greater wealth and comfort and lives to an old age (Becvar & Becvar, 2018; Becvar et al., 1997).

The final first-order cybernetic constructs include (a) communication and information processing, (b) relationship and wholeness, and (c) goals and purpose. The three cybernetic communication and information processing principles are the following: (a) one cannot not behave; (b) one cannot not communicate; and (c) the meaning someone makes of an experience is not the truth, but the unique meaning an individual has given to it. Relationship and wholes are expressed with the common phrase *the whole is greater than the sum of its parts*. Mathematically, this is expressed as $1 + 1 = 3$ (i.e., the two people and the relationship). In this sense, the person is viewed in the context of a relationship. Without the interactional component of the equation, the wholeness of an experience cannot be comprehended. Lastly, the goals and purpose of any system are created by the observer. This creation is communicated in a metalanguage (i.e., language that describes language; Becvar & Becvar, 2018; Becvar et al., 1997). In short, the literal content is less important when compared with the more complex patterns that accompany the process of communication (Bateson, 1972). For example, a family secret is less salient than the process the family undergoes to discover the truth.

SECOND-ORDER CYBERNETICS

As the clinical world moved from the first- to the second-order cybernetics perspective, there was an acknowledgment that the first-order cybernetics perspective implied that the clinician has been viewed as being independent of the family system being observed. The problem with this perspective is that clinicians practicing from the model appeared to think everything in the universe was connected except that of the family therapist. It is impossible to truly observe a system from the outside without influencing it. At the second-order level of cybernetics, the clinician's influence was included in the system they were attempting to observe (i.e., participant-observer). In short, the individuals, couples, and families that are being treated are affected by the clinician; consequently, the nature of family dynamics is influenced by the therapist (Becvar & Becvar, 2018; Becvar et al., 1997).

Two additional second-order cybernetic constructs are autopoiesis and structural determinism. While the notion of autopoiesis originated in biology, Maturana and Varela (1980) theorized that human systems (couples and families) are autopoietic in nature. Autopoiesis has to do with the way things relate within the system, and this phenomenon is a key aspect to understanding the nature of living systems. The most significant aspect of the autopoietic system is that it energizes and organizes itself and eventually achieves self-maintenance through internal and external processing. The internal structure of a family system determines what it can and cannot do. According to Becvar and Becvar (2018),

> [f]amily members create rules. These rules comprise a boundary by which the family system distinguishes itself and may be distinguished from the larger suprasystem of which it is a part. The family and the boundary require each other but do not cause each other (p. 31).

Similarly, structural determinism is centered on the philosophy that the system structure itself has limits and determines the range in which it demonstrates variations.

Four additional second-order cybernetic constructs are consensual domains, epistemology of participation, structural coupling, and nonpurposeful drift. The consensual domains have to do with couple and family interactions cocreating a particular reality for the system. Two domains include those in which we investigate (first-order) and the consensual domains we are a part of (second-order). As people engage in either process, they are influencing the creation of the consensual domain through the act of observation. The epistemology of participation has to do with the importance of surrendering to the cocreation of reality. It also asks system members to use caution with thinking there is only one right way to do something. Ultimately, any thought or conviction is subjective in nature. While structural coupling has to do with the ability of systems to coexist (i.e., compatibility, congruence), nonpurposeful drift has to do with the process of systemic mutual influence and potential (i.e., structure emerges as a function of systemic interaction). For example, every family has potential to change given its context (nonpurposeful drift); however, whether the parents can demonstrate the compatibility necessary to have a positive parenting and intimate partnership is idiosyncratic to the family in question (structural coupling; Becvar & Becvar, 2018; Becvar et al., 1997).

The final second-order cybernetic constructs included in this review will be reality as a multiverse, wholeness, and self-reference. This higher level of cybernetic theory changes the clinician's vantage point from a universe to that of a multiverse. From a multiverse view, we all live in a multiverse of many observer-dependent realities. For example, a multiverse perspective becomes evident when clinicians use a family sculpting technique. Specifically, each family member has a unique nuanced vision of how they see the family dynamics. None of the perceptions are invalid, just based on the unique experiences and presuppositions in the family. Similarly, the theoretical tenet of wholeness (i.e., interconnectedness of everyone) and self-reference (i.e., inclusion of the observer in the observed) becomes apparent when one considers that the observer (i.e., clinician) is now part of the perceived (i.e., family system). Given these factors, the clinician's perspective is ultimately subjective in nature (Becvar & Becvar, 2018; Becvar et al., 1997).

CONSTRUCTIONISM AND CONSTRUCTIVISM

According to Crotty (1998), constructionists focus on the collective generation and transmission of meaning, and therefore maintain a critical spirit, and have a foundation in sociology with a language-based perspective. Constructionism (i.e., social constructionism) is an epistemology created by American mathematician Seymour Papert (1928–2016). Papert described constructionism as a method of education that encourages people to build knowledge through actively engaging in constructing things in the world. Constructionism influences three major theoretical stances: constructivism, interpretivism, and critical inquiry (Limberg et al., 2021). Constructionists theorize that reality cannot be experienced objectively; they are created and perpetuated by the ruling class of people. These cultural constructions that form the norms, reality, and mores of any society are communicated through certain mediums, including, but not limited to, religion, education, laws, historical events, news and media, and politics. Consequently, the cultural narratives that create a sense of reality are filtered through the prepackaged thoughts of a society embedded into the minds of its citizens. In other words, reality that appears to be independently experienced by the population is inseparable from the stable and enduring cultural categories of knowledge that have created what we see and know about the world around us. If most knowledge is considered nothing more than cultural stories that are embedded in our language, information is always negotiable and able to be reconstructed; however, changing cultural stories takes considerable work and reprogramming. Furthermore, change in cultural thought can be scary and painful for many people who have become reliant on a particular way of living, thinking, and behaving (Gergen, 1991; Laird, 1995).

According to Becvar et al. (1997), the *Diagnostic and Statistical Manual of Mental Disorders,* Fifth Edition, Text Revision (*DSM-5-TR*; American Psychiatric Association, 2022), is merely the socially, economically, politically, and psychologically correct way for mental health professionals to think and talk about their clients and their presenting problems. In other words, this text is nothing more than a socially constructed narrative of problem patterns experienced by people in American society. Furthermore, the act of diagnosis can be defined as professional deficit-based observation and categorization. Can you imagine if the field went in the opposite direction and decided to focus on strength-based observation and categorization? There could be a new textbook entitled the *Diagnostic and Statistical Manual of Personal Strengths and Abilities.* This text would have categories of mental strengths, such as the positive self-affirming categorization and/or the patient and supportive categorization. What would happen if highly trained mental health professionals were taught to assess and diagnose these positive patterns in human behavior? Could there be a societal self-fulfilling prophecy of empowerment and improved mental health? The possibilities create a sense of curiosity in many mental health providers and clients. Certainly, major theoretical movements (e.g., postmodernism, positive psychology), certain humanistic theories (i.e., person-centered, the human validation process, Maslow's hierarchy of needs), and particular therapeutic techniques (e.g., reframing, exceptions, externalization) seem to be in favor of such a professional transformation and on undoing some of the damage caused by hurtful society-based labeling.

According to Crotty (1998), constructivism is a meaning-making experience within the individual's mind that encompasses the unique experience of that particular individual. Constructivism (i.e., social constructivism) is based on the educational learning and development theory of Swiss psychologist Jean Piaget (1896–1980). According to Limberg et al. (2021),

> [c]onstructivists believe that people construct their world based on the influence of several factors including: (a) the physical environment, (b) the social environment, (c), their culture, and (d) prior experiences. The truth within constructivism is in the individual's description of an event and how they make sense and meaning of an experience (p. 50).

Consequently, if practitioners take on a constructivist framework, they would be entering the world of narratives and stories and side-stepping the notion of absolute truth. From a constructivist perspective, truth may be real; however, it is inaccessible to humans and other living things. Instead, all that is known are constructions made through one's personal lens. This personal lens includes all life experiences, formal and informal teachings, and societal constructions. If one considers the construction of the *DSM* and diagnostic categories from a constructivist perspective, there is a surrender to the notion that there are no objectively treatable *DSM* structures and categories. In other words, the assessment and diagnosis of individual or systemic issues say more about the clinician, and the lens through which they see the world, than it says about the family they are treating (Becvar et al., 1997). In short, the truth in this particular experience is within the clinician's experience, description, and meaning-making experience of the client, not in their actual characteristics.

POSTMODERNISM

Postmodern family therapy is a more recent epistemologic framework of therapeutic practice. Postmodern therapeutic models include, but are not limited to, solution-focused brief therapy (SFBT), narrative therapy, and collaborative therapy. Among other theoretical tenets, postmodern family therapists consider clients to be the experts and focus on client strengths, therapeutic creativity and imagination, and counselor and client collaboration. SFBT is a postmodern form of therapy that was developed at the Milwaukee Brief Family Therapy Center in Wisconsin by American social worker and jazz musician Steve de Shazer (1940–2005) and his spouse South Korean social worker Insoo Kim Berg (1934–2007). Narrative therapy is a postmodern form of therapy developed by Australian social worker and family therapist Michael White (1948–2008) and New Zealand social worker and family therapist David Epston (b. 1940). Lastly, collaborative therapy is a postmodern approach to psychotherapy developed by American psychologist Harlene Anderson (b. 1942) and American psychologist Harold A. Goolishian (1924–1991).

According to Flaskas (1994), postmodernism is an oppositional epistemology. Specifically, it is an umbrella term that stands in direct opposition to modernism. In other words, postmodernism is standing in opposition to a knowable reality (i.e., modernism). Modernism is aligned with science, realism, objectivism, positivism, rationalism, and reductionism. This perspective provides a foundation for core mental health constructs such as healthy, unhealthy, normal personality, abnormal personality, compatible relationships, incompatible relationships, and the general role of the therapist as the expert and the client as the seeker of expertise. In contrast, postmodernists believe that reality is subjective in nature. Given this subjective nature, postmodernists question notions like universal truths, normal and abnormal personality, and the notion that a therapist is an expert. Furthermore, like second-order cyberneticians, postmodernists believe that we dwell in a multiverse (rather than a universe; Becvar et al., 1997).

The overarching epistemologic meaning of postmodernism is that all knowledge and ways of thinking should be questioned since they often benefit those in power. Postmodern approaches to therapy tend to be collaborative, developmental, creative, process-oriented, positive, nonlabeling, nonhierarchical, and reflective. Postmodernists promote thinking about issues in a variety of ways, including deconstructing vague concepts to empower individuals to understand the underlying meaning of cultural messages, encouraging individuals to engage in their own meaning-making process, and enabling others to help themselves achieve something tangible. Postmodernists believe all realities are based on personal, cultural, and linguistic constructions, and while they are created by privileged individuals and/or groups, they deeply impact and affect others living with them. The notion of truth is a key construct in the shaping of reality. According to Neimeyer and Bridges (2003),

> [t]ruth, in this view, is actually constituted by individuals and social groups and reflects the dominant social ideologies of the day, however fallible these turn out to be in the hindsight of later generations. For example, cultural assumptions about the appropriate roles of women or ethnic minorities, laws that prohibit and punish certain behavior, and even psychiatric diagnoses can all be considered historically situated (and changing) social constructions, but this does not mitigate their impact on those subjected to them (p. 275).

In addition to understanding the continuously changing nature of truth, postmodernists work hard to make apparent the often-covert elements taking place in social and political life. Practitioners operating from this perspective will work with clients to deconstruct cultural, family, and personal messages when they limit someone's ability to move forward.

The modernistic therapeutic staples of personality, assessment, and diagnosis all represent complications in a postmodern framework. Philosophically, from a postmodern perspective, personality is not a fixed set of stable traits. From this vantage point, the concept of self can be conceptualized as a way to organize past meaning-making experiences in an effort to adapt to the shifting social and cultural realities. More radical postmodern perspectives view personality as nothing more than a linguistic construction.

Similar to constructivists, postmodern therapists avoid diagnosis whenever possible. While all clinicians must engage in the diagnosis process to satisfy insurance companies and the managed healthcare system, helping professionals practicing from a postmodern perspective would prefer to reframe *DSM* diagnosis as a person's unique way of approaching a life problem. Instead of engaging in deficit-based observation (i.e., diagnosis), postmodern therapists would prefer to understand the client's unique way of coping or dealing with life challenges so they could develop multiple paths toward healing and hope. Similarly, clinical assessment typically entails the deliberate use of both biological (e.g., health screenings) and socially based (e.g., client contextual factors) assessments. This multipronged approach to assessment allows the clinician to attain a full picture of the client's issues and context, which allows for the cocreation of helpful pathways and solutions (Neimeyer & Bridges, 2003).

GESTALT THEORY AND THERAPY

One cannot describe gestalt therapy without mentioning the impact of Friedrich (Fritz) Perls (1893–1970). Fritz and his spouse Laura Perls first developed gestalt therapy in the 1940s. Fritz was a German-born psychiatrist who grew up in the bohemian scene in Berlin, Germany. He served in World War I, connected with Wilhelm Reich at his technical seminars in Vienna, served under Reich in Berlin, and later became associated with the Esalen Institute in Big Sur, California. Fritz's style was confrontational, charismatic, and dramatic. He challenged clients to gain awareness around what they were avoiding and encouraged them to take responsibility (Perls et al., 1994).

Gestalt is a holistic theory and practice in which clinicians argue that one cannot understand the parts of something as a method for understanding the thing as whole. In other words, organisms instinctively perceive whole patterns and not bits and pieces. The first step in describing gestalt therapy is to provide a definition. According to Perls et al. (1994), "[g]estalt therapy is a process of psychotherapy with the goal of improving one's contact in community and with the environment in general. This goal is accomplished through aware, spontaneous, and authentic dialogue between client and therapist. Awareness of differences and similarities is encouraged while interruptions to contact are explored in the present therapeutic relationship" (p. 17). Four important theoretical lines related to gestalt are (a) the organism/environment field, (b) the self, (c) the experience of contact and contact withdrawal, and (d) disturbances of functioning of self (Lobb & Lichtenberg, 2005).

Gestalt theory and therapy have been a major influence on the systemic approach to therapy and vice versa. While systems theory offers a theoretical foundation and security of a formal theory of therapy, gestalt theory and therapy opens practitioners up to the creative possibilities centered on walking the boundary between the known and the unknown. In short, the gestalt field theory describes a process not a system. Family systems pioneers Virginia Satir and Carl Whitaker are attached to the gestalt model (e.g., neurolinguistic programming, curiosity, asking *how* questions [avoiding *why* questions]), and many of systemic therapy's highly experiential interventions are reminiscent of gestalt simply because they are centered on movement, awareness, communication, and provoking change (e.g., enactments, reenactments, family sculpting, role-playing, humor). Theoretically, gestalt's *organismic self-regulation* and the systemic/cybernetic theoretical tenet of *homeostasis* are very similar. Additionally, both theories focus on change and the here and now within the therapeutic process. Within this brief overview of gestalt therapy and theory, theoretical tenets and skills will be reviewed and connected to the systemic paradigm.

The Organism and Environment Field

Kurt Lewin's (1951) field theory was an important influence on the contact-making theoretical tenets of gestalt therapy. Organismic (i.e., person, people) and field (i.e., environment) contact (i.e., something that happens between two or more people) and withdrawal from contact are central to the gestalt theory (Perls et al., 1994). Gestalt theorists often describe the importance of the contact boundary, which essentially means the place where people meet and withdraw from their environment. In comparing the organism/environment field theory and systems theories, Lobb and Lichtenberg (2005) described the gestalt field theory as "a relational product that functions best when our thinking is totally centered on the contact boundary and thus grasping both what is internal and what is external, both the self's needs or experiences and the environment's demands or conditions" (p. 26).

The Self

Within the gestalt literature, much attention is placed on the concept of *self*. One's inner construct of self is transformed and modified with every new interaction they have with another person. You may be wondering, "How does the concept of the self fit into the organism-environment field?" Gestalt views the self as a function (i.e., not a fixed structure), which means that instead of defining what it is, the focus is on what it does. The purpose of the self is to make contact with its environment. This contact is spontaneous, intentional, and creative (Lobb & Lichtenberg, 2005; Perls et al., 1994). From a gestalt field theory perspective, the self is partly organized around clusters of experiences, and the psychoanalytic terms *id*, *ego*, and *superego* (Köhler, 1940). The self as a function can emerge as a physiologic need that is activated by an internal excitation or by an external influence. For example, an adult who feels lonely could realize their desire for intimacy spontaneously from within their mind, or they might walk by someone they find attractive and suddenly feel a desire for intimacy.

The Experience of Contact and Contact Withdrawal

Practitioners often feel much confusion around the contact and withdrawal from contact theoretical tenets. Contact is made by seeing, hearing, smelling, touching, and moving. If you have optimal contact with the environment, change is inevitable. As the self makes contact with the environment, it eventually withdraws after the fullness of the encounter. According to Lobb and Lichtenberg (2005), contact has four phases: *forecontact* (i.e., self-activation or need), *contact* (i.e., the self expands toward the contact boundary), *final contact* (i.e., the whole self is at the contact boundary), and *postcontact* (i.e., the self diminishes and integration takes place). For example, Bryan is interested in finding a new job (i.e., forecontact) in his field and decides that it is time to update his resume. Bryan opens his resume, and edits and adds jobs, experiences, and certifications to his existing resume (i.e., contact). He reviews and edits it one final time and hits save (i.e., final contact).

Disturbances of Functioning of Self

A gestalt clinician does not theorize symptoms or behaviors as pathologic. The disturbances in the functioning of self are not a problem or a reflection of pathology. Instead, psychopathology and resistance are conceptualized as a creative adjustment to a difficult situation. Healthy contact is when people interact with nature and other people without losing their own individuality. Frequent interruptions of contact can lead to the accumulation of incomplete situations (i.e., unfinished business). A gestalt refers to the complete configuration or pattern of a set of elements. Gestalt practitioners believe organisms instinctively perceive whole present, not bits and pieces. Disturbances emerge as incomplete gestalt and habitually not experiencing the present fully (Perls et al., 1994).

Humans develop defenses that serve as disturbances to contact and loss of ego functioning. The six boundary disturbances, which are sometimes referred to as resistance, are introjection (i.e., indiscriminately allowing inputs from the environment to become part of self), projection (i.e., disowning certain aspects of ourselves and placing them on others), retroflection (i.e., inward treatment of ourselves of what we would like to have done to someone else), confluence (i.e., inability to withdraw due to the threat of nothingness), devaluation (i.e., make contact but devalue its importance), and deflection (i.e., avoiding direct contact in favor of partial contact). During the process of therapy, clients work to stay in the here and now, as the most important unfinished business will always emerge into consciousness. Unless dealt with, the unfinished business will interfere with present-centered awareness. This notion of unfinished business emerging is central to the gestalt figure formation process. As the gestalt practitioner and the client explore unexpressed thoughts, memories, and feelings that have not been addressed, they are tracking how some features of the environmental field emerge from the background and become the focus of the client's attention (Burley & Freier, 2004; Lobb & Lichtenberg, 2005; Perls et al., 1994).

GESTALT TECHNIQUES

According to Mackewn (1997), gestalt practitioners value the dialogical relationship centered on bringing their whole self to the contact boundary. This includes being fully present, authentic, and validating. This sense of validation represents the person-to-person (IThou) therapeutic stance and attempts to avoid the more objective (IIt) attitude (Buber, 1923). An additional key aspect of gestalt therapy is helping clients gain awareness through experiential techniques. The techniques in gestalt are centered on rules and games that create awareness and provoke change. Gestalt experiments, like the hot seat technique and empty chair technique, can increase client consciousness and awareness. Techniques like these allow clients to stay in the here and now, where unfinished business can emerge into consciousness and be resolved. In the following sections, the techniques of empty chair, hot seat, experiments, dream work, exaggeration, and making the rounds are reviewed.

The Empty Chair

The empty chair technique is a powerful experiential method that aids clients in integrating disowned aspects of their personality. This gestalt experiment creates insight and awareness by having the client imagine someone (i.e., part of themselves) sitting in the chair. The client would name the part of themselves in the chair and begin speaking with the empty chair in an effort to better understand and integrate aspects of their personhood. The client then sits in the other chair and continues the conversation, this time reversing roles (Burley & Freier, 2004; Lobb & Lichtenberg, 2005; Perls et al., 1994). For example:

Clinician: Name the part of yourself that keeps holding you back.

Client: Stupid Janet.

Clinician: Now put that part in the seat across from you. Tell Stupid Janet how you want her to change.

Clinician: Now change seats and be Stupid Janet and plead your case to Janet.

The Hot Seat

The hot seat is a gestalt group therapy technique that involves the client sitting in a chair in front of the practitioner and having an additional empty chair next to the client that symbolizes the presence of a significant other or a disowned part of the self. The clinician, the client, and the empty chair would essentially engage in individual therapy in front of the group. The therapist will prompt, ask questions, and invite the client to discuss their past. After the hot seat interaction, the other group members will provide feedback on how they were impacted and what they noticed, and will be encouraged to link their own similar experiences to the hot seat interaction (American Psychological Association, 2020). For example:

Clinician: It seems like part of you really wants to stay home and not pursue your college dreams and part of you does want to go.

Client: Yeah, I'm all mixed up.

Clinician: Okay, go ahead and name the part of yourself that wants to attend college.

Client: Brave.

Clinician: Now name the part of you that wants to stay home.

Client: Weak.

Clinician: Now become Brave and talk to Weak about what you think of him. (*Following this the clinician would facilitate group dialogue around the hot seat experience.*)

Experiments

Gestalt experiments are a method that shifts the focus of counseling from talking about a topic to an activity that will heighten the client's awareness and understanding through experience (Burley & Freier, 2004; Lobb & Lichtenberg, 2005; Perls et al., 1994). For example:

Client: I get so insecure when I try to talk to my husband about our finances because I never know what his reaction is going to be.

Clinician: Lisa, I would like you to close your eyes for a minute and imagine yourself sitting in your kitchen with your husband talking about your finances. I want you to imagine yourself as confident. As you imagine this, I want you to pay attention to all of your bodily sensations. What's going on for you?

A second gestalt experiment could be the following:

Client: I get extremely annoyed when people tell me I'm wrong, because I know in every situation I am always right. I'm basically invincible.

Clinician: Sally, would you do an experiment for me? I would like you to imagine a time when you were wrong about something. It could be anything at all. I want you to pay particular attention to how you felt in that moment.

Dream Work

This is the recreation of a dream and reliving it as if it were happening now. Dreams contain existential messages and represent conflicts, wishes, and key themes in our lives (Burley & Freier, 2004; Lobb & Lichtenberg, 2005; Perls et al., 1994). For example:

Client: I had a dream a few days ago about walking through a grocery store and being robbed.

Clinician: I want you to tell me about the dream as if it were happening now. What are you feeling, seeing, and doing in the moment?

Exaggeration

The client is asked to repeat and intensify a specific behavior to help bring about awareness of that behavior, thoughts, and emotions (Burley & Freier, 2004; Lobb & Lichtenberg, 2005; Perls et al., 1994). For example:

Client: I know that I am a good person, but sometimes I don't feel like it.

Clinician: Dan, I'd like you to say "I'm a good person" again. This time say it louder.

Client: I'm a good person!

Clinician: Again, louder!

A second exaggeration targeting a body movement could look like the following:

Clinician: Justin, I notice you've been tapping your feet throughout the whole session and that this is something you have always done, but rarely notice. I want you to tap your feet twice as loud and for three minutes to help you pay attention to and notice your movements and what's going on inside.

Making the Rounds

Group members are encouraged to go around to each of the other group members and say something that they usually do not express verbally (Burley & Freier, 2004; Lobb & Lichtenberg, 2005; Perls et al., 1994). For example:

Clinician: Kali, I remember you saying it's hard for you to give other people compliments, but that you would like to improve in this behavior. Would you mind saying a compliment to each member of the group?

A second could look like the following:

Clinician: Sam, I know you have mentioned that you're worried others in the group don't accept you. I would like you to address each member of the group and say, "I'm worried you won't accept me because_____."

ATTACHMENT THEORY

The importance of attachment and the caregiver infant interaction is certainly not a new concept. Sigmund Freud documented its importance over 100 years ago in his famous text *History of an Infantile Neurosis* (1918). The 1950s brought forth both primate (Harlow & Zimmermann, 1959) and rodent (Weininger et al., 1954) research that demonstrated the importance of maternal care and nurturance beyond food and routine care. Almost simultaneous to the animal- and rodent-based research, Rene Spitz and James Robertson explored the detrimental effects of child caregiver separation in orphaned and hospitalized youth (Robertson, 1952; Spitz, 1953). Their findings demonstrated increased depressive symptomology and a compromised recovery. Psychiatrist John Bowlby (1907–1990) and developmental psychologist Mary Ainsworth (1913–1999) collaborated on an observationally based (e.g., strange situation test) theory of infant attachment. Bowlby likened the importance of attachment to childhood survival and described humans as having preprogrammed biological caregiver proximity-seeking behavior. This bidirectional behavior created a sense of security within the child and ensured protection and ultimately survival (Sullivan et al., 2011).

There is a relationship between a child's primary caregiver's behavior and the child's ability to feel a sense of security in other relationships. Attachment is a relationship of interacting affection, long-lasting emotional connection, and physical closeness. A baby is born with innate behaviors which elicit a caregiver's response (e.g., smiling, crying, and clinging). These behaviors elicit a response in caregivers to comfort, protect, and feed the infant. Furthermore, these responses begin to create a blueprint in the baby's mind for the development of future relationships. Secure attachment emerges when the caregiver consistently provides warmth, nurturance, engagement, structure, and appropriate challenge. In a general sense, insecure attachment patterns emerge if there is a lack of predictability and/or responsiveness from a significant caregiver, or if they are deficient in the areas of nurturing, engagement, structure, and challenge. Early childhood attachment experiences can be altered; however, it typically takes effective treatment or a major life event to provoke a permanent change (Black & Flynn, 2020; Simeone-Russell, 2011; Sullivan et al., 2011).

Attachment is a bidirectional lifelong process. Thompson (1998) described attachment as a physically close, interacting, affectionate, and long-lasting emotional connection. Children's repeated interactions with caregivers give them a sense of their identity, how people should treat them, and how they should treat other people. This information creates an *internal working model* for future relationships. Secure attachment is when children feel protected by their caregivers. Repeated and predictable positive interactions between infants and caregivers provide a sense of security, predictability, identity, as well as a positive internal working model of healthy relationships (Ainsworth et al., 1978). Within a play therapy or strange situation assessment, securely attached children become upset as their caregiver leaves; however, they are happy upon their return. While securely attached children can connect to a certain degree with other adults, they prefer their primary attachment figure. Securely attached children are often seen as having high self-esteem, appropriate maturity, positive peer relationships, and a high level of self-reliance (Cherry, 2006; Cherry et al., 2014).

Children who experience harsh, punitive, and/or abusive parenting styles that are centered on lack of predictability and consistency often demonstrate an insecure attachment style. Repeated experiences with caregivers who have fractious relationships and provide inconsistent or abusive care may result in an internal working model that views relationships as unsafe and hurtful. This can create a large range of issues that emerge when engaging in future adult relationships, including, but not limited to, mistrustfulness, fear of intimacy, preference for isolation, anxious and clingy relational behavior, avoidance, and abusiveness.

Attachment Styles

When many clinicians consider the possibility of attachment issues, reactive attachment disorder (RAD) is what comes to mind. The *DSM-5-TR* describes RAD as "a pattern of markedly disturbed and developmentally inappropriate attachment behaviors, in which a child rarely or minimally turns preferentially to an attachment figure for comfort, support, protection, and nurturance" (American Psychiatric Association, 2022, p. 296). RAD emerges from inadequate, abusive, and pathogenic caregiving during infancy. In addition, most children diagnosed with RAD have suffered from child abuse or neglect and/or directly experienced frequent changes in primary caregiver. Common examples of unstable family environments include moving from orphanage to adoptive and/or temporary family settings, being placed and removed from various residential treatment centers (RTCs), and being elevated from RTC to prison settings. Unique behaviors associated with the disorder are extreme and antisocial behavior, an inability to attach or form relational bonds, and lack of conscience and empathy. Considerable misdiagnosis and comorbidity issues exist between RAD, attention deficit hyperactivity disorder (ADHD), oppositional defiant disorder (ODD), and conduct disorder (American Psychiatric Association, 2022).

Neglectful, absent, and unpredictable parents often foster the dismissive/avoidant attachment style within their children. These caregivers are often detached, unresponsive, and absent. Children exemplifying this attachment style tend to be distant, detached with others, and rarely display a sense of emotionality. When feeling a sense of fear, these children attempt to use their own personal resources to deal with it alone, and under most conditions will not engage in proximity-seeking behavior with caregivers (Ainsworth et al., 1978).

Inconsistent caregiving behavior tends to foster an anxious/ambivalent attachment style in children. In parenting contexts that foster an anxious/ambivalent style, caregivers oscillate between nurturing, attuned, and responsive to intrusive, insensitive, or unavailable. There does not appear to be a meaningful pattern within this parenting style other than the frequency in change. As a response, children in this caregiving context feel a sense of confusion, insecurity, and suspicion; however, instead of distancing themselves from caregivers (i.e., dismissive/avoidant), they cling to them in an effort to survive. Children with an anxious/ambivalent style behave randomly and impulsively in relationships. In addition, they tend to have difficult time trusting others, remain wary in new situations, and during the strange situation assessment they tend to become emotional and distressed even with the caregiver present (Ainsworth et al., 1978).

Neglectful and abusive caregiving environments produce a sense of fear and hostility. Children reared in this environment usually experience little to no parenting, poor parent/child interpersonal boundaries, inappropriate blurring of roles and boundaries, and immense contradictions and errors in communication. In reviewing the nuances of this parent child relationships, Main and Solomon (1986) described the disorganized/disoriented attachment style. Children emulating the disorganized/disoriented style of attachment demonstrate an inability or extreme difficulty attaching to others, appear to lack empathy, and experience very low self-esteem. Within the playroom, clinicians have observed the following behaviors that are symbolic of this attachment style: poor boundaries, dissociating, and rocking and freezing physical movements.

Many disorders that begin in childhood continue into adulthood (e.g., ADHD, ODD); attachment is no exception. While attachment, coping, and general relational styles may stay largely the same, the big change that takes place is the context and expectations of adult relationships. Adults with a more anxious and preoccupied-oriented attachment style will demonstrate an increase in proximity-seeking behavior (e.g., clinginess, overly pursuing, argumentative, overly dependent, possessive). This attachment style may become actualized within intimate relationships in a variety of ways, including frequent texting, controlling what the other partner does with whom, stream of conscious arguing that appears to have no end, and overpursuing a partner to engage in frequent intimate experiences. Adults with a more avoidant and dismissive relationship style will demonstrate a decrease in proximity-seeking behavior (e.g., avoidance, indifference, mistrust, distrustful of relationships, void of interpersonal dependency). This attachment style could manifest in the following ways: partner avoiding uncomfortable conversations, disinterest in intimacy, acts of extreme self-sufficiency, and ignoring a partner's needs. The fearful-disorganized strategy is a combination of the anxious and avoidant attachment styles and is characterized by a fearfulness and repeated relational seeking and rejecting behaviors (Mikulincer & Shaver, 2012; Palmer & Lee, 2008).

SUMMARY

It is so interesting to consider the theories that inspire an entire field. While this chapter did not explore the major models of couple, marriage, and family therapy (transgenerational, structural, etc.) or the various waves of psychotherapy (psychodynamic, behavioral, humanistic, cognitive), it did provide a breakdown of the key theories that have historically connected most with the field. Through review of the proper method of using a sole theory or mixing various theoretical orientations (e.g., integration, eclecticism, pluralism), social justice theories (e.g., feminism, RBF, the racial minority model), first- and second-order cybernetics, constructionism, constructivism, postmodernism, gestalt, and attachment, readers can start to feel the essence of being a couple, marriage, and family practitioner. As readers continue their journey into exploring the major models of family therapy and various contemporary issues and interventions, it is important to consider how these theories and beliefs have shaped the interventions and skills that are promoted in the field.

END-OF-CHAPTER RESOURCES

STUDENT ACTIVITIES

Exercise 1: Systems Theory and Cybernetics

Directions: Review the following information and answer the reflection questions:

This chapter goes over systems theory and cybernetics. Cybernetics is the study of principles governing goal-directed, self-regulating systems. Within this theory, there are two orders of cybernetics perspective. Both of these orders include constructs that help define the theory.

- What is the difference between first- and second-order cybernetics? Why is an understanding of both important to a clinician?
- What is the difference between positive and negative feedback loops?
- How do systems theory and cybernetics play into family boundaries?
- How does cybernetics help you as a clinician when working with clients?

Exercise 2: Article Review

Directions: Review the following instructions and answer the questions:

Go to your university's online EBSCO Database and find Academic Search Premier. Search and find an article focused on the minority stress model. Review the article in its entirety and answer the following questions related to how this model may best help you in your future work as a clinician.

- How would you best utilize your knowledge of the minority stress model to work with future clients?
- When working with a diverse client base, it is important to have an understanding of how individuals who are part of a community of color experience stress. How would knowledge of this model help with working with future clients?
- What aspects of minority stress model would help you with your work with clients?
- How does the minority stress model help you better understand yourself?

Exercise 3: Gestalt Theory and Techniques

Directions: Review the following instructions and create a mock plan for potential clients:

After reading through this chapter, you should have a basic understanding of some of the major aspects of the gestalt theory, as well as the techniques used within gestalt. Using your knowledge of gestalt theory and techniques, create a mock plan for potential future clients that you could use within a therapy session.

- How would knowledge of gestalt help you as a therapist?
- How would the gestalt techniques help your clients within your therapy sessions?
- Research this theory more in depth and describe how you could incorporate some of the theory and/or techniques into your preferred model of therapy.

Exercise 4: Constructionism and Constructivism

Directions: Review the following information and answer the reflection questions:

Constructionism or social constructionism is a method of education that encourages people to build knowledge through actively engaging in constructing things in the world. Constructivism, or social constructivism, is a theory that people construct their world based on the influence of factors within their life and mind. Both of these are methods that clinicians can choose to work from in their practice.

- How would working from one theory or the other influence your ability to help clients?
- In what aspects of the therapeutic process would you use a constructionist vantage point?
- In what aspects of the therapeutic process would you use a constructivist theoretical perspective?

Exercise 5: How to Be an Antiracist

Directions: Go to the following website: www.counseling.org/docs/default-source/resources-for-counselors/anti-racism-toolkit.pdf. Review the article in its entirety and answer the following questions related to how antiracism informs your future clinical practice:

- Review the sections on racism and macroracism and discuss three ways you can create psychoeducation on these topics in future therapy sessions.
- Describe three reflective methods that you can use to explore your subconscious for any underlying racism and bias. How can you use these methods in client homework or in-session work?
- When working with a parent, name a few strategies you can encourage them to use to encourage antiracist behavior in their children.

ADDITIONAL RESOURCES

HELPFUL LINKS

- "The Fine Line Between Integration or Eclecticism and Syncretism in New Therapists": https://dual-diagnosis.imedpub.com/the-fine-line-between-integration-or-eclecticism-and-syncretism-in-new-therapists.pdf
- "Integrative Psychotherapy Works": https://www.ncbi.nlm.nih.gov/pmc/articles/PMC4707273/
- "A Feminist Approach to Family Therapy": https://www.jssa.org/wp-content/uploads/2017/12/A-Feminist-approach-to-family-therapy-with-resources-packet.pdf

- "Feminist Therapy": https://www.psychologytoday.com/us/therapy-types/feminist-therapy

- "The Minority Stress Perspective": https://www.apa.org/pi/aids/resources/exchange/2012/04/minority-stress

- "Prejudice, Social Stress, and Mental Health in Lesbian, Gay, and Bisexual Populations: Conceptual Issues and Research Evidence": https://www.ncbi.nlm.nih.gov/pmc/articles/PMC2072932/

- "#MeToo Is at a Crossroads in America. Around the World, It's Just Beginning": https://www.washingtonpost.com/opinions/2020/05/08/metoo-around-the-world/

- "7 Positive Changes That Have Come From the #MeToo Movement": https://www.vox.com/identities/2019/10/4/20852639/me-too-movement-sexual-harassment-law-2019

- "The #MeToo Moment": https://www.nytimes.com/series/metoo-moment

- "Getting Tight—The Psychology of Cancel Culture": https://www.psychologicalscience.org/news/getting-tight-the-psychology-of-cancel-culture.html

- "What Is Cancel Culture?": https://www.psychologytoday.com/us/blog/the-science-behind-behavior/202007/what-is-cancel-culture

- "Constructivism as a Theory for Teaching and Learning": https://www.simplypsychology.org/constructivism.html

- "Constructivism: Definitions and Theorists": https://sites.google.com/site/constructivism512/Home/definitions-and-theorists

- "Gestalt Therapy Explained: History, Definition, and Examples": https://positivepsychology.com/gestalt-therapy/

- "What Is Attachment Theory?": https://www.simplypsychology.org/attachment.html

HELPFUL BOOKS

- Anderson, H. (1997). *Conversation, language, and possibilities: A postmodern approach to therapy*. Basic Books.

- Bateson, G. (1972). *Steps to an ecology of mind*. University of Chicago Press.

- Bateson, G. (1979). *Mind and nature: A necessary unity*. Dutton. Reprinted Bantam, 1988.

- Haley, J. (1973). *Uncommon therapy: The psychiatric techniques of Milton H. Erickson*. Norton.

- Hoyt, M. F. (Ed.). (1998). *The handbook of constructive therapies: Innovative approaches from leading practitioners*. Jossey-Bass.

- Martin, J., & Sugarman, J. (1999). *The psychology of human possibility and constraint*. State University of New York Press.

- Perls, F., Hefferline, R., & Goodman, P. (1994). *Gestalt therapy: Excitement and growth in the human personality*. Julian Press (original work published 1951).

- Schatzki, T. (2002). *The site of the social: A philosophical account of social life and change*. Pennsylvania State University Press.

HELPFUL VIDEOS

- Me Too: How It's Changing the World: https://youtu.be/ATYK2svJ6eM

- Family Systems #2: Cybernetics: https://www.youtube.com/watch?v=Fh3gzICZ3KA

- Cybernetics Theory: https://www.youtube.com/watch?v=k0kuTH_u8T4

- Social Constructionism: https://sociologydictionary.org/social-constructionism/

- What Is Constructionism?: https://www.youtube.com/watch?v=3kAclpwNvX4

- Constructivism in Psychology: Theories and Applications: https://study.com/academy/lesson/constructivism-in-psychology-definition-theories-approaches.html

- What Is Constructivism? (Definitions, Examples, Ontology, and Epistemology of Constructivism): https://www.youtube.com/watch?v=hR5LSwr6MFI

- Theories of Counseling—Gestalt Therapy: https://www.youtube.com/watch?v=9YZjZbIl4hc

- Postmodern Therapeutic Approaches: https://www.youtube.com/watch?v=WTxQmJExfes

- The Attachment Theory: How Childhood Affects Life: https://www.youtube.com/watch?v=WjOowWxOXCg

REFERENCES

Ainsworth, M. D. S., Blehar, M. C., Waters, E., & Wall, S. (1978). *Patterns of attachment: A psychological study of the strange situation.* Lawrence Erlbaum.

American Psychiatric Association (2022). *Diagnostic and statistical manual of mental disorders* (5th ed., Text Revision). American Psychiatric Association. https://doi.org/10.1176/appi.books.9780890425787

American Psychological Association. (2020). Hot-seat technique. In *APA dictionary of psychology*. Retrieved November 8, 2021, from https://dictionary.apa.org/hot-seat-technique

Barrett, M. J., Trepper, T. S., & Fish, L. S. (1990). Feminist-informed family therapy for the treatment of intrafamily child sexual abuse. *Journal of Family Psychology, 4*(2), 151–166. https://doi.org/10.1037/0893-3200.4.2.151

Bateson, G. (1972). *Steps to an ecology of mind: Collected essays in anthropology, psychiatry, evolution, and epistemology.* Granada Publishing.

Becvar, R. J., & Becvar, D. S. (2018). *Systems theory and family therapy: A primer.* Hamilton Books.

Becvar, R. J., Canfield, B. S., & Becvar, D. S. (1997). *Group work: Cybernetic, constructivist, and social constructionist perspectives.* Love Publishing Company.

Benito, M. J. (2018). The fine line between integration and eclecticism and syncretism in new therapists. *Dual Diagnosis: Open Access, 3.* https://dual-diagnosis.imedpub.com/the-fine-line-between-integration-or-eclecticism-and-syncretism-in-new-therapists.pdf

Black, L. L., & Flynn, S. (2020). *Crisis, trauma and disaster a clinician's guide.* Sage.

Braverman, L. (1988). *A guide to feminist family therapy.* Harrington Park Press.

Buber, M. (1923). *I and thou.* Clydesdale Press.

Burley, T., & Freier, M. C. (2004). Character structure: A gestalt-cognitive theory. *Psychotherapy: Theory, Research, Practice, Training, 41*(3), 321–331. https://doi.org/10.1037/0033-3204.41.3.321

Cherry, K. (2006, July 17). *How attachment theory works.* Verywell Mind. Retrieved November 9, 2021, from https://www.verywellmind.com/what-is-attachment-theory-2795337

Cherry, M. G., Fletcher, I., & O'Sullivan, H. (2014). Validating relationships among attachment, emotional intelligence and clinical communication. *Medical Education, 48*(10), 988–997. https://doi.org/10.1111/medu.12526

Christensen, A., & Doss, B. D. (2017). Integrative behavioral couple therapy. *Current Opinion in Psychology, 13,* 111–114. https://doi.org/10.1016/j.copsyc.2016.04.022

Cooper, M., & Dryden, W. (2016). *The handbook of pluralistic counselling and psychotherapy.* Sage.

Cooper, M., & McLeod, J. (2006). A pluralistic framework for counselling and psychotherapy: Implications for research. *Counselling and Psychotherapy Research, 7*(3), 135–143. https://doi.org/10.1080/14733140701566282

Crotty, M. J. (1998). *The foundations of social research: Meaning and perspective in the research process.* Sage.

Dentato, M. P. (2012, April). The minority stress perspective. *Psychology and AIDS Exchange Newsletter.* http://www.apa.org/pi/aids/resources/exchange/2012/04/minority-stress.aspx

Eylem, O., de Wit, L., van Straten, A., Steubl, L., Melissourgaki, Z., Danışman, G. T., de Vries, R., Kerkhof, A. J., Bhui, K., & Cuijpers, P. (2020). Stigma for common mental disorders in racial minorities and majorities a systematic review and meta-analysis. *BMC Public Health, 20*(1). https://doi.org/10.1186/s12889-020-08964-3

Flaskas, C. (1994). Exploring the therapeutic relationship, a case study. *Australian and New Zealand Journal of Family Therapy, 15*(4), 185–190. https://doi.org/10.1002/j.1467-8438.1994.tb01010.x

Freud, S. (1918). *From the history of an infantile neurosis.* Hogarth Press.

Gergen, K. J. (1991). *The saturated self: Dilemmas of identity in contemporary life.* Basic Books.

Gottman, J. M., & Silver, N. (2015). *The seven principles for making marriage work: A practical guide from the country's foremost relationship expert.* Harmony Books.

Harlow, H. F., & Zimmermann, R. R. (1959). Affectional response in the infant monkey. *Science, 130*(3373), 421–432. https://doi.org/10.1126/science.130.3373.421

Hill, M., & Ballou, M. (1998). Making therapy feminist. *Women & Therapy, 21*(2), 1–16. https://doi.org/10.1300/j015v21n02_01

Johnson, S. M. (2019). *The practice of emotionally focused couple therapy: Creating connection* (3rd ed.). Routledge/Taylor & Francis Group.

Kant, I., & Meiklejohn, J. M. D. (2009). *Critique of pure reason.* The Floating Press.

Köhler, W. (1940). *Dynamics in psychology.* Liveright.

Laird, J. (1995). Family-centered practice in the postmodern era. *Families in Society: The Journal of Contemporary Social Services, 76*(3), 150–162. https://doi.org/10.1177/104438949507600303

Lazarus, A. A. (1967). In support of technical eclecticism. *Psychological Reports, 21*(2), 415–416. https://doi.org/10.2466/pr0.1967.21.2.415

Lebow, J. (1997). The integrative revolution in couple and family therapy. *Family Process, 36*(1), 1–17. https://doi.org/10.1111/j.1545-5300.1997.00001.x

Levy, R., & Mattsson, M. (2019). The effects of social movements: Evidence from #metoo. *SSRN Electronic Journal.* https://doi.org/10.2139/ssrn.3496903

Lewin, K. (1951). *Field theory in social science: Selected theoretical papers* (D. Cartwright, Ed.). Harpers.

Lilienfeld, S. O. (2017). Microaggressions. *Perspectives on Psychological Science, 12*(1), 138–169. https://doi.org/10.1177/1745691616659391

Limberg, D., Guest, J. D., & Gonzales, S. K. (2021). History of research in the social sciences. In S. Flynn (Ed.), *Research design for the behavioral sciences: An applied approach* (pp. 43–70). Springer Publishing Company.

Lobb, M. S., & Lichtenberg, P. (2005). Classical gestalt therapy theory. *Gestalt Therapy: History, Theory, and Practice,* 21–40. https://doi.org/10.4135/9781452225661.n2

Luepnitz, D. A. (1989). *The family interpreted: Feminist theory in clinical practice.* Basic Books.

Mackewn, J. (1997). *Developing gestalt counselling: A field theoretical and relational model of contemporary gestalt counselling and psychotherapy.* Sage. https://doi.org/10.4135/9781446280461

Main, M., & Solomon, J. (1986). Discovery of an insecure-disorganized/disoriented attachment pattern. In T. B. Brazelton & M. W. Yogman (Eds.), *Affective development in infancy* (pp. 95–124). Ablex Publishing.

Maturana, H. R., & Varela, F. J. (1980). *Autopoiesis and cognition: The realization of the living.* D. Reidel Publishing Company.

Meyer, I. H. (2007). Prejudice and discrimination as social stressors. *The Health of Sexual Minorities,* 242–267. https://doi.org/10.1007/978-0-387-31334-4_10

Meyers, L. (2018, August 31). Talking about #MeToo. *Counseling Today.* https://ct.counseling.org/2018/08/talking-about-metoo/

Mikulincer, M., & Shaver, P. R. (2012). An attachment perspective on psychopathology. *World Psychiatry, 11*(1), 11–15. https://doi.org/10.1016/j.wpsyc.2012.01.003

Minuchin, S. (1974). *Families & family therapy.* Harvard University Press.

Neimeyer, R. A., & Bridges, S. K. (2003). Postmodern approaches to psychotherapy. In A. S. Gurman & S. B. Messer (Eds.), *Essential psychotherapies: Theory and practice* (pp. 272–316). Guilford Press.

Neukrug, E. (2015). *The world of the counselor: An introduction to the counseling profession*. Brooks/Cole.

Palmer, G., & Lee, A. (2008). Clinical update: Adult attachment. *Family Therapy Magazine, 7*, 36–42.

Perls, F. S., Hefferline, R. F., & Goodman, P. (1994). *Gestalt therapy: Excitement and growth in the human personality*. Souvenir Press.

Pierce, C. (1974). *Psychiatric problems of the Black minority* (Vol. 2, pp. 512–523). American Handbook of Psychiatry.

Robertson, J. (1952). *A two-year-old goes to hospital* [Film]. Concord Films.

Semlyen, J., King, M., Varney, J., & Hagger-Johnson, G. (2016). Sexual orientation and symptoms of common mental disorder or low wellbeing: Combined Meta-analysis of 12 UK population health surveys. *BMC Psychiatry, 16*(1). https://doi.org/10.1186/s12888-016-0767-z

Simeone-Russell, R. (2011). A practical approach to implementing theraplay for children with autism spectrum disorder. *International Journal of Play Therapy, 20*(4), 224–235. https://doi.org/10.1037/a0024823

Smith, W. A. (2008). Higher education: Racial battle fatigue. In R. T. Schaefer (Ed.), *Encyclopedia of race, ethnicity, and society* (pp. 615–618). Sage.

Spelman, B. (2021, July 5). *The effects cancel culture and 'collective bullying' has on mental health*. Private Therapy Clinic. https://theprivatetherapyclinic.co.uk/blog/the-effects-cancel-culture-has-on-mental-health/

Spitz, R. A. (1953). *Shaping the personality: The role of mother-child relations in infancy* [Film]. National Library of Medicine.

Stricker, G., & Gold, J.R. (1996). Psychotherapy integration: An assimilative, psychodynamic approach. *Clinical Psychology: Science and Practice, 3*, 47–58. https://doi.org/10.1111/j.1468-2850.1996.tb00057.x

Sue, D.W., Sue, D., Neville, H. A., & Smith, L. (2019). *Counseling the culturally diverse: Theory and practice* (8th ed.). John Wiley & Sons.

Sullivan, R., Perry, R., Sloan, A., Kleinhaus, K., & Burtchen, N. (2011). Infant bonding and attachment to the caregiver: Insights from basic and clinical science. *Clinics in Perinatology, 38*(4), 643–655. https://doi.org/10.1016/j.clp.2011.08.011

Tasca, G. A., Sylvestre, J., Balfour, L., Chyurlia, L., Evans, J., Fortin-Langelier, B., Francis, K., Gandhi, J., Huehn, L., Hunsley, J., Joyce, A. S., Kinley, J., Koszycki, D., Leszcz, M., Lybanon-Daigle, V., Mercer, D., Ogrodniczuk, J. S., Presniak, M., Ravitz, P., … Wilson, B. (2015). What clinicians want: Findings from a psychotherapy practice research network survey. *Psychotherapy, 52*(1), 1–11. https://doi.org/10.1037/a0038252

Thompson, R. A. (1998). Attachment and emotional understanding in preschool children. *Developmental Psychology, 34*(5), 1038–1045. https://doi.org/10.1037/0012-1649.34.5.1038

Tong, R. (2001). Towards a feminist global bioethics: Addressing women's health concerns worldwide. *Health Care Analysis, 9*(2), 229–246. https://doi.org/10.1023/a:1011390521518

Wampold, B. E., & Imel, Z. E. (2015). *The great psychotherapy debate: The evidence for what makes psychotherapy work* (2nd ed.). Routledge/Taylor & Francis Group.

Weininger, O., McClelland, W. J., & Arima, R. K. (1954). Gentling and weight gain in the albino rat. *Canadian Journal of Psychology/Revue Canadienne De Psychologie, 8*(3), 147–151. https://doi.org/10.1037/h0083606

Williams, M. T. (2019). Microaggressions: Clarification, evidence, and impact. *Perspectives on Psychological Science, 15*(1), 3–26. https://doi.org/10.1177/1745691619827499

CHAPTER 4

THE INTEGRATION OF FOUNDATIONAL COUNSELING AND SYSTEMIC SKILLS

LEARNING OBJECTIVES

After reading this chapter, you will be able to:

- ■ Identify session management.

- ■ Distinguish the details of cotherapy.

- ■ Recognize basic systemic therapy skills.

- ■ Describe the integration of invitational, attending, and influencing skills in systemic practice.

- ■ Recognize the core techniques associated with transgenerational, structural, strategic, experiential, solution-focused, narrative, cognitive behavioral family therapy, and emotion-focused theories.

INTRODUCTION TO SYSTEMIC AND COUNSELING SKILLS AND INTERVENTIONS

Family therapy pioneer Salvador Minuchin provided incredible insight into the acquisition of skills when he likened the training of family therapists to that of Samurai warriors (Minuchin & Fishman, 1981). Samurai apprentices would study, with extreme discipline, all the time-honored moves and skills until mastery was achieved. After 7 years of deep learning, they would relinquish the acquired techniques and skills to make room for their own personal style to emerge. This greatly resembles the training of couple, marriage, and family practitioners. After deeply learning microcounseling skills, general systemic therapy skills, and tradition-based systemic interventions, the therapist will emerge as an effective clinician who has acquired the skills and interventions of the profession. The next step is to return to one's core sense of self and reincorporate one's personhood and individual style. Given this evolution, you are encouraged to deeply learn the forthcoming chapter-based skills and interventions. Once they are deeply ingrained in your mind, let them go and reinvestigate and incorporate your own style of helping others.

As clinicians consider the various skills and techniques associated with systemic therapy and various theoretical traditions, it is important to remember two key points. First, therapy is a practice. Any practitioner's ability to execute a group of skills and techniques is evolving and grounded in practicing them for a long period of time. While clinicians work hard to acquire competencies, putting an enormous amount of pressure on oneself to do things "correctly" at all times is not helpful and can lead to serious errors, burnout, and unnecessary stress. A good way to think about the acquisition of competency is to view it as a lifelong process. While everyone improves in their own way, we never hit the apex of skill acquisition. There is always more to learn. The second important point to remember is that humans are not behavioral software. We do not all use the same skills and techniques in the same way. As long as nothing unethical is taking place, creativity and imagination with the understanding and execution of skills and techniques should be supported and celebrated.

Effective couple, marriage, and family practitioners constantly vacillate between using both core systemic skills and interventions and counseling microskills. Within this textbook, I differentiate the use of practical skills from complex interventions. Practical skills are typically straightforward techniques that cut across therapeutic approaches (atheoretical), or initially were used within a particular tradition but gradually were absorbed into general profession-based skills. Examples include structural family therapy's (SFT's) use of enactment and the use of reframing in the human validation process (i.e., Satir). While both of these skills were initially promoted in a particular theoretical camp (Minuchin, 1974; Satir & Baldwin, 1983; Watzlawick et al., 1974), they have become so widespread that they are considered part of general systemic therapy practice.

Complex interventions are often theoretically based, detailed, and part of a larger repertoire of theoretical techniques. While many clinicians may claim an eclectic or integrative therapeutic framework, most systemic *interventions* have their origins in a particular theoretical tradition (e.g., SFT's use of reenactment, emotionally focused therapy's [EFT's] use of heightening). On the other hand, there are many systemic *skills* that are less technical and cut across theoretical traditions. These skills include (a) joining, (b) actualizing the family's transaction patterns, (c) escalating conflict and stress, (d) defusing conflict, (e) paradoxical injunctions, (f) circular questioning, (g) communication training, (h) positive connotation reframing, (i) broadening and displacing the symptom, (j) emphasizing individual boundaries, (k) restructuring dysfunctional subsystem boundaries, (l) modeling, (m) advice giving, (n) in-session behavior prescriptions, and (o) out-of-session work (Patterson et al., 2018; Russell et al., 1984). While many systemic practitioners claim a theoretical home, they should all have practical and in-depth knowledge of the aforementioned general systemic skills.

Foundational counseling microskills are extremely important for all helping professionals to understand because they are key to developing a deeply rooted therapeutic alliance. In fact, all theoretical orientations acknowledge the power of the therapeutic relationship. For example, Harmon et al. (2005) reported four decades of empirical support for the power of the therapeutic relationship. According to Yalom (1980), the helper interacts with the client in a genuine fashion, conveys warmth in a non possessive manner, and tries to grasp the meaning of the client's life and experience to create a relationship of safety and acceptance. Counseling microskills that enhance the client–counselor relationship include invitational skills (e.g., nonverbal communication, encouragers, vocal tone, observation, and silence), attending skills (e.g., goal setting, open-ended questioning, closed-ended questioning, clarification, paraphrasing, summarizing, normalizing, and reflection of feeling), and influencing skills (e.g., advocacy, immediacy, challenging and pointing out discrepancies, feedback, reflecting meaning and values, reframing, interpretation, self-disclosure, psychoeducation, homework, and directives; Cormier et al., 2017; Flynn & Hays, 2015; Ivey et al., 2017; Young, 2016).

SESSION MANAGEMENT

Each therapeutic encounter is unique, and every session is different. Some sessions have a purpose (e.g., intake, assessment, termination), while others are centered on achieving treatment plan goals. Furthermore, relationships between counselors and clients vary so much that there is essentially no universal description of what a therapy session entails. While unique factors always exist, most sessions have both peaks and valleys. Phases of a therapy session often include particular aspects of each session (e.g., opening, working, and closing). In addition to understanding the essence of the phases of therapy, practitioners maintain multicultural competency, engage clients in a developmentally appropriate manner, and work hard to understand contextual issues that may serve as a benefit or a negative consequence within each phase of session.

Most sessions start with a more superficial feeling. During the opening phase of a therapeutic encounter, the clinician will often warmly greet the client, offer a summary of the previous session (if applicable), describe the outcomes of any homework, and apply a transition into the working part of the session. For example, many clients may discuss their drive to the session, a few minor stressful issues that came up during the week, or the outcome of out-of-session work. While it may be helpful to discuss some of these topics, many of the early-session discussion points will not be directly related to long-term and/or short-term goals. Certain theoretical orientations such as cognitive behavioral therapy (CBT) and dialectical behavioral therapy (DBT) may set the stage with clients taking part in a mood check (0–100 rating scale) or an outcome questionnaire to numerically assess their progress. After a few minutes of superficial discussion, the clinician may transition the client to a deeper aspect of the session with an invitation such as "Please tell me what you would like to work on today."

As the session progresses, the client will become increasingly dependent on the clinician and will ideally begin exploring the issues that directly pertain to their treatment plan goal(s). During the working phase of the session, the client typically explores relevant stories, provides internal introspection and insights, and describes issues related to the goals of treatment. During this phase, the clinician uses microcounseling skills to enhance the relationship, employs interventions centered on creating change, evaluates progress relative to goals, and may provide resources and referrals if necessary. As the session ends, the client will often return to a more superficial level (i.e., less dependent on the therapist) and discuss issues related to out-of-session work. Closing phase skills employed by clinicians often include bringing a timely end to the session, summarizing the session, handling unexpected end-of-session client behavior appropriately, and, if needed, cocreating plans for future sessions.

While there are many additional aspects to consider, three salient points relate to centering the client on the goals if they become less focused or are avoiding a topic, handling sudden end-of-session serious concerns, and using skills to address issues related to diversity and multiculturalism. At times, the initial reason for coming to therapy (i.e., referral) becomes the topic that is not addressed. As clinicians determine what is or is not important for discussion and the time frame for such disclosures, they consider the strength of the therapeutic alliance, client resistance, and the natural flow of therapy. For example, a clinician working with a family that has concerns around adolescent pornography use might notice that the family avoids the topic in the first three sessions. During the fourth session, the practitioner introspects on whether the therapeutic relationship with the family is strong enough for the therapist to break the ice and begin inquiring about the issue or the reason the topic is not being discussed. In many cases, difficult, taboo, and hurtful issues will be avoided until the clinician brings them up. Clinicians could also consider simply letting go of the desire to create an interaction with the client and simply allow it to happen on its own. Resistance is something that should be embraced, and if clients are not opening up about something it may be in their best interest not to do so, or they may be hesitant because the topic is undesirable to discuss (Shallcross, 2010).

A second common issue that emerges in session management is the client disclosing a very serious issue at the end of the session (i.e., dropping a last-minute bomb). This phenomenon falls into the category of time management and boundary issues (Howes & Spieker, 2008), and it is likely to come up frequently throughout one's career. The issue disclosed (e.g., early childhood abuse, death of a loved one, impending divorce) often requires a lot of time to unpack and fully understand; however, the clinician is in a bind because the session time has run out and the next client is waiting for their session. For example, during the final 5 minutes of the session, a client might inform the clinician, for the first time, that they experienced early childhood sexual abuse and believe that it is getting in the way of their ability to connect with their partner. Clinicians who find themselves in this situation must balance the need to empathize, unpack, and support their client with the need to properly manage the closure of the session. A clinician may offer a comment such as this: "I appreciate the bravery it took for you to state that in session today. That sounds like a terrifying experience that has deeply affected you and your ability to feel safe in relationships. While I would like to unpack this information further, our time has unfortunately ended. Let's place a bookmark on this issue and discuss it more thoroughly next week." Whatever the client's rationale for dropping such an important topic at the end of the session might be, if it does not pose an imminent threat to the client or others, most of the time the clinician will empathically wrap up the session and move on to their next appointment.

The final common issue that frequently emerges involves issues related to diversity and multiculturalism. Early-career practitioners can become confused when these issues impact their clinical work. Diversity and multicultural issues often manifest with clients suddenly shutting down, displaying a sense of mistrust or friction, not engaging in the session, or simply not returning to therapy. For example, during a session with an Asian American client, a Caucasian counselor begins advocating that she stand up for her beliefs with her father. While the counselor may have intended to be supportive and empowering, this suggestion has challenged the client because it does not acknowledge her family's and culture's beliefs that younger relatives ought to value the perspectives of elders and refrain from disagreeing or arguing with the older generation's perspectives. In response to this unintended cultural misstep, the client shuts down and stares at the floor. In this situation, the counselor is receiving important feedback and must manage the experience or risk hurting the therapeutic alliance. While every intervention must be tailored to the unique therapeutic experience and there is no universal intervention for such a situation, a possible response could be this: "I noticed that when I stated you should confront your father, you didn't respond and stared at the floor. I want to apologize if I stated something that was off base. I wonder if you wouldn't mind sharing with me how my encouragement affected you." Generally speaking, it is often helpful for a therapist to name what happened, empathize with the client's response, and provide a genuine disclosure around the situation. An important key point is for therapists to avoid pretending they are more knowledgeable than they are around an in-session cultural misstep (Williams et al., 2021).

Cotherapy

Cotherapy is a team approach to counseling in which two professionals work together to simultaneously apply therapy to a couple, family, network, or group. This approach was historically used by Alfred Adler (i.e., multiple therapy) and further popularized by contemporary experiential family therapy pioneers Carl Whitaker and Virginia Satir (Satir & Baldwin, 1983; Whitaker & Keith, 1983). Cotherapists essentially collaborate to strategically support the clients they serve. Each clinician provides a source of support for the other and frequently depends on the other during conjoint treatment. Aside from the benefits of collaboration and not working in isolation, cotherapy provides multiple perspectives on an issue, can motivate a group through cotherapy dialogue (e.g., discussing sensitive topics, gossip, and modeling effective decision-making), and can greatly increase the diversity in the room by incorporating practitioners from different contextual backgrounds (e.g., sex, race, ethnicity, age, ability, sexual orientation, gender identity). Lastly, due to the shared workload and support, cotherapy greatly reduces the likelihood of therapist burnout, compassion fatigue, and impairment. Not only does within-session support help with this factor, but if one of the cotherapists is sick or out of the office the other can cover for them (Roller & Nelson, 1991).

The first step in creating an effective cotherapy partnership is choosing the right cotherapist. According to Roller and Nelson (1991), the top criterion for choosing a cotherapist is being equal in openness and communication. Additional desirable qualities include willingness to discuss disagreements outside of session, to formulate treatment objectives, to engage in postsession processing, to differ openly, and to confront with empathy. Among other important factors, the authors found that clinicians preferred working with cotherapists who held similar values and theoretical leanings. The second step involves preparing for the upcoming session(s). Joining tasks are divided, and practitioners decide how they will make contact. For example, cotherapy preparation dialogue might look like this: "I'll attempt to deeply reflect Josh's feelings while you occasionally summarize key points we make. As for Rhonda, why don't you take the lead and I'll summarize?" A third step includes presession planning and roles. The responsibilities and authority of each therapist must be clearly established. For example, will both therapists speak at once, or will one speak as the other takes notes and occasionally interjects? Perhaps one cotherapist starts speaking while the other nods and occasionally offers paraphrases and summarizations.

While the benefits of cotherapy are evident, challenges exist. For example, financial challenges often arise. Therapists' time and workloads are often carefully reviewed by organizations and by private practitioners. Despite the benefits of cotherapy, administrators could possibly view the use of two therapists as unnecessary. Furthermore, if evident, cotherapist intimacy and sexual relationships can create difficult boundary issues for both counselors and clients (Storm et al., 1990). Roller and Nelson's (1991) Five Cs of Cotherapy Dilemmas provide a clear blueprint for what to avoid in cotherapy situations. The issues described include cotherapy competition, countertransference, confusion and lack of communication, lack of congruence, and codependency. Competition has to do with avoiding dominance and recognition in cotherapy. Countertransference is equated with cotherapists reenacting their own family-of-origin issues within the cotherapy dyad. Confusion and lack of communication is centered on not engaging in the processing and planning aspects of the cotherapy relationship. Lack of congruence has to do with disagreement about the presenting problem and/or the treatment plan. Lastly, codependency emerges when the cotherapists lose their identity as individuals.

Therapeutic gossip is a unique skill used in cotherapy. The essence of this skill is the dynamic that emerges when cotherapists talk to each other about what they are observing in front of the couple, group, network, or family to remain connected and to evoke a response. This technique allows the family/group members to regroup and get a feel for what is happening in the session (Roller & Nelson, 1991; Satir & Baldwin, 1983). For example, the dialogue between cotherapists might sound like the following:

Clinician A: I don't know about you, Chris, but I'm sensing something different about the family today.

Clinician B: Yeah, Alex, it seems something has happened that caused everyone to get quiet and uncomfortable around each other. Hmmm . . . I wonder what it could be.

Another example:

Clinician A: Shameika, I don't know about you, but I'm not satisfied with the depth the couple is going into.

Clinician B: Arjun, I know exactly what you mean. It seems like most weeks we get past this superficial stage quickly.

Clinician A: Shameika, something is certainly different. I just can't put my finger on it.

Reflection Team

Norwegian psychiatrist Tom Andersen created the intervention that is now known as the reflection team, or RT (Andersen, 1991). Andersen was trained in the Milan Systemic Approach (Selvini et al., 1979), and, as in the Milan Systemic Approach, one of the goals of RT is to offer multiple descriptions of the client's presenting issues and potential solutions. Practitioners who use RT engage in live supervision (e.g., behind a one-way mirror, digitally based center) with multiple experts. The purpose of RT is to exchange physical positions with a couple or family so the family members/ therapist(s) can observe a team of professionals reflecting on the family issues and consequently generating multiple descriptions of what is going on within and between the couple/family. The team shares its reflections speculatively, remains open to multiple possibilities and explanations, and allows clients to select those ideas that fit. After RT is finished, the counselor attends to the multiple descriptions of the problem, unpacks these descriptions, and invites reflection on relationships, differences, and implications of changed perspectives (Andersen, 1991; Chang, 2010).

The benefits of using RT include its effectiveness in alleviating many mental health issues (Kjellberg et al., 1995). It is promoted as a gold standard systemic technique (Hoffman, 1995) and can be used effectively with young children (Lax, 1989) and stepfamilies (Berger, 2000). Furthermore, Sells et al. (1994) found that clients greatly benefited from RT's use of multiple perspectives. Negative aspects of RT include the belief that it is essentially a technique that is missing a theoretical home, as well as the necessity for using a particular facility (i.e., live supervision center) and multiple people. In addition, one aspect of the intervention that is both positive and negative is the fact that there are so many variations of the intervention that there is no procedural consistency to properly use RT (Chang, 2010).

The following example highlights the ethos of the RT experience:

Clinician: As I mentioned, now we will change places with the team, and they will have a conversation about what they have seen and heard in our session. What they are saying is not "the way it is," just their perceptions. As you listen to the team's reflections, note what fits for you, what does not fit for you, what seems to be useful, and what jumps out at you. After they're done, we'll meet again for a few minutes to sort it all out.

After RT is completed, the clinician attends to the multiple descriptions of the problem, unpacks these descriptions, and invites reflection on relationships, differences, and implications of changed perspectives. For example:

> *Clinician:* Okay, there was a lot reflected on during the experience. I wonder what stood out to you as an area to focus on upfront.

FOUNDATIONAL SYSTEMIC SKILLS

As noted earlier, there are certain systemic skills and proficiencies that all couple, marriage, and family practitioners must learn. These include foundational systemic skills (Patterson et al., 2018; Russell et al., 1984) and microcounseling skills (Ivey et al., 2017; Young, 2016). Novice students are taught these skillsets during their graduate training. In the following sections, I expand on the work of Patterson et al. (2018) and Russell et al. (1984) to provide a concise definition and two brief examples of 15 common systemic skills: (a) joining, (b) actualizing the family's transaction patterns, (c) escalating conflict and stress, (d) defusing conflict, (e) paradoxical injunctions, (f) circular questioning, (g) communication training, (h) positive connotation reframing, (i) broadening and displacing the symptom, (j) emphasizing individual boundaries, (k) restructuring dysfunctional subsystem boundaries, (l) modeling, (m) advice giving, (n) in-session behavior prescriptions, and (o) out-of-session work. As you review the following descriptions and examples, please note that there is no universally correct way to use a particular skill. Skill use depends on a number of factors, including, but not limited to, context, diversity, privilege, clinician preference, and common factors. The forthcoming information is meant to provide a foundational description and a glimpse of how a particular systemic skill might be used in a clinical context.

Joining

Most theoretical schools discuss the importance of the therapeutic alliance. *Joining* is the systemic form of aligning and developing a relationship with individuals, couples, and families. The clinician starts by developing a relationship with all clients in the room. Next, the clinician adopts the family's language, style of communication, and affective range (i.e., mimesis). Furthermore, the clinician will accept the current family structure and accommodate to the family's norms and rules. For example:

> *Client:* I . . . ugh, I don't know what she wants. She always wants my attention but doesn't like cars, baseball, or anything I'm into.
>
> *Clinician:* You are saying that you care about things that she doesn't seem too interested in.
>
> *Client:* Yeah, you know . . . guy stuff.
>
> *Clinician:* What team do you watch?

Another example:

> *Client:* I hate my mom! She is always breathing down my neck about grades and becoming a doctor . . . I just want her to back the hell off!
>
> *Clinician:* You're so pissed off (client's language), and it's like you against the world . . . no one is on your side.
>
> *Client:* Hell, yeah . . . that's the way it has always been.

Actualizing the Family's Transactional Patterns

It can take an individual, couple, and/or family time to feel comfortable in a therapy session. This technique emphasizes the clinician disengaging or decentralizing from the system. This disengagement provides the opportunity for the couple or the family to interact in their normal manner, which will eventually allow for the emergence of typical communication and behavioral patterns. For example:

Client A: I'm just so discouraged with our relationship. All I want is for you to give me some respect. What is wrong with me and you?

Client B: See what I mean? . . . I . . . I just don't know what to do here.

Clinician: I think you do. Go ahead and respond as you normally do.

Client B: Okay. Just be quiet and deal. We can make it through this.

Another example:

Client B: Well, should we get a divorce? Is that what you are saying?

Client A: I don't know; I just don't know (tearfulness).

Client B: Well, this is where we always get stuck.

Clinician: Show me more about stuck . . . keep going.

Client B: I don't want to lose this relationship, but you need to make some big changes.

Client A: Forget it. You blame everything on me, so I just give up.

Escalating Conflict and Stress

While many clients may be looking for ways to reduce conflict or stress, there are times when clinicians may want to escalate the stress in the room. This skill is typically used to bypass or change the family's typical method of avoiding conflict or stress. A clinician can employ many methods to alter the family's typical behavior and increase stress and conflict, including, but not limited to, (a) blocking the typical way people communicate (e.g., not allowing typical interruptions), (b) stopping the family and having them focus on members and/or communication that typically gets glossed over, (c) creating enactments that are confrontational in nature, or (d) clinician aligning themselves with a family member or subsystem to create abnormal amounts of stress. For example:

Client A: I'm really, umm . . . I guess . . . angry with how you've treated me over the last few years. I'm sorry; I don't mean that. I'm just overreacting again.

Clinician: Juanita, I want you to stay with your anger and don't make light of it. You're feeling angry here.

Client A: Okay, here goes. I just want you to stop putting your work before your family in all circumstances.

Clinician: You're angry that you are always second place!

Client B: You're not always second . . . I mean, I love you and the girls, but work is just so all-encompassing. (The clinician in this example highlights an interaction the family typically glosses over and briefly aligns with the partner.)

Another example:

Client A: I think you need to spend more time with the girls.

Client C: Mom, I don't like it when you talk like this! What is wrong?

Clinician: Jenny, I can tell this is really different from what you're used to. Mom and Dad need to work this out right now.

Client B: Well, I would like to create a schedule, so things seem more equitable. (The clinician successfully blocks the child from interrupting this important dialogue and provides a concise rationale for doing so.)

Defusing Conflict

Many couples and families choose to come to therapy when there is chaos, high conflict, or when they are at the brink of divorce. Unfortunately, preventive mental health has a long way to go in the therapeutic world. Clinicians work hard to defuse conflict so people can hear one another, and sessions can be productive instead of extremely conflictual and defensive. Clinicians will actively stop explosive interactions that create a deep sense of hurt, mistrust, and suspicion. For example:

Client A: I'm sick of your lies and your cheating!

Client B: She is always accusing me of things I don't do.

Client A: Well, remember, you looked at that girl when we were driving one day, and I know the way you were looking at her. I know lots of girls probably want you, and you love that, don't you?

Clinician: Okay, I'm going to stop you right now. I can tell you are very afraid of being manipulated and you sound very suspicious of her behavior. I also know that we are not going to get anywhere if we just sit and yell at each other. Each of you desperately wants to be able to trust the other.

Client A: Trust has always been hard for me. (The clinician successfully stops the escalated conversation and reframes the issue in a positive way [working toward trust].)

Another example:

Client A: You know, Jason . . . you are such a little baby! Why don't you just step it up and propose to me? We've been together for how long now. Get a clue!

Clinician: You are very angry and disappointed that you have not been proposed to.

Client A: Uh huh.

Client B: Yeah, like talking to me like that will really encourage me to make a lifelong commitment.

Clinician: Okay, both members of the relationship stop looking at each other and turn your chairs so they're facing me. The new rule is, for right now, only talk to me when you feel those strong aggressive feelings toward each other. Agreed?

Client B: Sure.

Client A: Okay, I'll try.

Clinician: Amy, I want you to talk to me about the hurt you feel beneath some of that anger. (The clinician takes a more behavioral approach to stopping the conflict. Specifically, she encourages both clients to turn to her instead of each other until they reach a place where they can emotionally self-regulate.)

Paradoxical Injunctions

Very few skills both excite and terrify graduate-level trainees as much as the paradoxical injunction. This technique is directive in nature and typically involves the clinician providing encouragement to continue the undesirable behavior that is very difficult to change. When the client realizes they can increase the undesirable behavior voluntarily, they also become aware that they are in control of it and can choose to stop doing it. The technique typically involves reinforcing the behavior that the family or individual would like to change, suggesting to the individual or family that increasing the undesirable behavior will somehow lead to positive change, and consequently creating a paradox where the client is told to change by remaining unchanged. For example:

Client A: Suzie keeps acting up at home.

Client C: No, I don't.

Client B: I think she typically does it when Jen (spouse/mother) and I get into an argument.

Clinician: I think I understand what's taking place. So, it seems Suzie is the glue for this family. When the two of you argue, she acts out to stop the fight.

Client A: I never thought it was to stop the fight and keep us together. I just thought. . . .

Clinician: Suzie has established herself as the family peacemaker for the purpose of saving it. It is apparent that she is willing to sacrifice her own development to help protect her father from her mother's anger. Until this process is more fully understood, I believe it is important for Suzie to continue her caring and attention-seeking ways in order to help the family to stay together. (This is an example of a typical identified patient paradox.)

Another example:

Clinician: I would like to suggest something. This may sound strange, but I'd like to suggest it anyway. The next time Gary throws a temper tantrum, Jasmine, what I'd like you to do is to feel bad and act upset (everyone laughs). Just see if it works. Do you know the first sign?

Client A: I can hear his screams. He moans and groans and whines.

Clinician: At the moment when you see that he is going to have one of his weekly temper tantrums, instead of coddling him, I'd like you to become increasingly preoccupied about your own issues. Specifically, I'd like you to start to cry or start to complain about friends at school. (The clinician prescribes the client's problem to the family members to provoke change.)

Circular Questioning

This type of questioning is used to help inspire systemic introspection. Basically, one member of the family is asked to comment on or speculate about another family member's beliefs, feelings, and behavior. For example, "If your sister were to get married, who would miss her the most?" or "If I ask your father, will he agree with your sister or your mother?" or "John, what do you think has kept your mother from hearing your complaints?" A more in-depth example could include the following:

Client A: My mom would be so sad about the way that I treat my kids.

Clinician: If your mother were here today, what would she say about your parenting style?

Client A: I'm not sure, but it probably wouldn't be as harsh as the way Shawn criticizes me.

Client B: My two moms are always fighting about parenting stuff.

Clinician: When your moms are fighting, what is your sister doing?

Communication Training

One of the most common reasons for family and couple referrals is communication issues. Communication training involves creating a situation in session that requires new communication skills. This technique helps couples and families improve their communication through feedback, coaching and modeling new skills, and behavioral rehearsal. Clinicians will frequently encourage enactments that are structured to require applying new empathy and listening skills, exploring personal feelings, voicing negative feelings, providing mutual support, and exercising assertiveness. For example:

Clinician: Let's work on discussing the infidelity in a meaningful and direct way. Megan, without blaming and by using the "I statements" we previously discussed, please tell Janet what happened. Janet, all I want you to do is to listen to Megan and then let them know in your own way what you heard them say.

Client A: I am so sorry, Janet. I took Alice on a drive, and we parked near the barn. One thing led to another, and we ended up sleeping together.

Client B: I hear that you're sorry that you slept with Alice when I was out of town.

Another example:

Clinician: As a family, you are working on expressing more gratitude. John, I want you to turn your chair and face your mom. Mom, all I want you to do is listen to him for now. Now, in your own words, tell her one thing you're grateful she did this week.

Client A: Mom, I'm grateful you let me play my music in the morning before school.

Clinician: Now, Mom, please face John and let him know one thing you are grateful that he did this week.

Client B: John, I'm grateful you made your bed most mornings.

Clinician: Great job. Let's keep this going throughout the week. . . .

Positive Connotation Reframing

Reframing is about looking at the client's experience from a more positive angle. Clinicians will describe a family member's actions, communication, and/or behavior as positive, benevolent, and centered on good intentions. This reframing experience promotes the idea that there are positive, good, and noble reasons embedded into a family member's challenging behavior. For example:

Client: As you can see, Rishi is getting in trouble everywhere with everyone.

Clinician: I hear that you are upset by this. Rishi, I am impressed with how you have selflessly been the focus of the family so that no one will notice the parents' arguments.

Another example:

Client: We have a real problem with trust. We just cannot seem to let go of our fear of being used by one another.

Clinician: You both care so deeply about this relationship that you are willing to not fully love each other to protect it.

Broadening and Displacing the Symptom

Broadening and displacing the symptom is a systemic skill that expands clients' understanding of the family problem being centered on one member's actions or lack thereof. A common issue in families is scapegoating a particular family member for the majority of the problems. The goal is to shift this thinking to an awareness that others are contributing to the problems in direct and indirect ways. This could include expanding the definition of the family problem or temporarily moving the family problem from one family member to another. For example:

Client A: The problem in our family is Brian's behavior.

Clinician: Really? I wouldn't be so sure.

Client B: Well, the issues he's having in school are severe.

Clinician: I have no doubt that Brian is having severe issues; however, I think it is important to consider how the family as whole is playing into this problem.

Another example:

Clinician: A family is like a mobile. When one member is affected by something, it reverberates throughout the other members and consequently there are multiple reactions. So, Destiny's issue with eating may have something to do with how the family is responding or not responding and therefore allocating her a fixed role.

Emphasizing Individual Boundaries

This systemic skill emphasizes the autonomy that each family member has within the system. This creates a temporary sense of differentiation between family members in the session. Boundaries could include formulating rules around listening and speaking, such as expecting people to take turns speaking, encouraging family members to speak directly to each other and not about each other, requiring people to answer their own questions, encouraging unique perspectives about issues instead of allowing one member to be the spokesperson for the entire family, and acknowledging differences in developmentally appropriate child behaviors. For example:

Clinician: Go ahead and face her and tell her what you told me (encouraging family members to talk to each other, not about each other).

Another example:

Clinician: You sound like you are completely consumed with pleasing them. What do you want out of the relationship?

Restructuring Dysfunctional Subsystem Boundaries

A major aspect of systemic work is the restructuring of dysfunctional boundaries. Clinicians fix a variety of issues related to dysfunctional family rules, poor cohesion, inflexibility, coalitions, scapegoating, parentification, and problematic communication patterns. For example:

Client A: I spend most of my time with Mom talking to her about day-to-day stuff.

Client B: She talks to her mother about our relationship, and her mother coaches her on how to deal with me.

Clinician: Is this true?

Client A: Yes, unfortunately it is.

Clinician: The couple is trying to learn how to communicate. John, you shut down. Rachel, you ask your mom for advice and then attack.

Client B: Exactly!

Clinician: Well, let's reenact a recent argument. (The clinician uses a mix of positive connotation and restructuring subsystem boundaries, then leads into a reenactment.)

Another example:

Clinician: I need Justin to step out of the room.

Client C: Why? I hear this stuff all the time.

Clinician: I know this seems a little strange, but I believe that certain conversations should only happen between parents.

Client C: Fine. (Justin leaves the room.)

Clinician: Now, I need the two of you to work out together how you want to handle discipline in the family.

Modeling

Effective systemic practitioners work hard to practice what they preach. Specifically, clinicians model the same behavior they hope to see their individual clients, couples, families, networks, and groups demonstrate. For example, when working with caregivers and children, the clinician would demonstrate age-appropriate communication, temporarily taking over as a caregiver to demonstrate a parenting skill, modeling a healthy lifestyle, and initiating confrontations about inappropriate family behavior. For example:

Clinician: Janelle and Cindy, please observe my age-appropriate interactions with Michael. Michael, I can tell this is very upsetting to you and you are not ready to talk about it with anyone. When you are ready to talk, I'll be here to listen.

Another example:

Clinician: I can tell you really want to throw that ball at Dad, and that ball is not for throwing at people. If you want to throw something, you can throw a tissue in the trash can.

Advice Giving

Due to the therapeutic ethos of encouraging clients to make their own decisions, advice giving can be somewhat controversial in the helping professions. When it is used sparingly, however, advice giving can equip clientele with applicable family-related information, research, information on age-appropriate child behaviors and needs, and suggestions for parenting. For example:

> *Clinician:* I suggest you direct your child in a more specific way. Instead of saying "Clean up better," it is generally more effective to tell young children more specifically what you want cleaned up and where exactly they should put it.

Another example:

> *Clinician:* One way to become better at parenting is to read books. Since you want to move away from physical discipline, a book you could read is *Positive Discipline: A Classic Guide to Helping Children Develop Self-Discipline, Responsibility, Cooperation, and Problem-Solving Skills* (Nelsen, 2006). This is available at most online bookstores.

In-Session Behavior Prescriptions

A powerful and important part of systemic therapy is teaching in-session family-related skills to clients. This technique requires confidence, knowledge, and the ability to teach clientele in a direct and experiential manner. Clinicians indicate, teach, and experientially direct clientele how to communicate, parent their children, discuss sensitive issues calmly, and coparent. For example:

> *Clinician:* Instead of blaming Vanessa for all the problems in the relationship, I would like you to start the conversation by taking responsibility for your part in the problem and trust that she will accept her piece of the responsibility as well.

Another example:

> *Clinician:* Talk to your parent as if he or she were sitting in that chair. Now, sit in that chair and answer as your parent would.

Out-of-Session Work

Out-of-session work (i.e., homework) is very important for actualizing the behaviors and communication strategies learned during therapy. When the clinician is designating tasks to be completed at home, it is generally better to be specific (e.g., exact behavior, time frame) in describing what needs to be done. During the next session, clinicians should follow up on the out-of-session work. For example:

> *Clinician:* Over the next week, try to notice two times when you find yourself thinking negative thoughts about yourself and challenge those thoughts with a positive alternative. Report your experience to me next week.

Another example:

> *Clinician:* This week my hope is that you will randomly compliment John on something he does around the house. John, you are to notice when Beatriz appreciates you and report at our next session on how it felt to hear this compliment.

INVITATIONAL SKILLS IN SYSTEMIC PRACTICE

Counseling microskills are small therapeutic building blocks that are considered fundamental to the creation of a therapeutic relationship. Microskills can be combined with other theory-based skills and interventions as well as foundational systemic therapy skills. Invitational skills are what a clinician uses to invite clients to participate in the relationship. These skills include, but are not limited to, nonverbal communication, vocal tone, observation, encouragement, nonverbal communication, and silence (Ivey et al., 2017; Young, 2016). Invitational skills help create an atmosphere of comfort and strengthen therapeutic relationships. Furthermore, these foundational skills create an atmosphere that welcomes self-disclosure. Young (2016) aptly described the importance of self-disclosure when he stated, "It is not enough to think about one's life; it must be disclosed verbally or in writing. The act of disclosing . . . is the first step in the healing process" (p. 80). Invitational skills are synonymous with active listening in that they allow clients to fully describe a situation to you and to themselves. This foundational atmosphere is a key first step in the therapeutic process. Regarding multiperson therapy, everyone in the family, couple, group, and/or network should receive a similar invitational experience. This means that clinicians must actively bracket any bias, personal thoughts and feelings, and countertransference they have in relation to the clients in the therapeutic environment. In the following explanations, I briefly summarize and provide relevant examples of the most common invitational skills.

Nonverbal Communication and Vocal Tone

Nonverbal communication is a basic invitational skill that is critical to therapeutic success. This skill is somewhat in line with the previously described *joining* skill. The clinician must be culturally and contextually appropriate with eye contact, facial expression, posture, gestures, and spatial distance. Furthermore, the clinician must maintain an open and relaxed posture and dress professionally. The clinician flexibly uses variations in nonverbal communication to correspond to the client's cultural background. The following are a few examples of how this may look: (a) maintaining appropriate dress, (b) using multiculturally sensitive eye contact, and (c) maintaining a facilitative and open posture.

Nothing conveys a sense of understanding or an emotion as effectively as vocal tone. Clinicians use vocal tones that are appropriate for the session and goals. The clinician's vocal tone communicates caring, acceptance, and congruence with the context of the session. Finally, the vocal tone demonstrates a comprehension of multicultural nuances, and the clinician makes appropriate vocal quality adjustments whenever relevant.

Observation

Clinicians frequently observe their own verbal and nonverbal behaviors. These observations extend to anticipating individual, familial, and multicultural differences within the clientele. Furthermore, practitioners frequently notice normal breaks in eye contact, body shifts, changes in vocal tone, discrepancies in verbal statements, and discrepancies in nonverbal behavior (e.g., smiling while discussing a painful issue). During the therapeutic process, clinicians observe and convey awareness of differences in the clinician's and the client's verbal and nonverbal behaviors in key areas (e.g., client speech, grooming, posture, build, gait, hesitation, stammer).

Encouragers

Encouragers are small indicators that the clinician is in process with the client. This frequent encouraging creates an atmosphere of reassurance and support. The clinician uses nonverbal minimal encouragers including a natural body style of encouragement, congruency with the client's bodily movement, leaning forward, and head nodding.

Furthermore, the practitioner will frequently use verbal encouragers, including, but not limited to, "Oh? . . .," "So . . . ," "Then . . . ," "And . . . ," "Mm-hmm . . . ," "Uh-huh . . . ," "Tell me more," and repetition of keywords. For example:

Client: I want a better life.

Clinician: Uh-huh, tell me more.

Client: I just, just, uh . . . I don't know.

Clinician: (silence, gentle head nodding).

Client: It all centers on my job.

Another example:

Client: I hate my mother. She is always in my business and doesn't even understand what a personal boundary is.

Clinician: Personal boundary.

Client: Yeah, you know, just get out of my life.

Clinician: Mm-hmm.

Silence

The concept of using silence as a therapeutic technique often intimidates beginning clinicians. In fact, any gap or pause in conversation can be unsettling to both clinicians and clients. Clinicians use unfilled pauses or periods of silence to serve various functions in the counseling sessions (e.g., reducing their own level of activity, slowing down session pace, giving the client time to think, and returning responsibility to the client). Practitioners avoid the use of silence in the following situations: (a) after the client discloses something extremely personal, (b) when the clinician does not know what to say next, (c) when the clinician is afraid of saying something, or (d) because the client upset the clinician in some way. For example:

Client: I don't know. I'm just not sure what to do about it (tearful about recent breakup). I just . . .

Clinician: (attentive nonverbals and giving the client space to figure the issue out).

Another example:

Client: I am not sure what to talk about today.

Clinician: (attentive nonverbals and giving the client space to determine what to talk about in session).

ATTENDING SKILLS IN SYSTEMIC PRACTICE

Clinicians often wonder, "How can I effectively demonstrate to a client that I am listening?", "How can I develop a trusting relationship with a couple or family?", or "What are the ways clients can feel unheard?" Learning the core elements of attending skills can greatly increase one's ability to hear, validate, and create a sense of trust within one's therapeutic relationships. Attending skills enhance the relational aspects of contact within the therapeutic relationship. These skills include, but are not limited to, goal setting, open-ended questioning, closed-ended questioning, clarification, summarizing, normalizing, and reflection of feeling (Ivey et al., 2017; Young, 2016). In the following I briefly summarize and provide relevant examples of the most common attending skills. Please note that these skills cut across therapeutic formats (e.g., individual, couple, family, network, and group therapy).

Goal Setting

Most clinicians understand the importance of goal setting; however, most do not consider this to be a counseling skill per se. This is due to its use in most aspects of daily living, its use as a major element of the treatment planning process, and the evolving nature of therapeutic goal setting. Goal setting is a collaborative process in which the client(s) and the therapist turn the presenting issues into small and large goals. Clinicians demonstrate their ability to identify issues and themes that the client presents and then funnel them down to treatment goals. For example:

Client: Thanks to the flood, our family is officially homeless. My sister was nice enough to let us stay at her house for the weekend, but a family of five is just not sustainable for a small apartment like hers.

Clinician: I understand this has been a terrifying and extremely painful process for you and your family. Joe, it sounds like a short-term goal is to find you and your family housing. Have you started to explore the area for short-term rentals?

Client: Yes, we have one starting tomorrow.

Open-Ended Questioning

Open-ended questions are helpful for a number of reasons. Open-ended questioning can encourage client self-exploration, direct the conversation, help a session to begin, clarify issues, and help clients explore topics and new ideas. Perhaps the most important reason to use this technique is that open questions encourage client disclosure. Well-trained clinicians understand the types of questions to ask (i.e., questions that begin with *what, how, when, where, who, could, would*) and avoid overuse. For example:

Clinician: What aspect of relationships is hard?

Client: I just can't stand putting out more than I get back.

Clinician: How have you coped with being let down this long? (The clinician utilizes two open-ended questions to explore the client's relationship discomfort.)

Another example:

Client: I hate school and doing a bunch of work that really has nothing to do with my future goals.

Clinician: Could you describe for me your future goals?

Client: I want to be an expert plumber.

Clinician: What are some things about school that you do like? (The clinician uses two open-ended questions to explore the client's career interests and school issues.)

Closed-Ended Questioning

Closed-ended questions can be useful if the clinician needs a particular bit of information. Similar to open-ended questions, this technique should not be overused. If it is overused, clients can feel like they are being interrogated. Typically, closed-ended questions can be answered with a few words. This can be helpful in emergency situations (e.g., suicidal ideation, homicidal ideation, child abuse and neglect). When used correctly, close-ended questions begin with certain words such as *Are, Do, Can, Is,* and *Did,* and they can be answered with *Yes, No,* or another short response. For example:

Client: I want to just end it all.

Clinician: Are you suicidal?

Client: Yes.

Another example:

Client: I lost the court case on Friday.

Clinician: Did they give you jail time?

Client: No.

Clarification

Clinicians use this skill to encourage clients to elaborate on vague statements. Often, clients make comments that make sense to them but seem confusing to others. Clinicians ask their clients to elaborate on vague, ambiguous, or implied statements, with the request for clarification usually expressed as a question beginning with a phrase such as "Are you saying . . . ?" or "Could you try to describe that?" or "Can you clarify that?" Clarifications can also take the form of statements with a questioning intonation, such as "They are always talking about you?" For example:

Client: They always put me down and never give me a chance.

Clinician: When you say "they," who do you mean?

Client: My friends John and Pete.

Another example:

Client: Well, I mean, you know, he was getting too close to me. And I didn't want to do that but felt it was necessary.

Clinician: Are you saying you cheated on your husband to protect yourself?

Client: Yes!

Paraphrasing

Paraphrasing is helpful because it lets your client know that they have been heard. This is the first attending skill that requires the clinician to give a little bit of themselves to help a client gain a sense of clarity. Clinicians essentially rephrase the client's primary words and thoughts, paying selective attention to the content part of the message and translating the client's key ideas into their own words. For example:

Client: I've been having a terrible time with Joan. She just got promoted and seems to have a big head. She keeps telling me what to do. In fact, yesterday she said I wasn't doing a good job and that if I didn't improve, she'd fire me.

Clinician: Bob, you're saying that the new supervisor is giving you a terrible time and you're concerned she may fire you.

Another example:

Client: I'm doing okay. I don't know . . . I just don't have much to talk about today.

Clinician: You're doing pretty well, and you're not sure if you have anything to work on.

Summarizing

Summarizing requires the clinician to focus the content of the client's statements. The clinician works to distill the content of the conversation into an integrative whole. This whole can be a number of paraphrases, a summary of the entire session, or perhaps themes that have been expressed over multiple sessions. Summarizing ties together multiple elements of a client's message, identifying themes or patterns; this skill is used as a tool for feedback or as a focusing method for interrupting client "storytelling." For example:

Client: I just don't know why I'm here. Counseling seems to be really difficult, and I constantly feel like I'm digging up problems that need to stay buried.

Clinician: So far, you've been saying this counseling experience is painful, overwhelming, and at times lacks purpose.

Another example:

Client: I'm sure you're surprised that I'm here after last week. I guess I do have a bunch of things I should be working on.

Clinician: Last week you said you didn't want to be here, you see yourself as having nothing to work on, and didn't see the point of counseling, and today you say you're interested in the counseling process and admit that you have a lot to work on.

Normalizing

While we all have issues, sometimes clients feel there is something wrong with their thoughts or emotions when, in fact, their experiences are normative in nature. Normalizing is noting appropriately the commonality of issues without inappropriately minimizing important issues. This often starts with phrases like "It is normal" or "Most people would feel that way." For example:

Client: I have a lot of anxiety and fear around starting my new job. I just don't like how this feels.

Clinician: It's normal to feel overwhelmed when starting a new job . . . In fact, everybody who starts a new job experiences this feeling to a certain degree.

Another example:

Client: I haven't had any sexual relations with my partner, and I feel terrible about it.

Clinician: It's normal to want a better sex life . . . Most people want satisfaction in this area.

Reflection of Feeling

This is a key area for competency because it facilitates a client's movement from superficial contact to a deeper connection with the clinician. This is the verbal pragmatic embodiment of empathy. The clinician communicates their accurate understanding of the client's world. Reflection of feeling states succinctly the feeling and the content of the problem expressed by the client on the implied and stated level, adding to a paraphrase an emotional tone or feeling word (e.g., hurt, mad, sad, jealous, confused, terrified, and scared). In general, the fewer qualifiers are used, the more powerful the reflection of feeling. For example:

> *Client:* I'm so tired of everything. I'm working so hard. My kids need me to be a dad. My graduate program is so much work that I feel like I'm going to have a heart attack.

> *Clinician:* John, you're feeling torn. Part of you really wants to be close to your family and take care of those closest to you. The other part is trying to survive your graduate program.

Another example:

> *Client:* I'm going to miss him.

> *Clinician:* You're sad to be leaving him.

INFLUENCING SKILLS IN SYSTEMIC PRACTICE

Why would a clinician want to influence a client? Would humanistically oriented family therapists like Virginia Satir ever try to influence someone? These common questions can create confusion around a whole genre of therapeutic skills that create high-impact therapeutic experiences. It is important to note that the previously described invitational and attending skills also influence clients. The experience of being heard and empathized with is highly influential. The eight common influencing skills explored in this section are immediacy, challenging and pointing out discrepancies, feedback, reflection of meaning and values, interpretation, self-disclosure, psychoeducation, and directives (Ivey et al., 2017; Young, 2016). Please note that homework, advocacy, and reframing would also be considered influencing in nature; however, since they were described elsewhere, I will not define them again within this section.

Influencing involves practitioners using their own power and control to create some level of awareness and/or change in a client's life. When clinicians are influencing someone, they are briefly sitting in a position of power; however, since they are using their influence to help client(s), it is benevolent in nature. Influencing skills are commonly used to create proactive change in a client's life. These skills do involve a more hierarchical stance on the part of the clinician. This delicate balance of power requires special attention. Abuses of power are common ethical issues in the helping professions, so it is essential for clinicians to ensure they adhere to ethical and moral communicational issues when creating these experiences with their client(s).

Immediacy

Immediacy involves immediately disclosing something that is occurring between the clinician and the client. This acknowledgment can take the form of a statement or a self-disclosure. Immediacy is applied when a clinician immediately recognizes something in the here and now, verbally makes note of patterns and relational issues, and discusses currently experienced thoughts and emotions. For example:

Client: I don't know if there is anything I need to talk to you about today. I'm fine.

Clinician: Michael, I noticed that you came 5 minutes late, you don't appear to have anything to talk about, and you aren't making eye contact with me. This happened the last time I went on a vacation and we took a few weeks off.

Client: Yeah, I guess so. . . .

Clinician: I sense that you are upset with me.

Another example:

Client A: Things have gotten better between us this week.

Client B: I disagree, but at least we didn't fight.

Clinician: Alex, I sense that you feel defeated and are just biding your time.

Client B: Although I'm complying with Rachel's requests, the relationship feels dead.

Challenging and Pointing Out Discrepancies

People are often inconsistent and incongruent. At times, it can be helpful to point out discrepancies in attitudes and beliefs, thoughts and behaviors, emotions, and cognitions. The skill of challenging and pointing out discrepancies is applied when the practitioner describes discrepancies, conflicts, and mixed messages apparent in the client's feelings, thoughts, and actions. Clients can have a number of reactions to this technique, including denial, partial examination, full examination, and deciding to live with the inconsistency. For example:

Client: I guess so . . . I'm not really sure. I like the idea of happiness, yet I don't really see things the way you do.

Clinician: You find yourself having mixed reactions to what I said. One side of you wants to agree, while the other wants to fight and disagree.

Another example:

Client: Everything is going great with us.

Clinician: You say that things are better; however, your voice and expression suggest that perhaps you aren't there yet.

Feedback

Feedback essentially involves the clinician relaying concrete and honest reactions based on observation of a client's verbal and nonverbal behavior to foster awareness of how the client appears to others. For example:

Clinician: Jerome, look at the expression of happiness on Jennifer's face now that you have paid her a compliment. Your self-disclosure about feeling connected and safe caused this reaction.

Another example:

Clinician: Jada, I want you to notice how the rest of your family is looking at you right now. Your anger played a part in their negative reaction to you.

Reflection of Meaning and Values

Reflection of meaning has to do with what the clinician thinks is a key issue in the client's life. A reflection of meaning looks very much like a paraphrase but focuses on going beyond what the client expresses verbally. Descriptions of this skill often include the words *meaning, values, vision,* and *goals.* In short, reflecting meaning and values occurs when the clinician relays the underlying spoken or unspoken meanings (i.e., core experiences) accurately back to the client in a statement that extends beyond paraphrasing. For example:

> *Clinician:* What has dissatisfied you the most in your relationship?
>
> *Client:* I need to feel love and appreciation. Xavier just takes everything I do for granted.
>
> *Clinician:* You deeply value reciprocity in your relationship. It is important to be given verbal affirmation for what you do and who you are.

Another example:

> *Clinician:* What do you value in your life?
>
> *Client:* Not much . . . life sucks and so do my friends. I want to be close to people in my life; however, they would sell me out for a slice of pizza.
>
> *Clinician:* You find a lot of meaning in loyalty and friendship and have been disappointed by your friendships.

Interpretation

A client's message is not always straightforward. Sometimes they do not fully understand their own thoughts, feelings, and behaviors. In such cases, they may describe certain aspects of their life without noticing connections, patterns, and underlying thoughts. Interpretation is a skill that calls on a clinician to state their well-informed hunches on what the client is thinking, feeling, wishing, and implying. In short, interpretation identifies and reflects behaviors, patterns, goals, wishes, and feelings that are suggested or implied by the client's communication. The clinician uses intuition to make the implied client messages more explicit. For example:

> *Client:* I'm not sure what to say to her. We have kids, and I know that means we are meant to be together.
>
> *Clinician:* A big part of you wants to get out of this relationship, and the fact that you have children is the major thing keeping you with her.
>
> *Client:* Yeah, I suppose you're right.

Another example:

> *Client:* I hate how racist everyone is around here. The fact that I'm Native American doesn't mean shit to these people; however, they are the first ones to pimp me out on their website.
>
> *Clinician:* You are angry at yourself for allowing the administrators to take your picture and put it on their website. You feel used.

Self-Disclosure

In a general sense, we are constantly self-disclosing. Every word, posture, nonverbal behavior, and choice reflects a direct or indirect self-disclosure. Yet from a skills perspective, we focus specifically on overt, direct, and verbal self-disclosure. While self-disclosure by the clinician can be positive (e.g., increase trust, increase client's awareness of the universality of things), it can also be harmful if overused. In short, this skill must be used specifically to help a client through a situation, must relate directly back to the client's situation, and must also be used very judiciously so the dynamics in the therapeutic relationship do not suffer (e.g., the client starts to feel like the clinician). Clinically speaking, self-disclosure fosters rapport, promotes feelings of universality, increases therapeutic trust, and instills hope. Self-disclosure is not used for the clinician's own personal gain. For example:

> *Client:* I tried so hard to do the right thing, but I just couldn't seem to keep her happy.

> *Clinician:* Rich, I have been in a similar situation, and it took me a long time to realize that it wasn't my fault—that no matter what or how much I did, my partner still would have left.

Another example:

> *Client:* Even my own family can't stand me. I'm such a loser.

> *Clinician:* There have been times when I've also felt down on myself, so I can sense how discouraged you are. Sometimes criticism from someone close to me has made me feel even worse, although I'm learning how to value myself regardless of critical comments from those I care about.

Psychoeducation

Psychoeducation is an educational experience the clinician provides to a client for the purpose of awareness, clarification, goal achievement, and strategizing for success. The clinician discusses pragmatic behaviors involved in the new learning and helps the client plan how to generalize this information to daily life. For example:

> *Clinician:* One thing that has come up for us is your insecurity with being able to effectively listen to others. You should make eye contact with the person you are talking with, notice their nonverbal messages and match them, match their tone and volume. Now let's practice this together in a role-play. Go ahead and engage me in the topic of negotiating for a higher salary.

Another example:

> *Clinician:* Sometimes you really only look at things as having one potential outcome and it tends to come out the way you predict. In therapy we call this a *self-fulfilling prophecy*. So, when you say to me, "I know Dewayne will eventually cheat on me . . . they always do," you are simultaneously ignoring him, creating challenges in the relationship, and not meeting either of your needs for intimacy. Sometimes it can be really easy to blame everyone but yourself and pretend that people are constantly out to get you. What really is going on is that you have a script of what is happening in your life that you feel comfortable and safe with. This is actually shielding you from intimacy and keeping you safe by never giving anyone a chance to get close.

> *Client:* People are always screwing me over.

Directives

A final influencing skill is using directives. Effectively used directives can result in immediate change; however, the way in which the directive is used is at least as important as what is discussed. When directives are used occasionally, they can provide new options; however, overuse of this technique can rob clients of their freedom of choice. Practically speaking, a directive offers an explicit suggestion (e.g., "I suggest . . . ") and/or activity (e.g., role-play, empty chair) to the client, which provides new options without taking away the client's freedom of choice. Clinicians should also be careful to avoid giving advice. For example:

Clinician: It seems like one part of you really wants to stay home and not pursue your college dreams, and the other part of you does want to go.

Client: Yeah, I'm all mixed up.

Clinician: Okay, go ahead and name the part of yourself that wants to attend college.

Client: Brave.

Clinician: Now name the part of you that wants to stay home.

Client: Weak.

Clinician: Now become Brave and talk to Weak about what you think of him.

Another example:

Clinician: It sounds like this conversation was going well initially but took a bad turn when you started the blame game.

Client: Yes, I just don't know how to control myself.

Clinician: Let's return to that situation and play it out.

Client: Okay.

Clinician: I'll role-play Frank and you be yourself.

Client: Okay. Frank, I just don't understand why you don't take care of your daily home responsibilities.

Clinician: Here we go again, you're starting to blame me for everything.

MARRIAGE AND FAMILY THERAPY MODEL-BASED TECHNIQUES

Most techniques are grounded within theoretical models. This section reviews the core techniques associated with eight schools of thought. These techniques are frequently used to help families, couples, and individual clients. In addition, these models have a celebrated history within academia as well as marriage and family psychotherapy. The eight schools of thought are transgenerational family therapy, SFT, strategic family therapy, experiential family therapy, solution-focused therapy, narrative therapy, cognitive behavioral family therapy (CBFT), and EFT. While there are other important schools of thought that merit exploration, this sample represents eight of the most prominent traditions within the profession. The forthcoming model-based techniques were derived, in part, from Gehart (2017), Johnson (2019), Nichols and Davis (2020), Reiter (2013), Satir and Baldwin (1983), and Walsh and McGraw (2002). Please note that this textbook focuses on skills, techniques, and contemporary issues. For a deeper theoretical review of each of these traditions, please consider reviewing *Marriage and Family Therapy: A Practice-Oriented Approach* (Metcalf, 2018). Table 4.1 lists each model's founder(s), their contributions to family therapy, and a salient publication.

TABLE 4.1 FAMILY THERAPY LEADER, MODEL, CONTRIBUTION, AND SALIENT PUBLICATION

Contributor	Model	Contribution	Salient Publication
Murray Bowen	Transgenerational	Founder of transgenerational family theory and therapy	Bowen, M. (1966). The use of family theory in clinical practice. *Comprehensive Psychiatry, 7*(5), 345–374. https://doi.org/10.1016/S0010-440X(66)80065-2.
Michael Kerr	Transgenerational	Worked with Murray Bowen to develop transgenerational theory and therapy	Kerr, M. E., & Bowen, M. (1988). *Family evaluation: An approach based on Bowen theory*. W. W. Norton.
Philip Guerin	Transgenerational	Worked with Murray Bowen to develop transgenerational theory and therapy	Guerin, P. J., Jr., Fogarty, T. F., Fay, L. F., & Kautto, J. G. (1996). *Working with relationship triangles: The one-two-three of psychotherapy*. Guilford Press.
Betty Carter	Transgenerational	Developed an expanded perspective of family development within transgenerational theory	Carter, B., & McGoldrick, M. (1981). *The family life cycle: A framework for family therapy*. Gardner Press.
Monica McGoldrick	Transgenerational	Developed and popularized genograms in clinical settings	McGoldrick, M., Gerson, R., & Petry, S. (2008). *Genograms: Assessment and intervention*. W. W. Norton.
Salvador Minuchin	Structural	Developed structural family therapy	Minuchin S. (1974). *Families and family therapy*. Harvard University Press.
Charles Fishman	Structural	Worked with Salvador Minuchin and coauthored a techniques-oriented textbook with Minuchin	Minuchin, S., & Fishman, H. C. (1981). *Family therapy techniques*. Harvard University Press.
Braulio Montalvo	Structural	One of the developers of structural family therapy	Minuchin, S., Montalvo, B., Guerney, B., Jr., Rosman, B., & Schumer, F. (1967). *Families of the slums: An exploration of their structure and treatment*. Basic Books.
Bernard Guerney Jr.	Structural	Creator of relationship enhancement therapy, developed filial family therapy	Minuchin, S., Montalvo, B., Guerney, B., Jr., Rosman, B., & Schumer, F. (1967). *Families of the slums: An exploration of their structure and treatment*. Basic Books.
Bernice Rosman	Structural	Worked with Salvador Minuchin in developing structural family therapy	Minuchin, S., Baker, L., & Rosman, B. L. (1978). *Psychosomatic families: Anorexia nervosa in context*. Harvard University Press.
Florence Schumer	Structural	Worked with Salvador Minuchin in developing structural family therapy	Schumer, F. (1983). *Abnormal psychology*. Heath Publishing.

(continued)

TABLE 4.1 FAMILY THERAPY LEADER, MODEL, CONTRIBUTION, AND SALIENT PUBLICATION (CONTINUED)

Contributor	Model	Contribution	Salient Publication
John Weakland	Strategic (MRI)	Founder of brief and family therapy	Fisch, R., Weakland, J. H., & Segal, L. (1991). *The tactics of change: Doing therapy briefly.* Jossey-Bass.
Don Jackson	Strategic (MRI)	Pioneer of family and brief therapy, founder of the Mental Research Institute	Jackson, D. D. (1968). *Communication, family, and marriage: Human communication.* Science and Behavior Books.
Paul Watzlawick	Strategic (MRI)	Developed interactional view theory of communication	Watzlawick, P., Bavelas, J. B., & Jackson, D. D. (1967). *Pragmatics of human communication: A study of interactional patterns, pathologies and paradoxes.* W. W. Norton.
Richard Fisch	Strategic (MRI)	Developed brief therapy	Fisch, R., Weakland, J. H., & Segal, L. (1991). *The tactics of change: Doing therapy briefly.* Jossey-Bass.
Jay Haley	Strategic (Haley)	Founder of brief and family therapy, founder of strategic model of therapy	Haley, J., & Richeport-Haley, M. (1997). *The art of strategic therapy.* Routledge.
Cloe Madanes	Strategic (Haley)	One of the originators of strategic therapy	Madanes, C. (1991). Strategic family therapy. In A. S. Gurman & D. P. Kniskern (Eds.), *Handbook of family therapy* (Vol. 2, pp. 396–416). Brunner/Mazel.
Carl Whitaker	Experiential	Psychotherapy pioneer family therapist, codeveloped symbolic-experiential approach to therapy	Whitaker, C. A., & Bumberry, W. M. (1988). *Dancing with the family: A symbolic-experiential approach.* Routledge.
Virginia Satir	Experiential	Created the Satir change process model (i.e., communication and validation approach)	Satir, V. M. (1964). *Conjoint family therapy: A guide to theory and technique.* Science and Behavior Books.
Steve de Shazer	Solution-focused	Developer and pioneer of solution-focused brief therapy, founder of the Brief Family Therapy Center	de Shazer, S. (1985). *Keys to solution in brief therapy.* W. W. Norton.
Insoo Kim Berg	Solution-focused	Pioneer of solution-focused brief therapy	Berg, I. K. (1994). *Family-based services: A solution-focused approach.* W. W. Norton.
Yvonne Dolan	Solution-focused	Founder of the Institute for Solution-Focused Therapy	de Shazer, S., Dolan, Y., & Korman, H. (2012). *More than miracles: The state of the art of solution-focused brief therapy.* Routledge.

Eve Lipchik	Solution-focused	A pioneer of the solution-focused brief therapy approach	Lipchik, E. (2002). *Beyond technique in solution-focused therapy: Working with emotions and the therapeutic relationship.* Guilford Press.
Michael White	Narrative	Cofounder of narrative therapy	White, M., & Epston, D. (1990). *Narrative means to therapeutic ends.* W. W. Norton.
David Epston	Narrative	Cofounder of narrative therapy	White, M., & Epston, D. (1990). *Narrative means to therapeutic ends.* W. W. Norton.
Jill Freedman	Narrative	Codirector of Evanston Family Therapy Center, internationally acclaimed teacher of narrative therapy	Freedman, J., & Combs, G. (1996). *Narrative therapy: The social construction of preferred realities.* W. W. Norton.
Gene Combs	Narrative	Codirector of Evanston Family Therapy Center	Freedman, J., & Combs, G. (1996). *Narrative therapy: The social construction of preferred realities.* W. W. Norton.
Susan Johnson	Emotionally focused	Developed emotionally focused couples therapy	Johnson, S. M. (2004). *The practice of emotionally focused couple therapy: Creating connection.* Brunner-Routledge.
Les Greenberg	Emotionally focused	Originator and primary developer of emotionally focused therapy	Greenberg, L. S., & Goldman, R. N. (1988). *Emotion-focused couples therapy: The dynamics of emotion, love, and power.* American Psychological Association.
Aaron T. Beck	Cognitive behavioral family therapy	Founder of cognitive behavioral therapy	Beck, A. T., Rush, A. J., Shaw, B. F., & Emery, G. (1978). *Cognitive therapy of depression.* Guilford Press.
Frank Dattilio	Cognitive behavioral family therapy	Helped develop cognitive behavioral family therapy	Dattilio, F. M. (2001). Cognitive–behavior family therapy: Contemporary myths and misconceptions. *Contemporary Family Therapy: An International Journal, 23*(1), 3–18.

MRI, Mental Research Institute.

TRANSGENERATIONAL FAMILY THERAPY TECHNIQUES

Transgenerational family therapy (TFT) comprises seven core concepts: nuclear family emotional process, differentiation of self, family projection process, emotional cutoff, multigenerational transmission process, triangles, and emotional process in society. See Table 4.2 for a brief summary of the theoretical tenets of TFT as well as multicultural and feminist considerations. While all of these topics are important and warrant deep exploration, the foundation of TFT is the notion that unresolved fusions to one's family of origin must be resolved before a person can fully differentiate and mature in a healthy

TABLE 4.2 TRANSGENERATIONAL FAMILY THERAPY THEORETICAL TENETS

Theoretical Tenet	Explanation
Nuclear family emotional process	Lack of differentiation within a family constrains members' abilities to regulate emotionality and manage anxiety. This lack of differentiation creates excessive emotionality and/or fusion.
Differentiation of self	This is the degree to which family members balance their emotional and intellectual functioning in interpersonal relationships. It also refers to a person's ability to think, reflect, and not respond automatically to emotional pressures.
Family projection process	Parents transmit their lack of differentiation to their children. Overly fused children have difficulty adapting because of their focus on parental anxiety.
Emotional cutoff	This involves reducing or completely severing emotional contact with other family members. New relationships may become too important and centered on meeting unmet needs carried over from the family of origin.
Multigenerational transmission process	The family's emotional process is transmitted across multiple generations. Family members who are most involved in the family's fusion move toward a lower level of differentiation of self, while members who are least involved move toward higher levels of differentiation.
Triangles	Triangles are formed when significant relationships are heavily influenced by third parties. Triangulation fixes conflict in place, and the third party becomes a chronic diversion that undermines relationships.
Emotional process in society	The emotional process in society influences the emotional process in families. This concept takes into account various contextual factors (culture, gender, race, etc.).
Multicultural considerations	The construct of differentiation of self needs context because there are variations within and across cultures in the ways in which healthy connectedness and healthy separateness are defined.
Feminist critique	Bowen's concepts have been evaluated as possibly being centered on the nature of Western male socialization. Being autonomous, relying on reason, and goal directedness are salient to the nature of male socialization and neglect the ways women are typically socialized (e.g., to be nurturing and caring).

Note: This table provides a breakdown of key therapeutic tenets, multicultural considerations, and feminist critiques of the transgenerational family therapy model. Further reading is required for a comprehensive understanding of this approach.

Sources: Data from Gehart, D. R. (2017). *Mastering competencies in family therapy: A practical approach to theory and clinical case documentation* (3rd ed.). Brooks/Cole; Kağitçibasi, Ç. (1996). The autonomous-relational self: A new synthesis. *European Psychologist, 1*(3), 180–186. https://doi.org/10.1027/1016-9040.1.3.180; Lerner, G. (1986). *The creation of patriarchy*. Oxford University Press; Nichols, M. P., & Davis, S. D. (2020). *The essentials of family therapy*. Pearson Education; Reiter, M.D. (2013). *Case conceptualization in marriage and family therapy*. Pearson Education; Walsh, W. M., & McGraw, J. A. (2002). *Essentials of family therapy: A structured summary of nine approaches*. Love Publishing Company.

manner. The core TFT techniques explored in this section include genograms, emotional neutrality, factual questioning, didactic teaching, role-playing, and the empty chair.

Genogram

When most clinicians think about TFT techniques, they envision a powerful assessment method called the genogram. People have a natural curiosity in their familial patterns, and many individuals like to consider which aspects of their family they want to honor and stay loyal to and which they would like to get rid of. Genograms are visual representations of at least three generations of a family. Genograms organize a family's relational patterns and other contextual factors in a standardized manner. Clinicians use symbols to indicate family patterns and dynamics (e.g., triangles, cutoff, pathology). Multiple working genograms can represent specific factors (e.g., patterns of intimacy, religion) that affect a family. The following example demonstrates how a clinician might begin a genogram:

> *Clinician:* Today we are going to start working on an exciting project known as a genogram. A genogram is a visual representation of your current family and your family of origin several generations back. Included in this genogram are your family's basic demographics, relationship status between members, major events including illness, death, abortion, adoption, addictions, and mental illness. Lastly, the genogram will have references to communication styles and behaviors of members. The point of a genogram is to notice the various patterns in your family's history and whether you want to stay loyal to those patterns or if you want to change that family tradition. What questions do you have before we begin?

> *Client:* None really . . . this sounds helpful.

> *Clinician:* Okay, let's get started. We are going to work from your current family back in time. Tell me about yourself. What work have you done in your life?

Emotional Neutrality

A major theoretical tenet of the TFT model is to avoid responding automatically to emotional pressures. The skill of emotional neutrality demonstrates the clinician's ability to think, reflect, and use logical reasoning in the therapeutic relationship. Having emotional neutrality is the clinician's embodiment of healthy differentiation. The clinician can effectively facilitate change by remaining objective in session and staying de-triangulated from the system. By staying outside the emotionality of the family, the clinician can better resist the reactivity of triangulation and fusion. For example:

> *Client A:* Do you see what I mean? They cannot stop themself from being mean to us. They're just a creep.

> *Clinician:* You're angry about how Duante is talking to you.

> *Client A:* Absolutely; wouldn't you be?

> *Clinician:* The family is struggling with communication.

Another example:

> *Client A:* I'm glad we finally decided to come to counseling. Maybe you can help me fix her.

> *Clinician:* I'm interested in helping both of you fix your relationship.

Client B: Yeah, she's really scared now because someone is going to finally see how it is not just my fault.

Clinician: I believe that through the exploration of current issues and past ones we will find something helpful here.

Factual Questioning

One method that can often help reduce emotional reactivity is to frequently ask factual questions. Asking individuals factual questions in front of other family members can also have a de-triangulating effect and temporarily reduce fusion. By asking factual questions and having the clients turn and face the clinician while answering the questions, the counselor can reduce emotionality and reactivity. For example:

Client A: I just hate coming home from school lately (tearfulness); it is just too much to have to be around them.

Clinician: What do you mean by "too much"?

Client B: She's just whining again.

Clinician: I am going to keep my focus on Kim right now; however, I will come back to you. Kim, what do you mean by "too much"?

Another example:

Clinician: What exactly do you mean by "hopeless" in talking about the relationship?

Client: I'm just not sure I can ever trust him again.

Clinician: For you, what would it take to regain trust once it has been broken?

Client: I . . . I would need to see him honoring me for a long time.

Didactic Teaching

Clinicians who use a TFT model in practice are accustomed to teaching families about the various tenets of the model. Learning about important TFT theoretical constructs can help individuals begin to think more autonomously about the presenting problem and the part they are playing in it. Clinicians will teach families about the communication and behavioral patterns (e.g., triangulation, communication problems, social role patterns) that emerge within the genogram. For example:

Client: I'm just not sure what to do about the family issues. They seem unsolvable. We are just so volatile and at each other's throats.

Clinician: The family seems to be so tightly connected to one another that no one can see themselves as an individual. Families tend to function best when there is a level of closeness and separateness. No family is perfect, but each family will have a unique blend of unity and autonomy. When family members are too close to one another, it causes a tremendous amount of anxiety because as humans we are naturally programmed to become autonomous individuals. Additionally, when a family is too distant and there is no family identity, this can cause a sense of anxiety and loneliness. Does this make sense?

Another example:

Client: It is embarrassing to say this, but I have more in common with our son than I do with him. We are just strangers in the same house.

Clinician: Well, it is interesting that you mentioned your bond with Samuel. I want to talk to you briefly about a phenomenon called triangulation. When family members bond with one another against a third member, it's called triangulation. Triangulation can have a devastating effect on families because it sets up an "us against them" attitude that creates a lot of conflict, mistrust, and inappropriate relations with various family members. For example, Samuel and you have a bond that consists of you telling him information about your relationship with Dave. This puts Samuel in a very awkward position in that he is receiving inappropriate information about your relationship. Part of him is feeling bad and knows this is wrong, and another part of him feels privileged in receiving this typically confidential information.

Role-Playing

Have you ever heard the phrase "practice makes perfect"? If so, you can start to understand a few of the benefits of engaging in role-playing. This technique provides a pathway for understanding and perhaps changing communication patterns, family dynamics, and/ or relational behavior. This can be helpful with the differentiation process because clients can begin to test the waters and understand what it means to be defused. For example:

> *Clinician:* It sounds like you are having a difficult time confronting your grandfather.
>
> *Client:* Yes, it is extremely intimidating, and I don't want to hurt his feelings.
>
> *Clinician:* Let's practice what you might say to him.
>
> *Client:* Okay.
>
> *Clinician:* I'll role-play your grandfather and you be yourself.
>
> *Client:* I'm not sure I can...
>
> *Clinician:* Okay, how about we start with you playing your grandfather and I'll play you.
>
> *Client:* Sure, this sounds interesting.

Another example:

> *Clinician:* Instead of talking to me about what you want to say to Samantha, I want you to role-play it with her.
>
> *Client:* What do you mean?
>
> *Clinician:* Talk to her as if she were sitting in that chair.
>
> *Client:* Samantha, why don't you try in our relationship anymore?
>
> *Clinician:* Now sit in that chair and answer as Samantha would.
>
> *Client:* Brian, you're just overreacting. I do love you; it's just not that lusty phase we went through in the beginning. When are you going to grow up?

Empty Chair

We discussed the use of the empty chair technique in Chapter 3 of this textbook; however, that discussion was in reference to gestalt therapy. TFT would use this psychodrama technique to help clients differentiate and heal from past emotional cutoffs. From a TFT perspective, the more fully one integrates various parts of themselves, the more fully they can differentiate from their family of origin. The empty chair technique is a form of role-playing in which the individual works out aspects of themselves independently. Typically, this technique involves the individual speaking to the empty chair, with the clinician supporting and coaching them through the process. For example:

Clinician: It seems like part of you wants to press charges and the other just wants to drop it and move on.

Client: Yeah, I can't decide.

Clinician: Okay, go ahead and name the part of yourself that wants to press charges.

Client: Confident.

Clinician: Now name the part of you that wants to say drop it.

Client: Realistic.

Clinician: Now become Confident and talk to Realistic about what you think of her.

Another example:

Clinician: You have just been explaining how painful and difficult it was for you to choose to get an abortion. It seems that you feel a deep sense of shame and hurt, but you also feel it was the only realistic decision you could make at the time.

Client: Yes, it seemed to be the only legitimate choice I could live with, but now I'm having a hard time living with myself.

Clinician: Thank you for sharing these deeply personal feelings. I want to try something different to see if you can't come to more of a sense of acceptance of the decision you made or at least a deeper sense of self-awareness.

Client: That sounds good.

Clinician: I want you to start by naming the part of yourself that made the final choice to get an abortion.

Client: Only Option.

Clinician: Now name the part of yourself that feels regret and sadness around this decision.

Client: Selfish.

Clinician: Let's have Only Option discuss her thought process regarding the decision with Selfish. After this discussion, Selfish will have a chance to defend her position.

Client: Okay.

STRUCTURAL FAMILY THERAPY TECHNIQUES

SFT comprises five core concepts: family structure, subsystems, boundaries, adaptation to stress, and developmental family life stages. See Table 4.3 for a breakdown of SFT theoretical tenets as well as multicultural considerations and feminist critiques. While all of these theoretical tenets are important and should be explored deeply, the foundation of SFT is the theory of family structure, including, but not limited to, boundaries (diffuse/enmeshed and rigid), family hierarchy, subsystems, coalitions, patterns of interaction, and rules.

TABLE 4.3   STRUCTURAL FAMILY THERAPY THEORETICAL TENETS

Theoretical Tenet	Explanation
Family structure	Family structure refers to family behavioral patterns and how a family organizes itself. A healthy family structure is one in which there are clear boundaries around the system and its subsystems.
Subsystems	A family system can be further divided into subsystems. Subsystems are smaller units within the family system that consist of one or more individuals who have similar characteristics (e.g., age, gender, sexuality, family role) or are bonded in some way.
Boundaries	Boundaries symbolize family rules for who participates and to what extent. They are the invisible barriers that govern the contact that subsystems have with other subsystems and are necessary for a healthy family structure.
Adaptation to stress	Adaptability and cohesion toward stress are key characteristics of a family. There is a balance between maintaining emotional connectedness and supporting autonomy. If a family is unable to adapt to stress, the family structure is threatened.
Developmental family life stages	Families go through developmentally appropriate changes as they progress through the family life cycle. If families are not able to accommodate and adapt during these transition periods, the family system may experience stress.
Multicultural considerations	Clinicians using structural family therapy must be aware of cultural and ethnic differences as well as ethical guidelines related to family structure. Clinicians must consider how the client's culture dictates what the family structure should look like and what must be addressed to be culturally sensitive to the family.
Feminist critique	Structural family therapy investigates relational dynamics like power and hierarchy; however, this is typically in the context of relatedness between generations (e.g., executive and sibling subsystems). Issues related to power differences between partners should receive as much attention as those between different generations.

Note: This table provides a breakdown of key therapeutic tenets, multicultural considerations, and feminist critiques of the structural family therapy model. Further reading is required for a comprehensive understanding of the approach.

Sources: Data from Connell, C. (2010). Doing, undoing, or redoing gender? *Gender & Society, 24*(1), 31–55. https://doi .org/10.1177/0891243209356429; Gehart, D. R. (2017). *Mastering competencies in family therapy: A practical approach to theory and clinical case documentation* (3rd ed.). Brooks/Cole; Hare-Mustin, R. T. (1987). The problem of gender in family therapy theory. *Family Process, 26*(1), 15–27. https://doi.org/10.1111/j.1545-5300.1987.00015.x; Nichols, M. P., & Davis, S. D. (2020). *The essentials of family therapy*. Pearson Education; Reiter, M.D. (2013). *Case conceptualization in marriage and family therapy*. Pearson Education; Walsh, W. M., & McGraw, J. A. (2002). *Essentials of family therapy: A structured summary of nine approaches*. Love Publishing Company.

The core SFT techniques explored in this section include maintenance, mimesis, enactment, reenactment, and confirming statements. Please note that joining is a key skill within the SFT theoretical model; however, like many SFT skills and concepts, it has become a basic component of general systemic practice and thus was defined and described earlier in the chapter.

Maintenance

A key aspect of SFT is the constant maintenance techniques the practitioner provides to couples, families, and individuals. The clinician encourages specific communication and behaviors to increase optimal systemic functioning (e.g., cohesion and flexibility in individuals, subsystems, and coalitions). For example:

> *Client:* I'm just tired of being treated this way. I want to start living.
>
> *Clinician:* You want to start living.

Client: Yes, I'm in charge of my destiny and I don't need his approval to move forward.

Clinician: You're moving forward.

Another example:

Client A: I love you so much and I just want to start being sexual again.

Clinician: You want to embrace sexuality.

Client B: I'm feeling better, and I think if we try tonight maybe we can get back into a good sexual routine.

Clinician: Both partners want to embrace sexuality.

Mimesis

In using the technique of mimesis, the clinician copies the family's style of behaving, affective range, manners, and style of communicating. In short, the clinician adopts this style to try to fit in and adapt to the family environment. For example:

Client A: You know we're just not fancy people. I drove truck for the past 30 years and Jamie tended to the pigs and livestock. We have always worked, and since we both retired, we're not used to spending this much time around each other.

Clinician: I hear that you really feel worried about this change in your lifestyle. You were used to being out on the road for long periods of time and now you have to be around each other all the time.

Client B: Yeah, we both had our separate stuff and now we're always together. We've been together for 35 years now.

Clinician: Even though this is hard, you both have a lot of pride in your relationship.

Another example:

Client: I just pushed him once. I don't see what the big deal is. I wouldn't do it again, but I just need him to tell me what he is thinking more often!

Clinician: From your perspective, pushing him was a way to get him to tell you what he is thinking.

Client: I didn't even realize I was doing it until it was too late.

Clinician: You're saying this was an accident.

Client: Yep.

Clinician: The couple has the communication issue of Juanita being a verbal processor of emotion and Jose being an internal processor of information.

Client: Yeah, he can't stand it when I talk about my feelings . . . it's like he wants every comment to be perfect.

Enactment

Clinicians practicing SFT frequently use enactments to assist families. Directly discussing challenging topics in the clinician's presence can be healing and instructional. Clinicians will ask the individuals who are experiencing family conflict to discuss the issue in session. The clinician will take part in the enactment, manage the communication, ask for clarification, provide psychoeducation, increase/decrease intensity, and use the information learned from the enactment to map the family's structural patterns. For example:

Clinician: Raphael and Martha, the experiences that have brought you to therapy are obviously serious and provoke intense feelings for each of you. I could try to take care of your relationship, but experience suggests that you'll be better off if I help *you* do that. So, think of me as a conduit and a coach for your relationship. Martha, go ahead and look at Raphael and tell him what you think.

Client A: I'm just so upset with our relationship; I want to connect with you again.

Clinician: Is there anything else you need to tell him about the connection?

Client A: Well, we used to be so close. I just want to get back to that place again.

Clinician: Okay, Raphael, turn to her, look into her eyes, and talk to her about connecting.

Another example:

Clinician: Today, both of you are going to have a conversation about the anger and hurt you felt during the recent incident. Both of you mentioned that the recent conversation about personal possessions and what belongs to who was a complete disaster. John, I want you to talk with Suzie about your desire to have complete freedom to use each other's possessions. Suzie, I want you to talk about your anger at how disrespected you felt after John destroyed your favorite rug.

Client A: I'll start. Honey, I just want to get along and share our possessions. I think we'll be better off if we don't have all of these rules around who uses what.

Clinician: Is there anything more you'd like to discuss about this, John?

Reenactment

In using reenactment, the clinician asks the family to re-create a challenging situation and then enact it again with a successful outcome. This skill naturally creates positive self-efficacy around working together and solving problems. Furthermore, the technique creates a sense of awareness around what is possible. For example:

Clinician: The family is going to re-create what happened on Saturday night, starting at the very beginning. During this reenactment, I'm going to direct you on just what you could have done to make the situation different and more positive. I want you to talk frankly about my suggestions and let me know if what I'm saying is making sense. Okay, let's begin. Steve, I want you to walk in the door as if you just got home. Shannon, do you remember how you greeted him?

The following example provides a glimpse at the second half of a reenactment experience:

Clinician: Now that we have re-created the car ride, Dad, I want you to start the conversation with saying what you liked about dinner.

Client A: Okay, I really enjoyed the salad and discussing Melissa's band performance during dinner.

Clinician: Melissa, try to express some level of enthusiasm over the topic and let Dad know that you appreciate the support.

Client B: Okay, I'll try. Dad, thanks for coming to the performance and paying for my lessons all these years.

Clinician: Let's pause and reflect on what could have been different if the conversation had gone this way.

Confirming Statement

Confirming statements involves overtly stating a negative aspect of the individual or family, while absolving the parties involved from any responsibility for the negative behavior. For example:

Clinician: Addie, you seem to be quite immature. What have your parents done to keep you this way?

Client: They're never around, and when they are, Mom is useless. She completely relies on Dad for every decision.

Clinician: You act very dependent on your husband. What does he do to keep you this way?

Another example:

Clinician: You are very worried about what everyone thinks about you. How does your family promote this way of thinking?

Client: Well, I'm the firstborn, and everyone just assumes I'm always okay and I don't need any help.

STRATEGIC FAMILY THERAPY TECHNIQUES

Strategic family therapy comprises seven core concepts: family patterns, hierarchy, alliances and coalitions, communications, symptoms, power, and family life cycle. See Table 4.4 for a breakdown of strategic family therapy's theoretical tenets as well as multicultural considerations and feminist critiques. While all of the strategic theoretical concepts hold importance, the key aspects are that therapy should be brief, the role of intrapsychic processes should be downplayed, resistance should be bypassed, and change can occur suddenly. The core strategic family therapy techniques explored in this section include straightforward directives, one-down stance, restraining technique, paradoxical directives, pretend technique, ordeals, metaphorical tasks, devil's pact, empowering, and jamming.

Straightforward Directives

Strategic family therapy is known for using straightforward directives designed to promote change. These tasks create opportunities that change interactional sequences. Directives are presented in a manner that promotes completion and avoids resistance. While directives can take many forms, they typically present as suggestions and advice giving. For example:

Clinician: Face John and let him know how you felt about what happened.

TABLE 4.4 STRATEGIC FAMILY THERAPY THEORETICAL TENETS

Theoretical Tenet	Explanation
Family patterns	The patterns of family behavior create a sense of systemic organization. These patterns become highly predictable.
Hierarchy	Systemic hierarchy has to do with the level of influence a family member has over another. Vertically speaking, families function best when caregivers are in the executive subsystem and children are in the sibling subsystem.
Alliances and coalitions	Alliances and coalitions have to do with family members grouping together for a particular purpose (mother and daughter create a coalition to challenge grandfather). These alliances and coalitions can challenge the hierarchical status quo.
Communications	There are two levels of strategic communication: digital and analog. Digital communication is technical and has one reference point. Analog communication has many reference points, including the body, symbols, and family metaphors.
Symptoms	These are patterned behavior used to attain control over familial relationships.
Power	Power is the struggle to make rules in a family system. Some members flexibly welcome change, while others fight very hard to keep it from happening.
Family life cycle	The family undergoes a process of development through time (e.g., birth of first child, adolescents, and children leaving home). Movement from one developmental stage to the next can be a source of significant familial stress.
Multicultural considerations	The nature of many strategic family therapy interventions puts the clinician in the role of the expert. To ensure cultural competence, a practitioner of strategic family therapy must understand each family's cultural group, the internal reality of the family, and the clinician's own cultural self. If these conditions are met, the clinician can make informed and culturally appropriate choices about what to do and when to do it.
Feminist critique	Clinicians who use nuanced techniques designed to help families must also consider socially programmed sex roles that are reflected and reinforced within families. Without this awareness, interventions may inadvertently promote the sexist culture's status quo. To move beyond this issue, structural family therapy should augment its family-based theoretical assumptions with larger multicultural and gender-based theories.

Note: This table provides a breakdown of key therapeutic tenets, multicultural considerations, and feminist critiques of the strategic family therapy model. Further reading is required for a comprehensive understanding of the approach.

Sources: Data from Gehart, D. R. (2017). *Mastering competencies in family therapy: A practical approach to theory and clinical case documentation* (3rd ed.). Brooks/Cole; Guanipa, C. (2003). Sharing a multicultural course design for a marriage and family therapy programme: One perspective. *Journal of Family Therapy, 25*(1), 86–106. https://doi.org/10.1111/1467-6427.00236; Nichols, M. P., & Davis, S. D. (2020). *The essentials of family therapy.* Pearson Education; Penfold, P. S. (1989). Family therapy: Critique from a feminist perspective. *The Canadian Journal of Psychiatry, 34*(4), 311–315. https://doi.org/10.1177/070674378903400408; Reiter, M.D. (2013). *Case conceptualization in marriage and family therapy.* Pearson Education; Walsh, W. M., & McGraw, J. A. (2002). *Essentials of family therapy: A structured summary of nine approaches.* Love Publishing Company.

Client: John, I was upset when you disobeyed us and snuck out last night. I was afraid that you were going to be hurt.

Another example:

Clinician: I suggest you take time each morning to brush your teeth and hair if you are worried about your appearance.

Client: I see your point.

One-Down Stance

Strategic family therapists attempt to motivate individuals, couples, and families to change their behavior. Sometimes they use a nonauthoritarian position (i.e., one-down stance) to create motivation and reduce anxiety and resistance. For example:

> *Clinician:* When you say Alice is demanding, I'm not sure what you mean. Because I'm not part of your family and don't see you day-to-day, I am unfamiliar with this side of Alice's personality. Can you help me understand?

> *Client:* Sure. She has been overly demanding in regard to household chores. She needs everything perfect and will inspect the house to see just how well you've cleaned.

Another example:

> *Clinician:* You see, I'm not married to Bob, so you're the expert on his mood and what he needs to stay happy.

> *Client:* Yeah . . . but sometimes I'm not sure what he needs.

> *Clinician:* Well, you surely know more about Bob than I do.

Restraining Technique

Sometimes it is motivating to be restrained, slightly discouraged, or told to not try as hard as one imagines they must try. You might be wondering why it could be motivating to be restrained. That is a good question. First, people have pride, and often pride and courage internally motivate people to change. Second, if given the option, most people would prefer to change a negative situation as quickly as possible. Third, never underestimate someone's desire to prove themselves and to rise up to overcome a challenge. The strategic therapist understands these human dynamics and uses them to create change. The restraining technique is being used when a practitioner encourages client(s) not to change too fast or warns them to slow down or risk the possibility of relapse. The restraining technique also reinforces the clinician's one-down position. For example:

> *Client:* A lot of our problems stem from Dawn's drinking. She drinks two bottles of wine every night, and she and I both agree that starting this weekend she won't drink at all.

> *Clinician:* I wonder if Dawn will feel too overwhelmed and give up if she doesn't meet this goal right away.

Another example:

> *Client:* This past week Dawn reduced her drinking to one glass per night. I couldn't be happier, and I know things are changing for the better.

> *Clinician:* I wonder what it would be like if some of the beneficial changes you're seeing didn't meet your expectations tomorrow.

Paradoxical Directives

Paradoxical directives exaggerate the presenting problem and ultimately encourage family members to perform the symptomatic behavior in an extreme way, which could ultimately conclude in clients defying the directive or following the directive in an extreme way and eventually recoiling when things get out of control. A clinician should follow a series of strategic steps in delivering a paradoxical directive: (a) establish a deep sense of trust where change is expected, (b) define the family's presenting problem in a clear and concise manner, (c) set very specific and achievable objectives, (d) disqualify the current understanding of the issue, (e) deliver the paradoxical directive in a serious and honest manner, (f) encourage more of the problematic behavior, and (g) give the family complete credit for making the change. For example:

> *Clinician:* Counseling is about helping you, as a couple, establish trust following the infidelity. I will focus my efforts on reflecting your feelings and thoughts to one another and also encourage change. When I say "change," I mean changing faulty patterns of communications, boundary problems, etc. It seems that you and Adriana don't trust one another because of frequent manipulative behaviors, lying, and because of frequent infidelity.

> *Client A:* Yes, that is it. We don't trust each other for good reason.

> *Clinician:* Okay, so our goal is to increase trust through repeated risk-taking, sticking to our word during the risk time period, and through this behavior rebuilding the foundation of your relationship.

> *Client B:* There is absolutely no way this is going to work. Instead, every time when Fernando leaves or goes out with his friends, I will be worrying about what he is doing. I think we shouldn't take any risks for the next few years!

> *Client A:* I don't care what we do; I just want to be happy.

> *Clinician:* Adriana, it sounds like you won't feel safe with Fernando doing anything outside of the relationship. In fact, it sounds like you will be worried if you don't know what he is doing and who he is doing it with. Because Fernando is such a risk, I need you to not only worry about him when he goes out with his friends but I want you to increase your worrying to include anything he does out of the house or out of your sight.

> *Client B:* Okay. . . .

> *Clinician:* Fernando, I need you to call Adriana anytime you leave the house and describe to her, in great detail, all that you are doing out of the house.

> *Client A:* Okay. . . .

Another example:

> *Client:* I find myself constantly wondering if people are looking at me because there's something on my face.

> *Clinician:* I suggest you carry a small mirror and every time you have that thought, look at your face and see if there's something on it.

Pretend Technique

Strategically oriented clinicians subtly guide people to understand that they have control over things they think they cannot control. This sense of control allows important changes to take place. The pretend technique is a paradoxical intervention designed to encourage people to pretend to have a particular issue. This issue is in line with their referral for treatment. Because the behavior is centered on pretending, new awareness around the issue emerges. Specifically, it is now considered voluntary and consequently able to be changed. For example:

> *Client:* I can't control my anger.

> *Clinician:* Show me what it looks like at times when you can't control your anger.

Client: I'm so angry at you! You're a jerk and are causing me a lot of stress!

Clinician: I noticed you were angry. Did you feel angry?

Client: Yes, I sure did.

Clinician: Now you are looking at me very calmly and not mad at all.

Client: Yes, but . . . I. . . .

Clinician: This is something you can control.

Another example:

Client: Sometimes I just feel itchy and there's nothing I can do to stop it.

Clinician: Pretend like you're itchy right now, only this time try something to relieve the itchiness.

Client: Okay, I did it.

Clinician: Excellent job. Through experimenting with itchiness here in session you realized you can control it.

Ordeals

Ordeals is a systemic technique that heightens emotionality through the use of a directive-based paradox. The essence of this technique is to assign the family a task that makes having the issue more difficult than dropping it. For example:

Client: I can't stand my partner's coffee breath.

Clinician: Each morning, I want you to brew your partner's coffee.

Another example:

Client: I can't stand visiting my mother-in-law.

Clinician: Let's try something different. Every time you visit your mother-in-law, bring her flowers or another small gift.

Metaphorical Tasks

Assigning a metaphorical task provides families with a directive that symbolically relates to the presenting problem and thereby covertly facilitates change. For example:

Client A: My wife and I are having sexual problems.

Client B: Yeah, we cannot seem to get it together at nighttime.

Clinician: Okay, instead of focusing on sex, I want you to have a very large, well-prepared meal every evening around the time you would be having sex. After you make it together, sit down and slowly enjoy the meal while simultaneously engaging in rich conversation.

Another example:

Client A: She's always grumpy with me in the morning. We just cannot seem to get along.

Clinician: You both mentioned to me that you enjoy going for long walks on your own.

Client B: Yep, that's right.

Clinician: Okay, I want you to start going for short morning walks together this week. You should do it at least three times before our next session. Also, engage each other in an interesting topic during the walk.

Devil's Pact

A more appropriate name for this intervention could be "angel's pact" since it is likely to create a positive change in the family's life. The clinician asks the family to make a commitment to the practitioner without knowing what will be asked of them. The clinician informs the family that the task will be very demanding and it will test their resolve in fixing the presenting issue. Once they commit to the experience, the clinician will provide them with an important task that strategically helps the family. For example:

Clinician: I have a challenging task for you all to try. It might be helpful if you really want to resolve this issue, but first you must commit to doing it before I tell you what it is.

Client A: It is scary to trust you before you ask, but we did hire you to help our family.

Clinician: Right, so I need consensus before we can move forward. Also, I have to tell you upfront this task is incredibly time-consuming and may be difficult. Does the family agree?

Client A: Okay.

Client B: Sure.

Client C: Yep.

Clinician: You will have to start something called family rituals. This family seems to be lacking in connectedness, so during our time here today you need to decide on four weekly rituals that you will engage in over the next month.

Another example:

Clinician: It sounds like you're all having trouble agreeing on whether you want to solve this problem. If you do, I'd like you all to agree on completing a challenge I'm going to ask of you.

Client A: Yes, whatever you think will work.

Client B: Okay.

Clinician: As a family, I'd like you to write down all of the positive qualities your family possesses in regard to communication. On a separate list, I want you to brainstorm all of the communication difficulties you've been having and where you need improvement.

Empowerment

Strategic family therapists use empowerment to remind couples and families that while things might not be up to their standards, they must be doing something right or it would be a lot worse. This intervention connects with family pride and bolsters morale.

The family's sense of failure may be the result of holding unattainable expectations or trying too hard. For example:

Client: I just don't understand why things aren't getting better, since we're all working really hard on meeting our treatment goals.

Clinician: I noticed that you haven't indicated things are getting worse, so it seems as though you are doing something right.

Another example:

Client: It seems as though everything is getting worse since we started counseling.

Clinician: Sometimes families try so hard that when they don't see results right away it seems like a failure. Share with me some specific instances of positive change.

Jamming

Jamming is a technique that helps family members and couples work on demystifying unnecessary suspicion and lowering the impact of incessant criticism and defensiveness. With couples, this often comes up when one partner accuses the other of doing something that both agree was a poor decision (e.g., infidelity, dishonesty, insensitivity). When the inappropriate behavior is brought up, the partners launch into a barrage of accusations and defensiveness. The jamming intervention is used to decrease the behavior. To start, the clinician renounces any ability to determine who is right and who is wrong. After all, the clinician is not a judge nor a jury. Next, the clinician offers to assist in improving communication within the couple. The solution for this issue is to randomize the behavior that the clients are being accused of (i.e., sometimes deliberately engaging in the suspected behavior and sometimes not). Simultaneously, the accusers are asked to test the accuracy of their accusations while observing the randomized behavior. The clients must not discuss the experiment until the next session. The clinician is hopeful that this prescription will give less legitimacy to the suspected behavior, while liberating the defender from constantly defending themselves (i.e., the signal is jammed). For example:

Client A: I think Markus is cheating on me. I don't know why I think this—I just do. I know he's going to accuse me of being crazy, but I see how he looks at other women.

Client B: You are crazy. I am not cheating on you. I think you're mad because I feel free to appreciate beauty.

Client A: Jerk!

Clinician: It seems that Samantha thinks you cheated while you say you did not. I also hear some concern on Samantha's side about you looking at other women. There is absolutely no way to determine who is telling the truth and who is not, so Markus I need you to try something for me this week.

Client B: Okay, what?

Clinician: I need you to start looking at women you find attractive and those you do not. However, you may not discuss with Samantha which women you do find attractive. Samantha, I need you to write down the dates and times you notice Markus looking at other women and report back to me which attempts you think were authentic and which were not. Does that make sense to both of you?

COMMUNICATION AND VALIDATION FAMILY THERAPY TECHNIQUES

Communication/validation is an experiential family therapy that comprises four theoretical tenets: self-esteem, communication, family roles, and rules of the family. See Table 4.5 for a breakdown of communication/validation theoretical tenets. While all of these theoretical tenets are extremely important, a central tenet is the notion that humans have an innate capacity for nurturing, connectedness, and emotional expression. Suppressing these innate capacities is the root cause of most family dysfunctions. The core communication/validation techniques explored in this section are sculpting, family maps, reconstruction, humor, verbalizing presuppositions, and anchoring.

TABLE 4.5 COMMUNICATION AND VALIDATION FAMILY THERAPY THEORETICAL TENETS

Theoretical Tenet	Explanation
Individual self-esteem	Self-esteem is the holistic meaning and value that people place on their personhood. High self-esteem is associated with strong communication, while low self-esteem is associated with poor communication.
Communication	A key factor in influencing couples and families is communication. The way we communicate (e.g., congruent communication, incomplete communication) can be learned and unlearned.
Family roles	Roles are key factors in familial relationships. There is a mutual interaction that creates each role. Examples of roles include, but are not limited to, the blamer, the placater, the distractor, and the leveler.
Rules of the family	There are written and unwritten rules that govern all families. Rules can be rigid (i.e., nonnegotiable) or flexible (i.e., negotiable).
Multicultural considerations	Virginia Satir emphasized the unconditional acceptance of clients' cultural values (among other things), but she never discussed ethnic and racial differences and similarities between the therapist and the client. The clinician should understand and respect the specific norms and values of particular cultures (e.g., Hispanic values of familialism and respect).
Feminist critique	While Satir offers an extremely accepting and empathic approach, more directed gender-sensitive therapeutic efforts could increase the model's effectiveness—for example, unpacking gender stories in context and helping clients locate and identify their social locations.

Note: This table provides a breakdown of key therapeutic tenets, multicultural considerations, and feminist critiques of the communication and validation family therapy model. Further reading is required for a comprehensive understanding of the approach.

Sources: Data from Ashton, D., & Jordal, C. (2019). Re-visioning gender, re-visioning power: Equity, accountability, and refusing to silo. In M. McGoldrick & K. Hardy (Eds.), *Re-Visioning family therapy: Addressing diversity in clinical practice* (3rd ed., pp. 28–43). Guilford Press; Bermudez, D. (2008). Adapting Virginia Satir techniques to Hispanic families. *The Family Journal, 16*(1), 51–57. https://doi.org/10.1177/1066480707309543; Gehart, D. R. (2017). *Mastering competencies in family therapy: A practical approach to theory and clinical case documentation* (3rd ed.). Brooks/Cole; Nichols, M. P., & Davis, S. D. (2020). *The essentials of family therapy.* Pearson Education; Reiter, M.D. (2013). *Case conceptualization in marriage and family therapy.* Pearson Education; Satir, V., & Baldwin, M. (1983). *Satir step by step: A guide to creating change in families.* Science and Behavior Books; Walsh, W. M., & McGraw, J. A. (2002). *Essentials of family therapy: A structured summary of nine approaches.* Love Publishing Company.

Sculpting

Out of all of Virginia Satir's wonderful family therapy techniques, none have stood the test of time or inspired people more than family sculpting. This technique uses fantasy and role-play to provide symbolic awareness of how people in the family feel and experience their family's dynamics. Understanding the nuances of perceived family dynamics in the here and now is incredibly important. During a family sculpt, a family member or the clinician acts as a director and physically arranges the members of the family to represent their symbolic perception of what is taking place within the family. All family members will have a chance to create a sculpt. Following the initial sculpt, clinicians often do a second sculpt centered on family members cocreating a sculpt of how they would like their family to be symbolically. For example:

Clinician: We're going to try something different today. Specifically, there seems to be a lot of confusion about how people see the family and the current struggle. To increase our understanding, we are going to take part in an experiential activity where we symbolically represent the family dynamics with our bodies. For example, if I think my sister has a lot more power in the family than I do, I may have her standing while I kneel. Another example would be if I feel Mom and Dad fight a lot, I might have them pose with their dukes up. Everyone will have a chance to symbolically represent how they see the family dynamics. What questions do you have?

Client: What if I don't like the way someone represents something?

Clinician: Great question. During the sculpting exercise there will be no talking by the people being sculpted, and the sculptor will be polite and direct with the individuals being sculpted. We will all go through the experience, and following everyone's representation we will all process the experience together. After we go through sculpting the current family dynamics, we will all have an opportunity to sculpt the family to represent how we would like it to be in the future.

Family Maps

Family maps is Satir's version of a genogram, and it requires the cocreation of three maps. These maps include each parent's family of origin and the current family. For example:

Clinician: Today we are going to start working on an exciting project known as a family map. A family map is a visual representation of your current family and each parent's family of origin. Included in this family map are your family's basic demographics, relationship status between members, major events including illness, death, abortion, adoption, addictions, and mental illness. Lastly, the family map will include references to particular communication styles and behaviors of members. The point of a family map is to notice the various patterns in your family's history and whether you want to stay loyal to those patterns or change them. What questions do you have before we begin?

Client: None really . . . this sounds helpful.

Clinician: Okay, let's get started. We are going to work from your current family back in time. Tell me about yourself. What work have you done in your life?

Reconstruction

Experiential family therapy techniques are often connected to each other in a holistic manner. This technique uses the information from family maps to create awareness and possibly promote change. The technique of reconstruction is applied when the clinician essentially gathers unfinished business from the family's history and reenacts the event to find some level of closure. For example:

> *Clinician:* Okay, during this family map creation, several people mentioned the tremendous impact of finding out that Beverly had HIV. Specifically, all of you remember being in the car and sobbing and Mom being incredibly critical. Let's reconstruct that incident. Mom and Dad, go ahead and sit in these two chairs and let's pretend that these are the front seats in the car. Franklin and Shauntay, you sit in these two chairs behind your parents and pretend you are in the back seat of the car.

> *Client A:* This seems really weird!

> *Clinician:* It's normal to feel uncomfortable. This can be uncomfortable, and most families don't role-play regularly; however, the benefits are tremendous if you allow me to directly affect your communication process.

> *Client B:* Okay, let's just do it.

> *Clinician:* Right. Mom, pretend your phone rings and Beverly discloses this news. The rest of the family should try to handle this in a manner similar to how you responded 2 weeks ago.

Humor

It is no secret that humor and laughter cause a positive health response. Laughter and humor can be disarming, healing, and improve interpersonal connection. In the therapy room, humor can strengthen connections between the clinician and the family. Practitioners frequently use humor to encourage movement and to exaggerate family dynamics in a manner that decreases defensiveness. For example:

> *Client:* Why are women so needy? It's not like I always have the answer.

> *Clinician:* I want you to look over at Louise. What do you think her facial expression is communicating to you?

> *Client:* I'm in deep shit! (Everyone laughs.)

> *Clinician:* Bingo! I wonder how you could say that differently.

Another example:

> *Client A:* I'm not sure Brian knows how much his dad loves him.

> *Clinician:* Tell me more about this assumption.

> *Client A:* Well, I tell him I love him every day, hug him at least 3 times per day, and always tell him how handsome he is. I'm not sure Donald does any of that.

> *Clinician:* I'm impressed with your "I love you routine" (family laughs). Donald, how do you display your love to Brian?

Verbalizing Presuppositions

When this experiential technique is used, the clinician outwardly states the presuppositions embedded in a family's behavior. This gets back to the notion that one cannot *not* communicate or behave. Every communication and behavior has meaning. For example:

> *Clinician:* Chelsea, when Jim mentioned how much he cares for you and the boys, you put your hand on your heart and your legs moved closer to him. It is clear to me that you deeply care for Jim and desire his loving comments.

Another example:

> *Clinician:* It is clear to me that Sarah loves the family, as evidenced by her staying quiet. You see, Sarah knows the family is fragile right now, and by staying quiet she thinks she will not put the family at risk.

Anchoring

Anchoring is an example of an experiential technique that requires further training to be applied effectively. This technique helps connect emotions with touch, which makes the feeling more concrete for the individual. The clinician works with the client to create awareness around any physical responses to certain feelings. Essentially, the clinician assists the family member in associating a specific stimulus with the person's normal and expected emotional response. For example:

> *Clinician:* Okay, what we are going to do today is attempt to accentuate the present state of love you have for your child. During this exercise you are going to go into your imagination and picture caring scenes and experiences of Sam, and during the process Sam will touch your shoulder and say the word "Mom." Although this seems a bit different, the touch and words he utters will start to program your brain to respond in a positive manner to him. Does this make sense?

> *Client A:* Sure, I get it. It just might make me cry.

> *Clinician:* That is fine. I'm very comfortable with your tears. Okay, Martha, I want you to imagine you are on your vacation with Sam. Remember how happy you were to be near him and have that deep bonding. Remember how much fun it was to walk on the boardwalk together and watch him jump into the ocean. Sam, come here and touch your mom's shoulder and say the word "Mom."

> *Client B:* Mom.

> *Clinician:* Martha, now go ahead and look at Sam and feel what you feel inside.

SOLUTION-FOCUSED THERAPY TECHNIQUES

Solution-focused therapy is a postmodern therapy that comprises nine core concepts: solutions are the problem, complaint, exception, new solutions, types of clients, cooperation, therapeutic fit, rapid resolution, and meanings are negotiable. See Table 4.6 for a breakdown of solution-focused therapy theoretical tenets as well as multicultural considerations and feminist critiques. While all of these theoretical tenets are important and certainly warrant deep exploration, the foundation of solution-focused therapy is the notion that exceptions to the client's presenting problem(s) are the solutions. Essentially, people can behave in an effective manner but are often blocked by a negative and

TABLE 4.6 SOLUTION-FOCUSED THERAPY THEORETICAL TENETS

Theoretical Tenet	Explanation
Solutions are the problem	A key theoretical tenet of this model is that the presenting problem is not the actual problem. The solutions clients are using to solve the presenting problem are the real problems.
Complaint	Solution-focused practitioners use the word *complaint* to describe the presenting problem. This is simply the reason(s) the client(s) came to therapy.
Exception	Exceptions are the cornerstone of the solution-focused model. Exceptions are essentially any time the complaint does not happen.
New solutions	New solutions often emerge after the exceptions are noted. These are simply new ways of handling the complaint.
Types of clients	Clients can be categorized as *visitors* (i.e., clients who state they have no complaints), *complainants* (i.e., clients who expect a solution to the problem during therapy but are somewhat resistant), or *customers* (i.e., clients who want to work on the complaint).
Cooperation	Clinicians automatically consider clients to be cooperative and assume they have a desire for change. The clinician views the client as the expert on their problems.
Therapeutic fit	This refers to conveying empathy toward the client's situation in a nonthreatening and nonjudgmental manner.
Rapid resolution	This is the solution-focused belief that only a small amount of change is necessary for the change process to start. Following the initial spark, change occurs very quickly.
Meanings are negotiable	The important part of any clinical experience is the meaning that the client constructs around a phenomenon. The family that is engaging in treatment are the experts on the reality of their system.
Multicultural considerations	Solution-focused practitioners work hard to maintain a nonexpert, neutral, and equality-oriented therapeutic style. While this approach can be helpful, certain cultures and certain issues (e.g., dramatic conflict) require reassurance and direction. Clinicians should integrate multicultural theory whenever possible.
Feminist critique	The solution-focused therapy model fails to meet the feminist critique in a few key areas. The most salient critiques are centered on the model's focus on behavior change to the near exclusion of explanation and insight.

Note: This table provides a breakdown of key therapeutic tenets, multicultural considerations, and feminist critiques of the solution-focused family therapy model. Further reading is required for a comprehensive understanding of the approach.

Sources: Data from Dermer, S. B., Hemesath, C. W., & Russell, C. S. (1998). A feminist critique of solution-focused therapy. *The American Journal of Family Therapy, 26*(3), 239–250. https://doi.org/10.1080/01926189808251103; Gehart, D. R. (2017). *Mastering competencies in family therapy: A practical approach to theory and clinical case documentation* (3rd ed.). Brooks/Cole; Holyoake, D.-D., & Golding, E. (2012). Multiculturalism and solution-focused psychotherapy: An exploration of the nonexpert role. *Asia Pacific Journal of Counselling and Psychotherapy, 3*(1), 72–81. https://doi.org/10.1080/21507686.2011.651479; Nichols, M. P., & Davis, S. D. (2020). *The essentials of family therapy.* Pearson Education; Reiter, M.D. (2013). *Case conceptualization in marriage and family therapy.* Pearson Education; Walsh, W. M., & McGraw, J. A. (2002). *Essentials of family therapy: A structured summary of nine approaches.* Love Publishing Company.

narrow mindset. The core solution-focused therapy techniques explored in this section include deconstruction, change talk, exceptions, miracle question, and scaling.

Deconstruction

Solution-focused therapy works hard to deconstruct communication down to the basic nuts and bolts of what someone states. At times, people speak globally or generalize to the point that the message holds little significance. This technique can seem a lot like the attending skill of clarification discussed earlier in this chapter. In practicing this technique, the clinician encourages the client to go from general to specific in terms of describing the issues they are working on. Breaking down the problem into smaller issues may also make the problem appear less overwhelming and easier to deal with or overcome. For example:

Client: I had an affair because I was bored with my marriage.

Clinician: What specifically about your marriage are you bored with?

Another example:

Client: Parenting is too hard.

Clinician: Specifically, what is it about parenting that you find difficult?

Change Talk

Change talk is a technique that emphasizes the importance of change. Clients are asked to do something different or encouraged to use a response that differs from their existing repertoire. This directive is somewhat vague, allowing the client to choose a response that fits for them. This approach can circumvent client resistance that emerges from being told to do something that does not fit the client's frame of reference. For example:

Client: Denise is such a naughty kid.

Clinician: When you want to say that Denise is a "naughty kid," I want you to change your language and say, "Denise challenges my parenting skills."

Another example:

Clinician: Dad, this week I want you to "act" depressed three times.

Exceptions

Exceptions are a cornerstone technique in solution-focused therapy. This technique requires the client to consider times in which the problem did not exist, they successfully navigated an area of concern, or they successfully coped with a presenting concern. This technique assumes that most people experience and successfully cope with issues. Because of this, most people have their own solutions embedded in their memory. For example:

Client: Tommy has always tested my patience.

Clinician: Has there ever been a time that Tommy has not tested your patience?

Another example:

Client: Every parent gives in to their kids.

Clinician: Have you ever seen a parent not give in to their child?

Client: Yes.

Clinician: Tell me what that looked like.

Miracle Question

The miracle question is used to encourage clients to consider what their life would look like if everything was the way they want it to be. The information gathered from the miracle question is used by the clinician to create change, elicit solution-based information, and provide a map for meaningful change. The miracle question is presented like this: "Suppose that one night, while you were sleeping, there was a miracle, and this problem was solved." "How would you know? What would be different?" "How will your partner know without your saying a word to them about it?" For example:

> *Clinician:* Let's say that I have a magic wand, and I wave this magic wand and your marriage is perfect. What is the first thing that you would notice about your marriage that is different because this magic wand works?

Another example:

> *Clinician:* Ronnie, you have described the family as unsupportive and hurtful to you in many ways. I want you now to try something out with me. It's an experiment that is going to require you to use your imagination. So, here goes. You wake up tomorrow morning and open your eyes and you notice something is different. As you walk down the stairs you realize a miracle has occurred and everything is just the way you want it to be. Describe to all of us what is different in terms of support and family kindness.

Scaling

Scaling is a much-appreciated skill that practitioners from many diverse theoretical leanings borrow from solution-focused therapy. When using this technique, the clinician asks the family to provide a numerical rating regarding a particular situation. The scale is typically 1 to 10, with "1" being the worst it could be and "10" being as good as possible. The rating provides feedback to the clinician and other family members on how a particular individual views an experience. After the first number is provided, clinicians typically ask what it would take to go one number higher or lower. For example:

> *Clinician:* On a scale of 1 to 10, with 10 being the best and 1 being the worst, where would you rank your sex life with your wife?
>
> *Client:* 4.
>
> *Clinician:* Okay, what would it take to go to 5?

Another example:

> *Clinician:* On a scale of 1 to 10, with 1 being the least and 10 being the most, where would you rank your depression today?
>
> *Client:* 8.
>
> *Clinician:* Okay, an 8. Can you tell me what a 7 would look like?

NARRATIVE THERAPY TECHNIQUES

Narrative therapy is a postmodern therapy that comprises 10 core concepts: problems, storying of experience, language, dominant story, literary merit of a story, power, truths, lived experiences, problem-saturated description, and performance of stories. See Table 4.7 for a breakdown of narrative therapy's theoretical tenets as well as multicultural considerations and feminist critiques. While all of the narrative therapy concepts hold great importance, the narrative approach is primarily concerned with the ways people construct meanings and interpret their experiences. These interpretations and stories have a powerful influence on their lives. The core narrative therapy skills

TABLE 4.7 NARRATIVE THERAPY THEORETICAL TENETS

Theoretical Tenet	Explanation
Problems	The person is not the problem; the problem is the problem. From a narrative perspective, families and individuals influence and are influenced by the problem.
Storying of experience	Authoring stories occurs when clients organize their stories and give them meaning. People often shape their lives around the stories they author.
Language	Personal realities are socially constructed and represented through language.
Dominant story	People, families, and cultures all have dominant stories. Clients use their dominant stories as guiding metaphors.
Literary merit of a story	Literary merit is the subjective credibility of the various client narratives.
Power	This concept could include the power of the dominant narrative and the clinician's power to subjugate clients.
Truths	Truth is socially constructed by those in power and by everyday individuals. These truths often become the norms that people shape their lives around.
Lived experiences	Complete contact with reality is known as lived experience.
Problem-saturated descriptions	Problem-saturated descriptions are created when the client or family's sense of perception is dominated by the problem.
Performance of stories	These are the behaviors that people use to create meaningful stories. Clients creatively fill narrative gaps with new information attained through their imagination or witnessing. As the performances increase, so do their reauthoring experiences.
Multicultural considerations	From a multicultural perspective, narrative therapy must adapt to the specific cultural context in which it is being used. For example, certain collectivist cultures deeply value and respect authority, and therefore externalizing certain characteristics that were applied by elders or authorities may be incompatible with a client or family's culture.
Feminist critique	A major element of narrative therapy and theory is to practice from a perspective that empowers diverse groups including women. To increase the power of this approach with women, clinicians are encouraged to replace macrosystem-based misogynous cultural metaphors with narrative reauthoring self-narratives.

Note: This table provides a breakdown of key therapeutic tenets, multicultural considerations, and feminist critiques of the narrative therapy model. Further reading is required for a comprehensive understanding of the approach.

Sources: Data from Gehart, D. R. (2017). *Mastering competencies in family therapy: A practical approach to theory and clinical case documentation* (3rd ed.). Brooks/Cole; Johnson, S. M. (2019). *The practice of emotionally focused marital therapy: Creating connection.* Brunner-Routledge; Lee, J. (2008). Women re-authoring their lives through feminist narrative therapy. *Women & Therapy, 20*(3), 1–22, https://doi.org/10.1300/J015v20n03_01; Nichols, M. P., & Davis, S. D. (2020). *The essentials of family therapy.* Pearson Education; Reiter, M. D. (2013). *Case conceptualization in marriage and family therapy.* Pearson Education; Satir, V., & Baldwin, M. (1983). *Satir step by step: A guide to creating change in families.* Science and Behavior Books; Walsh, W. M., & McGraw, J. A. (2002). *Essentials of family therapy: A structured summary of nine approaches.* Love Publishing Company.

that will be explored in this section include presupposition of change, externalization, adopting a family's language, locating unique outcomes, restorying/reauthoring, and using the audience/witnessing.

Presupposition of Change

Clinicians use presupposition of change to inform clients about the inevitability of change. This change assumption creates a sense of energy around the intervention. For example:

Client A: I want to be a better friend with her, but I just get so angry at her irresponsible behavior. I don't know what else to do.

Client B: And I get angry at him for being so mean. I mean, I didn't sign up for this.

Clinician: The couple has suffered a lot at the hands of anger. Tell me when the couple was able to outsmart anger.

Another example:

Client A: I constantly take on more than I can handle.

Client B: That is how she controls us all.

Client C: Yeah, exactly.

Client D: It's like we feel bad asking anything of her because she quietly guilts and shames all of us.

Clinician: Mom, it sounds like the family has a story of a martyr who uses guilt and shame to control everyone.

Client A: I guess that's partly true.

Clinician: Can you tell me how you've protected your family from this martyr in the past?

Externalization

How helpful is it to internalize problems as part of oneself? According to narrative therapy, it is extremely unhelpful. Internalizing issues can create pathologizing, shaming, and scapegoating. Externalizing is the hallmark technique of the narrative approach. A narrative therapist will often have clients either externalize and diminish the powerful effects of negative labels, or for a period of time they may have clients personify the problem. Narrative therapists also externalize negative labels to disrupt the performance of the problem-saturated story. When externalizing is done in a thorough manner, it encompasses the history of the problem, mapping the problem, strategies of the problem, and exceptions to the problem. This level of externalizing can increase hope and decrease blame within a family. Externalizing a problem might look like the following example:

Client: So, this feels weird because everyone thinks I'm messed up for wetting the bed and it has always been that way.

Clinician: It can be a challenge, but I think Embarrassing Pee has been secretly sabotaging you for a long time. Just look how clever he is . . . your parents are sure that you're to blame.

Client: [giggles] Okay.

Clinician: I'm going to talk to Embarrassing Pee now. You know him better than anyone, so try to answer as accurately as possible. Embarrassing Pee, how long have you been a problem in Karl's life?

Client: As long as Karl has been alive. Well, actually I was more accepted when he was younger.

Clinician: Overall, how successful would you say you've been as a problem in Karl's life?

Next is an example of externalizing through mapping the problem:

Client: I'm just not sure I'll ever beat Evil Anger.

Clinician: Evil Anger, have you been able to have any effect on Lisa's social life or friendships?

Client: Oh yes, I've successfully ended most of her close friendships. . . . I'm okay with superficial friendships, but once someone gets too close, I destroy them.

Clinician: Are you able to have any impact on the way in which Lisa thinks?

Client: Sure, I keep her worried and suspicious of everyone's intentions. This keeps Lisa feeling unlovable and simultaneously keeps me in power.

In the next example, the clinician externalizes strategies of the problem:

Clinician: Codependent, currently how much control do you have over Samantha's life: 10%, 50%, 90%?

Client: Probably 50%. I mean, whenever she needs to be a disciplinarian or create some sort of boundary between her and John, I take over.

Clinician: Codependent, if Sam ever starts getting the upper hand, is there anything you do to put her back in her place?

Client: Yeah, I'm close friends with Poor Self-Esteem, and we tag team Sam whenever she starts feeling confident.

In the following example, the clinician externalizes exceptions to the problem:

Clinician: Drunken Bob, even though you've had an enormous impact on Bob's life, what has kept you from getting more control than you already have?

Client: His family and conscience keep getting in the way.

Adopting a Family's Language

As the narrative process begins, the clinician will attempt to connect with the family in different ways. One of the initial strategies will be to begin adopting the family's language. This occurs when the clinician begins to mirror the family's communication style, demonstrates a cognitive and empathic understanding of the issues, and provides a general sense of receptivity. For example:

Client A: Yeah, I'm such an idiot. I can't believe I'm still in this stupid marriage. We haven't gotten along in so long. I mean, she doesn't even like me.

Client B: I do like you at times . . . just not when Super Aggressive takes over.

Clinician: Fred, the current story for this relationship is that this arrangement is stupid and if you were less of an idiot, you would just end it.

Client A: You are only interested in assigning blame to Super Aggressive and its past reign of terror.

Another example:

Client: My life is slowly starting to come together . . . I mean, I feel free of the whole cheating thing. I'm not interested in keeping him under my thumb anymore.

Clinician: You're feeling calmer about the situation, and it sounds like you are about to pull up your thumb and take the pressure off of Mike.

Locating Unique Outcomes

The technique of locating unique outcomes is similar to the solution-focused exception technique. From a narrative perspective, locating unique outcomes refers to identifying experiences that are outside the dominant narrative of the client or the family. The three types of unique outcomes are historical (past events), current (current events), and future (possible future events). The clinician works with the client to map out various unique outcomes to challenge the dominant narrative and to serve the client's authoring and reauthoring experiences.

An example of a historical unique outcome could be the following:

Clinician: Although the family is invested in the story "You're always welcome home," there seems to be a discrepancy between this prominent story and what Jason described as the experience of being kicked out of the house when he was 15. I call this a subplot. What should we title this subplot?

Client: I suppose you could call it Limitation One.

An example of a current unique outcome could be the following:

Client A: The story of "We're overly close" is so relevant to our situation. I mean, what gives?

Client B: Yeah . . . but when Mom and Dad divorced, we needed each other.

Client C: Absolutely, and now we're finally coming to counseling and that would have never happened before.

Clinician: So, an exception to the current problematic story of "We're overly close" is the subplot of "Our closeness keeps us safe at times."

Client A: Absolutely!

A final example illustrates locating future unique outcomes:

Client A: I think we can change the story of "We're worse to the ones we love than to strangers."

Client B: I guess, but what are you going to do differently.

Clinician: You mean, "How are you going to keep outsmarting Meany Pants"?

Client B: Yeah, that's what I meant.

Client A: I just will have to keep practicing. I'm not going to be perfect or anything.

Clinician: If you continue to outsmart Meany Pants, what positive benefits can you foresee?

Restorying/Reauthoring

An individual or family is using restorying/reauthoring when they assign a new meaning to a narrative that was previously viewed as hurtful and/or oppressive. This allows the clients to move forward with a new story that allows them to feel empowered. If the clinician has successfully helped the family resist seeing the problem through the dominant story, it is called a unique redescription. An example of a unique redescription could look like the following:

Client A: I don't know if it is fair to keep blaming Bobby for all of these issues. I mean, he certainly took part, but maybe I did as well.

Client B: Yeah, maybe we need to think of the fact that we were dead broke. I mean, Jim just lost his job and we were collecting welfare and that was such a stress for everyone.

Client C: I know you say "for everyone," but it was just you and Mom fighting about that stuff and we were just worried because nobody knew what was going on besides you two.

Client B: I guess you're right.

Clinician: So, it sounds like the family has reauthored this issue. The old story was "The family is happy as long as Bobby is happy," and now this has been edited. What is the new story titled?

Client A: I think the accurate story is "When problems are evident, but no one talks about it, chaos occurs."

Client B: Yeah, "Unclear messages cause chaos."

An example of a traditional reauthoring experience could include the following:

Clinician: We've established that the issue we're working on is the story of "Should we stay, or should we leave"; however, the couple has been talking about how lack of trust can manipulate their relationship.

Client A: Yeah, along with our problem of indecision we both just have a hard time trusting anyone.

Client B: I guess we could call that story, "Trust manipulates our happiness."

Clinician: Okay, so in addition to the main story of "Should we stay or should we leave," there is this subplot of "Trust manipulates our happiness."

Using the Audience/Witnessing

Who are the potential audiences attached to the family's unfolding dominant narrative? What type of impact would these audiences have if they were invited to participate in the therapeutic process? The technique of using the audience or witnessing involves bringing important groups of individuals into the therapeutic process. The narrative-oriented clinician is constantly considering who the additional audiences are in the family's narrative. For example:

Clinician: So, as a couple you have chosen to become more collaborative and not allow competition to interfere with your love for one another. How will this new development affect your children? Even though this new story may be better in the long run, the family is very comfortable with business as usual. How will they deal with competition being removed from the couple and parental units?

Here is another example:

Clinician: The children have decided to protect Mom and Dad from triangulation and side-taking. This is a huge decision that will certainly have consequences. Mom and Dad, how do you plan on dealing with each other and the children without side-taking and triangulation in your life?

COGNITIVE BEHAVIORAL FAMILY THERAPY TECHNIQUES

Cognitive behavioral family therapy (CBFT) comprises six core theoretical concepts: classical conditioning theory, operant conditioning theory, social cognitive theory, cognitive appraisal theory, cognitive mediation model, and systems theory (Table 4.8). Practitioners using this theoretical school of thought to help people understand, identify, and change dysfunctional and disturbing thought patterns that negatively influence their behavior. CBFT combines interventions from cognitively and behaviorally oriented approaches within a family systems context. CBFT views a family problem as being embedded within the family system (Friedberg, 2006). Circular causal patterns among family members are identified as points for interventions that alter the perpetuating nature of the cycles (Dattilio & Epstein, 2021). Similar to the tenets of systems theory, CBFT posits that when one person within a family system changes, so will the other individuals within the system. There is an emphasis placed on cognitions playing a central role within a family system. Through changing family members' beliefs, there will also be a systemic change observed. Everyone within a client family is important and influential in the change of a family structure, and dysfunctional behaviors are not credited to one individual. Instead, they are conceptualized as a product of the overall family functioning. The most efficient way to enlist change in beliefs is by using techniques such as cognitive restructuring, downward arrow, validity testing, and role-playing (Dattilio & Epstein, 2021; Friedberg, 2006).

TABLE 4.8   COGNITIVE BEHAVIORAL THERAPY THEORETICAL TENETS

Theoretical Tenet	Explanation
Classical conditioning theory	A potent stimulus is combined with a neutral stimulus that results in pairing; the neutral stimulus then elicits the same response as the potent stimulus.
Operant conditioning theory	Reinforcement and punishment influence the frequencies in which people engage in behaviors. In family therapy, these reinforcers and punishers can be those family members give others for their actions.
Social cognitive theory	Observational learning is when an individual learns behavior indirectly from watching or listening to the experiences of others, leading to an increase or decrease in behaviors.
Social exchange theory	A high ratio of negative behaviors to positive behaviors engaged in via the interaction of people can lead to distress in relationships.
Cognitive appraisal theory	Individuals pay too much attention to negative incidents or cues and then overestimate the likelihood of the negative event happening again. Individuals then exaggerate the meaning or significance of the event.
Cognitive mediation model	Thoughts, feelings, and behaviors all interact and influence each other. These interactions are also influenced by an individual's schemas. When schemas are activated, faulty information processing occurs and spreads to selective attention, memory, and interpretation of experiences. Automatic thoughts then occur and perpetuate a cycle of emotional dysfunction and maladaptive behaviors.
Systems theory	The focus is on the interconnectedness of the family system and interpersonal processes within the family that influence each family member's functioning. Clinicians track interaction patterns and sequences and assess individual family member's psychological and physical health within the family context.

(continued)

TABLE 4.8 COGNITIVE BEHAVIORAL THERAPY THEORETICAL TENETS (*CONTINUED*)

Multicultural considerations	CBT is embedded with values supported by the dominant culture: assertiveness, independence, rationality, ability, and behavior change. This may not fit for cultures that value interdependence, collective decision-making, subtle communication, acceptance, and a less linear cognitive style. In addition, CBT has an individualistic orientation which may lead to an overemphasis on cognitive restructuring instead of environmental interventions.
Feminist critique	Feminist scholars critique CBT's overestimation of the importance of cognitive processes, pathologizing (i.e., problem-focused), and lack of emphasis on feelings. The negative cognitions present within the mind of the depressed may accurately depict the negative and undesirable nature of life. This is especially true for groups that have faced discrimination and a lack of equity.

CBT, cognitive behavioral therapy.

Note: This table provides a breakdown of key therapeutic tenets, multicultural considerations, and feminist critique of the cognitive behavioral family therapy model. Further reading is required for a comprehensive understanding.

Sources: Data from Gehart, D. R. (2017). *Mastering competencies in family therapy: A practical approach to theory and clinical case documentation* (3rd ed.). Brooks/Cole; Hays, P. A. (2009). Integrating evidence-based practice, cognitive–behavior therapy, and multicultural therapy: Ten steps for culturally competent practice. *Professional Psychology: Research and Practice, 40*(4), 354–360. https://doi.org/10.1037/a0016250; Nichols, M. P., & Davis, S. D. (2020). *The essentials of family therapy.* Pearson Education; Reiter, M. D. (2013). *Case conceptualization in marriage and family therapy.* Pearson Education; Safran, J. D. (1998). *Widening the scope of cognitive therapy.* Bookmart Press Inc.; Walsh, W. M., & McGraw, J. A. (2002). *Essentials of family therapy: A structured summary of nine approaches.* Love Publishing Company.

The Downward Arrow

The downward arrow technique helps identify family schemas that are resulting from maladaptive thought patterns. The clinician uses the downward arrow technique to help understand and alleviate the negative symptomology a client/family is feeling by identifying core beliefs and using CBT strategies to address them. The steps can include identifying the family schema, tracing the origins of the schema, pointing out the need for change, eliciting family members' acknowledgment to change, assessing the family's ability to make changes, implementing change, enacting new behaviors, and solidifying changes (Manhattan Center for Cognitive Behavioral Therapy, 2021). For example:

Client: I know I failed my test.

Clinician: What does it mean if you did?

Client: It means that I won't pass the class.

Clinician: What will happen if you don't pass?

Client: I won't graduate.

Clinician: What does it mean to you if you don't graduate.

Client: It means I am stupid!

Validity Testing

Validity testing is when the clinician challenges the validity of a client's or family's belief about a particular situation. This is typically done through asking the client to support their conclusions using objective evidence (Rice, 2015). For example:

Client A: I truly believe Sharon doesn't love me. She is always coming home late from work.

Client B: It isn't my fault. I do love you.

Clinician: Sharon, do you set your own work schedule?

Client B: No, my boss does.

Clinician: Frank, it really seems that Sharon is coming home late because that is when her shift ends. What evidence do you have to support the notion that she is deliberately coming home late to avoid you?

Cognitive Restructuring

Cognitive restructuring is when the clinician identifies maladaptive thought patterns and works with the client or family to change them to be more adaptive in nature. In addition, cognitive restructuring helps individuals more readily and accurately identify automatic thoughts and assumptions. Lastly, cognitive restructuring can assist individuals in developing a perspective that results in less emotional triggers and allows them to engage in more adaptive ways to meet their needs (Cognitive Behavioral Therapy Los Angeles, 2020). For example:

Client: I met with my manager yesterday and he had a lot to say about work this year.

Clinician: What were your thoughts around this meeting?

Client: I really thought I was doing a good job, but after the meeting I just felt defeated and stupid.

Clinician: What evidence do you have that supports the notion that you are defeated and stupid?

Client: Some of his comments were accurate.

Clinician: What doesn't support these hurtful comments?

Client: I have been selected for two awards this year, and this workplan review was abnormally critical.

Clinician: What balanced thought between these two extremes can you think of?

Client: My supervisor is probably harder on me because he knows my potential. I really think he wants me to succeed.

Role-Playing

Role-playing is a technique that is used to get the client/family to act out or reenact a response from a specific situation. With families, role-play can be used to change patterns of communication, act out common scenarios, and introduce new skills and ways of relating (Isaacson & Furrow, 2017). Role-playing helps increase the ability of clients who are struggling with social engagement. The clinician changes the emphasis from the client and places it on the role they are playing. Through role-play repetition, clients increase their sense of security regarding future social interactions (Hackett, 2011). For example:

Clinician: Kai, it seems that you and your daughter have had a terrible disagreement about chores this week.

Client: Yes, it has been extremely tough.

Clinician: Let's role-play the experience here in session. Kai, please face Alicia and start from when you told her to clean her room. Say it to her now as if you were at home.

EMOTIONALLY FOCUSED THERAPY TECHNIQUES

Emotionally focused therapy (EFT) comprises six core concepts: collaborative alliance, primacy of emotion in organizing attachment and relationship behaviors, the importance of attachment in perceived insecurity, problems maintained by the dominant emotional experience of each partner, identifying and delineating the negative interactive cycles, and change occurring when forming a new response and taking actions within the relationship. See Table 4.9 for a breakdown of EFT theoretical tenets as well as multicultural considerations and feminist critiques. While all EFT theoretical concepts are extremely important, EFT's primary theory stems from the theoretical cycle of emotional responsiveness and engagement that facilitates positive interactions, which in turn sustain safe and secure attachment. In this cycle, relational problems arise when attachment needs are unmet or insufficiently met. The core EFT techniques that will be explored in this section include the encounter, exploring and reformulating emotion, softening, evocative responding, heightening, empathic conjecture/interpretation, and personal/process disclosure.

The Encounter

The encounter is a key technique centered on directly healing emotional hurts. The clinician asks partners to turn to each other and share their thoughts, emotions, and past experiences. This step enables the clinician to create a safe and secure relationship in which attachment injuries can be understood and healed. The clinician encourages clients to understand the meaning of the various emotional responses expressed and encourages the couple to enact new behaviors based on new emotional experiences. For example:

Clinician: Can you tell him, "You do shut me out."?

Client A: This is all I can take, and I can't take you shutting me out again.

Client B: I understand.

Another example:

Client: I guess I feel ashamed about causing so much stress in the family, but it's very hard for me to. . . .

Clinician: This is the first time you've ever mentioned being ashamed. Could you tell him about that shame?

Exploring and Reformulating Emotions

This skill can involve reflecting feelings, paraphrasing key emotional experiences, asking questions, and exploring the client's emotional world. The clinician will explore emotions, offer empathic responses, and encourage clients to deeply explore

TABLE 4.9   EMOTIONALLY FOCUSED THERAPY THEORETICAL TENETS

Theoretical Tenet	Explanation
Collaborative alliance	An EFT therapeutic alliance is collaborative, nonpathologizing, respectful, and egalitarian in nature. The clinician and the client explore issues deeply, and during this in-depth process the client creates an effective dependency on the clinician.
Primacy of emotion in organizing attachment	Emotion is considered a powerful medium for change. The primacy of emotions is recognized in an individual's inner emotional experiences and interactional patterns, and it plays a key role in creating new cycles of interaction. These new cycles create secure relational attachment bonds.
Attachment and perceived insecurity	When clients demonstrate an insecure attachment, any perceived distance or separation in close relationships is interpreted as a threat to their sense of security. Strengthening insecure attachment bonds can restore a sense of emotional balance and protect people from a variety of health problems.
Delineating the negative interactive cycles	Through working with the couple, the clinician is able to identify and delineate the negative interactive style. Examples of these interactive styles include pursue/withdraw, withdraw/withdraw, attack/attack, complex cycles, and reactive pursue/withdraw.
Problems maintained by one's dominant emotional experience	EFT is the adult application of attachment theory. There is a universal need to form secure emotional and physical connections with caregivers. EFT conceptualizes adult intimate relationships as an extension of one's attachment to early caregivers. If the adult client's attachment style is insecure due to early life experiences, new emotional experiences are necessary for positive change to occur.
Forming a new response and taking actions within the relationship	After the EFT clinician shapes new cycles of positive interactions in which positive emotions arise and negative emotions can be regulated in new ways, the main task is to help create a secure attachment between the partners by creating a new emotional experience. These new and novel experiences now come from a place of security. The couple can rethink and solve previously unsolvable problems.
Multicultural considerations	EFT demonstrates a fair amount of cultural promise due to its emphasis on an open and curious stance, accessing vulnerability, and using the attachment frame. While these aspects of EFT seem very compatible with multicultural populations, EFT clinicians should practice educating clients on their respective culturally driven norms, values, and experiences regarding emotions in their relationship.
Feminist critique	EFT for couples needs to be adapted to the contemporary reality of gender ideology, sociocultural changes, contemporary economic reality, and the new intensified primacy of emotions in relationships.

EFT, emotionally focused therapy.

Note: This table provides a breakdown of key therapeutic tenets, multicultural considerations, and feminist critiques of the EFT model. Further reading is required for a comprehensive understanding of the approach.

Sources: Data from Gehart, D. R. (2017). *Mastering competencies in family therapy: A practical approach to theory and clinical case documentation* (3rd ed.). Brooks/Cole; Greenman, P. S., Young, M. Y., & Johnson, S. M. (2009). Emotionally focused couple therapy with intercultural couples. In M. Rastogi & V. Thomas (Eds.), *Multicultural couple therapy* (pp. 143–165). Sage. https://doi .org/10.4135/9781452275000.n8; Johnson, S. M. (2019). *The practice of emotionally focused marital therapy: Creating connection.* Brunner-Routledge; Vatcher, C.-A., & Bogo, M. (2001). The feminist/emotionally focused therapy practice model: An integrated approach for couple therapy. *Journal of Marital and Family Therapy, 27*(1), 69–83. https://doi.org/10.1111/j.1752-0606.2001.tb01140.x.

attachment-based emotions that they may have difficulty facing. The clinician's empathic responses stimulate client introspection. For example:

> *Clinician:* What keeps coming out as anger toward her for her behavior at work is coming from your core fear that the men at work will start to mean more to her than you.

Another example:

> *Clinician:* I can tell that part of you is very angry and you are very comfortable with the expression of anger. Also, everybody in the family seems both comfortable and intimidated by this part of you. I wonder if you're comfortable expressing the deep hurt and regret that is beneath this anger.

Softening

Couples do not often listen very carefully to one another when emotionality has been heightened and there is an accusatory tone to their partner's comments. The most common response to such behavior is defensiveness. When a clinician softens the critical partner's comments, there is increased responsiveness, and the other partner can empathically listen to what is being stated. Clinicians using an EFT orientation must explore, heighten, and soften emotions so that new dialogue can be created and attachment injuries can be addressed. For example:

> *Client:* I don't even know what to say about his behavior. I feel so . . . blown out of the water!
>
> *Clinician:* I can imagine how frustrating it is to be unsure how to express yourself. I wonder if you would allow me to add to your words some of the things I think I hear you saying.
>
> *Client:* Okay, let's hear it.
>
> *Clinician:* As I offer what I think I hear you saying, please pay close attention to what does and what doesn't fit your experience, and we will talk about it afterwards.
>
> *Client:* Sounds good.
>
> *Clinician:* I wonder if you might be trying to tell Jim "You are everything to me, and I feel so scared when I feel like I'm not the most important person to you"? Does that describe your experience?
>
> *Client:* It was accurate; however, I usually don't tell him things like "You are everything to me."

Another example:

> *Client:* I can't believe you are such a nasty bitch. Who would have an affair on the internet?
>
> *Clinician:* Josh, I can tell you are so angry. I want you to go ahead and take a look at Jeremiah. Do you think he really understands what you are saying right now?
>
> *Client:* Probably not, but I don't know what else to say.
>
> *Clinician:* Josh, I can tell you are so angry. Please take a look at Jeremiah. Jeremiah, I hear Josh saying he was very hurt to learn of your affair and he desperately wants to know why you had an intimate relationship with someone online.

Evocative Responding

The clinician offers open questions to expand a client's ability to understand certain emotional experiences. Using clear and concise examples, metaphors, and concrete language, the clinician begins to stimulate a client's action tendency, physical response, and related desires. For example:

> *Clinician:* What happens when you hear your husband talking like this, John? When he talks about feeling cornered and confined, how do you feel?

Another example:

> *Clinician:* What happened right there, Alan? Mary said that she has never felt taken care of in this relationship, and then you closed your lips and folded your arms across your chest.

Heightening

At times, the EFT-oriented clinician must heighten emotions to access the core attachment injuries and underlying messages. To heighten emotions, the clinician will use repetition, metaphors, encounter, and images. For example:

> *Clinician:* So, could you say that again, directly to her, that you do shut her out?
> *Client:* I do shut you out!

Another example:

> *Clinician:* It seems like this is so difficult for you, like climbing a cliff, so scary.
> *Client:* It is terrifying.

Empathic Conjecture/Interpretation

The clinician will sometimes offer a tentative guess at immediate, implicit client experience. This skill should be used judiciously and accurately. For example:

> *Client:* I'm not sure how to say it, but if she wanted me, I could tell she loved me. I mean daily.

> *Clinician:* I'm not sure I quite understand. Is it like, if she doesn't desire me every day, I've lost her? That's the signal you rely on to assure yourself that she's still here, that she wants you. Is that it?

Another example:

> *Clinician:* I think what you're trying to convey to Scott is, "I threaten the relationship, raise my voice, and even say mean things, not to hurt you, but to ensure that you love me." Is that it?

Personal/Process Disclosure

The clinician uses personal disclosure when they share relevant information about self. Process disclosure occurs when the clinician shares their own here-and-now reactions, intentions, or limitations. For example:

> *Client:* My partner of 20 years has recently left me for another man. I can't help but wonder if he didn't find me attractive anymore. I have been feeling so disgusted with myself. I keep wondering if I should have been doing things differently.

Clinician: Rich, I have been in a similar situation, and it took me a long time to realize that it wasn't my fault—that no matter what or how much I did, my partner still would have left. Does my experience have any usefulness to you?

Another example:

Client: I feel so down on myself. My partner is so mean to me, and often I think she's right. I really can't do much of anything well.

Clinician: There have been times when I've also felt down on myself, so I can sense how discouraged you are. Sometimes, too, hurtful comments from someone close to me has made me feel even worse, although I've learned how to value myself regardless of critical comments from those I care about.

SUMMARY

This chapter focused on understanding the skills and techniques used in couple, marriage, and family counseling. The chapter began with a review of management, cotherapy, and reflection teams. Next, readers were introduced to foundational systemic interventions and core counseling skills (i.e., invitational skills, attending skills, and influencing skills) and their relevance to systemic practice. The chapter concluded with a thorough review of interventions salient to the major schools of marriage and family therapy, accompanied by a concise breakdown of the theoretical tenets and leaders of each model. Students are encouraged to further hone their skills by applying model-specific and systemic interventions to the case studies included in the Student Activities section of the chapter.

END-OF-CHAPTER RESOURCES

 SPRINGER PUBLISHING CONNECT™ | A robust set of instructor resources designed to supplement this text is located at http://connect.springerpub.com/content/book/978-0-8261-8775-8. Qualifying instructors may request access by emailing **textbook@springerpub.com**.

STUDENT ACTIVITIES

Case Illustration and Questions 1: Vanessa, Tom, and Viola

Family Demographics:

- Mother/Partner: Vanessa, 22 years of age, cisgender woman, Hispanic, waitress, middle-class, born on the East Coast, United States
- Father/Partner: Tom, 30 years of age, cisgender man, Caucasian, military, middle-class, born in the Midwest, United States
- Daughter: Viola, 10 months of age, cisgender girl, biracial, middle-class, born on the East Coast, United States

Family Narrative and Presenting Problem:

Vanessa and Tom have been married for 3 years. Vanessa has been having a difficult time balancing home and work obligations. Tom has been having a difficult time adjusting to married life and parenthood. Tom mentions that he has a problem with how fixated Vanessa is on the baby, Vanessa's constant criticisms, and their inability to provide adequate childcare to their 10-month-old daughter Viola. Vanessa describes her relationship with Tom as chaotic at best. Vanessa wishes that Tom would take care of her instead of being so needy. She mentions that she is always comforting Tom regarding issues with his work, personal relationships, and feelings of inferiority. She says, "I just want him to be a man." The couple mentions that they adore their new child and feel that Viola is the only thing holding them together. They describe her as being an incredible amount of work and admit that this workload is far more than they could have ever predicted. Tom mentioned he has considered breaking up with Vanessa; however, he is often reminded of his own parents breaking up when he was child.

Observations:

- Couple seems very factual and monotone.
- Vanessa physically moves and stares at the floor when Tom mentions providing adequate childcare.
- The couple spends a lot of time looking at Viola (who is in a baby carrier, on the floor, sleeping).
- When Vanessa mentions "I just want him to be a man," Tom becomes tearful.

Questions:

- If you were to use a transgenerational theoretical model, what techniques would you use to create awareness and change?
- How will you point out nonverbals with this couple?
- How will you address the problem of workload at home?
- How do couple issues such as these connect with your personal feelings and life experiences? How will you bracket these experiences to best serve the couple?

■ What relational issues are the individuals and family currently dealing with?

■ When you inquire about the inadequate childcare, Tom mentions that when he goes on business trips Vanessa will go out to the bar after their child is asleep. What exactly will you say to this couple following this disclosure?

■ What are some paths you might take with this couple in provoking change?

Case Illustration and Questions 2: Darlene, Natalia, and José

Family Demographics:

■ Mother (single parent): Darlene, 42 years of age, cisgender woman, Hispanic, works in sales, middle-class, born on the East Coast, United States

■ Daughter: Natalia, 14 years of age, cisgender girl, Hispanic, high school student, middle-class, born on the East Coast, United States

■ Son: José, 7 years of age, cisgender boy, Hispanic, grade school student, middle-class, born on the East Coast, United States

Family Narrative and Presenting Problem:

Darlene brought her children into therapy and mentioned that the family is having trouble. Darlene seems very expressive about the problems her family is having. She describes herself as "being pulled in too many directions." She mentions that her son José has been acting up a lot lately and was given a written warning by the police for skateboarding in a restricted area. She adds that he is typically "a good kid" but recently has been hanging out with an older group of boys who are into skateboarding and a popular computer game that José spends countless hours playing. The computer game has begun to affect his schoolwork and dominates almost every conversation he has with Darlene and Natalia. Darlene mentions that this is only the tip of the iceberg. She describes her daughter Natalia as typically being "a great kid," yet Darlene feels Natalia has made some poor decisions lately. According to Darlene, Natalia recently sent a cell phone picture of her bare chest to a close friend as a joke. After the friend received the picture, she decided to send it to 15 of her closest friends, and the consequence of this was most of her class seeing a picture of her chest by the next day. According to Darlene, when Natalia came to school the next day, she received cruel notes and flirtatious looks from various peers. This was so devastating that Natalia spent the better part of a week in tears, locked up in her room, and entered a new high school the following week. In addition, Natalia mentions that her grandmother (the family matriarch) called her "a little slut" when she found out about the cell phone incident. She mentioned that she now hates her grandmother and feels like "a loser." José mentions that he is doing well, and he doesn't like hearing about Darlene and Natalia's issues. He describes their problems as "girl stuff."

Observations:

■ Darlene seems expressive with hands and body (i.e., moving forward at times and describing things with hand gestures). She dominates the session. Darlene seems hesitant to disclose too much about Natalia in front of José.

■ Natalia is nonexpressive and has a monotone voice. She begins to become tearful when the cell phone picture is brought up, and her tearfulness escalates when her grandmother is mentioned.

■ When Natalia and Darlene have a heated conversation, José interrupts by bringing up a positive issue or making a humorous comment (e.g., "You see what I have to deal with").

■ José seems to be well-adjusted and demonstrates an appropriate range of affect.

Questions:

- If you were to use a structural theoretical model, what techniques would you use to create awareness and change?

- How will you structure your time with this family? Will you see them together, separately, or something else?

- As you work with this family you notice that Darlene dominates most conversations and simultaneously complains about how quiet her kids are. How will you deal with this problematic communication pattern (i.e., double bind)?

- During the sessions you notice that Darlene and Natalia avoid discussing the incident involving the cell phone. They both seem embarrassed about the incident and change the topic to other issues. How would you work with this issue? Describe an intervention you might use to break the ice.

- José's issues seem to be ignored, and Darlene seems focused on Natalia. José mentions he would like to talk to you privately, and Darlene agrees that this might be best. You agree and meet with José. José seems very mature for his age and describes himself as having an anger problem. Further, he mentions that he was bullied at school for a long time; however, he has started fighting the bullies. So far it has worked, and he is now respected. How would you address this issue?

Case Illustration and Questions 3: Samantha and Tyler

Family Demographics:

- Partner: Samantha, age 27, cisgender woman, Caucasian, manager of franchise restaurant, student (accounting), middle-class, born in the Midwest, United States

- Partner: Tyler, age 32, cisgender man, Caucasian, athletic trainer at a local gym, student (nursing), middle-class, born on the East Coast, United States

Couple Narrative and Presenting Problem:

Samantha and Tyler have been together for approximately 7 years. They live in a small city working in their respective professional settings. They both mention wanting to stay together; however, they do not know how to make their relationship work. They have been having frequent arguments and they both feel the other has changed since they first met. In addition, they have different goals and expectations. Samantha is interested in taking their relationship to the next level. She wants the couple to consider buying a house, getting married, and having children in the next few years. Tyler has different goals and expectations for the couple. He would like to achieve a promotion at work and focus on completing his degree. He is passionate about attaining wealth before he has a child or gets married. Tyler mentions that Samantha is always giving him a hard time when he takes on extra responsibilities at work. Samantha describes herself as being terrified that Tyler is cheating on her and that he is addicted to working. Tyler mentions that he has never been with another woman, and he describes his sex drive as declining due to his exhaustion from the competing interests of work and school. Samantha mentions they have not had any intimacy for 8 weeks and she is becoming extremely unhappy with their relationship.

Observations:

- The couple is showing nonverbal signs of connection (sitting close together, pointing legs toward one another, and at times holding hands).

■ The couple seems to intellectualize most of their concerns, and they appear to be actively suppressing their feelings.

■ They both smile when the topic of their initial courtship is brought up.

Questions:

■ If you were to use a strategic theoretical model, what techniques would you use to create awareness and change?

■ When you ask Samantha how Tyler has changed, she says, "He's like a different person. In the beginning we spent a lot of time together, laughed, and had deep and meaningful conversations. Now Tyler does not talk to me very much, he never laughs, and he always wants to sleep when he gets home." What would you say to Tyler and Samantha regarding their relational interaction? How would you try to bring Tyler into the dialogue?

■ You determine that a major strength for this couple is their romantic courtship. How will you use this information to strengthen the couple's bond during this challenging time?

■ The couple has different opinions/values for how they should live and what their goals should be. When you bring up their values, Tyler mentions, "I know Samantha loves me and all . . . it's just that I think she's trying to limit my success." When you look over at Samantha, she seems unemotional and uninterested. How will you address this?

Case Illustration and Questions 4: Janet, Beth, Brandon, and Jason

Family Demographics:

■ Partner: Janet, 35 years of age, cisgender woman, Caucasian, sales, middle-class, born on the East Coast, United States

■ Partner: Beth, 40 years of age, cisgender woman, Caucasian, waiting tables, middle-class, born in the Midwest, United States

■ Son: Brandon, 4 years of age, cisgender boy, Asian, middle-class, born on the East Coast, United States (adopted)

■ Son: Jason, 10 months of age, cisgender boy, Caucasian, middle-class, born on the East Coast, United States (artificial insemination)

Family Narrative and Presenting Problem:

Janet and Beth have been together for approximately 7 years. They live in rural New Hampshire and are open about their relationship despite overt and covert discrimination. Both partners wanted children; however, Beth wanted to adopt, and Janet wanted to have a biological child. They initially adopted Brandon because Beth was ready to start dedicating herself to full-time parenting. At that point, Janet was more focused on her career and was angry with Beth for not taking her desires into consideration before adopting Brandon. The couple understood that Beth would be the primary caregiver and Janet would be a more peripheral influence on Brandon's life. More recently, Janet became ready to start parenting. She chose to go to a sperm bank and become artificially inseminated without consulting Beth regarding who the donor would be and when she would get the procedure. Approximately 19 months ago, Janet came home pregnant. She waited 3 months to tell Beth about the pregnancy, and this caused a major rift between the two of them. Jason was born 10 months ago, and Janet has spent all of her free time tending to the baby (i.e., breastfeeding, playing, adoring, and teaching). Beth feels they are not really a couple and should just break up. She thinks Janet is very manipulative and thinks her secretive behavior was an attempt to get back at her for adopting Brandon. Janet does not want to break up because she feels they finally have child-rearing in common and she would be lonely living in New Hampshire without Beth.

Observations:

- Both Beth and Janet seem jovial and frequently tease one another.
- The couple looks at each other frequently.
- They are not very forthright with you in regard to their feelings for each other.
- Janet leans forward toward Beth, while Beth leans back and has her arms and legs crossed.

Questions:

- If you were to use an emotionally focused therapy model, what techniques would you use to create awareness and change?
- How will you join with this couple?
- How will you discuss their fear of exposing their sexuality to you? How will you let them know you are an open-minded person who will not reject them due to their sexual orientation?
- The couple has demonstrated poor communication and manipulation. Describe these issues. How will you try to create connection within this couple despite the various issues?
- Develop a strength-based perspective. What does this couple have going for them?
- What are some personal and situational challenges adopted children face? What are some personal and situational challenges artificially inseminated children face?

Case Illustration and Questions 5: Marti, Eugene, Brenda, and Samuel

Family Demographics:

- Mother: Marti, 38 years of age, cisgender woman, Caucasian, part-time day care, middle-class, born on the East Coast, United States
- Father: Eugene, 40 years of age, cisgender man, Caucasian, systems analyst, middle-class, born on the East Coast, United States
- Daughter: Brenda, 10 months of age, cisgender girl, Caucasian, middle-class, born on the East Coast, United States
- Son: Samuel, 2 years of age, cisgender boy, Caucasian, middle-class, born on the East Coast, United States

Couple Narrative and Presenting Problem:

Marti and Eugene have been married for 5 years. Marti has given up her career as a social worker and private practitioner to take a part-time position in a day-care center so that she can spend more time with the children. Eugene has been offered a promotion and a significant raise in salary in his career as a systems analyst, and the change will necessitate moving several states away. Marti is unhappy with the prospect of relocating and believes that Eugene should turn down the promotion to stay in their current community. Marti asserts that she has given up her career to assume more childcare responsibility and has developed a strong support system of family and friends. She is happy with her work in the day-care center and believes that Eugene should consider the sacrifices she made early in their relationship. Eugene is angry and claims that he is the primary breadwinner, and that the family should go where he has the greatest opportunity to advance his career and improve the family's financial standing. The couple mentions that they have been having communication issues for a long time. Eugene mentions that he has argued many times with Marti and has decided to stop arguing and start ignoring her whenever she brings up volatile topics. Specifically, he mentions that he does not mind talking to Marti about these topics as long as she has a calm emotional affect. He further discloses that he does not trust himself with Marti when she is overly emotional.

Observations:

- Marti and Eugene constantly glare at you (the clinician) and rarely look to each other.
- Marti and Eugene do not have much change in vocal affect (all monotone).
- Both are nicely dressed and appear to have adequate grooming.
- When the topic of career advancement is mentioned, both individuals appear angry and become red in the face.

Questions:

- If you were to use a solution-focused therapy model, what techniques would you use to create awareness and change?
- How will you join with this couple?
- How will you point out nonverbal messages with this couple?
- How will you address the obvious power issues within the couple?
- How do power issues of this sort challenge your personal feelings and life experiences?
- What would you do if Marti looked at you (as the clinician) and said, "I need your help because I feel like I have no power in this relationship," and Eugene followed with "My wife can't see the forest past the trees . . . if she recognized the big picture, she'd be on board with the move"?
- What are some paths you might take with this couple in provoking change?

ADDITIONAL RESOURCES

HELPFUL LINKS

- "Bowen Family Systems Theory and Practice: Illustration and Critique": https://www.thefsi.com.au/wp-content/uploads/2014/01/Bowen-Family-Systems-Theory-and-Practice_Illustration-and-Critique.pdf
- "What Is Structural Family Therapy?": https://www.verywellmind.com/what-is-structural-family-therapy-5193068
- "Brief Strategic Family Therapy: An Intervention to Reduce Adolescent Risk Behavior": https://www.ncbi.nlm.nih.gov/pmc/articles/PMC3737065/
- "Remembering Family Therapist Guru Virginia Satir": https://www.psychologytoday.com/us/blog/progress-notes/201908/remembering-family-therapist-guru-virginia-satir

- "What Is Solution-Focused Therapy?": https://solutionfocused.net/what-is-solution-focused-therapy/

- "19 Best Narrative Therapy Techniques and Worksheets": https://positivepsychology.com/narrative-therapy/

- "What Is EFT?": https://iceeft.com/what-is-eft/

- "A Summary of Eight Counselling Microskills": https://www.counsellingconnection.com/index.php/2012/08/09/counselling-micro-skills-a-summary/

HELPFUL BOOKS

- Brown, C., & Augusta-Scott, T. (2006). *Narrative therapy: Making meaning, making lives.* Sage Publications.

- Greenber, L. S. (2002). *Emotion-focused therapy: Coaching clients to work through their feelings.* American Psychological Association.

- Ivey, A. E., Ivey, M. B., & Zalaquett, C. P. (2017). *Intentional interviewing and counseling: Facilitating client development in a multicultural society.* Thomson/Brooks-Cole.

- Johnson, S. M. (2019). *The practice of emotionally focused marital therapy: Creating connection.* Brunner-Routledge.

- Kerr, M. E., & Bowen, M. (1988). *Family evaluation: The role of the family as an emotional unit that governs individual behavior and development.* W. W. Norton.

- Lipchik, E. (2002). *Beyond technique in solution-focused therapy: Working with emotions and the therapeutic relationship.* Guilford Press.

- Lutz, A. (2014). *Learning solution-focused therapy: An illustrated guide.* American Psychiatric Publishing.

- McGoldrick, M., Gerson, R., & Petry, S. (2008). *Genograms assessment and intervention* (3rd ed.). W. W. Norton.

- Minuchin, S., & Fishman, C. (1981). *Family therapy techniques.* Harvard University Press.

- Minuchin, S., Nichols, M., & Wai-Yung, L. (2007). *Assessing families and couples. From symptom to system.* Pearson Education.

- Napier, A., & Whittaker, C. (1988). *The family crucible: The intense experience of family therapy.* HarperCollins.

- Payne, M. (2000). *Narrative therapy: An introduction for counselors* (2nd ed.). Sage.

- Satir, V., & Baldwin, M. (1983). *Satir step by step: A guide to creating change in families.* Science and Behavior Books.

- Walsh, W. M., & McGraw, J. A. (2002). *Essentials of family therapy: A structured summary of nine approaches.* Love Publishing Company.

HELPFUL VIDEOS

- What Is Emotionally Focused Therapy (or EFT)?: https://www.youtube.com/watch?v=xQCg-jC25fo

- Sue Johnson Emotionally Focused Couples Therapy (EFT) in Action Video: https://www.youtube.com/watch?v=xaHms5z-yuM

- What Is Narrative Therapy?: https://www.youtube.com/watch?v=GoMfpmTJ28c

- Role-Play: Solution Focused Therapy: https://www.youtube.com/watch?v=T33j_ZETzUs

- ■ Insoo Kim Berg Solution-Focused Family Therapy Video: https://www.youtube.com/watch?v=6Fe8D0hAQh0

- ■ Virginia Satir Therapy Video: https://www.youtube.com/watch?v=hLfaNQF7trs

- ■ Satir Family Therapy: https://www.youtube.com/watch?v=ql3mPOcX7kY

- ■ What Is Strategic Family Therapy?: https://www.youtube.com/watch?v=jPNT8C3A-wU

- ■ Strategic Couples Therapy Video: https://www.youtube.com/watch?v=6tku1SkU_9c

- ■ Structural Family Therapy Example: https://www.youtube.com/watch?v=bOrnOcHWXgA

- ■ Minuchin and Structural Family Therapy: https://www.youtube.com/watch?v=7UAuAheYrsk

- ■ Transgenerational Family Counseling: https://www.youtube.com/watch?v=2xrrcfqf2ew

REFERENCES

Andersen, T. (1991). *The reflecting team: Dialogues and dialogues about the dialogues.* W. W. Norton.

Ashton, D., & Jordal, C. (2019). Re-visioning gender, re-visioning power: Equity, accountability, and refusing to silo. In M. McGoldrick & K. Hardy (Eds.), *Re-visioning family therapy: Addressing diversity in clinical practice* (3rd ed., pp. 28–43). Guilford Press.

Berger, R. (2000). The goodness of fit between the reflecting team approach and stepfamilies' problems and issues. *Journal of Systemic Therapies, 19*(2), 43–55. https://doi.org/10.1521/jsyt.2000.19.2.43

Bermudez, D. (2008). Adapting Virginia Satir techniques to Hispanic families. *The Family Journal, 16*(1), 51–57. https://doi.org/10.1177/1066480707309543

Chang, J. (2010). The reflecting team: A training method for family counselors. *The Family Journal, 18*(1), 36–44. https://doi.org/10.1177/1066480709357731

Cognitive Behavioral Therapy Los Angeles. (2020). *Part 6: Cognitive restructuring to change your thinking.* Cognitive Behavioral Therapy Los Angeles. Retrieved April 25, 2022, from https://cogbtherapy.com/cognitive-restructuring-in-cbt#:~:text=Cognitive%20restructuring%20refers%20to%20the,or%20more%20skillful%20behavior

Connell, C. (2010). Doing, undoing, or redoing gender? *Gender & Society, 24*(1), 31–55. https://doi.org/10.1177/0891243209356429

Cormier, L. S., Nurius, P., & Osborn, C. J. (2017). *Interviewing and change strategies for helpers* (8th ed.). Cengage Learning.

Dattilio, F. M. (2001). Cognitive–behavior family therapy: Contemporary myths and misconceptions. *Contemporary Family Therapy: An International Journal, 23*(1), 3–18. https://doi.org/10.1023/A:1007807214545

Dattilio, F. M., & Epstein, N. B. (2021). Cognitive behavioral couple and family therapy. In A. Wenzel (Ed.), *Handbook of cognitive behavioral therapy: Applications* (Vol. 2, pp. 513–548). American Psychological Association. https://doi.org/10.1037/0000219-016

Dermer, S. B., Hemesath, C. W., & Russell, C. S. (1998). A feminist critique of solution-focused therapy. *The American Journal of Family Therapy, 26*(3), 239–250. https://doi.org/10.1080/01926189808251103

Flynn, S. V., & Hays, D. G. (2015). The development and validation of the comprehensive counseling skills rubric. *Counseling Outcome Research and Evaluation.* https://doi.org/10.1177/2150137815592216

Friedberg, R. D. (2006). A cognitive-behavioral approach to family therapy. *Journal of Contemporary Psychotherapy, 36*(4), 159–165. https://doi.org/10.1007/s10879-006-9020-2

Gehart, D. R. (2017). *Mastering competencies in family therapy: A practical approach to theory and clinical case documentation* (3rd ed.). Brooks/Cole.

Greenman, P. S., Young, M. Y., & Johnson, S. M. (2009). Emotionally focused couple therapy with intercultural couples. *In* M. Rastogi & V. Thomas (Eds.), *Multicultural couple therapy* (pp. 143–165). Sage. https://doi.org/10.4135/9781452275000.n8

Guanipa, C. (2003). Sharing a multicultural course design for a marriage and family therapy programme: One perspective. *Journal of Family Therapy, 25*(1), 86–106. https://doi.org/10.1111/1467-6427.00236

Hackett, D. (2011). Role-playing. In S. Goldstein & J. A. Naglieri (Eds.), *Encyclopedia of child behavior and development* (pp. 1278–1279). Springer. https://doi.org/10.1007/978-0-387-79061-9_2466

Hare-Mustin, R. T. (1987). The problem of gender in family therapy theory. *Family Process, 26*(1), 15–27. https://doi.org/10.1111/j.1545-5300.1987.00015.x

Harmon, C., Hawkins, E. J., Lambert, M. J., Slade, K., & Whipple, J. S. (2005). Improving outcomes for poorly responding clients: The use of clinical support tools and feedback to clients. *Journal of Clinical Psychology, 61*(2), 175–185. https://doi.org/10.1002/jclp.20109

Hays, P. A. (2009). Integrating evidence-based practice, cognitive–behavior therapy, and multicultural therapy: Ten steps for culturally competent practice. *Professional Psychology: Research and Practice, 40*(4), 354–360. https://doiorg.libproxy.plymouth.edu/10.1037/a0016250

Hoffman, L. (1995). Foreword. In S. Friedman (Ed.), *The reflecting team in action: Collaborative practice in family therapy* (pp. ix–xiv). Guilford.

Holyoake, D.-D., & Golding, E. (2012). Multiculturalism and solution-focused psychotherapy: An exploration of the nonexpert role. *Asia Pacific Journal of Counselling and Psychotherapy, 3*(1), 72–81. https://doi.org/10.1080/21507686.2011.651479

Howes, C., & Spieker, S. (2008). Attachment relationships in the context of multiple caregivers. In J. Cassidy & P. R. Shaver (Eds.), *Handbook of attachment: Theory, research, and clinical applications* (pp. 317–332). Guilford Press.

Isaacson, K., & Furrow, J. L. (2017). Role playing in couple and family therapy. In J. Lebow, A. Chambers, & D. Breunlin (Eds.), *Encyclopedia of couple and family therapy* (pp. 1–2). Springer. https://doi.org/10.1007/978-3-319-15877-8_94-1

Ivey, A. E., Ivey, M. B., & Zalaquett, C. P. (2017). *Intentional interviewing and counseling: Facilitating client development in a multicultural society.* Thomson/Brooks-Cole.

Kağitçibasi, Ç. (1996). The autonomous-relational self: A new synthesis. *European Psychologist, 1*(3), 180–186. https://doi.org/10.1027/1016-9040.1.3.180

Kjellberg, E., Edwardsson, M., Niemela, B. J., & Oberg, T. (1995). Using the reflecting process with families stuck in violence and child abuse. In S. Friedman (Ed.), *The reflecting team in action* (pp. 38–61). Guilford Press.

Lax, W. D. (1989). Systemic family therapy with young children in the family: Use of the reflecting team. In J. J. Zilbach (Ed.), *Children in family therapy* (pp. 55–74). Haworth.

Lee, J. (2008). Women re-authoring their lives through feminist narrative therapy. *Women & Therapy, 20*(3), 1–22. https://doi.org/10.1300/J015v20n03_01

Lerner, G. (1986). *The creation of patriarchy.* Oxford University Press.

Manhattan Center for Cognitive Behavioral Therapy. (2021, May 15). *How to use the downward arrow technique in CBT.* Retrieved April 25, 2022, from https://www.manhattancbt.com/downward-arrow-technique/

Metcalf, L. (2018). *Marriage and family therapy: A practice oriented approach* (2nd ed.). Springer Publishing Company.

Nelsen, J. (2006). *Positive discipline: A classic guide to helping children develop self-discipline, responsibility, cooperation, and problem-solving skills* [Rev.]. Ballantine.

Nichols, M. P., & Davis, S. D. (2020). *The essentials of family therapy.* Pearson Education.

Patterson, J., Williams, L., Edwards, T., Chamow, L., & Grauf-Grounds, C. (2018). *Essential skills in family therapy: From the first interview to termination* (3rd ed.). Guilford Press.

Penfold, P. S. (1989). Family therapy: Critique from a feminist perspective. *The Canadian Journal of Psychiatry, 34*(4), 311–315. https://doi.org/10.1177/070674378903400408

Reiter, M. D. (2013). *Case conceptualization in marriage and family therapy.* Pearson Education.

Rice, R. H. (2015). Cognitive-behavioral therapy. In: E. S. Neukrug (Ed.), *The SAGE encyclopedia of theory in counseling and psychotherapy* (Vol. 1, pp. 194–199). Sage.

Roller, B., & Nelson, V. (1991). *The art of co-therapy: How therapists work together.* Guilford Press.

Russell, C. S., Atilano, R. B., Anders, S. A., Jurich, A. P., & Bergen, L. P. (1984). Intervention strategies: Predicting family therapy outcome. *Journal of Marital and Family Therapy, 10*(3), 241–251. https://doi.org/10.1111/j.1752-0606.1984.tb00015.x

Safran, J. D. (1998). *Widening the scope of cognitive therapy.* Bookmart Press.

Satir, V., & Baldwin, M. (1983). *Satir step by step: A guide to creating change in families.* Science and Behavior Books.

Sells, S. P., Smith, T. E., Coe, M. J., Yoshioka, M., & Robbins, J. (1994). An ethnography of couple and therapist experiences in reflecting team practice. *Journal of Marital and Family Therapy, 20,* 247–266. https://doi.org/10.1111/j.1752-0606.1994.tb00114.x

Selvini, M. P., Boscolo, L., Cecchin, G., & Prata, G. (1979). Hypothesizing—circularity—neutrality: Three guidelines for the conductor of the session. *Family Process, 19*(1), 3–12. https://doi.org/10.1111/j.1545-5300.1980.00003.x

Shallcross, L. (2010, February 14). Managing resistant clients. *Counseling Today*. https://ct.counseling.org/2010/02/managing-resistant-clients/#

Storm, C. L., York, C. D., & Sheehy, P. T. (1990). Supervision of cotherapists. *Journal of Family Psychotherapy, 1*(1), 65–74. https://doi.org/10.1300/j085v01n01_06

Vatcher, C.-A., & Bogo, M. (2001). The feminist/emotionally focused therapy practice model: An integrated approach for couple therapy. *Journal of Marital and Family Therapy, 27*(1), 69–83. https://doi.org/10.1111/j.1752-0606.2001.tb01140.x

Walsh, W. M., & McGraw, J. A. (2002). *Essentials of family therapy: A structured summary of nine approaches*. Love Publishing Company.

Watzlawick, P., Weakland, J. H., & Fisch, R. (1974). *Change: Principles of problem formation and problem resolution*. W. W. Norton.

Whitaker, C. A., & Keith, D. V. (1983). Family therapy as symbolic experience. *International Journal of Family Psychiatry, 1*, 197–208.

Williams, M. T., Skinta, M. D., & Martin-Willett, R. (2021). After pierce and sue: a revised racial microaggressions taxonomy. *Perspectives on Psychological Science, 16*(5), 991–1007. https://doi.org/10.1177/1745691621994247

Yalom, I. D. (1980). *Existential psychotherapy*. Basic Books.

Young, M. E. (2016). *Learning the art of helping: Building blocks and techniques* (6th ed.). Merrill.

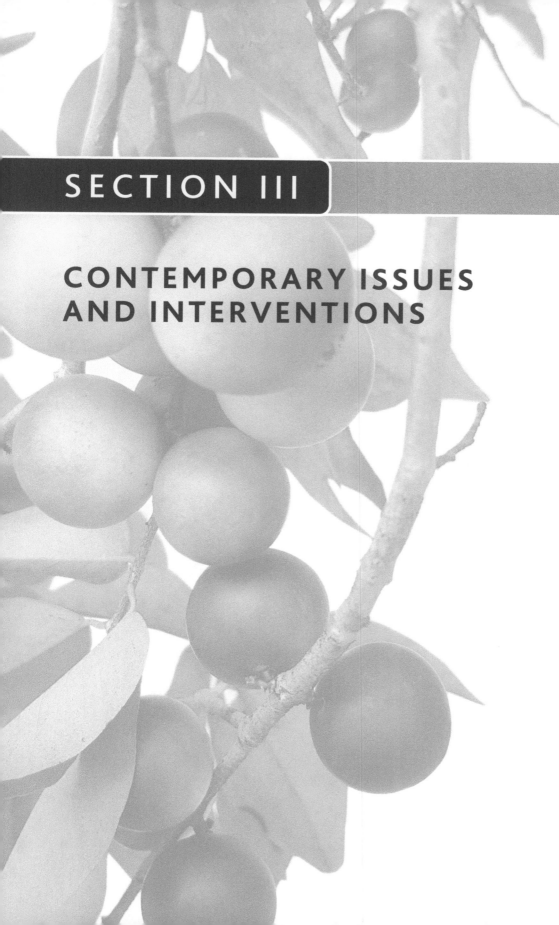

SECTION III

CONTEMPORARY ISSUES AND INTERVENTIONS

CHAPTER 5

RACISM, DISCRIMINATION, AND UNDERREPRESENTED FAMILIES

LEARNING OBJECTIVES

After reading this chapter, you will be able to:

- Identify family-based racism and discrimination.
- Demonstrate the skills for helping clients with racism stress management.
- Identify racial and ethnic socialization.
- Demonstrate the relevant skills and interventions for working with interracial couples.
- Recognize the skills and techniques for understanding and helping families cope with ethnic microaggressions.
- Identify homophobia and other issues relevant to the LGBTQIA+ population.
- Distinguish the relational and family experiences of families who adopt children.

INTRODUCTION TO CONTEMPORARY RACISM AND DISCRIMINATION

Black, Indigenous, and People of Color (BIPOC) are under threat in the United States and have been for a long time. This chapter will start by focusing briefly on the recent experiences that have deeply affected the African American/Black and Asian American and Pacific Islander (AAPI) communities. Please note, this chapter is centered on highlighting key contemporary issues related to racism and discrimination; it is not a comprehensive review of social justice and multiculturally based issues or populations. For a more comprehensive review, please consider reading Sue et al.'s (2019) textbook entitled *Counseling the Culturally Diverse: Theory and Practice*.

Voices From the Field

This chapter features sections entitled Voices From the Field. These sections explore multicultural, social justice, equity, diversity, and intersectionality issues from the perspective of clinicians representing a wide range of ethnic, racial, and national backgrounds. The purpose of adding quotes from individuals representing communities of color or who frequently serve diverse populations is to provide you, the reader, with cutting-edge social justice and multiculturally oriented skills, interventions, and clinical conceptualization. The four clinicians who took part in this chapter's Voices From the Field segments came from different life contexts, racial and ethnic backgrounds, and diverse intersections of cultural advantage and disadvantage. Participant background information is provided below:

Dr. Sherritta Hughes, a 43-year-old African American woman, is a licensed professional counselor and approved clinical supervisor. She is an associate professor at Georgian Court University, where she also serves as program director and lead therapist. Dr. Hughes has over 17 years of experience conducting professional counseling with a variety of client populations.

Ms. Alexandra Manigault, a 29-year-old biracial African American and Caucasian woman, is a licensed marriage and family therapist. Ms. Manigault provides clinic-based, trauma-informed treatment to help teens and families mitigate problematic sexual behavior.

Ms. Tahira Matthews, a 29-year-old African American woman, is a licensed associate counselor, national certified counselor, and certified school social worker. As a school social worker, Ms. Matthews serves as a liaison between the parents, the school, and the sending district; assists with crisis intervention; and provides direct counseling services to students and their families.

Ms. Yu-Wei Wang, a 26-year-old Taiwanese woman, is a marriage and family therapy candidate. Ms. Wang is a clinician specializing in individual, couple, marriage, and family therapy within an agency setting.

....

Participants were sent a questionnaire featuring eight open-ended questions regarding their experiences practicing in the field. Participant quotes are placed throughout the chapter to enhance the content. Participant questions are as follows:

- As clinicians, we have been trained to analyze and explore the nature and interconnectedness of families and couples. In your personal experience with this work, what are the effects of racism, bias, and/or hate on family units? Have you had the opportunity to use any skills and/or interventions that have helped to reduce the painful effects of racism, bias, or hate?

- Racism-related stress refers to the psychological distress related to experiences of racism. Unfortunately, this form of stress is unavoidable for many clients and professionals due to the prevalence of overt and covert racism and racist acts. How have you worked with clients to manage racism-related stress?

- As clinicians, we can work deeply with families in ways that give us a different look into their dynamics. Parents of BIPOC children are often tasked with the responsibility of providing them with racial and ethnic socialization. As clinicians, we can do something similar with our clients by intentionally addressing race-related stress and trauma. How have you used racial and ethnic socialization as a tool in the therapeutic process?

- BIPOC professionals may experience greater burnout due to racism/discrimination-related compassion fatigue and/or vicarious trauma. How has having to cope with this racism-related stress affected your work as a clinician?

- When microaggressions are perceived in therapy, they can interfere with the therapeutic process. Within your own work, how has your knowledge of ethnic and racial microaggressions aided you as a clinician? Conversely, does your inexperience with microaggressions ever come up during the therapeutic process?

- When working with clients, it is important to understand intersectionality to be able to fully comprehend their identity, levels of privilege, and disadvantage(s). It is also important to understand our own intersectional identities for the same reasons. How do you think your intersectional identity impacts your presence in the therapy room?

- When working with underrepresented families in therapy, it is important to address the barriers they face in order to obtain mental health treatment. How do you as a clinician ensure you are able to build trust and form relationships with clients who are part of underrepresented communities?

■ How has your work as a clinician differed when your clients are in an interracial relationship? How has a difference in privilege within these couples affected the work you do with them?

Black Lives Matter and Anti-Asian American and Pacific Islander Sentiment

This chapter begins with a review of the tragic death of Breonna Taylor at the hands of Louisville, Kentucky police. The March 2020 shooting and killing of Breonna Taylor, a Black woman and ED technician, and the subsequent nonindictment of the officers who shot Ms. Taylor, is a clear case of a tragic injustice that was influenced by systemic racism, discrimination, and nonaccountability within the Louisville Metro Police Department (LMPD), the state of Kentucky, and the country. On March 13, 2020, plain-clothed officers forced entry into Ms. Taylor's apartment to investigate alleged drug-related activities on the part of Kenneth Walker (Breonna's ex-boyfriend). When the officers breached the door, Mr. Walker fired a warning shot at the floor from a personal handgun. After this warning shot was fired, the officers responded by firing 32 rounds of ammunition into Ms. Taylor's dark apartment. Ms. Taylor was hit and killed by six bullets. The jury found that LMPD Detective Myles Cosgrove and Sergeant Jonathan Mattingly were justified in returning fire after they were shot at by Ms. Taylor's boyfriend. The combination of killing an unarmed and innocent Black woman and the lack of accountability for the firing officers has caused many to feel that this was a grave sense of injustice, discrimination, systemic racism, and bias. The issue for many is that nonuniformed police broke into Ms. Taylor's apartment, shot 32 rounds into the dark, and killed Ms. Taylor under the protection of a no-knock warrant. Ms. Taylor was not only an innocent victim of this approach to policing, but her death has gone largely unjustified and unaccounted for (Oppel et al., 2021).

The story of Ms. Taylor and the countless other Black people who have been brutalized by police has been made visible partly because of the Black Lives Matter (BLM) movement. BLM is a decentralized social movement started in 2013 with the hashtag *#BlackLivesMatter* and has gained an incredible amount of momentum in recent years. The BLM movement is centered on stopping racially motivated violence against Black people. The BLM movement was partly initiated because of the police brutality and shootings of Black people including, but not limited to, Trayvon Martin (1995–2012), Michael Brown (1996–2014), Eric Garner (1970–2014), Breonna Taylor (1993–2020), and George Floyd (1973–2020). According to Buchanan et al. (2020), the BLM movement may be the largest movement in U.S. history. The peak of the BLM movement was on June 6, 2020, when peaceful protestors turned out in approximately 550 locations across the United States. The authors note that the majority of the counties that have protested have been more than 75% White. This is likely a reflection of the public opinion regarding the BLM movement and its importance and a reflection of a country that was prepared for protesting due to the various policies (e.g., immigration, gun control, climate change) President Donald Trump and his allies promoted and/or defunded while in office (Buchanan et al., 2020).

Three important antecedents have added to the anti-Asian AAPI sentiment and the rise in hate crimes currently taking place in the United States: (a) the historical treatment of Asians in America (e.g., Page and Chinese Exclusion Acts, perpetual foreigner stereotype, 1871 massacre of 19 Chinese Americans in Los Angeles), (b) American leadership and scapegoating around the COVID-19 pandemic, and (c) the Atlanta area spa shooting on March 16, 2021 (Abrams, 2021; Arguelles, 2021). These events have at least partly led to a significant increase in incidents of hate and xenophobia within the AAPI community and the anti-Asian peaceful protests around the world. While these recent events are both tragic and terrifying, it is important to understand that the current spike in anti-AAPI sentiment is not new. During the 19th and 20th centuries, AAPI living in America were treated very poorly. Examples of this include, but are not limited to, frequent discrimination and racism, laws that taxed Chinese gold miners and forbade land ownership, the Chinese Exclusion Act of 1882, and the incarceration of over 120,000 Japanese Americans during World War II (Arguelles, 2021).

According to Campbell (2021), anti-Asian hate crimes in 2021 were up by 164% in the nation's largest cities and counties. Similarly, Venkatraman (2021) reported that 2020 showed a 73% increase in anti-Asian hate crimes in the United States. The increase in Asian hate seems to be partly stemming from comments made by former President Donald Trump and his allies, who falsely blamed Asian and Asian American communities for creating COVID-19. For example, racist rhetoric such as "China virus," "Kung flu," and "Wuhan virus" opened the door for a significant increase in AAPI racism, acts of discrimination, and cultural scapegoating. As anti-Asian sentiment steadily increased in 2020 and early 2021 due to the pandemic-related leadership issues, a tragic shooting spree on March 16, 2021, occurring at three separate spas in the metropolitan area of Atlanta, Georgia, took the lives of eight people, six of whom were Asian women. Although the perpetrator, Robert Aaron Long, was not accused of executing a hate crime, this event served as a powerful antecedent to anti-Asian protests in cities across the world (Abrams, 2021; Arguelles, 2021; Campbell, 2021; Venkatraman, 2021).

RACISM, DISCRIMINATION, AND UNDERREPRESENTED FAMILIES

Race, ethnicity, gender, gender identity, sexual orientation, religion, and culture are key conversations currently taking place around the world. It can be difficult for many people to discuss these issues because they may have a sense of fear that this topic could lead to uncomfortable and/or negative interpersonal experiences (e.g., sadness, discomfort, anger, guilt, shame, and awkwardness). Conversations of this sort could be especially uncomfortable for those who have benefited from cultural privilege and the current status quo. A percentage of individuals may enjoy a special cultural advantage due to factors like skin color, heritage, and socioeconomic status. You may be asking yourself, "Why would these individuals want to give up this unearned social status, power, and privilege?" The truth is many do not and will not unless they see a personal advantage in doing so. For example, most would not choose to be profiled by local police, want to be fearful of walking alone at nighttime, or be paid less than their colleagues. This is part of the reason clinicians are being trained to advocate and empower individuals who have experienced stigma, marginalization, bigotry, and hate (e.g., social justice).

Racism is a major issue affecting individuals and families today. Racism, hate, bigotry, and discrimination are persistent cultural issues that have led to widespread public condemnation. Despite public disapproval, when families and couples present for therapy with experiences of racism, discrimination, bigotry, and hatred, many clinicians feel confused about how to help. The bombardment of hurtful emotional experiences and the omnipresent effects of racism, bigotry, discrimination, and racial micro- and macroaggressions can cause clinicians to feel they are empathizing, empowering, and advocating for clients against an immense, multilayered system. Simultaneous to the confusion around how to help clients cope against an all-pervading system, many clients are presenting with a chronic state of racial battle fatigue due to experiencing the frequent attacks of micro- and macroracism and hatred. This sense of racial battle fatigue can cause physical and psychological exhaustion, among other negative effects (Sue et al., 2019).

Some clinicians assume that the general population wants racism, discrimination, bigotry, and hatred to disappear as much as they do. This is partly due to the professional, political, and social circles most clinicians live in; the ethos of multicultural and social justice training in clinical programs; and the humanistic/nonhatred-oriented professional literature. While the therapeutic world may stand in solidarity against such acts, the general population is a mixed bag (e.g., nonracist, ambiguous/neutral, racist). According to Sue et al. (2019), there are a number of reasons nonracist people fail to act against hatred, racism, bigotry, and discrimination, including "(a) the invisibility of modern forms of bias, (b) trivializing an incident as innocuous, (c) diffusion of responsibility, (d) fear of repercussions or retaliation, and (e) the paralysis of not knowing what to do" (p. 128).

Social justice scholars and advocates indicate that institutional, structural, and cultural racism have created a culture of White supremacy in the United States. These large-scale racist structures manifest as cultural policies, practices, and social arrangements. Huber and Solorzano (2014) created the term *macroaggression* to describe these racist-born policies and practices. One of the negative outcomes of macroaggressions is police brutality against people of color (POC). For example, according to Edwards et al. (2019), police violence is a leading cause of death of young Black men in the United States. The authors state that approximately 1 in every 1,000 Black men are killed by police. In addition to the brutal deaths of POC, policing communities of color in an unfair and unbalanced manner is one example of using power to maintain the structural inequalities between racial groups. Police racial profiling is an example of a frequent microaggression which creates a detrimental impact on POC, including physical and mental health issues (e.g., anxiety, paranoia).

Additional individual and large-scale *POC-specific* stressors like pay inequity, unusually large workloads compared with other cultural groups, discrimination in housing, and negative health issues are frequently correlated with poor intimate partnership outcomes (Pager & Shepherd, 2008; Randall & Bodenmann, 2009). These obvious forms of inequity add to the perceptions of social devaluing that many communities of color have (Steele et al., 2002). Furthermore, these issues, and others, can create a psychological response (e.g., anger, helplessness, fear, jealousy, frustration) and/or a physiologic reaction (e.g., immune, neuroendocrine, cardiovascular). These responses can relate to an immediate negative coping response (e.g., avoidance, alcohol use, passivity) and poor relationship outcome and/or quality (e.g., relational instability, avoiding a partner, overpursuing a partner, infidelity). Table 5.1 breaks down the definitions of key terms that will be explored in the chapter. Please explore the following International City/County Management Association (ICMA) website for a more comprehensive list of social justice terms and definitions: https://icma.org/glossary-terms-race-equity-and-social-justice.

VOICES FROM THE FIELD: SHERRITTA

Dr. Sherritta Hughes shared her experiences working with couples and families around racism, bias, and hate.

Experiences within the systems that families function within show up in the daily burdens that are carried by each generation of the family, including children, parents, and grandparents. The burdens carried often correlate to the lowering of psychological functioning that surfaces as frustration, pessimism, poor grades, and bad performance. People don't always open up about what is *really* wrong. The ideas about what is really wrong would call for such families to delve into vulnerable spaces of thought and narratives about how they were looked at like criminals,

TABLE 5.1   KEY TERMS AND DEFINITIONS

Racism	Prejudice, discrimination, or antagonism directed against a person or people on the basis of their membership in a particular racial or ethnic group, typically one that is a community of color or marginalized
Discrimination	The unjust or prejudicial treatment of different categories of people or things, especially on the grounds of race, age, or sex
Marginalization	The treatment of a person, group, or concept as insignificant or peripheral
Prejudice	A feeling toward a person based on their perceived group membership; the word is often used to refer to a preconceived evaluation or classification of another person based on that person's perceived characteristics
Bias	Prejudice in favor of or against one thing, person, or group compared with another, usually in a way considered to be unfair
Privilege	A special right, advantage, or immunity granted or available only to a particular person or group
Bigotry	Obstinate or unreasonable attachment to a belief, opinion, or faction; in particular, prejudice against a person or people on the basis of their membership of a particular group
Hatred	Intense dislike or ill will
Racial microaggressions	A statement, action, or incident regarded as an instance of indirect, subtle, or unintentional discrimination against members of a marginalized group
Racial macroaggressions	Refers to the power of institutional and structural forms of racism
Xenophobia	Dislike of or prejudice against people from other countries

Sources: Data from Huber, L. P., & Solorzano, D. G. (2014). Racial microaggressions as a tool for critical race research. *Race, Ethnicity, and Education*, 18, 297–320. https://doi.org/10.1080/13613324.2014.994173; Oxford University Press. (n.d.). Food. In *Oxford Advanced Learner's Dictionary*. Retrieved November 28, 2021, from https://languages.oup.com/.

second guessed, called unprofessional, not supported in class, and seem to be invisible. When I have clients with such lived experiences in our shared society, I have used what I now call culturally responsive mental wellness care. It's not empirically based, nor is it an approach you'll see in a textbook. However, it is what I have learned to use over my 17 years of clinical practice with clients who identify with collective cultural groups historically and presently marginalized, oppressed, and who have experienced racism, bias, and hatred across various life contexts. The method, if you will, is to create an intentional safe space with the client via asking various questions about life dynamics, using a model of dimensions of wellness. I help the client to hold space for the pain felt, asking where it comes from, about its impact on life and living. Also, through this method, I verbally acknowledge the validity in the narratives shared, highlighting the -isms, expressing that "It's okay to talk about that here." Across the dimensions of wellness, we discuss cultural food, holidays, values, ways of being, imposter syndrome, being the "only one," hair, community relations with politics, etc.

VOICES FROM THE FIELD: ALEXANDRA

Ms. Alexandra Manigault described her experience of working with a family that is struggling around race/ethnicity identity and adoption issues.

I currently am working with a family with two White parents and an adopted Mexican and Native American teenage boy. The teenage boy is becoming more interested in his biological heritage and has been in communication with biological family members and completed a 23 and Me DNA test. This has brought up some emotions both within himself and his parents around the teenager struggling with his self-image as he very obviously does not look like his parents or his peers. . . . The parents are struggling with hurt feelings as he is pushing away from them in order to be more engaged with his biological family. I have been working with the teenager around encouraging him to explore his heritage and encouraging him to include his parents during this process, so they don't feel excluded. I have also done some processing with the parents around their emotions of raising an adopted child and the impending feelings around knowing that eventually the teenager would want to explore his biological background.

VOICES FROM THE FIELD: TAHIRA

Ms. Tahira Matthews expanded on her experiences working with diverse couples and families and the role of generational trauma.

In my personal experience with families and couples, I have noticed that generational trauma presents more often than people may see. Within different cultures, families have their own way of doing things based on their own experiences whether it is for survival or pure love. For example, as a Black woman, I was taught in my household to not speak on things with others unless it was my immediate household and also to watch certain things I say around other races due to fear of being punished. I understand that the intention was to protect me; however, it impacted many of my relationships due to lack of trust in others because of what I was being taught in my own race. At my previous employment on APH (acute psychiatric hospital) unit, I implemented a culture/recovery group because many people were scared to talk about their experiences and did not understand the correlation between culture and mental health. When this was implemented, clients benefited from understanding their own values and beliefs and why they behaved the way they did.

VOICES FROM THE FIELD: YU-WEI

Similarly, Ms. Yu-Wei Wang provided an important example related to racism disclosure in the therapy room.

I remember when I first encountered racism issues in the therapy room, I had no idea how to deal with my client's intense pain and frustration. I thought there were some magic tools or miracle coping skills that could instantly take away the painful effects of racism, bias, or hate. After working with an Asian American client for 3 months, I was stressed that I didn't have the perfect tool to make them feel better. However, there was one session that my client told me that they appreciated how I provided the space for them to simply express and let out their emotions. The client stated, "You didn't rush to fix me or make me feel better, you just allowed me to talk about it. I don't think there is any place that allows me to talk about it without wanting me to get over it." Because of this experience and others, I have come to realize that providing space for clients to process might be the best tool of reducing their pain.

UNDERSTANDING THE EFFECTS RACISM HAS ON FAMILIES AND COUPLES

According to Priest et al. (2020), data from a large-scale series of research studies entitled Midlife in the United States National Longitudinal Studies (MIDUS I, II, and III) revealed that great racial discrimination equated to increased levels of family and intimate relationship strain, less family support, and decreases in both physical and mental health (Radler, 2014). In other words, the more racial discrimination POC experience, the less support their family provides to them, the higher the strain on their relationship or marriage, and the more physical health issues they contract as a result of their mental health issues. Given this vicious cycle and nonsupportive culture, POC who successfully sustain a longstanding family and/or relationship can seem extraordinary.

When society treats a particular group of people poorly, it has a ripple effect that spreads to all of their relationships. Examples of how macro-based issues play out in a member of a marginalized community's daily life include perceptions of being hated by others and/or society, experiencing racist policies and laws, and/or witnessing the privilege of other cultural groups. Furthermore, the construct of *stress spillover* (Buck & Neff, 2012) has been identified to describe the notion that daily negative social experiences spill over into the home/interpersonal relationship areas of one's life. Stress spillover can look different when present in families and cultures. Spillover might be evident for one individual as they project their insecurities onto other family members whom they target (i.e., scapegoating), while another person might burn out their partner by frequently using them as a quasi-counselor for processing their daily struggles.

The common and pervasive exposure to racism, discrimination, and hatred can create a state of chronic stress and anxiety for communities of color. Being in a state of chronic stress and anxiety is not conducive to cocreating healthy and stable interpersonal relationships. While not nearly enough, there has been some research and scholarship indicating the negative effects that daily racism and discrimination have on relationships. For example, the results of Bryant et al.'s study (2010) indicated discrimination in the African American community is likely to have a negative effect on relationships. In a recent study of 344 African American heterosexual couples, Lavner et al. (2018) found that racism and discrimination experiences were negatively associated with the effective functioning of relationships. Specifically, men described elevated levels of emotional aggression and relationship instability if they suffered increased levels of racism and discrimination in their daily lives. Comparably, women reported greater levels of physical aggression if they experienced higher levels of racial discrimination.

Like the Lavner et al. (2018) investigation, Doyle and Molix (2014) also found a negative relational effect in a sample of racially diverse participants who perceived daily discrimination. The 630 emerging majority participants in this investigation represented various ethnic and/or racial populations, including African American, Mexican, Dominican, and Puerto Rican. The results indicated the detrimental effects stigma and discrimination have on the intimate relationships of members of devalued groups. While more research is needed, this information provides evidence related to the relational challenges a racist culture can create. Many of us imagine that our relationship can serve as a safe haven from these negative influences; however, research demonstrates the negative relational, mental, and physical toll of living in a racist environment.

VOICES FROM THE FIELD: SHERRITTA

Dr. Sherritta Hughes shared her experiences around racial battle fatigue, the body's response to racial stress, and wellness strategies.

The first concept that comes to mind here is racial battle fatigue. This terminology was coined by psychologist Dr. William A. Smith. While many scholars are discussing this concept now, Smith introduced it as a psychological experience that occurs within African Americans when needing to operate or function in environments that are predominately European American. Racial battle fatigue is a framework that I've presented on at talks and conferences as what we as therapists and educators may use to increase our awareness of overt and covert racism in therapy, the workplace, among colleagues, the community, and in the classroom. For me, this is to open up the complexity of impact that racism has on the body, from a wellness perspective, whereby the stress hormones that are produced in the body and often prolonged in the body leading to chronic illness and significant aches and pains. I provide empirical research from the medical field that supports these factors as variables necessary to widen the scope of race talks and how racism hurts over the lifetime for many people, such as African Americans, Latinx immigrants, and Indigenous peoples of the Americas. I work with such clients from a stress-relief and relaxation modality to calm and retrain the body to respond to racism according to the stimuli that it is. According to Dr. Smith it's not PTSD [posttraumatic stress disorder] if the traumas are still occurring, hence I help clients to respond mentally and physically in ways that help them as opposed to hindering them.

VOICES FROM THE FIELD: ALEXANDRA

Ms. Alexandra Manigault described her experience of working with a biracial youth who struggles with self-image due to looking different from his peers.

The adopted teenage boy I previously mentioned struggles around not looking similar to his peers, and this issue has simultaneously increased his struggles with social anxiety. I have worked with the student on encouraging him to explore his heritage, which thus far has shown an increase in positive self-image and goals for the future around making connections with his biological family. The client has identified many ways of connecting with his peers through shared interests and activities, rather than solely focusing on how he does not look alike. The client also has been spending time with our program's history teacher in order to dig deeper into the history of his ancestry.

VOICES FROM THE FIELD: TAHIRA

Ms. Tahira Matthews provided information on her theoretical approach to working with clients around racism-related stress.

For clients who struggle to manage racism-related stress, I utilize CBT [cognitive behavioral therapy] to help them challenge their own distorted thoughts and to have a better understanding around one situation generalizing to other situations. With helping clients better understand the way they think and why they think that way, they were able to understand that they were creating their own stress in those moments.

VOICES FROM THE FIELD: YU-WEI

Ms. Yu-Wei Wang provided an important example related to client comfort and clinician preference in disclosing racism-related stress.

I think a stable therapeutic alliance is very essential when talking about racism-related issues and stress. One of my colleagues shared that she was working on depression and anxiety issues with an Asian American female client, and during her sessions she often feels like they are missing something. After checking in with her client, the client cried and shared that she hates working with White clinicians, but she feels too guilty to vocalize it. She shared that she wanted to process racism-related stress, but she does not feel comfortable to talk about those issues with a White therapist. After hearing that experience, I realized the importance of exploring the client's comfort with the therapist's racial and ethnic background. Surprisingly, I found out that clients tend to be more comfortable talking about racism and racial identity issues after talking about the dynamic in the session.

Racism, Stress Management, and the Body's Response to Stress

There has been an increased focus on understanding the unique mental health concerns brought on by racism and discrimination and how to help POC who are suffering. Williams (2018) aptly stated the key factor behind much of the stress and mental health concerns marginalized communities face on a daily basis:

> The dominant group devalues, disempowers, and differentially allocates desirable societal opportunities and resources to racial groups categorized as inferior. Supporting and buttressing the structure of racism is an ideology that is deeply embedded in the culture of the society, that provides the rationale for the ranking of groups (p. 467).

When individuals are targeted by racism and discrimination, they are often at least somewhat aware of what is happening to them. They often experience stressors that affect their physical and mental health. Given the unique and deeply pervasive nature of racism, discrimination, hatred, and bigotry, POC need to gain awareness of what is happening to them on a daily basis and create pathways for mental and physical well-being.

You may be wondering what happens to people when they experience frequent bouts of racism and discrimination. This is a great question with many answers depending on the context of the encounters. First, it is important to understand what can happen to one's body and mind when people consciously experience these negative and extremely hurtful messages. According to McEwen and Stellar (1993), *allostasis* is the way people physically react to a perceived threat, and *allostatic load* refers to the damage created by persistent physical stress. The trauma literature often describes the actualization of these terms as fight, flight, or freeze (Black & Flynn, 2021). This is what happens to people when they perceive threatening racist and discriminatory messages. During the allostasis process, the body begins preparing for conflict, including (a) the body system being flooded with hormones, (b) increase in blood pressure, (c) increase in heart rate, and (d) blood being diverted to the extremities. This body system response gives people a fast boost of energy so they can fight, flight, or freeze. Physically, POC who experience daily bouts of racism and discrimination are fraught with chemical wear and tear. The frequent stress (i.e., heavy allostatic load) overburdens the body's regulatory mechanisms, including the immune, endocrine, and circulatory systems. This can ultimately lead to hypertension, high blood pressure, an enlarged heart, and damage to the heart, kidneys, and other organs of the body (Black & Flynn, 2021; Greenberg et al., 2020; McEwen & Stellar, 1993).

The physical and mental toll of being discriminated against is massive and pervasive. During these extremely stressful experiences, the sympathetic nervous system activates the aforementioned fight, flight, or freeze reaction. This is when the stress hormone cortisol is released into the body. When the threat is highly elevated, excessive amounts of cortisol are released (American Psychiatric Association, 2013). Cortisol transforms fat into sugar so the body can respond. Frequent cortisol flooding creates cortisol resistance. This resistance causes proinflammatory cytokines to be frequently produced. Proinflammatory cytokines will then start attacking other cells and tissue, and the person in distress will begin having an overtaxed and overexcited immune system (Greenberg et al., 2020).

One of the scariest consequences of this overtaxation of the immune system is the shrinking of the hippocampus, which can cause emotional regulation problems (e.g., rage, excessive anxiety, preoccupation), inability to recognize a true threat (e.g., oversuspiciousness, paranoia), and hyperarousal, which often leads to disturbed sleep patterns. Among other health concerns, the overtaxed immune system will create a premature aging of cells, which could potentially shorten one's life span. In addition, the physical exertion brought on by these hurtful racist comments, microaggressions, and macroaggressions can cause POC to be at higher risk for other serious illnesses, including heart disease, diabetes, and COVID-19 (Black & Flynn, 2021; Greenberg et al., 2020; McEwen & Stellar, 1993).

VOICES FROM THE FIELD: SHERRITTA

Dr. Sherritta Hughes shared her experiences around microaggressions and the work she has done to ensure that she is not unintentionally contributing to further microaggressions in sessions.

Knowledge within this facet of racism has significantly aided the work that I do in a way that supports me being able to hear its covertness in narratives shared by, and at times missed by, clients. It is enlightening when I notice it out loud with a client who was aware of it, but surprised that I also heard it in the story dynamics being shared. My inexperience with certain microaggressions has revolved around LGBTQIA+ cultural groups and identities. At times, I want to think that I know, but I don't, and have often found myself internalizing mistakes in my language, whether real or imagined. No client has said that I hurt them by using a wrong pronoun, but I find myself possibly being overly empathic in creating safe spaces for gender inclusivity. Or in this way I'm simply being self-aware of otherness while at the same time experiencing imposter syndrome, second guessing if I'm doing this right or saying the right thing.

VOICES FROM THE FIELD: ALEXANDRA

Ms. Alexandra Manigault described her awareness of microaggressions and her ability to educate clients on them.

As a person with a BIPOC identity, I feel as though I am hyperaware of microaggressions, which has aided me in being able to manage engaging in those problematic behaviors. I also think it has helped me to educate my clients on what microaggressions are and why they are problematic.

VOICES FROM THE FIELD: TAHIRA

Ms. Tahira Matthews discussed her experience of microaggressions, client upbringing, and using microaggressions as a relationship-building phenomenon.

Knowledge of microaggression has aided me as a clinician to better serve all populations. I started in the field young, about 23 years old; an African American female who has lighter skin.

Many clients did not respect me due to age or race. This made the therapeutic process challenging as the first couple of sessions were all about rapport-building. I needed to separate my feelings about what they thought of my race and age and even competence, and remember that they are in therapy for a reason and my job is to educate and better serve them. As the years went on and my knowledge and experience grew regarding the nature of microaggressions, I understood that it all came down to their upbringing and their own experiences that skewed their own perceptions. When talking about the elephant in the room at times, some clients would feel comfortable because they knew they would be able to say what they felt and needed to at that moment.

VOICES FROM THE FIELD: YU-WEI

Ms. Yu-Wei Wang described clinical situations in which microaggressions emerged and her ability to understand the true intention behind what her clients stated.

An 8-year-old kid asked if I am good at math during our intake session. I was not able to tell if she asked because of the stereotype that all Asian people are good at math or if she was interested in math so she was trying to find some shared interests with me to build up the relationship. Instead of feeling offended by her, I found it easier to be curious about the meanings behind those sentences that may be labeled as microaggressions. It can be related to my limited experience in therapy practice, but most of the time when I experience microaggressions during the therapeutic process (e.g., "Where are you really from?" "I thought you would be more knowledgeable about arranged marriage."), my clients are genuinely asking questions or making comments because they are curious, not because they wanted to offend me. Instead of being attacked, the ability to be empathetic and be curious about where the comments came from has allowed me to use the experiences of microaggressions as ways to build alliance with my clients.

Methods of Stress Management

Oppressed groups and their families may experience extreme stress or racial trauma related to the constant barrage of hateful microaggressions, macroaggressions, racism, and discrimination they experience in society. To combat these issues and others, it is common to use community resources. Whether it is religion and spirituality, support networks, holistic healing and self-care, armoring, or shifting, clients should tailor their strategy to what works best for them. Remember, most people who experience a racist, discriminatory, or hateful act will not initially seek formal therapy, and for those who do your task is to help them return to a place of empowerment, equilibrium, safety, and control as soon as they are able.

Religion and Spirituality

In a general sense, those with a strong religious and spiritual practice can rise above stress by believing that there is a bigger picture and a higher purpose in life. Religion and spirituality are core coping strategies that can create a sense of meaning, hope, understanding, forgiveness, relieving of stress, and community for those experiencing discrimination, hatred, and racism. Religions and spiritual-based practices such as prayers, meditation, reciting scriptures, and singing/dancing can serve as important practices to help individuals cope (Holder et al., 2015).

Support Networks

Support networks can be informal (e.g., trusted friends, family) or formal (e.g., group therapy, network therapy). In a general sense, support networks assist people in not feeling isolated or invalidated when confronted by stressful situations. Having a circle of trusted friends, family, or community members to turn to when one is experiencing racism, discrimination, or hate can be extremely helpful and healing. Support networks can create a validating experience, a source of advice, and a place to gain access to resources (Holder et al., 2015).

Therapy and Holistic Healing

Receiving counseling after suffering discriminatory and racist experiences can be key to feeling a sense of relief. In addition to counseling, survivors of these stressful experiences can engage in holistic healing strategies designed to restore balance, including, but not limited to, breathing retraining, deep muscle relaxation, meditation, music, physical exercise, and yoga. Additionally, common strategies like taking a vacation and spending time with family can alleviate stress (Holder et al., 2015).

Armoring

Armoring is an example of a protective mechanism designed for hurtful social experiences. Believing in oneself and having a deep sense of pride in one's family, self, and culture are extremely helpful in protecting the self. According to Bell and Nkomo (1998), "[a]rmor is a form of socialization where a girl child learns the cultural attitudes, preferences, and socially legitimate behaviors for two cultural contexts" (p. 286). This internal sense of validation and pride can help communities of color feel a sense of dignity when confronted with racism and discrimination (Holder et al., 2015).

Shifting

The final coping skill reviewed is a skill known as shifting. According to Allison (2010), communities of color counter discriminatory stereotypes and hurtfulness by shifting their body, speech, perspective, and attire to keep colleagues confused as to who they are as a person or de-emphasizing racial differences with White people and POC (Holder et al., 2015).

VOICES FROM THE FIELD: SHERRITTA

Dr. Sherritta Hughes shared her experiences around burnout and cultural and social justice-oriented therapy and education.

As an African American with ancestors of North American slavery, I have truly experienced burnout over the last 18 months due to clientele increase at my practice, Hughes Integrative Wellness, Inc. For the first time in my career, a majority of the clients seeking services are adamantly requesting to see a Black therapist. As this is new to me, it is also exciting, and necessary to realize that culturally responsive mental health and wellness care is my ethical responsibility. It may sound simple, but empathy, unconditional positive regard, and congruence are vital. In essence, this Rogerian approach has led to validation of client problems as they are predominantly concerns around forms of racism and gender biases, such as microaggressions, and limited representation of cultural diversity. However, it has been very exhausting because I felt the need to turn no one away, especially since most of these clients had never sought mental healthcare in the past. My mind is overworked because many of their experiences have been mine as well. Also, as a counselor educator who is in the classroom, I bring many cases to class to discuss. The latter has been appreciated by most students of a predominantly European American student body, yet several of the students have reflected that they are tired of hearing about diversity, inclusion, racism, social justice, and other limitations of mental healthcare practices that are not culturally responsive.

VOICES FROM THE FIELD: TAHIRA

Ms. Tahira Matthews discussed her experience of racism-related stress and the lack of administrative support.

Having to cope with racism-related stress affected my work as a clinician because I felt as though the company I worked for did not show much compassion to the POC when things happened. I would talk about the racism-related stress with colleagues so we could support each other, but the lack of support from administration made it difficult at times. . . .

VOICES FROM THE FIELD: YU-WEI

Ms. Yu-Wei Wang explored her emotions, stress, and experiences during the week of George Floyd's murder.

The place where I did my internship provided free therapy for every client who was open to seeing interns. Therefore, I had the opportunity to work with people from different social statuses. I remember the week of George Floyd's murder, there were two extremely different dynamics in my sessions. Some clients were processing their grief and frustration with the system, and some clients were not aware of the ongoing issues. I remember that I was feeling emotional when my client sobbed in the session and my next client accused others of *overreacting*. It was a huge challenge for me to hear all of the different narratives while at the same time being aware of my own biases. It was difficult to be present and allow my clients to use the space and process. I remember feeling exhausted in those weeks where I constantly had to check in with my self-of-the-therapist and to challenge myself not to be triggered by clients who have the different beliefs than me. My supervisor constantly reminded me of the importance of self-care and to do things that I enjoy doing to make myself grounded and to differentiate myself from all the conflicting narratives.

THE IMPACT OF RACIAL AND ETHNIC SOCIALIZATION

Racial and ethnic socialization (i.e., the process through which children learn about race) has a major impact on communities of color, couples, and families. Racism, discrimination, and hatred greatly magnify the challenges of raising children today. Encounters with racism, discrimination, and hatred compromise childhood mental well-being, physical health, and educational outcomes (Tatum, 2017; Tran, 2014). Racial and ethnic socialization is the process where children acquire values, attitudes, and perceptions around their ethnic/racial group and how they see themselves as a member of the group (Rotherman & Phinney, 1987). Caregivers help children understand and cope effectively with their socialization. For communities of color, this includes coping with racism, discrimination, hatred, and privilege.

Racism-related stress refers to race-related interactions that occur between individuals, groups, and their environment, and the toll of these interactions on individuals' well-being and internal resources (Jones et al., 2020). These interactions include race-related life events, vicarious racism, microaggressions, chronic stress from systemic racism, collective experiences in culture and politics, and transgenerational transmission of historical racism. According to Osborne et al. (2021), statistics demonstrate approximately 90% of Black and African American youth indicate having experiences with racism before the age of 13. The systemic nature of racism creates deficits before a child is born. Lower quality healthcare during pregnancy, underfunded schools, exposure to violence, and parental stress contribute to further marginalizing POC (Jones et al., 2020).

Caregivers/parents of color have likely experienced a lifetime of racism, discrimination, and hatred, and the accompanying stress, trauma, and/or emotional wounds. Caregiver experiences with racism outside of the home have been identified as an antecedent to bad parenting outcomes with children (Braveman & Barclay, 2009; Tran, 2014). Bronfenbrenner (1979) and Bronfenbrenner and Ceci (1994) described the nature of human development as happening "in the midst of a vibrant, complex environment" (p. 14). Consequently, caregiver stress over racist experiences outside of the home can directly and indirectly affect children and adolescents. Clinicians work with caregivers to develop effective coping skills and parenting practices to create appropriate boundaries at home while finding healthy pathways for emotional release (e.g., counseling, exercise, meditation).

While it is important to avoid severely preoccupying children and adolescents with thoughts of racism and discrimination, most families of color talk to children about the historical, social, and political factors affecting race and ethnicity (i.e., ethnic and racial socialization). Wang et al. (2020) found that the use of ethnic and racial socialization created a sense of well-being and prosocial behaviors, and supports the development of a strong childhood racial identity. While the results of this investigation were dependent on the child's developmental stage and cognitive ability, the authors found that positive outcomes were dependent on four educational experiences, namely preparation for bias, socialization, egalitarianism, and promotion of a sense of mistrust. These conversations and socialization methods help children cope with the effects of racism and discrimination. Preparing children and adolescents for potential stressors and practicing ways to approach the situations and cope in a healthy manner can help build resilience. In adolescents, learning communication skills and building self-esteem are especially important as this is a time when they begin to identify and experience racism and racial barriers firsthand (Jones et al., 2020).

Couple, marriage, and family practitioners are in a unique position to help individuals and families cope with race-related stress (Jones et al., 2020). By identifying, processing, and validating race-related stress and introducing behavioral interventions (e.g., coping, racial socialization, social support) and cognitive interventions (e.g., progressive relaxation, mindfulness meditation, storytelling), clinicians can build a strong therapeutic alliance, increase client engagement, and aid their clients in learning new ways of coping and problem-solving. Racism is a pervasive systemic issue that requires extensive change outside of the counseling setting; however, clinicians can help individuals, couples, and families learn how to cope with the daily racial stressors in their surroundings.

VOICES FROM THE FIELD: SHERRITTA

Dr. Sherritta Hughes shared her experiences around sharing developmentally appropriate approaches and theories to understanding race, ethnic socialization, and oppression.

I have used a developmental approach to better understand where a client is in who they are becoming in a society that is often unapologetically marginalizing and oppressive. Specifically, I reach for the theoretical understanding and applications of Drs. Janet Helms, William Cross, Lewis Gordon, William Edward Burghardt Du Bois, and Clemmont Vontress, who all have discussed experiences of racial identity development, mostly from an existential perspective. I intentionally apply theorists who are not in textbooks that outline theories of personality for counseling and psychotherapy. This information is grounded in multidiscipline scholarly literature and the theories have expounded upon living experiences of what it means to be African American across time and in various contexts. I introduce these (people, theorist, and applications) to clients and provide space for the client to hold in order to explore themselves across time, contexts, and according to their narratives.

VOICES FROM THE FIELD: ALEXANDRA

Ms. Alexandra Manigault described her experience of encouraging clients to explore their heritage.

I have encouraged the student to spend time researching his heritage and building connections with those in his biological family.

VOICES FROM THE FIELD: TAHIRA

Ms. Tahira Matthews shared information on her approach to helping clients understand race and cultural norms, generational experiences of discrimination, and using information to create positive change.

I have utilized racial and ethnic socialization as a tool in therapy with African Americans by reciting the norms in Black families to them that are known in many generations, such as you go to church, you talk with your family, etc. I do this as a starting point to help them understand how that may have shaped their lives in the moment and they can accept the generational norms or make changes to it by doing things similarly but different, such as seeking help, reaching out to a support system, etc. Discrimination is real and so is racism, so it is important that POC or other backgrounds do understand that, but also have an understanding that they do not have to act in ways their parents might have.

VOICES FROM THE FIELD: YU-WEI

Ms. Yu-Wei Wang provided information on holding safe space, deeply listening to her clients, and encouraging a sense of self-care.

. . . I rarely use racial and ethnic socialization as a tool to normalize or address the trauma with them. I tend to provide the space for my clients to process their intense emotions. I enjoy focusing on self-care and self-compassion so they can love themselves by utilizing their internal strengths and values.

UNDERSTANDING INTERSECTIONALITY IN RELATIONSHIPS

Intersectionality centers on understanding an individual's intersecting identities and experiences to comprehend the intricacy of prejudices people experience. This is to honor the number of ways people are disadvantaged and advantaged within a given society. Common intersecting elements to consider include, but are not limited to, race, ethnicity, gender, sexual orientation, gender identity, religion, ability, socioeconomic status, and age. While this intersection can seem somewhat theoretical, it is meant to provide a snapshot of the uniquely tailored discriminatory experiences people may be dealing with in a particular society (Davids & Mitchell, 2017).

You may be wondering, "How does intersectionality affect people in intimate relationships?" Great question. The intersection of each partner will further intersect in an intimate relationship. In other words, couples should have an understanding of the multiple intersections and identities they and their intimate partner express. Couples and family practitioners should understand these intersections, so they can have awareness and appreciation of the multicultural, social justice, and holistic nature of a couple in therapy. In describing this phenomena, Akamatsu (2008) uses the label *multiplexity* to describe the notion that a partner in a relationship may be discriminated against or disadvantaged and simultaneously advantaged. For example, if a cisgender Black man who identifies as Christian and heterosexual comes to therapy, he may describe being discriminated against because of his race and simultaneously enjoying a sense of privilege because of sexual and religious affiliation. Now let's suppose he is married to a Muslim Black cisgender woman who comes from a wealthy family. She may feel culturally disadvantaged for being a woman, Black, and Muslim and simultaneously feel a sense of privilege around her family's socioeconomic status and her sexual orientation (Addison & Coolhart, 2015; Davids & Mitchell, 2017).

From a second-order cybernetics perspective, the clinician must also be considered with this viewpoint. How do the clinician's multiple identities and contextual variables interact with each partner in the relationship? The healing and change that take place within a therapeutic encounter can be seen as the interaction of the practitioner's and the family's cultural and personal constructions (Falicov, 2003). For example, the clinician may match up in a similar manner contextually with one spouse and, if they are not introspective, this may influence and bias their perception of the presenting problem (Addison & Coolhart, 2015).

VOICES FROM THE FIELD: SHERRITTA

Dr. Sherritta Hughes described the intentional work she engages in daily to better understand her clients.

At all times, I try to have a working awareness of who I am and who the clients are that I work with. In doing so, I am purposive in dialogue and questioning when it comes to my personal growth outside of sessions. Specifically, I read books by Gloria Jean Watkins (i.e., bell hooks; e.g., on love, teaching), Lawrence N. Houston (e.g., *Psychological Principles and the Black Experience*, 1990), and listen to lectures on YouTube by Father of Africana Studies Henry Clarke. As these scholars who I go to for strengthening my ethnic identity, I also check in with family, friends, and my spirituality to feed my identity because I, too, have found myself broken and fearful because of my experiences with racism in day-to-day life.

VOICES FROM THE FIELD: ALEXANDRA

Ms. Alexandra Manigault described her awareness of microaggressions and her ability to educate clients on them.

As a BIPOC raised in New England, I can identify that I have more privilege than someone of color or not who was raised in a less financially stable environment and that I had the support of family through college and graduate school. At the same token, I can also identify that I am a minority in my community, which can come with some feelings of discouragement or feeling like I have to go above and beyond to be taken seriously as a mental health professional.

VOICES FROM THE FIELD: TAHIRA

Ms. Tahira Matthews described the importance of her diverse clinical experience and of introspecting on her own experiences and assumptions.

My intersectional identity impacts my presence in the therapy room due to my experience working with many populations from different backgrounds, races, genders, and ages. I also am a minority, so I try to separate my own experience from others but also am able to empathize with some more than others. By working with different identities and levels of privilege, I am able to challenge some of my assumptions, learn from the clients, and be able to have more information that will help the next individual.

VOICES FROM THE FIELD: YU-WEI

Ms. Yu-Wei Wang described her intersectionality as an Asian woman from Taiwan and shared a clinical situation in which a Black client disclosed feeling safer with her due to her ethnicity and race.

Being insecure about my English language ability and being unfamiliar with the U.S.'s culture, I think my intersectional identity as an international student has a larger impact on my ethnicity and race. In other words, my insecurity of my own identity has limited my ability to reflect on my intersectional identities. But being an Asian female, I found it easier to build alliance with some of my clients. I once worked with a Black family (single mom and three children), when talking about her kids' relationships at school, the mother shared "You probably understand our situation as a minority." It was heartbreaking for me when I heard that comment, and I truly appreciate their trust. At that moment, I realized that being a non-White therapist, I am privileged in gaining the trust from my clients and building stronger alliances with them.

WORKING WITH UNDERREPRESENTED FAMILIES

The term *underrepresented families* refers to impoverished, marginalized community (e.g., racial, sexual), and/or ethnically diverse families that receive mental health services in disproportionately low numbers. According to Dickson et al. (2017), families that represent communities of color are less likely to seek mental health services. Furthermore, Chacko et al. (2016) found that education groups populated with POC suffer from poor retention. Le et al. (2010) discovered that when underrepresented family members do seek services, they are less likely to receive evidence-based interventions and often prematurely terminate (Organista et al., 1994). Given the immense cultural stress, lack of probability around seeking formal mental health services, and poor therapeutic retention rates, underrepresented families need advocacy and support.

An additional area that requires close attention during the therapeutic process is social class and classism. Underrepresented families are often deeply affected by social class and classism. Social class and contextual variables like gender, sexuality, race, ethnicity, and age are not personal characteristics derived within oneself. Instead, these contextual variables constitute a reflection of institutional and societal inequalities, privilege, and the associated power or lack thereof. Kliman (1998) described the manifestation of social class and class-based power structures as cultural hegemony. This hegemony is caused by people who create differential access to resources within sectors of society. Ultimately, classism reflects structural and societal privilege and/or disadvantage between groups of people.

By 1973, the American Psychiatric Association deleted homosexuality from the second edition of the *Diagnostic and Statistical Manual of Mental Disorders* (*DSM-II*; American Psychiatric Association, 1968). This formally ended the professional pathologizing of individuals identifying as lesbian, gay, bisexual, transgender, intersex, queer and/or questioning, asexual, and/or ally, plus (LGBTQIA+); however, it did not stop the mistreatment, hatred, and discrimination of individuals in these communities. Families where at least one member identifies as LGBTQIA+ represent between one and nine million in the United States (Linville & O'Neil, n.d.). While this population is growing, there is still widespread discrimination, harassment, assault, and hatred toward LGBTQIA+ individuals, couples, and families. Even greater negative consequences persist for individuals identifying on the intersection of LGBTQIA+ and an underprivileged and/or marginalized status (Barnett et al., 2019).

Phobia has a particular meaning in the helping professions that is centered on persistent and excessive fear; however, homophobia is somewhat different as it centers on a sense of fear and hatred toward members of the LGBTQIA+ communities. Homophobia (i.e., prejudice toward gay people), biphobia (i.e., prejudice toward bisexual [bi] people), and transphobia (i.e., prejudice toward transgender people) generally refer to a person who dislikes, hates, and/or tries to convert people who are not heterosexual (Frost & Meyer, 2009). Sometimes this hate is directed toward people who do not identify with the LGBTQIA+ community but appear to in some way (e.g., men who are considered effeminate). Lastly, according to Meyer and Dean (1998), internalized homophobia is "the gay person's direction of negative social attitudes toward the self" (p. 161). This is essentially a sense of self-hatred and poor self-awareness. All of the aforementioned phobic responses toward others and/or self are tremendously destructive to individuals, couples, and families.

Individuals who identify as LGBTQIA+ may feel a sense of internalized homophobia because they are rejected by their family and/or society. Internalized homophobia may result in an individual's desire to change their same-sex attraction and/or alter their gender identity. Conversion (i.e., reparative) therapy is a discredited, harmful, and unethical practice that attempts to remove someone's natural feelings of attraction to the same sex, increase someone's attraction to the opposite sex, and/or modify behavior to encourage identification with recorded birth sex. In addition to being unethical and unlawful in certain states, this is not an empirically validated treatment and the skills used are completely unregulated. Furthermore, conversion therapy has major social justice implications. In a society that already rejects and punishes individuals who identify as a sexual and/or gender minority, the existence of conversion therapy only further amplifies a sense of prejudice and self-hatred. Presently, conversion therapy has been banned in Canada and in the following states: California, Oregon, Illinois, Vermont, New Jersey,

New Mexico, Connecticut, Nevada, Rhode Island, Washington, Maryland, New Hampshire, Hawaii, Delaware, New York, Massachusetts, Colorado, Maine, and Washington DC (American Counseling Association, n.d.).

INTERRACIAL COUPLES AND FAMILIES

What does it mean to be in an intimate relationship with someone from another culture, race, or ethnicity? How will one's family's traditions continue with a partner from a different culture? What implications are there for raising children in an interracial family? These initial questions are important to consider as practitioners think about working with interracial couples and families. All couples, regardless of culture, must negotiate a variety of common issues, including, but not limited to, family rules, negotiating gender roles, creation of effective communication styles, decision-making authority, and attaining/maintaining a mutually satisfying emotional and sexual relationship. There are a tremendous number of potential positive aspects to interracial relationships. Examples include, but are not limited to, being introduced to a new culture, sharing one's own culture, traveling to new places, experiencing new food, and combining the benefits of two diverse parenting styles. Potential negative aspects to interracial relationships are linked to lower marital satisfaction (Bratter & King, 2008), more conflicts (Potter & Thomas, 2012), lower relational stability (Hohmann-Marriott & Amato, 2008), and contending with a racist culture (Leslie & Young, 2015).

Spickard (1992) defines *interracial couples* as "partners, married or not, of a different racial background" (p. 12). From a historical perspective, interracial relationships have been considered a cause of mental illness, inherently dysfunctional, unnatural, and against the law (Perry & Sutton, 2008; Villazor, 2018). Although the birth rate of mixed-race individuals has more than quadrupled since the 1970s (Laszloffy, 2008), racist and hateful societal norms (e.g., "birds of a feather should fly together"), strict legal prohibitions, hypodescent (i.e., the assignment of mixed-race children to the least privileged racial/ethnic group), stereotypic characterizations, and treatment (e.g., being labeled as their minority identifying race when looking for housing) have discouraged the intermixing of different ethnicities and races (Laszloffy, 2008; Perry & Sutton, 2008; Villazor, 2018). From a historical and contemporary perspective, interracial couples hide their relationships because they feel ostracized, fear rejection, and/or do not feel safe (Fusco, 2010). Furthermore, Brownridge (2016) found interracial couples to have more intimate partner violence when compared with same-race couples. This coupling of outside relational tension and discrimination with relational stress can create havoc to interracial couples and families.

VOICES FROM THE FIELD: SHERRITTA

Dr. Sherritta Hughes described her clinical strategies for working with underserved clients.

To assure that this barrier is reduced, I find myself developing the therapeutic alliance over the course of all sessions, but more intentionally within the first three to four sessions. In these sessions, we process and unpack who the client is, exploring deep questions about becoming, living, and in their preferred contexts. To do this, I use the Eight-Dimensional Wellness Model, which has eight life areas where the client is offered space to speak of themselves as pluralistic beings (i.e., all of their identities). I provide cultural-based homework assignments such as think about what your *It Factor* is, think about terms used and build upon them with personal meanings, etc. These activities are what I have found to be helpful in ensuring underrepresented clients come back, return week after week, open up and process in a manner that makes connection, develop autonomy, and explore levels of progress.

VOICES FROM THE FIELD: ALEXANDRA

Ms. Alexandra Manigault described her process for bracketing bias and encouraging her clients to explore their heritage.

I think that appropriately sharing experiences that I have had with clients and how I managed those situations can be encouraging and helpful as well as encouraging clients to explore their heritage. I also do my best to check my own biases at the door so to speak and not become reactive when clients discuss things from their point of view when it doesn't match up with mine. I also process with my supervisor if I am struggling with my own biases.

VOICES FROM THE FIELD: TAHIRA

Ms. Tahira Matthews reviewed some of her strategies for helping underserved families, and described her process around building a sense of trust, assessment, and care coordination.

With underrepresented families in therapy, I assess their needs and also ask them what their needs may be. I help ensure and build trust with families by providing psychoeducation on different resources that may benefit them, such as housing, financial opportunities, free childcare within the county. Once I assist with providing resources and case management, the family is more trusting because they understand I am trying to help them.

VOICES FROM THE FIELD: YU-WEI

Ms. Yu-Wei Wang provided insight into the therapeutic alliance and techniques she uses to build relationships with individuals representing underrepresented cultural groups.

I am an Asian therapist, I am part of an underrepresented culture group; when working with clients who come from the same culture as I do, I often start the session by saying "We might share the same skin color but that does not necessarily mean I completely understand your experience. There may be something that I can relate to, but I don't want to invalidate your feeling by pretending that I know everything." The dynamic in therapy sessions could be similar when working with underrepresented families from different cultures. Although the process of normalizing is essential for the families to understand that they are not in the situation alone, overnormalizing may be invalidating and create a hierarchy in the therapy room, which may limit clients' willingness to share their experience. I find it important to be aware of my own biases and be respectful and curious of my clients' narratives when it comes to building relationships with various communities.

SUMMARY

This chapter reviewed important contemporary issues, theories, and interventions/skills centered on working with underrepresented individuals, families, and couples. Topics explored included discrimination and racism, couple and family experiences of ethnic microaggression, racial and ethnic socialization, understanding homophobia and other issues relevant to same-sex couples, and interracial couple and family experiences. This chapter showcased sections entitled Voices From the Field. Voices From the Field are interview transcriptions from clinicians representing various cultural backgrounds. The information within this chapter will hopefully help to connect some of the key social justice literature with the voices of clinicians representing one or more communities of color.

END-OF-CHAPTER RESOURCES

A robust set of instructor resources designed to supplement this text is located at http://connect.springerpub.com/content/book/978-0-8261-8775-8. Qualifying instructors may request access by emailing textbook@springerpub.com.

STUDENT ACTIVITIES

Exercise 1: Understanding Intersectionality With Self and in Relationships

Directions: Review the following information and answer the reflection questions:

Intersectionality examines the interconnected nature of social categorizations that may encompass a person's identity, and it recognizes that everyone has their own unique experiences of discrimination and oppression based on their intersectional identity. Common intersecting elements to consider include, but are not limited to, race, ethnicity, gender, sexual orientation, gender identity, religion, ability, socioeconomic status, and age.

- Why is it important to consider intersectionality when working with clients instead of focusing on one or two aspects of their identity?

- What is your intersectional identity? Describe at least five elements of this identity.

- How would knowing more about your own identity help you as a clinician when working with clients?

Exercise 2: Researching Local Resources

Directions: Review the following instructions and compile local resources that could be helpful to your work as a clinician in the future:

As clinicians, we work hard to ensure our clients are fully supported within the therapy office and their community. When working with underrepresented clientele, this need for help can feel beyond our own scope of practice. The term *underrepresented families* refers to impoverished, marginalized community (e.g., racial, sexual), and/or ethnically diverse families who receive mental health services in disproportionately low numbers. Research the local resources around you that may be helpful when working with diverse clients in the future, including social communities, podcasts, books, shelter and housing resources, substance use programs, employment resources, and government assistance offices.

Exercise 3: Working With Clients From Different Cultures

Directions: Review the following instructions and create a mock plan for potential clients:

When working with clients, whether diverse populations, interracial couples/families, or those who grew up within a different culture from your own, it is important to be open and willing to learn more about other cultures and values to best understand our clients and their individual experiences.

- Create a mock plan for how to talk to clients about their experiences that validates them and does not put them in a position to completely educate you on their culture.

- Create thoughtful questions to ask that will help you understand your clients more thoroughly.

■ Create one multicultural counseling scenario in which you could warrant the use of immediacy.

■ Find resources (e.g., books, articles) on two different cultures to refer to when needed.

Exercise 4: Understanding the LGBTQIA+ Movement

Directions: Review online and library resources to answer the following prompts related to the LGBTQIA+ movement:

■ Create a detailed time line reflecting high-impact events that influenced the LGBTQIA+ movement.

■ Describe three events that set the stage for legalizing gay marriage in the United States.

■ How do constructs like homophobia and internalized homophobia affect LGBTQIA+ couples and families?

■ Name four reasons the practice of conversion (reparative) therapy can be damaging and hurtful to individuals who identify as LGBTQIA+.

Exercise 5: Article Review

Directions: Review the following instructions and answer the questions:

Go to your university's online EBSCO Database and find Academic Search Premier. Search and find an article focused on engaging in therapy with interracial families. Review the article in its entirety and answer the following questions related to serving this important population:

■ How do the authors describe this population and the contemporary issues affecting their well-being?

■ What, if any, specific techniques are promoted within the article?

■ Reflect on the experiences you have with interracial families (e.g., professional, family, friends, acquaintances). What areas do you need to strengthen to better serve interracial families?

ADDITIONAL RESOURCES

HELPFUL LINKS

■ "What to Know About Breonna Taylor's Death": https://www.nytimes.com/article/breonna-taylor-police.html

■ "Black Lives Matter": https://www.britannica.com/topic/Black-Lives-Matter

■ "With Racial Attacks on the Rise, Asian Americans Fear for Their Safety": https://www.npr.org/sections/health-shots/2021/10/13/1045746655/1-in-4-asian-americans-recently-feared-their-household-being-targeted-poll-finds

■ "A Reading List on Issues of Race": https://news.harvard.edu/gazette/story/2020/06/a-reading-list-on-issues-of-race/

■ "Discrimination and the Stress Response: Psychological and Physiological Consequences of Anticipating Prejudice in Interethnic Interactions": https://www.ncbi.nlm.nih.gov/pmc/articles/PMC3483920/

- "How Racism Is Bad for Our Bodies": https://www.theatlantic.com/health/archive/2013/03/how-racism-is-bad-for-our-bodies/273911/

- "Ethnic Socialization and Ethnic Identity Development Among Internationally Adopted Korean American Adolescents: A Seven-Year Follow-Up": https://www.ncbi.nlm.nih.gov/pmc/articles/PMC5722028/

- "Challenges of an Interracial Marriage From Society": https://www.verywellmind.com/interracial-marriage-challenges-2303129

- "Interracial Marriages Now More Common, But Not Without Challenges": https://www.cbsnews.com/news/interracial-marriages-now-more-common-but-not-without-challenges/

- "Canada Bans Conversion Therapy, a Practice Trudeau Calls 'Despicable and Degrading'": https://www.cnn.com/2021/12/09/americas/canada-conversion-therapy-ban/index.html

HELPFUL BOOKS

- Crotty, M. (1998). *The foundation of social research: Meaning and perspective in the research process*. Sage.

- Czarniawska, B. (2004). *Narratives in social science research*. Sage.

- Hall, E. T. (1989). *Beyond culture*. Doubleday.

- Lee, C. C. (2006). *Multicultural issues in counseling: New approaches to diversity* (3rd ed.). American Counseling Association.

- Ramirez, M. (1991). *Psychotherapy and counseling with minorities: A cognitive approach to individual and cultural differences*. Pergamon.

- Ramirez, M., III. (1999). *Multicultural psychotherapy: An approach to individual and cultural differences* (2nd ed.). Allyn & Bacon.

- Sue, D. W., & Sue, D. (2012). *Counseling the culturally diverse: Theory and practice* (6th ed.). Wiley.

- Sue, D. W., Carter, R. T., Casas, J. M., Fouad, N. A., Ivey, A. E., Jensen, M., LaFromboise, T., Manese, J. E., Ponterotto, J. G., & Vazquez-Nutall, E. (1998). *Multicultural counseling competencies: Individual and organizational development*. Sage.

HELPFUL VIDEOS

- A Living History of the LGBT Movement Since The 1800s: https://www.youtube.com/watch?v=Q1D65SxzojI

- Racism in America: https://www.apa.org/education-career/undergrad/diversity

- United Against Racism: https://www.youtube.com/watch?v=NDKOzFyes5Q

- Ask An Expert: Kay Sanders: https://www.youtube.com/watch?v=21-B0RuPZHw

- Race Socialization: https://www.youtube.com/watch?v=Gp-V--4KVH8

- Trauma and the Brain: https://www.youtube.com/watch?v=4-tcKYx24aA

- Understanding Trauma: Learning Brain vs Survival Brain: https://www.youtube.com/watch?v=KoqaUANGvpA

- Hate Crimes Against Asian Americans on the Rise: https://www.youtube.com/watch?v=BqDjZsnLE9M

- The Life Threatening Dangers of Gay Conversion Therapy: https://www.youtube.com/watch?v=HL5ThApf0IA

REFERENCES

Abrams, Z. (2021, September 1). How bystanders can shut down microaggressions. *Monitor on Psychology, 52*(6), 55. https://www.apa.org/monitor/2021/09/feature-bystanders-microaggressions

Addison, S. M., & Coolhart, D. (2015). Expanding the therapy paradigm with queer couples: A relational intersectional lens. *Family Process, 54*(3), 435–453. https://doi.org/10.1111/famp.12171

Akamatsu, N. (2008). Teaching White students about racism and its implications in practice. In M. McGoldrick & K. V. Hardy (Eds.), *Re-visioning family therapy* (2nd ed., pp. 413–424). Guilford Press.

Allison, A. (2010). (Re)imaging the afrocentric self: An organizational culture analysis of shifting. *The International Journal of Diversity in Organizations, Communities, and Nations: Annual Review, 10*(1), 89–98. https://doi.org/10.18848/1447-9532/cgp/v10i01/39799

American Counseling Association. (n.d.). *Conversion therapy bans*. Author. https://www.counseling.org/government-affairs/state-issues/conversion-therapy-bans

American Psychiatric Association. (1968). *Diagnostic and statistical manual of mental disorders* (2nd ed.). Author.

American Psychiatric Association. (2013). *Diagnostic and statistical manual of mental disorders* (5th ed.). https://doi.org/10.1176/appi.books.9780890425596

Arguelles, D. (2021, March 26). *From the gold rush to the COVID pandemic: A history of anti-Asian violence*. National Parks Conservation Association. https://www.npca.org/articles/2860-from-the-gold-rush-to-the-covid-pandemic-a-history-of-anti-asian-violence

Barnett, A. P., Del Río-González, A. M., Parchem, B., Pinho, V., Aguayo-Romero, R., Nakamura, N., Calabrese, S. K., Poppen, P. J., & Zea, M. C. (2019). Content analysis of psychological research with lesbian, gay, bisexual, and transgender people of color in the United States: 1969–2018. *The American Psychologist, 74*(8), 898–911. https://doi.org/10.1037/amp0000562

Barton, A. W., Beach, S. R., Bryant, C. M., Lavner, J. A., & Brody, G. H. (2018). Stress spillover, African Americans' couple and health outcomes, and the stress-buffering effect of family-centered prevention. *Journal of Family Psychology, 32*(2), 186–196. https://doi.org/10.1037/fam0000376

Bell, E. L., & Nkomo, S. M. (1998). Armoring: Leaming to withstand racial oppression. *Journal of Comparative Family Studies, 29*(2), 285–295. https://doi.org/10.3138/jcfs.29.2.285

Black, L. L., & Flynn, S. V. (2021). *Crisis, trauma, and disaster: A clinician's guide*. Sage.

Bratter, J. L., & King, R. B. (2008). "But will it last?": Marital instability among interracial and same-race couples. *Family Relations, 57*(2), 160–171. https://doi.org/10.1111/j.1741-3729.2008.00491.x

Braveman, P., & Barclay, C. (2009). Health disparities beginning in childhood: A life-course perspective. *Pediatrics, 124*(Suppl. 3), S163–S175. https://doi.org/10.1542/peds.2009-1100d

Bronfenbrenner, U. (1979). *The ecology of human development*. Harvard University Press.

Bronfenbrenner, U., & Ceci, S. J. (1994). Nature-nuture reconceptualized in developmental perspective: A bioecological model. *Psychological Review, 101*(4), 568–586. https://doi.org/10.1037/0033-295x.101.4.568

Brownridge, D. A. (2016). Intimate partner violence in interracial relationships. *Journal of Family Violence, 31*(7), 865–875. https://doi.org/10.1007/s10896-016-9809-z

Bryant, A. S., Worjoloh, A., Caughey, A. B., & Washington, A. E. (2010). Racial/ethnic disparities in obstetric outcomes and care: Prevalence and determinants. *American Journal of Obstetrics and Gynecology, 202*(4), 335–343. https://doi.org/10.1016/j.ajog.2009.10.864

Buchanan, L., Bui, Q., & Patel, J. K. (2020, July 3). Black Lives Matter may be the largest movement in U.S. history. *The New York Times*. https://www.nytimes.com/interactive/2020/07/03/us/george-floyd-protests-crowd-size.html

Buck, A. A., & Neff, L. A. (2012). Stress spillover in early marriage: The role of self-regulatory depletion. *Journal of Family Psychology, 26*(5), 698–708. https://doi.org/10.1037/a0029260

Campbell, J. (2021, May 5). *Anti-Asian hate crimes surged in early 2021, study says*. CNN. Retrieved December 13, 2021, from https://www.cnn.com/2021/05/05/us/anti-asian-hate-crimes-study/index.html

Chacko, A., Jensen, S. A., Lowry, L. S., Cornwell, M., Chimklis, A., Chan, E., Lee, D., & Pulgarin, B. (2016). Engagement in behavioral parent training: Review of the literature and implications for practice. *Clinical Child and Family Psychology Review, 19*(3), 204–215. https://doi.org/10.1007/s10567-016-0205-2

Davids, C. M., & Mitchell, A. M. (2017). Intersectionality in couple and family therapy. *Encyclopedia of Couple and Family Therapy*, 1–6. https://doi.org/10.1007/978-3-319-15877-8_1013-1

Dickson, K. S., Zeedyk, S. M., Martinez, J., & Haine-Schlagel, R. (2017). Examining ethnic disparities in provider and parent in-session participation engagement. *Journal of Children's Services, 12*(1), 47–58. https://doi.org/10.1108/jcs-12-2016-0022

Doyle, D. M., & Molix, L. (2014). How does stigma spoil relationships? Evidence that perceived discrimination harms romantic relationship quality through impaired self-image. *Journal of Applied Social Psychology, 44*(9), 600–610. https://doi.org/10.1111/jasp.12252

Edwards, F., Lee, H., & Esposito, M. (2019). Risk of being killed by police use of force in the United States by age, race–ethnicity, and sex. *Proceedings of the National Academy of Sciences, 116*(34), 16793–16798. https://doi.org/10.1073/pnas.1821204116

Falicov, C. J. (2003). Culture in family therapy: New variations on a fundamental theme. In T. L. Sexton, G. R. Weeks, & M. S. Robbins (Eds.), *Handbook of family therapy: The science and practice of working with families and couples* (pp. 37–55). Brunner-Routledge.

Frost, D. M., & Meyer, I. H. (2009). Internalized homophobia and relationship quality among lesbians, gay men, and bisexuals. *Journal of Counseling Psychology, 56*(1), 97–109. https://doi.org/10.1037/a0012844

Fusco, R. A. (2010). Intimate partner violence in interracial couples: A comparison to White and ethnic minority monoracial couples. *Journal of Interpersonal Violence, 25*(10), 1785–1800. https://doi.org/10.1177/0886260509354510

Greenberg, N., Docherty, M., Gnanapragasam, S., & Wessely, S. (2020). Managing mental health challenges faced by healthcare workers during COVID-19 pandemic. *BMJ*, m1211. https://doi.org/10.1136/bmj.m1211

Hohmann-Marriott, B. E., & Amato, P. (2008). Relationship quality in interethnic marriages and cohabitations. *Social Forces, 87*(2), 825–855. https://doi.org/10.1353/sof.0.0151

Holder, A. M., Jackson, M. A., & Ponterotto, J. G. (2015). Racial microaggression experiences and coping strategies of Black Women in corporate leadership. *Qualitative Psychology, 2*(2), 164–180. https://doi.org/10.1037/qup0000024

Huber, L. P., & Solorzano, D. G. (2014). Racial microaggressions as a tool for critical race research. *Race, Ethnicity and Education, 18*, 297–320. https://doi.org/10.1080/13613324.2014.994173

Jones, S. C. T., Anderson, R. E., Gaskin-Wasson, A. L., Sawyer, B. A., Applewhite, K., & Metzger, I. W. (2020). From "crib to coffin": Navigating coping from racism-related stress throughout the lifespan of Black Americans. *American Journal of Orthopsychiatry, 90*(2), 267–282. https://doi.org/10.1037/ort0000430

Kliman, J. (1998). Social class as a relationship: Implications for family therapy. In M. McGoldrick (Ed.), *Re-visioning family therapy: Race, culture, and gender in clinical practice* (pp. 50–61). Guilford Press.

Laszloffy, T. A. (2008). *The Black Academic's guide to winning tenure—Without losing your soul*. Lynne Rienner Publishers.

Lavner, J. A., Barton, A. W., Bryant, C. M., & Beach, S. R. H. (2018). Racial discrimination and relationship functioning among African American couples. *Journal of Family Psychology, 32*(5), 686–691. https://doi.org/10.1037/fam0000415

Le, B., Dove, N. L., Agnew, C. R., Korn, M. S., & Mutso, A. A. (2010). Predicting nonmarital romantic relationship dissolution: A meta-analytic synthesis. *Personal Relationships, 17*, 377–390. https://doi.org/10.1111/j.1475-6811.2010.01285.x

Leslie, L. A., & Young, J. L. (2015). Interracial couples in therapy: Common themes and issues. *Journal of Social Issues, 71*(4), 788–803. https://doi.org/10.1111/josi.12149

Linville, D., & O'Neil, M. (n.d.). *Same sex parents and their children*. American Association for Marriage and Family Therapy. https://aamft.org/Consumer_Updates/Same-sex_Parents_and_Their_Children.aspx

McEwen, B. S., & Stellar, E. (1993). Stress and the individual: Mechanisms leading to disease. *Archives of Internal Medicine, 153*(18), 2093–2101. https://doi.org/10.1001/archinte.153.18.2093

Meyer, I. H., & Dean, L. (1998). Internalized homophobia, intimacy, and sexual behavior among gay and bisexual men. In G. M. Herek (Ed.), *Stigma and sexual orientation: Understanding prejudice against lesbians, gay men, and bisexuals* (pp. 160–186). Sage Publications, Inc. https://doi.org/10.4135/9781452243818.n8

Oppel, R. A., Jr., Taylor, D. B., & Bogel-Burroughs, N. (2021). What we know about Breonna Taylor's case and death. *The New York Times*. Retrieved August 23, 2022, from https://www.nytimes.com/article/breonna-taylor-police.html

Organista, K. C., Muñoz, R. F., & González, G. (1994). Cognitive-behavioral therapy for depression in low-income and minority medical outpatients: Description of a program and exploratory analyses. *Cognitive Therapy and Research, 18*(3), 241–259. https://doi.org/10.1007/bf02357778

Osborne, K. R., Caughy, M. O. B., Oshri, A., Smith, E. P., & Owen, M. T. (2021). Racism and preparation for bias within African American families. *Cultural Diversity and Ethnic Minority Psychology, 27*(2), 269–279. https://doi.org/10.1037/cdp0000339

Pager, D., & Shepherd, H. (2008). The sociology of discrimination: Racial discrimination in employment, housing, credit, and Consumer Markets. *Annual Review of Sociology, 34*(1), 181–209. https://doi.org/10.1146/annurev.soc.33.040406.131740

Perry, B., & Sutton, M. (2008). Policing the colour line: Violence against those in intimate interracial relationships. *Race, Gender, & Class, 15*(34), 240–261. https://irep.ntu.ac.uk/id/eprint/6568

Potter, H., & Thomas, D. T. (2012). "We told you that's how they are": Responses to White women in abusive intimate relationships with men of color. *Deviant Behavior, 33*(6), 469–491. https://doi.org/10.1080/01639625.2011.636661

Priest, J. B., McNeil Smith, S., Woods, S. B., & Roberson, P. N. E. (2020). Discrimination, family emotional climate, and African American health: An application of the BBFM. *Journal of Family Psychology, 34*(5), 598–609. https://doi.org/10.1037/fam0000621

Radler, B. T. (2014). The Midlife in the United States (MIDUS) series: A national longitudinal study of health and well-being. *Open Health Data, 2*(1). https://doi.org/10.5334/ohd.ai

Randall, A. K., & Bodenmann, G. (2009). The role of stress on close relationships and marital satisfaction. *Clinical Psychology Review, 29*(2), 105–115. https://doi.org/10.1016/j.cpr.2008.10.004

Rotherman, M., & Phinney, J. (1987). Introduction: Definitions and perspectives in the study of children's ethnic socialization. In J. Phinney & M. Rotherman (Eds.), *Children's ethnic socialization: Pluralism and development* (pp. 10–28). Sage.

Spickard, P. R. (1992). The illogic of American racial categories. In M. P. P. Root (Ed.), *Racially mixed people in America* (pp. 12–23). Sage.

Steele, C. M., Spencer, S. J., & Aronson, J. (2002). Contending with group image: The psychology of stereotype and Social Identity Threat. *Advances in Experimental Social Psychology,* 379–440. https://doi.org/10.1016/s0065-2601(02)80009-0

Sue, D. W., Sue, D., Neville, H. A., & Smith, L. (2019). *Counseling the culturally diverse: Theory and practice* (8th ed.). John Wiley & Sons.

Tatum, B. D. (2017). *Why are all the Black kids sitting together in the cafeteria?: And other conversations about race.* Penguin Books.

Tran, A. G. (2014). Family contexts: Parental experiences of discrimination and Child Mental Health. *American Journal of Community Psychology, 53*(1-2), 37–46. https://doi.org/10.1007/s10464-013-9607-1

Venkatraman, S. (2021, October 25). *Anti-Asian hate crimes rose 73% last year, updated FBI data says.* NBCNews.com. Retrieved December 13, 2021, from https://www.nbcnews.com/news/asian-america/anti-asian-hate-crimes-rose-73-last-year-updated-fbi-data-says-rcna3741

Villazor, R. C. (2018, April 10). Problematizing the protection of culture and the insular cases. *Harvard Law Review.* https://harvardlawreview.org/2018/04/problematizing-the-protection-of-culture-and-the-insular-cases/

Wang, M.-T., Henry, D. A., Smith, L. V., Huguley, J. P., & Guo, J. (2020). Parental ethnic-racial socialization practices and children of color's psychosocial and behavioral adjustment: A systematic review and meta-analysis. *American Psychologist, 75*(1), 1–22. https://doi.org/10.1037/amp0000464

Williams, D. R. (2018). Stress and the mental health of populations of color: Advancing our understanding of race-related stressors. *Journal of Health and Social Behavior, 59*(4), 466–485. https://doi.org/10.1177/0022146518814251

CHAPTER 6

CONTEMPORARY ISSUES IN COUPLE AND MARRIAGE THERAPY

LEARNING OBJECTIVES

After reading this chapter, you will be able to:

- Identify changing views of marriage.
- Recognize issues caused by increased rates of infertility.
- Describe factors related to delayed motherhood.
- Identify adult attachment issues.
- Distinguish premarital issues and warning signs.
- Identify causes of marital and relationship distress.
- Recognize ways in which crisis and disaster affect relationships.
- Identify relational issues related to substance abuse.
- Recognize how financial stress affects relationships.
- Distinguish trends and factors related to infidelity.
- Identify the causes and effects of intimate partner violence.
- Recognize contemporary issues related to divorce conflict.
- Distinguish online issues affecting relationships.
- Describe the nuances of internet addiction.
- Identify clinical issues associated with sex addiction.

INTRODUCTION TO CONTEMPORARY ISSUES THAT AFFECT COUPLES AND MARRIAGES

The American Association for Marriage and Family Therapy (AAMFT) defines *marriage and family therapy* as "[a]n intervention aimed at ameliorating not only relationship problems but also mental and emotional disorders within the context of family and larger social systems" (AAMFT, n.d.-a, para. 13). As this definition implies, couples and families are affected by changes in norms, mores, politics, religion, laws, media, and other influencing factors that affect everyone who belongs to a society.

Family composition and attitudes regarding family life in the United States have changed dramatically over the past 45 years. According to Daugherty and Copen (2016),

> [t]hese changes have resulted from a delay in the age of first marriage, a steep rise and then decline in the divorce rate, a lower fertility rate, an increase in cohabitation, a higher proportion of births occurring outside of marriage and within cohabiting unions, and an increasing number of first births to older women (p. 1).

While it is beyond the scope of this chapter to dive deeply into the nuances of each of the above issues, I will touch base on a few of them.

The U.S. Supreme Court legalized same-sex marriage in all 50 states in 2015. According to the U.S. Census Bureau, there were approximately 568,000 same-sex married couples in the United States in 2019. This major legal and cultural change reflects a new and more inclusive era in American history. Partly because of the legalization of same-sex marriage, changing demographics of the United States, and increased awareness around multicultural, diversity, intersectional, and social justice issues, this era holds the promise of further acceptance of diversity, inclusivity, equity, and support for groups that have historically been marginalized. In short, recent family-oriented developments demonstrate a dramatic shift to embracing diversity, sexual minorities, gender equality, and a more inclusive view of the family unit and of family life. This view influences not only same-sex intimate partnerships but also includes same-sex partners' parenting practices, increased ethnic and racial equality and equity, increasing numbers of multiracial families, single parents building biological families, and a seemingly endless intersection of components of identity. The initial example of legalized same-sex marriage signals that clinicians must adapt to an ever-changing relational landscape or risk being viewed as incompetent or irrelevant. A few additional contemporary relational changes include increased divorce, cohabiting couples who do not marry, and children born to unmarried parents (Witeck, 2014).

THE CHANGING INTEREST IN MARRIAGE

Contemporary statistics demonstrate that fewer couples are getting married and increasing numbers are involved in long-term relationships outside of marriage (Centers for Disease Control and Prevention [CDC], n.d.-b). Statistics from the CDC (n.d.-b) reveal that marriage is steadily becoming less popular among Americans. According to the report, there were only 6.8 marriages per 1,000 people in the United States in 2019, a decrease from 8.2 marriages per 1,000 people in 2006. Similarly, the Pew Research Center analyzed marital trends in 2019 and discovered that only 53% of American adults (aged 25–54) were married, compared with 72% in 1960 and 67% in 1990.

Many individuals are opting for nonmarital relationship structures such as living together, common-law marriages, cohabitation contracts (i.e., living together agreements), civil unions, and domestic partnerships. You may be wondering about the characteristics and implications of each option. Table 6.1 breaks down each option and provides additional practical information. To start, simply living together is a nonlegalized method of cohabitation. Many couples are now opting to do this permanently, and despite the potential legal and financial benefits of marriage they are choosing not to get married. While short-term cohabitation with an intimate partner is not new, it is worth stating that couples may strategically use this noncontractual time frame to determine whether they are compatible and able to effectively live together, or they may regard living together simply as a premarriage arrangement (i.e., courtship). When couples live together, they generally do not have any property rights in the other partner's assets if they break up. In other words, if the couple calls it quits, each partner will not retain anything but their own property. This option may be appealing for those wanting to avoid the litigious ramifications of a contractual relationship structure (Nelson, 2014; Trost, 2016).

Cohabitation contracts are an additional nonmarital relationship structure. In a general sense, unmarried people who live together are cohabiting. A cohabitation contract specifies who gets what if the relationship falls apart. Like a prenuptial agreement, a cohabitation contract can be drawn up by an attorney and can describe who is legally entitled to what (e.g., division of finances, investments, assets, pets, child custody, child support, debt payment) if the couple breaks up. One important caveat is the need to clarify shared assets. Cohabitation contracts provide information on ownership rights in shared assets. Cohabitation contracts are essentially ownership blueprints that provide couples with a detailed synopsis of decision-making processes (Nelson, 2014; Trost, 2016).

Prior to the legalization of same-sex marriage, some states offered legal protection through civil unions and domestic partnerships. While same-sex couples now have the same marital rights as opposite-sex couples, domestic partnerships and civil unions are still recognized as alternatives to marriage. Civil unions refer to a legal relationship status available in some states. This status can be granted to same-sex or opposite-sex couples. While benefits can vary from state to state, the status generally provides partners with health coverage, property rights, adoption provisions, and tort claims. While this arrangement can be ideal for certain couples, it is important to note that civil unions do not confer tax or social security benefits or offer partners other significant benefits found in a marriage. Domestic partnerships in some states also offer limited rights to unmarried couples (Nelson, 2014; Trost, 2016). In general, domestic partnerships may be similar to civil unions, depending on the state or jurisdiction. A main difference is that civil unions are legally recognized and somewhat similar to marriage, whereas domestic partnerships are not legally considered similar to marriage (First Look Family Law, n.d.).

Alongside increasing rates of cohabitation, rising numbers of U.S. births are taking place outside of marriage. The proportion of births to unmarried parents rose from 18% in 1980 to a record high of approximately 40% in 2016 (Child Trends, 2018; Martin et al., 2009). These statistics are far more pronounced for families of color—approximately 69.4% of Black children are born to mothers who are not married (National Vital Statistics Report, 2019). One major reason for the increase in unwed births is the higher percentage of cohabitating mothers (Brown, 2010). Again, it appears that growing numbers of people are simply choosing not to get married, choosing to cohabitate, and choosing to raise children outside of marriage (Daugherty & Copen, 2016).

According to recent statistics, the U.S. divorce rate of approximately 50% is among the highest in the world, with second marriages demonstrating far poorer outcomes than first marriages (Daugherty & Copen, 2016). This statistic actually demonstrates a decline in the U.S. divorces between 2000 and 2022. Reports indicate that the decline is partly due to the lower number of millennials getting married (Olito, 2019). Scott et al. (2013) found that the most frequently reported contributors to divorce were *lack of commitment*, *infidelity*, and *conflict/arguing*. Scott et al. (2013), in their study of 52 divorced individuals, found that lack of relationship commitment was the most common contributing factor to divorce. Some couples described their marital commitment as diminishing gradually over time, while others indicated a sudden drop in commitment.

Scott et al. (2013) found that infidelity was the second most common contributor to divorce. Interestingly, although infidelity was described as a key reason for divorce, it was often viewed as a turning point in an already declining relationship.

The third most cited cause of divorce was conflict and arguing. Prior to making the decision to get a divorce, partners were involved in intense and frequent arguments that were accompanied by lack of support and connectivity. According to participants, as the conflicts escalated over time, there was also a general sense of poor communication.

INCREASED RATES OF INFERTILITY

Fertility—the ability to conceive children—has always been a key factor in the survival of the human species. As such, parenthood is one of the most salient and meaningful desires experienced by societies, cultures, couples, and individuals (Riskind & Patterson, 2010). Given the importance of fertility and parenthood, infertility is often considered a major life crisis for affected couples and individuals. The World Health Organization (2020) defines *infertility* as the inability to conceive within 1 or more years after engaging in regular unprotected sexual intercourse. Infertility is further defined as primary or secondary. Primary infertility is experienced by individuals who never get pregnant or conceive. Secondary infertility applies to individuals who have successfully conceived in the past but are no longer able to conceive.

Globally, infertility is a major health issue that affects 15% of couples of reproductive age—approximately 48 million couples and 186 million individuals (Kuohung & Hornstein, 2021; Sharlip et al., 2002; World Health Organization, 2020). According to Honarvar and Taghavi (2020), the prevalence of infertility has increased by approximately 50% from 1955 to the present. The Cleveland Clinic, a nonprofit American academic medical center based in Cleveland, Ohio, found that the risk factors for infertility in all genders include age (over 35 for women and 40 for men), diabetes, eating disorders, excessive alcohol and substance use, exposure to environmental toxins (e.g., lead or pesticides), excessive exercise, radiation therapy, sexually transmitted diseases (STDs), stress, smoking, and weight problems (Cleveland Clinic, 2020). Furthermore, over the past 40 years, global sperm counts have dropped by half (Levine et al., 2017). Potential causes of low sperm counts include environmental chemicals, increased rates of diabetes and obesity, and the trend to delay conceiving a child. Overall, infertility is on the rise, and the inability to reproduce can have enormous physical, emotional, financial, and sociocultural implications for couples.

Along with the rise in infertility is the rise in individuals and couples seeking therapy related to reproductive-based issues. Complex interpersonal and intrapersonal issues accompany infertility. According to Domar et al. (1993), difficulty in conceiving often creates serious emotional distress for individuals and couples. The authors compare the magnitude of this distress with being diagnosed with HIV, heart disease, or cancer. The distress often manifests as anxiety or depression.

Research has found gender differences in the way people cope with infertility stress. Early in treatment, women typically demonstrate more intense emotional responses regardless of which partner has the issue(s) around fertility. By contrast, men generally demonstrate negative emotions only if the infertility involves their own health issues (Nachtigall et al., 1992; Verhaak et al., 2005). Men who avoid or dismiss the topic often increase the feelings of stress experienced by their partners. Similarly, men often become more distressed when women are increasingly confrontative and upfront with their emotions surrounding infertility (Peterson et al., 2009). Lastly, when both partners experience feelings of shame and self-blame, they may become emotionally distant and unable to give or receive spousal support (Peterson et al., 2006).

Sexual and gender minority individuals (LGBTQIA+ individuals) face unique issues related to infertility treatment. These issues partly involve heteronormative biases and challenges related to insurance coverage for infertility-based concerns. According to Baptiste-Roberts et al. (2017), medical diagnoses often include heteronormative terms such as *couple* and *insemination*. This excludes the population of individuals who are single parents pursuing biological family building. In addition to the systemic marginalization and homophobic attitudes faced by LGBTQIA+ individuals, many insurance companies simply do not cover infertility treatment (Shanley & Asch, 2009). Individuals identifying as LGBTQIA+ are likely to use expensive services and technologies such as donor insemination, in vitro fertilization (IVF), and surrogacy (Bitler & Schmidt, 2012; Shanley & Asch, 2009). Many of these treatments require additional services such as working with a fertility professional, legal counsel, and mental health services. The out-of-pocket costs for these services can make access to procreation impossible for many.

DELAYED MOTHERHOOD

The increasing prevalence of delayed motherhood symbolizes a significant change for women in many Western societies. The average age when women in many Western countries have their first child has shifted to much later in life (Lemoine & Ravitsky, 2015; Wyndham et al., 2012). Delayed motherhood now stretches into the late 30s and 40s for women who have the privilege (e.g., ability to pay steep out-of-pocket fees for uninsured procedures) and ability to forego motherhood until their education, career, and other pertinent personal goals have been sufficiently achieved. For example, Matthews and Hamilton (2014) found that between 1973 and 2006 there was a sixfold increase in 35- to 39-year-old U.S. women giving birth, and between 1985 and 2012 there was a fourfold increase in 40- to 44-year-old women giving birth. Factors contributing to social acceptance of postponed motherhood include a cultural trend toward later parenthood, vast innovations in assisted reproductive technologies (ARTs), intense financial and career pressures on young adults, and widespread media promotion of unlimited reproductive autonomy for women (Daniluk & Koert 2012; Lemoine & Ravitsky, 2015; Miller, 2011; Wyndham et al., 2012). From a social justice perspective, women who wait until later in life to conceive a child are likely able to compete at a higher level within the workplace. While benefits associated with younger motherhood are prevalent, many young mothers observe their male colleagues and nonchildbearing/rearing female colleagues excel and surpass them in the workplace. With limited societal support for providing career and educational advancement options for young mothers, lack of professional advancement can seem like a cultural punishment for honoring an ideal biological fertility window. In addition to cultural norms and potential advantages of postponing motherhood, certain corporations appear to be financially incentivizing delayed motherhood so female employees can concentrate on their careers. For example, Apple, Google, and Facebook provide funding for egg freezing for women who are interested in concentrating on their corporate careers and delaying child-rearing until later in life (Duvander et al., 2005; Weller, 2017).

From a biological perspective, women are most fertile during their early to mid-20s (Lemoine & Ravitsky, 2015). Despite social pressure and incentives for delaying motherhood, investigations into child-rearing perceptions still demonstrate that many individuals believe that the late 20s are the ideal time to have children (Daniluk & Koert, 2012). In addition, evidence suggests that many older mothers (35–40 years of age) regret waiting until later in life to have children (Daniluk et al., 2012). While reproductive technologies can extend the female reproductive cycle, there are also health risks for both mothers and children when the biological window for reproduction is expanded in this manner.

Women who wait until an older age to have biological children run a variety of health risks, including ectopic pregnancy, fetal death and pregnancy loss, multiple births, preeclampsia (i.e., high blood pressure and organ damage), gestational diabetes, Cesarean delivery, and preterm delivery (Beemsterboer et al., 2006; Hoffman et al., 2019; Liu et al., 2011). In addition, fetuses and infant children of older mothers also face increased rates of health concerns, such as low birth weight, chromosomal abnormalities (i.e., extra, deleted, or duplicated chromosomes), cerebral palsy (i.e., impairment of child's ability to move and to maintain balance and posture), developmental delay, learning disability, sensory impairment (e.g., deafness, blindness), language delay, and attention and behavioral concerns (Deonandan, 2010; Hoffman et al., 2019; Liu et al., 2011). Lastly, delayed fatherhood also poses increased health risks for fetuses and infant children, including miscarriage, schizophrenia, and autism (Balasch, 2010; Wicks, 2021).

Individuals having children at an advanced maternal age experience a variety of issues related to infertility. As previously indicated, natural conception becomes more difficult as women age. According to Leridon (2004), the likelihood of conceiving within a 1-year time frame drops from 75% at age 30 to 44% at age 40. Given that more than half of older mothers have difficulties with conception, they tend to depend on ART to become pregnant. ARTs increase the hope that women can reproduce when they choose. While ARTs provide a hopeful option, they do not guarantee positive results. Similar to biological/natural conception, the effectiveness of ARTs decreases with maternal age. For example, according to Gunby et al. (2011), a 40-year-old woman who receives IVF or intracytoplasmic sperm injection (ICSI) has only an 11.4% rate of conception, compared with a 37.4% success rate for the same procedures in women 35 years of age and younger. Table 6.1 describes the ARTs (Medical News Today, n.d.).

TABLE 6.1 ASSISTED REPRODUCTIVE TECHNOLOGIES AND DESCRIPTIONS

Assisted Reproductive Technologies	Description
Artificial insemination	Directly inserting sperm into a woman's cervix, fallopian tubes, or uterus
In vitro fertilization	Extracting and fertilizing a woman's egg and transferring the resulting embryo into the uterus of the biological or surrogate mother
Intracytoplasmic sperm injection	Injecting a single sperm cell into the cytoplasm of a woman's egg
Preimplantation genetic diagnosis	Identifying genetic defects in embryos created through in vitro fertilization prior to pregnancy
Intrafallopian transfer	Using laparoscopic surgery to distribute gametes (egg and sperm cells) into a woman's fallopian tube
Frozen embryo transfer	Thawing previously frozen embryos and inserting them into a woman's uterus
Third-party reproductive technology	Inseminating sperm or implanting an egg/embryo into a surrogate mother

Note: The descriptions in the table only provide a brief definition of each procedure.

Source: Data from Medical News Today. (n.d.). *What to know about assisted reproductive technology*. https://www.medicalnewstoday.com/articles/assisted-reproductive-technology#types.

ADULT ATTACHMENT

As described in previous chapters, John Bowlby and Mary Ainsworth empirically investigated and theorized the biological attachment needs of human beings. While much of the literature and research focus on the attachment needs of children and infants, Bowlby (1988) theorized that human attachment needs remain present throughout one's life. As people develop and engage in adult intimate partnerships, there is a constant need for emotionally and physically receptive human contact. Throughout the human life span, individuals amass an internal working model of the nature and their success at obtaining sufficient proximity or comfort from their attachment figures, beginning with their caregivers and continuing with close friends and intimate partners (Simpson & Rholes, 2017). Adult internal working models are considered stable and are theorized to transfer between relationships; however, because these cognitive models are based on one's experiences with relationships, they can be altered based on new relational experiences (Agishtein & Brumbaugh, 2013).

Secure adult attachment relationships encompass a sense of trust, self-esteem, enjoyment of intimacy, and freely sharing feelings with others. Bowlby believed that the sense of security reflects how an individual has been treated across the life span. If the intimate relationship does not provide security, adults develop different attachment coping strategies that provide self-protection and reflect their internal processes. Most often, these strategies manifest as overly anxious or increasingly distant and avoidant attachment styles (Bowlby, 1988). The vulnerabilities of highly avoidant or anxious individuals emerge primarily when they encounter stressful relationally bound experiences that activate their internal working models (Simpson & Rholes, 2017). Examples could include physical, sexual, and emotional threats such as divorce, infidelity, and manipulation.

As individuals consider the notion of attachment throughout the life span, a common question might be, "Does my childhood attachment pattern translate directly into my adult life?" The answer is complicated. In short, adult attachment depends on many factors that happen between infancy and adulthood. These factors may involve the evolution of the parent–child relationship throughout adulthood, adult relationship experiences, and other relationships with friends and family members. For example, a person who appears preoccupied and anxious as a child may develop a secure attachment pattern as an adult. Conversely, a securely attached child may develop a dismissive and avoidant pattern in adulthood. While it is unclear whether early attachment styles predict future adult intimacy behaviors, they can help predict patterns of behavior in adulthood. If insecurity becomes a factor in adulthood, it typically manifests as anxious and preoccupied behavior or dismissive and avoidant behavior. At the core of anxious and preoccupied attachment coping strategies is a fear of interpersonal abandonment or rejection, an intense need for approval, and a tendency to overreact to negative feelings in order to receive intimate partner support and/or comfort. In comparison, a dismissive and avoidant attachment coping strategy is conceptualized as fear of intimacy, intense desire for self-reliance, a negative perception of others, and emotional withdrawal (Mikulincer & Shaver, 2012; Mikulincer et al., 2003; Wei et al., 2005).

Clinicians working with adults who demonstrate insecure attachment patterns will likely notice hyperactivation strategies (i.e., anxious and preoccupied attachment style) or deactivation strategies (i.e., dismissive and avoidant attachment style). Adults who demonstrate hyperactivation coping strategies are likely to show heightened emotional responses and to overreact to negative emotions. In relationships, this can manifest in a variety of ways, including, but not limited to, clingy behaviors (e.g., frequent and excessive texting), preoccupation with intimacy (e.g., frequent requests or encouragement for sex and/or intimacy), and hypervigilance around any perceived rejection (i.e., perceiving benign partner behavior as relational rejection). Adults who demonstrate deactivation coping strategies often appear emotionally detached, avoid intimacy and emotions, and frequently distance themselves from their intimate partner. In relationships, this can emerge in a plethora of ways, including, but not limited to, avoiding emotional engagement (e.g., not responding to a partner's text messages), inhibiting sexual arousal (e.g., avoiding sex), and becoming overly self-reliant (e.g., doing all chores and household projects alone; Mikulincer & Shaver, 2012; Mikulincer et al., 2003; Wei et al., 2005).

Findings on Cultural Attachment Patterns

Apart from early fieldwork in Uganda (Ainsworth, 1967), initial research into attachment patterns was centered on middle-class White families in the United States (Ainsworth, 1985). Consequently, more research was needed to determine whether attachment patterns transfer to different cultures. Fortunately, thanks to much research, there is now evidence that supports the presence of the attachment behavioral system in all people (van Ijzendoorn & Sagi-Schwartz, 2008). In other words, while parenting behavior and childhood attachment norms vary, both secure and insecure attachments occur in every culture (Rothbaum et al., 2000). Globally, there is consensus regarding the existence of three basic attachment styles: secure, avoidant, and anxious (Behrens et al., 2007). Furthermore, from a global perspective, the secure attachment style is the most common attachment pattern found in children of all cultures (van Ijzendoorn & Sagi, 1999). According to van Ijzendoorn and Bakermans-Kranenburg's (1996) meta-analysis of cross-cultural investigations into adult attachment, the worldwide adult attachment style averages are 24% avoidant, 58% secure, and 18% anxious.

While global patterns exist, clinicians who assess attachment styles must pay attention to cultural differences in child-rearing practices, culturally bound contextual influences, and variations in cultural norms and mores. Behavioral representations of a secure attachment pattern in infants can vary culturally. For example, White northern European U.S. caregivers tend to parent their children to become happy, confident, and assertive, while Puerto Rican mothers often parent children to become attentive, well-behaved, and calm (Carlson & Harwood, 2003; Harwood et al., 1999). Regarding attachment style, compared with global norms, African Americans tend to demonstrate a higher rate of the avoidant attachment style (Magai et al., 2001; Wei et al., 2004) and individuals from Japan show a higher rate of the anxious attachment style and a lower rate of the avoidant attachment style (Behrens et al., 2007; Takahashi, 1986).

PREMARITAL ISSUES AND WARNING SIGNS

Researchers have discovered over 24 factors that predict marital satisfaction. These factors can be clustered into three overarching categories: (a) individual traits (e.g., personality traits, emotional health, mental health issues, values, attitudes, and beliefs); (b) couple traits (e.g., communication style, conflict resolution ability, goals and values compatibility, and degree of acquaintance); and (c) personal and relational contexts (e.g., family background, existing children and previous marriage, family-of-origin relational history, age of marriage, and approval/disapproval of friendship network; AAMFT, n.d.-d). Individual traits that negatively affect marital satisfaction include difficulty with stress management, self-consciousness, anxiety, irritability, depression, hostility, impulsiveness, and emotional problems. For example, individuals who demonstrate anger and hostility often jump to conclusions, lose their temper, and make hurtful comments or display hurtful behaviors to their partners. These individuals do not often make good relational partners because their destructive behavior places their partner in a constant state of fear. Individual traits that can positively affect marital satisfaction include sociability, good physical health, conventionality, good interpersonal skills, high self-esteem, and flexibility (Jackson, 2009). For example, individuals who demonstrate good relational flexibility tend to effectively navigate the many relational, emotional, and contextual ups and downs couples frequently encounter.

Dr. John M. Gottman has engaged in an impressive and extensive amount of research to understand the premarital warning signs that can lead to separation or divorce. Gottman's (1999) textbook entitled *The Marriage Clinic: A Scientifically Based Marital Therapy* provides couple, marriage, and family practitioners with a blueprint for his approach and the tools to ensure effective outcomes. The central component of Gottman-oriented premarital counseling is building a *sound relationship house*. The sound relationship house theory is the foundation of the Gottman method. This theory uses a practical approach to help couples break through barriers to achieve higher levels of intimacy, awareness, connection, and understanding in their relationships. Other important aspects of Gottman's premarital therapy include creating love maps, promoting rituals of connection, learning communication skills, strengthening problem-solving skills, and increasing fondness and admiration (Gottman, 1999).

While hurtful comments, criticism, contempt, and abuse are toxic, destructive, and unfortunately present in many relationships, most nonabusive yet problematic relational behaviors are motivated by a partner's misguided and uninformed actions aimed toward keeping the relationship moving in a desirable direction. For example, a partner who attempts to make their partner jealous by attracting attention on the internet (flirtatious comments on Instagram, Facebook likes, etc.) may mistakenly believe that this strategy will keep their partner interested and motivated to be in the relationship or to want them sexually. Unfortunately, this behavior is more likely to result in emotional distancing, fear, mistrust, and/or retaliation.

Gottman's premarital warning signs (i.e., danger signs) that emerge when couples communicate about problems or conflicts are key to understanding relational pitfalls and impediments to relationship satisfaction. Gottman and his colleagues have identified nine danger signs that can lead to separation or divorce: (a) harsh startups; (b) the four horsemen of the apocalypse: criticism, defensiveness, contempt, and stonewalling; (c) flooding; (d) body language; (e) failed repair attempts; and (f) bad memories (Gottman, 1999, 1994; Gottman & Levenson, 1992). Table 6.2 provides concise definitions of these danger signs.

There is abundant evidence that the strongest predictor of relationship dissatisfaction and dysfunction is the way couples deal with conflict (Canary et al., 1995; Karney & Bradbury, 1995). Furthermore, partners may use positive or negative maintenance behaviors to control and maintain a preferred relationship condition and trajectory. While positive relational maintenance is associated with satisfaction (Canary & Dainton, 2003), negative relational maintenance behaviors lead to negative relational outcomes and dissatisfaction (Dainton & Gross, 2008; Goodboy & Bolkan, 2011). Six common negative relational maintenance behaviors are associated with destructive outcomes: (a) allowing a partner's overly controlling behavior to continue, (b) initiating hurtful conflict to control one's partner, (c) avoiding one's partner or evading discussion of a particular relational topic, (d) spying on one's partner to attain information, (e) engaging in infidelity, and (f) inducing jealousy (Dainton & Gross, 2008).

TABLE 6.2 GOTTMAN'S PREDICTORS OF BREAKUP OR DIVORCE, DESCRIPTION, AND EXAMPLE

Predictor of Breakup/Divorce	Description	Examples
Harsh startups	The couple's conflictual discussions begin with criticism, sarcasm, or negative comments.	"We have so many problems, I don't even know where to begin."
Criticism	A partner blames their partner's personal character for their relational problem(s). Criticism usually begins with "you."	"You are completely insensitive to my needs."
Defensiveness	One partner blames the other partner for the issue, thereby intensifying the conflict.	"I am not insensitive. I think about your needs all the time. You just never notice the good times."
Contempt	One partner behaves in ways that intentionally hurt the other partner (e.g., eye rolling, mockery, name calling, hostile humor).	"You don't care about me because you are a misogynistic pig."
Stonewalling	Partner stops responding and listening to their spouse (silence, looking away, disengagement, or leaving the room). This is often an attempt to control overwhelming emotions aroused by contempt.	"I'm not sure how to respond."
Flooding	Communication becomes so negative that it becomes too overwhelming to handle and communication ends.	"You are so negative, cynical, and controlling it is hardly worth talking to you."
Body language	Physically distressing bodily changes occur during flooding.	Examples include rapid heart rate, elevated blood pressure, and shortness of breath.
Failed repair attempts	When a couple escalates during a discussion, there is often an attempt to deescalate the tension in the conversation. Failed repair attempts are a predictor of breakup/divorce.	"Can we please talk about this later?"
Bad memories	Partners have a negative perspective on their past and do not talk about positive memories or success in dealing with challenges.	"I know this happened 18 years ago, but I just cannot seem to get over it."

Source: Data from Gottman, J. (1999). *The marriage clinic: A scientifically based marital therapy.* W. W. Norton & Company.

It is no secret that one of the most common reasons couples choose to come into therapy is to improve their communication. Communication is a cornerstone issue that can make or break a relationship. When communication is a problem, relationships suffer tremendously. Couples considering long-term relationships may be wondering how to identify signs of communication problems. Markman et al. (2001) identified communication danger signs that lead to relational dissatisfaction and distress: escalation (i.e., interactions that increase emotional intensity), invalidation (i.e., hurtful comments that debase an individual), withdrawal (i.e., checking out), and negative interpretations (i.e., believing a partner's motives are based on negative intent).

MARITAL AND RELATIONSHIP DISTRESS

Marital and long-term relationship distress has an enormous impact on couples and families. Emotions such as worry, anxiety, sadness, depression, and tension emerge within families when there is relational distress. The interconnectedness, interdependence, and hierarchical nature of most families creates a situation in which problems within the marital/relational dyad reverberate throughout all of the subsystems and individual family members. For example, if the couple/parents are frequently arguing, the children may present as overly anxious and needy, due in part to a general sense of insecurity.

As previously described, communication difficulty is a common presenting problem that couples come to therapy to repair. While it is true that couples who experience distress often present with negative patterns of communication, there are often multiple negative issues involved, and for most couples things have to get very bad before they will reach out for professional therapeutic help. Couples who experience severe relational distress tend to fight frequently, have lost a sense of affection for one another, stop having sex, do not consider their spouse to be a friend, appear completely alienated from one another, and express a significant amount of disappointment. Common issues that often create a sense of distress in relationships include, but are not limited to, substance abuse, gambling, loss of a child, raising children with special needs, lack of financial resources, infidelity, infertility, loss of employment, negative experiences with in-laws, and untreated mental illness (AAMFT, n.d.-c).

Marriages and long-term relationships are delicate, ever-changing, and developmentally transformative bonds. Marital distress has an enormous impact on society, adults, and children. According to Lebow et al. (2012), marital distress can affect people *emotionally*, *behaviorally*, and *cognitively*. Emotionally, individuals in distressed marriages often demonstrate negative emotions, do not have much emotional affection, and have difficulty with emotional self-regulation. From a behavioral perspective, individuals in distressed marriages may demonstrate negative communication patterns, have negative sexual issues, and display physical aggression. Cognitively speaking, individuals in distressed marriages tend to have negative attributions about their partner, to hold unrealistic expectations for their relationship, and to perceive their partner as being motivated by negative intentions.

Beyond general emotional, behavioral, and cognitive distress, distressed marriages have long been associated with increased mental health issues and psychological distress, which often manifest as anxiety and depression (Hawkins & Booth, 2005; Proulx et al., 2007; Whitton et al., 2007). Furthermore, distressed marriages and relationships are associated with increased risk of physical health issues such as heart disease, delayed wound healing, cancer, a variety of metabolic syndromes, chronic pain, and early mortality rates (Holt-Lunstad et al., 2010; Impett & Peplau, 2006; Kiecolt-Glaser et al., 2005; Orth-Gomér et al., 2000; Schmaling & Sher, 1997; Troxel et al., 2005).

While excessive conflict equates to negative relational outcomes, some conflicts are inevitable in any relationship. Throughout the life span, all relationships go through transitions that have the potential to create varying degrees of relational distress. Some common transitions that cause relationship distress include moving in together, marriage, career change, having children, adjusting to child developmental periods (e.g., adolescence, adulthood), transitioning children out of the home, and retirement. While these changes and transitions are common, they have the potential to create distress if partners lack flexibility or cohesion (Storaasli & Markman, 1990; Whiteman et al., 2007).

The COVID-19 global pandemic has had a tremendous impact on couples, affecting relational satisfaction, family life, health, education, and economic security in countries all over the world. The pandemic has caused many couples to feel stressed, isolated, financially insecure, and afraid. Pandemic issues that have caused high levels of stress include healthcare needs, fear of COVID-19 transmission and the subsequent decrease in intimacy, social isolation, mental health deterioration, lack of physical well-being, closure of many schools and additional childcare responsibilities, business closures and subsequent economic vulnerability, and job losses. Marital distress and dissatisfaction are particularly high among couples where spouses are unresponsive, hurtful, and prone to abusive behaviors. According to Boserup et al. (2020), cases of intimate partner violence (IPV) increased by 25% to 33% globally during the first phase of the global pandemic. Similarly, according to Maldonado-Rodriguez (2021), the National Commission on COVID-19 and Criminal Justice reported that the number of IPV incidents in the United States increased by 8.1%.

EFFECTS OF CRISIS AND DISASTER ON RELATIONSHIPS

Crises have the potential to disturb, ravage, and devastate people's lives. Recent history is replete with both crisis and disaster on an individual, couple, family, local, national, and global scale. Those who experience or witness crisis are affected at some level. The degree to which people are affected has to do with the duration, intensity, type, acuity of the fallout, and the speed at which response efforts occur. The Robb Elementary School shooting in Uvalde, Texas, on May 24, 2022, where 19 students and 2 teachers were shot and killed by 18-year-old Salvador Ramos; the Sandy Hook Elementary School shooting in Newtown, Connecticut, on December 14, 2012, where 20 students and 6 teachers and administrators were shot and killed by 20-year-old Adam Lanza; and the Las Vegas shooting on October 1, 2017, where 60 people were shot and killed and 411 were wounded by 64-year-old Stephen Paddock are but a few recent examples of large-scale human-initiated crises. While all crises exact a toll on observers, the various contextual factors, including the magnitude, intensity, human initiation, and the inclusion of the vulnerable population of young children, create an extremely sad, tragic, and horrific meaning around the previously stated examples. Additional factors that enhanced the horror of the explicated examples include lackluster police response efforts, lack of motives from the perpetrator, the use of semiautomatic rifles, and the unanswered questions due to the gunman's subsequent suicide or death due to shootout with police (Barron, 2012; Black & Flynn, 2020; Hayes, 2017; Pilkington, 2022).

While disasters have been taking place since the beginning of time, the disaster mental health research and literature is less well-developed when compared with the crisis literature. Disasters can range in category (e.g., human-initiated, nature-initiated, technology-initiated). For example, the COVID-19 global pandemic would be considered a nature-initiated disaster (i.e., caused by events that take place in nature), the 2022 Russian invasion of Ukraine would be considered a human-initiated disaster (i.e., deliberately or nondeliberately caused by people), and the 1986 Chernobyl plant nuclear meltdown in Ukraine would be considered a technology-initiated disaster (i.e., caused by technology failure). Whatever the category, the essence of a disaster is an abnormal event that is often catastrophic, spontaneous, and typically carries large-scale losses and devastation. Like crises, the context and meaning individuals ascribe to a disaster matter a great deal. Regarding context, disasters are broad in scope, have clear beginnings and ends, are either intentional or unintentional, have unique patterns in regard to response efforts, and there is much variability regarding whether or not disasters have an identifiable cause (Black & Flynn, 2020).

Do people typically experience trauma during the aftermath of a disaster or crisis? What predicts postdisaster/crisis resilience? These are important questions to consider when working with couples who have survived nature-based, human-based, and/or technology-based crises/disasters. In general, research (e.g., Bonanno et al., 2007; Butler et al., 2009) indicates that most individuals can and do successfully bounce back from crisis and disaster. While initial stress is a normal aspect of crisis and disaster, it is generally believed that people can resume normal functioning once the crisis and disaster have subsided (Black & Flynn, 2020). Although it is commonly understood that exposure to crisis and disaster can bring stress, posttraumatic stress disorder, acute stress disorder, and anxiety symptoms, there has been far less attention given to its effects on intimate relationships.

In light of recent events (e.g., the COVID-19 global pandemic, nature-based disasters, school shootings, war), it would seem short-sighted to discuss contemporary relational issues without describing the potentially destructive effects of crises and disasters on relationships. Specifically, postdisaster individual and collective traumatic response has always had a major impact on people's lives (see Black & Flynn, 2020). When disaster strikes, people navigate the challenges with the help of family members and close friends. Floods, wildfires, hurricanes, and mass migration have immense impact on the sense of equilibrium that many couples experience. For example, following a natural disaster, couples may experience scarce resources, inability to fulfill basic needs, displacement, and their own personal mental health issues. In addition to these issues, they will also experience their partner's reaction to these concerns. It would be a serious understatement to suggest that relationships and people suffer greatly when these events take place. In truth, people's lives are often devastated, and it can seem like a miracle when couples pull through a crisis or disaster with their relationship intact.

Social vulnerabilities include negative experiences related to society's contextual devaluing related to race/ethnicity, age, socioeconomic status, language, gender, and health. In a general sense, social vulnerabilities give rise to many negative relational outcomes, including physical, emotional, and sexual violence. IPV is one of the most destructive postcrisis relational experiences (First et al., 2017; Lauve-Moon & Ferreira, 2017). Research indicates an increase in IPV in postdisaster environments (Lauve-Moon & Ferreira, 2017; Schumacher et al., 2010). The potential for abuse is increased even further for those in devalued social vulnerability contexts (Enarson et al., 2006; First et al., 2017).

While classic scholarship suggests that crisis and disaster have the potential to increase relational dissatisfaction (e.g., Bodenmann, 1995; Story & Bradbury, 2004), more recently Williamson et al. (2021) discovered that couples may experience an initial boost or increase in relational satisfaction immediately before and after the disaster but then revert to predisaster functioning as the rescue period continues. Furthermore, scholarship (Cutter et al., 2003) indicates that social vulnerabilities place people at greater risk for negative outcomes following crisis and disaster.

The American Psychological Association has defined *resilience* as "the process of adapting well in the face of adversity, trauma, tragedy, threats or even significant sources of stress" (2014, para. 4). What protective factors can help couples pull through the immense challenges presented by crisis and disaster? Literature on this topic indicates that protective factors include, but are not limited to, the following: positive predisaster functioning, religion or spirituality, effective coping skills, advanced education, limited experience with trauma and loss, capacity for hope and optimism, and emotional stability. Furthermore, adaptive skills such as application of flexible, contextualized coping skills, seeking social support, positive reframing after the disaster, and meaning-making are regarded as greatly helpful in rebounding from crisis and disaster (Bosmans et al., 2013, 2015; Henslee et al., 2015; Shing et al., 2016).

Relational Teletherapy With Crisis and Disaster Survivors

As scientific technology evolves and coalesces with contemporary crisis and disaster clinical issues, clinicians must stay on the cutting edge of clinical advancements and their implications for more effective practice. Crisis and disaster survivors have more technology-oriented therapeutic options now than ever before. Contemporary trauma-based interventions could include teletherapy, online psychoeducation, virtual reality (VR) interventions, functional MRI (fMRI) output, eye movement desensitization and reprocessing (EMDR), and brainspotting (BSP; Black & Flynn, 2020). While technology-driven interventions are remarkable, most are conducted within an individual counseling context and some have yet to be formally adapted for online use (e.g., BSP).

The worldwide upheaval caused by the COVID-19 pandemic has created a massive restructuring in how therapeutic services are delivered. COVID-19 and subsequent variants have significantly changed the norms around therapeutic services. When the government shut down and citizens were required to quarantine, therapeutic services were made available via Health Insurance Portability and Accountability Act (HIPAA)-compliant telehealth options (e.g., Amazon Chime, Updox, VSee, Zoom for Healthcare, Doxy.me; Office for Civil Rights, 2021). The status quo for many clinicians has been in-person clinical practice, but the global pandemic changed the status quo and forced the clinical world into wide-scale telehealth adoption (Calkins, 2021).

While increasing adoption of telebehavioral healthcare is a burgeoning contemporary issue, different forms of telehealth have been available since the 1990s and states have passed unique laws and mandates regarding its use. Prior to the global pandemic, many insurance companies would not reimburse telehealth therapeutic services at parity with in-person therapy (i.e., in-person services received a higher reimbursement rate). The global pandemic created a situation in which states have mandated and insurers have approved expanded telehealth coverage. It is unknown whether or not this parity will continue postpandemic; however, it is clear that telehealth is here to stay (Calkins, 2021).

Online couple therapy (e.g., couple teletherapy, remote relational therapy) has been used with much greater frequency since the pandemic's official declaration on March 11, 2020. Greater than normal challenges affected relationships, including, but not limited to, financial strain, job loss, COVID-19 infection, increased time spent together at home, increased relational conflict, uncertainty about the future, and overall declines in mental health (Lebow, 2020; Pietromonaco & Overall, 2020; Stanley & Markman, 2020). These problems have created a great need for couple-based work; however, due to fear surrounding the possibility of virus transmission, individuals are hesitant to enter physical therapeutic settings, dislike therapy with face mask and social distancing protocols, or practitioners may simply not offer in-person sessions due to how the aforementioned issues affect them. All of these factors have created a situation where clinicians have either chosen or have been forced to establish and/or increase their ability to offer telehealth services to couples.

It is one thing to work with an individual client via computer; however, the intimate, systemic, and nonverbal nature of working with couples has the potential to create new challenges within the online therapeutic environment. After surveying 58 couple therapists, Hardy et al. (2021) provided initial information on clinicians' couple teletherapy experiences. Participants described the importance of (a) understanding and following current state laws and standards regarding telehealth practice, (b) having a sound clinical infrastructure (e.g., video, notes, secure physical space, reliable internet connection), and (c) intentionality around staying alert and focused during the therapeutic process. This sense of being alert and focused may have to do with the different internal stimulation a practitioner receives when conducting relational therapy via telehealth.

You may be asking, "How do we incorporate the latest cutting-edge trauma-based technology within a relational therapy practice context?" Great question. First, it is essential that clinicians find a secure and private space; have a computer with the appropriate HIPAA-compliant telehealth platform (e.g., Zoom for Healthcare, Doxy.me);

find a platform that will help with the management of their practice, including documentation, insurance, billing, and scheduling (e.g., SimplePractice); develop a fee scale; get on multiple insurance panels as an approved provider; network and market their services; and enhance and update their skillset with relevant professional development experiences. Lastly, it is important to consult the literature and colleagues to avoid major pitfalls associated with being an online practitioner. For example, Hertlein et al. (2015) reported the perceptions of 226 marriage and family counselors/therapists regarding online ethical issues associated with teletherapy. They identified concerns and barriers to growth, including (a) confidentiality, (b) impact on the therapeutic alliance, (c) licensing and liability concerns, (d) handling crises, and (e) training and educational constraints.

SUBSTANCE ABUSE

According to the National Center for Health Statistics (2021), substance overdose is the number one cause of accidental death in the United States. Substance abuse has been on the rise for quite some time; however, the COVID-19 global pandemic greatly exacerbated substance abuse issues. During the first year of the pandemic, there were over 100,000 fatal overdoses in the United States. This represents the highest overdose death toll ever recorded in a single year (Ahmad et al., 2022). According to an American Medical Association (2021) article entitled "Nation's Drug-Related Overdose and Death Epidemic Continues to Worsen," since the start of the COVID-19 pandemic every state in the United States has experienced an increase in substance-related overdose deaths. The epidemic is now monopolized by illicit forms of fentanyl, fentanyl analogs, and other illicit drugs (e.g., methamphetamines, prescription opioid, cocaine, and heroin) that are being contaminated with fentanyl.

According to Abramson (2021), COVID-19 and the accompanying stress and uncertainty has increased the demand for mental health and substance abuse services. Mental health issues (e.g., anxiety, depression), substance abuse (e.g., opioid, amphetamine abuse), and environmental issues (e.g., pandemic, stay-at-home orders) often overlap in a comorbid manner, and as a result many clients qualify for dual diagnoses. Stress, uncertainty, and isolation resulting from the global pandemic have created unique issues (e.g., quarantining, layoffs, social distancing, difficulty accessing prescription medications) that have increased the use of substances, especially opioids (e.g., fentanyl, heroin, oxycodone) and stimulants (e.g., amphetamines, cocaine, Ecstasy). Czeisler et al. (2020) reported that 13% of all American citizens began using substances or increased their current substance use during the initial phase of the pandemic. Social isolation, social distancing, and the resulting lack of access to prescription medications are also important issues to consider. This has greatly contributed to the increased use in synthetic opioids like fentanyl during the pandemic. While fentanyl is not an illegal street drug, it is much stronger than illicit drugs like heroin, and consequently the rate of death related to fentanyl misuse and abuse is much higher.

According to the Substance Abuse and Mental Health Services Administration (SAMHSA), the most common substance use disorders involve alcohol, cannabis, tobacco, stimulants, hallucinogens, and opioids. Statistics show that 165 million Americans (60.2%) aged 12 years or older currently abuse substances (National Center for Drug Abuse Statistics, 2022). The National Council on Alcoholism and Drug Dependence has described substance abuse and dependence as a *family disease* because addiction causes damage, dysfunction, and other systemic effects on the entire family (e.g., codependence, children of addicted parents, infidelity, financial damage, IPV, divorce).

According to the 2013 National Survey on Drug Use and Health, approximately 24.6 million people are in a marriage where one spouse is addicted to a substance. Scott et al. (2013) studied the reasons for divorce among 306 former couples and found that 34.6% of participants reported that substance abuse was a significant contributor to divorce. This study revealed that substance use was also a common *final straw* reason for divorce. Several additional research studies found that divorce and marital dissolution became more likely when substance use was present in the relationship for varied lengths of time (see Amato & Rogers, 1997; Collins et al., 2007; Wilsnack & Wilsnack, 1991).

Due to the damaging and interconnected effects of substance abuse and divorce on families, it may seem like common sense to say that alcohol and drugs are bad for relationships and greatly contribute to divorce. This is not a new problem, yet contemporary issues (e.g., synthetic opioid abuse, COVID-19) have increased the rates of use and abuse and have also created new contextual factors (e.g., stay-at-home orders, job insecurity) that have intensified the challenges involved. Lastly, the use and abuse of substances greatly increases one's susceptibility to COVID-19 infection. The National Institute on Drug Abuse (2021) stated that individuals with current and/or previous substance abuse disorder diagnosis are 1.5 times more likely to contract COVID-19 than those who do not use substances (Wang et al., 2021).

FINANCIAL STRESS

Given the unstable nature of local, national, and global economies, it is important to fully understand the impact of financial strain on contemporary couples. The past 15 years have brought on extreme financial challenges due to multiple crises. The COVID-19 global pandemic has forced many American families deep into a desperate financial struggle. According to the 2021 Prudential Financial Wellness Census Report, almost half (46%) of U.S. citizens self-report that they are struggling financially. These financial hardships are even more pronounced among Black Americans and female-headed households. Specifically, 52% of Black Americans and 42% of women have an annual household income under $30,000. While the pandemic is the latest crisis that has created immense financial instability, prior to the pandemic the worldwide economic crisis of 2008 created similar outcomes, including increased unemployment, diminished savings, increased debt, and reduced income (Moore & Palumbo, 2009).

Substantial disparities exist between couples in regard to race/ethnicity, socioeconomic status, and relational satisfaction. According to Bhutta et al. (2020), the 2019 Survey of Consumer Finances shows that the average American White family has eight times the wealth of the average African American/Black or Hispanic family. Furthermore, Black couples report lower levels of household income and marital quality compared with other racial and ethnic groups (Broman, 2005; DeNavas-Walt et al., 2013). Research on the effects of financial strain on couples of color demonstrates considerable emotional spillover that affects relational stability (e.g., arguments, IPV, separation/divorce; Falconier & Epstein, 2011).

Economic hardship and financial distress can have catastrophic effects on couples and families. When families face losing everything due to uncontrollable financial circumstances, they can manifest a variety of disturbing physical and emotional responses. These responses include anxiety, depression, posttraumatic stress, severe grief, alcohol or drug abuse, nightmares, panic, overwhelming levels of stress, confusion, feelings of detachment, feeling surreal, over- or undereating, inadequate or excessive sleep, diarrhea, nausea, and upset stomach (AAMFT, n.d.-b).

According to Papp et al. (2009), financial challenges are the most common focus of marital disagreement. Contemporary research provides information on wide-ranging detrimental effects of financial stress, including increased marital instability (Barton & Bryant, 2016), hostile behaviors and emotions between partners (Conger et al., 1994), negative health consequences (Kahn & Pearlin, 2006), and decreased marital satisfaction (Archuleta et al., 2011). In addition, perception of the quality of financial management has been shown to be closely related to marital satisfaction (Kerkmann et al., 2000), and the negative effects of financial strain have been empirically linked to marital distress (Kinnunen & Feldt, 2004; Robila & Krishnakumar, 2005). Given the numerous investigations linking financial status to the quality of a marriage and relational stability, it is essential for couple, marriage, and family practitioners to have a working knowledge of these issues.

INFIDELITY

According to Leeker and Carlozzi (2014) and Russell et al. (2013), approximately 11% to 25% of all married couples experience infidelity. In a general sense, infidelity is a secret and prohibited relationship that violates the understanding, vow, or agreement between two partners that neither will seek fulfilling emotional or sexual needs with someone outside of the partnership (Milne, 2011; Moller & Vossler, 2015). In contrast, a loyal relationship that is void of infidelity could be defined by an overt or covert promise, including maintaining a close intimate relationship that has both sexual and emotional fidelity (Manoochehr et al., 2019).

There are multiple types of infidelity that partners engage in, including sexual, emotional, and online infidelity. According to Guitar et al. (2017), sexual infidelity and emotional infidelity often occur simultaneously. Sexual infidelity involves engaging in physical and/or sexual intimacy with someone other than one's spouse. This could be engaging in the act of sex or sexually oriented behaviors. Emotional infidelity includes intimate emotions and thoughts for a person other than one's partner. This could involve expressing intimate thoughts, having passionate conversations, and engaging in emotional support for a variety of issues. In short, emotional infidelity involves being more devoted emotionally to someone outside the relationship than to one's partner. Lastly, online or cybersex infidelity is a type of infidelity that takes place online. This form of infidelity will be discussed later in the chapter.

Infidelity is regarded as a very serious relationship violation, only surpassed by physical abuse (Whisman et al., 1997). While many individuals engage in infidelity, those who do not are often deterred by unwillingness to breach relationship trust, a previously established commitment to a partner, religious values, moral standards, the prospect of marital harm, and risk of contracting an STD. Common reasons for involvement in infidelity include marital dissatisfaction, blurred boundaries in a close friendship, being physically separated from one's partner, and experiencing feelings of attraction for another person (Allen et al., 2005; Widerman & Allgeier, 1996). Factors that influence the destructive nature of infidelity include the degree of sexual or emotional involvement, duration of the affair, nature and extent of deception, and how/if the affair is disclosed (Allen et al., 2005).

While it would be convenient if the harmful effects of infidelity were exclusively experienced within the couple/marital relationship, they are not. The harmful repercussions of infidelity impact the immediate family, children, extended family, and friendship circles. Evidence suggests that marital infidelity is directly correlated with family suffering and conflict (Ben-Ami & Baker, 2012). When considering the experience between partners, the roots of the conflict and suffering are fear, anger, and mistrust (Mao & Raguram, 2009). This is partly why infidelity becomes such a strong predictor of relationship failure and/or divorce (Previti & Amato, 2004). For children and extended family, infidelity can bring about abrupt changes in the family structure, including divorce, separation, and coalitions. Children often feel betrayed, outraged, or extremely hurt by the parent who engages in infidelity (Nogales & Bellotti, 2009). Lastly, couples often cocreate many of their social circles. If information is spread to friendship groups, dynamics could change, and side-taking and scapegoating can occur. Furthermore, if divorce takes place, friendship groups may become divided among partners instead of shared.

INTIMATE PARTNER VIOLENCE

To say that IPV has pervasive and negative effects on cultures, families, and individuals would be an understatement. IPV has an enormous negative impact on individuals, couples, families, and society. On average, approximately 20 people per minute experience some form of physical abuse by an intimate partner in the United States. This equates to approximately 10 million people in any given year (Black et al., 2011; National Coalition Against Domestic Violence, 2020b). Furthermore, according to the National Coalition Against Domestic Violence (2020a), one in four women and one in nine men experience severe intimate partner physical violence, intimate partner sexual violence, and/or intimate partner stalking. Women between the ages of 18 and 24 are the most common victims of relational abuse. IPV accounts for 15% of all violent crimes (Truman & Morgan, 2014). Lastly, 72% of all murder-suicides involve an intimate partner; 94% of the victims of these murder-suicides are women (Violence Policy Center, 2020).

According to the CDC (2020), IPV is abuse and/or aggression that takes place within an intimate relationship. There is a lot of variability on how often IPV takes place and how severe it is; however, it is typically categorized as one of the following: physical violence, sexual violence, threats of sexual or physical violence, psychological or emotional violence, and stalking. When IPV happens to teenagers, it is often referred to as teen dating violence. While severe IPV can involve physical or sexual violence and could ultimately result in physical injury or death, IPV that involves psychological and emotional abuse (e.g., harassment, criticism, control, withholding of basic needs) is centered on power and control and is extremely painful. Survivors of IPV can experience a wide range of mental health issues, including, but not limited to, posttraumatic stress disorder, anxiety, suicide, substance use, and depression (CDC, n.d.-a; Karakurt et al., 2014). Table 6.3 summarizes the most common types of IPV and provides concise examples of each.

IPV is predictable and preventable. When individuals are educated on the nature of safe, nonviolent, healthy, and respectful relationships, they can make informed decisions to engage in these relationships and avoid unsafe, violent, and disrespectful relationships. Developing strong social support networks, positive relationships with caring others, and access to community resources can be extremely helpful in these situations. Accounts of IPV survivors and perpetrators have been used to describe warning signs within the relationship that could equate to later abuse (Lang, 2011; Short et al., 2000; Towler et al., 2020). While warning signs can be helpful, they are not always a predictor of future violence and abuse (Jory, 2004). Nonetheless, it is helpful to map out what some of these warning signs are so partners can work together on improving the health of their relationship or make an informed decision to end the relationship. The CDC provides a comprehensive list of these warning signs, including partner jealousy,

TABLE 6.3 TYPES OF INTIMATE PARTNER VIOLENCE AND EXAMPLES

Types of Intimate Partner Violence	Examples
Physical violence	Pushing, strangling, shaking, smacking, punching, burning, hitting with a weapon, using restraints, and physically dominating and controlling another person
Sexual violence	Physically forcing someone into unwelcome sexual activity, engaging in sexual activity with a person who is not able to understand the nature and condition of the encounter and/or cannot communicate whether they are interested in engaging in the sexual activity, and violent sexual contact
Threats of physical or sexual violence	Communicating the desire to cause death, disability, injury, or physical harm using words, gestures, and/or weapons
Psychological/emotional violence	Humiliating, controlling the victim's behaviors, withholding information, isolating the victim from friends and family, and denying access to money or other basic needs
Stalking	Repeated harassing or threatening behavior, including sending the victim unwelcome gifts, secretly following, destroying or threatening to destroy property, showing up at a victim's home or work, defamation of character, spreading rumors, or harassing the victim via the internet

Source: Data from Centers for Disease Control and Prevention. (n.d.). *Intimate partner violence.* Retrieved January 26, 2022, from https://www.cdc.gov/violenceprevention/intimatepartnerviolence/index.html.

possessiveness, tension, dominance and control by one partner over the other, family experience of economic stress, unhealthy family relationships and interactions, association with antisocial and aggressive peers, witnessing violence between parents as a child, history of experiencing poor parenting as a child, and history of experiencing physical discipline as a child (CDC, n.d.-a). It is important to note that evidence exists that these are more powerful predictors when found in a constellation or repeatedly engaged in (Murphy, 2013).

Race, ethnicity, and contextual factors disproportionately affect IPV rates. Communities of color (e.g., Black/African American, Hispanic/Latinx, Native American/Alaska Native, Asian American) and other marginalized groups are deeply affected by these issues due to economic instability, lack of safe childcare options, local violence, unsafe housing, and general physical and mental health disparities (Stockman et al., 2015). For example, several large-scale investigations (Campbell & Soeken, 1999; Cho, 2012; Tjaden & Thoennes, 2000) discovered that African American/Black women experienced more IPV than any other group of women. In addition, the *National Intimate Partner and Sexual Violence Survey* (NISVS) discovered that 40.9% of African American/Black women have experienced physical violence within an intimate relationship. This is nearly 10% more than White women (Black et al., 2011).

One additional issue that deeply affects women in communities of color is lack of economic independence. The financial dependence within abusive relationships can create and maintain a situation where victims cannot leave their abusive partners without risking extreme poverty, homelessness, loss of children, or other devastating consequences (Evans et al., 2020). In addition to the aforementioned issues, many ethnically/racially diverse victims of IPV may fear the professionals who are supposed to help and protect them (e.g., police, medical professionals, social workers). Due to the racist systemic issues present in society (e.g., police brutality, mass imprisonment, racial profiling), this fear is grounded in reality (Stockman et al., 2015; Sue et al., 2019).

The COVID-19 global pandemic brought an enormous amount of attention to IPV. According to Lausi et al. (2021), research reports indicate that since the start of the COVID-19 pandemic in 2019 there has been a significant increase in IPV. Quarantine, forced cohabitation, isolation due to stay-at-home orders, restricted movements, school closures and the accompanying increased childcare responsibilities, furloughs, layoffs, and arrangements to work from home have all created a situation that increases the rate and severity of IPV. While it may seem that the pandemic is solely to blame for the increase in IPV, there are interrelated consequences of factors such as isolation, stay-at-home orders, job loss, and household stress. For example, as family members spend more time in close quarters, household stress intensifies and family members use more household appliances and energy (e.g., oil, water, gas, food), which results in increased financial stress. Victims of IPV are at greater risk during periods of social distancing and stay-at-home orders because they are isolated from supportive family and social networks. Furthermore, there are barriers to reporting IPV during a pandemic. For example, due to the forced cohabitation, victims of IPV may not have a safe and private place where they can retreat in times of danger (Evans et al., 2020; Lausi et al., 2021).

REDUCING DIVORCE CONFLICT

Divorce is a common occurrence in the United States. As previously stated, about half of all U.S. first marriages end in divorce and approximately 67% of remarriages end in divorce (Copen et al., 2012; Kreider & Ellis, 2011). In terms of intervention, minimizing conflict during the divorce process is key. When partners separate and divorce, the nature of partner interaction varies. Regarding postdivorce conflict, 5% to 25% report high levels of conflict (Ottosen et al., 2017; Smyth & Moloney, 2017) and approximately 20% to 80% of divorced couples report some continuing conflict (Hutson, 2007; Symoens et al., 2014). Negative partner consequences associated with high-conflict divorces include reduced wellness; higher levels of anxiety, stress, and depression; poorer health outcomes, including cardiovascular risk; loss of emotional support; and financial depletion (Iveniuk et al., 2014; Lamela et al., 2016; Liu & Waite, 2014; Symoens et al., 2014).

Massive adjustments must take place when a marriage ends. Minimizing partner conflict, protecting children from tension and friction, and making sense of what becomes a new idea of normal for both partners and their children are top priorities when ending a marriage. Both partners could be experiencing a plethora of emotions, ranging from extreme hurt and fear to tremendous relief and happiness. While divorcing parents may not intend to involve children, poorly managed parental conflict and emotions can be extremely detrimental to a child's sense of security and stability. If the separation and divorce are not handled properly, children could experience behavioral issues such as anxiety, depression, social problems, poor academic performance, and substance abuse (Blaisure & Saposnek, n.d.).

It is normative to have moderate to high conflict in cases of divorce. This is especially true during the phase of the divorce that involves working with the court system. However, as time passes, most parents reach a new sense of homeostasis in their role as coparents. This new sense of equilibrium often involves creating two separate systems that the child can effectively live in. It is optimal for rules, expectations, disciplinary behaviors, daily routines, and household norms to be aligned in each system (Clarke-Stewart & Brenton, 2006). This creates a sense of safety, consistency, and predictability for the child. Furthermore, following the divorce, coparents typically develop agreements for parallel parenting (i.e., different rules and style of parenting for each caregiver) or cooperative parenting (i.e., conflict is low and parents communicate).

While the aforementioned positive divorce processes typically equate to success and less negative outcomes for children and divorcing partners, a percentage of separating and divorcing parents continue to have a relationship centered on hostility and high conflict (Hutson, 2007; Symoens et al., 2014). These couples often engage in IPV, child abuse and neglect, spousal name calling, seemingly endless arguments, numerous motions/litigations, attorney switching, denying a partner access to children, slandering the other partner/parent, and exaggerating or distorting memories (Baris, 2001). In addition, it has been theorized that the main issue that prolongs conflict in divorcing couples is hatred and viewing the former spouse as being unworthy of respect (Demby, 2009; Smyth & Moloney, 2017).

Children whose parents are involved in high-conflict separations and divorces are often unintentionally caught in the middle. Please note that when the phrase *caught in the middle* is used to describe a child's process in a divorce, it could signal a variety of inappropriate behaviors/roles, including, but not limited to, parentification, collusion, triangulation, secret informant, and/or witness. These new roles and expectations can create mixed reactions within children. On one hand, they may feel privileged and somewhat empowered to be brought into the parental subsystem for a period. On the other hand, they may feel they are betraying and teaming up against someone they love and care for (and who loves them).

Lack of safety and a sense of betrayal may accompany the massive boundary violation of being pulled out of the sibling subsystem and placed in the parental subsystem to be used in an inappropriate manner (e.g., *Mom's informant, Dad's personal counselor*). Due in part to child development issues, this betrayal and boundary violation may not be fully understood by the child until later in life. If a child chooses a side, this can create extreme alienation for the targeted caregiver. Furthermore, this mixed emotional experience can cause a great deal of turmoil within a child and could eventually lead to parent–child relationship issues such as weakened caregiver–child relationships, weakened relationships with extended family members, less frequent contact with a particular caregiver, caregiver villainization, creating false narratives about a caregiver's behavior, excessive praise for the nontargeted caregiver, intense dislike and hatred expressed toward the scapegoated caregiver, and refusal to visit or spend time with the targeted parent (Kelly & Ward, 2002). Furthermore, the toxic family atmosphere may cause children to develop instability or full mental health disorders.

THE INTERNET

Most Americans use the internet regularly. According to a 2019 Statistica report, the United States ranks third globally with regard to the number of internet users. This equates to approximately 312 million internet users. China and India are the only two countries that were reported to have more (Johnson, 2021). Martin's (2021) U.S. Census Bureau report entitled "Computer and Internet Use in the United States: 2018" provides information about American internet use. According to the report, 92% of all households had some form of computer (e.g., desktops, laptops, tablets, smartphones) and 85% had a broadband internet subscription, with 53% claiming to have *high connectivity*. Smartphones have taken the lead as the most common (84%) type of computer present in homes. The widespread use of internet and mobile communication technology has changed the nature of communication, intimacy, and general human social exchanges.

Engaging in meaningful relationships and social interactions influences many aspects of life, including social well-being, health, and mortality (Holt-Lunstad et al., 2010). The digital age has created opportunities for people to be more connected than ever before. Email, Twitter, Facebook, Instagram, Snapchat, YouTube, Digg, LinkedIn, blogs, and a variety of other online cultures offer new ways to keep people connected and informed. Online dating websites (e.g., eHarmony, Match) and mobile applications (e.g., Tinder, Bumble) serve as platforms to help strangers meet each other for the purpose of offline dating, intimacy, and the possibility of starting a relationship. There are different levels of comfort with the use of these online cultures. For example, digital natives such as Millennials, Generation Z, and Generation Alpha have grown up with computers, the internet, and other forms of technology, enabling them to consume and use digital information rapidly and comfortably. Individuals outside of these generations have varying degrees of comfort with the internet (or lack thereof). All of these platforms have their own unique rules, and the internet, like any other potentially addictive phenomenon, can be used in destructive (e.g., internet addiction, excessive pornography use) and hurtful (e.g., online bullying, spying, infidelity) manners.

Online Dating

Online dating is a powerful form of social connection and intimacy that appears to be here to stay. Dating is a form of interpersonal intimacy. In general, intimacy is one of the most important and fulfilling human experiences. Today, there are many websites and apps that facilitate social contact and intimacy between strangers for the purpose of dating. According to Rosenfeld et al. (2020), the most common method for couples to meet today is online. In fact, it is very common for contemporary generations to never approach someone in the physical world for a dating experience.

Online dating has created a situation where people can peruse a variety of potential partners with identity and anonymity. According to Anderson et al.'s (2020) report entitled "The Virtues and Downsides of Online Dating," dating sites and apps are used by approximately 30% of U.S. adults. Despite frequent reports of harassment, the report found that the overall dating experiences were helpful for users. On the positive side, the online dating world has been created to meet a variety of contemporary desires and lifestyle issues. First, given the fast pace of the world we all live in, people have limited time to go out and meet others in a more traditional manner (e.g., intermediation of friends, coffee shop, bar; Rosenfeld et al., 2020). Second, due to people's busy lives and limited social circles, they may have fewer opportunities for choosing intimate partners. Lastly, due to the wide proliferation of internet use in many aspects of life, it only seems normal to use it for dating as well (Anderson et al., 2020).

Millions of people use dating sites. For many digital natives, online dating and nonphysical communication have become the new forms of early relational courtship. This experience includes getting to know someone, providing details about oneself and one's life, and becoming vulnerable. While online dating can help a certain percentage of people find suitable partners, there are both challenges and harmful risks involved in this form of dating. According to AnKee and Yazdanifard (2015), deception (e.g., altering one's online picture to attract more people), unreliable matching methods (e.g., nonscientific algorithms, only asking members questions about themselves), short-lived relationships (because meeting virtually is an ineffective cognitive experience), threats to marriage (e.g., internet infidelity, increase in relational disposability), health risks related to increased sexual activity (e.g., increased risk of contracting STDs), racial prejudice (e.g., different demographic information producing incompatible algorithms), and scamming and privacy breaches (e.g., defrauding potential daters for a substantial amount of money) are all major risks and challenges associated with online dating.

Online Infidelity

The prevalence of online infidelity has increased for a variety of reasons, and the following are four common reasons: (a) accessibility and anonymity related to using the internet, (b) the convenient nature of online dating websites and apps, (c) internet-based intermittent reinforcement stimulating the neural reward pathways within the brain, and (d) the highly addictive nature of the online world creating behavioral dependence (Cooper, 1998; Dew et al., 2006; Hertlein & Piercy, 2006; Schneider, 2000a). According to Jones and Tuttle (2012), online infidelity can consist of any online interaction that includes emotions and behaviors that hurt one's current relationship and distract them from their committed partner. When people are suffering from relationship dissatisfaction, some will attempt to get their needs met online. In the process, they may deceive others by remaining anonymous and by not communicating that they are married or in a committed relationship. Behaviors that were once seemingly impossible due to personal inhibitions, lack of opportunity, and marital/local social controls suddenly become a possibility online (Leiblum & Döring, 2002).

Partners often desire a secure adult attachment and fidelity within their intimate relationships. Secure attachment is centered on being the main form of security, consistency, and emotional/physical support for a partner. According to Corley and Kort (2006), the destructive effect of infidelity has the potential to disturb the limbic resonance (i.e., the capacity for sharing deep emotional states arises from the limbic system of the brain) and partners may no longer have a sense of connectedness and the relationship is no longer viewed as a safe haven. When a partner suspects online infidelity, they are likely to seek confirmation and evidence through observing their partner's online activity and asking them about it. While a sense of online anonymity can be developed, internet activity leaves evidence (e.g., emails, old chats, search history). According to Johnson (2005), when cheating partners are confronted with evidence or questions related to potential infidelity, they often deny that they are engaging in the behavior, minimize and/or rationalize the cheating behavior, and/or initiate the marital dance of pursue/withdrawal or attack/defend. The various emotional dance routines will likely persist until the issues (e.g., attachment injuries) are addressed honestly and comprehensively.

While it goes without saying that infidelity can seriously disrupt the bond between partners, the addictive power of online infidelity and pornography use can create a situation where users are very reluctant to stop and face challenging negative consequences when they attempt to do so. In addition, if users are moving beyond their devices (e.g., solely social, emotional, and flirting encounters) and begin meeting people for physical encounters, they could develop sex addiction, online addiction, or contract STDs. Whether emotional or physical, all infidelities constitute a major relationship violation and betrayal (AAMFT, n.d.-e). Continued engagement in online dating, pornography, and masturbation can create a number of serious consequences, including isolation, loss of trust, and, for men, an inability to attain and sustain an erection with real-life sexual encounters. Research indicates men who frequently masturbate to pornography or other online content have difficulty with arousal, fear their own erectile dysfunction, avoid sex, and consequently experience severe emotional distress (Cooper et al., 2004; Schneider, 2000b).

Pornography Use in Adult Relationships

With increased use of the internet, proliferation of wireless devices, and widespread availability of internet connections, the online pornography industry has been skyrocketing. Hardcore pornography is now available to most people all of the time. While reliable information on the present-day total number of pornography sites is difficult to find, 10 years ago there were 2.5 million sites on the internet (Ogas & Gaddam, 2012). Given the industry's growth, there are probably a lot more today. According to IBISWorld, a site that gathers industry statistics, in 2022 the category of adult and pornographic websites in the United States represented a $856.2 million industry with 6.5% annual growth (IBISWorld, n.d.). An additional factor that has fueled this growth is the proliferation of nonprofessional pornography websites. These sites allow anyone to upload pornographic videos that people can watch for a low cost or for free. One example is the site Pornhub. In 2019 alone, this site had 42 billion visitors who anonymously perused free and/or low-cost downloadable porn videos (Leventry, 2020; Solano et al., 2020).

Pornography use becomes problematic when it becomes compulsive or obsessive, having negative effects on an individual's life. Frequent use of pornography has been linked to many negative outcomes, including, but not limited to, depression, social isolation (Manning, 2006), damaged relationships, marital separation, divorce (Reid & Woolley, 2006; Schneider, 2000b), sexual violence (Foubert et al., 2011), sexist feelings and actions toward women (Garcia, 1986), participation in infidelity and prostitution (Stack et al., 2004), a deep breach in trust between partners, and trauma for manipulated nonporn-using partners (Zitzman & Butler, 2009).

Given the widespread use of internet pornography, concerns have emerged regarding whether frequent use could represent addiction. According to Del Giudice and Kutinsky (2007), sexual addiction (Schneider, 1994) includes behaviors such as obsessive and compulsive pornography use. If frequent online pornography use truly constitutes a behavioral addiction, what level of use is considered addictive or problematic (Duffy et al., 2016; Harper & Hodgins, 2016)? It seems that part of the answer to this question is whether or not the pornography is being used to avoid and/or replace personal experiences such as emotions and thoughts (Hayes & Levin, 2012). If this is happening, the individual's capacity to engage in healthy (i.e., nonviolent, nonobjectifying) sexual experiences is greatly reduced or eliminated. If sexual addiction is indicated, the porn user will demonstrate issues involving cognitive, behavioral, and emotional dysregulation. These issues could greatly impair the individual's ability to engage in normal intimacy and could create dysfunctional love maps and unhealthy erotic templates (Schwartz & Southern, 2017). Despite this concern (Willoughby et al., 2019), pornography addiction and sex addiction have been controversially excluded from the *Diagnostic and Statistical Manual of Mental Disorders*, Fifth Edition (*DSM-5*; American Psychiatric Association, 2013).

While controversy exists on the addictive nature of online pornography, a 15-year review of research on the effects of pornography on couple relationship and intimacy demonstrates mixed results (Newstrom & Harris, 2016). The findings of this large body of research indicated the importance of communication between both partners regarding pornography use. Overall, when comparing pornography-viewing with nonpornography-viewing individuals, the research demonstrated lower rates of negative communication, higher rates of relationship dedication, and higher levels of relationship adjustment for individuals who did not use pornography. Couples who viewed pornography together reported higher levels of sexual satisfaction and comfort expressing their sexual desires in comparison with those who viewed it alone; however, there is evidence to suggest that these couples used the pornography to compensate for arousal difficulties and low self-esteem (Bergner & Bridges, 2002; Daneback et al., 2009; Newstrom & Harris, 2016).

Internet Addiction

Globally, the number of internet users is more than five billion. This equates to approximately 63% of the world's population (DataReportal, 2022). While there are many valuable aspects of internet use, excessive online activity has been linked to addictive behavior (Young, 1999). Internet addiction or overuse is essentially excessive and pathologic use of the internet. While the internet is an integral part of most people's lives, those with internet addiction cannot control their use and have strong cravings to constantly stay online despite the negative consequences. This loss of control eventually leads to distress, functional impairment in daily life, and a variety of mental and physical disorders (Young, 1999). Internet addiction has been associated with various psychological problems, including social anxiety, attention deficit hyperactivity disorder (ADHD), self-injury, loss of concentration, and sleep deprivation (Choi et al., 2009; Jang et al., 2008; Li et al., 2015). On the physical side of things, it has been associated with poor eyesight, carpal tunnel syndrome, headaches, dry eyes, poor sleep patterns, and backaches (Almukhtar & Alsaad, 2020; Anderson, 2001; Marazziti et al., 2017).

Addiction is a chronic biopsychosocial issue. Goodman (1990) described the source of addiction as a stimulus that renders a person powerless because it simultaneously provides pleasure and creates relief from interpersonal discomfort. Furthermore, Goodman added that the negative effects that ultimately come from addiction do not thwart continued use (i.e., unmanageability). A main reason for the substance, or in this case behavior (i.e., internet use), being so hard to stop is the influencing factors in one's life, including psychological (e.g., avoiding or escaping stress), social (e.g., frequent use of the internet by family members and friends), and environment (e.g., accessibility to everything on the internet via smartphone). Furthermore, internet overuse creates a complex neurologic pathway in the brain based on reward, reinforcement, memory, impulse control, and motivation (Psychology Today Staff, n.d.). More specifically, these changes include alterations to the area of the brain known as the prefrontal cortex (i.e., cortical) and limbic system (i.e., subcortical; American Psychological Association, n.d.).

Although evidence related to the addictive nature of the internet exists, it is not listed as a disorder within the *DSM-5* (American Psychiatric Association, 2013). In other words, internet addiction is not a supported mental health disorder within the *DSM*. The main reason for the exclusion of behavioral-based addictions like internet addiction, internet gaming addiction, online gambling addiction, internet pornography addiction, and sex addiction is the insufficient research on these topics and the difficulty of determining what amount of internet-based behavior would be considered addictive in nature (Yau & Potenza, 2015). While this situation can be challenging for those who suffer and need treatment, the inclusion of gambling disorder in the *DSM-5* provides hope that other behavioral addiction disorders will be included in future editions (American Psychiatric Association, 2013).

SEX ADDICTION AND COMPULSIVITY

According to Kavur et al. (2020), the prevalence of sexual addiction and compulsivity in America is 8.6% of the population. Sexual addiction has been defined as a serious issue involving frequent sexual behavior despite worsening of negative consequences to self and/or others (Case & Bailey, 2008). Fong (2006) described sexual compulsivity as the inability to control one's sexual behaviors, as evidenced by continuing sexual behavior despite the desire to stop and/or a range of negative consequences. It is differentiated from sexual addiction because sexual addiction also includes preoccupation, ritualization, and despair related to the sexually compulsive behavior. Schwartz and Southern (2017) further described sexual compulsivity as being "more about intimacy, attachment, and connection with self and others, and less about sex" (Schwartz & Southern, 2017, p. 237). Repetitive behaviors that may indicate sexual addiction include compulsive masturbation, simultaneous or repeated sequential affairs, pornography use, online sex, phone sex, multiple anonymous partners, unsafe sexual activity, partner objectification/demand for sex, frequenting strip clubs and adult bookstores, use of prostitution/escorts, sexual aversion/anorexia, attending erotic massage parlors, sexual paraphilias, and/or engaging in sexually offensive behavior (Case & Bailey, 2008).

When individuals engage in a lifestyle centered on sexual addiction and compulsivity, they typically demonstrate the following negative consequences and risky behaviors: increased rates of unsafe sexual practices, unwanted sexual partners, risky sexual encounters, sexually transmitted infections, decreased relationship satisfaction, risk of legal consequence, and unwanted pregnancy (Thomas et al., 2020). There is no known biological trigger for these disorders; however, medication side effects have provided information on the possible role of neurotransmitters. Available data suggest increased ventral striatal reactivity to sexual cues in individuals with sexual addiction and compulsivity issues. Further, the well-known sexual side effects of serotonin-modulating antidepressants and the hypersexual/impulse control behaviors suggest serotonergic and dopaminergic pathway involvement (Kavur et al., 2020).

A central issue affecting individuals with sexual addiction and compulsivity is the absence of the capacity to form a secure attachment. According to Weinstein et al. (2015), individuals with insecure attachment patterns may be looking for sexual activity devoid of emotional relationships. In comparison, individuals with secure attachment patterns can form healthy adult relationships and are unlikely to become addicted to sex. These individuals can limit and regulate their sexual activity much better than those with insecure attachment patterns. While attachment theory provides a helpful conceptualization, unfortunately addictive and compulsive sexual behavior does not have its own diagnostic category in the *DSM-5* (American Psychiatric Association, 2013), making it difficult to effectively diagnose and treat the condition.

SUMMARY

In this chapter, readers were introduced to a variety of key contemporary issues related to treating couples, including changing attitudes toward marriage, increased rates of infertility, delayed motherhood, adult attachment, premarital issues and warning signs, marital and relational distress, effects of crisis and disaster on relational issues, substance abuse, financial stress, infidelity, intimate partner violence, reducing divorce conflict, various online contemporary issues that affect relationships, and sex addiction and compulsivity. The main objective of this chapter was to describe the nuances of issues that affect today's couples. Specifically, throughout the chapter, readers were provided with contemporary examples, key information, and in-depth conceptualizations that accentuate the powerful effect of each issue on relationships.

END-OF-CHAPTER RESOURCES

 SPRINGER PUBLISHING CONNECT™ A robust set of instructor resources designed to supplement this text is located at **http://connect.springerpub.com/content/book/978-0-8261-8775-8.** Qualifying instructors may request access by emailing **textbook@springerpub.com.**

STUDENT ACTIVITIES

Exercise 1: Understanding Infertility Challenges Within Marginalized Communities

Directions: Review the following polycule (i.e., consensually nonmonogamous relationships) case and answer the questions provided:

Family Demographics:

- Partner: Li, 25 years of age, cisgender man, Asian, works in sales, middle-class, born in Chongqing, China
- Partner: Maya, 31 years of age, cisgender woman, Asian, works in advertising, middle-class, born on the East Coast, United States
- Partner: Frankie, 33 years of age, transgender man, Caucasian, works in data entry/analysis, middle-class, born on the East Coast, United States

Family Narrative and Presenting Problem:

Li, Maya, and Frankie have been living together for the past 3 years in a town in suburban New Jersey. Maya has been frustrated due to reproductive-based issues. Specifically, she and Li have been trying to get pregnant for the past 9 months with no success. Because of this situation, Maya has been having daily bouts of tearfulness and anger. Li has mostly avoided the pregnancy topic, engages in excessive video game playing, and frequently states, "It will happen if it's meant to." This is very unsettling to Maya. Maya seeks comfort and consultation from Frankie. Frankie empathetically responds to Maya and simultaneously supports Li's disconnection from the issue. When Maya complains about Li, Frankie explains that "There is no one right way to cope with infertility challenges." During this time, Frankie has complained to both Li and Maya about feeling like a "third wheel" and describes his role as the "family glue." Li largely ignores these comments from Frankie. Maya occasionally engages Frankie with intimacy, but states that due to her infertility challenges she feels helpless and has lost much of her sex drive. To determine their options for infertility treatment, Maya, Li, and Frankie visited their local hospital. When inquiring about the possibility of artificial insemination, the physician asked, "Who the father will be?" Maya stated that both Li and Frankie will be the child's future father. The physician responded to this with the following comment: "Aren't you a creative group." The physician then assertively clarified, "Who is the sperm donor going to be?" Maya tearfully pointed at Li. Following their visit to the hospital, they received information in the post regarding the procedure details and the price. In reviewing the cost of treatment, Li states that there is no way they can afford artificial insemination, and they should just call it off. Maya storms out of the room in an agitated manner. Frankie states, "Maybe if we save for a year, we can revisit this." Nobody responds to his comment.

Questions:

- If you were a clinician working this case, what communication challenges would you likely need to address?

- Frankie, Li, and Maya frequently experience polyphobia and occasionally homophobia in their daily lives. Please describe your reaction to their interaction with the local physician.

- According to the Federal Bureau of Investigation (n.d.), 16.7% of hate crimes in 2019 were related to the victim's sexual orientation or gender identity and 57.6% were related to the victim's race, ethnicity, and ancestry. Regarding hate crime offenses, intimidation accounts for 40% of all hate crimes tactics. Describe 5 to 10 common ways a racially/ethnically diverse polycule family might regularly experience intimidation.

- One of the challenging aspects of this case is the price of infertility treatments. Explore your community resources and determine if there are any known ways to reduce the price of infertility treatments for marginalized communities.

Exercise 2: Understanding the Differences and Similarities of Modern Versus Traditional Families

Directions: Review the following information and answer the questions provided:

Emerging couple, marriage, and family practitioners need to understand premarital issues and warning signs. When couples are considering marriage or long-term partnerships, they can work on these issues to improve their chances for relational success. Please review and respond to the following prompts:

- This chapter includes nine predictors of breakup/divorce. Consider and describe how knowledge of these predictors could help you to work effectively with premarital clients.

- Premarital counseling is not as popular as traditional couples counseling. Write down possible reasons couples might not seek premarital counseling and then describe why this work could be helpful for your future clients.

- Communication is often identified as the primary reason couples come into counseling. Describe two therapeutic interventions that you know of or are currently using in practice that may be helpful for enhancing couple communication.

Exercise 3: Article Review

Directions: Review the following information and answer the questions provided:

Go to your university's online EBSCO Database and find Academic Search Premier. Search and find an article focused on marital distress. Review the article in its entirety and answer the following questions related to marital distress and working with future clients:

- How does the article showcase the theory and interventions utilized to help clients who are working through marital distress?

- Crisis and disaster events often bring on a tremendous amount of marital distress. Describe how these stressful and potentially traumatic events may heighten the issues already present within your clients' intimate relationships.

■ Distress can increase during marriage as couples slowly grow apart. How would you work with clients to alleviate the negative patterns that can occur in the middle years of a marriage?

Exercise 4: Working With Specific Stressors in Couples Therapy

Directions: Review the following instructions and create a mock plan for potential clients:

After reading through this chapter, you should have acquired a basic understanding of some of the major stressors that come up when working with couples, such as dealing with crisis and disaster, substance abuse, infidelity, and financial stress. Using your knowledge of these stressors as well as the information provided in the chapter, create a mock treatment plan for potential future clients that you could use within a couple therapy session. How would your understanding of the effects of financial stress, for example, help you as a therapist? How would it help your clients within your therapy sessions? Research one of these issues in greater depth and then create a treatment plan, including couple objectives, short-term goals, and long-term goals.

Exercise 5: Intimate Partner Violence in Family Therapy

Directions: Review the following information and respond to the prompts provided:

Intimate partner violence (IPV) is abuse or aggression that occurs in intimate relationships. IPV can vary in frequency and severity. Helping clients who have been impacted by IPV or are currently working through it can be difficult for clients and clinicians alike. As therapists, it is important to have a plan in place for clients who are dealing with IPV. This chapter provides an overview of IPV; however, it is important for clinicians to do their own research on handling IPV in therapy.

■ Describe two techniques that can be helpful for survivors of IPV.

■ Reflect on how you might assist clients who have experienced IPV. Reach out to mentors and fellow clinicians to gain an understanding of how they help survivors of IPV.

■ Community resources can be extremely beneficial for individuals who are working through IPV issues in their relationship. Research your local community and find five resources that you could offer to future clients.

ADDITIONAL RESOURCES

HELPFUL LINKS

■ "Emotionally Focused Therapy With Diverse Couples": https://www.alongsideyou.ca/emotionally-focused-therapy-with-diverse-couples/

■ "Let's Talk Gender and Sexually Diverse Couples": https://relationshipinstitute.com.au/news/lets-talk-gender-and-sexually-diverse-couples/

■ "Professor Melody Brown Focuses on Intersectionality in Couple and Family Therapy": https://news.ucdenver.edu/professor-melody-brown-focuses-on-intersectionality-in-couple-and-family-therapy/

■ "Intersectionality, Cultural Attunement, and Emotionally Focused Couples Therapy": https://www.nikkilively.com/single-post/2017/04/30/intersectionality-cultural-attunement-emotionally-focused-couples-therapy

- "Your Attachment Style Influences the Success of Your Relationship": https://www.gottman.com/blog/attachment-style-influences-success-relationship/

- "An Adult Attachment Primer": https://www.therapyduo.com/resources/adult-attachment-primer/

- "Troubled Relationships: How to Identify Early Warning Signs": https://www.marriagefriendlytherapists.com/blog/troubled-relationships-how-to-identify-early-warning-signs-60

- "Family Therapy": https://www.mayoclinic.org/tests-procedures/family-therapy/about/pac-20385237

- "Marital Distress": https://aamft.org/Consumer_Updates/Marital_Distress.aspx

- "The Effects of Financial Stress on Marriage: Psychological and Physiological Impacts": https://www.suburbanfinance.com/effects-of-financial-stress-on-marriage/

- "Online Infidelity": https://aamft.org/Consumer_Updates/Online_Infidelity.aspx

- "What Is Online Infidelity?": https://www.psychologytoday.com/us/blog/love-digitally/201412/what-is-online-infidelity

- "Substance Abuse and Intimate Relationships": https://www.aamft.org/Consumer_Updates/Substance_Abuse_and_Intimate_Relationships.aspx

- "Infidelity": https://aamft.org/Consumer_Updates/Infidelity.aspx

- "After the Infidelity: Can Counseling Help?": https://www.psychologytoday.com/us/blog/suffer-the-children/201309/after-the-infidelity-can-counseling-help

- "Compulsive Sexual Behavior": https://www.mayoclinic.org/diseases-conditions/compulsive-sexual-behavior/symptoms-causes/syc-20360434

- "Signs of a Sex Addict": https://www.webmd.com/mental-health/signs-sex-addict

- "Addressing Intimate Partner Violence With Clients": https://ct.counseling.org/2019/06/addressing-intimate-partner-violence-with-clients/

- "Providing Services During the Coronavirus Pandemic": https://www.aamft.org/Events/Coronavirus-Telehealth-Update.aspx

- "Managing Conflict During Divorce": https://aamft.org/Consumer_Updates/Managing_Conflict_During_Divorce.aspx

HELPFUL BOOKS

- Capuzzi, D., & Stauffer, D. M. (2021). *Foundations of couples, marriage, and family counseling* (2nd ed.). Wiley.

- McGlodrick, M., & Hardy, V. K. (2019). *Re-visioning family therapy: Addressing diversity in clinical practice* (3rd ed.). Routledge.

- Hanna, M. S. (2018). *The practice of family therapy: Key elements across models* (5th ed.). Routledge.

- Metcalf, L. (2019). *Marriage and family therapy: A practice-oriented approach*. Springer Publishing Company.

- Nichols, M. P., & Davis, S. D. (2020). *Family therapy: Concepts and methods* (12th ed.). Pearson.

- Patterson, J., Williams, L., Edwards, M. T., Chamow, L., & Grauf-Grounds, C. (2018). *Essential skills in family therapy* (3rd ed.). Guilford Press.

HELPFUL VIDEOS

- What Is Intersectionality and Why Is It Important?: https://www.youtube.com/watch?v=3qhadch9oDo

- Signs Your Marriage Is Over and Not Worth Fighting For: https://www.youtube.com/watch?v=uTcgVGdu9RM

- Making Marriage Work—Dr. John Gottman: https://www.youtube.com/watch?v=AKTyPgwfPgg&t=18s

- Online Love and Infidelity: We're in the Game, What Are the Rules?: https://www.youtube.com/watch?v=gQGjAp4GXU4

- Love in the Age of Porn: https://www.youtube.com/watch?v=jblzls4Efx8

- Intimate Partner Violence: https://www.youtube.com/watch?v=vK3RhRwMwIg

- Sex Addiction: Diagnosis andTreatment: https://www.youtube.com/watch?v=2OlRBUC8FrE

- Impact of COVID-19 on Relationships: https://www.youtube.com/watch?v=p9iKTpgnB2Y

- How to Keep Relationships Strong During COVID-19: https://www.youtube.com/watch?v=hgqobcV1Muw

REFERENCES

Abramson, A. (2021, March 1). Substance use during the pandemic. *Monitor on Psychology, 52(2)*, 22. https://www.apa.org/monitor/2021/03/substance-use-pandemic

Agishtein, P., & Brumbaugh, C. (2013). Cultural variation in adult attachment: The impact of ethnicity, collectivism, and country of origin. *Journal of Social, Evolutionary, and Cultural Psychology, 7*(4), 384–405. https://doi.org/10.1037/h0099181

Ahmad, F. B., Rossen, L. M., & Sutton, P. (2022). *Provisional drug overdose death counts*. National Center for Health Statistics.

Ainsworth, M. D. (1985). Patterns of attachment. *The Clinical Psychologist, 38*(2), 27–29.

Ainsworth, M. D. S. (1967). *Infancy in Uganda: Infant care and the growth of love*. Johns Hopkins Press.

Allen, E. S., Atkins, D. C., Baucom, D. H., Snyder, D. K., Gordon, K. C., & Glass, S. P. (2005). Intrapersonal, interpersonal, and contextual factors in engaging in and responding to extramarital involvement. *Clinical Psychology: Science and Practice, 12*(2), 101–130. https://doi.org/10.1093/clipsy.bpi014

Almukhtar, N. M., & Alsaad, S. M. (2020). Quality of life in medical students with internet addiction. *Journal of Family Medicine and Primary Care, 9*(11), 5736. https://doi.org/10.4103/jfmpc.jfmpc_986_19

Amato, P. R., & Rogers, S. J. (1997). A longitudinal study of marital problems and subsequent divorce. *Journal of Marriage and the Family, 59*(3), 612–624. https://doi.org/10.2307/353949

American Association of Marriage and Family Therapy. (n.d.-a). *AAMFT social policies*. Retrieved January 26, 2022, from https://www.aamft.org/About_AAMFT/Pos_on_couples.aspx

American Association of Marriage and Family Therapy. (n.d.-b). *Financial distress & the family*. Retrieved January 26, 2022, from https://aamft.org/Consumer_Updates/Financial_Distress.aspx

American Association of Marriage and Family Therapy. (n.d.-c). *Marital distress*. Retrieved January 26, 2022, from https://aamft.org/Consumer_Updates/Marital_Distress.aspx

American Association of Marriage and Family Therapy. (n.d.-d). *Marriage preparation*. Retrieved January 26, 2022, from https://aamft.org/Consumer_Updates/Marriage_Preparation.aspx

American Association of Marriage and Family Therapy. (n.d.-e). *Online infidelity*. Retrieved January 26, 2022, from https://aamft.org/Consumer_Updates/Online_Infidelity.aspx

American Psychiatric Association. (2013). *Diagnostic and statistical manual of mental disorders* (5th ed.). https://doi.org/10.1176/appi.books.9780890425596

American Psychological Association. (n.d.). *Addictions*. American Psychological Association. Retrieved January 26, 2022, from https://www.apa.org/topics/substance-use-abuse-addiction

American Psychological Association. (2014). *The road to resilience*. American Psychological Association. http://www.apa.org/helpcenter/road-resilience.aspx

American Medical Association. (2021). *Issue brief: Nation's drug-related overdose and death epidemic continues to worsen*. American Medical Association Advocacy Resource Center. https://www.ama-assn.org/system/files/issue-brief-increases-in-opioid-related-overdose.pdf

Anderson, K. J. (2001). Internet use among college students: An exploratory study. *Journal of American College Health, 50*(1), 21–26. https://doi.org/10.1080/07448480109595707

Anderson, M., Vogels, E. A., & Turner, E. (2020, October 2). *The virtues and downsides of online dating*. Pew Research Center: Internet, Science, & Tech. https://www.pewresearch.org/internet/2020/02/06/the-virtues-and-downsides-of-online-dating/

AnKee, A. W., & Yazdanifard, R. (2015). The review of the ugly truth and negative aspects of online dating. *Global Journal of Management and Business Research: E Marketing, 15*(4), 31–36. https://globaljournals.org/GJMBR_Volume15/5-The-Review-of-the-Ugly.pdf

Archuleta, K. L., Britt, S. L., Tonn, T. J., & Grable, J. E. (2011). Financial satisfaction and financial stressors in marital satisfaction. *Psychological Reports, 108*(2), 563–576. https://doi.org/10.2466/07.21.PR0.108.2.563-576

Balasch, J. (2010). Ageing and infertility: An overview. *Gynecological Endocrinology, 26*(12), 855–860. https://doi.org/10.3109/09513590.2010.501889

Baptiste-Roberts, K., Oranuba, E., Werts, N., & Edwards, L. V. (2017). Addressing health care disparities among sexual minorities. *Obstetrics and Gynecology Clinics of North America, 44*(1), 71–80. https://doi.org/10.1016/j.ogc.2016.11.003

Baris, M. A. (2001). *Working with high-conflict families of divorce: A guide for professionals*. Jason Aronson.

Barron, J. (2012, December 14). Nation reels after gunman massacres 20 children at school in Connecticut. *The New York Times*. https://www.nytimes.com/2012/12/15/nyregion/shooting-reported-at-connecticut-elementary-school.html

Barton, A. W., & Bryant, C. M. (2016). Financial strain, trajectories of marital processes, and African American newlyweds' marital instability. *Journal of Family Psychology, 30*(6), 657–664. https://doi.org/10.1037/fam0000190

Beemsterboer, S. N., Homburg, R., Gorter, N. A., Schats, R., Hompes, P. G. A., & Lambalk, C. B. (2006). The paradox of declining fertility but increasing twinning rates with advancing maternal age. *Human Reproduction, 21*(6), 1531–1532. https://doi.org/10.1093/humrep/del009

Behrens, K. Y., Hesse, E., & Main, M. (2007). Mothers' attachment status as determined by the Adult Attachment Interview predicts their 6-year-olds' reunion responses: A study conducted in Japan. *Developmental Psychology, 43*(6), 1553–1567. https://doi.org/10.1037/0012-1649.43.6.1553

Ben-Ami, N., & Baker, A. J. L. (2012). The long-term correlates of childhood exposure to parental alienation on adult self-sufficiency and well-being. *American Journal of Family Therapy, 40*(2), 169–183. https://doi.org/10.1080/01926187.2011.601206

Bergner, R. M., & Bridges, A. J. (2002). The significance of heavy pornography involvement for romantic partners: Research and clinical implications. *Journal of Sex & Marital Therapy, 28*(3), 193–206. https://doi.org/10.1080/009262302760328235

Bhutta, N., Chang, A. C., Dettling, L. J., & Hsu, J. W. (2020). Disparities in wealth by race and ethnicity in the 2019 survey of Consumer Finances. *FEDS Notes, 2020*(2797). https://doi.org/10.17016/2380-7172.2797

Bitler, M. P., & Schmidt, L. (2012). Utilization of infertility treatments: The effects of insurance mandates. *Demography, 49*(1), 125–149. https://doi.org/10.1007/s13524-011-0078-4

Black, L. L., & Flynn, S. V. (2020). *Crisis, trauma, and disaster: A clinician's guide*. Sage.

Black, M. C., Basile, K. C., Breiding, M. J., Smith, S. G., Walters, M. L., Merrick, M. T., Chen, J., & Stevens, M. R. (2011). *The national intimate partner and sexual violence survey (NISVS): 2010 summary report*. National Center for Injury Prevention and Control, Centers for Disease Control and Prevention.

Blaisure. K., Saposnek, D. T. (n.d.). *Managing conflict during divorce*. American Association of Marriage and Family Therapy. Retrieved January 26, 2022, from https://aamft.org/Consumer_Updates/Managing_Conflict_During_Divorce.aspx

Bodenmann, G. (1995). A systemic-transactional conceptualization of stress and coping in couples. *Swiss Journal of Psychology/Schweizerische Zeitschrift für Psychologie/Revue Suisse de Psychologie, 54*(1), 34–49.

Bonanno, G. A., Galea, S., Bucciarelli, A., & Vlahov, D. (2007). What predicts psychological resilience after disaster? The role of demographics, resources, and life stress. *Journal of Consulting and Clinical Psychology, 75*(5), 671–682. https://doi.org/10.1037/0022-006X.75.5.671

Boserup, B., McKenney, M., & Elkbuli, A. (2020). Alarming trends in US domestic violence during the COVID-19 pandemic. *The American Journal of Emergency Medicine, 38*(12), 2753–2755. https://doi.org/10.1016/j.ajem.2020.04.077

Bosmans, M. W. G., Benight, C. C., van der Knaap, L. M., Winkel, F. W., & van der Velden, P. G. (2013). The associations between coping self-efficacy and posttraumatic stress symptoms 10 years postdisaster: Differences between men and women. *Journal of Traumatic Stress, 26*(2), 184–191. https://doi.org/10.1002/jts.21789

Bosmans, M. W. G., van der Knaap, L. M., & van der Velden, P. G. (2015). Personality traits as predictors of trauma-related coping self-efficacy: A three-wave prospective study. *Personality and Individual Differences, 76*, 44–48. https://doi.org/10.1016/j.paid.2014.11.052

Bowlby, J. (1988). *A secure base: Parent–child attachment and healthy human development.* Basic Books.

Broman, C. L. (2005). Marital quality in Black and White marriages. *Journal of Family Issues, 26*(4), 431–441. https://doi.org/10.1177/0192513x04272439

Brown, S. L. (2010). Marriage and child well-being: Research and policy perspectives. *Journal of Marriage and Family, 72*(5), 1059–1077. https://doi.org/10.1111/j.1741-3737.2010.00750.x

Butler, L. D., Koopman, C., Azarow, J., Blasey, C. M., Magdalene, J. C., DiMiceli, S., Seagraves, D. A., Hastings, T. A., Chen, X.-H., Garlan, R. W., Kraemer, H. C., & Spiegel, D. (2009). Psychosocial predictors of resilience after the September 11, 2001 terrorist attacks. *Journal of Nervous & Mental Disease, 197*(4), 266–273. https://doi.org/10.1097/nmd.0b013e31819d9334

Calkins, H. (2021). Online therapy is here to stay. *Monitor on Psychology, 52*(1), 78. https://www.apa.org/monitor/2021/01/trends-online-therapy

Campbell, J. C., & Soeken, K. L. (1999). Forced sex and intimate partner violence: Effects on women's risk and women's health. *Violence Against Women, 5*(9), 1017–1035. https://doi.org/10.1177/1077801299005009003

Canary, D. J., Cupach, W. R., & Messman, S. J. (1995). *Relationship conflict: Conflict in parent–child, friendship, and romantic relationships.* Sage.

Canary, D. J., & Dainton, M. (Eds.). (2003). *Maintaining relationships through communication: Relational, contextual, and cultural variations.* Lawrence Erlbaum Associates Publishers. https://doi.org/10.4324/9781410606990

Carlson, V. J., & Harwood, R. L. (2003). Attachment, culture, and the caregiving system: The cultural patterning of everyday experiences among Anglo and Puerto Rican mother–infant pairs. *Infant Mental Health Journal, 24*(1), 53–73. https://doi.org/10.1002/imhj.10043

Case, B., & Bailey, C. (2008). *Clinical updates for family therapists: Research and treatment approaches for issues affecting today's families.* American Association for Marriage and Family Therapists.

Centers for Disease Control and Prevention. (n.d.-a). *Intimate partner violence.* Retrieved January 26, 2022, from https://www.cdc.gov/violenceprevention/intimatepartnerviolence/index.html

Centers for Disease Control and Prevention. (n.d.-b). *Marriage and divorce.* Retrieved January 26, 2022, from https://www.cdc.gov/nchs/fastats/marriage-divorce.htm

Centers for Disease Control and Prevention. (2020). *Preventing intimate partner violence.* National Center for Injury Prevention and Control: Division of Violence Prevention. https://www.cdc.gov/violenceprevention/pdf/ipv/IPV-factsheet_2020_508.pdf

Child Trends. (2018). *Births to unmarried women.* Child Trends DataBank. Retrieved February 1, 2022, from https://www.childtrends.org/indicators/births-to-unmarried-women

Cho, H. (2012). Examining gender differences in the nature and context of intimate partner violence. *Journal of Interpersonal Violence, 27*(13), 2665–2684. https://doi.org/10.1177/0886260512436391

Choi, K., Son, H., Park, M., Han, J., Kim, K., Lee, B., & Gwak, H. (2009). Internet overuse and excessive daytime sleepiness in adolescents. *Psychiatry and Clinical Neurosciences, 63*(4), 455–462. https://doi.org/10.1111/j.1440-1819.2009.01925.x

Clarke-Stewart, A., & Brentano, C. (2006). *Divorce: Causes and consequences.* Yale University Press.

Cleveland Clinic. (2020). *Infertility causes.* Cleveland Clinic. Retrieved January 26, 2022, from https://my.clevelandclinic.org/health/diseases/16083-infertility-causes

Collins, D., Johnson, K., & Becker, B. J. (2007). A meta-analysis of direct and mediating effects of community coalitions that implemented science-based Substance Abuse Prevention Interventions. *Substance Use & Misuse, 42*(6), 985–1007. https://doi.org/10.1080/10826080701373238

Conger, R. D., Ge, X., Elder, G. H., Lorenz, F. O., & Simons, R. L. (1994). Economic stress, coercive family process, and developmental problems of adolescents. *Child Development, 65*(2), 541. https://doi.org/10.2307/1131401

Cooper, A. L. (1998). Sexuality and the internet: Surfing into the New Millennium. *CyberPsychology & Behavior, 1*(2), 187–193. https://doi.org/10.1089/cpb.1998.1.187

Cooper, A., Galbreath, N., & Becker, M. A. (2004). Sex on the internet: Furthering our understanding of men with online sexual problems. *Psychology of Addictive Behavior, 18*(3): 223–230. https://doi.org/10.1037/0893-164X.18.3.223

Copen, C., Daniels, K., & Vespa, J. (2012, March 22). *First marriages in the United States; data from the 2006–2010 national survey of family growth.* Centers for Disease Control and Prevention. https://stacks.cdc.gov/view/cdc/12055

Corley, M. D., & Kort, J. (2006). The sex addicted mixed-orientation marriage: Examining attachment styles, internalized homophobia and viability of marriage after disclosure. *Sexual Addiction & Compulsivity, 13*(2-3), 167–193. https://doi.org/10.1080/10720160600870737

Cutter, S. L., Boruff, B. J., & Shirley, W. L. (2003). Social vulnerability to environmental hazards. *Social Science Quarterly, 84*(2), 242–261. https://doi.org/10.1111/1540-6237.8402002

Czeisler, M. É., Lane, R. I., Petrosky, E., Wiley, J. F., Christensen, A., Njai, R., Weaver, M. D., Robbins, R., Facer-Childs, E. R., Barger, L. K., Czeisler, C. A., Howard, M. E., & Rajaratnam, S. M. W. (2020). Mental health, substance use, and suicidal ideation during the COVID-19 pandemic—United States, June 24–30, 2020. *MMWR: Morbidity and Mortality Weekly Report, 69*(32), 1049–1057. https://doi.org/10.15585/mmwr.mm6932a1

Dainton, M., & Gross, J. (2008). The use of negative behaviors to maintain relationships. *Communication Research Reports, 25*(3), 179–191. https://doi.org/10.1080/08824090802237600

Daneback, K., Træen, B., & Månsson, S. A. (2009). Use of pornography in a random sample of Norwegian heterosexual couples. *Archives of Sexual Behavior, 38*, 746–753. https://doi.org/10.1007/s10508-008-9314-4

Daniluk, J. C., & Koert, E. (2012). Childless Canadian men's and women's childbearing intentions, attitudes towards and willingness to use assisted human reproduction. *Human Reproduction, 27*(8), 2405–2412. https://doi.org/10.1093/humrep/des190

Daniluk, J. C., Koert, E., & Cheung, A. (2012). Childless women's knowledge of fertility and assisted human reproduction: Identifying the gaps. *Fertility and Sterility, 97*(2), 420–426. https://doi.org/10.1016/j.fertnstert.2011.11.046

Daugherty, J., & Copen, C. (2016). *Trends in attitudes about marriage, childbearing, and sexual behavior: United States, 2002, 2006–2010, and 2011–2013.* National Health Statistics Reports: 92. National Center for Health Statistics.

DataReportal. (2022). *Digital 2022 global digital overview.* https://datareportal.com/reports/digital-2022-global-overview-report

Del Giudice, M. J., & Kutinsky, J. (2007). Applying motivational interviewing to the treatment of sexual compulsivity and addiction. *Sexual Addiction & Compulsivity, 14*(4), 303–319. https://doi.org/10.1080/10720160701710634

Demby, S. (2009). Interparent hatred and its impact on parenting: Assessment in forensic custody evaluations. *Psychoanalytic Inquiry, 29*(6), 477–490. https://doi.org/10.1080/07351690903013959

DeNavas-Walt, C., Proctor, B. D., & Smith, J. C. (2013, September). *Income, poverty, and health insurance coverage in the United States: 2012* (Current Population Reports No. P60-245). U.S. Census Bureau. https://www.census.gov/library/publications/2013/demo/p60-245.html

Deonandan, R. (2010). The public health implications of assisted reproductive technologies. *Chronic Diseases in Canada, 30*(4), 119–124. PMID: 20946712.

Dew, B., Brubaker, M., & Hays, D. (2006). From the altar to the internet: Married men and their online sexual behavior. *Sexual Addiction & Compulsivity, 13*(2-3), 195–207. https://doi.org/10.1080/10720160600870752

Domar, A. D., Zuttermeister, P. C., & Friedman, R. (1993). The psychological impact of infertility: A comparison with patients with other medical conditions. *Journal of Psychosomatic Obstetrics and Gynaecology, 14*(Suppl), 45–52. PMID: 8142988.

Duffy, A., Dawson, D. L., & das Nair, R. (2016). Pornography addiction in adults: A systematic review of definitions and reported impact. *Journal of Sexual Medicine, 13*(5), 760–777. https://doi.org/10.1016/j.jsxm.2016.03.002

Duvander, A.-Z., Ferrarini, T., & Thalberg, S. (2005). *Swedish parental leave and gender equality—Achievements and reform challenges in a European perspective.* Institute for Futures Studies.

Enarson, E., Fothergill, A., & Peek, L. (2006). Gender and disaster: Foundations and directions. In H. Rodriguez, E. L. Quarantelli, & R. R. Dynes (Eds.), *Handbook of disaster research* (pp. 130–146). Springer Media.

Evans, M. L., Lindauer, M., & Farrell, M. E. (2020). A pandemic within a pandemic—Intimate partner violence during COVID-19. *New England Journal of Medicine, 383*(24), 2302–2304. https://doi.org/10.1056/nejmp2024046

Falconier, M. K., & Epstein, N. B. (2011). Couples experiencing financial strain: What we know and what we can do. *Family Relations: An Interdisciplinary Journal of Applied Family Studies, 60*(3), 303–317. https://doi.org/10.1111/j.1741-3729.2011.00650.x

Federal Bureau of Investigation. (n.d.). *Victims*. 2019 Hate Crime Statistics. Retrieved December 14, 2022, from https://ucr.fbi.gov/hate-crime/2019/topic-pages/victims

First, J. M., First, N. L., & Houston, J. B. (2017). Intimate partner violence and disasters. *Affilia, 32*(3), 390–403. https://doi.org/10.1177/0886109917706338

First Look Family Law. (n.d.). *What's the difference between civil union, domestic partnership, and marriage?* Retrieved January 26, 2022, from https://www.firstlookfamilylaw.com/Blog/CivilUnionDomesticPartnershipMarriage

Fong, T. W. (2006). Understanding and managing compulsive sexual behaviors. *Psychiatry (Edgmont), 3*(11), 51–58. https://pubmed.ncbi.nlm.nih.gov/20877518/

Foubert, J. D., Brosi, M. W., & Bannon, R. S. (2011). Pornography viewing among fraternity men: Effects on bystander intervention, rape myth acceptance and behavioral intent to commit sexual assault. *Sexual Addiction & Compulsivity, 18*(4), 212–231. https://doi.org/10.1080/10720162.2011.625552

Garcia, L. T. (1986). Exposure to pornography and attitudes about women and rape: A correlational study. *Journal of Sex Research, 22*(3), 378–385. https://doi.org/10.1080/00224498609551316

Goodboy, A. K., & Bolkan, S. (2011). Attachment and the use of negative relational maintenance behaviors in romantic relationships. *Communication Research Reports, 28*(4), 327–336. https://doi.org/10.1080/08824096.2011.616244

Goodman, A. (1990). Addiction: Definition and implications. *British Journal of Addiction, 85*(11), 1403–1408. https://doi.org/10.1111/j.1360-0443.1990.tb01620.x

Gottman, J. M. (1999). *The marriage clinic: A scientifically based marital therapy*. W. W. Norton & Company.

Gottman, J. M. (1994). *What predicts divorce? The relationship between marital processes and marital outcomes*. Lawrence Erlbaum Associates.

Gottman, J. M., & Levenson, R. W. (1992). Marital processes predictive of later dissolution: Behavior, physiology, and health. *Journal of Personality and Social Psychology, 63*(2), 221–233. https://doi.org/10.1037/0022-3514.63.2.221

Guitar, A. E., Geher, G., Kruger, D. J., Garcia, J. R., Fisher, M. L., & Fitzgerald, C. J. (2017). Defining and distinguishing sexual and emotional infidelity. *Current Psychology, 36*, 434–446. https://doi.org/10.1007/s12144-016-9432-4

Gunby, J., Bissonnette, F., Librach, C., & Cowan, L. (2011). Assisted reproductive technologies (ART) in Canada: 2007 results from the Canadian Art Register. *Fertility and Sterility, 95*(2). https://doi.org/10.1016/j.fertnstert.2010.05.057

Hardy, N. R., Maier, C. A., & Gregson, T. J. (2021). Couple teletherapy in the era of COVID-19: Experiences and recommendations. *Journal of Marital and Family Therapy, 47*(2), 225–243. https://doi.org/10.1111/jmft.12501

Harper, C., & Hodgins, D. C. (2016). Examining correlates of problematic internet pornography use among university students. *Journal of Behavioral Addictions, 5*(2), 179–191. https://doi.org/10.1556/2006.5.2016.022

Harwood, R. L., Schoelmerich, A., Schulze, P. A., & Gonzalez, Z. (1999). Cultural differences in maternal beliefs and behaviors: A study of middle-class Anglo and Puerto Rican mother–infant pairs in four everyday situations. *Child Development, 70*(4), 1005–1016. https://doi.org/10.1111/1467-8624.00073

Hawkins, D. N., & Booth, A. (2005). Unhappily ever after: Effects of long-term, low-quality marriages on well-being. *Social Forces, 84*(1), 451–471. https://doi.org/10.1353/sof.2005.0103

Hayes, C. (2017, October 2). Las Vegas shooting: Cops took more than an hour to storm gunman's room. *Newsweek*. https://www.newsweek.com/las-vegas-shooting-cops-took-more-hour-storm-gunmans-room-676198

Hayes, S. C., & Levin, M. E. (2012). Acceptance and commitment therapy as a unified model of behavior change. *The Counseling Psychologist, 40*(7), 976–1002. https://doi.org/10.1177/0011000012460836

Helgeson, V. S., Naqvi, J. B., Gary-Webb, T., & Korytkowski, M. (2021). Observed couple interactions among White and Black persons with type 2 diabetes. *Journal of Family Psychology, 35*(8), 1117–1127. https://doi.org/10.1037/fam0000857

Henslee, A. M., Coffey, S. F., Schumacher, J. A., Tracy, M., H. Norris, F., & Galea, S. (2015). Religious coping and psychological and behavioral adjustment after Hurricane Katrina. *The Journal of Psychology, 149*(6), 630–642. https://doi.org/10.1080/00223980.2014.953441

Hertlein, K. M., Blumer, M. L. C., & Mihaloliakos, J. H. (2015). Marriage and family counselors' perceived ethical issues related to online therapy. *The Family Journal, 23*(1), 5–12. https://doi.org/10.1177/1066480714547184

Hertlein, K. M., & Piercy, F. P. (2006). Internet infidelity: A critical review of the literature. *The Family Journal, 14*(4), 366–371. https://doi.org/10.1177/1066480706290508

Hoffman, R. M., Brummel, S. S., Britto, P., Pilotto, J. H., Masheto, G., Aurpibul, L., Joao, E., Purswani, M. U., Buschur, S., Pierre, M. F., Coletti, A., Chakhtoura, N., Klingman, K. L., Currier, J. S., & PROMISE (Promoting Maternal and Infant Safety Everywhere) 1077HS Team. (2019). Adverse pregnancy outcomes among women who conceive on antiretroviral therapy. *Clinical Infectious Diseases, 68*(2), 273–279. https://doi.org/10.1093/cid/ciy471

Holt-Lunstad, J., Smith, T. B., & Layton, J. B. (2010). Social relationships and mortality risk: A meta-analytic review. *PLoS Medicine, 7*(7). https://doi.org/10.1371/journal.pmed.1000316

Honarvar, N., & Taghavi, M. (2020). Relation of religious coping and depression levels in infertile women. *Iranian Journal of Psychiatry, 15*(2), 134–142.

Hutson, R. A. (2007). Child support and parental conflict in low-income families. *Children and Youth Services Review, 29*(9), 1142–1157. https://doi.org/10.1016/j.childyouth.2007.04.004

IBISWorld. (n.d.). *Adult & pornographic websites in the US—Market size 2005–2028*. Retrieved January 26, 2022, from https://www.ibisworld.com/industry-statistics/market-size/adult-pornographic-websites-united-states/

Impett, E., & Peplau, L. (2006). "His" and "Her" relationships? A review of the empirical evidence. In A. L. Vangelisti & D. Perlman (Eds.), *The Cambridge handbook of personal relationships* (pp. 273–291). Cambridge University Press. https://doi.org/10.1017/CBO9780511606632.016

Iveniuk, J., Waite, L. J., Laumann, E., McClintock, M. K., & Tiedt, A. D. (2014). Marital conflict in older couples: Positivity, personality, and health. *Journal of Marriage and Family, 76*(1), 130–144. https://doi.org/10.1111/jomf.12085

Jackson, J. B. (2009). *Premarital couple predictors of marital relationship quality and stability: A meta-analytic study* [Unpublished doctoral dissertation]. Brigham Young University.

Jang, K. S., Hwang, S. Y., & Choi, J. Y. (2008). Internet addiction and psychiatric symptoms among Korean adolescents. *Journal of School Health, 78*(3), 165–171. https://doi.org/10.1111/j.1746-1561.2007.00279.x

Johnson, J. (2021, January 27). *Number of internet users in the United States from 2000 to 2022*. Statista. Retrieved January 26, 2022, from https://www.statista.com/statistics/276445/number-of-internet-users-in-the-united-states/

Johnson, S. M. (2005). Broken bonds. *Journal of Couple & Relationship Therapy, 4*(2-3), 17–29. https://doi.org/10.1300/j398v04n02_03

Jones, K. E., & Tuttle, A. E. (2012). Clinical and ethical considerations for the treatment of cybersex addiction for marriage and family therapists. *Journal of Couple & Relationship Therapy, 11*(4), 274–290. https://doi.org/10.1080/15332691.2012.718967

Jory, B. (2004). The intimate justice scale: An instrument to screen for psychological abuse and physical violence in clinical practice. *Journal of Marital and Family Therapy, 30*(1), 29–44. https://doi.org/10.1111/j.1752-0606.2004.tb01220.x

Kahn, J. R., & Pearlin, L. I. (2006). Financial strain over the life course and health among older adults. *Journal of Health and Social Behavior, 47*(1), 17–31. https://doi.org/10.1177/002214650604700102

Karakurt, G., Smith, D., & Whiting, J. (2014). Impact of intimate partner violence on women's mental health. *Journal of Family Violence, 29*(7), 693–702. https://doi.org/10.1007/s10896-014-9633-2

Karney, B. R., & Bradbury, T. N. (1995). The longitudinal course of marital quality and stability: A review of theory, methods, and research. *Psychological Bulletin, 118*(1), 3–34. https://doi.org/10.1037/0033-2909.118.1.3

Kavur, M., Finlayson, A., & Cowan, R. (2020). Sexual addiction: A missed diagnosis. *Sexual Addiction & Compulsivity, 27*, 112–118. https://doi.org/10.1080/10720162.2020.1772156

Kelly, R. F., & Ward, S. L. (2002). Allocating custodial responsibilities at Divorce. *Family Court Review, 40*(3), 350–370. https://doi.org/10.1111/j.174-1617.2002.tb00846.x

Kerkmann, B. C., Lee, T. R., Lown, J. M., & Allgood, S. M. (2000). Financial management, financial problems and marital satisfaction among recently married university students. *Financial Counseling and Planning, 11*(2), 55–64. https://www.afcpe.org/news-and-publications/journal-of-financial-counseling-and-planning/volume-11-2/%EF%BB%BFfinancial-management-financial-problems-and-marital-satisfaction-%EF%BB%BFamong-recently-married-university-students/

Kiecolt-Glaser, J. K., Loving, T. J., Stowell, J. R., Malarkey, W. B., Lemeshow, S., Dickinson, S. L., & Glaser, R. (2005). Hostile marital interactions, proinflammatory cytokine production, and wound healing. *Archives of General Psychiatry, 62*(12), 1377. https://doi.org/10.1001/archpsyc.62.12.1377

Kinnunen, U., & Feldt, T. (2004). Economic stress and marital adjustment among couples: Analyses at the dyadic level. *European Journal of Social Psychology, 34*(5), 519–532. https://doi.org/10.1002/ejsp.213

Kreider, R., & Ellis, R. (2011, May). *Number, timing, and duration of marriages and divorces: 2009.* United States Census Bureau: Report Number P70-125. https://www.census.gov/library/publications/2011/demo/p70-125.html

Kuohung, W., & Hornstein, M. D. (2021). Treatments for female infertility. *UpToDate.* Retrieved March 10, 2022, from https://www.uptodate.com/contents/treatments-for-female-infertility

Lamela, D., Figueiredo, B., Bastos, A., & Feinberg, M. (2016). Typologies of post-divorce coparenting and parental well-being, parenting quality and children's psychological adjustment. *Child Psychiatry & Human Development, 47*(5), 716–728. https://doi.org/10.1007/s10578-015-0604-5

Lang, S. C. (2011). *The earliest warning signs of intimate partner violence* (Publication No. 3460488) [Doctoral dissertation, Capella University]. ProQuest Dissertations and Theses Global. https://www.proquest.com/docview/878168878

Lausi, G., Pizzo, A., Cricenti, C., Baldi, M., Desiderio, R., Giannini, A. M., & Mari, E. (2021). Intimate partner violence during the COVID-19 pandemic: A review of the phenomenon from victims' and help professionals' perspectives. *International Journal of Environmental Research and Public Health, 18*(12), 6204. https://doi.org/10.3390/ijerph18126204

Lauve-Moon, K., & Ferreira, R. J. (2017). An exploratory investigation: Post-disaster predictors of intimate partner violence. *Clinical Social Work Journal, 45*, 124–135. https://doi.org/10.1007/s10615-015-0572-z

Lebow, J. L. (2020). COVID-19, families, and family therapy: Shining light into the darkness. *Family Process, 59*(3), 825–831. https://doi.org/10.1111/famp.12590

Lebow, J. L., Chambers, A. L., Christensen, A., & Johnson, S. M. (2012). Research on the treatment of couple distress. *Journal of Marital and Family Therapy, 38*(1), 145–168. https://doi.org/10.1111/j.1752-0606.2011.00249.x

Leeker, O., & Carlozzi, A. (2014). Effects of sex, sexual orientation, infidelity expectations, and love on distress related to emotional and sexual infidelity. *Journal of Marital and Family Therapy, 40*(1), 68–91. https://doi.org/10.1111/j.1752-0606.2012.00331.x

Leiblum, S., & Döring, N. (2002). Internet sexuality: Known risks and fresh chances for women. In A. Cooper (Ed.), *Sex and the internet: A guidebook for clinicians* (pp. 19–45). Brunner-Routledge.

Lemoine, M.-E., & Ravitsky, V. (2015). Sleepwalking into infertility: The need for a public health approach toward advanced maternal age. *The American Journal of Bioethics, 15*(11), 37–48. https://doi.org/10.1080/15265161.2015.1088973

Leridon, H. (2004). Can assisted reproduction technology compensate for the natural decline in fertility with age? A model assessment. *Human Reproduction, 19*(7), 1548–1553. https://doi.org/10.1093/humrep/deh304

Leventry, A. (2020, January 3). *There were 42 billion visits to Pornhub last year—you were probably one of them.* Scary Mommy. https://www.scarymommy.com/42-billion-people-visited-pornhub-last-year

Levine, H., Jørgensen, N., Martino-Andrade, A., Mendiola, J., Weksler-Derri, D., Mindlis, I., Pinotti, R., & Swan, S. H. (2017). Temporal trends in sperm count: A systematic review and meta-regression analysis. *Human Reproduction Update, 23*(6), 646–659. https://doi.org/10.1093/humupd/dmx022

Li, W., O'Brien, J. E., Snyder, S. M., & Howard, M. O. (2015). Characteristics of internet addiction/pathological internet use in U.S. university students: A qualitative-method investigation. *PLoS One, 10*(2). https://doi.org/10.1371/journal.pone.0117372

Liu, H., & Waite, L. (2014). Bad marriage, broken heart? Age and gender differences in the link between marital quality and cardiovascular risks among older adults. *Journal of Health and Social Behavior, 55*(4), 403–423. https://doi.org/10.1177/0022146514556893

Liu, K., Case, A., Cheung, A. P., Sierra, S., AlAsiri, S., Carranza-Mamane, B., Case, A., Dwyer, C., Graham, J., Havelock, J., Hemmings, R., Lee, F., Liu, K., Murdock, W., Senikas, V., Vause, T. D. R., & Wong, B. C.-M. (2011). Advanced reproductive age and fertility. *Journal of Obstetrics and Gynaecology Canada, 33*(11), 1165–1175. https://doi.org/10.1016/s1701-2163(16)35087-3

Magai, C., Cohen, C., Milburn, N., Thorpe, B., McPherson, R., & Peralta, D. (2001). Attachment styles in older European American and African American adults. *The Journals of Gerontology: Series B: Psychological Sciences and Social Sciences, 56*(1), S28–S35. https://doi.org/10.1093/geronb/56.1.S28

Maldonado-Rodriguez, N., Crocker, C. V., Taylor, E., Jones, K. E., Rothlander, K., Smirl, J., Wallace, C., & van Donkelaar, P. (2021). Characterization of cognitive-motor function in women who have experienced intimate partner violence-related brain injury. *Journal of Neurotrauma, 38*(19), 2723–2730. https://doi.org/10.1089/neu.2021.0042

Manning, J. C. (2006). The impact of internet pornography on marriage and the family: A review of the research. *Sexual Addiction & Compulsivity, 13*(2-3), 131–165. https://doi.org/10.1080/10720160600870711

Manoochehr, P., Asmah, I., Jaafar, W. M. W., & Yusni, Y. (2019). *Infidelity in marital relationships*. Medwin Publishers. Retrieved January 31, 2022, from https://medwinpublishers.com/PPRIJ/PPRIJ16000200.pdf

Mao, A., & Raguram, A. (2009). Online infidelity: The new challenge to marriages. *Indian Journal of Psychiatry, 51*(4), 302. https://doi.org/10.4103/0019-5545.58299

Marazziti, D., Mucci, F., Vanelli, F., Renda, N., Baroni, S., & Piccinni, A. (2017). Prevalence of internet addiction: A pilot study in a group of Italian students. *European Psychiatry, 41*(S1), S248. https://doi.org/10.1016/j.eurpsy.2017.02.030

Markman, H., Stanley, S., & Blumberg, S. L. (2001). *Fighting for your marriage: Positive steps for preventing divorce and preserving a lasting love*. Jossey-Bass.

Martin, J. A., Kirmeyer, S., Osterman, M., & Shepherd, R. A. (2009). Born a bit too early: Recent trends in late preterm births. *Europe PMC: NCHS Data Brief, (24)*, 1–8. https://europepmc.org/article/MED/19922725

Martin, J. A., Hamilton, B. E., Osterman, M. J. K., & Driscoll, A. K. (2019). Births: Final data for 2018. *National Vital Statistics Reports, 68*(13), 1–46. U.S. Department of Health and Human Services. https://www.cdc.gov/nchs/data/nvsr/nvsr68/nvsr68_13-508.pdf

Martin, M. (2021, Apri 21). *Computer and internet use in the United States, 2018*. United States Census Bureau: Report Number ACS-49. https://www.census.gov/library/publications/2021/acs/acs-49.html

Matthews, T. J., & Hamilton, B. E. (2014, May 1). First births to older women continue to rise. *Europe PMC: NCHS Data Brief, (152)*, 1–8. https://europepmc.org/article/MED/24813228

Medical News Today. (n.d.). *What to know about assisted reproductive technology*. https://www.medicalnewstoday.com/articles/assisted-reproductive-technology#types

Mikulincer, M., & Shaver, P. R. (2012). An attachment perspective on psychopathology. *World Psychiatry, 11*(1), 11–15. https://doi.org/10.1016/j.wpsyc.2012.01.003

Mikulincer, M., Shaver, P. R., & Pereg, D. (2003). Attachment theory and affect regulation: The dynamics, development, and cognitive consequences of attachment-related strategies. *Motivation and Emotion, 27*, 77–102. https://doi.org/10.1023/A:1024515519160

Miller, A. R. (2011). The effects of motherhood timing on career path. *Journal of Population Economics, 24*, 1071–1100. https://doi.org/10.1007/s00148-009-0296-x

Milne, E. (2011). Marriage and the religion clauses. *St. John's Law Review, 85*, 1451–1482. https://scholarship.law.stjohns.edu/lawreview/vol85/iss4/3/

Moller, N. P., & Vossler, A. (2015). Defining infidelity in research and couple counseling: A qualitative study. *Journal of Sex & Marital Therapy, 41*(5), 487–497. https://doi.org/10.1080/0092623x.2014.931314

Moore, K., & Palumbo, M. (2009, December 10). *The finances of American households in the past three recessions: Evidence from the survey of consumer finances*. Finance and Economics Discussion Series Divisions of Research & Statistics and Monetary Affairs Federal Reserve Board. https://www.federalreserve.gov/pubs/feds/2010/201006/201006pap.pdf

Murphy, C. M. (2013). Social information processing and the perpetration of intimate partner violence: It is (and isn't) what you think. *Psychology of Violence, 3*(3), 212–217. https://doi.org/10.1037/a0033344

Nachtigall, R. D., Becker, G., & Wozny, M. (1992). The effects of gender-specific diagnosis on men's and women's response to infertility. *Fertility and Sterility, 57*(1), 113–121. https://doi.org/10.1016/s0015-0282(16)54786-4

National Center for Drug Abuse Statistics. (2022, January 21). *Drug abuse statistics [2022]*. Retrieved January 31, 2022, from https://drugabusestatistics.org/

National Center for Health Statistics. (2021). *Provisional drug overdose death counts*. National Vital Statistics System. https://www.cdc.gov/nchs/nvss/vsrr/drug-overdose-data.htm

National Coalition Against Domestic Violence. (2020a). *Domestic violence*. https://assets.speakcdn.com/assets/2497/domestic_violence-2020080709350855.pdf?1596811079991

National Coalition Against Domestic Violence. (2020b). *Statistics*. Retrieved January 31, 2022, from https://ncadv.org/STATISTICS

National Institute on Drug Abuse. (2021, January 13). *People with SUDs have increased risk for COVID-19 and worse outcomes*. NIDA Notes. https://nida.nih.gov/news-events/nida-notes/2021/01/people-with-suds-have-increased-risk-for-covid-19-worse-outcomes

Nelson, I. (2014). Recognition of civil unions and domestic partnerships as marriages in same-sex marriage states. *Minnesota Law Review, 98*(3), 1171–1209.

Newstrom, N. P., & Harris, S. M. (2016). Pornography and couples: What does the research tell us? *Contemporary Family Therapy, 38*, 412–423. https://doi.org/10.1007/s10591-016-9396-4

Nogales, A., & Bellotti, L. G. (2009). *Parents who cheat: How children and adults are affected when their parents are unfaithful*. Health Communications.

Office for Civil Rights. (2021, June 28). *Notification of enforcement discretion for telehealth remote communications during the COVID-19 nationwide public health emergency*. U.S. Department of Health and Human Services. https://www.hhs.gov/hipaa/for-professionals/special-topics/emergency-preparedness/notification-enforcement-discretion-telehealth/index.html

Ogas, O., & Gaddam, S. (2012). *A billion wicked thoughts: What the internet tells us about sexual relationships*. Plume.

Olito, F. (2019, January 30). *How the divorce rate has changed over the last 150 years*. Insider.com. https://www.insider.com/divorce-rate-changes-over-time-2019-1#the-divorce-rate-remained-steady-at-4-divorces-for-every-1000-americans-in-the-90s-but-slowly-declined-throughout-the-decade-12

Orth-Gomér, K., Wamala, S. P., Horsten, M., Schenck-Gustafsson, K., Schneiderman, N., & Mittleman, M. A. (2000). Marital stress worsens prognosis in women with coronary heart disease. *JAMA, 284*(23), 3008. https://doi.org/10.1001/jama.284.23.3008

Ottosen, M. E. H., Dahl, K., & Boserup, B. (2017, October 26). Parental conflicts after separation and divorce. *VIVE - Det Nationale Forsknings- Og Analysecenter for Velfærd*. https://www.vive.dk/en/publications/parental-conflicts-after-separation-and-divorce-6821/

Papp, L. M., Cummings, E. M., & Goeke-Morey, M. C. (2009). For richer, for poorer: Money as a topic of marital conflict in the home. *Family Relations, 58*(1), 91–103. https://doi.org/10.1111/j.1741-3729.2008.00537.x

Peterson, B. D., Newton, C. R., Rosen, K. H., & Skaggs, G. E. (2006). Gender differences in how men and women who are referred for IVF cope with infertility stress. *Human Reproduction, 21*(9), 2443–2449. https://doi.org/10.1093/humrep/del145

Peterson, B. D., Pirritano, M., Christensen, U., Boivin, J., Block, J., & Schmidt, L. (2009). The longitudinal impact of partner coping in couples following 5 years of unsuccessful fertility treatments. *Human Reproduction, 24*(7), 1656–1664. https://doi.org/10.1093/humrep/dep061

Pietromonaco, P. R., & Overall, N. C. (2020). Applying relationship science to evaluate how the COVID-19 pandemic may impact couples' relationships. *American Psychologist, 76*(3), 438–450. https://doi.org/10.1037/amp0000714

Pilkington, E. (2022, May 25). US reels after massacre in fourth-grade classroom leaves 21 dead. *The Guardian*. https://www.theguardian.com/us-news/2022/may/25/biden-reaction-uvalde-school-shooting

Previti, D., & Amato, P. R. (2004). Is infidelity a cause or a consequence of poor marital quality? *Journal of Social and Personal Relationships, 21*(2), 217–230. https://doi.org/10.1177/0265407504041384

Proulx, C. M., Helms, H. M., & Buehler, C. (2007). Marital quality and personal well-being: A meta-analysis. *Journal of Marriage and Family, 69*(3), 576–593. https://doi.org/10.1111/j.1741-3737.2007.00393.x

Psychology Today Staff. (n.d.). What is addiction? *Psychology Today*. Retrieved January 26, 2022, from https://www.psychologytoday.com/us/basics/addiction

Reid, R. C., & Woolley, S. R. (2006). Using emotionally focused therapy for couples to resolve attachment ruptures created by hypersexual behavior. *Sexual Addiction & Compulsivity, 13*(2-3), 219–239. https://doi.org/10.1080/10720160600870786

Riskind, R. G., & Patterson, C. J. (2010). Parenting intentions and desires among childless lesbian, gay, and heterosexual individuals. *Journal of Family Psychology, 24*(1), 78–81. https://doi.org/10.1037/a0017941

Robila, M., & Krishnakumar, A. (2005). Effects of economic pressure on marital conflict in Romania. *Journal of Family Psychology, 19*(2), 246–251. https://doi.org/10.1037/0893-3200.19.2.246

Rosenfeld, M. J., Thomas, R. J., & Hausen, S. (2020). Disintermediating your friends: How online dating in the United States displaces other ways of meeting. *Proceedings of the National Academy of Sciences, 116*(36), 17753–17758. https://doi.org/10.1073/pnas.1908630116

Rothbaum, F., Weisz, J., Pott, M., Miyake, K., & Morelli, G. (2000). Attachment and culture: Security in the United States and Japan. *American Psychologist, 55*, 1093–1104. https://doi.org/10.1037//0003-066x.55.10.1093

Russell, V. M., Baker, L. R., & McNulty, J. K. (2013). Attachment insecurity and infidelity in marriage: Do studies of dating relationships really inform us about marriage? *Journal of Family Psychology, 27*(2), 242–251. https://doi.org/10.1037/a0032118

Schmaling, K. B., & Sher, T. G. (1997). Physical health and relationships. In W. K. Halford & H. J. Markman (Eds.), *Clinical handbook of marriage and couples interventions* (pp. 323–345). John Wiley & Sons.

Schneider, J. P. (1994). Sex addiction: Controversy within mainstream addiction medicine, diagnosis based on the *DSM-III-R*, and physician case histories. *Sexual Addiction & Compulsivity, 1*(1), 19–44. https://doi.org/10.1080/10720169408400025

Schneider, J. P. (2000a). A qualitative study of cybersex participants: Gender differences, recovery issues, and implications for therapists. *Sexual Addiction & Compulsivity, 7*(4), 249–278. https://doi.org/10.1080/10720160008403700

Schneider, J. P. (2000b). Effects of cybersex addiction on the family: Results of a survey. *Sexual Addiction & Compulsivity, 7*(1-2), 31–58. https://doi.org/10.1080/10720160008400206

Schumacher, J. A., Coffey, S. F., Norris, F. H., Tracy, M., Clements, K., & Galea, S. (2010). Intimate partner violence and Hurricane Katrina: Predictors and associated mental health outcomes. *Violence and Victims, 25*(5), 588–603. https://doi.org/10.1891/0886-6708.25.5.588

Schwartz, M., & Southern, S. (2017). Recovery from sexual compulsivity. *Sexual Addiction & Compulsivity, 24*, 224–240. https://doi.org/10.1080/10720162.2017.1350229

Scott, S. B., Rhoades, G. K., Stanley, S. M., Allen, E. S., & Markman, H. J. (2013). Reasons for divorce and recollections of premarital intervention: Implications for improving relationship education. *Couple and Family Psychology: Research and Practice, 2*(2), 131–145. https://doi.org/10.1037/a0032025

Shanley, M. L., & Asch, A. (2009). Involuntary childlessness, reproductive technology, and social justice: The medical mask on social illness. *Signs: Journal of Women in Culture and Society, 34*(4), 851–874. https://doi.org/10.1086/597141

Sharlip, I. D., Jarow, J. P., Belker, A. M., Lipshultz, L. I., Sigman, M., Thomas, A. J., Schlegel, P. N., Howards, S. S., Nehra, A., Damewood, M. D., Overstreet, J. W., & Sadovsky, R. (2002). Best practice policies for male infertility. *Fertility and Sterility, 77*(5), 873–882. https://doi.org/10.1016/s0015-0282(02)03105-9

Shing, E. Z., Jayawickreme, E., & Waugh, C. E. (2016). Contextual positive coping as a factor contributing to resilience after disasters. *Journal of Clinical Psychology, 72*(12), 1287–1306. https://doi.org/10.1002/jclp.22327

Short, L. M., McMahon, P. M., Davis Chervin, D., Shelley, G. A., Lezin, N., Sloop, K. S., & Dawkins, N. (2000). Survivors' identification of protective factors and early warning signs for intimate partner violence. *Violence Against Women, 6*(3), 272–285. https://doi.org/10.1177/10778010022181840

Simpson, J. A., & Rholes, W. S. (2017). Adult attachment, stress, and romantic relationships. *Current Opinion in Psychology, 13*, 19–24. https://doi.org/10.1016/j.copsyc.2016.04.006

Smyth, B. M., & Moloney, L. J. (2017). Entrenched postseparation parenting disputes: The role of interparental hatred? *Family Court Review, 55*(3), 404–416. https://doi.org/10.1111/fcre.12294

Solano, I., Eaton, N. R., & O'Leary, K. D. (2020). Pornography consumption, modality and function in a large internet sample. *The Journal of Sex Research, 57*(1), 92–103. https://doi.org/10.1080/00224499.2018.1532488

Stack, S., Wasserman, I., & Kern, R. (2004). Adult social bonds and use of internet pornography. *Social Science Quarterly, 85*(1), 75–88. https://doi.org/10.1111/j.0038-4941.2004.08501006.x

Stanley, S. M., & Markman, H. J. (2020). Helping couples in the shadow of COVID-19. *Family Process, 59*(3), 937–955. https://doi.org/10.1111/famp.12575

Stockman, J. K., Hayashi, H., & Campbell, J. C. (2015). Intimate partner violence and its health impact on ethnic minority women. *Journal of Women's Health, 24*(1), 62–79. https://doi.org/10.1089/jwh.2014.4879

Storaasli, R. D., & Markman, H. J. (1990). Relationship problems in the early stages of marriage: A longitudinal investigation. *Journal of Family Psychology, 4*(1), 80–98. https://doi.org/10.1037/0893-3200.4.1.80

Story, L. B., & Bradbury, T. N. (2004). Understanding marriage and stress: Essential questions and challenges. *Clinical Psychology Review, 23*(8), 1139–1162. https://doi.org/10.1016/j.cpr.2003.10.002

Sue, D. W., Sue, D., Neville, H. A., & Smith, L. (2019). *Counseling the culturally diverse: Theory and practice* (8th ed.). John Wiley & Sons.

Symoens, S., Colman, E., & Bracke, P. (2014). Divorce, conflict, and mental health: How the quality of intimate relationships is linked to post-divorce well-being. *Journal of Applied Social Psychology, 44*(3), 220–233. https://doi.org/10.1111/jasp.12215

Takahashi, K. (1986). Examining the strange-situation procedure with Japanese mothers and 12-month-old infants. *Developmental Psychology, 22*(2), 265–270. https://doi.org/10.1037/0012-1649.22.2.265

Thomas, J., Katsikitis, M., Allen, A., & Kannis-Dymand, L. (2020). Desire thinking and metacognition associated with dysregulated sexuality. *Sexual Addiction & Compulsivity, 27*, 119–134. https://doi.org/10.1080/10720162.2020.1772155

Tjaden, P., & Thoennes, N. (2000). Prevalence and consequences of male-to-female and female-to-male intimate partner violence as measured by the National Violence Against Women Survey. *Violence Against Women, 6*(2), 142–161. https://doi.org/10.1177/10778010022181769

Towler, A., Eivers, A., & Frey, R. (2020). Warning signs of partner abuse in intimate relationships: Gender differences in young adults' perceptions of seriousness. *Journal of Interpersonal Violence, 35*(7-8), 1779–1802. https://doi.org/10.1177/0886260517696869

Trost, J. (2016). Marriage, cohabitation and LAT relationships. *Journal of Comparative Family Studies, 47*(1), 17–26. https://doi.org/10.3138/jcfs.47.1.17

Troxel, W. M., Matthews, K. A., Gallo, L. C., & Kuller, L. H. (2005). Marital quality and occurrence of the metabolic syndrome in women. *Archives of Internal Medicine, 165*(9), 1022–1027. https://doi.org/10.1001/archinte.165.9.1022

Truman, J. L., & Morgan, R. E. (2014, April). *Special report: Nonfatal domestic violence, 2003–2012.* U.S. Department of Justice, Office of Justice Programs, Bureau of Justice Statistics. https://bjs.ojp.gov/content/pub/pdf/ndv0312.pdf

van Ijzendoorn, M. H., & Bakermans-Kranenburg, M. J. (1996). Attachment representations in mothers, fathers, adolescents, and clinical groups: A meta-analytic search for normative data. *Journal of Consulting and Clinical Psychology, 64*(1), 8–21. https://doi.org/10.1037/0022-006x.64.1.8

van Ijzendoorn, M. H., & Sagi, A. (1999). Cross-cultural patterns of attachment: Universal and contextual dimensions. In J. Cassidy & P. R. Shaver (Eds.), *Handbook of attachment: Theory, research, and clinical applications* (pp. 713–734). The Guilford Press.

van Ijzendoorn, M. H., & Sagi-Schwartz, A. (2008). Cross-cultural patterns of attachment: Universal and contextual dimensions. In J. Cassidy & P. R. Shaver (Eds.), *Handbook of attachment: Theory, research, and clinical applications* (pp. 880–905). The Guilford Press.

Verhaak, C. M., Smeenk, J. M. J., van Minnen, A., Kremer, J. A. M., & Kraaimaat, F. W. (2005). A longitudinal, prospective study on emotional adjustment before, during and after consecutive fertility treatment cycles. *Human Reproduction, 20*(8), 2253–2260. https://doi.org/10.1093/humrep/dei015

Violence Policy Center. (2020, July 23). *Murder-suicide.* Retrieved January 31, 2022, from https://vpc.org/revealing-the-impacts-of-gun-violence/murder-suicide/

Wang, Q. Q., Kaelber, D. C., Xu, R., & Volkow, N. D. (2021). COVID-19 risk and outcomes in patients with substance use disorders: Analyses from electronic health records in the United States. *Molecular Psychology, 26*, 30–39. https://doi.org/10.1038/s41380-020-00880

Wei, M., Russell, D. W., Mallinckrodt, B., & Zakalik, R. A. (2004). Cultural equivalence of adult attachment across four ethnic groups: Factor structure, structured means, and associations with negative mood. *Journal of Counseling Psychology, 51*(4), 408–417. https://doi.org/10.1037/0022-0167.51.4.408

Wei, M., Vogel, D. L., Ku, T.-Y., & Zakalik, R. A. (2005). Adult attachment, affect regulation, negative mood, and interpersonal problems: The mediating roles of emotional reactivity and emotional cutoff. *Journal of Counseling Psychology, 52*(1), 14–24. https://doi.org/10.1037/0022-0167.52.1.14

Weinstein, A., Katz, L., Eberhardt, H., Cohen, K., & Lejoyeux, M. (2015). Sexual compulsion–relationship with sex, attachment and sexual orientation. *Journal of Behavioral Addictions, 4*(1), 22–26. https://doi.org/10.1556/JBA.4.2015.1.6

Weller, C. (2017, September 17). *What you need to know about egg-freezing, the hot new perk at Google, Apple, and Facebook.* Insider.com. https://www.businessinsider.com/egg-freezing-at-facebook-apple-google-hot-new-perk-2017-9

Whisman, M. A., Dixon, A. E., & Johnson, B. (1997). Therapists' perspectives of couple problems and treatment issues in couple therapy. *Journal of Family Psychology, 11*(3), 361–366. https://doi.org/10.1037/0893-3200.11.3.361

Whiteman, S. D., McHale, S. M., & Crouter, A. C. (2007). Competing processes of sibling influence: Observational learning and sibling deidentification. *Social Development, 16*(4), 642–661. https://doi.org/10.1111/j.1467-9507.2007.00409.x

Whitton, S. W., Olmos-Gallo, P. A., Stanley, S. M., Prado, L. M., Kline, G. H., St. Peters, M., & Markman, H. J. (2007). Depressive symptoms in early marriage: Predictions from relationship confidence and negative marital interaction. *Journal of Family Psychology, 21*(2), 297–306. https://doi.org/10.1037/0893-3200.21.2.297

Wicks, T. (2021). *Elevating Black pregnant voices for self-advocacy. Elevating Voices for Equity: Issues of Mental Health and Advocacy, 1*(1), 14. http://journalforequity.com/journalforequity/article/view/4

Wiederman, M. W., & Allgeier, E. R. (1996). Expectations and attributions regarding extramarital sex among young married individuals. *Journal of Psychology & Human Sexuality, 8*(3), 21–35. https://doi.org/10.1300/j056v08n03_02

Williamson, H. C., Bradbury, T. N., & Karney, B. R. (2021). Experiencing a natural disaster temporarily boosts relationship satisfaction in newlywed couples. *Psychological Science, 32*(11), 1709–1719. https://doi.org/10.1177/09567976211015677

Willoughby, B. J., Busby, D. M., & Young-Petersen, B. (2019). Understanding associations between personal definitions of pornography, using pornography, and depression. *Sexuality Research and Social Policy, 16*, 342–356. https://doi.org/10.1007/s13178-018-0345-x

Wilsnack, S. C., & Wilsnack, R. W. (1991). Epidemiology of women's drinking. *Journal of Substance Abuse, 3*(2), 133–157. https://doi.org/10.1016/s0899-3289(05)80033-1

Witeck, B. (2014). Cultural change in acceptance of LGBT people: Lessons from social marketing. *American Journal of Orthopsychiatry, 84*(1), 19–22. https://doi.org/10.1037/h0098945

World Health Organization. (2020, September 14). *Infertility*. World Health Organization. https://www.who.int/news-room/fact-sheets/detail/infertility

Wyndham, N., Marin Figueira, P. G., & Patrizio, P. (2012). A persistent misperception: Assisted reproductive technology can reverse the "aged biological clock." *Fertility and Sterility, 97*(5), 1044–1047. https://doi.org/10.1016/j.fertnstert.2012.02.015

Yau, Y. H., & Potenza, M. N. (2015). Gambling disorder and other behavioral addictions. *Harvard Review of Psychiatry, 23*(2), 134–146. https://doi.org/10.1097/hrp.0000000000000051

Young, K. S. (1999). Internet addiction: Symptoms, evaluation, and treatment. In L. VandeCreek & T. L. Jackson (Eds.), *Innovations in clinical practice* (Vol. 17). Professional Resource Press.

Zitzman, S. T., & Butler, M. H. (2009). Wives' experience of husbands' pornography use and concomitant deception as an attachment threat in the adult pair-bond relationship. *Sexual Addiction & Compulsivity, 16*(3), 210–240. https://doi.org/10.1080/10720160903202679

CHAPTER 7

COUPLE AND MARRIAGE THERAPY SKILLS AND INTERVENTIONS

LEARNING OBJECTIVES

After reading this chapter, you will be able to:

- ■ Identify skills for helping couples experiencing infertility.
- ■ Identify skills related to adult attachment.
- ■ Identify skills for engaging in premarital therapy.
- ■ Demonstrate skills for helping couples handling marital and relationship distress.
- ■ Recognize the techniques for helping couples experiencing the effects of crisis and disaster.
- ■ Identify skills for relational issues related to substance abuse.
- ■ Recognize skills for assisting couples experiencing financial stress.
- ■ Demonstrate skills for helping couples recovering from infidelity.
- ■ Identify skills related to helping couples engaging in intimate partner violence.
- ■ Recognize contemporary issues related to divorce conflict.
- ■ Distinguish the various clinical skills related to online addiction.
- ■ Identify the clinical skills associated with sex addiction.
- ■ Recognize the assessment measures used to analyze contemporary couple therapy issues.

INTRODUCTION TO COUPLE AND MARRIAGE INTERVENTIONS AND SKILLS

It is important to understand the skills and interventions that are most helpful and relevant in assisting couples as they work through various issues. According to Eysenck's (1952, 1961) famous and controversial empirical studies, psychotherapy does not assist with recovery from neurotic disorders. In fact, Eysenck found that an inverse correlation between psychotherapy and improvement exists (i.e., the more therapy one receives, the less likely they are to recover). Since that time, the helping professions have been increasingly focused on demonstrating evidence-supported treatment using well-designed empirically based investigations. Today, couple, marriage, and family practitioners efficaciously treat a wide variety of mental health disorders (e.g., depression, anxiety, bipolar disorder, trauma) with a wide array of interventions. The overall goal of this chapter is to provide important interventions related to the contemporary couple/marriage issues previously reviewed in this book, including infertility, adult attachment, premarital issues and warning signs, marital distress, crisis and disaster, substance abuse, financial stress, infidelity, intimate partner violence (IPV), divorce conflict, online addiction, and sex addiction.

Therapeutic skills and interventions are important because they can assist the practitioner in forming a strong therapeutic relationship with the client, create awareness, decrease mental health symptomology, and help the therapist and the client achieve agreed-upon goals. While the benefits are evident, learning the art and science of therapy requires a lot of work. Clinicians must first understand what the skills entail and why they are used. This is typically accomplished through reading textbooks and articles, using a skill description, exploring a series of tangible examples, through supervision and supervised practice, attending a training program, or attending relevant sessions at conferences. Next, it is helpful to further enhance one's understanding of a skill by reviewing a case study or watching a digital recording of a therapist using the skill in a mock/real session. Third, a common phase of training is practicing skills with a fellow clinician or supervisor. This can be done in a variety of ways, including, but not limited to, a mock counseling session or through fast-paced skill enhancement opportunities in which a fellow clinician or supervisor will provide the same opportunity repeatedly so the clinician can gain competency. Lastly, after reviewing materials, attending trainings, and witnessing therapy in action, the clinician will begin to incorporate the skill(s) in their therapeutic work with clients.

At the core, counseling, therapy, and psychotherapy are a practice. There is no apex of clinical ability because we are always growing, developing, adapting, and changing. Clinicians are intentional about learning from experience and gaining awareness through practice. In addition to the technical understanding of the core skills used in helping individuals heal from contemporary relational issues, it is important for clinicians to engage in *reflective practice* and *reflective thinking* throughout their training and clinical practice (Rosin, 2015). Reflective practice is similar to the construct of self-awareness, and is an essential skill for couple, marriage, and family practitioners to use when advancing their understanding of a relational issue, conceptualizing the nuances of a particular case, developing pertinent skills and interventions, and developing a sense of professional competency (Collins et al., 2010). Reflective practice could be described as the deliberate process of enhancing one's clinical acumen through learning from practice and making the implicit explicit (Black & Flynn, 2021). Reflective thinking is not passive, is intentional, and creates a sense of purposefulness and curiosity (Dewey, 1933). When engaging in reflective practice and thinking, clinicians are constantly enhancing their understanding of skills they used, familiarizing themselves with each skill, integrating the skills into their preferred theoretical tradition, and critiquing their skill-based performance.

Most helping professionals desire to be very good at what they do. The number of traits, skills, and other factors that contribute to being an effective couple, marriage, and family practitioner is incalculable. In a general sense, professionals should work hard to continuously develop their strengths and try to enhance areas in need of further refinement. While improvements can be made in every area of professional practice, all helping professionals bring their own unique blend of talent and ability to any clinical encounter. For example, some practitioners demonstrate excellent skill delivery, while others are extremely effective at clinical assessment, and a third group may demonstrate incredible relationship-building skills. Additionally, in terms of factors that contribute to excellent clinical work, professional factors like personal characteristics, common factors, theoretical orientation, level of multicultural orientation (e.g., cultural humility, cultural opportunities, cultural comfort), humility and ability to critique one's therapeutic work, management of countertransference, and deliberate practice (engaging in intentional exercises to enhance clinical skill and ability) all play a major role in engaging in highly effective therapy (Shaw et al., 2020).

Voices From the Field

This chapter features sections entitled Voices From the Field. These sections explore multicultural, social justice, equity, diversity, and intersectionality issues from the perspective of clinicians representing a wide range of ethnic, racial, and national backgrounds. This chapter will feature professional counselors who identify as LGBTQIA+. The purpose of adding quotes from individuals representing one or more communities of color or who frequently serve diverse populations is to provide you, the reader, with cutting-edge social justice and multiculturally oriented skills, interventions, and clinical conceptualization. The two individuals who took part in the Voices From the Field process came from different life contexts, different regions of the United States, and diverse intersections of cultural advantage and disadvantage. Participant information is provided in the following:

Dr. Harvey Peters is a 31-year-old White cisgender man who identifies as gay/queer. He is a nationally certified counselor and an assistant professor of counselor education at The George Washington University. In addition to his work as a faculty member, Dr. Peters has worked with queer couples on a variety of contemporary issues over the past 10 years.

Ms. Jennifer Kassing is a 38-year-old White cisgender woman who identifies as gay. She is a licensed mental health counselor and nationally certified counselor. Ms. Kassing has engaged in a broad range of clinical experiences with diverse populations throughout her career.

Participants were sent a questionnaire featuring seven open-ended questions regarding their experiences practicing in the field. Participant quotes are placed throughout the chapter to enhance the content. Participant questions are as follows:

- Our work as helping professionals provides opportunities to understand and explore the experiences that couples endure. In your personal experience with this work, what are the effects of infertility on couples? Have you had the opportunity to use any therapeutic methods that can help to reduce the painful experiences related to infertility and/or infertility treatment? What, if any, unique issues emerge for couples who identify as LGBTQIA+?

- Internet-related issues (e.g., social media, internet dating apps, internet addiction, pornography) have had a powerful impact on couples. Unfortunately, this form of stress can feel unavoidable for many couples due to the prevalence of the internet in daily life. How have you worked with couples to manage internet-related issues? What, if any, unique issues emerge for couples who identify as LGBTQIA+?

- Marital/long-term relationship distress is a common issue for any population of people. When considering your work with LGBTQIA+ couples, describe a few unique issues that come up in session? How has having to cope with discrimination and hate affected the couples in your clinical practice who identify as LGBTQIA+?

- Infidelity is a common destructive relationship issue for any population of people. When considering infidelity within the LGBTQIA+ population, describe a few unique issues that often come up in session.

- As clinicians, we have the ability to work deeply with couples in ways that give us a different look into their relational dynamics. When a couple is moving toward divorce and wants your assistance with minimizing divorce conflict, what strategies have you utilized? Have you had to adjust your techniques when working with individuals who identify as LGBTQIA+?

- Professional helpers who work with the LGBTQIA+ population may experience burnout, compassion fatigue, and/or vicarious trauma due to frequently witnessing their clients' firsthand experiences with bias, hatred, and discrimination. How has having to cope with this discrimination-related stress affected your work as a clinician?

- When working with couples, intimate partner violence can emerge during counseling or might be present in the relationship prior to treatment. Can you name an instance where intimate partner violence affected an LGBTQIA+ couple you were conducting counseling with? From your experience, what unique factors influence intimate partner violence with couples who identify as LGBTQIA+?

HELPING COUPLES STRUGGLING WITH INFERTILITY

Fertility challenges are invisible to outsiders and difficult to understand unless one has experienced them directly. While all infertility experiences and narratives are unique, partners who experience these issues are going through a loss of something that they had hoped for and expected but have never directly experienced. This is somewhat different from losing something that one had (e.g., death of a loved relative), but no longer has. Specifically, it is the extreme sadness and disappointment associated with not experiencing a common vision or dream that one had hoped for over a long period of time.

Discussions of fertility problems are taboo and hidden, and many who experience infertility are silent about the process they have endured (e.g., medication schedules, side effects, embryo transfer) and/or do not have the vocabulary to discuss the issues at hand. Furthermore, infertility can put an enormous strain on a relationship and cause a number of emotional issues for one or both partners, including emotional trauma, a deep sense of grief, emotional withdrawal, feeling hopeless and defeated, depression, anxiety, and stress related to severe financial strain due to the cost of treatment (McBain & Reeves, 2019). Relationship challenges include, but are not limited to, emotional distance, poor communication, stress on the sexual relationship, blaming each other, marital dissatisfaction, and turning away from each other during a time of need (Chow et al., 2016; Donarelli et al., 2016; McBain & Reeves, 2019).

These issues are coupled with disillusionment around the dreams each partner had about having a biological family, becoming a parent and a grandparent, passing on one's genes (i.e., genetic legacy), and the loss women experience around becoming pregnant and giving birth (e.g., ultrasound visits, baby shower, announcing the news to family members). If the couple chooses not to adopt, this could mean missing out on multiple expected stages of life. When working with individuals who are affected by infertility, it is very likely that the practitioner will need to engage in grief therapy. While every infertility experience is unique, couples may experience the five common themes associated with grief and loss: denial, anger, bargaining, depression, and acceptance (Kübler-Ross, 1970). While grief and loss are common, people experience these phases and unique emotions around infertility in different ways.

While Kübler-Ross's and similar phase/stage models are very helpful, the field of grief counseling has greatly expanded to include models associated with all major theoretical orientations and other unique models that have been heavily promoted in the literature, including, but not limited to, adaptive grieving styles (Doughty, 2009), attachment theory (Stroebe, 2002), constructivism (Neimeyer et al., 2002), and the dual process model (Servaty-Seib, 2004). Given the wide variety of interventions and theories centered on grief counseling, remember that regardless of the model used it is important to keep the therapeutic work centered on the specific issues associated with infertility.

Infertility counseling is centered on helping couples endure the physical, cognitive, and emotional pain that occurs throughout the treatment process. Many clinicians ask themselves, "How do you help a couple or person heal from an invisible issue that is very difficult to discuss and causes enormous emotional pain?" First, clinicians need to understand the fertility nomenclature (see Chapter 6) so they can understand what clients are discussing, are aware of treatment options, and/or so they can provide education to clients and family members. This factual information is combined with the demographic, cultural, and contextual factors associated with the couple experiencing infertility distress. Additionally, it is very important to convey a sense of accurate empathy to clients. In order to encourage the couple/client to believe that you fully understand their pain, it is helpful to use their language, accurately reflect their pain, and sit in their pain with them (i.e., do not minimize, encourage hope, or avoid deeper exploration). For example:

> *Clinician*: Samantha, you feel so sad and empty after receiving the infertility diagnosis. Brad, you haven't said much and appear to be somewhat in denial about the situation. Please tell me more.

Next, clinicians work hard to validate the loss that couples feel when they cannot have a biological child or the loss of the ideal conception narrative (e.g., passionate sex vs. sterile hospital environment, medication). This validation is so important given the enormous amount of pain, confusion, and disappointment the couple may be feeling. For example:

Clinician: Robert, you felt so defeated by not being able to engage in passionate sex that eventually led to conception. Julia, you feel furious that things turned out this way and I can tell that it is painful for you to discuss the specifics.

For couples who were eventually able to have a biological baby or who chose to adopt, clinicians could combine this deep validation with a sense of gratitude for the baby (Chow et al., 2016; Donarelli et al., 2016; McBain & Reeves, 2019). For example:

Clinician: While the couple is grateful for Arianna, I can sense some sorrow around letting go of the initial vision of a biological child.

Lastly, because of the unpredictable nature of infertility issues, partners, especially men, are encouraged not to attempt to engage in any problem-solving. Instead, couples are encouraged to reach for each other during these emotional and hurtful experiences. For example:

Clinician: Juanita, please speak directly to Megan about your fears. Megan, try to listen and continue holding her hand while she's talking.

VOICES FROM THE FIELD: HARVEY

Dr. Harvey Peters shared his experiences working with couples who struggle with infertility and identify as LGBTQIA+.

Within the queer communities, understanding the within-group differences of infertility is essential given the various access, opportunities, and structures that can support or hinder the infertility process. For example, understanding how intersectional social locations, such as affectional orientation, gender identity, race, socioeconomic status, education level can help understand the emotional and relational toll, implications, and needs of couples. When I have worked with queer couples experiencing infertility, I have often integrated the use of emotionally focused therapy with Worden's tasks of mourning, bibliotherapy, and advocacy to assist in the complicated practice of processing thoughts and emotions, meaning-making, and decision-making informed by theory, intersecting identities, and cultural self. Some issues that can occur involve financial concerns, lack of family or queer community support, nonaffirmative and oppressive systems and healthcare, and navigating decisions around family planning.

VOICES FROM THE FIELD: JENNIFER

Ms. Jennifer Kassing shared her experiences working with couples experiencing infertility issues and provides a detailed account of how she helps couples identifying as LGBTQIA+.

Many women, and sometimes men, see this (infertility) as a personal defect and the pressure to have biological children is high. Along with processing the grief, sadness, and anger, it is important to help couples find acceptance and develop a practical plan of action. Also, I help couples learn how to manage conflict and stress, and how to stay connected and keep their emotional bank account in the positive. Also, it is important to help couples learn how to navigate various medical systems and deal with the stress and strain that come from this process. I utilize Gottman interventions with all my couples. Regarding the effects of infertility, couples experience stress and strain, doubt, grief, anger, sadness, frustration, and increased relational conflict. Also, it can have practical effects, such as lack of resources (e.g., money and time) and difficulty finding access to fertility doctors and follow-up care. These can be added stressors for couples. In working with the one gay couple, we also engaged in safety planning, which is a common practice when working with LGBTQIA+ persons and is done for a variety of reasons, including being aware of and understanding the possible discrimination they may face and planning for how to handle a situation that could leave them feeling emotionally or physically unsafe. Also, I help them learn how to handle and develop resiliency around microaggressions and other forms of rejection. In addition, working with the couple to find a provider who specializes in providing medical services to LGBTQIA+ couples and finding a support system for other LGBTQIA+ parents is important. These aren't specific interventions or methods necessarily, but they are strategies I often utilize with my gay, lesbian, and trans clients. Also, I frequently use Gottman methods to help the couple stay connected through conflict, times of high stress, and through disappointments or setbacks. There can be familial pressure or rejection, so learning how to cope with this is key to my work. Sometimes LGBTQIA+ people don't have a strong support system, so embarking on a fertility journey can feel lonely without the proper support system. So, growing this support system is vital.

HELPING COUPLES HEAL FROM ATTACHMENT INJURIES

Due to its salience and relevance in treating couple-based attachment injuries, this section will focus primarily on certain aspects of the practice of emotionally focused therapy (EFT). For a complete review of the emotionally focused couple therapy modality, clinicians and graduate students should consider reading *The Practice of Emotionally Focused Couple Therapy: Creating Connection, Third Edition* (Johnson, 2019). Couple-based attachment injuries are typically caused by the perception that one has been betrayed, abandoned, or there has been a major breach in trust by an intimate partner (i.e., attachment figure; Johnson et al., 1998, 2001). This injury, or negative relational experience, becomes recurring, and couples come to be stuck in a negative interactional cycle. The cycle can become rigid and has the potential to escalate into a serious relationship distress and/or gridlock (Makinen & Johnson, 2006).

It is important to note that when authors and clinicians discuss interactional cycles, they are attempting to describe a relational dance that includes many variations (e.g., attack–defend, pursue–distance, attack-attack). These negative interactional styles are centered on blocking relationship repair attempts, and they create a scenario that makes it very difficult for partners to respond during times of urgent need, further damaging the attachment bond (Simpson & Rholes, 1994). Johnson (2002) labeled the severe consequences of these damaged attachment bonds as *small t traumas* (i.e., less intense trauma that changes how we see ourselves and/or the world). Regarding the negative consequences, when attachment injuries occur, injured partners become burdened with a variety of emotional experiences, including avoidance, numbing, disturbing memories, hypervigilance, and feelings of betrayal (Enright & Fitzgibbons, 2000; Hargrave, 2004).

After detecting an attachment injury, clinicians work with couples to establish a secure attachment bond with high levels of trust, commitment, relational satisfaction, and support (Kirkpatrick & Davis, 1994; Mikulincer, 1998). The clinician can help alleviate the couple's sense of insecurity and start building the therapeutic alliance by educating them on the nature of attachment injuries and/or normalizing their interactions (e.g., dance) as typical coping skills that many couples use to try to feel a sense of connection. For example:

Clinician: Jasper, your frustration is evident, and I can tell this sense of forcefulness we've been discussing is your attempt to keep the relationship going in a positive direction. Toby, you haven't said much and when you discussed the nature of your interaction you mentioned feeling overwhelmed and shut down. The two of you are engaging in a pursuer–distancer relationship dynamic.

While this has been challenging, I want to let you know it is a normal way of coping with the challenges we've been discussing. Although this is something we're going to spend a lot of time working on, this sort of thing is common.

A first step in helping couples heal from an attachment injury includes the clinician developing a strong therapeutic alliance with the couple. Next, the clinician will often begin working with the couple on forgiveness, faith, and trust. Forgiveness is a complicated interaction that involves validation, mending emotional hurts, and increasing the couple's sense of trust. Additionally, forgiveness is healthy both for those doing the forgiving and for those being forgiven (Gordon et al., 2000). Next, cocreating a sense of faith and trust in one's partner can generate the optimal atmosphere for working on deep attachment injuries. This, along with forgiveness, will change the couple's feelings of uncertainty and will help them relax and calm their fears and insecurities about the relationship.

As the couple calms, relaxes, and becomes more open, a therapeutic priority is to help the injured partner communicate to the other partner. For example:

Clinician: Pierre, while you didn't show it outwardly, you really thought you lost Alex to Sam. You felt betrayed.

Next, the clinician will help the other partner hear and reflect back the injured partner's hurt and pleas for reassurance. The practitioner is helping the party that caused the attachment injury to respond in a caring manner and to take responsibility for whatever took place. For example:

Clinician: Alex, you feel a great deal of shame around how you treated Pierre. It sounds like you want him to know that you're sorry, things are safe, and you want the relationship to be the same as it was before.

This example showcases how important it is for the clinician to uncover any feelings of shame, hurt, and fear during the therapeutic process and to encourage responsibility-taking. Reframing and softening these feelings allow the injured partner to express the profound emotional hurt they feel in a nondefensive manner.

While mapping out the entire EFT therapeutic model is beyond the scope of this chapter, the attachment injury resolution model showcased in Table 7.1 is extremely relevant to working with couples on their attachment injuries (Makinen & Johnson, 2006).

TABLE 7.1 THE ATTACHMENT INJURY RESOLUTION MODEL, DESCRIPTIONS, AND EXAMPLES

Attachment Injury Phase	Description	Clinical Examples
Recognizing the marker of an attachment injury	Emotionally, the hurt partner discusses the events in which they experienced the attachment injury that damaged their belief in the relationship. When discussing the event, the injured party deeply expresses their emotions. The other partner discounts, refuses to accept, or minimizes the occurrence and their partner's accompanying emotional pain and takes a defensive stance.	*Client A:* Vanessa, you cheated on me with Simon. I'm not sure where to go from here. I don't know if I can be with a cheater like you. *Client B:* I admit to cheating. I am interested in explaining myself to you. I love you and never intended to hurt you. That incident wasn't such a big deal to me. *Clinician:* Vanessa, you hear Marcel's concern and let him know you love him. It sounds like the affair didn't mean much to you and you are ready to make amends.

(continued)

TABLE 7.1   THE ATTACHMENT INJURY RESOLUTION MODEL, DESCRIPTIONS, AND EXAMPLES (*CONTINUED*)

Attachment Injury Phase	Description	Clinical Examples
Differentiation of affect	The injured partner maintains psychological contact with the attachment injury and begins to describe its effect and how the incident relates to current levels of relational security. The other partner begins to understand and comprehend the significance of the experience.	*Clinician:* Stay with that feeling of hurt. *Client A:* We have always been honest with each other. I understand I'm not perfect, but I think we can be honest with each other. *Client B:* My affair was so selfish. I'm sorry for not putting us first. *Clinician:* Marcel, you are reaching for a sense of security. Vanessa, you are supporting Marcel by taking responsibility for the dishonesty.
Reengagement	The injured partner cautiously engages in a more integrated formulation of the attachment injury and opens up by expressing sorrow and concern regarding the loss of the attachment security. The other partner becomes more emotionally engaged and empathically recognizes their responsibility and expresses regret and remorse.	*Clinician:* Marcel, how are you feeling about what Vanessa just said? *Client A:* I am worried that things will go well for a while and then Vanessa will begin cheating on me again. I don't think she can change. I'm also concerned my forcefulness played into this. *Clinician:* Vanessa, I noticed you slowly nodding your head. When Marcel mentioned concern that you might not change, you sighed. *Client B:* Marcel, I really love you and I am sorry for my mistake. I wish I didn't do it.
Forgiveness and reconciliation	The injured partner asks for reassurance and compassion that were inaccessible at the time of the injury. The other partner responds in a thoughtful manner, which acts as a remedy to the attachment injury.	*Clinician:* Marcel, what do you need from Vanessa? *Client A:* I just want to be loved. I want her to be near me and hold me. *Client B:* I love you and will always be here for you.

HELPING COUPLES THROUGH PREMARITAL THERAPY

Many people have asked themselves, "Why aren't there more cultural efforts to teach people effective relationship skills prior to marriage or long-term cohabitation?" While education and therapy are not required prior to marriage, they can be extremely helpful to take part in. One of the best ways to handle negative premarital warning signs or other concerning relationship issues is through premarital therapy. Engaging in premarital therapy can be very helpful in increasing relationship satisfaction and reducing marital distress. The general goal of any premarital counseling experience is to identify any areas of conflict before they become a serious marital issue and to *teach* couples effective communication skills and strategies for handling relational conflict. This form of therapy can be offered in a variety of formats, and many clinicians choose to see the couple together, while others prefer to start the therapeutic relationship with individual sessions. According to Carroll and Doherty's (2003) classic meta-analytic review of research centered on the effectiveness of premarital prevention programs, couples can expect 30% increase in relationship quality and interpersonal skills if they engage in premarital therapy.

In general, couples attend premarital analyses and evaluate various aspects of their relationship and develop relevant skills to help navigate the various relationship challenges that emerge throughout a long-term relationship. While all premarital counseling experiences are unique, some common experiences that clinicians provide couples include addressing relational strengths, relationship weaknesses/concerns, goals, coping mechanisms, identifying couple warning signs and helpful strategies, and identifying common relationship issues that cause tension for most couples and their potential solutions. In addition, premarital education is extremely important in helping couples strategize for long-term relational success. According to Stanley (2001), there are five ways premarital education helps couples: (a) space to reflect on important marital decisions, (b) educating partners on the work and commitment required for a successful marriage, (c) destigmatizing the helping process and normalizing reaching out for future couple counseling opportunities, (d) reducing the risk of divorce, and (e) providing immediate improvement in relationship quality.

There are a number of high-quality premarital therapy programs available on the mental health marketplace, including the Gottman method, insight-oriented marital therapy, behavioral marital therapy, EFT, and psychodynamic couples therapy. Within these comprehensive programs, there are typically a vast number of topics covered. Some of the most common areas include finances, children, intimacy, communication, conflict resolution, roles in marriage, commitment, financial management, sexuality, parenting expectations, values and religion, and partners' families of origin (Stahmann & Salts, 1993). In addition, most programs offer couples premarital inventories (e.g., PREPARE/ENRICH, RELATE relationship assessments) to help them learn about their relationship style and ability, predict relational success, and make informed marital decisions (Larson et al., 2002). For over 35 years, Drs. John and Julie Gottman have been researching and engaging in clinical practice around premarital warning signs and premarital therapy (Gottman et al., 1998; Gottman & Levenson, 2000). Given their impact in the field, this section will focus primarily on understanding the Gottman approach to premarital therapy.

As previously stated, the Gottman method has a tremendous amount of empirical support as a treatment method and additional empirical evidence demonstrating its effectiveness as a premarital therapy (Barnacle & Abbott, 2009; Hicks et al., 2004). For a complete review of the Gottman method for helping couples, clinicians and graduate students should consider reading *The Marriage Clinic: A Scientifically Based Marital Therapy* (Gottman, 1999). To start, the Gottman method engages partners in a detailed assessment of their areas of conflict to tailor-fit premarital encounters. One area that the Gottman method explores is the ratio of positive to negative interactions. Gottman-oriented practitioners consider a high ratio of negative to positive interactions as the strongest predictor of a dysfunctional relationship. When assessing premarital relational compatibility and level of conflict, the Gottman-oriented practitioner is constantly considering whether the couple is maintaining the five (or more) positive interactions to every one negative interaction ratio that is symbolic of a stable and happy marriage (Gottman & Levenson, 2000).

As treatment begins, couples will be introduced to the theory of the Sound Marital House (SMH; Gottman & Levenson, 2000). The SMH theory promotes the notion that there are seven elements to a happy marriage/long-term cohabitation. These elements (floors of the house) are the following: (a) build love maps that maintain awareness of a significant other's world, (b) share fondness and admiration as these are deposits into the partner's emotional bank account, (c) turn toward instead of away from one's partner and accept their bids for emotional connection, (d) maintain a positive perspective about the relationship, (e) manage conflict and accept the other partner's influence, (f) make life dreams come true and support each other's life goals, and (g) create shared meaning and build a shared sense of purpose. These factors are described to couples as stories of a house that need foundational stability to support the upper floors (Gottman & Levenson, 2000). At the center of Gottman's SMH theory are the methods used to build a sense of relational trust, love, and loyalty in one's relationship. Couples are unable to move through the SMH levels until there is a basic sense of trust, loyalty, and commitment in the relationship. The methods clinicians use to encourage these positive interactive feelings include, but are not limited to, (a) each partner focusing on creating a deep sense of trustworthiness in the relationship, (b) each partner working hard to increase their partner's well-being, (c) each partner committing to the shared responsibility of building trust in every interaction, (d) avoiding negative relationship comparisons, and (e) minimizing any thoughts on a partner's negative qualities and constantly reminding one's self of all of the positive qualities the other partner has (Gottman & Levenson, 2000).

The SMH describes healthy marriages/long-term cohabitations as being free of the many Gottman-based dysfunctional relational patterns described in Chapter 6 (e.g., stonewalling, contempt, harsh startups). Table 7.2 provides the levels of the SMH theory, concise descriptions, and clinical skill examples.

TABLE 7.2   GOTTMAN'S SOUND MARITAL HOUSE THEORY, DESCRIPTION, AND CLINICAL EXAMPLE

Sound Marital House Level	Description of the Level	Premarital Therapy Examples
Build love maps	This refers to the depth of knowledge each partner has into their spouse's psychological world.	*Clinician:* Janet, describe for me two of Michael's friends. What are they like?
Share fondness and admiration	Effective partnerships have an in-depth level of respect, appreciation, and friendship.	*Clinician:* Jerome, when you mentioned your love for Alphonso, he moved his chair closer to you and uncrossed his arm. There is so much love here.
Turn toward instead of away	To create a stronger bond and friendship, couples make bids for their partner's attention. The key is to turn toward these bids and keep growing the intimate connection.	*Clinician:* April, you seemed surprised by Mark's random act of kindness and the two of you have been laughing and staring at each other this entire session.
Positive sentiment override	The establishment of positive relational feelings can create a barrier that serves as a positive sentiment override protecting the couple from most negative relational conflicts.	*Clinician:* Raphael, the critical comment that Jill made would have typically set you off. How were you able to take it in stride?
Manage conflict	To effectively manage conflict, healthy couples openly discuss the issue and address solvable problems with clear solutions, and partners can self-sooth if conflict emerges.	*Clinician:* Samantha, you and Jacquie openly discussed the issues that caused that uncomfortable silence on the way to church. It seems like you are on the same page with things once again.
Support life dreams together	In healthy marriages/long-term partnerships, couples work hard to support each other's life dreams and aspirations.	*Clinician:* Stephen, you demonstrate your love for Meredith when you tell her how proud you are that she completed the rigorous nursing program.
Create shared meaning	A collective narrative is created that brings a sense of togetherness to the partnership. This narrative is created through rituals and traditions, consensus on marital roles, articulating goals, and agreement on relationship values.	*Clinician:* The couple values being thrifty so they can save money for adventures and traveling that they deeply enjoy.

Source: Data from Gottman, J. (1999). *The marriage clinic: A scientifically based marital therapy.* W. W. Norton & Company.

HELPING COUPLES EXPERIENCING MARITAL AND RELATIONSHIP DISTRESS

Marital and long-term relationship distress is a common problem that spouses/partners experience in a variety of different ways. In the United States, divorce continues to be a massive cultural issue affecting approximately 50% of first marriages and a much higher percentage of second marriages (Daugherty & Copen, 2016). Perfect compatibility is a myth, and all couples work hard to endure the ups and downs associated with a relationship. Whether the issue has to do with communication, unrealistic expectations, lack of intimacy, or financial challenges, couples often experience frequent bouts of distress related to long-term partnerships. During these stressful interactions, spouses negotiate, argue, problem-solve, reflect on potential solutions, and consider whether they are working with a solvable problem. When spouses reach an impasse, experience an attachment injury, and/or experience gridlock, they are likely experiencing a great deal of relational distress (Lebow et al., 2012). Couple, marriage, and family practitioners are a helpful resource for reducing marital/relational distress.

There are many couples-based treatments for marital distress, including, but not limited to, the Gottman method, behavioral couples therapy, and emotionally focused couples therapy. While there are many options for clinicians to consider, the goal of this section is to review general skills and treatment considerations. A first important step in reducing a couple's relational distress is to spread the symptom to the system. Couples are notorious for scapegoating their partner for problems in the relationship and simultaneously avoiding any responsibility-taking. Cancio-Bello and Rudes (2020) recommended three macrosteps to help decrease this behavior: (a) decreasing the couple's anxiety through the clinician remaining neutral, (b) taking a step back and taking a more macroview of the couple's problems, and (c) continually highlighting the reciprocity in the maintenance of the problem. For example:

> *Clinician:* Beth, I notice when Angela becomes quiet and defensive, you start blaming her for the problems in the relationship. Angela, occasionally you intentionally shut down when Beth is irritating you.

Encouraging clients to see their part in the interaction is an important first step to reducing relationship distress.

While this can seem like common sense to most clinicians, effective treatments for marital distress are centered on validation and acceptance of the other person. After taking a more macroview of the issue, clinicians can help partners introspect on their process and manage their emotions toward their partner. Cancio-Bello and Rudes (2020) described the process of looking at oneself and acknowledging the reciprocal nature of the relationship distress and openly considering and working on negative relational patterns. In other words, couples cannot entertain the idea that they can fix their relationship if they believe that their partner is completely at fault for the present distress. Following the aforementioned self-awareness, clinicians empathically guide couples to begin considering the many ways they contribute to the reciprocal nature of the relationship distress. Following this awareness, the couple begins to work on the reciprocal nature of the issue through strategically engaging in new relational behavior. For example:

> *Clinician:* Angela, I noticed that when Beth became quiet and reflected, you didn't become forceful. You are actively using the information you've been gathering to better support Beth.

As the couple begins to accept and validate one another and consider the new awareness they have around their own relationship behavior, they often feel a sense of empowerment through effectively managing their differences.

Psychoeducation and homework around avoiding marital distress can be extremely helpful for couples coming into couples therapy. A first step can be for clinicians to encourage spouses to increase the supportive behaviors they do for one another and to report back about how the experiences went. A key factor with this behavioral intervention is for the clinician to make sure the intervention is specific and time-sensitive, and to provide couples with appropriate operant conditioning. For example:

> *Clinician:* Frank, it sounds like work has been monopolizing your time with Ivory. You're looking for ways to improve the small amount of quality time you have together. One activity that keeps coming up is going for casual walks together in the morning. Between now and our next session, I would like you to ask Ivory to go for a walk on two mornings. To ensure that it happens, talk to her a few days beforehand so she can schedule it. At the beginning of our next session, I will ask you how the walk went (Association for Behavioral and Cognitive Therapies, 2021).

The Speaker and Listener Technique

Communication skills training can be helpful in treating couples' marital/relational distress. Many practitioners use a version of the speaker and listener technique to increase the couple's overall relational satisfaction and reduce the likelihood of divorce. The speaker and listener technique is a structured communication directive. The speaker and listener technique has been heavily endorsed by the Prevention and Relationship Enhancement Program (PREP; Markman et al., 2010) and many behavioral couple therapy programs for decades (Cornelius et al., 2007). While research findings (Markman & Rhoades, 2012) suggest this technique is extremely helpful, it has come under criticism (see Carlson et al., 2014; Gottman et al., 1998). While controversy exists, the speaker and listener technique is a foundational intervention for couples seeking treatment around communication issues and for couples who need to discuss issues that are too difficult to talk about without a structured intervention.

While there are many variations on how to use this technique, the essence of the couple speaker and listener technique is one person serving as a listener who paraphrases back to the speaker the thoughts and feelings they stated. The speaker clearly states their position with a variety of "I" statements. After the speaker finishes their dialogue, the partners will switch roles (i.e., the listener becomes the speaker and the speaker becomes the listener). Regarding relational distress, this technique would ideally be used with one of the serious issues that brought the couple into therapy and causes the most pain (Cornelius et al., 2007; Markman et al., 2010; Wood, 2010). The goal of this technique is to facilitate a mutual understanding and to ensure each partner feels heard. To accomplish this, clinicians will instruct clients on how to engage in active listening and when to validate their partner's thoughts and feelings. According to Wood (2010), this intervention is extremely helpful for couples who need to process topics that are too difficult to talk about. She suggests that the speaker and listener technique provide the necessary structure that slows down the conversation, creates emotional regulation, and provides a platform for clients to discuss issues that are important to them (Cornelius et al., 2007; Markman et al., 2010; Wood, 2010).

According to Markman et al. (2010), the speaker and listener technique is a safe method that assists couples in clearly discussing issues that are difficult. A few general rules include the following: (a) the speaker has the floor, (b) ensure equality in role sharing, (c) avoid problem-solving, (d) speak for yourself, (e) be brief, (f) stop and allow the listener to paraphrase, (g) only paraphrase what you heard, (h) ask the listener to not argue, and (i) engage in active listening. The following is an example of one way to use the speaker and listener technique. Many of the rules are centered on communication issues and errors. Furthermore, negative communication styles are a major cause of marital/relational distress. Table 7.3 breaks down the destructive couple communication styles and clinical interventions (Hammond, 1978). Practitioners help couples avoid these dysfunctional forms of communication.

TABLE 7.3 DESTRUCTIVE COUPLE COMMUNICATION STYLES, DESCRIPTIONS, AND INTERVENTIONS

Name of Communication Style	Description	Interventions
Overgeneralization/lack of specificity	Partner's criticisms are vague and multiple problems are introduced simultaneously.	Clinician encourages partners to avoid using overgeneralization words (always, never, all) and promotes describing specific behaviors.
Dominating, interrupting, and not listening	Partner does not listen or provide active listening, frequently interrupts, and does not empathize.	Clinician encourages partners to listen, maintain eye contact, empathize, summarize partner's comments, and nonverbally convey interest.
Gunnysacking	Partner stores up grievances acquired throughout the relationship, not resolving them when they first occur, and eventually bombards their partner with these issues at once.	Clinician encourages partners to discuss concerns when they initially come up and refrain from engaging in multiple criticisms based on current and historical content.
Mind reading/speaking for partner	Partner interprets the other partner's behavior, makes assumptions about their thoughts and feelings without confirming, jumps to a conclusion, and possibly speaks for them based on these assumptions.	Clinician encourages partners to check in with each other about what the other is going through and urges partners to speak for themselves.
Judgment, blame, attack, and rejection	Partner attacks and rejects the other in an intense and upset manner and this results in negative consequences (name calling, sarcasm, contempt, "you" statements).	Clinician encourages and/or uses rules to enforce the use of "I" statements and encourages partners to avoid name calling and contempt.
Coercion/manipulation	Partner controls the other partner through concealing motives and manipulation, and instead of expressing genuine feelings plays a variety of toxic roles to get what they want.	Clinician encourages partners to avoid controlling and manipulative communication, and advocates for a safe relationship built on trust and honesty.
Taken for granted	Partner expects a variety of things to be provided (meals, sex, chores, money), but does not show appreciation or gratitude.	Clinician encourages partners to express appreciation, gratitude, and politeness, and to inquire about their partner's feelings before deciding.
Concentration on negatives	Partner ignores their partner's pleasing behaviors, primarily focuses on the negative behaviors, and does not use encouragement.	Clinician encourages partners to focus on what their partner is doing right, attend to pleasing behaviors frequently, and deemphasize strategies of discouragement.

(continued)

TABLE 7.3 DESTRUCTIVE COUPLE COMMUNICATION STYLES, DESCRIPTIONS, AND INTERVENTIONS (*CONTINUED*)

Name of Communication Style	Description	Interventions
Replaying ancient history	Partner reprocesses past conflictual behaviors and arguments and seeks justification for their rightness.	Clinician encourages partner to stop serving as the relationship historian and to avoid attempting to justify past experiences.
Intellectualization and avoidance of feelings	Partner does not express emotions, but does express rationalizations, justification, and thoughts.	Clinician encourages partners to reflect on gender roles and other reasons they avoid emotions and creates situations in which partner's feelings are expressed.
Overemotionality	Partner overdramatizes and overexaggerates their views to get attention, attain sympathy, or for blackmailing and overpowering their partner.	Clinician helps partners to realize this emotionality is taking place and encourages self-reflection and provides guidance toward new ways of communication.
Avoidance of conflict	Partner avoids dealing with conflicts and substitutes an unhealthy role, such as the placater or the nice guy.	Clinician encourages partners to avoid extreme suppression of conflict, and extreme attacking or venting, and encourages the expression of constructive negative emotions.

Source: Data from Hammond, C. D. (1978). *Destructive couple communication styles.* Upper Island Assessment Resources Services.

The Speaker and Listener Technique Example

Clinician: Today we are going to try something new and carefully discuss one of the most stressful issues you came to therapy with. Specifically, we are going to be discussing the infidelity that nearly drove you to divorce. This method requires each of you to face each other and to avoid arguing, accusing, and problem-solving. One person will serve in a speaker role and describe their issues related to the past infidelity, while the other partner will listen and paraphrase back what they heard. While speaking you are to use the "I" statements we previously discussed and avoid accusing and saying hurtful comments to your partner. What questions do you have about this? *Client A:* Who should start? *Client B:* Probably you. *Clinician:* Either of you can start. I'll be sure to coach you around your role and remind you of any of the rules as we process the infidelity. Rachel, please start. *Client A:* I'm not sure where to start. I am still confused about why you cheated on me. What happened? *Client B:* It sounds like you're confused about why I did what I did. *Clinician:* Great job. Rachel, what else do you want to say to Felix? *Client A:* Nothing right now. I just want to hear what he has to say. *Clinician:* Okay, Rachel, you'll switch to the listener role, and Felix, you'll engage in the speaker role. Felix, feel free to speak when you're ready.

VOICES FROM THE FIELD: HARVEY

Dr. Harvey Peters shared his experiences working with couples who struggle with relationship and/or marital distress and identify as LGBTQIA+.

It is important that counselors examine a queer couple's chronosystem (i.e., historical experiences that impact the contexts of the other experiences), as there are likely many overlapping common issues (e.g., communication, lack of trust, unresolved hurt, not growing together, lack of intimacy), as well as unique queer-specific issues, such as familial, community, and societal disapproval or oppression. Other issues may involve having different affectional orientations (e.g., gay and bisexual, pansexual and lesbian), navigating spaces built for hetero-sexual couples and families or the single environment of queer culture, and loss of queer spaces and connections. For coping with discrimination and hate, queer couples and families are resil-ient and have often grown up in an environment and system where it is the norm. Thus, it can be important that couples and families address and/or revisit the impact this has on the couple or family because it can go overlooked or be minimized by one or multiple members of a couple or throuple, which can build up and have relational implications.

VOICES FROM THE FIELD: JENNIFER

Ms. Jennifer Kassing shared her experiences working with LGBTQIA+ couples experiencing relationship distress and how much of it can come from outside hurtful, discriminatory, homophobic, and sociopolitical phenomena.

The unique issues that come up include family-of-origin stress and lack of support and accep-tance, specifically related to sexuality or gender identity. Ostracism from family of origin or friend groups. Discrimination within the family of origin, greater society, workplace settings, etc. Political topics arise and create stress. For example, the fear and anxiety that arise at the thought of gay marriage or second-parent adoptions being taken away are high, especially as of late. Gender roles or roles within the home and family can be points of stress at times as well. Sometimes in heterosexual relationships, gender roles are better defined. This is not always the case for LGBTQIA+ couples. Having to cope with these things has affected couples in many ways. A lot of my LGBTQIA+ couples suffer from depression and anxiety more often, struggle with sleep issues, substance issues (marijuana use is high here, where it's legal), and couples can struggle to find ways to work together as a team. Suicidality is higher among my LGBTQIA+ clients, which reflects what I notice with couples in my own practice. An example that comes to mind is a queer/trans couple I work with. The trans partner endured discrimination and trans-phobia at work on several occasions over several years and recently quit. They did this without speaking with their spouse, which caused an increase in conflict, but the spouse felt torn. Spe-cifically, they supported the departure given the discrimination endured by their partner, and wanted to be supportive, but the abruptness put them in a difficult financial situation.

HELPING COUPLES EXPERIENCING CRISIS AND DISASTER

Humans are unique and each person experiences, processes, and recovers from trauma in a different manner. If a couple experiences a crisis or disaster, each partner likely ex-periences it in a different manner. One partner might demonstrate a sense of resilience and process the experience immediately, while the other partner could find it very dis-tressing and experience serious traumatization. While the trauma and stress associated with a crisis or disaster can be detrimental to relationships, they can also lead some couples to experience an increase in intimacy and relational growth (Laughlin & Rusca, 2020). While variability exists, when crisis and/or disaster strike, relationships can become extremely strained. For couples who survive a serious disaster, relocation, fi-nancial hardships, finding community resources, childcare, entering a new educational setting, and the increase in isolation and alone time can be an enormous stress (Sluzki, 1992). This can lead to serious mental health concerns, including, but not limited to, sui-cide, posttraumatic stress disorder (PTSD), complex trauma, and anxiety. An example demonstrating the relationship between crisis and mental health took place during the 2008 U.S. financial crisis when suicide rates increased by 3% to 8% (Reeves et al., 2012).

Little is known about the impact of crises and disasters on marital and long-term relationships. Some evidence exists regarding the effects of different types of crises and/or disasters on the partnership. For example, the trauma associated with terrorist attacks has been found to trigger couples to engage in more intimacy, while natural disasters tend to create chronic stress that seriously disrupts marriages (Lowe et al., 2012). Other findings suggest that the impact of crises and disasters on communities of color is associated with poor marital adjustment, conflict, marital distress, poverty, unemployment, loss of income, and divorce (Conger et al., 2002, 2003; Lowe et al., 2012). One well-cited consequence of crisis and disaster can be trauma (American Psychiatric Association, 2022; True et al., 1993; Yehuda et al., 1998). Single-incident trauma, PTSD, and complex trauma produce symptoms and can increase destructive behaviors that can have a major impact on relationships, including chronic anger, frequent arguments, insomnia, intrusive nightmares and flashbacks, difficulty concentrating, risky behavior, self-injury, worsening of mental health issues, IPV, and substance abuse (Ford, 2009; Herman, 1992; van der Kolk, 2005). Relationally speaking, trauma survivors have demonstrated a decrease in sexual activity and relationship satisfaction, and an inability to express emotion. Lastly, individuals diagnosed with PTSD have demonstrated higher divorce rates than those without the disorder (Cook et al., 2004).

Treating Traumatized Couples

Clinicians begin any trauma-based work by establishing a deep and empathic therapeutic relationship with the couple. General trauma treatment for adult couples is long term, intense, and empowering. Herman (1997) postulated three general phases associated with healing from trauma: *safety, remembrance and mourning,* and *reconnection.* Herman considers safety to be the most important stage of treatment. She urges clinicians to reestablish a sense of safety within the client and in relation to others, including their intimate partner. This includes developing a deep connection with the therapist, creating a plan aimed at self-care and healing, and referrals to appropriate treatment providers when necessary. Remembrance and mourning have to do with unpacking the trauma story and recollections. The client will decide what parts of the trauma experience they want to explore and how deep they will dive into the trauma narrative. Trauma narratives might start as fragments or distorted recollections and slowly transform into a coherent whole. When clients start to grieve the losses associated with the traumatic event, they experience an all-permeating profound sense of grief. The clinician frequently reflects the client's pain and affirms a position of moral solidarity with the survivor. Lastly, Herman's reconnection phase is similar to adaptation and encourages the individual or couple to engage and incorporate new self-esteem-increasing experiences. This could include encouraging the clients to engage in new supportive coping skills, groups, and classes (Herman, 1997).

According to Pollock (2014), clinicians encourage traumatized survivors to reach out to their intimate partners to discuss their experience of trauma and the resulting symptoms. The author states that when partners are clued into their significant other's process with trauma, they will understand how to help them and will be less likely to attempt to try to help them in an unwanted or unneeded manner. For example:

> *Clinician:* Stephen, please tell your partner how you would like him to help you.
>
> *Client:* Brian, could you please just hold my hand and listen to me?

Additionally, clinicians are also urged to remind the client to communicate openly in treatment about any stressors, triggers, and symptoms. This is so the clinician understands how to help clients heal and so their partner can gain awareness into their personal process with trauma. Lastly, a key factor is the maintenance of hope. When the couple maintains hope that their relationship can survive the trauma, they both can become focused on putting the time and effort into helping the traumatized person heal.

Pollock (2014) poignantly described the role of the nontraumatized partner in treatment. Partners should understand that healing from trauma takes time and that they should avoid trying to help or fix their partner's symptomology. Clinicians should encourage nontraumatized partners to work on listening in a supportive and nonjudgmental manner. Clinicians should remind clients of the common symptoms that survivors of crisis, disaster, and trauma experience and to try not to react negatively when they emerge. A key factor is to avoid assumptions and ask the traumatized partner what they want. For example:

> *Clinician:* Roberta, it seems like your guesses about Beth's needs are not on target. Could you try to ask her what she needs?

> *Client:* I noticed that you were getting angry. Is there anything I can do to help you feel more comfortable?

Lastly, nontraumatized partners should consider engaging in their own therapy and/or self-care. When both partners have a strong sense of wellness, a lot of positive work can be done.

While working through the stages of trauma, couples must be provided with psychoeducation. Couples need to be educated on the effects of crisis, disaster, and trauma. Specifically, unprocessed trauma can often affect people neurologically, creating a fight, flight, or freeze state. These neurologic states can create symptoms of hypervigilance, avoidance, flashbacks, negative sleep patterns, learning issues, attention problems, memory limitations, and cardiophysiologic issues (American Psychiatric Association, 2022; Black & Flynn, 2021). Table 7.4 provides well-known trauma symptoms, a brief description, and examples. Clinicians should consider using this table as a guide when conducting the psychoeducation portion of their treatment. As clinicians review the symptoms, descriptions, and examples with couples, they should inform partners that many of these behaviors happen without any warning and in situations that most would experience as nonthreatening. Partners should be reminded that their partners may be triggered by something and fall into one of these states and suddenly appear unstable, agitated, and irrational.

This section highlighted the general process of working with couples who have suffered from the negative impact of crisis, disaster, and trauma. While the skills and issues presented will be helpful to couple, marriage, and family practitioners working with couples, those who wish to specialize in treating trauma, complex trauma, and PTSD should strongly consider employing one of the empirically based gold standard trauma treatments, including, but not limited to, trauma-focused cognitive behavioral therapy (TF-CBT), prolonged exposure (PET), cognitive processing therapy (CPT), cognitive behavioral therapy (CBT), psychological debriefing, critical incident stress debriefing (CISD), eye movement desensitization and reprocessing (EMDR), art-assisted therapy, and brainspotting (BSP). While couple therapy options are limited with the aforementioned approaches, TF-CBT and CPT can be offered in a group counseling context (CATS Consortium, 2007; Ebert et al., 2012; Karlin et al., 2010). While the aforementioned treatments may not include special provisions for couples, they are excellent choices for helping individual adults, adolescents, and children experience relief from the powerful symptoms of trauma.

TABLE 7.4 TRAUMA SYMPTOMS, DESCRIPTIONS, AND EXAMPLES

Symptom	Description	Examples
Fight	The amygdala signals an emergency and an excessive amount of the hormone cortisol is released, creating agitation and aggressive symptoms which are used to fight a perceived threat.	Raising one's voice, physically acting out, sobbing, shaking, and violence directed at self or others
Flight	The amygdala signals an emergency and an excessive amount of the hormone cortisol is released, turning into anxiety, panic, and a desire to flee from a perceived threat.	Fleeing from a situation, appearing overwhelmed, experiencing a sense of mistrust, and panicking over something seemingly benign
Freeze	The amygdala signals an emergency, an excessive amount of the hormone cortisol is released, the body becomes deactivated and numb, and the individual begins accumulating energy and internal resources to avoid painful trigger or memory.	Disengaging from a conversation, shutting down, appearing uninterested, silence, oversleeping, disinterest in typical activities, and substance use
Hypervigilance	This refers to intense hyperarousal and an exaggerated state of awareness.	Hyperaware of perceived danger, frequently scanning surroundings, and inability to make effective decisions
Flashbacks	This refers to sudden and unexpected reexperience of past traumatic incident in the present.	Reliving what previously happened, intrusive images and thoughts, panicking at a real or symbolic reminder, and nightmares
Negative sleep patterns	These are sleep disturbances caused by hyperarousal patterns and elevated stages of vigilance.	Sleep disturbances, awoken by every noise, difficulty getting to sleep, sleeping lightly, persistent insomnia, night terrors, nightmares, and sleep paralysis
Memory limitations	Memory loss used as a method to help survivors cope with the painful trauma symptoms.	Inability to remember traumatic event, difficulty accurately recalling time/date/location, and difficulty differentiating between true memories, dreams, and fantasies
Attention problems	Trauma causes difficulty in effectively sustaining and focusing attention, resulting in fragmented and incomplete memory coding.	Difficulty focusing on assignments, recalling events, paying attention in class or at work, and understanding detailed messages
Cardiophysiology	Trauma can negatively affect the body and mind in a manner that leads to problematic cardiovascular risks.	Blood pressure problems, an overactive nervous system, obesity, cardiovascular disease, hypertension, poor immune system, and hyperlipidemia

Sources: Data from American Psychiatric Association. (2022). *Diagnostic and statistical manual of mental disorders* (5th ed., text revision). https://doi.org/10.1176/appi.books.9780890425787; Black, L. L., & Flynn, S. V. (2021). *Crisis, trauma, and disaster: A clinician's guide.* Sage.

HELPING COUPLES EXPERIENCING SUBSTANCE ABUSE

Substance use and abuse is and has always been destructive to relationships and families. While this is not a new problem, the substances being abused are changing (fentanyl, oxycodone, other synthetic opioids; Wang et al., 2021). Furthermore, in 2015 the National Center for Chronic Disease Prevention and Health Promotion reported that excessive drinking alone caused 88,000 deaths annually in the United States. While accidents, alcohol poisoning, and other dramatic side effects happen all the time, many of the deaths reported were related to issues like liver disease, high blood pressure, heart disease, and cancer. Intimate relationship issues around substance use and abuse are unique. Dynamics play out in different ways depending on the couple. Substances use and abuse often negatively affects intimate relationships, family functioning, and parenting duties; however, there is a lot of variability involved in how each partner perceives the effects of substance use and the destructive consequences the abuse has on their intimate relationship and the family. Lastly, partners may have discrepant levels of motivation to attain sobriety.

While couples therapy can be helpful in reducing substance use and abuse, it is also very helpful in assisting with secondary problems that may have emerged due to substance use. For example, couples who struggle with one or both partners' addiction can frequently experience IPV, infidelity, lack of employment stability, legal problems, imbalance in household duties, partner overfunctioning to ensure the family is functioning well, sexual dysfunction, marital distress, negative role-modeling to children, and lack of adequate child supervision (Fals-Stewart et al., 2009; Morrissette, 2010). Central to all relational problems that emerge due to substance use and abuse is the deterioration of trust, communication, and cohesiveness in the partnership. Couples therapy can be extremely helpful in assisting partners in supporting each other in completing normal and expected aspects of relational functioning, as well as the achievement of sobriety. It is important to note that the destructive relational behaviors associated with substance use and abuse need to be addressed directly in treatment, not overlooked due to the clinical focus on substance use reduction (Hartney, 2020).

While substance abuse support groups such as Alcoholics Anonymous, Narcotics Anonymous, and Al-Anon can be extremely helpful in assisting the partner who is addicted reduce their triggers, substance use, and symptoms, relational therapy is extremely beneficial in healing the relationship or marriage that has suffered the brunt of the toxicity brought on by the substance abuser's behavior. Additionally, couple, marriage, and family practitioners assist clients by recognizing the enabling behavior that the nonaddicted partner or family member demonstrates that keeps the destructive cycle of addiction continuing. In situations where both members of a relationship are suffering from addiction, it can be extremely difficult for either partner to stop their addictive behavior due to the dual enabling behaviors (Zimmerman, 2018). In this case, relational therapy can assist partners in breaking out of the destructive prison of addiction (Landau-North et al., 2011; Zimmerman, 2018).

Behavioral Couples Therapy for Substance Abuse Disorders

Behavioral couples therapy for substance use disorders (BCT-SUD) is a theoretically based, manualized treatment for substance use and abuse that has been researched and used in high frequency over the past 40 years (Lam et al., 2009). Presently, BCT-SUD is the approach to couples' substance abuse treatment that has the most empirical validation (Fletcher, 2013; O'Farrell & Clements, 2012; Ruff et al., 2010). According to BCT-SUD, couple and family member interactions with the substance-abusing person can encourage an increase in substance use. There is a reciprocal relationship between the couple's interactions and the status of the addiction. If the relationship is in distress, the individual has a much higher likelihood of maintaining their addiction. On the other hand, if the couple has relational satisfaction and effective communication, there is a much lower likelihood of relapse (Fletcher & MacIntosh, 2018; O'Farrell & Clements, 2012).

The BCT-SUD model has several nonmutually exclusive phases of treatment. These phases include (a) the *engagement phase*, which determines if the couple has the motivation and commitment to succeed in treatment; (b) the *active phase*, where the practitioner helps manage the substance-abusing partner's addiction and improve the relationship; and (c) the *recovery phase*, which is ongoing. The active phase is where the clinician works on intensive behavioral skill-building with the couple. This often includes encouragement of a caring behavior (e.g., encouraging awareness and support of positive behavior), incorporation of caring days (e.g., intentionally noticing the positives), communication skills training (e.g., "I" statement usage, understanding nonverbal communication), and conflict resolution skills (e.g., intentionally using time-out; Klostermann & Mignone, 2019).

The recovery contract (RC) is the most prominent method of treatment. This requires the couple to identify positive and supportive activities that center on short- and long-term substance abuse recovery. Self-help activities include things like group counseling, church groups, retreats, and mutually beneficial couple activities that do not involve substance use. The RC also involves trust discussions aimed at the substance-using partner discussing their intentions of staying sober and offering gratitude for their partner's support (Klostermann & Mignone, 2019). For example:

> *Clinician:* The two of you have been doing such a great job engaging treatment. Michael, you have been sober for 23 days. How would you feel about engaging in a trust discussion?

> *Client A:* Sure, let's do it. Samantha, I have been sober for 23 days and I commit to remain sober for the next week. Thank you so much for being there for me. I love you and appreciate you.

> *Client B:* Great job, Michael. Thank you.

Emotionally Focused Couple Therapy for Addiction

While the same level of empirical validation or history in the field does not exist in the EFT couple's addiction treatment camp as does in the behavioral therapy field, in 2011 Landau-North et al. proposed a model for treating addiction through working with couples in an EFT format. According to Landau-North et al. (2011),

> . . . the ultimate goal of the EFT therapist working with an addicted couple is to help the addict substitute an "addiction" to emotional connection with a loved one for his or her attachment to a negative obsession with drugs, alcohol, or activities such as gambling or internet porn (p. 194).

Secure attachment can enhance a couple's ability to engage in resilient coping. EFT practitioners encourage partners to turn to each other with the goal of cocreating a safe haven in their relationship free of substance use and abuse.

When using the EFT framework to help with substance use and abuse, the stages are slightly different. Stage 1 would also include the EFT practitioner conceptualizing the addictive behavior as a key component of the couple's attachment interactive cycle. Furthermore, practitioners are to frame the addiction as an element of the negative cycle that couples fight together, and prior to moving to stage 2 of the process the addiction must be contained (i.e., not actively engaging in heavy substance use). Stage 2 includes reframing the addictive responses as attachment needs and fears. Within this stage, the couple's feelings regarding the addictive behavior and unmet attachment needs (e.g., fear, sadness, abandonment) are deeply explored using encounters. For example:

> *Clinician:* Beth, you started the session with discussing your anger around Anthony's drinking. Now turn to him and described the fear and helplessness beneath the anger.

Lastly, stage 3 involves consolidation and applying innovative solutions to the historical problems. During this stage, the clinician encourages the couple to create a new narrative about the addiction problems, the impact it had on their life, and how the attachment issues still emerge, and to detail a carefully detailed prevention plan (Landau-North et al., 2011). For example:

> *Clinician:* So far, you have engaged in multiple conversations around the heroin, its control over your life, and the purpose of reconciliation. You are fearful that things won't work out but are willing to try again. Let's discuss a plan in case relapse occurs.

HELPING COUPLES EXPERIENCING FINANCIAL STRESS

Individual characteristics, contextual background, history, and cultural differences all play a part in how couples handle financial stress. There are many situations that cause couples to feel a sense of financial strain. Some examples include high levels of debt, unexpected loss of income, surprise financial responsibilities, different spending habits, foreclosure, bankruptcy, and poverty. There are also additional financial challenges that are connected to an individual's personal decisions. Some of these issues include, but are not limited to, gambling, mismanagement of money, poor planning, impulsive financial decisions, frequent overspending, and reckless spending to feel a sense of emotional relief. While these issues are often brought on by poor decision-making and behavioral addiction, large-scale issues like economic recession, the COVID-19 global pandemic, floundering national economy, and credit card fraud/identity theft are largely out of the couple's personal control, yet can be equally devastating to their relationship (Richardson et al., 2013). When couples suffer from financially stressful issues, they often seek professional help; however, given the mix of needs (e.g., financial advising, relational therapy, childcare), there is often confusion on what path of professional support to seek.

Given the diversity in the types of knowledge required to attain competency as a financial and therapeutic provider, different pathways toward competency have been developed. When couples come into counseling for financial services, they are often offered four pathways moving forward: (a) financial training with a therapist; (b) cotherapy that includes a couple, marriage, and family practitioner and a financial advisor; (c) a referral to a financial advisor; and (d) a structured program that targets multiple couples simultaneously (Falconier, 2015; Falconier & Epstein, 2011). Whatever pathway a clinician chooses to follow should be in line with their professional competence and training.

Becoming a certified financial therapist requires additional training and education. The Association for Financial Counseling and Planning Education (AFCPE) is an organization in the United States established to train accredited financial counselors (AFC). Beyond the general education requirements, candidates must pass the accreditation exam, submit letters of recommendation, and pay a fee. To ensure proper continuing education, AFCs must complete 30 continuing education units biannually (Association for Financial Counseling & Planning Education, 2022). An additional organization that supports the training of financial therapists is the Financial Therapy Association. Clinicians interested in increasing their financial therapy competency should consider taking part in the Financial Therapy Association's many trainings and/or conferences through its website: https://financialtherapyassociation.org.

In addition to gaining personal competency as a financial advisor, practitioners can develop an interdisciplinary approach to their work with one of the models that advocate for therapy with couple, marriage, and family practitioner and a financial advisor (Gale et al., 2012). For example, Gale and colleagues (2009) developed a method called relational financial therapy, which employs cotherapists where one serves as the financial counselor and the other as the couple therapist. This method combines the practitioner's skills to provide both psychoeducation around the financial issues and couples therapy around negative relational issues that accompanied the previous and current financial stress. While interdisciplinary models such as this are somewhat ideal, they take a good deal of planning and strategizing prior to meeting with the couple, and regarding the couple's expenditure two professionals will cost more money than seeing one (Falconier & Epstein, 2011).

An additional approach that should be considered is for the couple, marriage, and family practitioner to work on the relational dynamics and financial stress coping skills, and to refer the couple to a financial counselor to deal directly with financial management and incompatibilities (Falconier & Epstein, 2011). This approach is probably the most typical and is used when the clinician has little to no training on financial management. While this certainly can be a positive option, the financial planner will largely focus on financial factors and avoid therapy and any consideration of the couple's relationship. While all of the aforementioned options have their strength, the interdisciplinary method is probably the most effective in providing the breadth and depth of help couples need in terms of relational therapy and financial advising; however, it is costly for the couple. Additionally, it is quite common that individuals seeking couples therapy for financial stress do not have funds for simultaneously hiring two professionals for weekly appointments.

To help reduce cost, structured programs that target multiple couples simultaneously have been created. TOGETHER and Couples Coping Enhancement Training are two psychoeducational programs that have been designed to help couples suffering from financial strain (Bodenmann, 1997; Falconier, 2015). These structured programs assist couples by increasing their financial health and by working on communication and coping skills as financially strained couples work together to get back on their feet financially and relationally. For example, TOGETHER educates couples on the harmful effects that financial stress can have on their families and personal health, works with participants to increase their ability to problem-solve together, clarifies roles and beliefs around financial matters, helps develop a repertoire of coping skills to improve couples' ability to adapt to the ever-changing financial environment, and of course teaches effective financial management skills (Falconier, 2015).

Session Dynamics

As couple, marriage, and family practitioners engage clients in relational sessions around the financial stress, they will observe both verbal and nonverbal behaviors. At times, partners (especially men) will have a difficult time directly stating their emotional concerns. This is partly due to finances being tethered to the family's sense of pride. Clinicians constantly observe couples' verbal and nonverbal behavior for cues that they are having an emotional response. When they observe these emotional interactions, they inquire as to what thoughts they are having (Baucom et al., 1998; Joo, 2008). For example:

> *Clinician:* Samuel, as you were describing your homelife, I noticed you quickly changed the subject and looked down when discussing family meals. I wonder what worried you at that moment.

> *Client:* Just frustrating that I can't afford the same quality and quantity of food we used to have.

As couples begin working with a clinician around financial difficulties, it may become clear that their issues are more than simply financial mismanagement. Often, issues like conflicting financial standards, mistrust over spending habits and impulses, and lack of intimacy due to breaches in trust can emerge. It is essential that clinicians bring attention to these issues and facilitate improvement in communication around these topics (e.g., "I" statements, the speaker and listener technique, enactments, re-enactments). Additionally, creating meaningful dialogue around each partner's role that led to the present challenges may increase intimacy and relational satisfaction. As couples engage in conversations around past events, it will likely become clear that financial decision-making that worked during one stage of life may not be relevant to the present situation (Baucom et al., 1998; Joo, 2008). For example:

> *Clinician:* It appears that when you both first met you each had separate bank accounts.

> *Client A:* Yes, that's correct. It was nice.

> *Clinician:* While that was satisfying, you now realize that it might be time for a change.

> *Client B:* It's time to open a joint account and stop acting like babies.

> *Client A:* Yeah, we also need to learn how to negotiate around joint spending. She's so stubborn.

As couples consider these new ways of collaborating around finances, clinicians must collaborate with them on progressive homework experiences. For example, a progressive series of weekly homework assignments might include the following: (a) meet with a financial advisor together, (b) open a joint account, (c) make decisions on weekly allowances, (d) discuss roles (e.g., bill payer, investments), and (e) create a relapse plan for partners who engage in problematic spending habits (Baucom et al., 1998; Joo, 2008). For example:

> *Clinician:* It sounds like you've made the decision to open a joint bank account. Please report back to me about your process of meeting with the banker and opening the account together next week.

HELPING COUPLES RECOVER FROM INFIDELITY

Infidelity (e.g., extradyadic involvement, affair, extramarital affair) is a serious relationship violation that involves one or both partners breaking their agreed-upon marital/relational contract and attaining emotional and/or sexual contact from a third party. Infidelity has been identified as the most common reason for divorce

(Allen et al., 2008; Girard et al., 2020). Infidelity frequently happens in both troubled and happy relationships and the dynamics surrounding it are often diverse and unique. According to Haney and Hardie (2014), infidelity is a traumatic and incomprehensible experience that creates immediate cognitive dissonance, emotional upheaval, and complex grief.

Investigations have assessed the prevalence of infidelity. According to research, 18% to 49% of men and 12% to 31% of women commit infidelity (Glass & Wright, 1997; Weeks & Fife, 2014; Wiederman, 1997; Wiederman & Hurd, 1999). In addition to its presence, infidelity is one of the most difficult issues for a couple, marriage, and family practitioner to help couples with. It is an issue that is difficult for couples to talk and be honest about, and the betrayed partner can experience a significant amount of trauma. While it may be difficult to treat, it is not uncommon. Investigations indicate that 50% to 65% of couples entering counseling described infidelity as their reason for coming to treatment (Atkins et al., 2001). Infidelity is regarded as an issue that is influenced by causality myths and cultural narratives, including the following: (a) love will see us through, (b) infidelity emerges due to an imperfect marriage, (c) affairs are cocreated by incompatibility, and (d) infidelity happens because there is a poor relational fit (Pittman & Wagers, 2005). These causality narratives have the potential to retraumatize the betrayed partner, who is not to blame for the other partner's behavior.

It is normative for disclosures of infidelity to bring on negative and intense emotions, distance, panic, and cognitive dissonance. While most relationships survive infidelity, the consequences of infidelity can range from deep emotional hurt to trauma. According to Phillips (2020), due to the similarities between PTSD and infidelity, therapists have relabeled infidelity-based PTSD as *postinfidelity stress disorder*. Further, Phillips described postinfidelity stress as including PTSD symptoms such as ruminating thoughts, depression, health issues, erratic behaviors, and sleep problems. Not only is a clinician helping the couple through this relational violation, they are also likely treating symptoms of PTSD within the betrayed partner.

While partners who commit infidelity rarely come out and indicate the full reason for the betrayal, common reasons partners engage in infidelity include relational dissatisfaction, low self-esteem, loneliness, unmet needs, unhappiness, inability to communicate, slowly falling out of love, death of a family member or loved one, and infatuation or lust (Hasenecz, 2010). While the person who committed the infidelity can feel a great deal of fear, confusion, shame, and regret, the betrayed partner who was cheated on can experience a sense of excruciating pain, grief, anger, and trauma (Glass, 2002). While hope for reconciliation exists, Rogers and Amato (1997) identified infidelity as the primary cause for divorce. When couples choose to stay together, they need to deconstruct what happened, heal any resulting attachment injury or trauma, and resolve any ambivalence within the relationship. Alternatively, couples may choose to dissolve the partnership and hopefully move toward a peaceful separation.

There is a lot of variability and many unique factors involved in infidelity; however, patterns have been identified. Gender patterns around reengaging with a partner and processing infidelity have been identified in research. One gender difference is around emotional attachment to the person they are having an affair with. Men tend to compartmentalize infidelity and the person they are having an affair with, and this is typically why they can seem as if they are in a happy marriage or relationship while having extramarital affair. Alternatively, women tend to get more emotionally attached to their affair partners and are less likely to engage in an affair unless they are already having a problematic relationship with their current partner. This can be a challenge if women are wanting to become reoriented to marriage as apathy and ambivalence can be a major hurdle that stands in the way of reconnection. Regarding reactions, men tend to be more hurt when women engage in sexual infidelity, and women tend to be more hurt by emotional infidelity (Prins et al., 1993; Shackleford et al., 2000; Tsapelas et al., 2011).

While many theories provide special parameters around the treatment of infidelity, this section breaks down general considerations. First, most couple, marriage, and family practitioners will work in a conjoint format when partners enter therapy with issues around infidelity; however, in situations where one partner is extremely agitated or confused about moving forward as a couple, they may encourage individual counseling prior to conjoint treatment (American Association for Marriage and Family Therapy, n.d.). When couples enter treatment, it is extremely important to avoid any causality assumptions directed toward the betrayed partner (Haney & Hardy, 2014). Instead, the practitioner must empathize with the betrayed partner while not rejecting the partner who engaged in infidelity. Next, clinicians encourage an ethos of acceptance and validation around the feelings of the betrayed partner (Glass, 2002). The initial sessions are more about gaining awareness, creating safety, and generating a sense of soothing around the emotional wounds caused by infidelity. It is important for clinicians to move at a slower pace at this point of treatment to provide adequate space for the grieving and betrayed spouse to process their feelings and the associated trauma, gather important information, decide if they can forgive their partner and move forward with the relationship, and avoid any false forgiveness (Glass, 2002; Haney & Hardy, 2014). While many relationships can heal and even become stronger following the disclosure of infidelity, it is important for clinicians to take their time and work through the emotional hurt; otherwise the betrayed partner could be inadvertently retraumatized.

As previously stated, many models exist (e.g., EFT, Gottman method, CBT) for helping couples heal from infidelity. While review of every model is beyond the scope of this textbook, Alsaleem's (2017) method will be briefly explored. Alsaleem (2017) developed a method for helping couples heal from emotional and sexual infidelity and the resulting trauma. The method is called systematic affair recovery therapy (SART). The main goal of the SART method is provide information on seven major milestones couples heal from as they process infidelity. These milestones are the following: (a) setting the stage for healing, (b) getting the story, (c) acknowledging the impact, (d) choosing a path, (e) creating a plan of action, (f) implementation and healing pains, and (g) sustainability.

Alsaleem's (2017) SART method provides a framework for processing the trauma with clients. Two important skills that are promoted within the SART model are defining the infidelity and telling the affair story. It is important to define infidelity thoroughly and correctly early in treatment. Once consensus has been achieved around the definition, appropriate interventions can be utilized. A second important step in Alsaleem's work is discussing the *affair story*. In this model, the clinician encourages the offending partner to fully disclose the affair story. This is to demonstrate that the offending partner is capable of being open and honest. During the affair story, the betrayed partner is encouraged to ask any questions that come to mind (Alsaleem, 2017; Phillips, 2020).

Infidelity recovery can be an intense and lengthy experience. It is typically longer for couples who want to reconcile. Experts suggest that healing from infidelity can often take place within 2 years (Good Therapy Team, 2018). While the SART model is a helpful contemporary method, Table 7.5 describes the typical phases of infidelity treatment, their descriptions, and clinical examples.

TABLE 7.5 INFIDELITY PHASES, DESCRIPTIONS, AND EXAMPLES

Infidelity Phase	Description	Examples
Preinfidelity	Every person and relationship is unique; therefore, it is important to understand the nature of the relational or marital contract (e.g., monogamy, polyamory) and any current or prior mental health issues affecting the partners.	*Clinician:* Brian, tell us about your family history regarding relationships. Specifically, please let us know if there are any past negative family issues like the challenges you and Jill have been discussing.
Trauma	This is the tumultuous and highly emotional period that follows the discovery of infidelity. The betrayed partner often feels trauma, anger, vengefulness, loss and grief, and rage. The other partner often feels fear, regret, shame, and guilt.	*Clinician:* Habibat, I can tell you feel deeply hurt and angry that Jeanette had an affair. You feel completely betrayed.
Clarification of issues	While the emotional instability is still present, the couple starts to examine the issues and events that led to the affair. While the betrayed partner may have contributed to past issues, the clinician works hard to ensure the other partner does not blame the betrayed partner for the infidelity.	*Clinician:* Robert, I can tell that Suzanne's constant texting and disinterest in sex were both frustrating to you. While I understand how upset this made you, it is important to remember that Suzanne never agreed that you could sleep with other women.
Addressing the issue	The couple's emotions stabilize, and they begin to work on the identified issues that led to infidelity. The couple goes beyond the act and discusses issues that are foundational to the relationship.	*Clinician:* It sounds like you were first tempted to engage with Sophia at last year's Christmas party, but you only got serious about it when she friended you on Facebook and began liking all your photos.
Creation of a new relationship	The couple either makes changes and cocreates a new relationship or chooses to end the relationship. The clinician helps the couple take an active role in their relationships so they can express dissatisfaction without engaging in infidelity.	*Clinician:* It sounds like you have decided to stay together and are trying to change a few things in the relationship. Although Joyce hasn't reached forgiveness, it seems like both of you want to try again.
Sustaining the change	Once treatment ends, the couple either attempts to live the new cocreated relationship style and reaches out for follow-up appointments whenever necessary or decides to separate/divorce.	*Clinician:* Julia and Sam, it has been wonderful getting to know both of you and working through the infidelity. I want to encourage both of you to keep working on the positive coping skills we discussed. If you would like to come in for a follow-up session, please don't hesitate to reach out to me.

Sources: Data from Glass, S. P. (2002). Couple therapy after the trauma of infidelity. In A. S. Gurman & N. S. Jacobson (Eds.), *Clinical handbook of couple therapy* (pp. 488–507). Guilford Press; Haney, J. M., & Hardie, L. (2014). Psychotherapeutic considerations for working with betrayed spouses: A four-task recovery model. *Australian and New Zealand Journal of Family Therapy, 35*(4), 401–413; Hasenecz, N. (2010). Grandparents of children with autism—support, caregiving, and advocacy. *Social Work Today, 10*(5), 18.

VOICES FROM THE FIELD: HARVEY

Dr. Harvey Peters shared his experiences working with couples who struggle with infidelity and identify as LGBTQIA+.

When considering infidelity, I have experienced several themes in my work with queer couples and families, such as the development of affectional and sexual rules and boundaries that have not been successfully discussed and unpacked. For example, a couple who has an open marriage is flexible in their rules, but they have not been proactive in exploring and developing rules, boundaries, and/or channels of communication to navigate the complex and dynamic nature of this, which has resulted in miscommunication and infidelity. Another important consideration includes understanding the history and current culture concerning how affection, sexuality, and non/monogamy are positioned in the queer community, and how community members may or may not care about another's relational status, rules, or boundaries.

VOICES FROM THE FIELD: JENNIFER

Ms. Jennifer Kassing shared her experiences working with LGTQIA+ couples experiencing infidelity and her experience of couples working through this painful issue.

I'm not sure I've noticed any unique issues related to infidelity within my LGBTQIA+ couples outside of partners seeming to endure more stress and relationship distress and being willing to work through the infidelity more often. But this is a small sample size, so I am not sure if this is actually the case or just coincidental to the couples I've worked with. I utilize Gottman methods interventions, interventions specific to their research and literature for treating affairs and trauma.

HELPING COUPLES WHO HAVE EXPERIENCED INTIMATE PARTNER VIOLENCE

According to Heyman et al. (2015), IPV includes hurting an intimate partner through physical, sexual, and psychological/emotional violence or abuse. According to Black (2011), IPV affects approximately 36% of women and 29% of men. The first step in treating IPV is assessing for it. The concern with IPV is that it is often hidden, and couples are rarely forthright with its prevalence. In general, the literature indicates that IPV takes place on a continuum. For example, on the severe side of the continuum, physically violent partners may engage in one or more of the following behaviors: punching, kicking, stabbing, and threatening partner with a weapon. On the less severe side of the physical abuse continuum lie behaviors such as slapping, shoving, and pushing (O'Leary et al., 1989; Stith & Rosen, 2005).

While there is variability in severity, clinicians should be aware that minor altercations can lead to more serious violence. Given this factor, it is essential that clinicians do not minimize any physical altercation no matter how benign (Aldarondo & Straus, 1994). Beyond physical violence, IPV includes sexual assault and emotional abuse (e.g., extreme criticism, control, harassment, withholding basic needs; Karakurt et al., 2014). For example:

Clinician: Tell me what happened during the argument.

Client A: Paul lost his cool, punched a hole in the wall.

Clinician: Was there anything else that happened?

Client B: I ended up pushing her away from me when she got too close.

Clinician: Paul, it sounds like you destroyed part of a wall in your home and used some physical aggression toward Jennifer. I just want to remind you, even when you become emotional, it is never okay to push or physically intimidate Jennifer.

While IPV models for couples therapy have been created (e.g., Stith et al., 2011), conjoint treatment for IPV is generally not recommended, has the potential for poor therapeutic outcomes, and could create a more dangerous situation for the victim. First, during initial sessions, it is quite common for abusive partners to scapegoat the victimized partner for the abuse. The emotions and accusatory behaviors could carry forward to the home environment and the abusive partner could engage in subsequent retaliatory behavior. Second, the abused partner may feel too afraid and uncomfortable to effectively disclose the violence, and consequently nothing changes. Lastly, if the abused partner is not immediately empathized with and dissolved of any blame, they could believe they are at fault for the abusive behavior (Stith & Rosen, 2005).

Some couples may not associate the more benign forms of IPV with violence. Clinicians who suspect this might be taking place should ask specific questions related to potential altercations. For example, "Does your partner ever shove, slap, or push you?" or "Do you ever feel fearful that your partner will get physical with you?" (Stith & Rosen, 2005). If the clinician determines there is physical aggression in the relationship, they should inquire about the severity, chronicity, and frequency of the behavior. The abused partner should be asked about their thoughts and predictions for how dangerous the relationship is and if they believe their partner's physical violence will escalate (Stith & Rosen, 2005; Weisz et al., 2000). Since it is possible that the abused partner will underestimate the situation, the victim's testimony is only one piece of information that the clinician uses to assess the dangerousness of the relationship. For example:

Clinician: Rachel, you have mentioned several times that you feel afraid of Rebecca when she starts drinking. Does she ever get physical with you?

Client A: Well, sometimes we start wrestling or she pushes me around but nothing big.

Clinician: It sounds like there is physical aggression in the relationship. I want you to know that this is something I take very seriously. How intense does the pushing and wrestling become? Describe it for me.

IPV is typically not centered on the need to physically injure someone; it is more about the need for one partner to have power and control over the other. Once there has been an indication of IPV, clinicians should further assess to see if there are any factors present that would greatly increase the risk of serious and/or lethal violence, including, but not limited to, guns or other weapons in the home, presence of substance abuse, depression, suicidality, emotional abuse, psychological abuse, and history of violence in the family of origin. Furthermore, protective factors like family and social support should be assessed during the initial sessions as they can serve as a group who will protect the victim (Karakurt et al., 2014; Stith & Rosen, 2005). For example:

Clinician: Jamal, you appear to be unable to control your anger and rage regarding Kai's disclosure. Clearly, the house is not a safe place when you are in this state. I know you mentioned that you have a gun collection and that you drink a lot. Until things calm down and you are a safe person to live with, I would like to make plan to secure your guns in a different location and I would ask you to refrain from drinking. Kai, do you have another place you can stay tonight and possibly for the next few days?

If couples have gone through a judicial process around IPV, the perpetrator will likely be sent to a set treatment dictated by state standards (Butters et al., 2021; Messing et al., 2015; Williston et al., 2015). State guidelines impose certain elements of treatment, including treatment type, length of engagement, and theory utilized by the clinician (Butters et al., 2021). According to Butters et al. (2021), many states require perpetrators to engage in a feminist-based psychoeducational group experience called the Duluth model (Murphy & Eckhardt, 2005) or a CBT approach (Miller et al., 2013). The Duluth model and CBT are most commonly used to treat intimate violence perpetrators and have garnered the most empirical support (Arias et al., 2013; Butters et al., 2021). Another common method of educating the victim and the perpetrator is through a tool called the Power and Control Wheel (National Center on Domestic and Sexual Violence, 2014). Figure 7.1 presents the Power and Control Wheel.

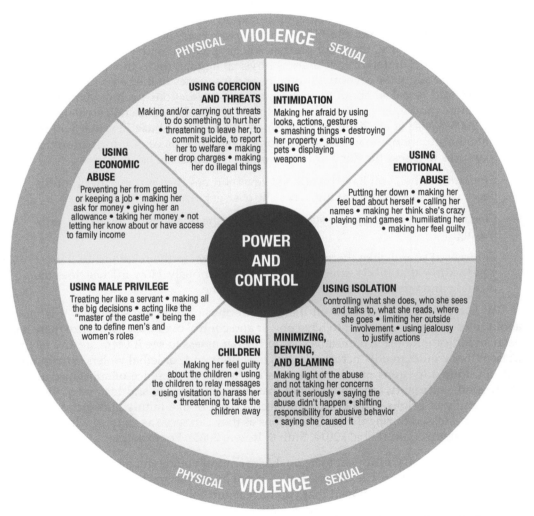

FIGURE 7.1 The Power and Control Wheel. This figure illustrates the eight elements of power and control in the context of intimate partner violence (National Center on Domestic and Sexual Violence, 2014).

Source: Domestic Abuse Intervention Programs, 202 East Superior Street, Duluth, Minnesota 55802, 218-722-2781, www .theduluthmodel.org.

According to Pender (2012), the Duluth model is a feminist psychoeducation method that is centered on the idea that patriarchy, male gender socialization, and privilege are at the core of IPV. Like the Power and Control Wheel, the Duluth model suggests that abusive men seek to control and have power over their partners. The original Duluth model initially focused solely on treatment and reeducation of male perpetrators of IPV and did not include special provisions for women perpetrators or LGBTQIA+ couples (Eisikovits & Edelson, 1989). The Duluth model is a nontherapeutic group treatment designed to be 28 weeks in length (Pender, 2012). The group format is centered on digital reenactments, role-plays, individual plans, and logs (Pence & Paymar, 1993; Pender, 2012). The client engagement is centered on confronting male perpetrators during treatment, addressing their thoughts about women, and bringing awareness to the normalization of treating women in controlling and violent ways (Eisikovits & Edelson, 1989).

The CBT form of IPV treatment is offered in an individual and group therapeutic format. CBT serves as an alternate to the Duluth model; however, in recent years, the Duluth model has incorporated many CBT interventions into their model (Butters et al., 2021). The CBT model targets thoughts and behaviors that influence the perpetration of IPV. According to Murphy and Eckhart (2005), CBT for IPV is centered on anger management, functional analysis of abusive behaviors, identification of factors that contribute to relapse, cognitive restructuring, encouraging awareness raising, responsibility-taking behaviors, and development of communication skills.

VOICES FROM THE FIELD: HARVEY

Dr. Harvey Peters shared his experiences working with couples who struggle with IPV and identify as LGBTQIA+.

It is important the counselors understand the prevalence of IPV within the queer community and how it can appear differently than other nonqueer couples. For example, how masculinity and femininity, affectional orientation, gender identity and expression, age, and relational and trauma history may influence a couple's experience with IPV as well as a counselor's implicit or myside bias when assessing and treating such issues. Some factors that may influence IPV may be previous family and dating history, substance use, level of internalized homophobia and transphobia, age and financial status, distal and proximal stressors, and multiplistic forms of oppression. I worked with a cross-racial queer cisgender female couple where one partner identified as bisexual and the other lesbian. One partner identifies as lesbian and has been out and dating women since she was in college, and the other partner was recently divorced and dating women for the first time, despite a long history of attraction. The bisexual female was engaging in emotional and physical forms of violence when she was drinking. She was dealing with and surviving the impact of being in a heterosexual relationship with an abusive man coupled with her own internalized homophobia and lack of family and community support. Thus, she was abusing her partner emotionally and physically. This resulted in the couple seeking both individual and couples counseling. In couples counseling, they were working on learning about the cycle of violence, the window of tolerance, and how to effectively cope and address a long history of trauma. This was also while supporting the couple with other related tasks.

VOICES FROM THE FIELD: JENNIFER

Ms. Jennifer Kassing shared her experiences working with LGBTQIA+ couples experiencing IPV and her unique experience with contextual issues that surrounded IPV incidents in the LGBTQIA+ community.

The gay (two women) couple I referred to earlier who divorced due to one partner developing a substance use disorder also had several instances of domestic violence. I also worked with a gay male couple who had several instances of domestic violence as well. This landed one male in the hospital because of his injuries and another time led to a car accident. Specifically, one male left after a conflict erupted and the other took chase and ended up crashing his car. I haven't seen anything unique specifically lead to violence, but the way it's handled and discussed can be different. The violence that occurred with the male couple mentioned above was often related to jealousy, but that's not unique to LGBTQIA+ couples. There can be a hesitancy to discuss IPV given gender and sexual identity stereotypes and being taken seriously by law enforcement. For example, regarding the female couple mentioned above, it took several instances and police reports by one partner to get the other partner arrested. Males are often seen as the aggressors, so this could have contributed to why it took several occurrences before the police would formally intervene. This could be completely unrelated to their gender or sexuality, but the one partner felt it had everything to do with their sexuality and not being taken seriously as women and a lesbian couple. The final incident involved a knife and their infant child, so the one partner was finally arrested. Something to note, LGBTQIA+ couples endure more stress and discrimination overall, so this added stress may also be a factor within IPV, as stress affects the ability to emotionally regulate.

HELPING COUPLES MINIMIZE DIVORCE/SEPARATION CONFLICT

Divorce and separation begin to emerge long before the official legal documents are signed. Conflict between divorcing partners is common, and as couples begin to go down the path of divorce issues like yelling, insults, belligerence, criticism, contempt, defensiveness, and stonewalling are all quite common (Birditt et al., 2010; Gottman & Levenson, 2000). Anger and self-doubt are also normal emotions to experience during a divorce. Not only can partners feel anger toward each other, they often hold on to anger because they are not prepared to detach from their partner and they secretly hope that their partner will return, forgive them, and see things from their perspective. Once partners let go of their anger, they begin to detach from their spouse and the hope of reconciliation. Couples can experience an enormous sense of loss when they divorce. Issues like feeling like they lost a best friend, spending less time with their children, not collaborating with celebrating their child's special experiences together (e.g., birthdays, Christmas, tooth fairy, bar mitzvah), financial insecurity, not participating in family traditions (e.g., bedtime routines, ice cream night), and change of home all hit suddenly and are extremely painful for everyone involved (Harvey & Fine, 2006).

The emotional and legal process of divorce/separation can also take enormous amount of time, energy, bravery, and money. Two people need the bravery to admit that the relationship has failed and to put the hopes and aspirations of being a married couple or in a serious committed relationship in the past. The adjustments and confusion can be even more intense when children are involved. Poorly managed conflict can bring a considerable amount of distress to children. When parents hurt each other emotionally, psychologically, or physically, the effects are extremely detrimental to children. Examples of common hurtful and harmful parenting behaviors that caregivers engage in with children during divorce include (a) having children send messages to the other parent, (b) interrogating children about what the other parent does, (c) making false statements about the other parent's interest or love for the child, and (d) stating derogatory things about the other parent to the children. When children are put through a process like this, they can experience a variety of negative consequences, including parentification, poor social adjustment, increased interest in substance use, increased risk-taking behavior, and poor school performance (Blaisure & Saposnek, n.d.).

As partners begin to accept that the divorce is happening, acknowledge the role they played in the relationship's demise, and start to establish the new rules of engagement, they can begin to work toward feeling a sense of happiness again. While most divorces bring some tension, after approximately 3 years postdivorce, most partners engage in a new normative coparenting, parallel parenting, or cooperative parenting arrangement (Braver et al., 2006). Despite their best efforts, many couples maintain a sense of hostility and anger toward each other. Partners in these situations can be assisted through therapeutic treatment, including, but not limited to, mediation (Sbarra & Emery, 2006) and collaborative divorce (Fagerström et al., 1997). These are empirically based options for couples who have already decided to end their marriage. Sometimes partners can have a mixed agenda (i.e., one person wants to stay together, while the other wants a divorce or separation). In these situations, couple, marriage, and family practitioners can utilize discernment counseling (Doherty, 2011).

Mediation

While therapy can be helpful, many couples may prefer the more structured and short-term divorce mediation. Divorce mediation includes a neutral third party that provides a platform for couples to negotiate their interests on identified topics and to reach an agreement regarding distribution of assets and liabilities, child and spousal support amounts, income tax, insurance, and other important factors. Mediation can also be done in abbreviated formats that focus on one salient issue (e.g., custody, financial matters). Mediation is typically short in duration, lasting anywhere between 1 and 10 sessions. Each session is approximately 90 minutes in length. The essence of mediation is self-determination decision-making authority. Following the mediation experience, the mediator will create a memorandum of understanding (MOU) that details the various elements of the agreement. The partners will have their respective attorneys review the MOU prior to agreeing and signing (Blaisure & Saposnek, 2007; Sbarra & Emery, 2006).

Mediators do not influence the content being discussed; however, they do typically control and manage the mediation process. Mediation is centered on the notion that certain elements of the divorce's decision-making process should be conducted in a calm, rational, problem-solving manner. Regarding professional background, mediators are typically mental health clinicians or attorneys by trade. Additionally, mediator qualifications are typically indicated in states' court rules (Blaisure & Saposnek, 2007). Mediation has many theoretically based models, including, but not limited to, transformative mediation (i.e., partners are transformed to recognize and respect each other's perspective; Folger & Bush, 1994), evaluative mediation (i.e., the mediator guides parties toward time-honored outcomes; Lowry, 2004), therapeutic mediation (i.e., encourages empathic emotional expression between partners in an effort to more smoothly arrive at consensus; Irving & Benjamin, 2002; Pruett & Johnston, 2004), and strategic mediation (i.e., uses strategies to encourage a quick and nonemotional resolution; Kressel, 2007).

Collaborative Divorce

Collaborative divorce was created as a method to move through the phases of divorce without resorting to hurtful court battles, unthoughtful court-endorsed parenting plans, the lingering bickering and disputes that follow divorce court-based decision, and as a structured nonadversarial method that seeks to protect children from the toxicity of court-based, high-emotion divorces (Alba-Fisch, 2016). According to Blaisure and Saposnek (2007), the essence of collaborative divorce is that the divorcing couple co-creates a written contract centered on finalizing the divorce outside of court-based litigation. The process begins with each spouse meeting with a mental health coach who helps them determine if they are truly interested in a nonadversarial divorce and their willingness to negotiate with a coach. Next, qualified couples meet for a number of four-way problem-solving meetings that include two collaborative attorneys and the spouse they are representing. These trained collaborative attorneys work to support their respective clients in negotiations leading to agreement. The discussions are based on disclosing all relevant information in a straightforward and honest manner. If the couple indicates the desire to move toward litigation, both collaborative attorneys are immediately terminated.

An important element of the collaborative divorce is the behavior code that divorcing spouses need to agree to prior to engaging in the process. The essence of this code is engaging with their partner in a courteous, honest, and transparent manner. There is a special provision centered on not involving the children in the divorce proceedings or stating hurtful comments about the other partner. Lastly, spouses are to act in good faith on all matters agreed upon and documented in the signed contract. While this can seem like an enormous challenge while experiencing the emotional hurt of divorce, the entire team is centered on achieving these elements of the behavioral code (Alba-Fisch, 2016).

Discernment Counseling

According to Doherty et al. (2011), discernment counseling emerged due to research findings indicating that many couples who had not fully agreed and settled on the notion of attaining a divorce filed for divorce prematurely due to a sense of ambivalence and fear that the relationship would eventually fall apart. The lack of systematic methods aimed at assessing spousal ambivalence about divorce and/or reconciliation was an additional factor that set the stage for the discernment counseling model. Couples who engage in couples therapy often present with one partner interested in divorcing and the other partner invested in making the marriage work (i.e., mixed-agenda couples). Couples in this situation are divided on what the nature of the relationship should be moving forward. The aim of discernment counseling is to provide couples a short-term therapeutic platform to decide to divorce or to continue working on the relationship with the aid of a trained couple, marriage, and family practitioner. The ultimate goal of this model is to help the couple achieve greater clarity on the direction of their relationship through meaningful conversations and with each person taking responsibility for their part of the problem (Doherty, 2011).

VOICES FROM THE FIELD: HARVEY

Dr. Harvey Peters shared his experiences working with couples who are working toward divorce or separation and identify as LGBTQIA+.

When working with couples looking to split up or divorce, I treat the process like a treatment plan wherein we coconstruct rules and goals with accompanying objectives, interventions, and timelines with additional attention given to the process. I have found that this has supported me in successfully supporting queer couples in the concluding of their marriage or relationship as they know it. I also look to assess how they envision their relationship in the short- and long-term because it is not uncommon for queer persons to remain friends or acquaintances with their ex-partner or their associated queer friends and community. Other factors to consider are their sense of safety and protections (e.g., transgender, lesbian, and gay rights), family and community reaction and level of support (born into or chosen), and other legal related concerns (e.g., custody, issues with law). Using symbolic-experiential family therapy, I have developed experiential and creative arts interventions tailored to the queer couple to aid in this process, such as creating an individual and an ex-couple vision board and having them role-play potential situations and issues, followed by exploring and unpacking these in counseling.

VOICES FROM THE FIELD: JENNIFER

Ms. Jennifer Kassing shared her experiences working with LGBTQIA+ couples who are working toward divorce and/or breaking up.

I've had several couples over the last 11 years move toward divorce. The shift that I try to make going from couples therapy and "divorce therapy" is to increase my objectivity. I continue to utilize Gottman methods as it pertains to communication and expression of complaints and needs. We have very structured conversations and steer clear of blame and bringing up past issues. I try to keep them present- and future-focused. There is time for the processing of emotions related to the divorce, and there are times when they can do this together; however, in my experience, emotions are high, so it's ineffective. There are also practical discussions pertaining to future planning (e.g., parenting, housing, financials) where I might introduce psychoeducation or provide resources. To be honest, I've had just a handful of couples work together when their relationship gets to this point. Typically, it becomes so contentious that they are unable to even engage in divorce therapy. It usually devolves into blaming and arguing so we end the therapeutic relationship. I've had one LGBTQIA+ couple divorce. This was due to one partner developing a substance use disorder, so I am not sure I noticed any unique issues. One thing that I have heard gay couples express though, not when approaching divorce, but just in general, is that they feel more pressure to make the marriage work due to stereotypes. In particular, the stereotype that gay men are mostly nonmonogamous and only interested in sex. They don't want to perpetuate this stereotype. I've also heard couples talk about needing to "make it work" so that society can see that gay couples are "real" couples who can have successful and happy marriages. What I have gathered from this is that there is some pressure these couples have felt to be a representative for all gay/queer couples.

HELPING COUPLES WHO ARE STRUGGLING WITH INTERNET ADDICTION

Problematic use of the internet (i.e., internet addiction disorder [IAD], problematic internet use [PIU], or iDisorder) has the potential to ruin relationships and careers, and due to the sedentary nature of screen time can prove detrimental to one's physical health. Excessive internet use and the detrimental effects it has on couples is a difficult issue to treat because it does not carry the same social stigma as other behavior addictions (e.g., gambling, sex). In fact, the use of internet is encouraged, legitimized, and simply considered a normal part of everyday life. The pathologic nature of internet use emerges when people spend many hours engaging in nonwork-related activities online (e.g., video games, social media, internet surfing; Cash et al., 2012; Czincz & Hechanova, 2009). These issues affect people by changing their overall mood, increasing rumination about their need to use the internet and other online media platforms, inability to control internet engagement, the need for more internet engagement to attain the same level of satisfaction, the presence of withdrawal symptoms when not engaging on the internet, and diminishing relationships and effectiveness at work (Beard, 2005; Cash et al., 2012).

Individuals who are addicted to the internet and other media experience a variety of rewards when engaged in the various applications. Specifically, similar to other behavioral addictions, the internet works as a variable ratio reinforcement schedule (VRRS). Furthermore, engaging in various online applications creates unpredictable and variable reinforcement schedules (Young & Abreu, 2011). As if this powerful reinforcement of internet was not enough, when the online reinforcement is further enhanced by additional stimulation commonly experienced during nonstructured online activities, the addictive nature is much stronger. These additional stimulating experiences provide a significant amount of mood enhancement. Examples include sexual stimulation from online pornography, the immersive graphics and character identification that takes place while using video games, the increase or decrease in money from online gambling, and the intimacy-based fantasy that takes place when using dating sites (Amichai-Hamburger & Ben-Artzi, 2003; Young & Abreu, 2011).

People who use the internet excessively are regarded as having an impulse control disorder. The following are common traits: (a) regards the internet as very important and precedes all other activities behaviorally and cognitively; (b) the internet modifies the individual's mood (e.g., euphoria); (c) need for an increase in technology due to tolerance; (d) presence of internet withdrawal symptoms (e.g., tension, irritability); (e) conflict (e.g., arguments, deception, social withdrawal); and (f) relapse (Chattopadhyay et al., 2020; Griffiths, 2000; Hollander & Stein, 2006). Regarding relationships, Muusses et al. (2015) found that partners where one member has compulsive internet use issues had significant relationship challenges, including the partner with internet addiction being perceived as having low self-control and the nonaddicted partner feeling a sense of mistrust toward the partner with internet addiction.

Despite the fact the *Diagnostic and Statistical Manual of Mental Disorders*, Fifth Edition, Text Revision (*DSM-5-TR*; American Psychiatric Association, 2022), does not indicate a formal diagnosis for internet addiction, there are certain types of internet addiction that have received attention in the professional literature, including internet gaming disorder (i.e., addiction to online video games; Przybylski & Weinstein 2017), internet gambling addiction (i.e., addiction to online gambling; Gainsbury, 2015), cybersex addiction (i.e., addiction to online relationships; Wéry & Billieux, 2017), and compulsive information-seeking addiction (i.e., addiction to seeking online information; Cash et al., 2012). One important question is whether or not the person with the IAD is addicted to the internet or to the experience found on the internet (e.g., gambling app). Information like this would prove valuable in guiding treatment.

Regarding treatment, there is not much scholarship or research available to help couples specifically. There is general agreement that complete avoidance of the internet should not be the goal of treatment. The goals should be more in line with helping partners find a sense of balance and control with their internet use (Petersen et al., 2009). Young (1999) provided a few helpful CBT strategies that have stood the test of time. Young's strategies include encouraging the client to disrupt their normal schedule with different times for internet usage, preplanning events that require the client to get off the internet, setting goals related to time online, avoiding apps that the client cannot control themselves on, creating reminder cards indicating the detrimental effects of internet addiction, developing a personal inventory of things the client previously engaged in before using the internet, entering a support group, and engaging in couple and family therapy.

While there is an absence of best-practice methods for treating internet addiction in couples therapy, general guidelines include educating the couple on the addictive nature of the internet, reducing any blame, enhancing communication around the historical issues that had been taking place prior to the internet addiction, and encouraging the nonaddicted spouse to serve in a sponsorship role if the addicted partner begins relapse (Peukert et al., 2010). The following is a couples therapy clinical encounter where the partner's compulsive internet use has negatively affected her family:

Clinician: Francesca, welcome back. How have things been going with your compulsive internet use?

Client: Not so good. Last week my internet service provider had an outage. Because of this I was irritable to Paul and not so nice to the kids. Once the internet was back on again, I felt a deep sense of relief.

Clinician: You're feeling guilty about your anger and connecting with Paul and the kids.

Client: Pretty much.

Clinician: How else has the internet been affecting your time spent with others?

Client: In general, I like being online more than I like being with other people, and I am always online more than I have to be.

Regarding treatment via a specific modality, scholars have explored and identified theoretical, multimodal, and inpatient internet recovery programs, including motivational interviewing (Miller, 2010), reality therapy (Jong-Un, 2007), acceptance and commitment therapy (Twohig & Crosby, 2010), CBT (Widyanto & Griffiths, 2006), and the reSTART Program (Cash et al., 2012). While very few studies exist, there is more research supporting the use of CBT compared with any other approach (Widyanto & Griffiths, 2006). CBT group therapy could provide very positive results. Wölfling et al. (2009) found group therapy to be particularly powerful in creating a sense of intrinsic motivation to reduce the amount of time spent online and with the identification of conditions that sustain the internet usage. This method is a mix of exposure therapy, psychoeducation, and learning new behaviors. While CBT is extremely helpful, Orzack and Orzack (1999) encouraged the use of a multimodal method including CBT, couple and family therapy, case management, and psychopharmacotherapy to properly treat the complexities of internet addiction.

VOICES FROM THE FIELD: HARVEY

Dr. Harvey Peters shared his experiences working with couples who struggle with internet issues and identify as LGBTQIA+.

When working with queer couples experiencing internet-related issues, I have first sought to understand the individual and coupled experiences and narratives associated with the potential issue. It is essential to understand a queer couple's values, beliefs, and practices regarding internet-related issues because the issue cannot be understood from a single narrative or the dominant culture. I first try to get a comprehensive and holistic understanding of the issues to aid in my ability to support queer couples. Moreover, the dearth of sexual and relational scripts and education for queer couples and families further complicates the process and impact. Some unique issues that can emerge for queer couples include their dating history and socialization into the queer culture, values, and beliefs about dating and sexuality, position on non/monogamy, and agreed-upon rules and boundaries. I find that queer couples have a range of unspoken histories, rules, and traumas that have not been successfully communicated and integrated into their rules, practices, and boundaries. Thus, the couple must work to construct an ecological and relational third space conducive to both partners.

VOICES FROM THE FIELD: JENNIFER

Ms. Jennifer Kassing shared her experiences working with LGBTQIA+ couples who are working toward divorce and/or breaking up.

Social media, email, and *screen time* are often the topic of conflict for many couples I work with. I've had a handful of couples who've dealt with internet porn issues as well. Generally, it's the man in a heterosexual relationship. Two of the couples I worked with chose to divorce in response to these issues. I generally refer the male partners to a sex therapist or someone who specializes in porn addiction for individual help, to accompany couples therapy. I utilize addictions research with this specific presenting concern, but also Gottman methods and EFT. On a practical level, we discuss the need that's being met by the use or overuse of internet-based applications. We set practical goals and I utilize psychoeducation regarding the link between screen time and depression and anxiety. I have worked with several couples where one partner plays computer or console video games for long periods of time, resulting in conflict. Again, this is typically a male counterpart, gay, straight or trans. Also, the work–life balance and being too connected to work emails are other frequent issues, more so with my high-achieving couples. Again, a lot of practical solutions and brief discussion on why these behaviors might be occurring, and then utilizing couples therapy methods such as Gottman methods or EFT to assist the couple in discussion and reconnection. Often this will become a perpetual problem, so assisting the couple in learning how best to manage it is the better strategy, as opposed to creating a situation where one or both partners have to quit using technology. I don't recall utilizing anything different with LGBTQIA+ couples regarding internet issues. The one thing that does come up often is that these outlets (games, email, social media, friend-finder apps) provide a social group for the person, and if they are from a marginalized group it helps them find community. This makes the desire to reduce these behaviors low, which can further impact the relationship dynamics. I have a queer/trans couple that I work with who both have robust internet-based lives. Conflict surrounding this topic typically arises when their connection is not strong or following conflict in another area. Again, I utilize Gottman methods or EFT to help them manage stress, conflict, and improve communication and deepen their connection.

HELPING COUPLES WITH SEXUAL ADDICTION AND COMPULSIVITY

Prior to reviewing treatment options for sexual addiction and compulsivity, it is important to define sexual addiction, sexual compulsivity, and acting out, and describe the various issues around diagnosis. Case and Bailey (2007) define *sexual addiction* as a persistent and increasing pattern of sexual behavior that endures despite harmful outcomes to self and others. *Sexual compulsivity* is "the inability to control one's sexual behaviors as evidenced by continuing sexual behavior despite the desire to stop or negative consequences. . ." and ". . . is differentiated from sexual addiction which also includes preoccupation, ritualization, and despair related to the sexually compulsive behavior" (Case & Bailey, 2007, p. 192). *Acting out* occurs when an individual engages in sexual behavior that is part of their sexual addiction. This act is outside the boundaries of a healthy sexual behavior. Since addictive and/or compulsive sexual behavior does not have its own diagnostic category in the *DSM-5-TR*, it can be diagnosed as a subcategory of another mental health condition, such as an impulse control disorder or a behavioral addiction. Additionally, if paraphilias are present, a diagnosis of a paraphilia is warranted (American Psychiatric Association, 2022; Case & Bailey, 2007; Kavur et al., 2020).

According to Kavur et al. (2020), 8.6% of people in the United States suffer from sexual addiction and compulsivity; however, without an official diagnosis within the *DSM-5-TR*, it becomes a difficult issue to effectively treat and becomes an expensive treatment since it will not be covered under most insurance policies. The current etiologic perspective on sexual addiction and compulsivity is centered on neurobiology. Specifically, the combination of the side effects of serotonin-modulating antidepressants and the hypersexual/impulse control behaviors suggest serotonergic and dopaminergic pathway involvement. Furthermore, available neurobiological data suggest an increase in ventral striatal reactivity to sexual cues in individuals with compulsive sexual behavior compared with those without (Kavur et al., 2020). Common behaviors (i.e., acting-out behaviors) demonstrated by those with sexual addiction and compulsivity include, but are not limited to, compulsive masturbation, simultaneous or repeated sequential affairs, frequent pornography use, cybersex, phone sex, multiple anonymous partners, unsafe sexual activity, partner objectification/demand for sex, strip clubs and adult bookstores, use of prostitution/escorts, sexual aversion/anorexia, frequenting massage parlors, sexual paraphilias, and/or sexually offensive behaviors (Case & Bailey, 2007).

According to O'Hara (2012), male sexual addiction and compulsivity are typically centered on men objectifying their partners. Men typically prefer little emotional involvement. In comparison, women sex addicts tend to use sex for power, control, and attention. Psychologically, women sex addicts demonstrate a constant interaction between addiction and codependency. They tend to engage in fantasy sex, seductive role sex, trading sex, and pain exchange. Additionally, Shimoni et al. (2018) researched sex addiction and gender and found gender-based differences in people presenting with sexual addiction and compulsivity. A sample of 186 men and 81 women were administered the Sexual Addiction Screening Test (SAST), the Big Five Personality Index, and a demographic questionnaire. Researchers discovered a higher frequency of male sex addicts compared with female. In addition, their research indicated that men were more open to sexual experiences and were less neurotic. Personality factors also contributed to the variance in sex addiction. Specifically, openness to experiences and neuroticism positively correlated with SAST scores, while conscientiousness had a negative correlation with SAST scores. Lastly, greater neuroticism was associated with higher SAST scores in men but not in women.

According to Schwartz and Southern (2017), "recovery from sexual compulsivity involves integration of various psychotherapy components needed to address underlying trauma, repetition compulsion, developmental roadblocks, compulsive behavioral reenactments, emotion dysregulation, and intimacy disorder" (p. 226). Individuals demonstrating sexual addiction and compulsivity issues experience a lot of shame, denial, and minimization of their sexual behaviors. Consequently, it is important that early in treatment there is a clear definition about what sobriety (i.e., not being addicted to sex) entails since complete abstention from all sexuality is typically not the goal of treatment. This is especially true if the client is in a relationship. In addition, sexual addiction and compulsivity can be the result of early beliefs around sex within one's family of origin, so genogram work related to intimacy, sexuality, and the expression of love could be very pertinent to treatment. Individuals demonstrating sex addiction tendencies also frequently experience emotional, sexual, or physical abuse early in life. Consequently, another important aspect of treatment is to provide space for partners to explore these issues.

According to Schwartz and Southern (2017), the following treatment options have been found to be effective in the treatment of sex addiction: internal family systems, gestalt therapy, schema therapy, EMDR, body work, EFT, and Sexaholics Anonymous (SA). Regarding medications, selective serotonin reuptake inhibitors (SSRIs; e.g., citalopram), naltrexone, and anticonvulsants (e.g., topiramate, valproic acid) have been found to be effective in reducing symptoms (Kavur et al., 2020). Attachment theory and therapy can also be helpful in conceptualizing and recovering from sexual addiction and compulsivity. Given that individuals who are addicted to sex are often searching for sexual activity without any emotional relationship, they are more likely to be characterized by avoidant or anxious attachment styles. In contrast, individuals with secure attachment styles are expected to have low chances of becoming addicted to sex since they have a healthy internal working model and can regulate and limit their sexual activity (Weinstein et al., 2015). Clinicians practicing from an attachment lens can use this information to create a secure professional relationship with their client, and consequently reduce sex addiction symptomology and/or the chance of relapse.

The main goals of treating sexual addiction and compulsivity are centered on assisting the client in managing their sexual compulsivity and/or addiction in a healthy manner and to also help people reconnect within their relationships. This often includes guiding partners on creating healthy attachments to others. When working with couples to restore trust after one partner discloses their sexual acting out, there are two focuses. The first step is for the offending partner to focus on apologizing to the other partner by completely acknowledging their harmful behaviors. This acknowledgment is important and often very difficult since a characteristic related to sexual addiction is the presence of shame surrounding sexual behaviors. The offending partner must also develop empathy for the partner they have affected. The work of the betrayed partner should be centered on the acknowledgment that their partner has hurt them and understanding that the behavior is not the person, but simply the behavior, and to pledge to discontinue "punishment" of the offending partner (Hughes, 2012).

ASSESSING CONTEMPORARY COUPLE THERAPY ISSUES

Assessment measures are extremely helpful to use when engaging in couple, marriage, and family therapy. Assessment measures are one aspect of evidence-based practice, and help clinicians track client progress, attain a comprehensive understanding of their clients, attain better treatment outcomes, home in on the exact problem the couple is having, and respond quickly to new problems. Assessment in couples therapy evaluates the conjoint and individual functioning of the couple and their environment, and helps guide the course of treatment. Assessment allows the clinician to collect the relevant information that informs the clinician about the course of treatment and intervention goals, and enhances the practitioner's understanding of the scope, nature, and severity of the presenting problem (Kenny, 2020). While the practicality and importance of assessment are clear, research suggests that the majority of therapists in the United States do not use any assessment intervention when beginning a new therapeutic relationship with a couple. Additionally, evidence suggests that most of their assessments come from the verbal clinical interview as opposed to an empirically based assessment (Lavee & Avisar, 2006).

While depending on clinical judgment and intuition is a normative part of clinical practice, empirically validated assessments assist clinicians in enhancing the accuracy and success of a couple's treatment. Furthermore, clinical assessment assists clinicians in avoiding ethical pitfalls (e.g., inferential bias, attribution error, reconstructive memory; Finn, 2015). This final section of the chapter reviews two empirically based assessments for each of the contemporary couples therapy issues previously reviewed. Table 7.6 breaks down the name of the contemporary issues and the name of the assessments, and provides one pertinent reference. Most of these assessments are affordable, are easily accessible, and greatly enhance the sometimes-confusing world of couples therapy.

TABLE 7.6 CONTEMPORARY COUPLES THERAPY EMPIRICAL ASSESSMENTS AND RELATED REFERENCES

Contemporary Issue	Assessment Name	Reference
Infertility	Fertility Problem Inventory (FPI)	Newton, C. R., Sherrard, W., & Glavac, I. (1999). The fertility problem inventory: Measuring perceived infertility-related stress. *Fertility and Sterility*, 72(1), 54–62. https://doi.org/10.1016/S0015-0282(99)00164-8.
Infertility	Fertility Quality of Life (FertiQoL)	Boivin, J., Takefman, J., & Braverman, A. (2011). Development and preliminary validation of the fertility quality of life (FertiQoL) tool. *Human Reproduction*, 26(8), 2084–2091. https://doi.org/10.1093/humrep/der171.
Adult attachment	Adult Attachment Scale (AAS)	Collins, N. L., & Read, S. J. (1990). Adult attachment, working models, and relationship quality in dating couples. *Journal of Personality and Social Psychology*, 58(4), 644–663. https://doi.org/10.1037/0022-3514.58.4.644.
Adult attachment	Adult Attachment Interview (AAI)	George, C., Main, M., & Kaplan, N. (1985). *Adult Attachment Interview (AAI)* [Database record]. APA PsycTests. https://doi.org/10.1037/t02879-000.
Premarital warning signs	RELATE	Busby, D. M., Holman, T. B., & Taniguchi, N. (2001). RELATE: Relationship evaluation of the individual, family, cultural, and couple contexts. *Family Relations*, 50, 308–316. https://doi.org/10.1111/j.1741-3729.2001.00308.x.
Premarital warning signs	PREPARE/ENRICH	Olson, D. H. (1996). *PREPARE/ENRICH counselor's manual*. Life Innovations.
Marital/relational distress	Marital Distress Scale (MDS)	Delphi, P. P., & Nithyanandan, D. V. (2020). Psychometric properties of marital distress scale. *Aegaeum Journal*, 8(3). http://aegaeum.com/gallery/agm-j-2537.108-ff.pdf.
Marital/relational distress	Couples Satisfaction Index (CSI)	Funk, J. L., & Rogge, R. D. (2007). Testing the ruler with item response theory: Increasing precision of measurement for relationship satisfaction with the Couples Satisfaction Index. *Journal of Family Psychology*, 21, 572–583. https://doi.org/10.1037/0893-3200.21.4.572.
Crisis and disaster	PTSD Checklist for DSM-5 (PCL-5)	Blevins, C. A., Weathers, F. W., Davis, M. T., Witte, T. K., & Domino, J. L. (2015). The Posttraumatic Stress Disorder Checklist for DSM-5 (PCL-5): Development and initial psychometric evaluation. *Journal of Traumatic Stress*, 28, 489–498. https://doi.org/10.1002/jts.22059.
Crisis and disaster	Impact of Event Scale-Revised (IES-R)	Beck, J. G., Grant, D. M., Read, J. P., Clapp, J. D., Coffey, S. F., Miller, L. M., & Palyo, S. A. (2008). The Impact of Event Scale –Revised: Psychometric properties in a sample of motor vehicle accident survivors. *Journal of Anxiety Disorders*, 22, 187–198. https://doi.org/10.1016/j.janxdis.2007.02.007.
Substance abuse	Alcohol Use Disorder and Associated Disabilities Interview Schedule-V (AUDADIS-V)	Hasin, D. S., Greenstein, E., Aivadyan, C., Stohl, M., Aharonovich, E., Saha, T., Goldstein, R., Nunes, E. V., Jung, J., Zhang, H., & Grant, B. F. (2015). The Alcohol Use Disorder and Associated Disabilities Interview Schedule-5 (AUDADIS-5): Procedural validity of substance use disorders modules through clinical re-appraisal in a general population sample. *Drug and Alcohol Dependence*, 148, 40–46. https://doi.org/10.1016/j.drugalcdep.2014.12.011.
Substance abuse	Adult Substance Abuse Subtle Screening Inventory-Fourth Edition (SASSI-4)	Lazowski, L. E., Kimmell, K. S., & Baker, S. L. (2016). *The Adult Substance Abuse Subtle Screening Inventory-4 (SASSI-4) user guide & manual*. The SASSI Institute.

(continued)

TABLE 7.6 CONTEMPORARY COUPLES THERAPY EMPIRICAL ASSESSMENTS AND RELATED REFERENCES (CONTINUED)

Contemporary Issue	Assessment Name	Reference
Financial stress	APR Financial Stress Scale	Heo, W., Cho, S., & Lee, P. (2020). APR Financial Stress Scale: Development and validation of a multidimensional measurement. Journal of Financial Therapy, 11(1), 2. https://doi.org/10.4148/1944-9771.1216.
Financial stress	Incharge Financial Distress and Financial Well-Being Scale	Prawitz, A., Garman, E. T., Sorhaindo, B., O'Neill, B., Kim, J., & Drentea, P. (2006). Incharge financial distress/financial well-being scale: Development, administration, and score interpretation. Journal of Financial Counseling and Planning, 17(1), 34–50. https://doi.org/10.1037/t60365-000.
Infidelity	Attitude Toward Cheating (ATC) Scale	Gardner, W. M., & Melvin, K. B. (1988). A scale for measuring attitude toward cheating. Bulletin of the Psychonomic Society, 26(5), 429–432. https://doi.org/10.3758/BF03334905.
Infidelity	Affair–Spouse's Comprehensive Worksheets	Affair–Spouse's Comprehensive Worksheets. (2001). The fourteenth mental measurements yearbook. Buros Institute of Mental Measurements.
Intimate partner violence	Conflict Tactics Scales-2 (CTS2)	Straus, M., Hamby, S., Boney-McCoy, S., & Sugarman, D. (1996). The Revised Conflict Tactics Scales (CTS2): Development and preliminary psychometric data. Journal of Family Issues, 17(3), 283–316. https://doi.org/10.1177/019251396017003001.
Intimate partner violence	Domestic Violence Screening Instrument-Revised (DVSI-R)	Williams, K. R., & Grant, S. R. (2006). Empirically examining the risk of intimate partner violence: The revised Domestic Violence Screening Instrument (DVSI-R). Public Health Reports, 121, 400–408. https://doi.org/10.1177/003335490612100408.
Divorce conflict	Divorce Conflict Scale (DCS)	Hald, G. M., Strizzi, J. M., Ciprić, A., & Sander, S. (2020). The divorce conflict scale. Journal of Divorce & Remarriage, 61(2), 83–104. https://doi.org/10.1080/10502556.2019.1627150.
Divorce conflict	Revised Conflict Tactics Scale-2 (CTS2)	Straus, M. A., Hamby, S. L., Boney-McCoy, S., & Sugarman, D. B. (1996). The Revised Conflict Tactics Scales (CTS2): Development and preliminary psychometric data. Journal of Family Issues, 17(3), 283–316. https://doi.org/10.1177/019251396017003001.
Online addiction	Internet Addiction Test	Young, K. S. (1998). Internet addiction: The emergence of a new clinical disorder. CyberPsychology & Behavior, 3(1), 237–244. https://doi.org/10.1089/cpb.1998.1.237.
Online addiction	Pornography Consumption Inventory (PCI)	Reid, R. C., Li, D. S., Gilliland, R., Stein, J. A., & Fong, T. (2011). Reliability, validity, and psychometric development of the pornography consumption inventory in a sample of hypersexual men. Journal of Sex and Marital Therapy, 37, 359–385. https://doi.org/10.1080/0092623X.2011.607047.
Sex addiction	PATHOS Questionnaire	Carnes, P. J., Green, B. A., Merlo, L. J., Polles, A., Carnes, S., & Gold, M. S. (2012). PATHOS: A brief screening application for assessing sexual addiction. Journal of Addiction Medicine, 6(1), 29–34. https://doi.org/10.1097/ADM.0b013e3182251a28.
Sex addiction	Sexual Addiction Screening Test-Revised (SASTR)	Carnes, P., Green, B., & Carnes, S. (2010). The same yet different: Refocusing the sexual addiction screening test (SAST) to reflect orientation and gender. Sexual Addiction & Compulsivity, 17(1), 7–30. https://doi.org/10.1080/10720161003604087.

DSM-5, Diagnostic and Statistical Manual of Mental Disorders, Fifth Edition; PTSD, posttraumatic stress disorder.

SUMMARY

In this chapter, readers were introduced to a variety of conceptualization details, skills, and techniques related to treating a diversity of contemporary issues affecting today's couples, including infertility, adult attachment, premarital issues and warning signs, marital distress, crisis and disaster, substance abuse, financial stress, infidelity, intimate partner violence, divorce conflict, online addiction, and sex addiction. The main objective of this chapter was to describe the skills and assessments for conceptualizing and treating couples suffering from these issues. Specifically, throughout the chapter, readers were provided with the essence of the contemporary issue, key skills and interventions, assessment measures, and in-depth conceptualizations that accentuate the powerful skills and techniques clinicians can utilize when treating couples suffering from one of the key contemporary issues.

END-OF-CHAPTER RESOURCES

STUDENT ACTIVITIES

Exercise 1: Working With Couples in Premarital Therapy

Directions: Review the following information and use the content from this textbook to answer the prompts:

For many clients, attending couples therapy can create a sense of fear around possible divorce, embarrassment for past behavior, and hearing critical and hurtful comments from their partner. Premarital therapy has been viewed as an extremely beneficial form of treatment. It can be one of the best ways to handle negative relationship issues and can help with increasing relationship satisfaction and decreasing marital distress.

- How does premarital therapy differ from more traditional couples counseling?
- What are the important interventions to keep in mind when engaging in premarital therapy?
- How does the Sound Marital House theory fit into premarital counseling and help in working with couples?

Exercise 2: Article Review

Directions: Review the following instructions and answer the questions:

Go to your university's online EBSCO Database and find Academic Search Premier. Search and find an article focused on substance abuse in couples work. Review the article in its entirety and answer the following questions:

- What important goals for couples therapy were mentioned throughout the article?
- How does Alcoholics Anonymous, Narcotics Anonymous, and/or Al-Anon fit into couples therapy for people diagnosed with substance use disorder?
- What couples therapy interventions seemed like they could be helpful in your future practice?

Exercise 3: Working With Infidelity

Directions: Review the following instructions and respond to the follow-up questions:

In couples work, infidelity is a common theme for clients coming into therapy for the first time. Infidelity can happen in both troubled and happy relationships. It can be very difficult for clients to work through disclosures of infidelity, and helping them work through this is an important aspect of couples work.

- What patterns have been identified when working with clients who are dealing with infidelity?
- Which theory do you think would be most helpful for you when working with a couple suffering from the effects of infidelity?

■ What specific techniques do you believe would be best utilized in order to address the manner in which infidelity has impacted clients?

Exercise 4: Understanding Intimate Partner Violence

Directions: Review the following instructions and respond to all questions and prompts:

Children who are exposed to adult violent behavior at home develop a number of problems, including (but not limited to) (a) mental health disorders; (b) hearing, learning, speech, intellectual, and language disabilities; and (c) poor educational, employment, and criminal justice outcomes. In addition, children exposed to IPV have an increased risk of committing IPV in their future relationships (Ravi & Black, 2022).

Review the following article related to children's exposure to IPV:

■ Ravi, K. E., & Black, B. M. (2022). The relationship between children's exposure to intimate partner violence and an emotional–behavioral disability: A scoping review. *Trauma, Violence, & Abuse, 23*(3), 868–876. https://doi.org/10.1177/1524838020979846

As a couple, marriage, and family practitioner, you will need to engage in a safety planning process for children and adults who survive IPV. Review the following helpful resources that can be used with future victims/survivors:

■ Family Violence Research Group, UNCG Department of Counseling and Educational Development: http://www.dvsafetyplanning.org

■ National Coalition Against Domestic Violence (NCADV): http://www.ncadv.org

■ National Network to End Domestic Violence (NNEDV): http://www.nnedv.org

■ For legal information: http://womenslaw.org/

Assessments and screening tools are key to understanding the nature of IPV. Please review the following assessment measures. Information and reviews can be found within your university's EBSCO *Mental Measurement Yearbook With Tests in Print* search engine.

■ Child–Parent Psychotherapy (CPP) Screener: https://childparentpsychotherapy.com/providers/tools-and-resources/cppscreener/

■ Hurt, Insult, Threaten, and Scream (HITS) Screening Tool: https://www.ctcadv.org/files/4615/6657/9227/HPO_HITS_Screening_Tool_8.19.pdf

Please read the following two articles for a comprehensive review of the factors surrounding IPV:

■ Galovski, T. E., Werner, K. B., Weaver, T. L., Morris, K. L., Dondanville, K. A., Nanney, J., Wamser-Nanney, R., McGlinchey, G., Fortier, C. B., & Iverson, K. M. (2022). Massed cognitive processing therapy for posttraumatic stress disorder in women survivors of intimate partner violence. *Psychological Trauma: Theory, Research, Practice, and Policy, 14*(5), 769–779. https://doi-org.libproxy.plymouth.edu/10.1037/tra0001100

■ Mechanic, M. B., Weaver, T. L., & Resick, P. A. (2008). Risk factors for physical injury among help-seeking battered women: An exploration of multiple abuse dimensions. *Violence Against Women, 14*(10), 1148–1165. https://doi.org/10.1177/1077801208323792

Exercise 5: Mock Plan for Minimizing Divorce Conflict

Directions: Review the following information and come up with a mock plan for working with couples on minimizing divorce conflict:

After reading through this chapter, you should have a basic understanding of some of the skills related to contemporary issues that emerge during couples therapy, including divorce conflict. Using your knowledge of managing divorce conflict, as well as the information from the chapter, create a mock plan for future clients that you could use within a therapy session. Consider the following questions and prompts as you create your plan:

- How would knowledge of mediation and communication skills-based psychoeducation help with this presenting issue in couples work?

- How could supplemental individual therapy help your clients, individually and collectively, as they process the divorce?

- Research divorce conflict more in depth and then create a treatment plan for a couple seeking divorce therapy. Be sure to include objectives, short-term goals, and long-term goals.

ADDITIONAL RESOURCES

HELPFUL LINKS

- "Adult Attachment Relationships": https://www.aamft.org/Consumer_Updates/Adult_Attachment_Relationships.aspx

- "Fertility Issues": https://www.goodtherapy.org/learn-about-therapy/issues/infertility

- "Marital Distress": https://aamft.org/Consumer_Updates/Marital_Distress.aspx

- "Premarital Counseling": https://www.goodtherapy.org/learn-about-therapy/modes/premarital-counseling

- "What Is Financial Counseling? (+ Couples Financial Therapy)": https://positivepsychology.com/financial-counseling-couples/

- "The Benefits of Couples Therapy While Separated": https://www.verywellmind.com/benefits-of-couples-therapy-while-separated-4161245

- "Infidelity": https://aamft.org/Consumer_Updates/Infidelity.aspx

- "Addressing Intimate Partner Violence With Clients": https://ct.counseling.org/2019/06/addressing-intimate-partner-violence-with-clients/

- "Behavioral Couples Therapy for Substance Abuse: Rationale, Methods, and Findings": https://www.ncbi.nlm.nih.gov/pmc/articles/PMC2851021/

- "It's Not About Sex": https://ct.counseling.org/2011/12/its-not-about-sex/

- "Internet Addiction": https://www.goodtherapy.org/learn-about-therapy/issues/internet-addiction

HELPFUL BOOKS

- Bowlby, J. (1988). *A secure base*. Basic Books.

- Dattilio, F. M. (2010). *Cognitive behavioral therapy with couples and families: A comprehensive guide for clinicians*. Guilford Press.

- Johnson, S. M. (2008). *Hold me tight: Seven conversations for a lifetime of love*. Little Brown.
- Mendenhall, T., Lamson, A., Hodgson, J., & Baird, M. (Eds.). (2018). *Clinical methods in medical family therapy*. Springer Publishing Company.
- O'Farrell, T., & Fals-Stewart, W. (2006). *Behavioral couple therapy for alcoholism and drug abuse*. Guilford Press.

HELPFUL VIDEOS

- Couples and Infertility Psychotherapy: https://www.youtube.com/watch?v=w7Jv9ZHA4qU
- Attachment Theory in Practice: EFT With Individuals, Couples, and Families: https://www.youtube.com/watch?v=4nSAxTC4BaI
- Making Marriage Work: https://www.youtube.com/watch?v=AKTyPgwfPgg
- Infidelity: Steps to Surviving an Affair: https://www.youtube.com/watch?v=uZUZtZEeid0
- Sue Johnson Explains Attachment Theory in 9 Minutes: https://www.youtube.com/watch?v=nZrr_ckIMpU
- Couples Therapy for Addictions: A Cognitive-Behavioral Approach: https://www.youtube.com/watch?v=Ij1MVE2D4Oc
- Therapy for Domestic Abuse Survivors: https://www.youtube.com/watch?v=53waCW9ir-k
- Crisis Counseling Skills: https://www.youtube.com/watch?v=528pfiNJt7o&t=89s
- Dr. Jordan Peterson Helps a Couple on the Brink of Divorce: https://www.youtube.com/watch?v=o_mR1pIbvoY
- What You Need to Know About Internet Addiction: https://www.youtube.com/watch?v=vOSYmLER664
- Couple's Therapy and Sexual Addiction: https://www.youtube.com/watch?v=-EQAWR6n7Fs

REFERENCES

Alba-Fisch, M. (2016). Collaborative divorce: An effort to reduce the damage of divorce. *Journal of Clinical Psychology, 72*(5), 444–457. https://doi.org/10.1002/jclp.22260

Aldarondo, E., & Straus, M. A. (1994). Screening for physical violence in couple therapy: Methodological, practical, and ethical considerations. *Family Process, 33*(4), 425–439. https://doi.org/10.1111/j.1545-5300.1994.00425.x

Allen, E. S., Rhoades, G. K., Stanley, S. M., Markman, H. J., Williams, T., Melton, J., & Clements, M. L. (2008). Premarital precursors of marital infidelity. *Family Process, 47*(2), 243–259. https://doi.org/10.1111/j.1545-5300.2008.00251.x

Alsaleem, T. H. (2017). *Infidelity: The best worst thing that could happen to your marriage: The complete guide on how to heal from affairs*. Illuminare Creations.

American Association for Marriage and Family Therapy (n.d.). *Infidelity*. Retrieved April 26, 2022, from https://aamft.org/Consumer_Updates/Infidelity.aspx

American Psychiatric Association. (2022). *Diagnostic and statistical manual of mental disorders* (5th ed., text revision). https://doi.org/10.1176/appi.books.9780890425787

Amichai-Hamburger, Y., & Ben-Artzi, E. (2003). Loneliness and internet use. *Computers in Human Behavior, 19*(1), 71–80. https://doi.org/10.1016/S0747-5632(02)00014-6

Arias, E., Arce, R., & Vilariño, M. (2013). Batterer intervention programs: A meta-analytic review of effectiveness. *Psychosocial Intervention, 22*(2), 153–160. https://doi.org/10.5093/in2013a18

Association for Behavioral and Cognitive Therapies. (2021, April 8). *Marital distress: Fact sheet— ABCT—association for behavioral and cognitive therapies.* Retrieved April 26, 2022, from https:// www.abct.org/fact-sheets/marital-distress/

Association for Financial Counseling & Planning Education. (2022, April 20). *AFCPE®: For financial counselors, coaches, and educators.* Author. Retrieved April 26, 2022, from https://www .afcpe.org/

Atkins, D. C., Baucom, D. H., & Jacobson, N. S. (2001). Understanding infidelity: Correlates in a national random sample. *Journal of Family Psychology, 15*(4), 735. https://doi .org/10.1037/0893-3200.15.4.735

Barnacle, R., & Abbott, D. A. (2009). The development and evaluation of a Gottman-based premarital education program: A pilot study. *Journal of Couple & Relationship Therapy, 8*, 64–82. https://doi.org/10.1080/15332690802626734

Baucom, D. H., Shoham, V., Mueser, K. T., Daiuto, A. D., & Stickle, T. R. (1998). Empirically supported couple and family interventions for marital distress and adult mental health problems. *Journal of Consulting and Clinical Psychology, 66*(1), 53. https://doi.org/10.1037/0022 -006X.66.1.53

Beard, K. W. (2005). Internet addiction: A review of current assessment techniques and potential assessment questions. *Cyber Psychology & Behavior, 8*, 7–14. https://doi.org/10.1089/ cpb.2005.8.7

Birditt, K. S., Brown, E., Orbuch, T. L., & McIlvane, J. M. (2010). Marital conflict behaviors and implications for divorce over 16 years. *Journal of Marriage and Family, 72*(5), 1188–1204. https:// doi.org/10.1111/j.1741-3737.2010.00758.x

Black, L. L., & Flynn, S. V. (2021). *Crisis, trauma, and disaster: A clinician's guide.* Sage.

Black, M. C. (2011). Intimate partner violence and adverse health consequences: Implications for clinicians. *American Journal of Lifestyle Medicine, 5*(5), 428–439. https://doi.org/ 10.1177/1559827611410265

Blaisure, K., & Saposnek, D. (2007). Clinical update: Reducing divorce conflicts. *Family Therapy Magazine, 6*(4), 44–52.

Blaisure, K., & Saposnek, D. T. (n.d.). *Managing conflict during divorce.* American Association for Marriage and Family Therapy. Retrieved April 26, 2022, from https://aamft.org/ Consumer_Updates/Managing_Conflict_During_Divorce.aspx

Bodenmann, G. (1997). Dyadic coping—A systematic-transactional view of stress and coping among couples: Theory and empirical findings. *European Review of Applied Psychology, 47*, 137–140. https://www.zora.uzh.ch/id/eprint/63651/

Braver, S. L., Shapiro, J. R., & Goodman, M. R. (2006). Consequences of divorce for parents. In M. A. Fine & J. H. Harvey (Eds.), *Handbook of divorce and relationship dissolution* (pp. 313–337). Lawrence Erlbaum Associates.

Butters, R. P., Droubay, B. A., Seawright, J. L., Tollefson, D. R., Lundahl, B., & Whitaker, L. (2021). Intimate partner violence perpetrator treatment: Tailoring interventions to individual needs. *Clinical Social Work Journal, 49*(3), 391–404. https://doi.org/10.1007/s10615-020-00763-y

Cancio-Bello, G., & Rudes, J. (2020, July 14). The marital paradox. *Counseling Today.* https:// ct.counseling.org/2020/07/the-marital-paradox/

Carlson, R. G., Guttierrez, D., Daire, A. P., & Hall, K. (2014). Does the frequency of speaker-listener technique use influence relationship satisfaction? *Journal of Psychotherapy Integration, 24*(1), 25–29. https://doi.org/10.1037/a0035971

Carroll, J. S., & Doherty, W. J. (2003). Evaluating the effectiveness of premarital prevention programs: A meta-analytic review of outcome research. *Family Relations, 52*(2), 105–118. https:// doi.org/10.1111/j.1741-3729.2003.00105.x

Case, B. T., & Bailey, E. C. (2007). Sexual addiction and compulsivity. *Clinical Update in Family Therapy Magazine, 14*(1).

Cash, H., Rae, C. D., Steel, A. H., & Winkler, A. (2012). Internet addiction: A brief summary of research and practice. *Current Psychiatry Reviews, 8*(4), 292–298. https://doi.org/10 .2174/157340012803520513

CATS Consortium. (2007). Implementing CBT for traumatized children and adolescents after September 11: Lessons learned from the Child and Adolescent Trauma Treatments and Services (CATS) project. *Journal of Clinical Child and Adolescent Psychology, 36*(4), 581–592. https://doi .org/10.1080/15374410701662725

Chattopadhyay, S., Kumar, M., Singh, O. P., & Talukdar, P. (2020). Effect of internet addiction on marital life. *Industrial Psychiatry Journal, 29*(2), 268–271. https://doi.org/10.4103/ipj .ipj_76_19

Chen McCain, S. L., Lolli, J. C., Liu, E., & Jen, E. (2019). The relationship between casino corporate social responsibility and casino customer loyalty. *Tourism Economics, 25*(4), 569–592. https://doi.org/10.1177/1354816618808077

Chow, K.-M., Cheung, M.-C., & Cheung, I. K. M. (2016). Psychosocial interventions for infertile couples: A critical review. *Journal of Clinical Nursing, 25*(15-16), 2101–2113. https://doi.org/10.1111/jocn.13361

Collins, S., Arthur, N., & Wong-Wylie, G. (2010). Enhancing reflective practice in multicultural counseling through cultural auditing. *Journal of Counseling & Development, 88*(3), 340–347. https://doi.org/10.1002/j.1556-6678.2010.tb00031.x

Conger, R. D., Neppl, T., Kim, K. J., & Scaramella, L. (2003). Angry and aggressive behavior across three generations: A prospective, longitudinal study of parents and children. *Journal of Abnormal Child Psychology, 31*(2), 143–160. https://doi.org/10.1023/A:1022570107457

Conger, R. D., Wallace, L. E., Sun, Y., Simons, R. L., McLoyd, V. C., & Brody, G. H. (2002). Economic pressure in African American families: A replication and extension of the family stress model. *Developmental Psychology, 38*(2), 179. https://doi.org/10.1037/0012-1649.38.2.179

Cook, J. M., Schnurr, P. P., & Foa, E. B. (2004). Bridging the gap between posttraumatic stress disorder research and clinical practice: The example of exposure therapy. *Psychotherapy: Theory, Research, Practice, Training, 41*(4), 374. https://doi.org/10.1037/0033-3204.41.4.374

Cornelius, T. L., Alessi, G., & Shorey, R. C. (2007). The effectiveness of communication skills training with married couples: Does the issue discussed matter? *The Family Journal, 15*(2), 124–132. https://doi.org/10.1177/1066480706297971

Czincz, J., & Hechanova, R. (2009). Internet addiction: Debating the diagnosis. *Journal of Technology in Human Services, 27*(4), 257–272. https://doi.org/10.1080/15228830903329815

Daugherty, J., & Copen, C. (2016). Trends in attitudes about marriage, childbearing, and sexual behavior: United States, 2002, 2006–2010, and 2011–2013. *National Health Statistics Reports,* (92), 1–10. https://pubmed.ncbi.nlm.nih.gov/27019117/

Dewey, J. (1933). *How we think: A restatement of the relation of reflective thinking to the educative process.* D.C. Heath & Co.

Doherty, W. J. (2011). In or out: Treating the mixed-agenda couple. *Psychotherapy Networker, September–October,* 45–50, 58.60. https://www.semanticscholar.org/paper/In-or-out%3A-Treating-the-mixed-agenda-couple-Doherty/b5aee89a3a708cfd76d351d0379a72a1772407da

Doherty, W. J., Willoughby, B. J., & Peterson, B. (2011). Interest in marital reconciliation among divorcing parents. *Family Court Review, 49*(2), 313–321. https://doi.org/10.1111/j.1744-1617.2011.01373.x

Donarelli, Z., Kivlighan, D. M., Jr., Allegra, A., & Coco, G. L. (2016). How do individual attachment patterns of both members of couples affect their perceived infertility stress? An actor–partner interdependence analysis. *Personality and Individual Differences, 92*, 63–68. https://doi.org/10.1016/j.paid.2015.12.023

Doughty, E. A. (2009). Investigating adaptive grieving styles: A Delphi study. *Death Studies, 33*(5), 462–480. https://doi.org/10.1080/07481180902805715

Ebert, L., Amaya-Jackson, L., Markiewicz, J. M., Kisiel, C., & Fairbank, J. A. (2012). Use of the breakthrough series collaborative to support broad and sustained use of evidence-based trauma treatment for children in community practice settings. *Administration and Policy in Mental Health and Mental Health Services Research, 39*(3), 187–199. https://doi.org/10.1007/s10488-011-0347-y

Eisikovits, Z. C., & Edelson, J. L. (1989). Intervening with men who batter: A critical review of the literature. *Social Service Review, 63*, 384–414. https://doi.org/10.1086/603710

Enright, R. D., & Fitzgibbons, R. P. (2000). *Helping clients forgive: An empirical guide for resolving anger and restoring hope.* American Psychological Association.

Eysenck, H. J. (1952). The effects of psychotherapy: An evaluation. *Journal of Consulting Psychology, 16*(5), 319–324. https://doi.org/10.1037/h0063633

Eysenck, H. J. (1961). Personality and social attitudes. *The Journal of Social Psychology, 53*, 243–248. https://doi.org/10.1080/00224545.1961.9922122

Fagerström, K. O., Tejding, R., Westin, Á., & Lunell, E. (1997). Aiding reduction of smoking with nicotine replacement medications: Hope for the recalcitrant smoker? *Tobacco Control, 6*(4), 311–316. https://doi.org/10.1136/tc.6.4.311

Falconier, M. K. (2015). Together—A couples' program to improve communication, coping, and financial management skills: Development and initial pilot-testing. *Journal of Marital and Family Therapy, 41*(2), 236–250. https://doi.org/10.1111/jmft.12052

Falconier, M. K., & Epstein, N. B. (2011). Couples experiencing financial strain: What we know and what we can do. *Family Relations, 60*(3), 303–317. https://doi.org/10.1111/j.1741-3729 .2011.00650.x

Fals-Stewart, W., Lam, W. K. K., & Kelley, M. L. (2009). Behavioral couple therapy: Partner-involved treatment for substance-abusing women. In K. T. Brady, S. E. Back, & S. F. Greenfield (Eds.), *Women and addiction: A comprehensive handbook* (pp. 323–338). Guilford Press.

Finn, S. E. (2015). Therapeutic assessment with couples. *Pratiques Psychologiques, 21*(4), 345–373. https://doi.org/10.1016/j.prps.2015.09.008

Fletcher, K. (2013). Couple therapy treatments for substance use disorders: A systematic review. *Journal of Social Work Practice in the Addictions, 13*(4), 327–352. https://doi.org /10.1080/1533256X.2013.840213

Fletcher, K., & MacIntosh, H. (2018). Emotionally focused therapy in the context of addictions: A case study. *The Family Journal, 26*(3), 330–340. https://doi.org/10.1177/1066480718795125

Folger, J. P., & Bush, R. A. B. (1994). Ideology, orientations to conflict, and mediation discourse. In J. P. Folger & T. S. Jones (Eds.), *New directions in mediation: Communication research and perspectives* (pp. 3–25). Sage.

Ford, S. (2009). Is the failure to respond appropriately to a natural disaster a crime against humanity—The responsibility to protect and individual criminal responsibility in the aftermath of Cyclone Nargis. *Denver Journal of International Law and Policy, 38*, 227. https://doi .org/10.2139/ssrn.1437785

Gainsbury, S. M. (2015). Online gambling addiction: The relationship between internet gambling and disordered gambling. *Current Addiction Reports, 2*(2), 185–193. https://doi.org/10.1007/ s40429-015-0057-8

Gale, J., Goetz, J., & Bermudez, M. (2009). Relational financial therapy. *Family Therapy Magazine, 8*(5), 25–29.

Gale, J., Goetz, J., & Britt, S. (2012). Ten considerations in the development of the financial therapy profession. *Journal of Financial Therapy, 3*(2). https://doi.org/10.4148/jft.v3i2.1651

Girard, A., Connor, J. J., & Woolley, S. R. (2020). An exploratory study of the role of infidelity typologies in predicting attachment anxiety and avoidance. *Journal of Marital and Family Therapy, 46*(1), 124–134. https://doi.org/10.1111/jmft.12371

Glass, S. P. (2002). Couple therapy after the trauma of infidelity. In A. S. Gurman & N. S. Jacobson (Eds.), *Clinical handbook of couple therapy* (pp. 488–507). Guilford Press.

Glass, S. P., & Wright, T. L. (1997). *Reconstructing marriages after the trauma of infidelity*. John Wiley & Sons.

Good Therapy Team. (2018, January 6). *Affair recovery*. GoodTherapy. Retrieved April 26, 2022, from https://www.goodtherapy.org/learn-about-therapy/issues/infidelity/recovery

Gordon, K. C., Baucom, D. H., & Snyder, D. K. (2000). The use of forgiveness in marital therapy. In M. E. McCullough, K. I. Pargament, & C. E. Thoresen (Eds.), *Forgiveness: Theory, research, and practice* (pp. 203–227). Guilford Press.

Gottman, J. (1999). *The marriage clinic: A scientifically based marital therapy*. W. W. Norton & Company.

Gottman, J. M., Coan, J., Carrère, S., & Swanson, C. (1998). Predicting marital happiness and stability from newlywed interactions. *Journal of Marriage and the Family, 60*, 5–22. https://doi .org/10.2307/353438

Gottman, J. M., & Levenson, R. W. (2000). The timing of divorce: Predicting when a couple will divorce over a 14-year period. *Journal of Marriage and the Family, 62*(3), 737–745. https://doi .org/10.1111/j.1741-3737.2000.00737.x

Griffiths, M. (2000). Internet addiction—time to be taken seriously? *Addiction Research, 8*(5), 413–418. https://doi.org/10.3109/16066350009005587

Hammond, C. D. (1978). *Destructive couple communication styles*. Upper Island Assessment Resources Services.

Haney, J. M., & Hardie, L. (2014). Psychotherapeutic considerations for working with betrayed spouses: A four-task recovery model. *Australian and New Zealand Journal of Family Therapy, 35*(4), 401–413. https://doi.org/10.1002/anzf.1073

Hargrave, T. D. (2004). Families and forgiveness: A theoretical and therapeutic framework. *The Family Journal: Counseling and Therapy for Couples and Families, 2*, 339–348. https://doi .org/10.1177/1066480794024007

Hartney, E. (2020). *The 11 official criteria for addiction/substance use disorder*. Very Well Mind. https:// library.plymouth.edu/az.php

Harvey, J. H., & Fine, M. A. (2006). Social construction of accounts in the process of relationship termination. In M. A. Fine & J. H. Harvey (Eds.), *Handbook of divorce and relationship dissolution* (pp. 189–199). Psychology Press.

Hasenecz, N. M. (2010). Grandparents of children with autism—Support, caregiving, and advocacy. *Social Work Today, 10*(5), 18. https://www.socialworktoday.com/archive/092310p18.shtml

Herman, J. L. (1992). Complex PTSD: A syndrome in survivors of prolonged and repeated trauma. *Journal of Traumatic Stress, 5*(3), 377–391. https://doi.org/10.1002/jts.2490050305

Herman, J. L. (1997). *Trauma and recovery* (Rev.). BasicBooks.

Heyman, R. E., Slep, A. M. S., & Foran, H. M. (2015). Enhanced definitions of intimate partner violence for *DSM-5* and *ICD-11* may promote improved screening and treatment. *Family Process, 54*(1), 64–81. https://doi.org/10.1111/famp.12121

Hicks, M. W., McWey, L. C., Benson, K. E., & West, S. H. (2004). Using what premarital couples already know to inform marriage education: Integration of a Gottman model perspective. *Contemporary Family Therapy, 26*(1), 97–113. https://doi.org/10.1023/B:COFT.0000016915.27368.0b

Hollander, E., & Stein, D. J. (Eds.). (2006). *Clinical manual of impulse-control disorders.* American Psychiatric Association Publishing.

Hughes, B. (2012). Sexual addiction: Diagnosis and treatment in clinical practice. *BMC Proceedings, 6*(4), 1. https://doi.org/10.1186/1753-6561-6-S4-P33

Irving, H. H., & Benjamin, M. (2002). *Therapeutic family mediation: Helping families resolve conflict.* Sage.

Johnson, S. M. (2002). *Emotionally focused couple therapy with trauma survivors: Strengthening attachment bonds.* Guilford Press.

Johnson, S. M. (2019). *Attachment theory in practice: Emotionally focused therapy (EFT) with individuals, couples, and families.* Guilford Press. https://www.guilford.com/books/Attachment-Theory-in-Practice/Susan-Johnson/9781462538249

Johnson, S. M., Maddeaux, C., & Blouin, J. (1998). Emotionally focused family therapy for bulimia: Changing attachment patterns. *Psychotherapy: Theory, Research, Practice, Training, 35*(2), 238. https://doi.org/10.1037/h0087728

Johnson, S. M., Makinen, J. A., & Millikin, J. W. (2001). Attachment injuries in couple relationships: A new perspective on impasses in couples therapy. *Journal of Marital and Family Therapy, 27*(2), 145–155. https://doi.org/10.1111/j.1752-0606.2001.tb01152.x

Jong-Un, K. (2007). A reality therapy group counseling program as an internet addiction recovery method for college students in Korea. *International Journal of Reality Therapy, 26*(2), 3–9. https://www.proquest.com/scholarly-journals/reality-therapy-group-counseling-program-as/docview/214442706/se-2

Joo, S. (2008). Personal financial wellness. In J. J. Xiao (Ed.), *Handbook of consumer finance research.* Springer Nature. https://doi.org/10.1007/978-0-387-75734-6_2

Karakurt, G., Smith, D., & Whiting, J. (2014). Impact of intimate partner violence on women's mental health. *Journal of Family Violence, 29*(7), 693–702. https://doi.org/10.1007/s10896-014-9633-2

Karlin, B. E., Ruzek, J. I., Chard, K. M., Eftekhari, A., Monson, C. M., Hembree, E. A., Resick, P. A., & Foa, E. B. (2010). Dissemination of evidence-based psychological treatments for posttraumatic stress disorder in the Veterans Health Administration. *Journal of Traumatic Stress, 23*(6), 663–673. https://doi.org/10.1002/jts.20588

Kavur, M., Finlayson, A., & Cowan, R. (2020). Sexual addiction: A missed diagnosis. *Sexual Addiction & Compulsivity, 27*, 112–118. https://doi.org/10.1080/10720162.2020.1772156

Kenny, A. C. (2020, December 18). *A case for therapeutic assessment with couples.* Society for Couple and Family Psychology. https://www.apadivisions.org/division-43/publications/blog/practice/therapeutic-assessment

Kirkpatrick, L. A., & Davis, K. E. (1994). Attachment style, gender, and relationship stability: A longitudinal analysis. *Journal of Personality and Social Psychology, 66*(3), 502. https://doi.org/10.1037/0022-3514.66.3.502

Klostermann, K., & Mignone, T. (2019). Behavioral couples therapy for substance use disorders. *Social Behavior Research and Practice, 3*(1), 25–27. https://doi.org/10.17140/SBRPOJ-3-113

Kressel, K. (2007). The strategic style in mediation. *Conflict Resolution Quarterly, 24*(3), 251–283. https://doi.org/10.1002/crq.174

Kübler-Ross, E. (1970). *On death and dying.* Collier Books/Macmillan Publishing Company.

Lam, W. K. K., Fals-Stewart, W., & Kelley, M. L. (2009). Parent training with behavioral couples therapy for fathers' alcohol abuse: Effects on substance use, parental relationship, parenting, and CPS involvement. *Child Maltreatment, 14*(3), 243–254. https://doi.org/10.1177/1077559509334091

Landau-North, M., Johnson, S. M., & Dalgleish, T. L. (2011). Emotionally focused couple therapy and addiction. In J. L. Furrow, S. M. Johnson, & B. A. Bradley (Eds.), *The emotionally focused casebook: New directions in treating couples* (pp. 193–217). Routledge/Taylor & Francis Group.

Larson, J. H., Newell, K., Topham, G., & Nichols, S. (2002). A review of three comprehensive premarital assessment questionnaires. *Journal of Marital and Family Therapy, 28*(2), 233–239. https://doi.org/10.1111/j.1752-0606.2002.tb00360.x

Laughlin, C. F., & Rusca, K. A. (2020). Strengthening vicarious resilience in adult survivors of childhood sexual abuse: A narrative approach to couples therapy. *The Family Journal, 28*(1), 15–24. https://www.doi.org/10.1177/1066480719894938

Lavee, Y., & Avisar, Y. (2006). Use of standardized assessment instruments in couple therapy: The role of attitudes and professional factors. *Journal of Marital and Family Therapy, 32*(2), 233–244. https://doi.org/10.1111/j.1752-0606.2006.tb01602.x

Lebow, J. L., Chambers, A. L., Christensen, A., & Johnson, S. M. (2012). Research on the treatment of couple distress. *Journal of Marital and Family Therapy, 38*(1), 145–168. https://doi.org/10.1111/j.1752-0606.2011.00249.x

Lowe, S. R., Rhodes, J. E., & Scoglio, A. A. (2012). Changes in marital and partner relationships in the aftermath of hurricane Katrina: An analysis with low-income women. *Psychology of Women Quarterly, 36*(3), 286–300. https://doi.org/10.1177/0361684311434307

Lowry, L. R. (2004). Evaluative mediation. In J. Folberg, A. Milne, & P. Salem (Eds.), *Divorce and family mediation: Models, techniques, and applications* (pp. 72–91). Guilford Press.

Makinen, J. A., & Johnson, S. M. (2006). Resolving attachment injuries in couples using emotionally focused therapy: Steps toward forgiveness and reconciliation. *Journal of Consulting and Clinical Psychology, 74*(6), 1055. https://doi.org/10.1037/0022-006X.74.6.1055

Markman, H. J., & Rhoades, G. K. (2012). Relationship education research: Current status and future directions. *Journal of Marital and Family Therapy, 38*(1), 169–200. https://doi.org/10.1111/j.1752-0606.2011.00247.x

Markman, H. J., Stanley, S. M., & Blumberg, S. L. (2010). *Fighting for your marriage: A deluxe revised edition of the classic best-seller for enhancing marriage and preventing divorce.* Jossey-Bass.

McBain, T. D., & Reeves, P. (2019). Women's experience of infertility and disenfranchised grief. *The Family Journal, 27*(2), 156–166. https://doi.org/10.1177/1066480719833418

Messing, J. T., Ward-Lasher, A., Thaller, J., & Bagwell-Gray, M. E. (2015). The state of intimate partner violence intervention: Progress and continuing challenges. *Social Work, 60*(4), 305–313. https://doi.org/10.1093/sw/swv027

Mikulincer, M. (1998). Attachment working models and the sense of trust: An exploration of interaction goals and affect regulation. *Journal of Personality and Social Psychology, 74*(5), 1209. https://doi.org/10.1037/0022-3514.74.5.1209

Miller, M., Drake, E., & Nafziger, M. (2013, January). *What works to reduce recidivism by domestic violence offenders?* (Document No. 13-01-1201). Washington State Institute for Public Policy.

Miller, N. H. (2010). Motivational interviewing as a prelude to coaching in healthcare settings. *Journal of Cardiovascular Nursing, 25*(3), 247–251. https://doi.org/10.1097/JCN.0b013e3181cec6e7

Morrissette, P. J. (2010). Couples at the crossroads: Substance abuse and intimate relationship deliberation. *The Family Journal, 18*(2), 146–153. https://doi.org/10.1177/1066480710364476

Murphy, C. M., & Eckhardt, C. I. (2005). *Treating the abusive partner: An individualized cognitive-behavioral approach.* Guilford Press.

Muusses, L. D., Kerkhof, P., & Finkenauer, C. (2015). Internet pornography and relationship quality: A longitudinal study of within and between partner effects of adjustment, sexual satisfaction and sexually explicit internet material among newly-weds. *Computers in Human Behavior, 45*, 77–84. https://doi.org/10.1016/j.chb.2014.11.077

National Center for Chronic Disease Prevention and Health Promotion. (2015). *Excessive alcohol use: Preventing a leading risk for death, chronic disease, and injury.* Centers for Disease Control and Prevention.

National Center on Domestic and Sexual Violence. (2014). *Power and Control Wheel.* https://www.thehotline.org/identify-abuse/power-and-control/

Neimeyer, R. A., Prigerson, H. G., & Davies, B. (2002). Mourning and meaning. *American Behavioral Scientist, 46*(2), 235–251. https://doi.org/10.1177/000276402236676

O'Farrell, T. J., & Clements, K. (2012). Review of outcome research on marital and family therapy in treatment for alcoholism. *Journal of Marital and Family Therapy, 38*(1), 122–144. https://doi.org/10.1111/j.1752-0606.2011.00242.x

O'Hara, S. (2012). *How are female sex addicts different than males?* PsychCentral. https://psychcentral.com/blog/how-are-female-sex-addicts-different-from-males#1

O'Leary, K. D., Barling, J., Arias, I., Rosenbaum, A., Malone, J., & Tyree, A. (1989). Prevalence and stability of physical aggression between spouses: A longitudinal analysis. *Journal of Consulting and Clinical Psychology, 57*(2), 263. https://doi.org/10.1037/0022-006X.57.2.263

Orzack, M. H., & Orzack, D. S. (1999). Treatment of computer addicts with complex co-morbid psychiatric disorders. *CyberPsychology & Behavior, 2*(5), 465–473. https://doi.org/10.1089/cpb.1999.2.465

Pence, E., & Paymar, M. (1993). *Education groups for men who batter: The Duluth model.* Springer Publishing Company.

Pender, R. L. (2012). ASGW best practice guidelines: An evaluation of the Duluth model. *The Journal for Specialists in Group Work, 37*(3), 218–231. https://doi.org/10.1080/01933922.2011.632813

Petersen, K. U., Weymann, N., Schelb, Y., Thiel, R., & Thomasius, R. (2009). Pathologischer Internetgebrauch–Epidemiologie, Diagnostik, komorbide Störungen und Behandlungsansätze [Pathological internet use—Epidemiology, diagnostics, co-occurring disorders and treatment]. *Fortschritte der Neurologie-Psychiatrie, 77*(5), 263–271. https://doi.org/10.1055/s-0028-1109361

Peukert, P., Sieslack, S., Barth, G., & Batra, A. (2010). Internet- und Computerspielabhängigkeit: Phänomenologie, Komorbidität, Ätiologie, Diagnostik und therapeutische Implikationen für Betroffene und Angehörige [Internet- and computer game addiction: Phenomenology, comorbidity, etiology, diagnostics and therapeutic implications for the addictives and their relatives]. *Psychiatrische Praxis, 37*(5), 219–224. https://doi.org/10.1055/s-0030-1248442

Phillips, L. (2020, April 1). Recovering from the trauma of infidelity. *Counseling Today.* https://ct.counseling.org/2020/04/recovering-from-the-trauma-of-infidelity/

Pittman, F. S., III, & Wagers, T. P. (2005). Teaching fidelity. *Journal of Clinical Psychology, 61*(11), 1407–1419. https://doi.org/10.1002/jclp.20190

Pollock, G. (2014). Sarah Kofman's father's pen and Bracha Ettinger's mother's spoon: Trauma, transmission and the strings of virtuality. In P. Harvey, E. Casella, G. Evans, H. Knox, C. McLean, E. B. Silva, N. Thoburn, & K. Woodward (Eds.), *Objects and materials* (pp. 180–190). Routledge.

Prins, K. S., Buunk, B. P., & VanYperen, N. W. (1993). Equity, normative disapproval and extramarital relationships. *Journal of Social and Personal Relationships, 10*(1), 39–53. https://doi.org/10.1177/0265407593101003

Pruett, M. K., & Johnston, J. R. (2004). *Therapeutic mediation with high-conflict parents: Effective models and strategies.* Guilford Press.

Przybylski, A. K., & Weinstein, N. (2017). A large-scale test of the goldilocks hypothesis: Quantifying the relations between digital-screen use and the mental well-being of adolescents. *Psychological Science, 28*(2), 204–215. https://doi.org/10.1177/0956797616678438

Ravi, K. E., & Black, B. M. (2022). The relationship between children's exposure to intimate partner violence and an emotional–behavioral disability: A scoping review. *Trauma, Violence, & Abuse, 23*(3), 868–876. https://doi.org/10.1177/1524838020979846

Reeves, A., Stuckler, D., McKee, M., Gunnell, D., Chang, S. S., & Basu S. (2012). Increase in state suicide rates in the USA during economic recession. *Lancet, 38,* 1813–1814. https://doi.org/10.1016/S0140-6736(12)61910-2

Richardson, T., Elliott, P., & Roberts, R. (2013). The relationship between personal unsecured debt and mental and physical health: A systematic review and meta-analysis. *Clinical Psychology Review, 33*(8), 1148–1162. https://doi.org/10.1016/j.cpr.2013.08.009

Rogers, S. J., & Amato, P. R. (1997). Is marital quality declining? The evidence from two generations. *Social Forces, 75*(3), 1089–1100. https://doi.org/10.2307/2580532

Rosin, J. (2015). The necessity of counselor individuation for fostering reflective practice. *Journal of Counseling & Development, 93*(1), 88–95. https://doi.org/10.1002/j.1556-6676.2015.00184.x

Ruff, S., McComb, J. L., Coker, C. J., & Sprenkle, D. H. (2010). Behavioral couples therapy for the treatment of substance abuse: A substantive and methodological review of O'Farrell, Fals-Stewart, and colleagues' program of research. *Family Process, 49*(4), 439–456. https://doi.org/10.1111/j.1545-5300.2010.01333.x

Sbarra, D. A., & Emery, R. E. (2006). In the presence of grief: The role of cognitive-emotional adaptation in contemporary mediation. In M. A. Fine & J. H. Harvey (Eds.), *Handbook of divorce and relationship dissolution* (pp. 553–602). Taylor and Francis.

Schwartz, M., & Southern, S. (2017). Recovery from sexual compulsivity. *Sexual Addiction & Compulsivity, 24,* 224–240. https://doi.org/10.1080/10720162.2017.1350229

Servaty-Seib, H. L. (2004). Connections between counseling theories and current theories of grief and mourning. *Journal of Mental Health Counseling, 26*(2), 125–145. https://doi.org/10.17744/mehc.26.2.p9aukha7v8fqkc9g

Shackleford, W. P., Proctor, F. M., & Michaloski, J. L. (2000). *The neutral message language: A model and method for message passing in heterogeneous environments.* National Institute of Standards and Technology. https://tsapps.nist.gov/publication/get_pdf.cfm?pub_id=823366

Shaw, G., Whelan, M. E., Armitage, L. C., Roberts, N., & Farmer, A. J. (2020). Are COPD self-management mobile applications effective? A systematic review and meta-analysis. *NPJ Primary Care Respiratory Medicine, 30*(1), 1–10. https://doi.org/10.1038/s41533-020-0167-1

Shimoni, L., Dayan, M., Cohen, K., & Weinstein, A. (2018). The contribution of personality factors and gender to ratings of sex addiction among men and women who use the internet for sex purpose. *Journal of Behavioral Addictions, 7*(4), 1015–1021. https://doi.org/10.1556/2006.7.2018.101

Simpson, J. A., & Rholes, W. S. (1994). Stress and secure base relationships in adulthood. In K. Bartholomew & D. Perlman (Eds.), *Attachment processes in adulthood* (pp. 181–204). Jessica Kingsley Publishers.

Sluzki, C. E. (1992). Transformations: A blueprint for narrative changes in therapy. *Family Process, 31*(3), 217–230. https://doi.org/10.1111/j.1545-5300.1992.00217.x

Stahmann, R. F., & Salts, C. J. (1993). Educating for marriage and intimate relationships. In M. E. Arcus, J. D. Schvanevedlt, & J. J. Moss (Eds.), *The handbook for family life education* (Vol. 2, pp. 33–61). Sage.

Stanley, S. M. (2001). Making a case for premarital education. *Family Relations, 50*(3), 272–280. https://doi.org/10.1111/j.1741-3729.2001.00272.x

Stith, S. M., McCollum, E. E., & Rosen, K. H. (2011). *Couples therapy for domestic violence: Finding safe solutions* (Vol. 278). American Psychological Association.

Stith, S. M., & Rosen, K. H. (2005). Intimate partner violence. In R. H. Coombs (Ed.), *Family therapy review: Preparing for comprehensive and licensing examinations* (pp. 301–321). Lawrence Erlbaum Associates.

Stroebe, M. S. (2002). Paving the way: From early attachment theory to contemporary bereavement research. *Mortality, 7*(2), 127–138. https://doi.org/10.1080/13576270220136267

True, W. R., Rice, J., Eisen, S. A., Heath, A. C., Goldberg, J., Lyons, M. J., & Nowak, J. (1993). A twin study of genetic and environmental contributions to liability for posttraumatic stress symptoms. *Archives of General Psychiatry, 50*(4), 257–264. https://doi.org/10.1001/archpsyc.1993.01820160019002

Tsapelas, I., Fisher, H. E., & Aron, A. (2011). Infidelity: When, where, why. In W. R. Cupach & B. H. Spitzberg (Eds.), *The dark side of close relationships II* (pp. 175–195). Routledge/Taylor & Francis Group.

Twohig, M. P., & Crosby, J. M. (2010). Acceptance and commitment therapy as a treatment for problematic internet pornography viewing. *Behavior Therapy, 41*(3), 285–295. https://doi.org/10.1016/j.beth.2009.06.002

Van der Kolk, B. A. (2005). Developmental. *Psychiatric Annals, 35*(5), 401. https://doi.org/10.3928/00485713-20050501-06

Wang, Q. Q., Kaelber, D. C., Xu, R., & Volkow, N. D. (2021). COVID-19 risk and outcomes in patients with substance use disorders: Analyses from electronic health records in the United States. *Molecular Psychiatry, 26*(1), 30–39. https://doi.org/10.1038/s41380-020-00880-7

Weeks, G. R., & Fife, S. T. (2014). *Couples in treatment: Techniques and approaches for effective practice.* Routledge.

Weinstein, A., Katz, L., Eberhardt, H., Cohen, K., & Lejoyeux, M. (2015). Sexual compulsion—Relationship with sex, attachment and sexual orientation. *Journal of Behavioral Addictions, 4*(1), 22–26. https://doi.org/10.1556/JBA.4.2015.1.6

Weisz, A. N., Tolman, R. M., & Saunders, D. G. (2000). Assessing the risk of severe domestic violence: The importance of survivors' predictions. *Journal of Interpersonal Violence, 15*(1), 75–90. https://doi.org/10.1177/088626000015001006

Wéry, A., & Billieux, J. (2017). Problematic cybersex: Conceptualization, assessment, and treatment. *Addictive Behaviors, 64*, 238–246. https://doi.org/10.1016/j.addbeh.2015.11.007

Widyanto, L., & Griffiths, M. (2006). "Internet addiction": A critical review. *International Journal of Mental Health and Addiction, 4*(1), 31–51. https://doi.org/10.1007/s11469-006-9009-9

Wiederman, M. W. (1997). Extramarital sex: Prevalence and correlates in a national survey. *The Journal of Sex Research, 34*(2), 167–174. https://doi.org/10.1080/00224499709551881

Wiederman, M. W., & Hurd, C. (1999). Extradyadic involvement during dating. *Journal of Social and Personal Relationships, 16*(2), 265–274. https://doi.org/10.1177/0265407599162008

Williston, S. K., Taft, C. T., & VanHaasteren, K. O. (2015). Military veteran perpetrators of intimate partner violence: Challenges and barriers to coordinated intervention. *Aggression and Violent Behavior, 21*, 55–60. https://doi.org/10.1016/j.avb.2015.01.008

Wölfling, K., Bühler, M., Lemenager, T., Mörsen, C., & Mann, K. (2009). Gambling and internet addiction: Review and research agenda. *Der Nervenarzt, 80*(9), 1030–1039. https://doi.org/10.1007/s00115-009-2741-1

Wood, J. (2010). *Why have sex? A cross sectional investigation of the reasons men and women engage in sex within heterosexual couple relationships* [Unpublished doctoral dissertation]. University of Guelph.

Yehuda, R., McFarlane, A., & Shalev, A. (1998). Predicting the development of posttraumatic stress disorder from the acute response to a traumatic event. *Biological Psychiatry, 44*(12), 1305–1313. https://doi.org/10.1016/S0006-3223(98)00276-5

Young, K. S. (1999). Internet addiction: Evaluation and treatment. *BMJ, 319*(S4). https://doi.org/10.1136/sbmj.9910351

Young, K. S., & de Abreu, C. N. (2011). *Internet addiction: A handbook and guide to evaluation and treatment.* John Wiley & Sons.

Zimmerman, E. R. (2018). Preoccupied attachment as predictor of enabling behavior: Clinical implications and treatment for partners of substance abusers. *Clinical Social Work Journal, 46*, 48–56. https://doi.org/10.1007/s10615-018-0645-x

CHAPTER 8

CONTEMPORARY ISSUES IN FAMILY THERAPY

LEARNING OBJECTIVES

After reading this chapter, you will be able to:

- ■ Identify trends in U.S. family life.
- ■ Distinguish what a contemporary family is like.
- ■ Identify racism and intersectionality in family practice.
- ■ Describe family cohesion and flexibility.
- ■ Identify issues relevant to blended families and stepfamilies.
- ■ Recognize contemporary issues related to multiracial families.
- ■ Identify the effect of obesity on families.
- ■ Recognize contemporary practices of parenting.
- ■ Identify family issues reflecting the influence of the internet.
- ■ Recognize the nuances of child abuse and neglect.
- ■ Recognize the issues that arise when grandparents are raising grandchildren.
- ■ Distinguish the challenges involved in grieving the death of a child.

INTRODUCTION TO CONTEMPORARY ISSUES IN FAMILY PRACTICE

The contemporary family is constantly changing. This section reviews some of the latest U.S. family-oriented statistics gathered by leading U.S. government organizations. Please note that this information reflects a range of years, and due to sampling issues and how the government defines certain constructs (e.g., family, household) the explicated percentages may appear to be in error. Having two married parents residing in the same house was the norm in America for many generations; however, according to the U.S. Census Bureau (2021c), 25% of all children now reside in single-parent households. This percentage is three times the percentage of U.S. families headed by single parents during the 1960s (U.S. Census Bureau, 2021c). Similarly, blended families (i.e., families with stepparents, stepsiblings, or half-siblings) comprise approximately 40% of all married couples in the United States. This statistic is even more pronounced for families in certain communities of color. For example, 60% of U.S. Black/African Americans live in stepfamily structures (Stewart & Limb, 2020).

Modern families have a broad range of incomes and expenditures. According to the 2021 U.S. Census, 24% of U.S. children were raised in families that had a stay-at-home mother, and 1% of U.S. children were raised by stay-at-home fathers (U.S. Census Bureau, 2021b). According to the U.S. Department of Housing and Urban Development, the national median family income in the United States in 2021 was $79,900, which represents an increase over the national median family income in 2020 of $78,500. Families that decide to raise children are engaging in an expensive endeavor. According to the Lino et al. (2017), the average family spends approximately $13,000 annually per child. By the time a child reaches 18 years of age, this equates to a quarter million dollars of expenditures per child.

The latest U.S. Census Bureau report (2021a) indicated that 37 million adults (15%) 18 years of age and over live alone. Furthermore, the percentage of adults living with an unmarried partner has increased 7% to 8% over the past 10 years. In 2021, 50% of all U.S. adults lived with a spouse. This was a decrease from 2020's statistic of 52% (U.S. Census Bureau, 2021a). According to the Centers for Disease Control and Prevention (CDC), the median income for families led by a single mother in 2019 was approximately $48,098. This was well below the 2019 median income of $102,308 for married couples. Regarding the decision to get married, in 2021 34% of adults 15 years of age and over were unmarried. This percentage was very high compared with 1950, when 23% of adults were unmarried. Similarly, in 1947 the estimated median age to marry for the first time was 23.7 for men and 20.5 for women. In 2021, the median age of marriage has risen to 30.4 for men and 28.6 for women (U.S. Census Bureau, 2021a).

Defining a Family

Attempting to define what constitutes a family can be a difficult and contentious task. Culturally bound family definitions can influence access to resources such as education, insurance, and mental healthcare, and family definitions have implications for what types of behavior are considered socially acceptable versus abnormal. In some circumstances, governments will provide a definition of family. For example, the U.S. Census Bureau (n.d., para. 22) defines a *family* as ". . . a group of two people or more (one of whom is the householder) related by birth, marriage, or adoption and residing together." Similar to governments, organizations can create their own definitions of family. The National Center for Cultural Competence (2007) provided a more diverse, culturally sensitive, and nuanced definition: "Family is an enduring relationship, whether biological or non-biological, chosen or circumstantial, connecting a child/youth and parent/caregiver through culture, tradition, shared experiences, emotional commitment and mutual support" (para. 4). While these definitions have their strengths, it is important to emphasize that a same-sex or opposite-sex couple that live together, are married, or are engaged in some form of cohabitation agreement constitutes a family. In other words, while children can make wonderful additions to a family, they are not a necessary component of a family.

Anthropologists and sociologists have long discussed and debated the proper way to describe a family and its relationship to society. Early definitions and descriptions were centered on the normative and widespread utilization of a family in every culture.

For example, in 1949 American anthropologist George P. Murdock described the family as *universal*. Murdock described the four key functions of a family as economic, sexual, reproductive, and educational. The universality of a family is further emphasized by the fact that families are found in more societies than any other social unit (e.g., religious communities, education organizations). Murdock (1949) added to his theory by hypothesizing that societies are created and maintained by families, and without the family unit societies would not exist and/or thrive.

Even though a family is the vital social unit of most human societies, today the shape and composition of this system vary widely. While classic definitions of family comprise parents and children, contemporary definitions are much more inclusive. Today, a family could be a couple, single-parent household, blended family, biracial family, LGBTQIA+ parents and children, single parents pursuing biological family building, grandparents raising grandchildren, individuals or groups of people with household pets, and people who are not related by birth or marriage. Plenty of people consider their friendship group to be family, while others simply add supportive nonrelatives to their family as they choose. It seems that (a) personal choice, (b) acceptance of diversity and intersectionality, (c) flexibility in who takes on various roles, and (d) use of modern technology are important aspects of the 21st-century family.

UNDERSTANDING HOW RACISM AND INTERSECTIONALITY AFFECT FAMILIES

The recent and tragic deaths of people of color such as Trayvon Martin (1995–2012), Michael Brown (1996–2014), Eric Garner (1970–2014), Breonna Taylor (1993–2020), George Floyd (1973–2020), and countless others sparked one of the largest nationwide protests in history centered on ending racial inequality, systemic racism, police brutality and violence, and inequity. Conversations about race, ethnicity, gender, gender identity, sexual orientation, religion, and culture are taking place around the world. While macro-level protests, demonstrations, social movements, media campaigns, calls for criminal justice reform, and sociopolitical agendas are pushing forward important cultural change, family units are coping with the macro-political issues at home in their own unique ways.

Given the fact that systemic inequality (e.g., employment, housing, and healthcare inequality) and racism (e.g., police profiling and brutality) continue to affect communities of color in the United States, Dana-Ain Davis (2020) described the clinical responsibility of checking in with parents of young children around the significance of vital parent–child conversations related to racism, privilege, and implicit bias. These conversations are both important and healing, as encounters with racism, discrimination, and hatred can harm a child's physical and psychological well-being (Tatum, 2017; Tran, 2014). Davis suggested that helping children process their feelings and thoughts related to events covered in the news media can temper the effects of racial trauma and/or poor emotional outcomes. Socialization regarding racial and ethnic bias usually occurs within family units when caregivers/parents of color initiate what is often referred to as *the talk* (Hughes et al., 2006). This parent–child interaction typically happens more than once and often includes a discussion of how to cope with racism, discrimination, hatred, and inequity (Rotheran & Phinney, 1987). For example, following racially charged police-related violence, investigations into family dynamics revealed that Black caregivers have important conversations with their children regarding specific homicides (Thomas & Blackmon, 2015; Threlfall, 2016). In comparison, White caregivers have been found to be less likely to engage in race-related conversations with their children and often default to a problematic colorblindness (i.e., "race is irrelevant") philosophy (Loyd & Gaither, 2018; Pahlke et al., 2012).

Individuals with happy and healthy social lives tend to live longer and experience less wear and tear than those with strenuous and less supportive relationships. When society targets and discriminates against a particular population of people, a ripple effect spreads throughout families and affects all of their relationships. For communities of color experiencing daily bombardments of microaggressions, racism, oppression, hatred, and lack of equity, there can be significant distress ranging from emotionality over hurtful microaggressions to full-blown posttraumatic stress disorder (PTSD) from overt racism and discrimination. In addition to experiencing adverse mental health consequences, when communities of color are constantly threatened their experiences can manifest as negative physical health issues (e.g., heavy allostasis load, hypertension, high blood pressure, enlarged heart, and damage to the heart, kidneys, and other organs of the body; Black & Flynn, 2021; Greenberg, 2020; McEwen & Stellar, 1993) as well as negative family functioning.

According to Buck and Neff (2012), stress spillover occurs when an individual absorbs hurtful, racist, and derogatory comments throughout their daily life, and the negative and stressful emotions spill over to affect their family and other important relationships. The relational consequences of spillover can range from spousal and parent–child arguments and criticism to intimate partner violence and child abuse and neglect (Doyle & Molix, 2014). In addition, Priest and colleagues found that Black American adults who experienced racial discrimination suffered from increased family strain and decreased family support, and inadequate levels of family support, empathy, and connection led to physical and mental health problems (Priest et al., 2020).

Neighborhoods, police, educational institutions, and employment all look very different when one is not part of a culture's privileged and/or dominant population. Instead of experiencing police as supportive and positive protectors of the common good, there can be fear and suspicion that police are out to punish, arrest, and imprison anyone who is not part of the privileged social class. While children who belong to the dominant/privileged culture may experience history class as a factual timeline of historical events, children of color may demonstrate various degrees of mistrust in what is being described in class due to cultural bias, racist societal underpinnings, and their own family-based ethnic/racial socialization process. When looking for employment, most White people assume that there is a normative wage range associated with certain types of work and levels of experience, while communities of color often fear they are being paid less due to the color of their skin.

Systemic racism (i.e., structural racism) is extremely insidious and creates social and health determinants that negatively affect communities of color at the neighborhood, economic, educational, and healthcare levels. Systemically speaking, all of these social factors spill over and reverberate throughout the family. Communities of color often live in neighborhoods that suffer from *socioeconomic deprivation*. This deprivation includes relatively low social standing (e.g., high unemployment rate), substandard physical value (e.g., low-income houses for sale, graffiti), and low economic status (e.g., low educational level, low income level) of the neighborhoods in which they reside (Galobardes et al., 2007). Beyond the neighborhood, communities of color often experience *economic inequality*—being trapped in perpetual poverty with no known way of escaping. Inequality includes the uneven distribution of money and wage growth in a culture, with disparities negatively affecting communities of color (e.g., unequal pay, unaffordable healthcare, no retirement options; Gould, 2020). Ethnic and racial *educational disparities* occur when children of certain communities of color consistently score lower than average on standardized tests (e.g., reading and math), have high rates of school dropout and/or failure to graduate, have a much lower percentage involved in gifted and/or talented programs, and have a high percentage of negative behavioral markers (e.g., frequent detention, suspension, and expulsion; American Psychological Association, 2012). Lastly, *differential access to healthcare* encompasses gaps in access, quality, and affordability of medical care. According to Riley (2012),

> [a]s a nation, we have an abundance of healthcare facilities, cutting edge technologies, and pharmacotherapeutics and other assets that are the envy of the world, but which are not accessible for a myriad of reasons to all segments of the population (p. 167).

Intersectionality

Systemically oriented therapists frequently consider the multiplicity of any human experience. Dimensions of multiplicity reflect the interplay of power and oppression within relationships. Families that come in for treatment have different relational structures with various degrees of mutually reinforcing privilege and oppression. From a family context perspective, families differ in size, composition, cultural beliefs, values, acculturation, membership criteria, sex, gender, ethnicity, race, sexuality, expression of gender, ability, and religious affiliation. When there is a disruption or change within the various family contextual factors, there can be a reverberation that creates change in various familial relationships. Contemporary literature has explored the nature of intersectionality as a method for understanding the intricate and overlapping ways in which identity, disparity, and social justice come together to demonstrate unique sources of privilege and oppression (Curtis et al., 2020). While it is extremely important to understand singular variables that create a sense of oppression, inequity, and marginalization (e.g., living in a sexist society and being a woman, living in a racist society and being non-White), it is helpful to glean a comprehensive understanding of multiple intersections affecting an individual and/or family. For example, this could include understanding the interaction between race, sexuality, religion, and gender in comprehending one's cultural experience with privilege and oppression.

There are challenges in viewing separate aspects of an individual's identity in isolation. Chantler (2005) described the concern with creating false contextually oppressive hierarchies in relationships (e.g., paying attention to gender while ignoring race). Intersectionality emphasizes the complexity of multiple combinations of power and oppression in relationships. For example, let's say a family comprises two opposite-sex parents/partners who identify as a Black man and a Hispanic woman. Now let's imagine the couple has two biological female children. One of the children has been diagnosed with a learning disability. As one can see from this example, the family has various intersections of privilege and oppression. On the privileged side of things, the couple benefits from their sexual orientation (i.e., heteronormativity), their ability to conceive biological children (i.e., bias against those with infertility issues), and their use of a culturally accepted relational contract (i.e., marriage). In addition, the man benefits from the privilege of living in a patriarchal culture. From the perspective of oppressive contextual variables, both spouses represent marginalized communities of color (i.e., racism and discrimination), the wife and children are oppressed as a result of the sexist/patriarchal culture (i.e., sexism), and the daughter diagnosed with a learning disability is further disenfranchised for having a disability (i.e., ableism).

FAMILY COHESION AND FLEXIBILITY

Couple, marriage, and family practitioners have sought to establish empirical credibility for understanding, assessing, and treating families. It would be incomplete to discuss research on family systems without discussing the prominence and importance of Olson's circumplex model. The circumplex model of marital and family systems, which is referred to as the circumplex model throughout this section, was developed in 1979 by David H. Olson and associates to understand family functioning using the dimensions of relational flexibility and cohesion (Franklin et al., 2001). In general, this model conceptualizes flexibility, cohesion, and communication as the basic blueprints for all family interactions (Olson, 2000). The circumplex model is empirically supported by more than 1,200 studies conducted over approximately 40 years (Olson, 2011). Because of the salience of the circumplex model, the prevalence of its dimensions, and the model's connection to basic family systems, it is always an important contemporary consideration for practitioners serving families, parents, couples, and children.

The key aspect of the circumplex model is family adaptability. When family and couple/marital systems form, the members cocreate power structures, roles, and relationship rules in response to situational and developmental influences and stressors. Adaptability is centered on the ability of a family system to balance flexibility and stability over time. Systems that have unhealthy high levels of change are labeled chaotic, while systems with low ability to change are called rigid. According to the model's founder, "balanced levels of cohesion and flexibility are most conducive to healthy family adaptability. Conversely, unbalanced levels of *cohesion* and *flexibility* (very low or very high levels) are associated with problematic family functioning" (Olson, 2011, p. 65).

You may be asking yourself, "What is meant by family flexibility?" That is a great question. In general, *family flexibility* refers to the amount of role and rule change that is possible in a family system (see Table 8.1). Remember that flexibility is not about having too much or too little flexibility; it is about maintaining a balance. In other words, both stability and change are needed in healthy couple and family relationships. The ability to allow for change and/or stability when needed is what creates healthy family structures. When a family system is too rigid (i.e., lacking flexibility), family members will have difficulty adjusting and responding to normative change. They essentially cling or remain loyal to an outdated or ineffective style of behaving. This change could be developmentally oriented (e.g., emergence of adolescence and family inability to adjust

TABLE 8.1 CIRCUMPLEX MODEL FLEXIBILITY DIMENSIONS

Dimension	Leadership	Discipline	Role Structure	Level of Change
Chaotic (unbalanced)	No leadership	Erratic	Severe role-shifting	Frequent changes
Flexible (balanced)	Shared leadership	Democratic	Role-sharing	Change when needed
Structured (balanced)	Occasionally shared	Quasi-democratic	Stable roles	Change when demanded
Rigid (unbalanced)	Authoritarian	Strict	Roles rarely change	Rarely changes

Sources: Data from Olson, D. H. (2000). Circumplex model of marital and family systems. *Journal of Family Therapy, 22*(2), 144–167. https://doi.org/10.1111/1467-6427.00144; Olson, D. (2011). Faces IV and the circumplex model: Validation study. *Journal of Marital and Family Therapy, 37*(1), 64–80. https://doi.org/10.1111/j.1752-0606.2009.00175.x.

rules), imposed from the outside (e.g., in denial about a spouse being fired from their job), or may emerge internally within individual family members (e.g., a child demonstrates issues related to a learning disability and the family does not accept or seek school-based assistance). On the other hand, too much flexibility can create a sense of chaos. Chaos occurs when a family has no firm stance or shared agreements that govern their actions. For example, child punishments change based on how the caregiver feels rather than on a set of rules or family expectations. While some flexibility is helpful, all families thrive when they have healthy standards and traditions. Overall, the circumplex model postulates that flexibly structured families find a healthy balance between rigidity and chaos with regard to their rules and roles (Olson, 2000, 2011).

The next logical question is "What is meant by family cohesion?" *Family cohesion* has been described as the emotional connection (i.e., bonding) that family members have with one another (Olson et al., 1982). Family cohesion is further assessed by the degree and types of connections between members, the nature of boundaries within the family, and the extent to which members have shared interests (see Table 8.2). To maintain family health, there needs to be a balanced level of cohesion. In general, this involves independence and togetherness. Too much cohesion can result in *enmeshment*, which equates to extreme levels of closeness, dependence, and a lack of personal identity and boundaries. Enmeshed families require an extreme amount of loyalty and provide little opportunity for disagreement, private space, or relationships outside of the family system. Families that demonstrate too much separateness (i.e., lack of cohesion) are *disengaged*. The members of these families are distant, avoidant of closeness, and focused on their own activities and experiences. There is little loyalty or commitment to family interests, and members do not depend on each other or take responsibility for each other. Optimal family cohesion is exhibited when families have a balance between separateness (e.g., individual interests, desires, goals) and connectedness (e.g., caring, family loyalty, traditions, family interest). In short, an optimal level of family cohesion falls between family disengagement and enmeshment (Olson, 2000, 2011).

Communication is the third dimension of the circumplex model, and Olson (2000, 2011) views communication as a potential facilitator of family flexibility and cohesion. The two types of communication that are included in this model are positive communication skills and negative communication skills. Olson considers positive communication to be centered on using empathy, reflective listening, supportive comments, and

TABLE 8.2 CIRCUMPLEX MODEL COHESION DIMENSIONS

Dimension	Nature of I–We	Closeness	Degree of Loyalty	Dependence
Disengaged (unbalanced)	I	Distant	Very little loyalty	Independence
Separated (balanced)	I–We	Low/intermediate closeness	Low/intermediate loyalty	Interdependence (higher independence)
Connected (balanced)	I–We	Intermediate/high closeness	High loyalty	Interdependence (higher dependence)
Enmeshed (unbalanced)	We	Very high closeness	Very high loyalty	High dependence

Sources: Data from Olson, D. H. (2000). Circumplex model of marital and family systems. *Journal of Family Therapy*, 22(2), 144–167. https://doi.org/10.1111/1467-6427.00144; Olson, D. (2011). Faces IV and the circumplex model: Validation study. *Journal of Marital and Family Therapy*, 37(1), 64–80. https://doi.org/10.1111/j.1752-0606.2009.00175.x.

sharing of family members' changing needs and preferences. All of these skills are aimed at maintaining balanced family cohesion and flexibility. Negative communication skills might include double messages, criticism, defensiveness, and minimizing other family members' ability to share their feelings and thoughts. Olson described negative communication as something that decreases balanced family cohesion and flexibility.

One assumption that the circumplex model relies upon is that families go through cycles of change in response to shifts and adjustments in daily life, different environmental challenges, and specific needs of family members. For example, a couple's relationship changes when a baby arrives, a teenager must be parented differently from an 8-year-old child, and when children leave the nest there will likely be a new level of closeness between the couple/parents. Furthermore, the circumplex model helps families understand and engage in first-order change (i.e., behavioral level) and second-order change (i.e., changes in the system's rules; Becvar & Becvar, 2013). Effective families surrender to the notion that change must occur at certain junctures. Some of this change may be superficial or behavioral (i.e., first-order change). For example, two sisters frequently argue and have a sense of hostility toward each other. To stop the arguing and hostility, they decide to stop discussing areas of disagreement and begin spending more time alone in their rooms. This example showcases a first-order change (behavioral) in which the arguing stops, but the sisters likely still harbor hostility toward each other. Family change can, at times, be deep-rooted and geared toward rule change (i.e., second-order change). While it seems like first- and second-order changes are different and separate, they often work in tandem. Specifically, first-order change often sets the stage for the more sustainable second-order change. A second-order change that could emerge from the previously showcased first-order change scenario could be the following example: While the sisters are in their separate rooms, one sister begins texting silly images to the other sister and they both laugh. This creates a new series of systemic changes, including frequent texting, conversations centered on fun and teasing, and deeper discussions about life. Simultaneously, for the time being, the sisters are no longer arguing or harboring hurtful feelings toward each other (Olson, 2000, 2011; Olson et al., 1982).

BLENDED AND STEPFAMILIES

According to the Pew Research Center (2015), recent Census Bureau data indicate that 16% of U.S. children are living in blended families. In addition, in 2011, 42% of Americans indicated that they have close step relationships (Pew Research Center, 2015). Blended families have become culturally normative. According to *Oxford Advanced Learner's Dictionary* (n.d.), *blended families* are broadly defined as families that consist of two parents (i.e., a couple) and their children from their relationship and all former relationships. *Stepfamilies* are defined as systems comprising a couple and a child or children that are formed from remarriage of widowed or divorced persons. While definitions are helpful, it is important to note that many stepcouple marriages symbolize an initial marriage for one or both partners. One noted difference between stepfamilies and blended families made by some organizations is the notion that blended families assume that the parents in the current marital/relational arrangement have their own child or children (Australian Bureau of Statistics, 2003). Others do not make this distinction and simply use the terms *blended family, stepfamily,* and *remarried family* interchangeably (Papernow, 2018).

Blended families can be as diverse and intersectional as any other modern relational structure. Simple stepfamilies are created when only one partner in the newly formed dyad brings a child or children. Complex stepfamilies are created when both partners bring a child or children (Papernow, 2018). Contextually speaking, blended families can vary in size, composition, cultural beliefs and values, acculturation, membership criteria, ethnicity, race, sexuality, expression of gender, ability, religious affiliation, and socioeconomic status, among other variables. Each of the aforementioned contextual factors could be further expanded and deepened. For example, consider sexuality and those who identify as a particular sexual identity. In general, *sexual and gender minorities* are defined as a group whose sexual identity, orientation, and/or practices differ from the cultural majority. In the United States, the cultural majority in terms of sexuality would include heterosexual, cisgender, and nonintersex individuals. Identities that could qualify as a sexual minority include, but are not limited to, those who identify as lesbian, gay, bisexual, transgender, queer, intersex, asexual, questioning, two-spirit, gender variant, swingers, polyamorists, and those engaging in bondage, discipline, dominance and submission, sadomasochism, and other related interpersonal dynamics (BDSM; Math & Seshadri, 2013).

According to the American Psychological Association (2019), prior to remarrying and/or engaging in a new blended family structure, families need to carefully plan living arrangements, address financial issues, and resolve any lingering concerns from the previous marriage. While children often do not wish to leave their childhood home, it may be optimal for remarried couples to move into a new home because it becomes "theirs" (i.e., not the one attached to the first-time family). Newly remarried couples should also establish clear rules and boundaries around finances. The primary concern is how or if each partner's finances will be shared with the other. Couples who use the *one-pot* method more often report a higher degree of satisfaction than couples who keep separate bank accounts. Lastly, once people enter a new marriage or some form of long-term cohabitation arrangement, there can be considerable emotional turmoil in the previously created family. The issues primarily stem from feelings of hurt and anger because the children and ex-spouse recognize that reconciliation with their primary caregiver and/or previous partner is not possible. Another common challenge arises if the new stepparent attempts to parent children in an overly hierarchical and authoritarian manner (Papernow, 2018).

While all family structures face major challenges, there are unique issues that affect blended families. First, blended families are not first-time families, and the caregivers who initially created attachment-based relationships with their children are partly replaced with a stepparent who may have no attachment, history, or relationship with the children. The previous parenting structure may have dissolved due to breakup (cohabiting couples), divorce, or death. While initial excitement and hopefulness exist in blended families, these new relationship structures are generally not successful and/or sustainable. Hetherington's (1993) classic 20-year longitudinal study, which followed 450 families who experienced divorce or remarriage, found that 60% to 73% of all marriages involving children from previous relationships end in divorce. Furthermore, as previously stated, about half of all U.S. first marriages end in divorce and approximately 67% of subsequent marriages end in divorce (Kreider & Ellis, 2011).

Papernow (2013) described five major challenges faced by blended families in navigating their newly formed relationships: (a) rigid insider/outsider positioning; (b) child-based issues involving loyalty binds, loss, and change; (c) division of parenting tasks between parents and stepparents; (d) creation of a new family culture when a previous one is already in place; and (e) maintaining the ex-parent as part of the family. Stepparents are not part of the first-time family that children were born into, nor do most of them have a shared history with the children, and they did not cocreate early attachment-based relationships with the children. In first-time families, the children are often born to individuals who are in an intimate relationship, and in healthy families caregivers and children are biologically driven to establish attachment-based relationships. Furthermore, research demonstrates that even when the situation and the people involved are positive and healthy, successfully cocreating, stabilizing, and developing a working blended family can take 3 to 6 years (Papernow, 2013). For families that have emotional, psychological, substance, and/or relational difficulties, the process can take much longer or never be completed. For stepparents, this can create a relational phenomenon known as the *stuck outsider*. The stepparent is essentially an outsider to the already powerful parent, ex-spouse, and child bond. Furthermore, the parent from the first family can turn into the *stuck insider*, struggling with divided loyalty and feeling emotionally and psychologically torn between the children and the new spouse (Papernow, 2018).

While entering a new relationship/marriage can be exciting for adults, children rarely have the same experience. Although adults may conceptualize leaving the first family and starting the new blended family as a win, a child will often view the new situation as a loss (Cartwright, 2008). According to van Eeden-Moorefield and Pasley (2013), although stepfamily adjustment is somewhat difficult for all children, the adaptation generally is smoother for boys than girls. It is particularly difficult for preadolescent girls. According to the American Psychological Association (2019), research suggests that in general children 10 years of age and under are more open to forming a positive relationship with a stepparent, while young adolescents (ages 10–14) appear to have the biggest stepfamily adjustment challenges. Adolescents aged 15 and over are generally less invested in stepfamily life because they are (a) going through the adolescent individuation process, (b) forming their own identities outside the family, and (c) naturally need less parenting.

Part of the reason children and adolescents often have a difficult time adjusting within a stepfamily has to do with their feelings of abandonment and the loyalty binds to their mother or father. Even if the situation in the first family was challenging and hurtful, children may feel that any effort to create positive relational growth with the stepparent means being disloyal to their parent and the legacy of the first-time family. Because of these challenges, stepchildren may be perceived as behaving badly, scheming, being defensive, or colluding. While children feel upset, insecure, and disappointed about the presence of the new stepparent in their life and the removal of the other parent, the stepparent often feels they are being scapegoated by the children, that they will never gain relational ground with them, and that they are uncertain what their role should be in the stepfamily (Cartwright, 2008; Ganong & Coleman, 2017; Papernow, 2018).

Forming a blended family is much different from forming a family where no previous children or marriage is involved. Children can feel anger, abandonment, awkwardness, and/or distress in response to their parent's devotion of time, energy, and intimacy to the new spouse. During this process, a key factor is the parent maintaining their role as the caregiver, disciplinarian, nurturer, and hierarchical figure in the family (Ganong & Coleman, 2017; Papernow, 2018). The stepparent's task is to start a supportive, trusting, and caring relationship with each of the children. Instead of rushing in to fulfill the role of a parent or a caregiver, they need to be more like a friend, camp counselor, or big brother/sister. They can also help the family by supporting their spouse through helping with household tasks, monitoring the children and reporting on their behavior, and empowering the first-family parent to achieve their goals for the family. One of the biggest mistakes a new stepparent can make is to engage the children as an authoritarian caregiver. Not only will this tactic elicit immediate rejection and resentment from the stepchildren, but it often permanently damages the stepparent's relationship with the stepchildren (Ganong & Coleman, 2017; Papernow, 2018).

According to Papernow (2018), the third challenge arises when parenting tasks create a divide between the stepparent and the first-family parent (i.e., within the new couple). Stepparenting requires a unique dance with the original parent. For example, if the stepparent quickly begins engaging with children in a firm and discipline-oriented parenting style, the parent and the stepparent can become divided. This divide is centered on the parent's loyalty to their children and to the new spouse. As the stepparent becomes increasingly harsh and firm with the children, the first-family parent becomes more permissive and protective of the children. This firming up and softening up parenting dance is toxic to the children and to the relationship between the spouses. In a general sense, families are healthier and happier when parents incorporate an authoritative parenting style (nurturing, engaging, and structured, with developmentally appropriate expectations; Bray, 1992), and if the first-family parent retains all of the responsibilities around child discipline.

The next challenge involves creating a new family dynamic while the previous family culture is still in place. According to Papernow (2018), the goal for an emerging blended family is to establish new rules, traditions, daily responsibilities, and values very slowly while simultaneously honoring and respecting what had previously been established within the first-family culture. The gradual movement toward change while maintaining a shared understanding about the previous and current family is guided by the first-family parent–children and supported and understood by the stepparent. Following the divorce, children typically have an optimal level of adjustment when the parent who has moved out of the house has a positive relationship with them and visits frequently and consistently. Unfortunately, once the divorced nonresidential caregiver remarries, their level of contact with their children often decreases. This can cause a great deal of sadness and sense of abandonment in the children.

The last potential challenge and necessary condition that Papernow (2018) describes has to do with parenting harmony. It may seem like common sense to state that children thrive when their parents and stepparents demonstrate low levels of conflict and high levels of cohesion with each other. This includes maintaining consistent interaction and a secure attachment with the parents of their first family, effective coparenting between separated ex-spouses, positive/collaborative relations between the ex-spouse and the stepparent, and continued involvement from the ex-spouse in the child's life (Ganong & Coleman, 2017; Papernow, 2018).

MULTIRACIAL FAMILIES

The term *multiracial* is a very broad socially constructed category that may carry different meanings depending on the historical timeline, political agenda, and context of its use (Harris & Sim, 2002; Rockquemore & Laszloffy, 2005). In 2000, the U.S. Census began allowing people to label themselves as belonging to more than one racial category. This symbolized the growing population of mixed-race individuals in the United States and the increased level of acceptance for individuals identifying as having more than one racial background. From a population growth perspective, the number of mixed-race individuals is growing rapidly: 7 million in 2000, 9 million in 2010, and 33.8 million in 2020 (276% increase). According to Henriksen and Maxwell (2016), multiracial individuals are the fastest growing population in the United States. This segment of the population is predicted to increase by 26 million individuals between 2014 and 2060 (Colby & Ortman, 2015). Furthermore, U.S. Census data confirm that between 2000 and 2016 the percentage of married interracial households grew from 7.4% to 10.2% (Rico et al., 2018; U.S. Census Bureau, 2021a).

While most individuals have some level of cultural mixing at some point in their family's history, not many describe themselves as multiracial, multiethnic, or biracial (Bradt, 2010; Laszloffy, 2005; Roth, 2005). Townsend et al. (2012) described the lack of acknowledgment around interracial individuals, couples, and families as partly related to the historical social and legal pejorative and racist prohibitions around identifying as *mixed race*. Practices like antimiscegenation laws (i.e., a law declaring it is illegal to marry outside of one's race), hypodescent (i.e., assigning mixed-race individuals the racial identity of the parent with the lowest social status), and the one-drop rule (i.e., people automatically labeled as their minority heritage, no matter the percentage) lend credence to this claim (Bradt, 2010; Laszloffy, 2005; Roth, 2005). Interracial marriage is a marital union involving people from different racial groups or racialized ethnicities. Due to pejorative political practices such as the antimiscegenation law, interracial marriages were prohibited and illegal in places like the United States, Nazi Germany, and apartheid-era South Africa (Downing et al., 2005). While this practice ended in the United States in 1967 due to a Supreme Court decision (see *Loving v. Virginia*), contemporary mixed-race couples and families have faced enormous amounts of discrimination, racism, and hate.

Racial groups in the United States have historically been categorized and conceptualized as being biologically distinct from each other. This is somewhat related to the historical notion of five separate races: African, Asian, European, Native American, and Oceanian (Chou, 2017; Laszloffy, 2005). According to Chou (2017), from a biological and social science framework, race is a social construct rather than a biological attribute. Genetically speaking, scientists have not been able to find trademark alleles or any other genetic evidence consistent for a single group of humans but not present in others. This and other evidence suggest that race has no biological basis. In short, scientifically speaking, research (Rosenberg et al., 2002) indicates that there is so much ambiguity between races and deviation within racial groups that the notion of biologically separate races is a myth, and the only truth is the notion that race is a socially created and employed construct.

According to Finney et al. (2020), multiracial individuals experience a variety of negative interpersonal and intrapersonal experiences, including identity confusion, identity purgatory, and social marginality. They frequently experience three types of microaggressions: microassault, microinsult, and microinvalidation.

Identity confusion often occurs because integrating multiple racial heritages into a unified whole is a very difficult process. Racial identity development should involve a variety of factors, including, but not limited to, (a) engaging in cultural and ethnic conversations within the family, (b) helping a child understand their unique racial identity, (c) permitting a child to mingle and socialize with children from different racial and ethnic heritages, (d) meeting role models during activities sponsored by people with diverse heritage, and (e) creating a family that has "interracial" as part of the family identity (McRoy & Freeman, 1986).

Identity purgatory is feeling tormented due to not having successfully integrated one's multiple racial and ethnic identities and levels of intersection. These levels of intersection and identity can create a mix of societal oppression and advantage that causes confusion and affects multiracial individuals by causing them to feel like they must "choose" a single racial and ethnic background to identify with. Exploring, integrating, and acknowledging one's multiracial and multiethnic identity are key first steps toward resolving this issue. Multiracial families, children, and adults do not have to decide to belong to only one of the racial or ethnic groups that make up their racial and ethnic ancestry; instead, they can integrate these intersectional identities to create a unified whole (Finney et al., 2020; Lucas, 2017).

Part of the identity purgatory experienced by many multiracial families, children, and adults has to do with understanding where they fit. Social marginality is very much a focal point for adolescents who often feel a sense of rejection and dismissal by both majority and minority populations (Gibbs, 1987). This can be more pronounced for individuals who appear physically and cosmetically as if they belong to a particular group and for individuals who appear to be of mixed racial and/or ethnic heritage (Finney et al., 2020; Gibbs, 1987; Lucas, 2017). White parents of multiracial children often need help understanding the various challenges (e.g., microaggressions, macroaggressions, identity purgatory, social marginalization, racism) that their mixed-race child/adolescent may be experiencing.

Multiracial families support children and adolescents by initiating racial and ethnic socialization conversations. Families have important conversations centered on helping members understand social experiences such as racism, hatred, prejudice, and privilege. These conversations explore what it is like to be racially oppressed and advantaged in certain circumstances (Lucas, 2017). According to Sebring (1984), it is essential to help adolescents understand how they may be internalizing damaging societal messages, biases, and beliefs.

Microaggressions may be inflicted intentionally or unintentionally and can leave a lasting mark on multiracial individuals. Marginalized children, families, and adults frequently contend with three types of microaggressions: microassaults, microinsults, and microinvalidations. Microassaults are deliberate verbal, nonverbal, and/or environmental attacks meant to exhibit discriminatory sentiments (e.g., yelling racist slurs, prohibiting marginalized communities from doing business with you). Microinsults are unconscious and unintentional remarks that are disrespectful and callous (e.g., assuming people of color do not know a piece of information, intentionally walking on the other side of the street). Microinvalidations are remarks that dismiss the reality and lived experiences of targeted groups (e.g., "They're not *really* racist"; Finney et al., 2020; Sue et al., 2019).

CONTEMPORARY PARENTING

Parenting is a foundational, controversial, and frequently evolving area of systemic work. Throughout this section, the terms *parent* and *caregiver* are used interchangeably in reference to the primary caregiver(s) of the child or children in a family. Additionally, the words *parent, parents, children,* and *child* are used frequently and interchangeably to refer to any number of parents or children in a family.

The following U.S. statistical information is based on the *2020 Current Population Survey*, a survey cosponsored by the U.S. Bureau of Labor Statistics and the U.S. Census Bureau. Compared with previous decades, fewer households in the United States currently consist of parents with children living at home. Over the most recent decade, the number of parents living with children declined from approximately 66.1 million in 2010 to 63.1 million in 2020. The marital status of parents changed less over the past 10 years. In 2020, 78% of U.S. parents were married, compared with 77% in 2010. In 2020, unmarried and cohabitating parents made up 7% of parents living with children under 18. Parents living without a partner accounted for 15% in 2020. Mothers and fathers had different living conditions in 2020, and 70% of mothers and 87% of fathers living with children under 18 were married. Furthermore, mothers more frequently lived without a partner (23%) compared with fathers (6%). The 2020 median age for first-time marriages was 28.1 for women and 30.5 for men—a significant increase from the 1947 median ages of 20.5 for women and 23.7 for men. Lastly, a quarter (25%) of U.S. children under the age of 15 lived in a married-couple family that had a stay-at-home mother, while 1% had a stay-at-home father.

Parents can vary in a number of ways, including, but not limited to, cultural beliefs, values, interests, acculturation, sex, gender, ethnicity, race, sexuality, expression of gender, nationality, ability, and religious affiliation. While each parent has their own contextual variables and identity, caregivers try to cohesively merge their beliefs, values, and interests as they collaborate to provide the foundation of their family and guide their children through their journey to adulthood.

When individuals who identify as LGBTQIA+ become parents, they face a society that often does not understand, accept, or support them. Individuals identifying as LGBTQIA+ become parents in a variety of ways, including donor insemination, surrogacy, previous heterosexual relationships, and foster parenting. In 2019, the U.S. Census Bureau (2021c) reported that there were 980,000 same-sex households in the United States. Approximately 58% of same-sex households were headed by married couples and approximately 42% by unmarried adults. Same-sex married couple households were much more likely to have children than unmarried same-sex couple households. Overall, compared with opposite-sex married couples, same-sex couples were about half as likely to have children.

The practice of parenting has been described as the specific behaviors that caregivers utilize to socialize their children (Darling & Steinberg, 1993). According to the *Encyclopedia of Psychology* (Kazdin, 2000), parenting practices around the world share three core goals: transmitting cultural values, preparing children to lead productive adult lives, and ensuring that children are safe and healthy. Broadly speaking, regarding the practice of parenting, there are two basic macro-parenting dimensions: *parental support* and *parental control* (Kuppens & Ceulemans, 2019).

The warm, responsive, nurturing, and engaging nature of the parent–child relationship is referred to as parental support (Cummings et al., 2000). Research indicates that parents who provide positive support to their children prevent substance abuse, depression, delinquency, and problems with externalizing behaviors (Barnes & Farell, 1992; Bean et al., 2006; Shaw et al., 1994).

Parental control has to do with caregivers behaviorally and psychologically controlling their children. Behaviorally speaking, parents attempt to control their children through reinforcement and punishment strategies, rules, contingency management, setting expectations, and monitoring (Barber & Harmon, 2002; Maccoby et al., 1990; Steinberg, 1990). Modest amounts of behavioral control have been associated with positive child outcomes, while insufficient behavioral control (e.g., neglect, abandonment, insufficient supervision) and excessive behavioral control (e.g., physical punishment, developmentally inappropriate expectations, obsessive monitoring) have been associated with negative outcomes, including, but not limited to, deviant behavior, parentification, depression, and anxiety (Coie and Dodge, 1998; Galambos et al., 2003). Psychological control involves trying to control a child through manipulation of thoughts, emotions, and feelings. This type of control is almost always associated with negative child developmental outcomes (e.g., depression, regression, failure to thrive, conduct disorder; Barber et al., 2005; Kuppens & Ceulemans, 2019; Kuppens et al., 2013).

Experts indicate that the most common goals for parenting include raising a well-adjusted, adequately developed, self-regulating, emotionally intelligent, and giving child (Davis et al., 2015; Joussemet et al., 2014; Moilanen et al., 2015). Perron (2018) describes the four Cs of parenting: care, consistency, choices, and consequences.

Care refers to the parent's ability to convey acceptance, warmth, and valuing to a child. For example, a parent might say: "Wow, I appreciate all of the hard work you put into your drawing. I'll bet you are happy about the way it turned out!"

Consistency refers to creating a safe and predictable environment. Because of the number of variables involved in any situation, exact consistency may be impossible to achieve; however, creating a mostly consistent environment greatly enhances the expression of care. For example, a parent might tell a child: "I understand you're interested in extending your video game time by 10 minutes; however, we have thought carefully about this and agree that it is important to stick with your normal bedtime."

Choices create a sense of autonomy and provide an opportunity for children to solve their own problems. This could involve the child making the wrong choice and struggling to find the right option. In a general sense, people learn to solve their own problems when they know they have choices. For example, a parent might say: "It sounds like you don't want to brush your teeth. You can choose to brush your teeth before bedtime reading or after. What would you like to do?"

Consequences are the results of choices. Natural consequences happen outside of parental influence. They are implemented by society, people, or nature. In this sense, negative consequences are not punishment—they are simply natural occurrences. For example, a child who eats too much might have an upset stomach. Other consequences of negative behavior are determined by parents. For example, a parent might ask: "Are you making a good choice? When you chose to swear, you chose to go to bed an hour early. It's your choice" (Cline, 2009; Perron, 2018).

Parenting Styles

There are seemingly endless ways to raise a child. Interactions with parents heavily influence children's morals, values, principles, and conduct. Different parenting styles are associated with different child outcomes. Five common parenting styles have been identified: authoritative, authoritarian, permissive, rejecting, and uninvolved (Baumrind, 1971; Masud et al., 2019; Olson et al., 2004). Depending on the culture, race, ethnicity, and nationality of the parents and children, these styles can manifest in idiosyncratic ways.

To start, let's consider the authoritative parenting style. Authoritative parenting, also referred to as democratic parenting, is characterized by warmth, appropriate child–parent boundaries, nonpunitive discipline (e.g., using time-out or grounding instead of physical punishment), using rules and reasoning to create a sense of obedience, promoting healthy self-regulation within children, and maintaining consistency between statements and actions across time (Baumrind, 1991; Moilanen et al., 2015). Children of authoritative parents typically exhibit energetic and friendly behavior, self-reliance, and a cheerful disposition. They tend to cope well with stress and are achievement-oriented (Baumrind, 1971; Masud et al., 2019; Olson et al., 2004). Researchers have identified several key attributes of authoritative parents that promote healthy child well-being, including affiliation, structure, and autonomy support (Joussemet et al., 2014).

Authoritarian parents lack warmth and a sense of nurturing, stress inflexible adherence to the rules they set (e.g., "Obey just because we said so"), emphasize the power and influence of their role, and use physical (i.e., corporal) punishment for child indiscretions. Furthermore, these parents tend to place high demands on their children while showing little responsiveness to their child's needs. Overall, authoritarian parenting has been negatively critiqued for being too controlling and retaliatory (Olivari et al., 2015). Children raised with this parenting style tend to be unhappy, demonstrate a sense of moodiness, are very sensitive to stressful situations, and are generally unfriendly (Baumrind, 1971; Masud et al., 2019; Olson et al., 2004).

Permissive parents, who are sometimes labeled laissez-faire parents, are too lax and demonstrate rule inconsistency in guiding their child's behavior. At times, these parents demonstrate overly lenient expectations regarding acceptable child behaviors and accountability (Olivari et al., 2015). Instead of parents overseeing the family, these parents raise children who are often in control of the family. This can easily lead to problematic family dynamics (e.g., collusion, parentification). Children of permissive parents demonstrate overbearing, defiant, and impulsive-aggressive behaviors (Baumrind, 1971; Masud et al., 2019; Olson et al., 2004).

Rejecting parents invalidate, push away, or reject their children. Parents demonstrating this style do not pay attention to their children and have many rules for how they should behave. These parents rarely show warmth and affection and tend to be dismissive of children's needs. Their children do not feel loved and nurtured; however, they are expected to behave according to strict familial rules. The consequences of this parenting style include immaturity and psychological problems (e.g., depression, anxiety, stress; Baumrind, 1971; Masud et al., 2019; Olson et al., 2004).

Uninvolved parents frequently ignore the needs of their children. Parents who exhibit this style of parenting tend to pay some attention to their children's needs as long as it does not interfere with their activities and goals. These parents offer little nurturing or emotional support, do not utilize a particular type of discipline, and are generally detached from their children. Uninvolved parents do not provide consistent rules or expectations. This style of parenting produces children who are loners, have difficulty self-regulating their emotions, are low achievers, and are self-sufficient due to necessity (Baumrind, 1971; Masud et al., 2019; Olson et al., 2004).

Metaphorical Parenting Styles

What is it about heavy machinery (e.g., helicopter, lawnmower, bulldozer, snowplow) and animals (e.g., tigers and panda bears) that causes scholars to associate them with a contemporary style in parenting? Within this section, a few contemporary parenting trends and styles are reviewed.

The helicopter parenting style is demonstrated when parents take an excessive and overprotective interest in the life of their child. The image of a hovering helicopter implies that there is continuous control over the child, although there is no direct interference in the child's life. The helicopter parent attempts to protect their child from difficult, harsh, and potentially dangerous situations that might arise. This parenting style gives the child covert and overt messages of weakness and low self-worth (i.e., they feel like they cannot do things without help). Similar to an actual helicopter, this parent makes a lot of noise. The type of noise is typically centered on making excuses for their child, taking responsibility for their child's behavior, and simultaneously complaining about all they do for their child. This type of parenting also robs children of experiencing natural consequences and uses guilt as a teaching method (Casillas et al., 2020; Srivastav & Mathur, 2020).

As times change, so do parenting styles. The novel metaphor of the helicopter no longer does this parenting style justice. If the field continues to conceptualize parents as vehicles, the helicopter is not proactive enough and would even be slightly on the passive side regarding the parenting styles being implemented today. Contemporary parents are often described as lawnmower parents, bulldozer parents, or snowplow parents. These parents do not simply hover and watch over their children (i.e., helicopter parent); instead, they deliberately clear all obstacles out of their children's path. While this clearing of life's obstacles may temporarily relieve their child of a challenge, it also deprives children of the opportunity to learn how to fight for resources, cope with barriers, handle disappointments, and deal with obstacles. Machines like bulldozers, lawnmowers, and snowplows are also metaphorically dangerous to those who get in their way. The metaphorical message is that these big, sturdy, and dangerous machines clear away obstacles (e.g., peers, teachers, parents, community members; Miller & Bromwich, 2019).

Turning from machinery to the animal kingdom to provide parenting metaphors, tiger parents are described as authoritarian in nature. These parents are strict, demanding, forceful, and have extremely high expectations for their children. They work extremely hard to drive their children toward success. The main goal of a tiger parent is future academic and financial success for their children. Tiger parents are highly focused on embedding a sense of motivation and self-control within their children. Tiger parents may encourage children to engage in events that could conclude with their children receiving awards and/or recognition, especially if the activities relate to future career and/or academic success. Instead of hanging out with friends and family or going to sleepovers, these children are often expected to maintain a strict schedule of activities that can contribute to their future success. While tiger parents do not focus on punishment and frequently praise their children, these children often have low self-esteem and feel they will never perform well enough to meet their parents' expectations. Because of the myriad of expectations and responsibilities placed on these children at a young age, they often do not have the opportunity to view the world from their own vantage point (Chua, 2011; Kim et al., 2013).

The panda parenting style is demonstrated when a caregiver creates a strong relationship with their children, gently guides children toward developmentally appropriate goals, and provides children with opportunities to do things their own way. This is similar to the authoritative style of parenting. Panda parents provide space for their children to develop their own standards and beliefs. They provide structure for their children, but within the daily structure there are abundant opportunities for children to explore the world on their own. Children of panda parents tend to be self-sufficient and independent, yet they know how to ask for help when they need it (Patel, 2019).

The Impact of Culture on Parenting

Parents in various cultures face a number of issues when raising children. According to Sanvictores and Mendez (2021),

> [t]he definition of culture refers to a pattern of social norms, values, language, and behavior shared by individuals. As a result, parents are affected by their culture. When it comes to self-regulation, parenting approaches vary across cultures concerning promoting attention, compliance, delayed gratification, executive function, and effortful control (p. 1).

Common parenting goals across cultures include (a) raising healthy youth, (b) ensuring youth are adequately developed, (c) making sure youth are emotionally intelligent, (d) helping youth become self-regulating, and (e) ensuring that youth demonstrate behaviors that show support of others (Davis et al., 2015; Joussemet et al., 2014; Moilanen et al., 2015). From a cross-cultural perspective, parents create an emotional climate in their home by modeling behaviors, thoughts, and feelings that reflect the family's culture and greater society (Olivari et al., 2015).

While there are some universal parenting practices that span cultures, people from different cultures raise their children in a variety of ways. Cultural backgrounds have a significant impact on the family unit. It is important for children to understand their culture and to feel secure with understanding cultural messages transmitted by their parents. For example, sometimes children are raised in homes that have parents from two different cultures. Children from these families can experience a substantial amount of diversity and intersectionality, yet parents may have to make compromises regarding the continuation of a particular culture practice regarding regular familial happenings (e.g., food, bedtime, routines, discipline, sleeping arrangements).

The balance of warmth and control often looks very different depending on one's culture. For example, in the United States, high levels of parental control are viewed negatively, while in certain Asian cultures parental control is correlated with parental warmth (Deater-Deckard et al., 2011). Similarly, autonomy looks very different depending on cultural norms. Autonomy is reflected in parenting when a child is encouraged to independently explore the environment and to express their thoughts and feelings, and when parents demonstrate empathy and regard for a child's own thoughts, emotions, and goals (Perron, 2018). Autonomy appears to be a highly supported family value in European countries (Olivari et al., 2015), and research suggests that Asian families exert higher levels of parental control than European families do (Joussemet et al., 2014).

Human development is often viewed differently across cultures. Culturally based parenting practices have been linked with protecting youth from the development of mental health disorders (e.g., conduct disorder, substance abuse disorder; Coard et al., 2007). Current parenting behaviors and values must be contextually and culturally understood. For example, acculturating families may have a variety of relational values within the home. These values could manifest as parents demonstrating a collectivistic relational structure and children engaging in an individualistic relational structure (Gershoff et al., 2010), potentially creating a significant disconnect within the family unit. While parents may demonstrate inhibition and subjugation (collectivist), children may lean toward assertiveness and independence (individualist).

Postdivorce Coparenting

As previously stated, first-marriage divorce rates hover around 50%, with second marriages demonstrating far higher percentages of divorce (Daugherty & Copen, 2016). To ensure a cordial and cooperative coparenting relationship, most states in the United States require separating spouses to participate in some form of divorce education program (Pollet & Lobreglia, 2008). Coparenting occurs when ex-spouses collaborate with each other on their ongoing efforts to raise children and coordinate their postdivorce childcare activities (Markham et al., 2007; Sobolewski & King, 2005). Coordinating responsibilities between ex-spouses, establishing norms around multiple living environments, and introducing new partners/spouses into the family (i.e., repartnering) can turn coparenting into a multilayered iterative experience. According to Russell et al. (2016), both divorced and married partners can engage in coparenting; however, coparenting ex-spouses can experience particular issues, including, but not limited to, feelings of sadness, anger, and hurt following the end of the marriage; experiencing both emotional and physical distance from the other caregiver; raising children in separate homes; challenges with the legal ramifications of a divorce; and general animosity over the postmarriage situation (Fischer et al., 2005; Jamison et al., 2014).

Former spouses are encouraged to create and sustain a collaborative and supportive coparenting structure. If former spouses begin to work with one another around (a) effectively coordinating various childcare activities, (b) participating in frequent communication to assist in ensuring positive childcare environments, and (c) working hard to minimize potential conflicts, they are engaging in *cooperative coparenting* (Adamsons & Pasley, 2006; Ahrons, 2007; Sobolewski & King, 2005). Cooperative coparenting (e.g., perfect pals, cooperative colleagues) has been found to reduce familial and ex-spouse conflict (Ahrons, 2011), enhance positive feelings between ex-spouses (Beckmeyer et al., 2017), increase the desires for both parties to continue coparenting (Beckmeyer et al., 2017), and support parent–child relationships (Adamsons & Pasley, 2006). While cooperative coparenting may appear to be key to ensuring a positive postdivorce outcome for children, Nielsen's (2017) review of 44 empirically based studies revealed that parent–child subsystem relationship quality was a stronger predictor of future child outcomes.

Although cooperative coparenting results in the best overall outcomes for ex-spouses and children, many divorced couples engage in less effective styles, including conflicted, disengaged, and mixed coparenting (Beckmeyer et al., 2014). When parents engage in frequent conflict, have minimal communication around the needs of their children, and achieve very little caregiving coordination, this pattern of interaction is labeled as conflicted coparenting (Maccoby et al., 1990) or parallel coparenting with conflict (Amato et al., 2011). It is called *parallel* because the parents are not completely disengaged from each other, yet they do not appear to have the ability to communicate without conflict. Disengaged coparenting occurs when the coparents stop communicating about most aspects of their child's life, including coordinating childcare (Amato et al., 2011). Lastly, a mixed coparenting style (Maccoby et al., 1990) has been conceptualized as having a high degree of both communication and conflict.

OBESITY

The World Health Organization (WHO; 2021) has defined *obesity* as irregular or extreme fat accumulation that may damage health. The CDC (n.d.) defines *obesity* as a body mass index (BMI) of 30 or higher, as estimated from weight and height. Weight that is higher than what is considered healthy for a given height is described as overweight or obese (CDC, n.d.). Individuals are considered obese when their weight is 20% or more above normal weight (CDC, n.d.). Obesity has become a global epidemic in recent decades, with at least 2.8 million annual deaths each year resulting from people being overweight or obese (WHO, 2021). Obesity is second only to smoking as a leading preventable cause of death in the United States (Goldman, 2020; Kushner & Manzano, 2002). Childhood obesity has been recognized as a pediatric condition for over 60 years, and it impacts children regardless of sex, age, race, ethnicity, and any other contextual variables (Federal Interagency Forum on Child and Family Statistics, 2007).

According to the American Medical Association (AMA; 2013), the epidemic of obesity is a preventable, multifactorial, and multifaceted disease affecting an enormous portion of the population. Due in part to several decades of obesity-related healthcare concerns, the AMA (2013) has officially recognized obesity as a chronic disease that needs medical attention. Similarly, due to the high percentage of children experiencing obesity (i.e., 31.7% of youth above the 85th percentile for BMI), policy makers have declared childhood obesity to be a critical public health threat (Ogden et al., 2012). The nature of the threat has to do with the rise in obesity across the nation and the growing prevalence of associated chronic diseases (e.g., high blood pressure, type 2 diabetes, high cholesterol, coronary heart disease). In 1950, the National Obesity Society was created to help people clinically manage obesity. Following its initial iteration, the organization has changed its name five times. The Obesity Medicine Association is the current name of this organization (Kyle et al., 2016).

According to WHO (2021), worldwide obesity has nearly tripled since 1975. Findings from the CDC support the notion that obesity is a serious health threat in the United States. According to the CDC, approximately 42% of U.S. adults were obese in 2017 and 2018. Obesity rates were highest in adults between 40 and 59 years of age; within this age range, the rates were 46.4% for men and 43.3% for women. Some demographic groups are affected by obesity more than others. Non-Hispanic Black adults (49.6%) had the greatest age-adjusted incidence of obesity, followed by Hispanic adults (44.8%), non-Hispanic White adults (42.2%), and non-Hispanic Asian adults (17.4%). Obesity rates were highest among non-Hispanic Black women at 56.9%. Higher education and income appear to protect people from obesity, with college graduates demonstrating lower rates of obesity (just under 28%) than individuals without a college degree. Lastly, men and women with higher incomes had lower rates of obesity: 29.7% for women and 31.5% for men.

Child and adolescent obesity rates have increased over the past four decades. According to WHO (2021), globally over 340 million children and adolescents aged 5 to 19 were overweight or obese in 2016. In addition, from a worldwide perspective, 39 million children under the age of 5 were overweight or obese in 2020. During 2017 and 2018, the CDC collected data on U.S. children and adolescents between 2 and 19 years of age. According to Fryar et al. (2020), the overall prevalence of obesity among U.S. youth 2 to 19 years of age was 19.3% (i.e., approximately 14.4 million youth). More specifically, the rate of obesity was 13.4% among U.S. youth 2 to 5 years of age, 20.3% among those 6 to 11 years of age, and 21.2% among those 12 to 19 years of age. The CDC also collected data on youth of color during 2017 and 2018. According to the CDC report, obesity prevalence was 25.6% among Hispanic children, 24.2% among non-Hispanic Black children, 16.1% among non-Hispanic White children, and 8.7% among non-Hispanic Asian children (Fryar et al., 2020).

Since the 1950s, the prevalence of obesity has increased throughout the United States and around the world. This increase in obesity includes all ages, races, ethnic groups, genders, educational levels, and socioeconomic status (Mitchell et al., 2011; Wang et al., 2004). You may be wondering why obesity is increasing worldwide. The three leading contributors to obesity and/or being overweight are diet, lack of exercise, and physical/social environment. In other words, people are not exercising enough, not eating an appropriate diet, and living in an environment where food is inexpensive, plentiful, and served in very large portions, and there is rarely a need to engage in activities that involve frequent and substantial energy outflow (e.g., exercise, hunting food, finding/making shelter, moving from one place to another; CDC, 2022; Hill et al., 2000).

Additional issues that contribute to obesity include (a) the combination of high calorie intake and low physical activity, (b) the high prices associated with healthy food, (c) sedentary work environments, (d) stress and emotional issues, (e) family history, (f) genetics, (g) disease (e.g., thyroid problems, polycystic ovary syndrome, Cushing syndrome), and (h) effects of community of color membership and low income (Drewnowski & Specter, 2004; Mitchell et al., 2011; Wang et al., 2004). Part of the reason that low-income youth and youth of color are affected more than average is the pattern of frequent ingestion of cheap and unhealthy foods and spending less time outside playing. According to Drewnowski and Specter (2004), the cheaper the food is, the more likely it is to contain high levels of sugar and fat. The authors add that humans are biologically driven to consume particular foods (e.g., foods high in caloric density and sugar) that are currently cheap and easily accessible. Lastly, low-income communities and/or communities of color might reside in neighborhoods that are unsafe for outdoor play due to violence, traffic, and other issues, and consequently are less likely to go outside for physical activity (Mitchell et al., 2011).

According to Ward et al. (2019), by the year 2030 one in every two U.S. adults will be obese. Ward et al.'s research indicates that the rate of obesity in 29 states will be higher than 50% of the statewide population and will not be lower than 35% of the population in any state. Given this prediction, the physical and mental health needs of this group will be vast. Physical issues include, but are not limited to, increased vulnerability to all causes of death, high blood pressure, high low-density lipoprotein cholesterol, low high-density lipoprotein cholesterol, high triglycerides, type 2 diabetes, coronary heart disease, stroke, gallbladder disease, osteoarthritis, sleep apnea, a variety of cancers, and body pain with difficulties in physical functioning.

While most of the physical problems associated with obesity could have their own comorbid mental health issues, there are a few mental health factors that are unique to individuals with obesity. These disorders and issues include, but are not limited to, depression, eating disorders, anxiety, substance abuse, and low self-esteem (Sarwer & Polonsky, 2016). In addition to meeting the criteria for mental health disorders, individuals who suffer from obesity are deeply affected by stigma and discrimination. In short, social and family issues that can deeply affect obese and/or overweight individuals include (a) discrimination in employment, education, and healthcare settings; (b) verbal victimization, fat shaming, and name calling; (c) rejection by family and friends; (d) delayed academic achievement and reduced social ability; and (e) frequent identification of obesity as a lifestyle choice (as opposed to a protected disability; Ogden et al., 2013; Sarwer & Polonsky, 2016).

FAMILY ISSUES RELATED TO INTERNET USE

According to the CDC (2022), 65.7% and 64.6% of boys and girls (ages 2–17) engage in 2 hours or more of recreational screen time per weekday. This percentage does not include time spent doing homework. Developmentally speaking, screen time has increased for both boys and girls across the life span: 47.5% (more than 2 hours of daily screen time) for children 2 to 5 years of age and 80% (more than 2 hours of daily screen time) for youth 12 to 17 years of age. The COVID-19 global pandemic and the ensuing stay-at-home mandates, required/optional online learning, and social distancing requirements drastically increased reliance on screens and digital media for nearly all aspects of the lives of youth (e.g., leisure, social interaction, learning). According to a large-scale ($N = 5,412$), cross-sectional, and culturally diverse survey conducted by Nagata et al. (2022), early in the COVID-19 global pandemic, the total mean daily screen use was 7.70 hours per day for participants aged 10 to 14—more than doubling the prepandemic estimate of 3.8 hours per day. This high level of internet use has adverse implications for children and adolescents' well-being, mental health, physical health, and safety.

Parents are concerned about the potential dangers and negative effects of screen time on their children and adolescents. When parents reflect on their childhood and think about time spent outside in nature, in their neighborhood, playing sports, or walking to friends' houses, they may feel concerned and fearful about the sedentary, addictive, and hypnotic nature of a lifestyle that incorporates a lot of screen time. Concerned parents often become worried about the physical impact (e.g., obesity, sleep problems), potential for victimization by predatorial and bullying individuals (e.g., sex trafficking, sexual abuse, online bullying), mental health effects (e.g., depression, fear of missing out, body-image issues), and other issues related to staring at a screen for long periods of time. They may also be worried about the effects of different types of screen activity (e.g., high-stimulation apps, gaming, chat rooms). Examples of online activity that often creates concern include programs/games demonstrating violence and risk-taking behavior, social media that attracts cyberbullying and predators, sexual content, programming that incorporates substance use, negative advertising aimed at children and adolescents, chat rooms with adult users who attempt to coerce youth into illegal sexual activity, and misleading and/or inaccurate online content (American Academy of Pediatrics [AAP], 2016; Fairclough, 2021; WHO, 2019).

Parents also consider the potential positive benefits of certain online programs that are educational and/or prosocial in nature. When the internet is used moderately, examples of activities that could benefit youth include pursuing knowledge through educational internet programs, improving manual dexterity by playing video games, and socializing through texting and video conferencing with friends and family. Furthermore, some parents may feel concerned that adolescents who do not engage in screen use may suffer from social isolation and will be poorly equipped for the digital world.

While the internet is not going away and adolescents require more independence than children do, it is still the parents' job to decide how much time teens spend online (e.g., "No screen time after 8:00 p.m."). In addition to establishing specific expectations, parents should set a good example by modeling appropriate screen usage. Many arguments and concerns can be ameliorated if computers are kept in a common area where the online content being utilized can be monitored by the caregivers (Fairclough, 2021).

WHO (2019) has published screen time and physical activity guidelines for children under the age of 5, recommending no screen time for children under 2 years of age and less than 1 hour per day for children 2 to 5 years of age. The AAP (2016) recommends no screen time for children under 18 months, except for video chatting. In addition, the American Psychological Association recommends that children 2 to 5 years of age have 1 hour or less of daily screen time (Pappas, 2022).

The AAP (2016) recommends that parents review all online content their child is accessing. This review can take place beforehand, or parents can watch shows, review apps, and play games with children to ensure the content is appropriate. Parents should ensure that online, app, and television-based content children are watching is age-appropriate, does not include adult sexual content, does not contain gratuitous violence, and is not saturated with fast-paced and distracting media. In households that include children of any age, parents should turn off the television and other devices when they are not being used, avoid screens during mealtimes, and ensure that children stop engaging in screen time 1 hour before bedtime. While exceptions exist (airplane flights, dental procedures), media should not be the only way to soothe children. Depending on screen time to soothe or calm down a child can prevent children from developing their own capacity for self-regulation and cause parents to become dependent on the internet as a babysitter whenever they want to focus on another task or take a break from parenting (AAP, n.d., 2016).

The AAP (2016) has developed a family media plan for older children and adolescents. This information focuses primarily on establishing limits and boundaries around screen time. Adolescent screen time often includes school homework and project completion, watching television shows, streaming videos, creating art or music online, gaming, connecting with peers via social media, and watching fast-stimulation online content (e.g., TikTok). While expectations for parental involvement change as children reach adolescence, parents continue to set limits and maintain awareness around what their teenagers are engaging in online. Due to the addictive nature of the internet, apps, and gaming, adolescents can spend far too much time online. This fixation with screens can create or exacerbate a sedentary lifestyle and lead to disengagement from in-person social activities, physical illness, and mental health issues (APP, 2016; Fairclough, 2021; WHO, 2019). Table 8.3 lists a number of internet-based parenting concerns, describes each issue, and summarizes pertinent best-practice standards.

TABLE 8.3   PARENTS' BEST-PRACTICE STANDARDS FOR CHILD INTERNET USE

Child Internet Use Issue	Description of Issue	Best-Practice Standards
Physical concerns	Negative physical effects of internet use on children, including obesity, sleep problems, etc.	Limitations and boundaries on screen time can encourage healthy habits with internet usage in children. WHO (2019) recommends no screen time for children under 2 years of age and less than 1 hour per day for children 2 to 5 years of age.
Predatorial concerns	Safety concerns surrounding predators on the internet, including social media, chat rooms with adult users, grooming youth for in-person encounters, sex trafficking, and sexual assault	The AAP (2016) recommends that parents talk to their children about the dangers and review all online content their child is accessing. Significant protective factors are parental involvement, supervision, and using the internet in a common area.
Bullying concerns	Concerns that internet use increases bullying of vulnerable children, including social media and online bullying	The AAP (2016) recommends that parents review all online content their child is accessing. Parental monitoring of internet usage and ensuring that the internet is accessed in a common area of the household can help reduce the likelihood that bullying will occur without the parents' knowledge.
Mental health concerns	Adverse effects of internet use on children's mental health, including an increase in depression, fear of missing out, body-image issues, anxiety, and feelings of inadequacy	The AAP (2016) recommends that parents review all content their child is engaging in. Setting limits around screen time can be helpful due to the addictive nature of internet sites, apps, and gaming. Parents can also turn off screens when not in use and avoid screens during mealtimes and before bedtime.
Online activity concerns	Concerns of possible adverse effects of internet-based activities on children's physical health, mental health, and safety; for example, children may be negatively affected by programs/games demonstrating violence and risk-taking behavior	The AAP (2016) recommends that parents review all online content their child is engaging in to ensure that all content is age-appropriate, does not include adult sexual content or violence, and does not rely heavily on fast-paced and distracting media.
Limiting screen use concerns	Concerns that restricting screen time may cause children to suffer from social isolation and be poorly equipped for the digital world	The AAP (2016) has developed a family media plan for older children which focuses on setting limits and boundaries for screen time. Parents can also demonstrate healthy boundaries with internet use for their children by being selective with their own usage.

AAP, American Academy of Pediatrics; WHO, World Health Organization.

Sources: Data from American Academy of Pediatrics. (n.d.). *Family media use plan.* HealthyChildren.org. Retrieved March 9, 2022, from https://www.healthychildren.org/English/media/Pages/default.aspx; World Health Organization. (2019). *Guidelines on physical activity, sedentary behavior and sleep for children under 5 years of age.* https://apps.who.int/iris/handle/10665/311664.

Outcomes Associated With Increased Screen Time

Evidence exists that parents rarely create firm boundaries around screen time. Chen and Adler (2019) collected data on 1,327 child participants via time diaries in 1997 and 2014. According to the findings, U.S. children aged 2 and under averaged 3 hours and

3 minutes of screen time per day in 2014. This was a major increase from 1997, when this age group had an average screen time of 1 hour and 19 minutes per day. Similarly, 3- to 5-year-olds engaged in 2 hours and 28 minutes of daily screen time in 2014. An interesting secondary finding of this investigation is that in 1997 *screen time* was defined as time spent watching television, playing video games, viewing videotapes, and engaging in home-based computer activity. The 2014 information described screen time in a more robust manner to include viewing television programs, videotapes, and digital video discs, and using game devices, computers, cell phones, smartphones, tablets, electronic readers, and children's learning devices. This is a good reminder that much of the screen time technology used today is relatively new. For example, first-generation iPhones were introduced in 2007 and iPads in 2010.

Walsh et al. (2018) investigated brain development, body movement, and screen usage with 4,524 U.S. children aged 8 to 11 years from 20 separate sites. The overall results demonstrated that meeting the 24-hour movement recommendations increased global cognitive ability. Furthermore, the results indicated that maintaining boundaries around recreational screen time improved cognitive ability and sleep time. A separate study using the same data set and age range indicated a combination of excessive screen time and inadequate sleep was correlated with childhood impulsivity (Guerrero et al., 2019). In summary, the aforementioned investigations found that lengthy screen usage was correlated with poor cognitive ability, shortened and disrupted sleep time, and impulsivity in children aged 8 to 11.

Stiglic and Viner (2019) conducted a systematic review of electronic databases to collect and analyze data indicating connections between child and adolescent screen time and any negative effects on health and well-being. The researchers found moderately strong correlational evidence between increased screen time and increased rates of obesity/adiposity and depressive symptoms. In addition, moderate evidence was discovered for an association between screen time and higher energy intake, a decrease in quality of healthy diet, and poorer quality of life.

Similarly, Goldfield et al. (2016) developed a cross-sectional study investigating the relationship between duration of screen time on different devices (e.g., computers, smartphones, video games) and depressive symptomology in a sample of 358 overweight and obese adolescents (aged 14–18). The researchers found that depressive symptomology was strongly associated with total screen time. Furthermore, while recreational computer time and video games were associated with depressive symptomology, television use was not significantly correlated.

Child and Adolescent Pornography Use

Internet pornography is centered on viewing, downloading, and observing videos and photographs of people engaging in sexual behavior. The sexual behaviors demonstrated in online pornography include, but are not limited to, sex (vaginal and anal), oral sex, masturbation, and a variety of sexual fetishes (Peter & Valkenburg, 2016). Because the internet is always available from virtually anywhere, pornography is constantly being globally disseminated in an accessible, affordable, and anonymous manner (Cooper, 1998). There are three basic fears regarding child and adolescent use of pornography, involving (a) easy access to pornography by children and adolescents, (b) the nature and content of pornography, and (c) the youth's inability to separate pornographic fantasy from the facts surrounding sexuality and sexual relationships (Wright & Štulhofer, 2019).

It is impossible to accurately determine the number of youth who view pornography intentionally due to the lack of online regulations, frequency of pornography-oriented pop-ups, widespread distribution of misleading spam and advertisements, mistyping of nonpornographic websites, and transmission of unsolicited explicit messages (Chen et al., 2013; Flood, 2007; Ševčíková, Šerek, Barbovschi & Daneback, 2014). Estimated rates of youth accidentally being exposed to internet pornography range from 19% to 32% (Hardy et al., 2013; Mitchell & Wells, 2007). One large-scale investigation (Wolak et al., 2007) revealed that 34% of 10- to 17-year-old participants deliberately searched and viewed internet pornography, while only 2% to 5% of boys and 1% of girls (ages 10–11) indicated intentional pornography use. These findings demonstrate that older youth tend to engage more frequently in intentional online pornography use, and younger youth usually stumble onto pornography sites accidentally.

There is a great deal of variability in research findings on pornography use among children and adolescents. First, pornography use among children under the age of 10 is relatively unexplored in the scholarly literature (Rothman et al., 2017). Regarding gender differences, it appears that males use internet pornography much more frequently than females do. One study (Ybarra et al., 2011) explored pornography use in youth 12 to 17 years of age and found that, of the 15% of intentional pornography users, 66% were male and 39% were female. Similarly, a large-scale pornography exposure study conducted by Andrie et al. (2021) found that, of the 10,930 adolescents interviewed (across six European countries), there was a sizable gender difference in exposure to pornography, with 76.5% of males stating they had witnessed pornography (40% indicating at least once per week), compared with only 42.9% of females admitting to watching pornography (8.9% indicating at least once per week).

Research has identified factors that increase the likelihood of youth pornography use. First, aside from contextual and psychosocial factors, one of the main indicators of youth-based pornography use is having unsupervised internet access on their phones or a computer in their bedroom (Hornor, 2020). This essentially increases the likelihood of pornography use due to opportunity and privacy. Other risk factors include male gender (Andrie et al., 2021), lower socioeconomic status (Hardy et al., 2013), identifying as bisexual or gay (Luder et al., 2011), living in a single-parent household (Ybarra & Mitchell, 2005), and having a sensation-seeking personality style (Peter & Valkenburg, 2016), rule-breaking tendencies (Hasking et al., 2011), weak attachment with caregivers (Ybarra & Mitchell, 2005), and being generally dissatisfied with their lives (Peter & Valkenburg, 2016). Lastly, youth tend to view pornography if they have undergone various interpersonal and psychosocial experiences, including social deviance (i.e., rule-breaking, norm-breaking; Hasking et al., 2011), parental divorce (Peter & Valkenburg, 2016), bullying and cyberbullying (Shek & Ma, 2014), and less family investment in religion (Peter & Valkenburg, 2016).

While many correlational risk factors are associated with youth pornography use, there are also protective factors that serve as a barrier to child and adolescent pornography use. First and foremost, a significant protective factor is parent involvement, supervision, and using the internet in a common area (e.g., not in the bedroom alone; Hornor, 2020). Additional protective factors include belief and engagement with religion, higher educational level of parents, higher socioeconomic status, greater investment and engagement with school, and healthier family relationships (Brown & L'Engle, 2009; Mesch, 2009).

Online Predators

Perhaps the most frightening aspect of the internet is the potential for a child or adolescent to be victimized by an online predator. Frequent media coverage of online/cyber predators can make the internet feel like a dangerous place for children and adolescents (Wolak, Finkelhor, Mitchell, & Ybarra, 2008). Many parents deeply fear online predators and work hard to protect their children or adolescents from sharing their identity and other information (e.g., profile pictures, personal information, social media information) online. Common internet-based platforms and devices used by online predators to make contact, socialize, and eventually exploit children and adolescents include social media sites, cell phones, chat rooms, video game consoles, apps and app-based video games, and instant messaging. These platforms allow predators to access potential victims in an anonymous, distant, and discreet manner to increase the opportunity for deception and manipulation (Wolak, Finkelhor, Mitchell, & Ybarra, 2008; Wolak & Finkelhor, 2013). Regarding deception, Quayle et al. (2014) found that online predators pretend to be much younger in many different areas (e.g., profile, name, physical appearance, hobbies, interests). This deception is part of an illegal strategy to lure unsuspecting youth into sexual conversations with people who appear to be of a similar age.

Predators often prefer the online environment because it provides an anonymous platform for becoming acquainted with potential victims without any community-based safeguards in place (e.g., concerned parents, teachers, police, other youth; McAlinden, 2006). The most common age range for targets of online victimization is between 13 and 17 years. Investigations show a greater likelihood of victimization for girls, youth identifying as LGBTQIA+, and those with existing psychological vulnerabilities such as a history of physical or sexual abuse, early childhood traumatization, and a diagnosis of depression (De Santisteban et al., 2018; Winters et al., 2017; Wolak & Finkelhor, 2013; Wolak et al., 2013). Online predators also take advantage of characteristics (i.e., risk factors) that make youth susceptible to manipulation and deceit. Most of these risk factors involve communication of personal information, developmentally normal youth behavior, and idiosyncrasies unique to particular youth, including, but not limited to, (a) youth who send personal information (e.g., name, age, telephone number, email address) to strangers when requested; (b) youth who demonstrate normal curiosity about intimacy; (c) youth seeking attention and affection from people they do not know; (d) youth with poor parental relationships; (e) youth who chat online with strangers about sex and sexual content; (f) youth who engage in risky behavior; (g) delinquent youth; and (h) youth who suffer from sadness, loneliness, shyness, or a lack of social skills (Beebe et al., 2004; Mitchell et al., 2007; Peter et al., 2005; Sun et al., 2005; Wolak et al., 2003).

The two common types of predators are *contact-driven* and *fantasy-driven* offenders (Briggs et al., 2011). According to Briggs et al. (2011), contact-driven offenders spend a short amount of time online and seduce and manipulate a child or adolescent to meet them offline as soon as possible. Fantasy-driven offenders spend a considerable amount of time grooming and engaging with minors online before ever considering meeting in person (if they ever do). Studies have indicated that the average amount of time fantasy-driven offenders spend grooming children online is between 32.9 and 180 days (Briggs et al., 2011; De Santisteban et al., 2018). In addition to the characteristics described in these common offender profiles, many offenders have criminal histories, desire power in relationships, seek admiration from naïve victims, want to reexperience adolescence, are fearful of adult relationships, have a low level of education, and feel inadequate in key areas. Offenders who are child molesters may exhibit anger, curiosity, impulsiveness, and a tendency to become behaviorally addicted to sexually exploiting youth (De Santisteban et al., 2018; Hines & Finkelhor, 2007; Lanning, 2002).

Motivated adult predators use the internet to increase their interactions with minors, operate multiple scenarios, and engage with multiple potential targets simultaneously (Winters et al., 2017). According to Wolak, Finkelhor, Mitchell, and Yabarra (2008), most crimes involving online predators are perpetrated by adult men who use the internet to meet youth and seduce them into sexual encounters. If caught, offenders are often charged with *statutory rape* with victims who are too young to consent to sex. Every state in the United States has a law indicating that youth below a particular age are too young to consent to intercourse; however, many states have their own unique age of consent, exemption around peer relationships within a particular age range, and increased severity of punishment for crimes involving younger children, intoxicated youth, and those that involve a trusted adult (e.g., priest, teacher, relative; Davis & Twombly, 2000; Glosser et al., 2004; Norman-Eady et al., 2003).

To reduce the potential for exploitation by online predators, parents can teach their children and adolescents a few basic rules for online activity: (a) never trade or post a photograph of yourself; (b) never offer personal information to strangers; (c) never share passwords with others; (d) never meet someone in person without parental permission and supervision; (e) never reply to a hostile email, message, post, or text; and (f) discuss hurtful and scary communication with a trusted adult. Further, parents should take other measures to guide their child or adolescent toward appropriate online behavior. Preventive measures should include spending time together looking at websites, keeping computers and other screens in common areas of the house that lend themselves to monitoring, bookmarking sites that are child favorites, and taking one's child/adolescent seriously if they report any scary or inappropriate online exchanges. Parents and other stakeholders should watch for potential warning signs that a child or adolescent might be engaging in an online predatorial experience, including, but not limited to, spending a large amount of time online, particularly at night; receiving phone calls or unsolicited gifts in the mail from unknown people; immediately turning off their device whenever a parent or another adult enters the room; and withdrawing from normal family life (Ben-Joseph, n.d.).

According to Wolak, Finkelhor, and Mitchell (2008), youth who have risk factors for internet-initiated sex crimes may not be open to parental advice and/or supervision. In addition, youth who demonstrate many of the risk factors may be alienated from their parents, enjoy the initial fantasy-based internet experiences with the predator, are victims of child abuse and/or neglect, or are questioning their sexual orientation and feel afraid to disclose this to their parent(s). Because of these issues and others, the best strategy may be to reach out directly and indirectly to the youth with media, peers, and/or authorities.

One final recommendation for preventive approaches is to address the developmentally appropriate and normal sexual feelings, urges, and curiosities that many adolescents have (Wolak, Finkelhor, & Mitchell, 2008). Wolak, Finkelhor, and Mitchell (2008) described the unrealistic nature of approaches that ignore developmentally appropriate sexual urges and curiosities and instruct youth to immediately tell a parent or trusted adult about internet-initiated sexual advances. Instead of only being instructed to immediately notify adults, youth should also be instructed on predatorial dynamics, seduction, grooming, and other ways in which online predators manipulate and exploit children and adolescents. Specifically, they should be informed about how online predators are aware of the sexual vulnerability of youth and use this to groom, exploit, and eventually engage in illegal in-person sexual contact.

CHILD ABUSE AND NEGLECT

Approximately 40 million children worldwide are abused annually (Butchart et al., 2006). Child maltreatment, including physical abuse, sexual abuse, psychological abuse, and neglect, is a very serious global public health issue. A meta-analysis of 244 self-reported studies conducted in different countries provided the following estimates of global prevalence of child maltreatment: physical abuse, 22.6%; emotional abuse, 36.3%; physical neglect, 16.3%; and emotional neglect, 18.4% (Stoltenborgh et al., 2015). The Children's Bureau published the 30th edition of the *Child Maltreatment Report* in 2019. According to the 2019 edition of the report, at least one in seven U.S. youth have experienced child abuse and/or neglect. Additionally, in 2019, 1,840 U.S. children died due to abuse and/or neglect. The number of fatalities represents a 60-person increase from 2018. Regarding child protective service investigations, in 2019 approximately 656,000 U.S. children were determined to be victims of maltreatment. The most common type of maltreatment was neglect (61.0%), followed by physical abuse (10.3%; U.S. Department of Health and Human Services et al., 2020). More recently, WHO (2021) reported that the increased stress, school closures, loss of financial security, and social isolation resulting from the COVID-19 global pandemic had increased the risk of child abuse and neglect.

According to the CDC (2020) report entitled *Trends in U.S. Emergency Department Visits Related to Suspected or Confirmed Child Abuse and Neglect Among Children and Adolescents Aged <18 Years Before and During the COVID-19 Pandemic, United States, January 2019–September 2020*, the pandemic created child abuse trends that require greater analysis to be fully understood (Swedo et al., 2020). While COVID-19 brought many challenging and/or negative issues that had the potential to fan the flames of abuse (e.g., loss of income/job, increased stress, living in close quarters for long periods of time, increased schooling and childcare responsibilities, increased substance use), official reports from child protective service agencies suggest that child abuse and neglect decreased nationally by 20% to 70% during 2019 and 2020 (Peterman et al., 2020). This decline has been attributed to less contact with people and professionals outside the home (e.g., teachers, counselors, physicians) who serve as mandated reporters (Welch & Haskins, 2020). While reports were down, the number of ED visits related to child abuse and neglect were up. Specifically, according to the CDC, children and adolescents under 18 years of age experienced a 2.1% increase in ED visits in 2019 and a 3.2% increase in ED visits in 2020. Closer examination of the statistics reveals that the largest increase occurred among children aged 0 to 4 years (3.5% in 2019 and 5.3% in 2020), compared with children aged 5 to 11 years (0.7% in 2019 and 1.3% in 2020), and adolescents aged 12 to 17 years (1.6% in 2019 vs. 2.2% in 2020; CDC, 2020).

Children are never responsible for being abused or neglected; however, they do unfortunately become victims of the terrible emotional and psychological pain that results from their experiences with maltreatment. According to Fortson et al. (2016), child abuse and neglect has lifelong effects on one's physical health, mental health, and sense of wellness if left untreated. The authors further add that childhood violence heightens the risks of harm, future aggression, victimization and perpetration, polysubstance abuse, sexually transmitted diseases, brain damage, lack of interest in higher education, and lack of employment prospects. A mix of relational (e.g., lack of family cohesion, family substance use), individual (e.g., child disability, child abuse history), community (e.g., community violence, higher poverty rates), and societal (e.g., war, pandemic) issues influence child abuse and neglect (CDC, n.d.).

Risk factors for child maltreatment have been provided by the CDC (n.d.). These risk factors should be considered when working with families that present with aggressive and/or violent behavior. These include (a) child disability and cognitive delay; (b) social isolation; (c) parents' ignorance of child development and parenting; (d) lack of family cohesion; (e) family substance abuse; (f) parental stress and distress; and (g) having young, single, and nonbiological parents. Three additional major risk factors deserve further exploration: negative parenting issues and styles, poverty, and previous experiences of being abused and/or neglected.

Caregivers and/or parents are the most frequent perpetrators of child victimization (U.S. Department of Health & Human Services et al., 2020). This parent-initiated abuse represents a pathologic relationship that significantly deviates from basic child-rearing standards (Cicchetti & Toth, 2005).

Certain parenting styles are associated with abuse potential. Specifically, harsh or authoritarian and permissive parenting styles are closely associated with abuse (Darling & Steinberg, 1993; Rodriguez, 2010), while the uninvolved parenting style is the most closely associated with neglect (Kuppens & Ceulemans, 2019).

The second factor that contributes to child abuse and neglect is the family's socioeconomic status. Abuse is five times higher among children in lower socioeconomic groups than those in higher socioeconomic groups (U.S. Department of Health & Human Services et al., 2020). In addition, among low-income families, those with family exposure to substance use have been shown to exhibit the highest rates of child abuse and neglect (Ondersma, 2002). Parenting styles are a cluster of attitudes related to how parents express themselves to children and the way they create an environment to raise their children (Darling & Steinberg, 1993). It has been discovered that children who grow up in families with lower socioeconomic status tend to have parents who raise them with harsher and more punitive authoritarian techniques (Haskett et al., 1995; Rodriguez, 2010). As such, poverty is a reliable predictor of child abuse and neglect. While most families with low socioeconomic status do not abuse or neglect their children, poverty does create a heightened risk because it is often comorbid with other influencing elements, such as extreme stress, substance abuse, lower education, harsh disciplinary practices, and occupational turmoil (Haskett et al., 1995; Hoffman, 2008; Rodriguez, 2010). Furthermore, mental health issues, parental expectations, and available resources are often negatively affected by poverty (Roubinov & Boyce, 2017).

The third factor that increases the risk of child abuse is being a victim of parental abuse during childhood. A violence orientation during the formative years of childhood is a key factor in what many people consider to be the cycle of abuse (CDC, n.d.). Specifically, research suggests that a sizable percentage of individuals who have been physically abused, sexually abused, or neglected engage in child violence, act out sexually toward children, and neglect children (Glasser et al., 2001; Kaufman & Zigler, 1987; Pears & Capaldi, 2001). Data from the National Longitudinal Study of Adolescent Health in the United States found that parents who reported being physically abused during their childhood were five times more likely to be reported as physically abusive parents than those who were not abused as youth (Kim et al., 2009). Kim et al. also discovered that parents who reported being neglected during childhood were 2.6 times more likely to neglect their own children than were those who were not neglected. Similarly, Glasser et al. (2001) found that, for male participants, having been sexually victimized as a child was a strong predictor of becoming a perpetrator as an adult. These investigations clearly point to a victim-to-victimizer cycle for physical abuse, sexual abuse, and neglect. While this pattern exists for some, it is important to note that many child maltreatment victims/survivors do not become perpetrators of abuse or neglect. Additionally, while the trend is prevalent in many studies, Salter et al. (2003) conducted a longitudinal study on 224 males who were survivors of child sexual abuse and discovered that only 11.6% became future child sex offenders.

Types of Child Abuse and Neglect

WHO (2022) defines child maltreatment as "all types of physical and/or emotional ill-treatment, sexual abuse, neglect, negligence and commercial or other exploitation, which results in actual or potential harm to the child's health, survival, development or dignity in the context of a relationship of responsibility, trust or power" (para. 1).

Similarly, *Psychology Today* (2021) defines *child abuse and neglect* as sexual, physical, or emotional pain inflicted on youth. Child abuse often involves actions such as hitting, inappropriate sexual contact, and name calling; however, inaction (i.e., neglect) can cause a great deal of damage as well. Child abuse can manifest in at least four different ways: neglect, physical abuse, psychological abuse, and sexual abuse (Gonzalez et al., 2021). Protecting children from abuse and neglect is not a new endeavor. In fact, the Child Abuse Prevention and Treatment Act (CAPTA) was passed in 1974, bringing national attention to the maltreatment of children and adolescents. As of 1986, all U.S. states had created a legal infrastructure that requires mandated reporting within pertinent professions, including mental health professionals, nurses, social workers, and teachers (Black & Flynn, 2021).

Physical Abuse

Child physical abuse involves intentional, unintentional, or threatened harm to a child by an adult. This abuse is typically nonaccidental, and its initiation can range from emotional and chaotic outbursts to a controlled, nonemotional pattern of ritualized abuse (Wolfe, 1999). There are a lot of variabilities and varieties in the types and signs of physical abuse. Evidence of physical abuse includes unexplained welts, bruises, and abrasions on certain areas of the body (e.g., lips, mouth, face, torso, back, buttocks, thighs). Burning is the second type of physical abuse. Signs of burning include unexplained surface burns from a lighter, cigar, or cigarette, or immersion burns that have unique design patterns (e.g., sock-like, glove-like, doughnut-shaped). Additionally, unexplained lacerations and abrasions to the eyes, lips, mouth, or gums are very rare, are uncommon, and are often signs of abuse. Lastly, unexplained broken or fractured bones should be investigated as there is typically a well-known and documented reason for this type of childhood injury (Fraenkel et al., 2004).

A topic relevant to physical abuse is the use of corporal punishment (e.g., spanking) to discipline a child. Historically, briefly striking a child for punishment was widely accepted in many cultures, and currently it is legally allowed in many states in the United States. While this practice is often tolerated, there is a growing body of research suggesting that corporal punishment leads to many negative issues (e.g., anxiety, behavioral issues, depression, aggression; Afifi et al., 2012; Gershoff, 2008). In addition, the AAP and the American Psychological Association denounce corporal punishment and consider it harmful and unwarranted. Lastly, Smith (2012) reported that globally 30 countries have completely banned the use of corporal punishment in any setting.

Sexual Abuse

Any sexual activity with a person who cannot or is not able to give consent is considered sexual abuse. Child sexual abuse is any form of sexual behavior between an adult and a child/adolescent. This includes any form of penetration (penile, digital, with an external object), fondling of a child's genitals and breasts, exposing the genitalia, or commercially exploiting a child through pornography or prostitution (Black & Flynn, 2021; Finkelhor, 1979). Clinicians must be aware of their state's laws regarding age of consent and statutory rape. Statutory rape is a federal crime in which an individual attempts to engage in a sexual act with a person who is at least 4 years younger and is between the ages of 12 and 16 years. At the state level, there is variability regarding age of consent standards. An interactive map is available here: www.ageofconsent.net/states.

Behavioral signs of child sexual abuse could include, but are not limited to, abdominal pain, bedwetting, challenges with walking or sitting, pain, and itching in the genital area. Other physical signs include child, preteen, or teenage anal or genital bruising, bleeding, sexually transmitted disease, urinary tract infection, and pregnancy. Unexplained withdrawal from physical activities, refusing to change clothes, unusual demands for privacy, marked change in eating or sleeping patterns, public masturbation, unusual sexual behavior, nightmares and unusual fears, and reports of sexual assault are behavioral indicators of sexual abuse (Black & Flynn, 2021; Capstick & Fraenkel, 2004; Finkelhor, 1979).

Emotional Abuse

Emotional abuse is often experienced concurrently with some other types of abuse. In other words, these categories of abuse are not often mutually exclusive. For example, when a child is physically abused (e.g., through hitting, kicking, burning, punching), the injury is often accompanied by emotional and psychological abuse (e.g., yelling, name calling, demoralizing speech). Emotional abuse can deeply compromise a youth's psychological health. While all abuse creates some sort of emotional hurt, serious emotional abuse leaves little external evidence, carries an extremely painful toll, and can affect victims for a long period of time. Examples include close confinement (e.g., locking a child in a small space, restraining a child to a bed), emotional and verbal assault (e.g., hurtful name calling, repeated insults, derogatory comments), and other general areas of emotional abuse (e.g., denying food, assigning extreme responsibilities). Signs of emotional abuse include speech disorders, failure to thrive, lags in physical development, emotional detachment, sudden changes in emotional regulation, age-inappropriate interpersonal boundaries, age-incongruent vocabulary, poor performance in school, social withdrawal, and impaired social skills. Lastly, parents may emotionally abuse youth by exposing them to drugs, alcohol, prostitution, assault, theft, and gambling (Black & Flynn, 2021; Capstick & Fraenkel, 2004; Finkelhor, 1979).

Neglect

Neglect is considered an act of omission in which a caregiver ignores a child's basic needs for a significant period. In general, caregivers who engage in neglect do not provide the bare necessities that help a child live a healthy life. Physical and emotional neglects are the most common types; however, many different forms of neglect are identified in the literature (e.g., medical neglect, educational neglect). A few of the most common types of physical neglect include refusing to provide medical or mental healthcare to a child; withholding food, clothes, and shelter; and not keeping up with a child's basic hygiene (e.g., dental care). A few examples of emotional neglect include withholding affection, engaging in chronic family violence, and allowing adolescents to use alcohol and drugs. Indicators of child neglect are desperately affectionate behavior, stealing money or other necessities, not attending school, inability to gain weight, and unattended physical problems or medical needs (Black & Flynn, 2021; Capstick & Fraenkel, 2004; Dubowitz et al., 1993; Finkelhor, 1979).

GRANDPARENTS RAISING GRANDCHILDREN

Nationally, it has become common for grandparents to serve as foster or surrogate parents for their grandchildren. In the United States, approximately 7.9 million children are living with grandparents or other relatives, with 2.65 million (4%) of youth living in grandfamilies with neither parent present (Annie E. Casey Foundation Kids Count Data Center, 2020). Additionally, it appears that the number of children being raised by grandparents in the United States is on the rise. For example, in 2005 a total of

2.5 million children were being raised by grandparents, and in 2015 the number had risen to 2.9 million children (Wiltz, 2016). Further, between 1970 and 2012, the number of children living in grandparent-headed U.S. households nearly doubled (Ellis & Simmons, 2014). When a child or children are raised by a grandparent or grandparents, the living arrangement could be called a grandfamily, skipped generation household, grandparent household, or grandparent kinship care. Whatever label is placed on the arrangement, the essence is the same: grandparents are raising their grandchildren.

When grandparents raise grandchildren, their engagement with the caretaking process can range from being completely and legally responsible for all aspects of the caretaking process (i.e., custodial grandparents), or partly and informally responsible for helping with child-rearing duties. Demographically speaking, custodial grandparents are often female, unmarried, younger than 60, and less educated (Ellis & Simmons, 2014). Grandparents can be asked to step into the parental role for a plethora of reasons, including, but not limited to, family crises, parental death, parental imprisonment, divorce, poverty, war, child protective service child removal, urban migration, teenage pregnancy, child disability, divorce, military deployment, abandonment, and death (Hayslip et al., 2017). While there are many reasons for taking on the family custodial parent role later in life, grandparents who raise grandchildren are maintaining the child's connection with the family of origin, living in communities the youth is familiar with, maintaining cultural traditions, and creating a sense of safety with other family members by serving as an essential social support (Generations United, 2018).

Socioeconomic status, race, and ethnicity are relevant singular and/or intersectional factors for grandfamilies. Grandparents often have a limited or fixed income, and the lack of sufficient financial resources is often a significant source of stress (Roe & Minkler, 1998). Most custodial grandparents are also part of the workforce and contribute partly or entirely to the financial aspects of raising grandchildren. Despite their late-in-life participation in the workforce, according to Turner's (2020) analysis of the CDC, 17% of these families live in poverty. Fields (2003) indicated that, in comparison with parent-led households, grandfamilies with a primary caregiver present were twice as likely to be living in poverty.

Regarding race and ethnicity, it can be normative for families of color to depend on grandparents to raise grandchildren. If primary caregivers are unavailable, it can be a great cultural strength for grandparents to take on a major or minor role with raising grandchildren. Unfortunately, when caregivers/parents of color cannot take care of their children, grandparents are often expected to parent without sufficient resources (e.g., finances, education, support from other relatives, support from society). Regarding race, American Indian/Alaskan Native, Hispanic, and Black grandfamilies are overly represented. However, due to cultural issues (e.g., the opioid epidemic), the number of White grandfamilies has increased (Ellis & Simmons, 2014; Livingston & Parker, 2010). Lastly, Dolbin-MacNab and Few-Demo (2018) aptly stated that the intersectional nature of race, class, age, and gender often creates greater risk for negative outcomes and further marginalization of grandfamilies.

Parenting Concerns With Being Raised by Grandparents

According to Lent and Otto (2018), grandparents who raise grandchildren report a deep sense of meaning in their contributions and a deepening of their relationship with grandchildren. However, raising grandchildren later in life (often with little support) can bring serious challenges. Specifically, grandparents may face enormous obstacles as they strive to effectively prepare children, monitor child health and wellness, and safeguard their own well-being. To add to the immense responsibility associated with childcare, many parenting practices and standards, educational guidelines, and health values and principles may have changed from years ago when grandparents were raising their own children. Specifically, grandparent caregiving challenges include (a) difficulties with maintaining discipline in the home, (b) difficulty meeting their grandchildren's educational and social needs, (c) difficulty understanding technology and the extensive use of computers and technology for school work, (d) maintaining the health of grandchildren, (e) personal emotional and psychological distress from the burden of raising children later in life, (f) personal physical health issues due to the increased amount of work combined with natural age-related issues, and (g) the added financial burden of raising grandchildren (Caputo, 2000; Fuller-Thomson, 2005; Fuller-Thomson et al., 1997; Hayslip & Kaminski, 2008; Neely-Barnes et al., 2010; Peterson, 2017; Yoo & Russell, 2020).

Aside from feelings of resentment, exhaustion, declining mobility, and discontentment with having to engage in the parenting role at an unexpected period of life (Jendrek, 1994), custodial and less formal grandparenting arrangements often suffer from multiple social and structural stressors. For example, grandparents may have challenges with contemporary U.S. family values regarding limit-setting and discipline techniques. Research demonstrates that some grandparents may be more lenient with their grandchildren than they were with their own children (Sampson & Hertlein, 2015). On the other hand, researchers have also found that grandparents' disciplinary procedures may be harsher and more likely to include outdated methods of corporal punishment (Zolotor et al., 2011).

When grandparents begin parenting grandchildren, they quickly realize how much has changed since they were parents. Two significant areas of concern are educational standards and social expectations. The complex educational, social, and extracurricular demands of raising grandchildren could include the following challenges: difficulties with mathematical comprehension, lack of confidence in learning new technology, unfamiliarity with internet platforms and social media, feeling alienated from parent–teacher meetings, feelings of isolation from younger parents, and having little in common with their grandchildren's friends (Giarrusso et al., 2000; Lee at al., 2019; Pittman & Boswell, 2007; Strom & Strom, 2000). Table 8.4 provides a summary of the major challenges faced by grandparents raising grandchildren.

TABLE 8.4   COMMON GRANDPARENTING DIFFICULTY AREAS AND EXAMPLES

Grandparenting Difficulty Area	Descriptions and/or Examples
Legal issues	Obtaining custody/guardianship, enrollment in school, accessing medical care, custody disputes
Financial issues	Difficulty with financially supporting housing, food, clothing, automobile
Parenting practices	Difficulty understanding parental discipline strategies, child development, contemporary childhood problems
Physical and mental health	Limited energy, physical health problems, neglecting their health due to a lack of financial resources, significant issues with anxiety and depression
Social	Less personal time, less time with one's partner and/or friends, inability to socialize and difficulty relating to younger parents and children
Family relationships	Resentment toward absent parents, desire to protect their grandchildren from parents' issues, difficulty setting limits with their grandchildren's parents
Accessing services	Unawareness of the range of family services available, issues with accessing services due to a variety of barriers, feeling disrespected and judged by service providers

Source: Data from Dolbin-MacNab, M., & Stucki, D. (2022). *Grandparents raising grandchildren*. Grandparents. Retrieved March 9, 2022, from https://www.aamft.org/Consumer_Updates/grandparents.aspx.

Due to the bidirectional relationship in any parenting arrangement, it is also important to consider the grandchild and their internal experiences in grandfamilies. According to an American Association for Marriage and Family Therapy (AAMFT) Consumer Report, youth raised by grandparents may have a variety of mental health, academic, emotional, and developmental challenges as a result of their experiences with their parents (not grandparents), including ". . . depression, anxiety, ADHD [attention deficit hyperactivity disorder], physical health problems, learning disabilities, poor school performance, developmental delays, and aggression. Grandchildren may also experience feelings of anger, rejection, and guilt" (Dolbin-MacNab & Bradford, n.d., para. 12). Due, in part, to the variability in initial caregiver issues, there is little consistency regarding the degree of intensity that the issue presents itself within grandchildren. This report also indicates that visits from parents can be difficult, unpredictable, and unstable. Children are often confused as to why their parent cannot spend more time with them. Lastly, grandchildren may feel disconnected from their grandparents in key areas, including, but not limited to, social relationships, technology, leisure activities, fashion, school, and household chores (Dolbin-MacNab & Stucki, 2022).

Opioid Abuse and Grandparents Raising Grandchildren

Nationally, highly addictive opioids have been responsible for approximately 70% of accidental drug overdoses (Wilson et al., 2020), making opioid overdose the leading cause of death in the United States (Feder et al., 2018). Opioids include painkillers (e.g., oxycodone, codeine, morphine, hydrocodone), synthetic opioids (e.g., fentanyl, carfentanil), and illegal drugs (e.g., heroin). Many of the people who misuse opioids or die from opioid overdoses are parents (Feder et al., 2018). Due to excessive use of opioids by expecting mothers, every 15 minutes an infant with prenatal exposure to opioids is born (Honein et al., 2019). The presence of opioid misuse and abuse creates an increased risk of future child abuse, child removal from home, and children being temporarily or permanently placed with alternative caregivers (Radel et al., 2018).

Initial evidence seems to suggest that the opioid epidemic has greatly contributed to the increased number of grandparents raising grandchildren in the United States (Dolbin-MacNab & O'Connell, 2021). Generations United (2018), in its survey on programs that assist grandparents raising grandchildren, concluded that 70% of grandfamilies were negatively impacted by parental opioid abuse. Furthermore, states with the highest rates of opioid prescriptions also had the largest numbers of grandparents raising grandchildren (Anderson, 2019). Sepulveda and Williams (2019) found that between 2007 and 2017 the percentage of youth being removed from homes and placed with relatives increased by 26% to 33%. Research into the child welfare system has revealed that parental substance abuse and misuse has greatly increased the number of children entering the foster care system and the number of youths removed from their parents' home and placed in the homes of relatives (Sepulveda & Williams, 2019).

PARENTAL GRIEF AFTER THE DEATH OF A CHILD

Grieving the death of a child of any age is beyond devastating. Most people cannot even fathom the idea of losing a child or ever recovering from such a loss. Truly, grieving the death of a child has no end (Woodgate, 2006). A caregiver going through this extreme pain feels as if a major part of the parent and family has died. While the prospect of losing a child is difficult to consider and conceptualize, children die every day, and parents, family, and friends attempt to understand, make meaning of, and grieve this immense loss in their own unique ways. While all bereavements can create stress, the bereavement and grieving process that parents endure when they lose a child can create extremely intense and enduring feelings of stress and pain (Bonanno, 2001; Fish, 1986; Martinson et al., 1991).

According to the CDC, in 2020 there were 3,529 deaths among U.S. children aged 1 to 4 years and 5,623 deaths among aged 5 to 14 years. The CDC (2020) elaborated on the leading causes of death for each age range (see Table 8.5). Globally speaking, WHO (2021) described substantial global reductions in childhood mortality in 2020. The total global child death numbers in 2020 include approximately 37 deaths per 1,000 live births globally and 5.0 million deaths in children under the age of 5. These figures demonstrate a major improvement in comparison with statistics gathered 20 years earlier. In 1990, WHO (2021) reported 93 deaths per 1,000 births globally and 12.6 million deaths in children under the age of 5 (WHO, n.d.).

Everyone grieves a loss in their own unique way. While most literature and research point to the extreme amount of pain and devastation experienced by surviving family members after the death of a child (Bartel, 2020; Cacciatore et al., 2014; Meij et al., 2008), the grieving process manifests differently in each person. For example, one member of a grieving family may spend a month becoming tearful on a daily basis, while another member of the family may cry for 1 day for 5 straight hours, and a third member of the same family may find a sense of release in singing a song that reminds them of the deceased. Because of the individuality of the grieving process, there is no "right" or "wrong" way to grieve the loss of a child.

While there are no set patterns for familial reactions to losing a child, the grief process could include guilt, anger, denial, shock, hopelessness, isolation, cognitive distortions, and a wide array of other possible grieving experiences. The major predictors of the family's future ability to cope and continue pushing forward are the health of family communication, cohesiveness, and flexibility. In short, when family members can adapt to change and communicate well with each other, their relationship may survive undamaged, but if these elements are unhealthy or weak the family may become fragmented (Bartel, 2020; Cacciatore et al., 2014; Meij et al., 2008).

Although unique grieving methods exist, the weight of the death of a child can create a state of unbearable horror that lasts a very long time for the family (Meij et al., 2008). The thought of a child's life ending so quickly, burying or cremating a child well before their predicted time of death, and the shock and disbelief around the family member being permanently gone can challenge core beliefs and assumptions about the world and

TABLE 8.5   CDC INFORMATION ON LEADING CAUSES OF CHILD MORTALITY

Age Range (Years)	Leading Cause 1	Leading Cause 2	Leading Cause 3
1–4	Accidental	Congenital malformation, deformations, chromosomal abnormalities	Assault (homicide)
5–9	Accidental	Cancer	Congenital malformation, deformations, chromosomal abnormalities
10–14	Accidental	Intentional self-harm (suicide)	Cancer

CDC, Centers for Disease Control and Prevention.

Source: Data from Centers for Disease Control and Prevention, National Center for Health Statistics. (2022, February 1). *FastStats—Child health.* Retrieved March 9, 2022, from https://www.cdc.gov/nchs/fastats/child-health.htm

completely dysregulate a parental subsystem (Klaassen, 2010). The untimely death of a child also creates temporary turmoil within most family systems. Specifically, trauma and deep sadness over the loss can create issues with family system rules, roles, and boundaries. For example, parents may briefly relate to each other in a much different manner (e.g., easily angered, harsh startups, quiet and defensive) following a child's death. If there is little awareness and empathy in regard to the partner's grieving process, this disconnection can create marital/long-term relationship problems.

Many models have been created to depict the process and/or stages within the grieving process. For example, the dual process model (Stroebe & Schut, 1999) is a bereavement theory that describes the importance of vacillating between loss-oriented coping (i.e., continued focus on the painful loss and death of the child) and restoration-oriented coping (i.e., adapting to the new normal and engaging in normal daily activities). This model postulates the importance of spending time together and the need for silence and distance when caregivers grieve the death of a child (Hooghe et al., 2012). In addition to partners supporting each other, there is evidence suggesting the importance of emotional support from friends, colleagues, and social networks during the bereavement process (Hooghe & Dassonneville, 2018).

Research findings indicate that coping with bereavement within the family can be supported by family members maintaining a relationship with the deceased, engaging in private rituals and practices around the deceased, and cocreating a sense of meaning in regard to the child's life and death (Granados et al., 2009; Gudmundsdottir & Chesla, 2006; Keesee et al., 2008). According to Davies (2004), families that maintain a bond with the deceased can sustain a healthy grieving process. The *bonds theory* purports that maintaining an interactive relationship with the deceased can create higher levels of acceptance and adaptability. For example, continuing to have casual and serious conversations with the deceased is considered a method for maintaining a bond with the deceased.

Creating a sense of connection with the deceased can also be greatly enhanced by engaging in rituals and practices centered on the deceased (Bartel, 2020). This process also enhances the family's ongoing relational connections. This could include rituals like saying a family prayer regarding the deceased family member at the same time every night or setting the child's favorite spot at the dining room table (Gudmundsdottir & Chesla, 2006). Lastly, recovery from most crises, including the death of a child, can be aided through engaging in a thorough meaning-making process (Keesee et al., 2008). Questions that could set the stage for a helpful meaning-making process in the family might include the following: "What do you remember most about the deceased family member?", "What meaning can you take away from their death?", or "What aspects of the deceased are you most grateful for tonight?"

SUMMARY

In this chapter, readers were introduced to a variety of key contemporary issues related to treating families, including the effects of racism and intersectionality on families, family cohesion and flexibility, blended and stepfamilies, multiracial families, contemporary parenting issues, obesity, various contemporary family issues regarding the internet, child abuse and neglect, grandparents raising grandchildren, and parental grief after the death of a child. The main objective of this chapter was to describe the nuances of these issues that affect today's families. Specifically, throughout the chapter, readers were provided with contemporary examples, key information, and in-depth conceptualizations that accentuate the powerful effect each contemporary issue has on families.

END-OF-CHAPTER RESOURCES

 SPRINGER PUBLISHING **CONNECT™**

A robust set of instructor resources designed to supplement this text is located at http://connect.springerpub.com/content/book/978-0-8261-8775-8. Qualifying instructors may request access by emailing textbook@springerpub.com.

STUDENT ACTIVITIES

Exercise 1: Parenting Styles

Directions: Review the following information and answer the reflection questions:

The way that parents interact with their children can heavily influence the child's morals, values, principles, and conduct. Various parenting styles are associated with different child outcomes. Classic parenting styles include authoritative, authoritarian, permissive, rejecting, and uninvolved. This categorization does not include metaphorical parenting styles such as helicopter, snowplow, tiger, and panda parenting styles. When working with parents and families, it is important to understand how a particular parenting style can affect children, parents, and the family.

- Compare and contrast the five common parenting styles described in the chapter.

- Consider why the metaphorical parenting styles may be more common today. What societal, family, and political factors may contribute to these styles? Consider how you would work with these factors when helping families.

- When working with families, it is important to be able to distinguish cultural norms from idiosyncratic parenting issues that could be detrimental to children. Consider how you would broach this topic with parents in session and how you would adapt the conversation to support enhancing the various parenting styles.

Exercise 2: Article Review

Directions: Review the following instructions and answer the questions:

Go to your university's online EBSCO Database and find Academic Search Premier. Search and find an article focused on how child abuse and neglect is addressed within the helping professions. Review the article in its entirety and answer the following questions related to the effects of child abuse and neglect on children and families.

- What are the factors that contribute to child maltreatment that are highlighted in the article and in this chapter?

- What are the long-term negative effects of child maltreatment on the child and on the family system?

- Describe a tentative plan you could create based on the information within this chapter and the article to ensure that you are able to effectively work with families affected by child maltreatment in an ethical and supportive way.

Exercise 3: Working With Different Family Structures

Directions: Review the following instructions and respond to the follow-up questions:

When working with family systems, it is important to acknowledge the different forms that a family can take. The traditional nuclear family, while still very much in place, is no longer the only cultural standard for what a family can be. Stepfamilies have become much more common in the United States and will most likely be part of your future client caseload.

- How do you think working with blended and stepfamilies will differ from working with a nuclear family system? What family system theory could you add to the information from this chapter to promote positive therapeutic outcomes?

- While family systems change and come in all different shapes and sizes, many are not fully acknowledged by youth. How would you work to understand a child's or adolescent's idea of their true family?

- Consider how you would adapt three of the family-based interventions that you have learned about or used in the past to incorporate into a blended family structure. Provide three examples.

Exercise 4: Internet Use With Children and Families

Directions: Review the following information and create a sample plan that may be used in working with families:

As the internet is more frequently used in everyday life, parents and families are struggling to determine how their children can safely engage in internet use. Parents may be considering a limit on screen time, monitoring screen time use, putting internet protection software in place to ensure certain websites are not accessed, and having important conversations with their child about online safety. Creating a plan for media use may help families establish concrete boundaries and expectations regarding children's internet use.

- Using www.healthychildren.org/MediaUsePlan, create a sample family media plan based on your parenting values.

- Using this type of plan can help parents and families think about the purpose behind internet use with children and create rules and goals that are in line with their family's values. Spend time exploring the media use plan you created so you can understand how families can get the most out of using it.

Exercise 5: Understanding Weight Stigma

Directions: Review the following information and answer the reflective questions:

Obesity can have a deeply negative effect on individual's lives, including (but not limited to) health concerns (e.g., high blood pressure, type 2 diabetes, gallbladder disease, sleep apnea, cancer, and coronary heart disease), mental health issues (e.g., depression, anxiety, substance use, and eating disorders), and societal stigma (e.g., themes in advertisement, body-shaming culture, misuse/overuse of the BMI, and weight-based discrimination). Within clinical practice, couple, marriage, and family practitioners have to carefully empower and validate clients suffering from the negative consequences of obesity, while doing their best not to play into the hurtful fat-shaming messages promoted within the U.S. culture. Recently, counselors have been forthright about dismantling fatphobia in their clinical practice.

Review the following article: Bray, B. (2022, November 30). Pushing back against fatphobia. *Counseling Today*, https://ct.counseling.org/tag/body-image/

- At times, clients will come to counseling with the goal of losing weight. These individuals may have been given feedback from their medical provider or dietitian to lose weight. Describe the boundaries and role a therapist should play when working with obese individuals who have a goal of losing weight.

- If a client describes feeling a sense of shame and disgust with their body, how can helpers promote positive self-esteem and body awareness?

- How can helping professionals help equip and empower clients suffering from obesity to combat the hurtful and negative body-size messages that they experience culturally?

ADDITIONAL RESOURCES

HELPFUL LINKS

- "Racial Justice Resources for MFTs": https://www.aamft.org/AAMFT/ENHANCE_Knowledge/Racial_Justice_Resources/Press_Info/racial_resources_resources_for_mfts.aspx?hkey=9df773fe-d48a-4fc8-9249-9f4801c7c7f8

- "'This Ish Is Exhausting': Acknowledging the Emotional Labor of Black MFTs": https://higherlogicdownload.s3.amazonaws.com/AAMFT/b49ef514-ecc1-460d-976b-b929d8024102/UploadedFiles/ubfcXMcT4q4nIQDHrkln_Armstrong.pdf

- "Understanding Intersectional Identities": https://www.psychologytoday.com/us/blog/understanding-the-erotic-code/201906/understanding-intersectional-identities

- "The Olson Circumplex Model: A Systemic Approach to Couple and Family Relationships": https://psychology.org.au/publications/inpsych/2011/february/sanders

- "Circumplex Model of Marital and Family Systems": https://www.uwagec.org/eruralfamilies/ERFLibrary/Readings/CircumplexModelOfMaritalAndFamilySystems.pdf

- "Family Lifestyle Dynamics and Childhood Obesity: Evidence From the Millennium Cohort Study": https://www.ncbi.nlm.nih.gov/pmc/articles/PMC5971431/

- "Causes of Obesity": https://www.cdc.gov/obesity/childhood/causes.html

- "Stepping Up to the Challenge": https://ct.counseling.org/2019/05/stepping-up-to-the-challenge/

- "Seven Essential Facts About Multiracial Youth": https://www.apa.org/pi/families/resources/newsletter/2013/08/multiracial-youth

- "Parenting Styles": https://www.apa.org/act/resources/fact-sheets/parenting-styles

- "Internet Addiction": https://www.goodtherapy.org/learn-about-therapy/issues/internet-addiction

- "Child Abuse and Neglect Prevention": https://www.cdc.gov/violenceprevention/childabuseandneglect/index.html

- "Grandparents Raising Grandchildren": https://www.aamft.org/Consumer_Updates/grandparents.aspx

- "Grieving the Loss of a Child": https://aamft.org/Consumer_Updates/Grieving_the_Loss_of_A_Child.aspx

HELPFUL BOOKS

- Abela, A., & Walker, J. (2013). *Contemporary issues in family studies: Global perspectives on partnerships, parenting and support in a changing world*. Wiley-Blackwell.

- American Association for Marriage and Family Therapy. (2005a). *Clinical updates for family therapists: Research and treatment approaches for issues affecting today's families* (Vol. 1). Author.

- American Association for Marriage and Family Therapy. (2005b). *Clinical updates for family therapists: Research and treatment approaches for issues affecting today's families* (Vol. 2). Author.

- American Association for Marriage and Family Therapy. (2008). *Clinical updates for family therapists: Research and treatment approaches for issues affecting today's families* (Vol. 3). Author.

- American Association for Marriage and Family Therapy. (2011). *Clinical updates for family therapists: Research and treatment approaches for issues affecting today's families* (Vol. 4). Author.

- Capuzzi, D., & Stauffer, D. M. (2021). *Foundations of couples, marriage, and family counseling* (2nd ed.). Wiley.

- Hanna, M. S. (2018). *The practice of family therapy: Key elements across models* (5th ed.). Routledge.

- McGlodrick, M., & Hardy, V. K. (2019). *Re-visioning family therapy: Addressing diversity in clinical practice* (3rd ed.). Routledge.

- Robe, P. A., Wubbolding R. E., & Carlson, J. (2012). *Contemporary issues in couples counseling: A choice theory and reality therapy approach*. Routledge.

HELPFUL VIDEOS

- Challenges and Rewards of a Culturally-Informed Approach to Mental Health: https://www.youtube.com/watch?v=VrYmQDiunSc&t=122s

- Circumplex Model: https://www.youtube.com/watch?v=Kmcv5QAkFCE

- How to Succeed as a Step Family: A Psychologist Explains: https://www.youtube.com/watch?v=XmPKDTZ2cy8

- Interracial Families: The New Normal: https://www.youtube.com/watch?v=-ZKvfZZ3kUE

- "Blended Families"—AAMFT Podcast—Episode 32: https://www.youtube.com/watch?v=KGIxRvVsc3g

- Dr. Fatima Cody Stanford on COVID Complications From Obesity: https://www.youtube.com/watch?v=9yzQmf7QI7Y

- Internet Safety: https://www.youtube.com/watch?v=GX2hnJhmnQg

- Internet Safety Part 1: https://www.youtube.com/watch?v=fm0V08nPMCA

- What Are Child Abuse and Neglect?: https://www.youtube.com/watch?v=6kcKX2In0B0

- The Neurobiology of Child Abuse and Neglect: https://www.youtube.com/watch?v=CKjEJT5rXRE

- Raising Children for a Second Time, 'Grandfamilies' Struggle During the Pandemic: https://www.youtube.com/watch?v=CInufouwJQE

- If You've Ever Lost a Child, Watch This: https://www.youtube.com/watch?v=SuGtD5kTXVo

REFERENCES

Adamsons, K., & Pasley, K. (2006). Coparenting following divorce and relationship dissolution. In M. A. Fine & J. H. Harvey (Eds.), *Handbook of divorce and relationship dissolution* (pp. 241–261). Lawrence Erlbaum Associates.

Afifi, T. O., Mota, N. P., Dasiewicz, P., MacMillan, H. L., & Sareen, J. (2012). Physical punishment and mental disorders: Results from a nationally representative us sample. *Pediatrics, 130*(2), 184–192. https://doi.org/10.1542/peds.2011-2947

Ahrons, C. R. (2007). Family ties after divorce: Long-term implications for children. *Family Process*, *46*(1), 53–65. https://doi.org/10.1111/j.1545-5300.2006.00191.x

Ahrons, C. R. (2011). Commentary on "reconsidering the 'good divorce.'" *Family Relations*, *60*(5), 528–532. https://doi.org/10.1111/j.1741-3729.2011.00676.x

Amato, P. R., Kane, J. B., & James, S. (2011). Reconsidering the "good divorce." *Family Relations*, *60*(5), 511–524. https://doi.org/10.1111/j.1741-3729.2011.00666.x

American Academy of Pediatrics. (n.d.). *Family media use plan*. HealthyChildren.org. Retrieved March 9, 2022, from https://www.healthychildren.org/English/media/Pages/default.aspx

American Academy of Pediatrics. (2016). Media use in school-aged children and adolescents. *Pediatrics*, *138*(5), e20162592. https://doi.org/10.1542/peds.2016-2592

American Medical Association. (2013). AMA adopts new policies on second day of voting at annual meeting. http://www.ama-assn.org/ama/pub/news/news/2013/2013-06-18-new-ama-policies-annual-meeting.page

American Psychological Association. (2012). *Ethnic and racial disparities in education: Psychology's contributions to understanding and reducing disparities*. Retrieved March 9, 2022, from https://www.apa.org/ed/resources/racial-disparities

American Psychological Association. (2019, August 23). *Making stepfamilies work*. https://www.apa.org/topics/families/stepfamily

Anderson, L. (2021, October 28). *The opioid prescribing rate and grandparents raising grandchildren: State and county level analysis*. Census.gov. Retrieved March 10, 2022, from https://www.census.gov/library/working-papers/2019/demo/SEHSD-WP2019-04.html

Anderson, L. (2019, April 11). *The opioid prescribing rate and grandparents raising grandchildren: State and county level analysis* (Working Paper Number SEHSD-WP2019-04). U.S. Census Bureau. Retrieved March 9, 2022, from https://www.census.gov/library/working-papers/2019/demo/SEHSD-WP2019-04.html

Andrie, E. K., Melissourgou, M., Gryparis, A., Vlachopapadopoulou, E., Michalacos, S., Renouf, A., Sergentanis, T. N., Bacopoulou, F., Karavanaki, K., Tsolia, M., & Tsitsika, A. (2021). Psychosocial factors and obesity in adolescence: A case-control study. *Children*, *8*(4), 308. https://doi.org/10.3390/children8040308

Annie E. Casey Foundation Kids Count Data Center. (2020). *Children in kinship care in the United States (2017–2019)*. https://datacenter.kidscount.org/data/tables/10455-children-in-kinship-care#detailed/1/any/false/1985,1757/any/20160,20161

Australian Bureau of Statistics. (2003). *Family characteristics, Australia*. https://www.abs.gov.au/how-cite-abs-sources

Barber, B. K., & Harmon, E. L. (2002). Violating the self: Parental psychological control of children and adolescents. In B. K. Barber (Ed.), *Intrusive parenting: How psychological control affects children and adolescents* (pp. 15–52). American Psychological Association. https://doi.org/10.1037/10422-002

Barber, B. K., Stolz, H. E., Olsen, J. A., Collins, W. A., & Burchinal, M. (2005). Parental support, psychological control, and behavioral control: Assessing relevance across time, culture, and method. *Monographs of the Society for Research in Child Development*, *70*(4), i–147. http://www.jstor.org/stable/3701442

Barnes, G. M., & Farrell, M. P. (1992). Parental support and control as predictors of adolescent drinking, delinquency, and related problem behaviors. *Journal of Marriage and the Family*, *54*(4), 763–776. https://doi.org/10.2307/353159

Bartel, B. T. (2020). Families grieving together: Integrating the loss of a child through ongoing relational connections. *Death Studies*, *44*(8), 498–509. https://doi.org/10.1080/07481187.2019.1586794

Baumrind, D. (1971). Current patterns of parental authority. *Developmental Psychology*, *4*(1, Pt.2), 1–103. https://doi.org/10.1037/h0030372

Baumrind, D. (1991). The influence of parenting style on adolescent competence and substance use. *The Journal of Early Adolescence*, *11*(1), 56–95. https://doi.org/10.1177/0272431691111004

Bean, R. A., Barber, B. K., & Crane, D. R. (2006). Parental support, behavioral control, and psychological control among African American Youth. *Journal of Family Issues*, *27*(10), 1335–1355. https://doi.org/10.1177/0192513x06289649

Beckmeyer, J. J., Coleman, M., & Ganong, L. H. (2014). Postdivorce coparenting typologies and children's adjustment. *Family Relations*, *63*(4), 526–537. https://doi.org/10.1111/fare.12086

Beckmeyer, J. J., Ganong, L. H., Coleman, M., & Markham, M. S. (2017). Experiences with coparenting scale: A semantic differential measure of postdivorce coparenting satisfaction. *Journal of Family Issues*, *38*(10), 1471–1490. https://doi.org/10.1177/0192513X16634764

Becvar, D. S., & Becvar, R. (2013). *Family therapy: A systemic integration*. Pearson.

Beebe, T. J., Asche, S. E., Harrison, P. A., & Quinlan, K. B. (2004). Heightened vulnerability and increased risk-taking among adolescent chatroom users: Results from a statewide school survey. *Journal of Adolescent Health, 35,* 116–123. https://doi.org/10.1016/j.jadohealth.2003.09.012

Ben-Joseph, E. P. (Ed.). (n.d.). *Online safety.* Nemours KidsHealth. Retrieved March 7, 2022, from https://kidshealth.org/en/parents/net-safety.html

Black, L. L., & Flynn, S. V. (2021). *Crisis, trauma, and disaster: A clinician's guide.* Sage.

Bonanno, G. A. (2001). Grief and emotion: A social–functional perspective. In M. S. Stroebe, R. O. Hansson, W. Stroebe, & H. Schut (Eds.), *Handbook of bereavement research: Consequences, coping, and care* (pp. 493–515). American Psychological Association. https://doi.org/10.1037/10436-021

Bradt, S. (2010, December 9). One drop rule persists: Biracials viewed as members of their lower-status parent group. *The Harvard Gazette.* https://news.harvard.edu/gazette/story/2010/12/one-drop-rule-persists/

Bray, G. A. (1992). Pathophysiology of obesity. *The American Journal of Clinical Nutrition, 55*(2), 488S–494S. https://doi.org/10.1093/ajcn/55.2.488s

Briggs, P., Simon, W. T., & Simonsen, S. (2011). An exploratory study of internet-initiated sexual offenses and the chat room sex offender: Has the internet enabled a new typology of sex offender? *Sexual Abuse: Journal of Research and Treatment, 23*(1), 72–91. https://doi.org/10.1177/1079063210384275

Brown, J. D., & L'Engle, K. L. (2009). X-rated: Sexual attitudes and behaviors associated with U.S. early adolescents' exposure to sexually explicit media. *Communication Research, 36*(1), 129–151. https://doi.org/10.1177/0093650208326465

Buck, A. A., & Neff, L. A. (2012). Stress spillover in early marriage: The role of self-regulatory depletion. *Journal of Family Psychology, 26*(5), 698–708. https://doi.org/10.1037/a0029260

Butchart, A., Harvey, A. P., Mian, M., & Fürniss, T. (2006). *Preventing child maltreatment: A guide to taking action and generating evidence.* World Health Organization, International Society for Prevention of Child Abuse and Neglect. https://apps.who.int/iris/handle/10665/43499

Cacciatore, J., Lacasse, J. R., Lietz, C. A., & McPherson, J. (2014). A parent's tears: Primary results from the traumatic experiences and resiliency study. *OMEGA—Journal of Death and Dying, 68*(3), 183–205. https://doi.org/10.2190/om.68.3.a

Capstick, C., & Fraenkel, P. (2004). Child abuse and neglect. In R. H. Coombs (Ed.), *Family therapy review: Preparing for comprehensive and licensing exams* (pp. 393–411). Lahaska Press.

Caputo, R. K. (2000). Grandparents and coresident grandchildren in a youth cohort. *Journal of Family Issues, 22*(5), 541–556. https://doi.org/10.1177/019251301022005001

Cartwright, C. (2008). Resident parent–child relationships in stepfamilies. In J. Pryor (Ed.), *The international handbook of stepfamilies: Policy and practice in legal, research, and clinical environments* (pp. 208–230). John Wiley & Sons.

Casillas, L. M., Elkins, S. R., Walther, C. A., Schanding, G. T., & Short, M. B. (2020). Helicopter parenting style and parental accommodations: The moderating role of internalizing and externalizing symptomatology. *The Family Journal, 29*(2), 245–255. https://doi.org/10.1177/1066480720961496

Centers for Disease Control and Prevention. (n.d.). *Defining adult overweight and obesity.* Author. Retrieved March 10, 2022, from https://www.cdc.gov/obesity/basics/adult-defining.html

Centers for Disease Control and Prevention. (2020). *Supplementary figure: Trends in U.S. Emergency Department visits related to suspected or confirmed child abuse and neglect among children aged <18 years before and during the COVID-19 pandemic—United States, January 2019–September 2020.* Retrieved March 9, 2022, from https://stacks.cdc.gov/view/cdc/98213

Centers for Disease Control and Prevention. (2022, January 20). *CDC releases updated maps of America's high levels of inactivity.* Retrieved March 11, 2022, from https://www.cdc.gov/media/releases/2022/p0120-inactivity-map.html

Chantler, K. (2005). From disconnection to connection: 'Race', gender and the politics of therapy. *British Journal of Guidance & Counselling, 33,* 239–256. https://doi.org/10.1080/03069880500132813

Chen, A.-S., Leung, M., Chen, C.-H., & Yang, S. C. (2013). Exposure to internet pornography among Taiwanese adolescents. *Social Behavior and Personality: An International Journal, 41*(1), 157–164. https://doi.org/10.2224/sbp.2013.41.1.157

Chen, W., & Adler, J. L. (2019). Assessment of screen exposure in young children, 1997 to 2014. *JAMA Pediatrics, 173*(4), 391. https://doi.org/10.1001/jamapediatrics.2018.5546

Chou, V. (2017, April 17). *How science and genetics are reshaping the race debate of the 21st century.* Harvard University: Science in the News. https://sitn.hms.harvard.edu/flash/2017/science-genetics-reshaping-race-debate-21st-century/

Chua, A. (2011). *Battle hymn of the tiger mother.* Bloomsbury Publishing.

Cicchetti, D., & Toth, S. L. (2005). Child maltreatment. *Annual Review of Clinical Psychology, 1*(1), 409–438. https://doi.org/10.1146/annurev.clinpsy.1.102803.144029

Cline, F. W. (2009). *All about consequences.* Love and Logic.

Coard, S. I., Foy-Watson, S., Zimmer, C., & Wallace, A. (2007). Considering culturally relevant parenting practices in intervention development and adaptation. *The Counseling Psychologist, 35*(6), 797–820. https://doi.org/10.1177/0011000007304592

Coie, J. D., & Dodge, K. A. (1998). Aggression and antisocial behavior. In W. Damon & N. Eisenberg (Eds.), *Handbook of child psychology: Social, emotional, and personality development* (pp. 779–862). John Wiley & Sons.

Colby, S. L., & Ortman, J. M. (2015, March). *Projections of the size and composition of the U.S. population: 2014 to 2060.* U.S. Census Bureau. Retrieved March 8, 2022, from https://mronline.org/wp-content/uploads/2019/08/p25-1143.pdf

Cooper, A. (1998). Sexuality and the internet: Surfing into the new millennium. *Cyberpsychology & behavior, 1*(2), 187–193. https://doi.org/10.1089/cpb.1998.1.187

Cummings, E. M., Davies, P. T., & Campbell, S. B. (2000). *Developmental psychopathology and family process: Theory, research and clinical implications.* Guilford Press.

Curtis M. S., M. G., Ellis, É. M., Ann, S., Dai, Y. Y., & Bermúdez, J. M. (2020). Intersectionality within family sciences and family therapy journals from 2010 to 2020. *Journal of Family Theory & Review, 12*(4), 510–528. https://doi.org/10.1111/jftr.12399

Darling, N., & Steinberg, L. (1993). Parenting style as context: An integrative model. *Psychological Bulletin, 113*(3), 487–496. https://doi.org/10.1037/0033-2909.113.3.487

Daugherty, J., & Copen, C. (2016). Trends in attitudes about marriage, childbearing, and sexual behavior: United States, 2002, 2006–2010, and 2011–2013. *National Health Statistics Report, 92,* 1–10. https://pubmed.ncbi.nlm.nih.gov/27019117/

Davies, R. (2004). New understandings of parental grief: Literature review. *Journal of Advanced Nursing, 46*(5), 506–513. https://doi.org/10.1111/j.1365-2648.2004.03024.x

Davis, A. N., Carlo, G., & Knight, G. P. (2015). Perceived maternal parenting styles, cultural values, and prosocial tendencies among Mexican American youth. *The Journal of Genetic Psychology, 176*(4), 235–252. https://doi.org/10.1080/00221325.2015.1044494

Davis, D.-A. (2020). Reproducing while Black: The crisis of Black Maternal Health, obstetric racism and assisted reproductive technology. *Reproductive Biomedicine & Society Online, 11,* 56–64. https://doi.org/10.1016/j.rbms.2020.10.001

Davis, N.S., & Twombly, J. (2000). *State legislators' handbook for statutory rape issues.* American Bar Association, Center on Children and the Law.

De Santisteban, P., Del Hoyo, J., Alcázar-Córcoles, M. Á., & Gámez-Guadix, M. (2018). Progression, maintenance, and feedback of online child sexual grooming: A qualitative analysis of online predators. *Child Abuse & Neglect, 80,* 203–215. https://doi.org/10.1016/j.chiabu.2018.03.026

Deater-Deckard, K., Lansford, J. E., Malone, P. S., Alampay, L. P., Sorbring, E., Bacchini, D., Bombi, A. S., Bornstein, M. H., Chang, L., Di Giunta, L., Dodge, K. A., Oburu, P., Pastorelli, C., Skinner, A. T., Tapanya, S., Tirado, L. M., Zelli, A., & Al-Hassan, S. M. (2011). The association between parental warmth and control in thirteen cultural groups. *Journal of Family Psychology, 25*(5), 790–794. https://doi.org/10.1037/a0025120

Dolbin-MacNab, M. L., & Bradford, D. S. (n.d.). *Grandparents raising grandchildren.* American Association for Marriage and Family Therapy. https://www.aamft.org/Consumer_Updates/grandparents.aspx

Dolbin-MacNab, M. L., & Few-Demo, A. L. (2018). Grandfamilies in the United States: An intersectional analysis. In V. Timonen (Ed.), *Grandparenting practices around the world* (pp. 189–208). Policy Press.

Dolbin-MacNab, M. L., & O'Connell, L. M. (2021). Grandfamilies and the opioid epidemic: A systemic perspective and future priorities. *Clinical Child and Family Psychology Review, 24*(2), 207–223. https://doi.org/10.1007/s10567-021-00343-7

Dolbin-MacNab, M. L., & Stucki, B. D. (2022). *Grandparents raising grandchildren.* American Association for Marriage and Family Therapy. https://www.aamft.org/Consumer_Updates/grandparents.aspx

Downing, K. E., Nichols, D. P., & Webster, K. (2005). *Multiracial America: A resource guide on the history and literature of Interracial Issues.* The Scarecrow Press.

Doyle, D. M., & Molix, L. (2014). How does stigma spoil relationships? Evidence that perceived discrimination harms romantic relationship quality through impaired self-image. *Journal of Applied Social Psychology, 44*(9), 600–610. https://doi.org/10.1111/jasp.12252

Drewnowski, A., & Specter, S. E. (2004). Poverty and obesity: The role of energy density and energy costs. *The American Journal of Clinical Nutrition, 79*(1), 6–16. https://doi.org/10.1093/ajcn/79.1.6

Dubowitz, H., Black, M., Starr, R. H., & Zuravin, S. (1993). A conceptual definition of child neglect. *Criminal Justice and Behavior, 20*(1), 8–26. https://doi.org/10.1177/0093854893020001003

Ellis, R., & Simmons, T. (2014, October). *Coresident grandparents and their grandchildren: 2012.* U.S. Census Bureau. Retrieved March 8, 2022, from http://thenorrisgroup.com/learning/files/media_manager/original/17.pdf

Fairclough S. J. (2021). Adolescents' digital screen time as a concern for health and well-being? Device type and context matter. *Acta Paediatricia, 110*(7). https://doi.org/10.1111/apa.15843

Feder, K. A., Mojtabai, R., Musci, R. J., & Letourneau, E. J. (2018). U.S. adults with opioid use disorder living with children: Treatment use and barriers to care. *Journal of Substance Abuse Treatment, 93*, 31–37. https://doi.org/10.1016/j.jsat.2018.07.011

Federal Interagency Forum on Child and Family Statistics. (2007, July). *America's children: Key national indicators of well-being.* Retrieved March 11, 2022, from https://www.childstats.gov/pdf/ac2007/ac_07.pdf

Fields, J. (2003, May 31). *Children's living arrangements and characteristics: March 2002. Current population reports.* ERIC. Retrieved March 11, 2022, from https://eric.ed.gov/?id=ED480459

Finkelhor, D. (1979). What's wrong with sex between adults and children? Ethics and the problem of sexual abuse. *American Journal of Orthopsychiatry, 49*(4), 692–697. https://doi.org/10.1111/j.1939-0025.1979.tb02654.x

Finney, N., Tadros, E., Pfeiffer, S., & Owens, D. (2020). Clinical implications for multi-racial individuals. *American Journal of Family Therapy, 48*(3), 271–282. https://doi.org/10.1080/01926187.2019.1709581

Fischer, T. F. C., De Graaf, P. M., & Kalmijn, M. (2005). Friendly and antagonistic contact between former spouses after divorce: Patterns and determinants. *Journal of Family Issues, 26*(8), 1131–1163. https://doi.org/10.1177/0192513X05275435

Fish, W. C. (1986). Differences of grief intensity in bereaved parents. In T. A. Rando (Ed.), *Parental loss of a child* (pp. 415–428). Research Press.

Flood, M. (2007). Exposure to pornography among youth in Australia. *Journal of Sociology, 43*(1), 45–60. https://doi.org/10.1177/1440783307073934

Fortson, B., Klevens, J., Merrick, M., Gilbert, L., & Alexander, S. (2016). *Preventing child abuse and neglect: A technical package for policy, norm, and programmatic activities.* National Center for Injury Prevention and Control Division of Violence Prevention. Retrieved March 9, 2022, from https://www.cdc.gov/violenceprevention/pdf/can-prevention-technical-package.pdf

Fraenkel, P., Sheinberg, M., & True, F. (2004). *Making families safe for children: Handbook for a family-centered approach to intrafamilial child sexual abuse.* Sex Abuse Project, Ackerman Institute for the Family.

Franklin, C., Streeter, C. L., & Springer, D. W. (2001). Validity of the faces IV family assessment measure. *Research on Social Work Practice, 11*(5), 576–596. https://doi.org/10.1177/104973150101100503

Fryar, C. D., Carroll, M. D., & Afful, J. (2020). *Prevalence of overweight, obesity, and severe obesity among children and adolescents aged 2–19 years: United States, 1963–1965 through 2017–2018.* National Center for Health Statistics: Health E-Stats. https://www.cdc.gov/nchs/data/hestat/obesity-child-17-18/obesity-child.htm

Fuller-Thomson, E. (2005). Grandparents raising grandchildren in Canada: A profile of skipped generation families (Working paper no. 132). SEDAP, McMaster University.

Fuller-Thomson, E., Minkler, M., & Driver, D. (1997). A profile of grandparents raising grandchildren in the United States. *The Gerontologist, 37*(3), 406–411. https://doi.org/10.1093/geront/37.3.406

Galambos, N. L., Barker, E. T., & Almeida, D. M. (2003). Parents do matter: Trajectories of change in externalizing and internalizing problems in early adolescence. *Child Development, 74*(2), 578–594. https://doi.org/10.1111/1467-8624.7402017

Galobardes, B., Lynch, J., & Smith, G. D. (2007). Measuring socioeconomic position in Health Research. *British Medical Bulletin, 81–82*(1), 21–37. https://doi.org/10.1093/bmb/ldm001

Ganong, L., & Coleman, M. (2017). Studying stepfamilies: Four eras of family scholarship. *Family Process, 57*(1), 7–24. https://doi.org/10.1111/famp.12307

Generations United. (2018). *All in together: Creating places where young and old thrive.* Author. https://www.gu.org/resources/all-in-together-creating-places-where-young-and-old-thrive/

Gershoff, E. T. (2008). *Report on physical punishment in the United States: What research tells us about its effect on children.* Phoenix Children's Hopsital, Child Abuse Prevention. http://www.nospank.net/gershoff.pdf

Gershoff, E. T., Grogan-Kaylor, A., Lansford, J. E., Chang, L., Zelli, A., Deater-Deckard, K., & Dodge, K. A. (2010). Parent discipline practices in an international sample: Associations with child behaviors and moderation by perceived normativeness. *Child Development, 81*(2), 487–502. https://doi.org/10.1111/j.1467-8624.2009.01409.x

Giarrusso, R., Feng, D., Silverstein, M., & Marenco, A. (2000). Primary and secondary stressors of grandparents raising grandchildren: Evidence from a national survey. *Journal of Mental Health and Aging, 6*(4), 291–310.

Gibbs, J. T. (1987). Identity and marginauty: Issues in the treatment of biracial adolescents. *American Journal of Orthopsychiatry, 57*(2), 265–278. https://doi.org/10.1111/j.1939-0025.1987.tb03537.x

Glasser, M., Kolvin, I., Campbell, D., Glasser, A., Leitch, I., & Farrelly, S. (2001). Cycle of child sexual abuse: Links between being a victim and becoming a perpetrator. *The British Journal of Psychiatry, 179*(6), 482–494. https://doi.org/10.1192/bjp.179.6.482

Glosser, A., Gardiner, K., & Fishman, M. (2004, December 15). *Statutory rape: A guide to state laws and reporting requirements*. Office of the Assistant Secretary for Planning and Evaluation, Department of Health & Human Services. Retrieved March 8, 2022, from https://ccoso.org/sites/default/files/import/Statutory-Rape---guide-to-reporting.pdf

Goldfield, G. S., Murray, M., Maras, D., Wilson, A. L., Phillips, P., Kenny, G. P., Hadjiyannakis, S., Alberga, A., Cameron, J. D., Tulluch, H., & Sigal, R. J. (2016). Screen time is associated with depressive symptomatology among obese adolescents: A hearty study. *European Journal of Pediatrics, 175*(7), 909–919. https://doi.org/10.1007/s00431-016-2720-z

Goldman, D. (2020, January 28). *Obesity, second to smoking as the most preventable cause of U.S. deaths, needs new approaches*. USC Dornsife College News RSS. https://dornsife.usc.edu/news/stories/3153/tackling-obesity-needs-new-approaches-says-health-economist/

Gould, E. (2020). *Black-White wage gaps are worse today than in 2000*. Working Economics [Blog], Economic Policy Institute.

Granados, S., Winslade, J., De Witt, M., & Hedtke, L. (2009). Grief counseling groups for adolescents based on re-membering practices. *Journal of School Counseling, 7*(43). https://eric.ed.gov/?id=EJ886148

Greenberg, N. (2020). Mental health of health-care workers in the COVID-19 era. *Nature Reviews Nephrology, 16*, 425–426. https://doi.org/10.1038/s41581-020-0314-5

Gonzalez, D., Bethencourt Mirabal, A., & McCall, J. D. (2021). Child abuse and neglect. *StatPearls* [Internet]. https://www.ncbi.nlm.nih.gov/books/NBK459146/

Gudmundsdottir, M., & Chesla, C. A. (2006). Building a new world: Habits and practices of healing following the death of a child. *Journal of Family Nursing, 12*(2), 143–164. https://doi.org/10.1177/1074840706287275

Guerrero, M. D., Barnes, J. D., Chaput, J.-P., & Tremblay, M.-S. (2019). Screen time and problem behaviors in children: Exploring the mediating role of sleep duration. *International Journal of Behavioral Nutrition and Physical Activity, 16*, 105. https://doi.org/10.1186/s12966-019-0862-x

Hardy, S. A., Steelman, M. A., Coyne, S. M., & Ridge, R. D. (2013). Adolescent religiousness as a protective factor against pornography use. *Journal of Applied Developmental Psychology, 34*(3), 131–139. https://doi.org/10.1016/j.appdev.2012.12.002

Harris, D. R., & Sim, J. J. (2002). Who is multiracial? Assessing the complexity of lived race. *American Sociological Review, 67*(4), 614–627. https://doi.org/10.2307/3088948

Haskett, M. E., Scott, S. S., & Fann, K. D. (1995). Child abuse potential inventory and parenting behavior: Relationships with high-risk correlates. *Child Abuse & Neglect, 19*(12), 1483–1495. https://doi.org/10.1016/0145-2134(95)00107-4

Hasking, P. A., Scheier, L. M., & ben Abdallah, A. (2011). The three latent classes of adolescent delinquency and the risk factors for membership in each class. *Aggressive Behavior, 37*(1), 19–35. https://doi.org/10.1002/ab.20365

Hayslip, B., & Kaminski, P. (2008). *Parenting the custodial grandchild implications for clinical practice*. Springer Publishing Company.

Hayslip, B., Smith, G. C., Montoro-Rodriguez, J., Streider, F. H., & Merchant, W. (2017). The Utility of the family empowerment scale with custodial grandmothers. *Journal of Applied Gerontology, 36*(3), 320–350. https://doi.org/10.1177/0733464815608492

Henriksen, R. C., Jr., & Maxwell, M. J. (2016). Counseling the fastest growing population in America: Those with multiple heritage backgrounds. *Journal of Mental Health Counseling, 38*(1), 1–11. https://doi.org/10.17744/mehc.38.1.01

Hetherington, E. M. (1993). An overview of the virginia longitudinal study of divorce and remarriage with a focus on early adolescence. *Journal of Family Psychology, 7*(1), 39–56. https://doi.org/10.1037/0893-3200.7.1.39

Hill, J. O., Melanson, E. L., & Wyatt, H. T. (2000). Dietary fat intake and regulation of energy balance: implications for obesity. *The Journal of Nutrition, 130*(2S Suppl.), 284S–288S.

Honein, M. A., Boyle, C., & Redfield, R. R. (2019). Public Health Surveillance of prenatal opioid exposure in mothers and infants. *Pediatrics, 143*(3). https://doi.org/10.1542/peds.2018-3801

Hines, D.A., & Finkelhor, D. (2007). Statutory sex crime relationships between juveniles and adults: A review of socialscientific research. *Aggression & Violent Behavior, 12*, 300–314. https://doi.org/10.1016/j.avb.2006.10.001

Hoffman, B. (2008). The science and politics of reducing child victimization. *Journal of Contemporary Criminal Justice, 24*(2), 103–113. https://doi.org/10.1177/1043986208315475

Hooghe, M., & Dassonneville, R. (2018). Explaining the Trump vote: The effect of racist resentment and anti-immigrant sentiments. *PS: Political Science& Politics, 51*, 528–534. https://doi.org/10.1017/S1049096518000367

Hooghe, M., Marien, S., & de Vroome, T. (2012). The cognitive basis of trust. The relation between education, cognitive ability, and generalized and Political Trust. *Intelligence, 40*(6), 604–613. https://doi.org/10.1016/j.intell.2012.08.006

Hornor, G. (2020). Child and adolescent pornography exposure. *Journal of Pediatric Health Care, 34*(2), 191–199. https://doi.org/10.1016/j.pedhc.2019.10.001

Hughes, D., Rodriguez, J., Smith, E. P., Johnson, D. J., Stevenson, H. C., & Spicer, P. (2006). Parents' ethnic-racial socialization practices: A review of research and directions for future study. *Developmental Psychology, 42*(5), 747–770. https://doi.org/10.1037/0012-1649.42.5.747

Hurt, R. T., Kulisek, C., Buchanan, L. A., & McClave, S. A. (2010). The obesity epidemic: challenges, health initiatives, and implications for gastroenterologists. *Gastroenterology & hepatology, 6*(12), 780–792. https://www.ncbi.nlm.nih.gov/pmc/articles/PMC3033553/

Jamison, T. B., Coleman, M., Ganong, L. H., & Feistman, R. E. (2014). Transitioning to postdivorce family life: A grounded theory investigation of resilience in coparenting. *Family Relations: An Interdisciplinary Journal of Applied Family Studies, 63*(3), 411–423. https://doi.org/10.1111/fare.12074

Jendrek, M. P. (1994). Grandparents who parent their grandchildren: Circumstances and decisions. *The Gerontologist, 34*(2), 206–216. https://doi.org/10.1093/geront/34.2.206

Joussemet, M., Mageau, G.A. & Koestner, R. (2014). Promoting optimal parenting and children's mental health: A preliminary evaluation of the how-to parenting program. *Journal of Child and Family Studies, 23*, 949–964. https://doi.org/10.1007/s10826-013-9751-0

Kaufman, J., & Zigler, E. (1987). Do abused children become abusive parents? *American Journal of Orthopsychiatry, 57*(2), 186–192. https://doi.org/10.1111/j.1939-0025.1987.tb03528.x

Kazdin, A. E. (2000). *Encyclopedia of psychology.* American Psychological Association, Oxford University Press.

Keesee, N. J., Currier, J. M., & Neimeyer, R. A. (2008). Predictors of grief following the death of one's child: The contribution of finding meaning. *Journal of Clinical Psychology, 64*(10), 1145–1163. https://doi.org/10.1002/jclp.20502

Kim, M. J., Tajima, E. A., Herrenkohl, T. I., & Huang, B. (2009). Early child maltreatment, runaway youths, and risk of delinquency and victimization in adolescence: A mediational model. *Social Work Research, 33*(1), 19–28. https://doi.org/10.1093/swr/33.1.19

Kim, S., Wang, Y., Orozco-Lapray, D., Shen, Y., & Murtuza, M. (2013). Does "tiger parenting" exist? Parenting profiles of Chinese Americans and adolescent developmental outcomes. *Asian American Journal of Psychology, 4*(1), 7–18. https://doi.org/10.1037/a0030612

Klaassen, D. W. (2010). *Spiritual and relational dimensions of parental grieving* [Doctoral thesis, University of British Columbia]. University of British Columbia Theses and Dissertations. https://open.library.ubc.ca/soa/cIRcle/collections/ubctheses/24/items/1.0053677

Kreider, R., & Ellis, R. (2011). *Number, timing, and duration of marriages and divorces: 2009.* Census.gov. Retrieved March 9, 2022, from https://www.census.gov/library/publications/2011/demo/p70-125.html

Kuppens, S., & Ceulemans, E. (2019). Parenting styles: A closer look at a well-known concept. *Journal of Child and Family Studies, 28*, 168–181. https://doi.org/10.1007/s10826-018-1242-x

Kuppens, S., Laurent, L., Heyvaert, M., & Onghena, P. (2013). Associations between parental psychological control and relational aggression in children and adolescents: A multilevel and sequential meta-analysis. *Developmental Psychology, 49*(9), 1697–1712. https://doi.org/10.1037/a0030740

Kushner, R. F., & Manzano, H. (2002). Obesity pharmacology: Past, present, and future. *Current Opinion in Gastroenterology, 18*(2), 213–220. https://doi.org/10.1097/00001574-200203000-00011

Kyle, T. K., Dhurandhar, E. J., & Allison, D. B. (2016). Regarding obesity as a disease: Evolving policies and their implications. *Endocrinology and Metabolism Clinics of North America, 45*(3), 511–520. https://doi.org/10.1016/j.ecl.2016.04.004

Lee, J., Lee, A., Lee, D., Jung, H. Y., Kim, S. G., & Lee, S. I. (2019). Suicidal ideation of the elderly according to their involvement in grandchild care. *Psychiatry Investigations, 16*(8):625–628. https://doi.org/10.30773/pi.2019.06.06

Lanning, K. V. (2002). Law enforcement perspective on the compliant child victim. *The APSAC Advisor, 14*(2), 4–9.

Laszloffy, T. A. (2005). *Raising biracial children*. AltaMira Press.

Lent, J., & Otto, A. (2018). Grandparents, grandchildren, and caregiving: The impacts of America's substance use crisis. *Generations, 42,* 15–22. https://www.jstor.org/stable/26591697#metadata_info_tab_contents

Lino, M., Kuczynski, K., Rodriguez, N., and Schap, T. (2017, January). Expenditures on children by families, 2015. Miscellaneous publication no. 1528-2015. U.S. Department of Agriculture, Center for Nutrition Policy and Promotion.

Livingston, G., & Parker, K. (2010). *Since the start of the great recession, more children raised by grandparents*. Pew Research Center.

Loyd, A. B., & Gaither, S. E. (2018). Racial/ethnic socialization for White youth: What we know and future directions. *Journal of Applied Developmental Psychology, 59,* 54–64. https://doi.org/10.1016/j.appdev.2018.05.004

Lucas, S. L. (2017). Reflection: How multiracial lives matter 50 years after *Loving. Creighton Law Review, 50*(3), 719–724. https://readingroom.law.gsu.edu/faculty_pub/2517

Lucas, C., & Washington, S. (2020, October). *Understanding systemic racism in the United States: Educating our students and ourselves*. American Occupational Therapy Association. https://www.aota.org/-/media/Corporate/Files/Publications/CE-Articles/CEA_October_2020.pdf

Luder, M. T., Pittet, I., Berchtold, A., Akré, C., Michaud, P. A., & Surís, J. C. (2011). Associations between online pornography and sexual behavior among adolescents: Myth or reality?. *Archives of Sexual Behavior, 40*(5), 1027–1035. https://doi.org/10.1007/s10508-010-9714-0

Maccoby, E. E., Depner, C. E., & Mnookin, R. H. (1990). Coparenting in the second year after divorce. *Journal of Marriage and Family, 52*(1), 141–155. https://doi.org/10.2307/352846

Markham, M. S., Ganong, L. H., & Coleman, M. (2007). Coparental identity and mothers? cooperation in coparental relationships. *Family Relations, 56*(4), 369–377. https://doi.org/10.1111/j.1741-3729.2007.00466.x

Martinson, I. M., Davies, B., & McClowry, S. (1991). Parental depression following the death of a child. *Death Studies, 15*(3), 259–267. https://doi.org/10.1080/07481189108252429

Masud, H., Ahmad, M. S., Cho, K. W., & Fakhr, Z. (2019). Parenting styles and aggression among young adolescents: A systematic review of literature. *Community Mental Health Journal, 55,* 1015–1030. https://doi.org/10.1007/s10597-019-00400-0

Math, S. B., & Seshadri, S. P. (2013). The invisible ones: Sexual minorities. *The Indian Journal of Medical Research, 137*(1), 4–6. https://www.ncbi.nlm.nih.gov/pmc/articles/PMC3657897/

McAlinden, A. M. (2006). 'Setting'em up': Personal, familial and institutional grooming in the sexual abuse of children. *Social & Legal Studies, 15*(3), 339–362. https://doi.org/10.1177/0964663906066613

McEwen, B. S., & Stellar, E. (1993). Stress and the individual: Mechanisms leading to disease. *Archives of Internal Medicine, 153*(18), 2093–2101. https://pubmed.ncbi.nlm.nih.gov/8379800/

McRoy, R. G., & Freeman, E. (1986). Racial-identity issues among mixed-race children. *Children & Schools, 8*(3), 164–174. https://doi.org/10.1093/cs/8.3.164

Meij, L. W.-D., Stroebe, M., Schut, H., Stroebe, W., Van Den Bout, J., van der Heijden, P. G. M., & Dijkstra, I. (2008). Parents grieving the loss of their child: Interdependence in coping. *British Journal of Clinical Psychology, 47*(1), 31–42. https://doi.org/10.1348/014466507X216152

Mesch, G. S. (2009). Parental mediation, online activities, and cyberbullying. *CyberPsychology & Behavior, 12*(4), 387–393. https://doi.org/10.1089/cpb.2009.0068

Miller, C. C., & Bromwich, J. E. (2019, March 16). How parents are robbing their children of adulthood. *The New York Times*. https://www.nytimes.com/2019/03/16/style/snowplow-parenting-scandal.html

Mitchell, K. J., Finkelhor, D., & Wolak, J. (2007). Youth internet users at risk for the most serious online sexual solicitations. *American Journal of Preventive Medicine, 32*(6), 532–537. https://doi.org/10.1016/j.amepre.2007.02.001

Mitchell, K. J., & Wells, M. (2007). Problematic internet experiences: Primary or secondary presenting problems in persons seeking mental health care? *Social Science & Medicine, 65*(6), 1136–1141. https://doi.org/10.1016/j.socscimed.2007.05.015

Mitchell, N. S., Catenacci, V. A., Wyatt, H. R., & Hill, J. O. (2011). Obesity: Overview of an epidemic. *Psychiatric Clinics of North America, 34*(4), 717–732. https://doi.org/10.1016/j.psc.2011.08.005

Moilanen, K. L., Rasmussen, K. E., & Padilla-Walker, L. M. (2015). Bidirectional associations between self-regulation and parenting styles in early adolescence. *Journal of Research on Adolescence, 25*(2), 246–262. https://doi.org/10.1111/jora.12125

Murdock, G. P. (1949) *Social structure*. Macmillan.

Nagata, J. M., Cortez, C. A., Cattle, C. J., Ganson, K. T., Iyer, P., Bibbins-Domingo, K., & Baker, F. C. (2022). Screen time use among US adolescents during the COVID-19 pandemic. *JAMA Pediatrics, 176*(1), 94. https://doi.org/10.1001/jamapediatrics.2021.4334

National Center for Cultural Competence. (2007). *A guide for advancing family-centered and culturally and linguistically competent care*. National Center for Cultural Competence, Georgetown University Center for Child and Human Development. https://nccc.georgetown.edu/documents/fcclcguide.pdf

Neely-Barnes, S. L., Carolyn Graff, J., & Washington, G. (2010). The health-related quality of life of custodial grandparents. *Health & Social Work, 35*(2), 87–97. https://doi.org/10.1093/hsw/35.2.87

Nielsen, L. (2017). Re-examining the research on parental conflict, coparenting, and custody arrangements. *Psychology, Public Policy, and Law, 23*(2), 211–231. https://doi.org/10.1037/law0000109

Norman-Eady, S., Martino, P., & Reinhart, C. (2003). *Statutory rape laws by state*. Connecticut General Assembly, Office of Legislative Research.

Ogden, C. L., Carroll, M. D., Kit, B. K., & Flegal, K. M. (2012). Prevalence of obesity and trends in body mass index among US children and adolescents, 1999–2010. *JAMA, 307*(5), 483–490. https://doi.org/10.1001/jama.2012.40

Ogden, C. L., Carroll, M. D., Kit, B. K., and Flegal, K. M. (2013). Prevalence of obesity among adults: United States, 2011–2012. National Center for Health Statistics Data Brief, no. 131. National Center for Health Statistics.

Olivari, M. G., Wahn, E. H., Maridaki-Kassotaki, K., Antonopoulou, K., & Confalonieri, E. (2015). Adolescent perceptions of parenting styles in Sweden, Italy and Greece: An exploratory study. *Europe's Journal of Psychology, 11*(2), 244. https://doi.org/10.5964/ejop.v11i2.887

Olson, D. (2011). Faces IV and the circumplex model: Validation study. *Journal of Marital and Family Therapy, 37*(1), 64–80. https://doi.org/10.1111/j.1752-0606.2009.00175.x

Olson, D. H. (2000). Circumplex model of marital and family systems. *Journal of Family Therapy, 22*(2), 144–167. https://doi.org/10.1111/1467-6427.00144

Olson, D. H., Gorall, D. M., & Tiesel, J. W. (2004). *Faces IV package*. Life Innovations.

Olson, D. H., Russell, C. S., & Sprenkle, D. H. (1983). Circumplex model of marital and family systems: VI. Theoretical update. *Family Process, 22*(1), 69–83. https://doi.org/10.1111/j.1545-5300.1983.00069.x

Ondersma, S. J. (2002). Predictors of neglect within low-SES families: The importance of substance abuse. *American Journal of Orthopsychiatry, 72*(3), 383–391. https://doi.org/10.1037/0002-9432.72.3.383

Oxford Advanced Learner's Dictionary. (n.d.). Blended family. In Oxford Learners Dictionaries.com. https://www.oxfordlearnersdictionaries.com/us/definition/english/blended-family

Pahlke, E., Bigler, R. S., & Suizzo, M. A. (2012). Relations between colorblind socialization and children's racial bias: Evidence from European American mothers and their preschool children. *Child Development, 83*(4), 1164–1179. https://www.jstor.org/stable/23255686

Papernow, P. L. (2013). *Surviving and thriving in stepfamily relationships: What works and what doesn't*. Routledge.

Papernow, P. L. (2018). Therapy with clients in stepfamily relationships: What individual, couple, child, and family therapists need to know. *Family Process, 57*(1), 25–51. https://doi.org/10.1111/famp.12321.

Pappas, S. (2022, June 30). What do we really know about kids and screens? *Monitor on Psychology, 51*(3), 42. https://www.apa.org/monitor/2020/04/cover-kids-screens

Patel, A. (2019, June 25). *'Panda parenting' is all about giving children more freedom - but does it work?* Global News. https://globalnews.ca/news/5428832/what-is-panda-parenting/

Pears, K. C., & Capaldi, D. M. (2001). Intergenerational transmission of abuse: A two-generational prospective study of an at-risk sample. *Child Abuse & Neglect, 25*(11), 1439–1461. https://doi.org/10.1016/s0145-2134(01)00286-1

Perron, N. C. (2018). The four Cs of parenting. *The Family Journal, 26*(1), 48–55. https://doi.org/10.1177/1066480717753014

Peter, J., & Valkenburg, P. M. (2016). Adolescents and pornography: A review of 20 years of research. *The Journal of Sex Research, 53*(4-5), 509–531. https://doi.org/10.1080/00224499.2016.1143441

Peter, J., Valkenburg, P. M., & Schouten, A. P. (2005). Developing a model of adolescent friendship formation on the internet. *CyberPsychology & Behavior, 8*, 423–430. https://doi.org/10.1089/cpb.2005.8.423

Peterman, A., Potts, A., O'Donnell, M., Thompson, K., Shah, N., Oertelt-Prigione, S., & Van Gelder, N. (2020). *Pandemics and violence against women and children* (Vol. 528). Center for Global Development.

Peterson, T. L. (2017). Changes in health perceptions among older grandparents raising adolescent grandchildren. *Social Work in Public Health, 32*(6), 394–406. https://doi.org/10.1080/19371918.2017.1327389

Pew Research Center. (2015, December 17). *The American family today.* Pew Research Center's Social & Demographic Trends Project. Retrieved March 11, 2022, from https://www.pewresearch.org/social-trends/2015/12/17/1-the-american-family-today/

Pittman, L. D., & Boswell, M. K. (2007). The role of grandmothers in the lives of preschoolers growing up in urban poverty. *Applied Developmental Science, 11*(1), 20–42. https://doi.org/10.1207/s1532480xads1101_2

Pollet, S. L., & Lombreglia, M. (2008). A nationwide survey of mandatory parent education. *Family Court Review, 46*, 375–394. http://doi.org/10.1111/j.1744-16172008.00207x

Priest, J. B., McNeil, S., Woods, S. B., & Roberson, P. N. E. (2020). Discrimination, family emotional climate, and African American health: An application of the BBFM. *Journal of Family Psychology, 34*(5), 598–609. https://doi.org/10.1037/fam0000621

Psychology Today. (2021, December). *Child abuse.* Retrieved March 11, 2022, from https://www.psychologytoday.com/us/conditions/child-abuse

Quayle, E., Allegro, S., Hutton, L., Sheath, M., & Lööf, L. (2014). Rapid skill acquisition and online sexual grooming of children. *Computers in Human Behavior, 3*, 368–375. https://doi.org/10.1016/j.chb.2014.07.005

Radel, L., Baldwin, M., Crouse, G., Ghertner, R., & Waters, A. (2018). *Substance use, the opioid epidemic, and the child welfare system: Key findings from a mixed methods study.* Office of the Assistant Secretary for Planning and Evaluation.

Rico, B., Kreider, R., Anderson, L., Raley, K., & Cavanagh, S. (2018, April). Examining change in the geographic distribution of interracial and interethnic married couple households: 2000 to 2016. In *PAA 2018 annual meeting.* Population Association of America.

Riley W. J. (2012). Health disparities: Gaps in access, quality and affordability of medical care. *Transactions of the American Clinical and Climatological Association, 123*, 167–174.

Roberts, S. O., Bareket-Shavit, C., Dollins, F. A., Goldie, P. D., & Mortenson, E. (2020). Racial inequality in psychological research: Trends of the past and recommendations for the future. *Perspectives on Psychological Science, 15*(6), 1295–1309. https://doi.org/10.1177/1745691620927709

Rockquemore, K. A., & Laszloffy, T. (2005). *Raising biracial children.* Rowman & Littlefield.

Rodriguez, C. M. (2010). Parent-child aggression: Association with child abuse potential and parenting styles. *Violence and Victims, 25*(6), 728–741. https://doi.org/10.1891/0886-6708.25.6.728

Roe, K. M., & Minkler, M. (1998). Grandparents raising grandchildren: Challenges and responses. *Generations: Journal of the American Society on Aging, 22*(4), 25–32. https://www.jstor.org/stable/44873306

Rosenberg, N. A., Pritchard, J. K., Weber, J. L., Cann, H. M., Kidd, K. K., Zhivotovsky, L. A., & Feldman, M. W. (2002). Genetic structure of human populations. *Science, 298*(5602), 2381–2385. https://doi.org/10.1126/science.1078311

Roth, W. D. (2005). The end of the one-drop rule? Labeling of multiracial children in Black intermarriages. *Sociological Forum, 20*(1), 35–67. https://doi.org/10.1007/s11206-005-1897-0

Rotheram, M., & Phinney, J. S. (1987). Definitions and perspectives in the study of children's ethnic socialization. In J. S. Phinney & M. Rotheram (Eds.), *Children's ethnic socialization: Pluralism and development* (pp. 117–133). Sage.

Rothman, E. F., Paruk, J., Espensen, A., Temple, J. R., & Adams, K. (2017). A qualitative study of what us parents say and do when their young children see pornography. *Academic Pediatrics, 17*(8), 844–849. https://doi.org/10.1016/j.acap.2017.04.014

Roubinov, D. S., & Boyce, W. T. (2017). Parenting and SES: Relative values or enduring principles? *Current Opinion in Psychology, 15*, 162–167. https://doi.org/10.1016/j.copsyc.2017.03.001

Russell, L. T., Beckmeyer, J. J., Coleman, M., & Ganong, L. (2016). Perceived barriers to postdivorce coparenting: Differences between men and women and associations with Coparenting Behaviors. *Family Relations, 65*(3), 450–461. https://doi.org/10.1111/fare.12198

Salter, D., McMillan, D., Richards, M., Talbot, T., Hodges, J., Bentovim, A., Hastings, R., Stevenson, J., & Skuse, D. (2003). Development of sexually abusive behaviour in sexually victimised males: A longitudinal study. *The Lancet*, *361*(9356), 471–476. doi: 10.1016/S0140-6736(03)12466-X

Sampson, D., & Hertlein, K. (2015). The experience of grandparents raising grandchildren. *Grandfamilies: The Contemporary Journal of Research, Practice and Policy*, *2*(1), 4. https://scholarworks.wmich.edu/grandfamilies/vol2/iss1/4

Sanvictores, T., & Mendez, M. D. (2021). Types of parenting styles and effects on children. *StatPearls* [Internet]. https://www.ncbi.nlm.nih.gov/books/NBK568743/

Sarwer, D. B., & Polonsky, H. M. (2016). The psychosocial burden of obesity. *Endocrinology and Metabolism Clinics*, *45*(3), 677–688. https://doi.org/10.1016/j.ecl.2016.04.016

Sebring, D. L. (1984). Considerations in counseling interracial children. *Journal of Non-White Concerns in Personnel and Guidance*, *13*(1), 3–9. https://doi.org/10.1002/j.2164-4950.1984.tb00308.x

Sepulveda, K., & Williams, S. C. (2019, February 26). *One in three children entered foster care in 2017 because of parental drug abuse*. Child Trends. https://www.childtrends.org/blog/one-in-three-children-entered-foster-care-in-fy-2017-because-of-parental-drug-abuse

Ševčíková, A., Šerek, J., Barbovschi, M., & Daneback, K. (2014). The roles of individual characteristics and liberalism in intentional and unintentional exposure to online sexual material among European youth: A multilevel approach. *Sexuality Research and Social Policy*, *11*(2), 104–115. https://doi.org/10.1007/s13178-013-0141-6

Shaw, D. S., Keenan, K., & Vondra, J. I. (1994). Developmental precursors of externalizing behavior: Ages 1 to 3. *Developmental Psychology*, *30*(3), 355–364. https://doi.org/10.1037/0012-1649.30.3.355

Shek, D. T., Yu, L., & Ma, C. M. (2014). The students were happy, but did they change positively? *International Journal on Disability and Human Development*, *13*(4), 505–511. https://doi.org/10.1515/ijdhd-2014-0348

Smith, B. L. (2012, April). The case against spanking. *Monitor on Psychology*, *43*(4), 60. https://www.apa.org/monitor/2012/04/spanking

Sobolewski, J. M., & King, V. (2005). The importance of the coparental relationship for nonresident fathers' ties to children. *Journal of Marriage and Family*, *67*(5), 1196–1212. https://doi.org/10.1111/j.1741-3737.2005.00210.x

Srivastav, D., & Mathur, M. L. (2020). Helicopter parenting and adolescent development: From the perspective of mental health. In L. Benedetto, & M. Ingrassia (Eds.), *Parenting—Studies by an ecocultural and transactional perspective*. IntechOpen. https://doi.org/10.5772/intechopen.93155

Steinberg, L. (1990). Autonomy, conflict, and harmony in the family relationship. In S. S. Feldman & G. R. Elliott (Eds.), *At the threshold: The developing adolescent* (pp. 255–276). Harvard University Press.

Stewart, S. D., & Limb, G. (2020). *Stepfamilies: Multicultural perspectives*. Cognella.

Stiglic, N., & Viner, R. M. (2019). Effects of screentime on the health and well-being of children and adolescents: a systematic review of reviews. *BMJ Open*, *9*(1), e023191. https://doi.org/10.1136/bmjopen-2018-023191

Stoltenborgh, M., Bakermans-Kranenburg, M. J., Alink, L. R., & van IJzendoorn, M. H. (2015). The prevalence of child maltreatment across the globe: Review of a series of meta-analyses. *Child Abuse Review*, *24*, 37–50. https://doi.org/10.1002/car.2353

Stroebe, M., & Schut, H. (1999). The dual process model of coping with bereavement: Rationale and description. *Death Studies*, *23*(3), 197–224. https://doi.org/10.1080/074811899201046

Strom, R. D., & Strom, S. K. (2000). Meeting the challenge of raising grandchildren. *The International Journal of Aging and Human Development*, *51*(3), 183–198. https://doi.org/10.2190/fr92-egw2-vevu-p8cr

Sue, D. W., Sue, D., Neville, H. A., & Smith, L. (2019). *Counseling the culturally diverse: Theory and practice* (8th ed.). John Wiley & Sons.

Sun, P., Unger, J. B., Palmer, P. H., Gallager, P., Chou, C-P., Baezconde-Garbanati, L., Sussman, S., & Johnson, C. A. (2005). Internet accessibility and usage among urban adolescents in Southern California: Implications for web-based health research. *CyberPsychology & Behavior*, *8*, 441–453. https://doi.org/10.1089/cpb.2005.8.441

Swedo, E., Idaikkadar, N., Leemis, R., Dias, T., Radhakrishnan, L., Stein, Z., Chen, M., Agathis, N., & Holland, K. (2020). Trends in US emergency department visits related to suspected or confirmed child abuse and neglect among children and adolescents aged <18 years before and during the COVID-19 pandemic—United States, January 2019–September 2020. *Morbidity and Mortality Weekly Report*, *69*(49), 1841. https://doi.org/10.15585/mmwr.mm6949a1

Tatum, B.D. (2017). *Why are all the Black kids sitting together in the cafeteria? And other conversations about race*. Basic Books.

Thomas, A. J., & Blackmon, S. K. M. (2015). The influence of the Trayvon Martin shooting on racial socialization practices of African American parents. *Journal of Black Psychology, 41*(1), 75–89. https://doi.org/10.1177/0095798414563610

Threlfall, J. M. (2016). Parenting in the shadow of Ferguson: Racial socialization practices in context. *Youth & Society, 50*(2), 255–273. https://doi.org/10.1177/0044118x16670280

Townsend, S. S. M., Fryberg, S. A., Wilkins, C. L., & Markus, H. R. (2012). Being mixed: Who claims a biracial identity? *Cultural Diversity and Ethnic Minority Psychology, 18*(1), 91–96. https://doi.org/10.1037/a0026845

Tran, A. G. T. T. (2014). Family contexts: Parental experiences of discrimination and child mental health. American Journal of *Community Psychology, 53*(1–2), 37–46. https://doi.org/10.1007/s10464-013-9607-1

Turner, T. (2020, July 31). *Taking care of yourself while raising your grandchildren*. Retire Guide. https://www.retireguide.com/guides/self-care-raising-grandchildren/

United Advocates for Children of California. (2005). *Definition of family*. Retrieved May 11, 2022 from www.cognitivetherapynyc.com/child.asp

U.S. Census Bureau. (n.d.). *Subject definitions: Family*. https://www.census.gov/programs-surveys/cps/technical-documentation/subject-definitions.html#family

U.S. Census Bureau. (2021a). *Annual America's families and living arrangements*. https://www.census.gov/newsroom/press-releases/2021/families-and-living-arrangements.html

U.S. Census Bureau. (2021b). *Census Bureau releases new estimates on America's families and living arrangements*. https://www.census.gov/newsroom/press-releases/2021/families-and-living-arrangements.html

U.S. Census Bureau. (2021c, November 22). *Historical living arrangements of children*. Retrieved March 9, 2022, from https://www.census.gov/data/tables/time-series/demo/families/children.html

U.S. Department of Health & Human Services, Administration for Children and Families, Administration on Children, Youth and Families, & Children's Bureau. (2020). *Child Maltreatment 2018*. Available from https://www.acf.hhs.gov/cb/research-data-technology/statistics-research/childmaltreatment

van Eeden-Moorefield, B., & Pasley, B. K. (2013). Remarriage and stepfamily life. *In G. W. Peterson & K. R. Bush (Eds.), Handbook of marriage and the family* (pp. 517–546). Springer Science + Business Media. https://doi.org/10.1007/978-1-4614-3987-5_22

Walsh, J. J., Barnes, J. D., Cameron, J. D., Goldfield, G. S., Chaput, J. P., Gunnell, K. E., Ledoux, A. A., Zemek, R. L., & Tremblay, M. S. (2018). Associations between 24 hour movement behaviours and global cognition in US children: a cross-sectional observational study. *The Lancet. Child & Adolescent Health, 2*(11), 783–791. https://doi.org/10.1016/S2352-4642(18)30278-5

Wang, S. S., Brownell, K. D., & Wadden, T. A. (2004). The influence of the stigma of obesity on overweight individuals. *International Journal of Obesity and Related Metabolic Disorders: Journal of the International Association for the Study of Obesity, 28*(10), 1333–1337. https://doi.org/10.1038/sj.ijo.0802730

Ward, Z. J., Bleich, S. N., Cradock, A. L., Barrett, J. L., Giles, C. M., Flax, C., Long, M. W., & Gortmaker, S. L. (2019). Projected U.S. state-level prevalence of adult obesity and severe obesity. *New England Journal of Medicine, 381*(25), 2440–2450. https://doi.org/10.1056/nejmsa1909301

Welch, M., & Haskins, R. (2022, March 9). *What covid-19 means for America's child welfare system*. Brookings. Retrieved March 9, 2022, from https://www.brookings.edu/research/what-covid-19-means-for-americas-child-welfare-system/

Wilson, N., Kariisa, M., Seth, P., Smith, H., & Davis, N. L. (2020). Drug and opioid-involved overdose deaths—United States, 2017–2018. *MMWR. Morbidity and Mortality Weekly Report, 69*(11), 290–297. https://doi.org/10.15585/mmwr.mm6911a4

Wiltz, T. (2016, November 2). *Why more grandparents are raising children*. The Pew Charitable Trusts. https://www.pewtrusts.org/en/research-and-analysis/blogs/stateline/2016/11/02/why-more-grandparents-are-raising-children.

Winters, G. M., Kaylor, L. E., & Jeglic, E. L. (2017). Sexual offenders contacting children online: an examination of transcripts of sexual grooming. *Journal of sexual aggression, 23*(1), 62–76. https://doi.org/10.1080/13552600.2016.1271146

Wolak, J., Evans, L., Nguyen, S., & Hines, D. (2013). Online predators: Myth versus reality. *New England Journal of Public Policy, 25*(1), 1–11. https://scholarworks.umb.edu/nejpp/vol25/iss1/6/

Wolak, J., & Finkelhor, D. (2013). Are crimes by online predators different from crimes by sex offenders who know youth in-person?. *Journal of Adolescent Health, 53*(6), 736–741. https://doi.org/10.1016/j.jadohealth.2013.06.010

Wolak, J., Finkelhor, D., & Mitchell, K. J. (2008). Is talking online to unknown people always risky? Distinguishing online interaction styles in a national sample of youth internet users. *CyberPsychology & Behavior, 11*(3), 340–343. https://doi.org/10.1089/cpb.2007.0044

Wolak, J., Finkelhor, D., Mitchell, K. J., & Ybarra, M. L. (2008). Online "predators" and their victims: Myths, realities, and implications for prevention and treatment. *The American Psychologist, 63*(2), 111–128. https://doi.org/10.1037/0003-066X.63.2.111

Wolak, J., Mitchell, K. J., & Finkelhor, D. (2003). Escaping or connecting? Characteristics of youth who form close online relationships. *Journal of Adolescence, 26*(1), 105–119. https://doi.org/10.1016/s0140-1971(02)00114-8

Wolak, J., Mitchell, K. J., & Finkelhor, D. (2007). Unwanted and wanted exposure to online pornography in a national sample of youth internet users. *Pediatrics, 119*(2), 247–257. https://doi.org/10.1542/peds.2006-1891

Wolfe, D. A. (1999). *Child abuse: Implications for child development and psychopathology.* Sage.

Woodgate, R. L. (2006). Living in a world without closure: Reality for parents who have experienced the death of a child. *Journal of Palliative Care, 22*(2), 75–82. https://pubmed.ncbi.nlm.nih.gov/17265659/

World Health Organization. (n.d.). *Child mortality and causes of death.* Retrieved March 9, 2022, from https://www.who.int/data/gho/data/themes/topics/topic-details/GHO/child-mortality-and-causes-of-death

World Health Organization. (2019). *Guidelines on physical activity, sedentary behavior and sleep for children under 5 years of age.* Author. https://apps.who.int/iris/handle/10665/311664.

World Health Organization. (2020). *Global status report on preventing violence against children 2020.* Author. https://www.who.int/publications/i/item/9789240004191external icon

World Health Organization. (2021). *Obesity and overweight.* Retrieved March 9, 2022, from https://www.who.int/news-room/fact-sheets/detail/obesity-and-overweight

World Health Organization. (2022, September 19). *Child maltreatment.* Author. https://www.who.int/news-room/fact-sheets/detail/child-maltreatment

Wright, P. J., & Štulhofer, A. (2019). Adolescent pornography use and the dynamics of perceived pornography realism: Does seeing more make it more realistic? *Computers in Human Behavior, 95*, 37–47. https://doi.org/10.1016/j.chb.2019.01.024

Ybarra, M. L., & Mitchell, K. J. (2005). Exposure to internet pornography among children and adolescents: A national survey. *Cyberpsychology & Behavior, 8*(5), 473–486. https://doi.org/10.1089/cpb.2005.8.473

Ybarra, M. L., Mitchell, K. J., Hamburger, M., Diener-West, M., & Leaf, P. J. (2011). X-rated material and perpetration of sexually aggressive behavior among children and adolescents: Is there a link? *Aggressive Behavior, 37*(1), 1–18. https://doi.org/10.1002/ab.20367

Yoo, J., & Russell, D. W. (2020). Caring for grandchildren and grandparents' physical and mental health changes. *Journal of Child and Family Studies, 29*(3), 845–854. https://doi.org/10.1007/s10826-019-01618-y

Zolotor, A. J., Theodore, A. D., Runyan, D. K., Chang, J. J., & Laskey, A. L. (2011). Corporal punishment and physical abuse: Population-based trends for three-to-11-year-old children in the United States. *Child Abuse Review, 20*(1), 57–66. https://doi.org/10.1002/car.1128

CHAPTER 9

FAMILY THERAPY SKILLS AND INTERVENTIONS

LEARNING OBJECTIVES

After reading this chapter, you will be able to:

- Demonstrate skills for helping enhance family cohesion and adaptability.
- Identify skills related to working with blended and stepfamilies.
- Identify skills for engaging with multiracial families.
- Identify skills for helping parents.
- Recognize the techniques for helping families struggling with obesity.
- Distinguish the various clinical skills related to the internet.
- Identify mandatory reporting skills for assisting with child abuse and neglect.
- Recognize skills for assisting grandparents raising grandchildren.
- Demonstrate skills for helping families grieve the death of a child.
- Recognize the assessment measures used to analyze contemporary family therapy issues.

INTRODUCTION TO FAMILY THERAPY INTERVENTIONS AND SKILLS

Family therapy engages systems to promote healing, change, connection, understanding, and development. When couple, marriage, and family practitioners engage systems (e.g., couples, parents, siblings, families), they are forming a picture of the systemic elements that influence family members at the cognitive, emotional, and behavioral levels. An important element of this engagement is observing and assessing factors like family role assignment (e.g., golden child, scapegoat, leader, peacemaker), contextual elements (e.g., race/ethnicity, age, gender, sexuality, socioeconomic status), life cycle stage (e.g., raising adolescents, retirement), subsystems (e.g., sibling subsystem, parental subsystem), coalitions, patterns of interaction/communication (e.g., pursuer/distancer, distancer/distancer), flexibility and cohesion, degree of openness and closedness, hierarchy, mental health disorders, and the family as a whole. When training clinicians, supervisors and instructors work hard to teach their supervisees each of these elements individually and how they interact to determine a family's level of functioning. For example, through observing and assessing the composition of the subsystems, family role assignments, and the presence of coalitions, clinicians can determine whether the family is impacted by issues like parentification, scapegoating, and cross-generational coalitions. Once clinicians understand the interconnected nature of family systems, they examine how their own presence in the family encounter has changed the system.

It is important to remember that many psychological issues emerge during childhood within one's family, and while these issues are hurtful during childhood they can emerge in different ways later in life (e.g., attachment insecurity, depression, anxiety, entitlement, repression). To understand how these individual issues came to be, the family must be viewed holistically. The holistic nature of a family's structure and the interactions between members can provide the blueprints for how family dynamics create a sense of mental illness within an individual family member. Systemic practitioners must observe key interactions to fully understand a system's functioning. In other words, the interaction between a subsystem, the family as a whole, and relevant systems outside of the family all play a part in the functioning of the individual family members and in the hierarchy, cohesiveness, and flexibility of the family. For example, the parental subsystem may be affected by the school system when a report card indicates their child has a failing grade in a class. This reverberates from the parental subsystem to the sibling subsystem (e.g., parents seem distressed and frequently inquire into homework completion), and eventually to the individual child (e.g., serious discussion, commitment to after-school study sessions). After this incident, the parents begin checking in more frequently regarding their children's grades.

While observing and assessing these family dynamics, emerging clinicians recognize they are part of the system (i.e., cybernetics of cybernetics) and are instructed on how to alter the various interactional patterns so the issue that brought the family into therapy is no longer present (Becvar & Becvar, 2013). During this change-oriented process, family members experience a great deal of *awareness*, *empathy*, and *understanding*. While awareness can come from many places, the clinician often uses their own presence and influence to create new levels of awareness within the family. This might be something as benign as sitting closer to a particular family member during a session and providing them with individual attention through a series of thoughtful questions (i.e., alignment), or something as intensive as having family members engage in an enactment to discuss a critical concern. Regarding empathy, most clinicians are very thoughtful, inquisitive, and empathic when working with clients. Throughout their systemic training, they undergo a comprehensive preparation experience so they can provide both invitational and attending skills throughout every interaction they have with families (Ivey et al., 2017; Young, 2016). These microcounseling skills are used so frequently that they essentially become part of a clinician's personhood. Lastly, understanding occurs frequently during most sessions. At times, practitioners create interventions that are centered on understanding (e.g., genogram, role-play, paradoxical injunction, enactment). Interventions such as these are often structured and somewhat directive. On different occasions, practitioners might create understanding through smaller skills (e.g., circular questioning, clarification, open-ended questioning). These interactions tend to happen frequently and fluidly throughout most sessions.

Voices From the Field

This chapter features sections entitled Voices From the Field. These sections explore multicultural, social justice, equity, diversity, and intersectionality issues from the perspective of clinicians representing a wide range of ethnic, racial, and national backgrounds. This chapter will feature clinicians who identify as East Asian and White. The purpose of adding quotes from individuals representing one or more communities of color or who frequently serve diverse populations is to provide you, the reader, with cutting-edge social justice and multiculturally oriented skills, interventions, and clinical conceptualization. The three individuals who took part in the Voices From the Field process came from different life contexts, different regions of the United States, and diverse intersections of cultural advantage and disadvantage. Participant information is provided in the following:

Mr. Long Hin Siu is a 29-year-old East Asian cisgender man. He is a licensed clinical mental health counselor and a licensed mental health counselor who serves diverse communities in Vermont as an adult staff counselor.

Mr. James "Jim" Thomas is a 64-year-old White cisgender man. He is a licensed marriage and family therapist who serves diverse communities in Colorado as a marriage and family therapist.

Mr. Michael Lopez-Jensen is a 52-year-old White cisgender man. He is a licensed clinical social worker who serves diverse communities in Colorado as a clinical social worker.

Participants were sent a questionnaire featuring eight open-ended questions regarding their experiences practicing in the field. Participant quotes are placed throughout the chapter to enhance the content. Participant questions are as follows:

- As clinicians, we have been trained to analyze and explore the nature and interconnectedness of families. In your personal experience with this work, what are the effects of racism, bias, and/or hate on family units? Have you had the opportunity to use any skills and/or interventions that have helped to reduce the painful effects of racism, bias, or hate?

- When microaggressions are perceived in therapy, they can interfere with the therapeutic process. Within your own work, how has your knowledge of ethnic and racial microaggressions aided you as a clinician? Conversely, does your inexperience with microaggressions ever come up during the therapeutic process?

- Navigating the ups and downs of stepfamily life can be a major challenge for any family. When stepfamilies fully or partly identify as Black, Indigenous, and People of Color (BIPOC), this can bring additional challenges. What issues have you noticed with the diverse stepfamilies you have engaged with? What interventions have you used to help diverse stepfamilies find a sense of cohesion?

- Children and adults who come from multiracial families may have a hard time understanding where they fit. They can feel pressured into fully identifying with a particular aspect of their ethnic/racial ancestry and disregard other aspects. How have you encouraged multiracial children and/or adults to integrate these intersectional identities? What techniques would you recommend to other clinicians?

- Counseling parents and/or parent education are important modalities for anyone who works with families. When considering your work with BIPOC parents, please name a few common issues that come up that are unique to these populations. Are there any unique objectives you review relevant to parent education?

- There are a lot of family-based concerns regarding the appropriate amount of screen time and/or type of internet content to allow children and adolescents to engage in. Many parents have concerns about how different internet-based activities may affect a child's health, mental health, and safety. For example, programs/games demonstrating violence and risk-taking behavior. What, if any, screen time/internet use patterns and trends are you noticing with your work with BIPOC families?

- Child maltreatment, including physical abuse, sexual abuse, psychological abuse, and neglect, is a very serious global public health issue. What unique considerations need to be given when child abuse and neglect emerges in BIPOC families? From a parent education perspective, what information have you found to be most helpful to BIPOC parents?

- Nationally, it has become common for grandparents to serve as foster or surrogate parents for their grandchildren. When grandparents raise grandchildren, their engagement with the caretaking process can range from being completely and legally responsible for all aspects of the caretaking process (i.e., custodial grandparents), or partly and informally responsible for helping with child-rearing duties. From your experience, what common problems emerge when BIPOC grandparents raise grandchildren? What, if any, interventions have you used to help this population?

INFLUENCING FAMILY COHESION AND ADAPTABILITY

Olson et al.'s (1970, 1983) circumplex model conceptualizes cohesion (i.e., degree of emotional bonding), adaptability (i.e., ability to balance stability and change), and communication as the core exchanges that encompass all family interactions. Given the prominence and importance of these issues in all family functioning, it is critical for couple, marriage, and family practitioners to receive thorough training in identifying these factors and influencing various family issues to create a sense of balance. Healthy family functioning is conceptualized as having balanced levels of cohesion (e.g., interdependence, closeness) and adaptability (e.g., ability to change when necessary, stable roles), while unhealthy family interaction has unbalanced levels of cohesion (e.g., little closeness, very high closeness) and/or adaptability (e.g., too much change, too little change). One additional key area in Olson's (2000) circumplex model is the facilitating skill of communication. This includes factors like listening ability, self-disclosure, and demonstrating a sense of respect. Balanced cohesion and flexibility are key ingredients to effective family communication.

Couple, marriage, and family practitioners are relational experts that use skills, interventions, and their personhood to cocreate change in families. A variety of skills and techniques can be used to develop a deeper emotional bond (i.e., cohesion) in a family. The following example demonstrates a common family scenario where a family is too disengaged from one another. The clinician uses several foundational family skills including defusing conflict, joining, and enactment to help the family connect more deeply. For example:

Clinician: The family appears exhausted today. Everybody is slouched and quiet. What's going on?

Client A: Beth and Jill have been avoiding each other up in their rooms.

Client B: They just don't get along very well.

Clinician: Beth and Jill, this is something that is really affecting your mom and dad. Beth, please talk to me about what's going beneath the silence you're demonstrating here in session (*defusing conflict*).

Client C: I just can't stand how Jill steals all my stuff. She's just so annoying!

Clinician: You're so angry about Jill stealing your stuff. It's normal to feel hurt when someone close to you takes your things without asking (*joining*).

Client C: Yeah and mom and dad don't do anything about it.

Clinician: Beth, go ahead and face your mom and tell her what you told me. Talk to Mom about how disrespected you feel and how you want new family rules addressing the stealing behavior (*enactment*).

While the above example and skills are common and foundational, it clearly demonstrates the clinician's attempt to create enhanced family cohesion (i.e., bonding). Specifically, a common method for enhancing family cohesion is through defusing the emotional conflict, cocreating structured communication experiences, and identifying and changing household rules so family members understand the expected behavior (i.e., second-order change). The family cohesion will be further contextualized and enhanced as different family members speak and identify what they think the issues are. Once a new rule is identified, further therapeutic effort is needed to develop a consistent routine as the family implements the rule into their daily life. Within this particular example, notice that the clinician avoided siding with the child against the parents. Instead, the clinician explored communication through an enactment. No matter what the clinician believes about the parents, it is important to avoid blaming, criticizing, or siding with the children against the parents. Part of maintaining homeostasis and a sense of cohesion is preserving the family hierarchy through supporting the parental subsystem. If parent education or confrontation is necessary, the clinician would ask the children to leave the session temporarily or schedule a parental consultation session for another day.

Couple, marriage, and family practitioners also use a variety of skills and techniques to enhance a family's adaptability. Families run into major issues when they demonstrate too little adaptability and become overly rigid or become so adaptable that a sense of family chaos emerges. The next clinical example demonstrates a common family scenario where the family's sense of adaptability is too chaotic. The clinician uses a combination of emphasizing individual boundaries, modeling, and restructuring dysfunctional subsystem boundaries to help the family incorporate greater structure. For example:

> *Clinician:* It seems like Brian has selflessly taken on the role of the family memory bank and spokesperson. Everyone in the room has stayed silent while Brian provided unique responses for every person. Let's go around the room and ask what each family member thinks about the rules regarding curfew (*emphasizing individual boundaries*).

> *Client A:* I think the kids need to have the same curfew as other kids their age, so 10:00 p.m. seems reasonable.

> *Client B:* I generally agree with Robin; however, I am open and flexible if there is a situation worthy of exception.

> *Client C:* 10:00 p.m. is way earlier than when my other friends need to be home, so I think it kind of sucks.

> *Clinician:* Samuel, I can tell the curfew is pretty discouraging. If you would like to discuss your thoughts on a preferable time frame, I'll be here to listen (*modeling*).

> *Client D:* What's the point? It's not like our parents actually give a shit.

> *Clinician:* Brian, you're very angry by what has been said. It can be hard to listen to everyone's own perspective when you are accustomed to fixing everything yourself. Robin and Justina, it seems like Brian needs some parenting and support around his role in all of this. Given what's been said, what should happen next? (*restructuring dysfunctional subsystem boundaries*).

The above example demonstrates the clinician's ability to help a family develop greater structure. This particular family was demonstrating a sense of chaos as one of the children appeared to manage and speak for every member of the family. The clinician used the common and foundational family skills of emphasizing individual boundaries, modeling, and restructuring dysfunctional subsystem boundaries. In addition, the family's sense of chaos was managed by frequently reinforcing the appropriate hierarchy, empathizing with the family memory bank/spokesperson, and providing a structured experience where everyone shares their perspective about the situation. Engaging in a process where Brian no longer manages and speaks for all other family members is an example of second-order change. Furthermore, asking the two moms if they would parent and support Brian is an example of the clinician supporting the appropriate family hierarchy and moving Brian back to the sibling subsystem. Lastly, modeling to the parents appropriate communication skills and boundaries with youth and managing the family democratically by asking for everyone's perspectives will hopefully provide a helpful road map for future encounters.

HELPING BLENDED AND STEPFAMILIES

Working with stepfamilies can be an enormous challenge, and due to inadequate professional preparation the guidance offered by clinicians could be misleading and/or harmful. Papernow (2018) has determined five stepfamily clinical patterns that practitioners need training in: (a) insider and outside positions; (b) struggling with loyalty binds, losses, and change; (c) the divide of separated parents; (d) building a new culture while respecting the old culture; and (e) ex-spouses as part of the family. An important and common challenge that practitioners frequently navigate is how to help a parent develop a strategy for providing attention to their children as well as their partner to prevent feelings of alienation or of being seen as an intruding outsider. This balancing act requires a lot of energy and communication, which can be a surprise to many remarrying parents who mistakenly believe that marrying a new partner will bring much desired relief from the stress of being a hard-working single parent.

Within stepfamilies, the biological parent often wants to emphasize caring and understanding for all of their children regardless of first-family origin. In comparison, stepparents are often more focused on setting limits and boundaries with nonbiological children. This creates an unpredictable and dichotomous environment for the child and can also pull the stepcouple into opposite corners, creating tremendous discord in the relationship (e.g., the biological parent being more loyal to their children vs. the stepparent being interested in getting their needs met in the relationship). Papernow (2018) points out that first-time parents often fight as much as stepparents; however, the content of the arguments is very different, with first-time parents often arguing about things like finances and with stepparents often arguing about child-rearing. Navigating the blending of two familial structures is a key developmental task for stepfamilies that clinicians should be prepared to address. What feels like home to one part of the family may feel foreign, and even offensive, to the other. As a result, stepfamily life, especially early on, can be filled with misunderstandings and unwelcome surprises that, if not understood as being natural and a normal part of the stepfamily development, can result in feelings of anger, betrayal, and strife.

The general clinical approach to supporting stepfamilies includes (a) psychoeducation, (b) interpersonal interventions/practices, and (c) addressing intrapsychic family-of-origin factors (Papernow, 2018). Providing psychoeducation around the various issues that emerge in stepfamilies is key to successful outcomes. Practitioners who specialize in step/blended family work understand the professional literature that specifies what works and what does not work around this important familial issue. Chapter 8 reviews many of the contemporary issues related to this topic; for a more comprehensive review, consider reading Papernow's "Empathic Joining" (2016) and "Clinical Guidelines for Working With Stepfamilies: What Family, Couple, Individual, and Child Therapists Need to Know" (2018). The following is an example of how a clinician might use psychoeducation in a stepfamily context:

> *Clinician:* You seem confused as to whether to force the family to get along together as a whole or to spend time with each child alone. It is important that you allow family connection to develop in a natural way. In other words, although it can be difficult, you shouldn't strain to blend.

The next area of focus in Papernow's (2018) model for working with stepfamilies is interpersonal connection. It is important for clinicians to encourage stepfamilies to turn toward each other, instead of pulling apart. This phase of treatment is much more process-oriented. The clinician encourages families to lean toward each other and engage in more satisfying and supportive connection. At this phase, Papernow either teaches family members basic skills (e.g., take a breath, cultivate positives) or encourages stepfamilies to shape experiences of connection (i.e., joining to build empathic connections). The following is an example of a clinician teaching a stepcouple skills:

> *Clinician:* I notice that you are starting to get a little more stressed with this conversation. Let's stop the discussion and take a few deep and steady breaths. As you breathe, I want you to consider where the stress and/or anger is coming from and try to let it go.

Shaping a couple's experience of connection is demonstrated in the following example:

> *Clinician:* Let's discuss the issue that happened this weekend. Brad, what would you like Susan to know about the discipline issue?
>
> *Client A:* I feel like the kids have no discipline and are extremely lazy.
>
> *Client B:* They are just at a tough stage of adolescence. It's very tumultuous for them right now.
>
> *Clinician:* Brad, every time you criticize the children, Rebecca runs to their rescue. How can you say things in a way that cultivates more collaboration?

The last phase of Papernow's (2018) model has to do with intrapsychic family-of-origin work. The third phase is implemented when the initial two phases do not produce positive results. For example, the stepcouple may continue demonstrating a high level of reactivity despite learning new skills and processing their feelings. At this point, the exploration of family-of-origin wounds and legacies becomes the focus of the session. According to Papernow (2018),

> [s]tuck insider and outsider positions evoke strong feelings in all humans. However, for stepparents who grew up feeling disregarded, unprotected, or abandoned, this challenge can be especially painful. Likewise, parents who could not please their own parents will feel much more triggered by their partner's complaints (p. 32).

For example:

> *Clinician:* It seems like something very deep-rooted may be at play here. Amanda, how was your childhood? What was your parent's relationship like?
>
> *Client A:* My father always loved me, but my mom gave me the role of the perfect child, so I wasn't allowed to have any feelings or imperfections.

VOICES FROM THE FIELD: LONG HIN

Mr. Long Hin Siu shared his experiences working with stepfamilies and the particular skills that he has found helpful.

Some issues I noticed include the relationship issues between the stepparent and the biological parent. The adaptation of diverse stepfamily can be affected by the relationship with members that are outside the unit. The genogram is a very powerful tool in addressing such issues in my experiences. A systemic approach using circular questioning is also a very helpful technique in finding a sense of cohesion as the members can begin to explore with each other about their own perspectives on the family and situations that bring them into the therapeutic room. Often, talking of their own experience, even though it can be messy, is a very therapeutic process that fosters cohesion through understanding of each other.

VOICES FROM THE FIELD: JIM

Mr. James Thomas shared his experiences working with BIPOC stepfamilies and immigrant families and reflected on how much he has learned from his work.

In my experience, BIPOC stepfamilies fare as well or better than many primarily White stepfamilies. BIPOC stepfamilies embrace and accept this diverse family form. To be quite honest, I learned a great deal about family formation, cohesion, and strengthening bonds from BIPOC stepfamilies as well as from immigrant families when I worked at Denver Children's Home for 12 years.

VOICES FROM THE FIELD: MICHAEL

Mr. Michael Lopez-Jensen shared his thoughts on interracial couples and increasing awareness within White partners.

I like Killian's work on interracial couples. I think many White people with partners or family members of color tend to minimize racist incidents and need to work to overcome their blind spots.

HELPING MULTIRACIAL FAMILIES

Treating multiracial families and individuals can be difficult due to the society operating largely on a monoracial paradigm. Consequently, multiracial individuals often feel isolated and disconnected from their racial heritage (Seto et al., 2021). Furthermore, parenting multiracial children is a process that is fraught with challenges due to the context in which the parenting takes place. The pervasive ideology of *color-blindness* leads to identity erasure among multicultural children by denying differences that are an essential part of multiracial and multiethnic identity. In contrast, Brunsma and Porow (2017) indicated that youth develop optimal racial identity when parents supported the racial backgrounds of both sides of the family. Unfortunately, both parents and children likely experience frequent microaggressions (e.g., "What are you?") and will possibly inherit some degree of their parents' own attitudes toward the races and cultures. As clinicians, it is important to convey to parents that youth are absorbing the meta-messages they are hearing about their identities from their parents, family, and other major areas of daily living (e.g., school, sports). Simply acknowledging these messages brings important awareness to the issues. Once awareness has been achieved, parents can address them with their children.

Rather than operating under a color-blind ideology that denies racial difference, studies have found that parents who operate under a *liberation ideology* (i.e., fighting against racism) are more likely to have children who are equipped to handle racism and prejudice and develop their own positive multiracial identity (Rockquemore et al., 2006). Parents should reflect and discuss their own racial identity formation with their children. This is part of open communication and learning, understanding one's ancestry, and the formation of one's own identity development. Part of the conversation should be centered on *the talk*. Boyd-Franklin and Bry (2001) described *the talk* as a racial etiquette script where Black families socialize their children for survival. During this talk, Black children are taught White people's expectations of Black people and how to act when around White people in order to best protect themselves. This discussion can also be extremely helpful for children from racial backgrounds, including those from multiracial families. During treatment, clinicians facilitate these conversations and help parents and children explore their racial identities. It is important that White practitioners listen and respond with humility and validation during these conversations. Lastly, a multidimensional approach to self-care, including having a diverse and accepting support network, allows for conversations and learning around race and racial identity to continue throughout treatment and life (Seto et al., 2021).

When working with multiracial families, it is important to understand how discrimination may affect them and how they may be experiencing it from multiple directions within their family as well as from society. Discrimination can cause ruptures in families and put stress on close interpersonal relationships. Clinicians can help normalize and affirm such experiences as stressful and offer coping strategies. Open dialogue about race is a mitigating factor against the negative effects of discrimination and can improve self-esteem while validating individual experiences (Bennett & Duchesne, 2020). Atkin and Jackson (2021) identified three strategies for parents supporting their multiracial children: (a) connection support (i.e., parent–child interactions that validate and assure the child of the strength of their relationship despite racial, cultural, and phenotypical differences), (b) discrimination support (i.e., standing up for children against discrimination practices, being present when talking about discrimination, and preparing children for racial discrimination), and (c) multiracial identity expression support (i.e., encouraging children to identify with both cultures and providing freedom to choose).

Clinicians encourage parents to instill pride in their child's racial identity. One area of strength and pride could be the bicultural competence and the ability to effectively navigate multiple cultural contexts without relinquishing their cultural identity (LaFromboise et al., 1993). Additionally, practitioners can provide psychoeducational information to parents on key concepts (e.g., monoracial paradigm, the one-drop rule) to improve their ability to provide discrimination support. Regarding multiracial identity expression support, practitioners can help parents engage in conversations with their multiracial children, providing them with choices regarding their racial identification. Lastly, practitioners can also role-play with families about how to address monoracism in different contexts. Narrative therapy strategies can be used to help the family reconstruct a multiracial family identity (Seto et al., 2021). For example:

Clinician: We've established that the issue we're working on is the story of "Should we allow others to keep defining our heritage or should we accurately define it ourselves"; however, the family has been talking about how trust can manipulate your experiences within the family.

Client A: Yeah, along with our problem of indecision, we both just have a hard time trusting anyone.

Client B: I guess we could call that story "Trust manipulates our ability to cocreate a new narrative regarding our family multiracial identity."

Clinician: Okay, so in addition to the main story, there is this subplot of "Trust manipulates our ability to cocreate a new narrative regarding our family multiracial identity."

Solution-focused techniques allow for elucidation of family strengths, cocreation of effective change, and fostering of family/client empowerment (De Jong & Miller, 1995; Edwards & Pedrotti, 2004). Specific techniques that could be beneficial to multiracial families include, but are not limited to, exceptions, coping questions, and scaling (De Jong & Miller, 1995). For example:

Clinician: On a scale of 1 to 10, with 1 being the least and 10 being the most, where would you rank your depression today?

Client A: An 8.

Clinician: Okay, an 8. Can you tell me what a 7 were to look like? (*scaling*)

Client A: I wouldn't be constantly thinking about the awful shit that went on during my childhood.

Clinician: How did you overcome these terrible experiences of discrimination when you were still so young? (*coping question*)

Client A: I always felt alone, and I just kept pulling myself up by my own bootstraps.

Clinician: You have such resilience. Was there ever a time when you depended on another person for support? (*exception*)

Client A: Occasionally I spoke to my mom about stuff that happened at school. She was always there for me, but she could only help so much.

Clinician: Through your own resilience and your mom's occasional support, you were able to survive an environment steeped in racism.

Client A: At times I thought I would go insane, but just like my kids, I always had my family to support me.

VOICES FROM THE FIELD: LONG HIN

Mr. Long Hin Siu shared his experiences working with families that have experienced racism, bias, and hate.

In my experience, the effect of racism occurs in a multigenerational context in which both the quality of the relationship of the multiracial couple and their families are affected in a negative way. Depending on the age of the couple, younger multiracial couples and their families often struggle with boundary issues in which families, in this case parents, often assert their thoughts and attempt to manage behaviors of the younger couple; for more mature couple, their issues are often associated with dealing with holiday anxieties as they are often fazed with troublesome and difficult decision-making. These often affect the relationships not only between the couple, but their own relationship with their respective family. Helping in situations like this can be challenging and tricky. Specifically, in working with intergenerational problems, I find that Bowen's Transgenerational Family Therapy can be very helpful through assisting couples and families as they navigate their sets of challenging issues. I help clients by using psychoeducation of the generational influences affecting the family, encouraging the understanding of respective family members, and through the differentiation of self. I also find that the strategic family approach, which focuses on behavioral responses and changes, is helpful in assisting couples and families prepare for situational anxieties such as holiday anxieties.

VOICES FROM THE FIELD: JIM

Mr. James Thomas shared his own diversity-related self-reflections; experiences working with couples and families from a variety of background who have experienced racism, bias, and hate; and reflections on how society can heal from the destructive effects of racism, hate, marginalization, discrimination, and prejudice.

First and foremost, I want to say that in answering these questions I do not intend in any way to speak for people of color and members of the LGBTQ community about their lived experiences. The inherent limit of my experiences and input as a White male person. So much of what I share reflects cross-cultural therapy experiences, learning from a cultural humility place, and attempts at a closer, deeper understanding through study, discussion, and ongoing practices of looking within at my own biases, blind spots, strengths, and weaknesses in cross-cultural awareness and competency.

Given that, implicit bias, overt racism, and the deeply embedded structural and systemic racism in the United States profoundly impact families, couples, communities, and the individuals suffering the ill effects of oppression and marginalization. Walking out into a world where some core aspect of your being triggers reactivity, avoidance, or aggression from others leaves a person in threat on a consistent basis. Stereotype threat alone puts the nervous system on alert and requires use of resources, energy in the person's brain to try to deal with or reduce the threat.

How it impacts families, in my experience, directly relates to how connected the family's relationships are in the face of racism. To venture out from a safe haven at home and in community to a world of bias and racism and back to that secure base differs greatly from a person whose own family stresses make the family system stressed, in conflict, or chaotic. So as a family and couples' therapist, it behooves us to acknowledge the impact of racism and to make multiple invitations at many levels for clients to discuss this with us.

Healthy cultural suspicion may exist when a therapist from a different ethnic background asks about lived experience in the world of racism and other forms of discrimination and prejudice. So, over time, family's responses led me to seek to be more open, vulnerable, and available in these discussions. An academic or clinically distant approach by myself as a White male therapist is left open to interpretation. Better to speak to my own ethnicity, to share that I seek to understand without requiring clients and their families to teach me about racism. This bridging of cultural differences within a therapy relationship may be a small bit of racial healing. Leveling, by saying overtly, openly, that as a White person I may be missing something key about your experience in this "argument with your wife," "conflict at work," "trauma responses in your family in the face of the George Floyd murder," and so on is a start.

However, the solution to reducing the painful effects of racism, bias, and hate lies as much in society and the whole of us as it does in each individual. The impact of hate, that we as a nation formed in such a violent manner, needs to be addressed both within therapeutic relationships and in the larger social-political sphere. It strikes me as so odd, painful, and sorrowful that we as nation do not make reparations for racism. So perhaps the task of every therapist is to look at where we sit in that larger cultural reality of ongoing racism, bias, and hate. Where does their family system, their community exist in this? Where is my heart in terms of looking at bias and hate within me as a person and professional? Being alert, learning, and consistently investigating and surfacing my own cultural bias are of utmost importance. Every time I imagine I have arrived at a more culturally humble, competent place, it turns out to be simply a false summit in a lifelong journey. But the higher I climb, the more that I yearn to bridge differences in as many aspects of my work and life as possible. That is the work for the therapist, or for me as a therapist. How can I remove the barriers to love and understanding within me, to paraphrase Rumi, across differences?

In therapy, there have been a good number of cross-cultural communications between me as therapist, as human, with families, couples, and individuals of color that included sharing of the impacts of racism on the family, couple, or individual. It has been important to honor and lean into the risk a client takes in opening up to a therapist whose skin color matches so many of those whose hands and voices have caused harm on many levels. And for me to take my own risks by both showing up for all who come to my office with my fullest, most open, loving heart, experience, strength, and hope while looking for signs and inviting feedback about how racism's legacy in the present, bias, and more may be impacting the work in the room, now, in this moment.

More recently in my career, more focused on couples therapy work, I have many bicultural couples come to my practice. Particularly with couples with one White partner and a BIPOC partner, exploring whether there is communication at a deep level about the experience of the BIPOC partner of racism on an ongoing basis is very helpful. Fostering vulnerable talk of family member experiences of racism, sexism, anti-GLBTQ hatred, and other stressors that arise from ethnicity, orientation, gender identity, and other socially marginalized aspects of self, if it is not already occurring, is one small way therapy can help mitigate against the ongoing devastating impacts of racism.

VOICES FROM THE FIELD: MICHAEL

Mr. Michael Lopez-Jensen provided his experiences around helping families who have experienced racism, bias, and hate.

Racism, bias, and/or hate can impact family units in so many ways: health disparities, stress from educational and legal systems, family tensions when family members disagree about whether or not an incident or run-in was racist, biased, or hateful. Skills and interventions I have used include placing responsibility for the hate on the perpetrator, not on the victim; helping family members with more social power understand and believe family members who encounter bias and racism; helping victims of hate feel empowerment through social action, artistic expression, or community support.

VOICES FROM THE FIELD: LONG HIN

Mr. Long Hin Siu shared his experiences and thoughts around microaggressions, biculturalism, and what to do if they are present in therapy.

Microaggressions are certainly picked up in the therapeutic process. Being a minority, personally, has aided me to have a broader understanding and clearer vision of microaggression due to bicultural experiences. With biculturalism, a person might be able to see and experience a conflicted cultural value where each respected culture would see themselves as correct. A harmless example: wearing shoes in the house. In East Asian culture, it is practically disrespectful and perceivably ethically "wrong" to be wearing outside shoes inside one's house or residence, whereas in the West this isn't a problem at all. A bicultural individual like myself might have experienced a conflicted cultural value like such that has aided me in being slightly more sensitive to microaggression in the therapeutic process. In the intergenerational family approach, psychoeducation on the differences and the influences on families and couples in different generations can alleviate some of the suffering in microaggression through developing empathetic understanding for other members in the unit. Microaggression sometimes can be unintended. Using open-ended questioning to seek the understanding of the intention of the microaggressive statement or behavior and to foster behavioral changes can be helpful in the therapeutic process.

VOICES FROM THE FIELD: JIM

Mr. James Thomas shared his experiences and thoughts around microaggressions, misattunements, and cross-cultural offenses, and his reflections on his own personal privilege.

When I first started in the field, and for many years after, what we now see as microaggressions were viewed as misattunements or being offensive to a client or family. Perhaps a metaphor might have been used that culturally the family found upsetting, dystonic, or rude. Knowing that cross-cultural offenses and misattunements need to be expected, I asked individuals, couples, and families for feedback, to let me know if how I showed up harmed them or was not useful. The lens of microaggressions helps as it puts the burden more on me as therapist to be thoughtful in all ways. How might what I as a White male therapist say, don't say, do or don't do be experienced by the person or persons in my office? My fear in my career is the times when I engaged in a microaggression, and I did not recognize, and the client or family did not feel safe to tell me. The times when a client or family told me my words, actions, or assumptions were harmful have been incredible learning opportunities. They take me out of a privileged veil, a comfort zone, and remind me of the omnipresent, pervasive existence of racism.

VOICES FROM THE FIELD: MICHAEL

Mr. Michael Lopez-Jensen reflected on his own racial background, personally committing microaggressions in therapy, and his process with taking responsibility, apologizing, and changing.

As a White clinician, I have certainly committed microaggressions in session. When this happens, I strive to take responsibility, to apologize, and to make behavioral changes. When clients of color speak in therapy about microaggressions, my role is to believe, validate, and confirm. I like Ijeoma Oluo's work on racism—paraphrased as "if the person of color thinks it was racist, it was racist." I believe people of color when they share their experiences. I have a responsibility to challenge White clients who may be committing microaggressions in therapy or in their daily lives. When I learn of this, I suggest resources that may be helpful in educating clients or seeing the impact of their actions.

VOICES FROM THE FIELD: LONG HIN

Mr. Long Hin Siu provided his thoughts and experiences around identity strengthening when working with children from multiracial families.

Helping the children understand that being different is "fine and okay" and normalizing, as appropriate, the child's differences. Identity development, in my experience, has been key and the most important focus within this type of therapeutic process. Strengthening the children's identification with both sides of the ancestries through a positive lens and developing and strengthening the interests in cultural activities for the families as a unit can also be helpful.

VOICES FROM THE FIELD: MICHAEL

Mr. Michael Lopez-Jensen provided resources when asked about supporting multiracial children.

Heritage camps, role models outside the family, the work of multiracial artists and writers.

HELPING PARENTS

Parenting is a bidirectional relationship a caregiver engages in for the purpose of effectively raising a child. Parents provide children with a safe, secure, empathic, and nurturing relationship that extends through all of the future developmental stages of their life. A happy and secure childhood provides the knowledge, values, attitudes, and behaviors necessary to become an adult and make a positive societal contribution. Furthermore, through engaging youth in a securely attached relationship (i.e., providing nurturing, engagement, structure, and developmentally appropriate expectations; Bray, 1992), parents are setting the stage for security and safety in future relationships. While factors like nurturing, engagement, safety, consistency, predictability, and structure all create more well-developed children, youth gain a strong self-concept through struggles and achievements (i.e., not constant praise). Concentrating and solving a problem also increase youth self-esteem, self-efficacy, and positive internal self-talk. Lastly, while positive reinforcement is used much more frequently in parenting, when children make mistakes or misbehave, effective parents hold them accountable (Gullotta & Adams, 2005; Kazdin, 2005). Table 9.1 provides a list of parenting dos and don'ts that can be used with any parent counseling experience. Specifically, the list provides the parent/caregiver with helpful information and examples that can quickly enhance positive parenting outcomes.

Therapeutic efforts involving parents can take place in a variety of formats, including parent education, parent counseling, parent consultation, or as an adjunct to a form of child/adolescent counseling (e.g., parent–child interaction therapy, play therapy, filial therapy) and as an important part of family therapy. As couple, marriage, and family practitioners begin working frequently with parents, they will undoubtedly discover a large variety of experiences. These experiences range from happiness and self-fulfillment to complete frustration and concern. Parenting is hard work, and because of this clinicians start every encounter with a deep sense of empathy, acceptance, and attentive listening. As you begin working with parents, they may inquire as to your personal experience raising children. Parents have these questions for a variety of reasons, so it is important to answer the question directly and honestly. For example:

> *Clinician:* I hear that you're curious as to whether I have my own kids. I do not have children. Despite not having my own, I do believe I can help you meet your parenting goals; however, you will be the best judge of that.

While training, supervision, and expertise are vitally important to working with parents, if you do not know something simply admit it (Sommers-Flanagan, 2012).

According to Sommers-Flanagan (2012), it is extremely helpful to ask parents why their child is engaging in a particular manner. Attaining the parents' perspective is important due to emotions like guilt and shame. In other words, they might never discuss the issue because they feel ashamed about what happened. To help them feel less insecure and/or shameful, clinicians should consider incorporating a strengths-based approach to their work and avoid criticism and critiques. Clinicians should ensure that they do not criticize parents in front of their children. During situations in which growth-oriented feedback needs to be provided, children should be instructed to leave the room temporarily or the parents could come in for a separate meeting on a later date. Lastly, because parenting is so personal and requires a good deal of work to successfully adjust, all advice and homework assignments should be followed by the clinician observing the client's reaction. For example:

> *Clinician:* Janice, for this week I want you to deliberately refrain from crying in front of your Jacquie. This is so she does not absorb your sense of anxiety and think of it as her own. What are your thoughts on this?

TABLE 9.1 PARENTING DOS AND DON'TS

Parenting Issues	Parenting Dos	Parenting Don'ts
Child accountability	**Do** hold children accountable, refuse to argue, incorporate empathy, integrate consequences for actions, incorporate choices.	**Don't** excuse inappropriate behavior, worry about being seen as mean, try to be inconsistent, act in an emotional or impulsive manner.
Child struggle and achievement	**Do** encourage respect and responsibility, encourage children to solve their own problems.	**Don't** provide constant praise, do it for them, aid unless they ask for it, compare them with other youth.
Parental anger and emotions	**Do** avoid anger, remain in control of your emotions, set limits with empathy and understanding.	**Don't** argue with children, express uncontrolled emotionality, get upset with children if you never set the limit they violated.
Providing choices	**Do** frequently offer choices within limits, ensure the choices are something you can live with, allow children to make the wrong choice, ensure child safety, allow the child to present their own choices.	**Don't** make one of the choices a punishment, make the choice for them (unless they take a long time), make a choice you can't live with, correct the child when they make the wrong choice, give more than two choices, allow them to take a long time.
Providing empathy	**Do** provide empathy often, be empathic prior to engaging in any punishment, make the empathy clear and concise, repeat the same empathic response repeatedly.	**Don't** avoid empathy, blame, argue, or act in an angry manner, use empathy in a sarcastic manner, have negative nonverbal behavior while being empathic.
Providing reinforcements	**Do** use this more than punishment, use parent statements, use hugs and pats on the back, use when you want a child to repeat a behavior, allow for natural reinforcers whenever appropriate.	**Don't** use as a bribe, overuse praise, use if you want to discourage a behavior, always count on natural reinforcers, use reinforcements for things a child does naturally.
Providing punishments	**Do** use sparingly, have clear and consistent rules, teach them in a calm and clear manner, use when you want to discourage your child from repeating a behavior, allow for natural consequences whenever appropriate, remain calm, hear them out.	**Don't** overuse, always count on natural consequences, yell or become angry, use corporal punishment, punish children for limits you have not set.
Child adherence to rules	**Do** be direct, be clear, provide age-appropriate instructions, give instructions one at a time, keep the explanation concise, discuss the fairness of the rule, allow children to process what you've said, provide as many specifics as possible, ensure the child knows why the rules exist and the consequence for breaking them, provide reminders, criticize the action not the child if a rule is broken.	**Don't** be vague, assume that a child knows the rules unless you've told them, use a consequence that hasn't been reviewed by the child, assume the child knows an outdated rule has changed, discourage questions and child expression, assume they won't need reminders, wait or place too much time between the rule being broken and the consequence.
Family meetings	**Do** encourage all family members to attend and participate, schedule at a routine time, discuss one topic a time, use "I" messages, make decisions via consensus.	**Don't** meet at random times, have meetings unless everyone is present, attempt to solve multiple problems simultaneously, discourage participation, engage in unilateral decision-making.

(continued)

TABLE 9.1 PARENTING DOS AND DON'TS (*CONTINUED*)

Parenting Issues	Parenting Dos	Parenting Don'ts
Time-outs	**Do** specify the rule, give a warning, provide the time-out in an immediate manner, provide time-out in a calm and controlled way, lead the child back to time-out if they refuse to stay, make time-out brief, require children to demonstrate calm and quiet before being released.	**Don't** allow second chances, engage in negotiations, take a long time to pass between the behavior and providing the time-out, put children in a time-out location that has a lot of stimulating objects and toys, allow any type of interaction or play while in time-out, use time-out to punish, combine time-out with negative tone of voice, humiliation, or for a long duration.

Sources: Data from Baldwin, J. D., & Baldwin, J. I. (2000). *Behavior principles in everyday life*. Prentice Hall; Cline, F. W. (2009). *All about consequences*. Love and Logic; Golden, C. O., & Kazdin, A. E. (2005). *Parent management training: Treatment for oppositional, aggressive, and antisocial behavior in children and adolescents*. Oxford University Press.

According to Leppma and Schimmel (2019), parent education involves a number of steps (e.g., curriculum creation, screening, cost, format) and is frequently offered in a group format. While there are manualized curriculums centered on parent education, manualized instructions are not necessary for effective results (Kaminski et al., 2008). The Centers for Disease Control and Prevention (CDC; 2009) indicated five major components of most parent education programs: (a) requiring caregivers to engage in parenting practices during session (i.e., actively using the new technique with their child in session), (b) helping parents understand emotional communication techniques (i.e., actively encouraging parents to use relationship-building skills to enhance connection to their child), (c) encouraging positive parenting communication (i.e., promoting positive interaction regarding normal family occurrences), (d) encouraging consistent responding (i.e., discipline, communication, and rules all need to be consistent), and (e) teaching parents how to effectively use time-out (i.e., parents learn how to use it appropriately and consistently; CDC, 2009; Kaminski et al., 2008; Leppma & Schimmel, 2019). One long-standing parent education program is parent management training (PMT).

PMT is a common treatment for youth diagnosed with attention deficit hyperactivity disorder, oppositional defiant disorder, disruptive mood dysregulation disorder, intermittent explosive disorder, conduct disorder, and other dysfunctional externalizing behavior. According to Kazdin (2005), PMT was developed in the 1960s and is centered on four interrelated theoretical components: learning theory, a variety of principles, specific skills, and assessment and evaluation. PMT is centered on training parents to use positive and open communication, creating a structured environment, setting rules and boundaries, and consistency with rules and boundaries. Family dysfunction is described as having a lack of cohesion, conflict, low parental skills, and dysfunctional externalizing behavior. PMT is widely used with parents and/or caregivers. During treatment, parents are taught strategies for handling a variety of behavioral issues and the parent–child relationship. Many stakeholders are involved in PMT, including the therapist (i.e., leader, coach), parent(s), child/adolescent, daycare workers, and teachers. PMT coaches parents to work effectively with a variety of child problems and behaviors, and encourages child prosocial behaviors. Parent skill interventions include positive reinforcement, social reinforcement, nonviolent and consistent discipline, effective monitoring and supervision, and constructive family problem-solving (Gullotta & Adams, 2005; Kazdin, 2005).

VOICES FROM THE FIELD: LONG HIN

Mr. Long Hin Siu shared his experiences working with BIPOC parents and how to cocreate an accurate understanding about various issues.

Parents have anxieties about their own incompetence and anxieties about their children's future. Though these seem to be common issues faced by any parents, in my experience, BIPOC parents might be challenged by issues that are caused by a systemic issue where immense hopelessness and helplessness and anxiety experiences can be consuming. When grandparents are an option, in my experience, I find that their wisdom or words can be helpful to BIPOC parents. In addition, pointing to helpful statistics (factual ones) to foster better understanding of the issues that are concerning has helped as parents tend to understand their concerns better and can distinguish emotionally charged news that represents many from their local statistics.

VOICES FROM THE FIELD: JIM

Mr. James Thomas shared his experiences working with BIPOC parents from a strengths-based perspective and described his method of creating a shared sense of hope in the family while simultaneously preparing them for the realities of racism.

BIPOC parents face the challenge of both generating hope in their children while simultaneously preparing them for the harsh realities of racism. Parents of children of color send their precious children out into a world mixed with possibilities, pitfalls, and danger. From teaching how to deal with police interactions to dealing with discrimination (overt and covert) in school or work, I see these parents balancing competing needs. First and foremost, with BIPOC parents, I approach their family situation, family strengths and stresses, and their parenting approach from a place of humility and curiosity. It's essential for the therapist to learn from parents, caretakers, kin, and others raising the children or adolescents the values, the context and the reasons behind their parenting approaches. Secondly, I seek to not make any negative assumptions about BIPOC families and parents. In providing in-home therapy, and working with families in a day treatment program, over and over again, the larger system seemed to start from a place of negative assumptions. It was as if BIPOC families needed to earn respect and trust, whereas White families in the system started with a blank slate or positive assumptions. So, for me, I find it of utmost importance to send clear welcoming signals to all families, but particularly those who differ from me culturally and in any other way. Therapists who believe in families, believe in the bonds in a family, and work with them collaboratively provide better services. Thus, bridging differences, acknowledging real life stressors created by ongoing systemic racism for families, being open about my innate privilege, asking for feedback, not expecting these families to "teach me about racism," and showing up as authentically as possible can help build a stronger therapy alliance. Then and only then, when the family tells the therapist that the relationship is developing, trust is present, would I begin to provide therapy interventions per se. And then, there is a consistent checking on my own part and then overtly with a family about whether a particular approach or intervention is congruent with their family values and goals.

VOICES FROM THE FIELD: MICHAEL

Mr. Michael Lopez-Jensen provided his experiences around helping BIPOC parents equip their children for living in a racist American culture.

Equipping children to deal with racist American culture, particularly in educational and legal system settings. Finding support with other BIPOC parents, encouraging an informed consumer approach to finding the right schools, communities, etc.

HELPING FAMILIES WITH OBESITY

According to the World Health Organization (2021), obesity is a global epidemic resulting in 2.8 million deaths per year. The U.S. Department of Health and Human Services (2020) depicted obesity as the most serious health threat of the 21st century. According to the CDC (2017), 41.9% of U.S. adults aged 20 and older are obese. Similarly, youth display very concerning statistics with regard to rates of obesity, including those 2 to 5 years of age showing 12.7% rate of obesity, 6 to 11 years of age with 20.7% rate of obesity, and 12 to 19 years with 22.2% rate of obesity. Obesity is clearly an epidemic. In addition to the negative physical health issues (e.g., high blood pressure, type 2 diabetes, high cholesterol, coronary heart disease), clinicians should be aware of the enormous stigma obese/overweight individuals endure. Research has indicated that approximately 25% of people diagnosed as overweight or obese have mental health concerns (Simon et al., 2006). A significant factor related to the emergence of mental health issues is the persistent and hurtful discrimination they experience on a daily basis.

Among the most significant and hurtful issues are the misconceptions and the negative and derogatory stereotypes that often follow individuals diagnosed with obesity. Obese adults and youth can be inaccurately identified as lazy, lacking self-discipline, ignorant, unmotivated, immoral, and less successful (Polinko & Popovich, 2001; Puhl & Brownell, 2001; Warchal & West, 2013). These negative and inaccurate stereotypes and generalizations can lead to a variety of hate-based marginalization, including wage and employment discrimination, college admissions, and access to healthcare and mental health services (Warchal & West, 2013). Furthermore, youth can face enormous challenges, including, but not limited to, bullying, peer rejection, hurtful comments, jokes, and social isolation (Robinson, 2006; Warchal & West, 2013). These painful experiences during youth can negatively affect the victim in many ways, including, but not limited to, exclusion from peer social experiences, poor self-esteem, body-image issues, poor academic performance, higher rates of activity restrictions, and higher levels of relational victimization (Pearce et al., 2002).

As clinicians begin working with obese and/or overweight clientele, they should collect information on the amount of bias and discrimination the individual, couple, or family has experienced at various points in their life. In addition, clinicians should self-reflect and introspect on their own bias, values, beliefs, and feelings related to obesity and any bias they may harbor. If they realize they hold any negative attitudes or beliefs related to this population, they must seek their own therapy, supervision, and additional training, and should refer the client, couple, or family to a safe, accepting, and affirming clinician who can ensure they will do no harm (Warchal & West, 2013).

Clinicians who work with individuals diagnosed with obesity should be sure not to overstep their ethical boundaries by offering any specific dietary prescription or exercise advice. While general recommendations that are available freely to the public can be provided, clinicians should avoid encouraging any specific diet or exercise regimen. Professionals such as registered dietitians, exercise specialists, nutritionists, physicians, and certified health coaches would be more appropriate to make recommendations around nutrition, exercise, and specific diet plans. Similar to the preparation needed to become a helping professional, proficiency in the practice and science of health and nutrition takes years of training. If questions emerge that are outside of a clinician's professional competency, it is important to refer the client to the appropriate community-based resource (Murphy, 2013).

There is surprisingly very little research and literature on therapeutic interventions and techniques for assisting obese clientele. This is especially concerning given the enormous negative impact it can have on people. Some scholarship describes the importance of therapist self-reflection on potential bias toward obese individuals and the importance of the clinician leading by example (i.e., demonstrating good physical health; Murphy, 2013). There has been some research into a few interventions, including (a) motivational interviewing to assess the client's readiness for change (Prochaska & DiClemente, 1983); (b) the transtheoretical model of change to work on decision, self-efficacy, and temptation (Prochaska & Dilemente, 1983); and (c) mindfulness interventions to enhance quality of life and psychological flexibility (Lillis et al., 2009). One area that has consistently garnered positive empirical support for clinical effectiveness is behavioral treatment packages for obesity (Brownell, 2000; Volpp et al., 2008; Wadden et al., 2005; Wing, 2008).

Comprehensive behavioral treatment has been seen as a gold standard treatment for weight loss since the 1980s (Mellin et al., 1987). Whitlock et al. (2010) examined existing data related to behavioral, pharmacologic, and surgical weight management treatment for obese and/or overweight youth. Whitlock et al. (2010) discovered that research suggested behavioral interventions are effective in treating obesity. Furthermore, the authors discovered that behavioral interventions with pharmacologic treatment can be helpful in treating very obese adolescents. Within their investigation, Whitlock et al. (2010) defined behavioral interventions as including the alteration of food intake, increasing physical movement, frequent family involvement in treatment, and use of cognitive behavioral therapy. In other words, behavioral interventions have been described as dietary, family, behavioral treatments, and physical activity (Jacob & Isaac, 2012; Pratt et al., 2011).

Philosophically, behavioral therapy has two main assumptions related to the management of obesity, namely problematic eating and exercise rituals, and maladaptive behaviors can be enhanced with particular interventions leading to weight loss. From a lifestyle management perspective, factors like calorie restriction, increasing total physical activity, reduction in sedentary lifestyle, and reduction in unhealthy eating patterns are all key to weight management (Jacob & Isaac, 2012). Table 9.2 provides a breakdown of some of the most common behavioral treatment strategies for weight loss (Bandura, 1977; Brownell, 2000; Volpp et al., 2008; Wadden et al., 2005; Wing, 2008).

One additional way that couple, marriage, and family practitioners can assist clients is by helping them understand inexpensive pathways to attaining healthy food. Food insecurity is paradoxically connected to obesity (Dhurandhar, 2016). It can be described as the lack of ability to find healthy food options due to scarcity of resources (University of Texas at San Antonio [UTSA], 2019). The U.S. Department of Agriculture Economic Research Service (n.d.) described food insecurity as "reports of reduced quality, variety, or desirability of diet. Little or no indication of reduced food intake" (para. 4). Data from 2016 indicate that there were 15.6 million households identified as food-insecure. This equates to 12.3% of all U.S. homes. Geographic areas known as "food deserts" are often hit the hardest. Food deserts are typically urban or rural areas where people do not have proper access to supermarkets that provide good-quality fresh food (UTSA, 2019). While individuals living in these communities have access to a variety of food, most of that food is unhealthy.

Helping professionals are in a good position to advocate for, educate, and assist clients and families suffering from food insecurity. First, clinicians should screen all clients for the presence of food insecurity. There are screening tools designed to quickly measure the presence of food insecurity (see Bickel et al., 2000; Hager et al., 2010). Second, clinicians should educate clients on healthier ways of coping during times when there is a lack of food. For example, clinicians can collaborate with a registered dietitian or nutritionist and provide education on coping strategies that assist with prioritizing quality of food over quantity (Patil et al., 2017). When assisting clients who have food insecurity, clinicians can provide very helpful information, including information on negative health consequences, educational materials on healthy eating habits, and referral

TABLE 9.2   BEHAVIORAL TECHNIQUES FOR TREATING OBESITY

Behavioral Technique	Brief Description
Self-monitoring	The client self-monitors by keeping a food diary or activity log. The food diary includes everything the client eats, the calories consumed, and the place the food was eaten.
Stimulus control	The client controls the stimuli around eating, including the type of food purchased, reducing the amount of food served, using smaller plates, limiting distractions (e.g., computer, television) while eating, and decreasing the proximity of food.
Goal setting	The client sets realistic weight loss goals over specific periods of time (e.g., weeks, months, year).
Behavioral contracting	This refers to use of operant conditioning to reward good behavior. Positive reinforcers could be financial or nontangible.
Social support	Social support increases the long-term effects of behavioral modification. The supporters could be one of the following: a spouse, family members, network therapy, or through group therapy.
Meal replacement	The client replaces one or two daily meals with liquid or healthy replacement meal.
Slower eating	The client slows the pace of eating or consumes water in between meals so the body can process the client's sense of fullness.
Education	The client engages in nutritional education, including a dietitian's directions for creating a structured meal plan.
Increasing physical activity	The client slowly increases daily physical activity that meets long- and short-term goals.

Source: Data from Jacob, J. J., & Isaac, R. (2012). Behavioral therapy for management of obesity. *Indian Journal of Endocrinology and Metabolism, 16*(1), 28.

pathways. Lastly, various reputable organizations provide pertinent online information and resources, including, but not limited to, Feeding America, No Kid Hungry, and the American Hospital Association (Patil et al., 2018). This information, along with pertinent community referrals, should be provided to all clients demonstrating food insecurity.

HELPING FAMILIES EXPERIENCING ISSUES WITH THE INTERNET

Excessive screen viewing and internet use has become a common global family problem (CDC, 2022). While these problems are having a massive global impact, screen use and extensive access to the internet are relatively new issues. In most clinical settings, issues like texting, social media, screen time, and gaming are identified as issues for virtually all children, adolescents, and families. While research is scant, there are findings related to how screen time affects youth sleep, weight, aggression, attention, mental health, and neurologic development (Gehart, 2020; Kamenetz, 2018; Knell et al., 2019; McCain & Campbell, 2018; Robinson et al., 2017; Swing et al., 2010). Family therapy, parent counseling, psychoeducation, family meetings, and use of third-party parental control apps have been found helpful in reducing screen time usage and viewing of inappropriate sites and images among youth (Bahadur et al., 2021; Gehart, 2020).

Couple, marriage, and family practitioners help families by providing important information about the negative effects of screen use. Sometimes this comes in the form of psychoeducation and consensus about family rules. For example:

Clinician: One thing that has come up for us is your fear that the screens are re-placing you as parents. You should consider making boundaries around when the daughters are allowed to use devices. First, when do you think they should put the devices away?

Client A: Since they usually start homework around 7 p.m. I think that would be a good time to turn their cell phones in.

Clinician: How about the weekend? Some families have different rules around weekend technology use.

Client B: I think they can start using technology on the weekend around 4 p.m.

Table 9.3 breaks down a number of contemporary issues and relevant research-based reference (Gehart, 2020). This information should be shared with families so they can understand the evidence backing up certain internet/screen time-based concerns.

TABLE 9.3   INTERNET ISSUE, DESCRIPTION OF PROBLEM, AND EMPIRICAL REFERENCE

Issue	*Description*	*References*
Sleep	Decrease in youth sleep time is directly linked with increase in time in front of a screen and social media use. This negatively affects the brain and the consolidation of memories.	Carter, B., Rees, P., Hale, L., Bhattacharjee, D., & Paradkar, M. S. (2016). Association between portable screen-based media device access or use and sleep outcomes. *JAMA Pediatrics, 170,* 1202–1208.
Obesity	Spending a lot of time online or in front of screens decreases the amount of time engaging in physical activity. A lack of physical activity is a common antecedent to negative problems with weight management.	Robinson, T. N., Banda, J. A., Hale, L., Lu, A. S., Fleming-Milici, F., Calvert, S. L., & Wartella, E. (2017). Screen media exposure and obesity in children and adolescents. *Pediatrics, 140*(Suppl 2), S97–S101. https://doi.org/10.1542/peds.2016-1758K.
Attention issues	The amount of time spent online and the speed of images flashing on the screen negatively affect the attention span of people of all ages. The more an individual watches fast-paced internet, the more difficult it is to pay attention to nonscreen and slow-paced activities.	Swing, E. L., Gentile, D. A., Anderson, C. A., & Walsh, D. A. (2010). Television and video game exposure and the development of attention problems. *Pediatrics, 126,* 213–221.
Desensitization to violence	Violent video gaming and online content have been connected to increased aggression and decreased sensitivity to the suffering of others in youth.	Hull, J. G., Brunelle, T. J., Prescott, A. T., & Sargent, J. D. (2014). A longitudinal study of risk-glorifying video games and behavioral deviance. *Journal of Personality and Social Psychology, 107*(2), 300–325.
Personality disorders	While screen time is not the cause of mental health disorder, narcissism has been correlated with issues like engaging in various social media platforms, high frequency of selfie postings, and fixation on the number of followers.	McCain, J. L., & Campbell, W. K. (2018). Narcissism and social media use: A meta-analytic review. *Psychology of Popular Media Culture, 7*(3), 308–327.
Brain development	There have been brain differences among those who engage in over 7 hours of total screen time per day. Lower language and reasoning test scores were associated with youth engaging in more than 2 hours of screen time per day.	U.S. National Institutes of Health. (2019). *The adolescent brain cognitive development study.* https://www.abcdstudy.org.

Source: Data from Gehart, D. R. (2020). Screening screen time: Evidence-informed guidelines for parenting in the digital age. *Family Therapy Magazine, 19*(1). https://ftm.aamft.org/screening-screen-time-evidence-informed-guidelines-for-parenting-in-the-digital-age/

Interventions centered on internet addiction previously described and presented in Chapters 6 and 7 can also be applied to families having issues with screen time. These interventions include cognitive behavioral therapy (Young, 1999), motivational interviewing (Miller & Rollnick, 2002), and reality therapy (Jong-Un, 2007). In addition, couples and families should be provided with helpful referral sites, including, but not limited to, the Center for Internet Addiction Recovery (www .netaddiction.com) and Virtual Addiction (www.virtual-addiction.com). Lastly, most screen-time issues can be addressed in a collaborative family homework assignment. For example:

Clinician: It seems like we've come to the conclusion that the family is going to be creating a more structured screen-time setup.

Client A: Yes, what do you have in mind?

Clinician: It seems like we've already come up with an initial structure to implement. The two older sisters, Maya and Faith, have cell phones; however, their usage has too been high. So, for this week, Maya and Faith will hand in their cell phones at 8 p.m. during the weekdays.

Client B: Okay, that should be a good start for the two teenagers. What about Michael?

Clinician: As a 5-year-old, Michael doesn't really need much screen time and it isn't all that healthy for him. The two of you discussed a movie and a few early morning cartoons during the weekend.

Client A: That seems reasonable to me.

Client B: Sounds good.

Clinician: Okay, let's agree to follow these rules this week. I will check in during our next session to see how it went.

VOICES FROM THE FIELD: JIM

Mr. James Thomas shared his experiences and thoughts around working with systems, families, and youth around screen time.

The big data and my experience would indicate that the problem of screen time for our youth in the U.S. cuts across racial, socioeconomic, and other lines. Schools with omnipresent cell phones suffer across our educational system. Humbly, I do not see the amount of use, which likely is inordinately high in general terms for our youth, to differ substantially from family to family. Indeed, the data on smartphones across some 46 countries in the recently released survey indicated that smartphones became ubiquitous with adolescent depression and anxiety increase.

THE MANDATORY REPORTING OF CHILD ABUSE AND NEGLECT

What could be more important than rescuing a child from an abusive environment? Child abuse and neglect reporting could be the most important and high-impact technique a clinician provides. While all states have child abuse laws, they all differ in scope and content. In all states, helping professionals are mandated reporters of child maltreatment. Mandated reporting is when an individual or agency is required by state law to report any instance where there is reasonable cause to suspect child abuse and neglect. Most states define a child to be anyone under the age of 18. In most states, failure of a mandated reporter to notify the appropriate statewide child protection agency of an instance of child abuse and neglect results in a misdemeanor. While reporting is required, the decision to retain or remove the child from their home is the responsibility of the child welfare agency, not the clinician (Black & Flynn, 2021). Information on relevant state-by-state mandated reporting statutes can be found on the Child Welfare Information Gateway website: www.childwelfare.gov/topics/systemwide/laws-policies/state. Please review your state laws and policies so you can ethically manage your practice.

An important aspect of mandated reporting includes the client(s) understanding of the limits to confidentiality at the beginning of treatment. All informed consent documents should clearly spell out the state statutes around the limits of confidentiality (e.g., child abuse and neglect, suicidal ideation, homicidal ideation, elderly abuse). This is so clients understand the limits of privacy, rules and procedures of therapy, and ethical leanings of practitioners, and so they are not surprised when the clinician informs a third party after the disclosure of a critical incident. It is also best practice to have clients read, sign, and discuss the limits of confidentiality prior to treatment. Most states require clinicians to inform child protective services of any suspicion of child abuse and neglect; however, clinicians do not have to be certain that the suspected child abuse and/or neglect has taken place in order to report it to the specified third party. When describing the requirements for disclosing child abuse and neglect, most states use terms like *reasonable suspicion, reasonably suspected,* or *reasonable cause to suspect.* This language is partly to ensure that clinicians will not be held liable for a good-faith report. Additionally, child abuse and neglect must be reported regardless of when it occurred (e.g., a 13-year-old reports being molested at the age of 4; Black & Flynn, 2021).

The following is an example of a typical mandatory reporting discussion with a client. While this small example may make the mandatory reporting process appear straightforward, it is typically one of the most difficult tasks that clinicians engage in. In fact, underreporting suspicion of child maltreatment has been a long-standing problem in the helping professions (Kenny & McEachern, 2002). Despite a clinician's best intentions to provide support and empathy, this breach of confidentiality drastically changes the in-session dynamics in a way that can cause clients to feel a deep sense of fear, anger, and shame. For example:

> *Clinician:* Rebecca, what you mentioned just now falls under child abuse. Specifically, the behavior of hitting your child with a closed fist is legally prohibited. As you probably remember from our first session, I am a state-mandated reporter of child abuse and neglect. At this point, I need to report what you mentioned to child protection services.

> *Client:* I do remember that conversation about the limitations of confidentiality. I just didn't think this constituted abuse.

> *Clinician:* I understand that you're confused and I know you deeply care and love your son. While I am going to communicate with child protective services, I want you to know that I am still committed to working with you and helping you achieve your goals. Child protective services has a great deal of information on appropriate and safe parental discipline. I'm also happy to discuss this with you here in session.

If the clinician suspects that the child's safety and/or life is presently in danger from the abusing party, or if they determine that informing the perpetrator of the child abuse and/or neglect report will likely create retaliatory behavior toward the child or adolescent, they should avoid informing the parents and report directly to child protective services and/or the local police. If there is any confusion about the procedures to implement given the nature of a particular situation, clinicians are encouraged to contact their state's child protective services department directly to ask questions. If the child has told the clinician about violence between adults in the household, that violence can also increase the potential danger to the child and should be noted on the report (Durborow et al., 2018).

The next step is for the clinician to collaborate with their state's child protective services agency and the family in question to ensure the welfare of the child or adolescent. In most states, there is a child protective services central intake office where clinicians are sent to discuss the situation firsthand with a trained employee. They may be asked a variety of questions, including, but not limited to, the following: the exact date and time of the incident, the nature of what was observed by the clinician, and the exact words, if any, that a child used to describe what happened. Following the oral report, the reporting clinician will likely be required to provide a variety of information about the victim, the incident, and the abusive environment they are in. If a full investigation takes place, much more information could be required, including, but not limited to, (a) the name and address of the child suspected of being abused and/or neglected; (b) the name and address of the person responsible for the child's welfare; (c) specific information indicating neglect or the nature and extent of the child's injuries, including any evidence of previous injuries; (d) the identity of the person or persons suspected of being responsible for the abuse and neglect; and (e) the identity of other children and adults currently residing in the household in question (Durborow et al., 2018; U.S. Department of Health and Human Services et al., 2018).

After the aforementioned information has been collected, the statewide child protective services agency will be in touch with the reporting clinician when/if needed. Throughout the mandatory reporting process, clinicians need to maintain clear and detailed documentation of all relevant events that transpire. It is very helpful to use and document the results of an empirically validated measure to further understand the nature of the abuse and neglect. A common empirically validated instrument is the 160-item assessment called the Child Abuse Potential Inventory (CAPI; Milner, 1986). Clinicians also need to be aware of the age of consent factors within the United States. There are a lot of nuances within various state laws. Fortunately, the Rape, Abuse, and Incest National Network (RAINN) put together a very comprehensive guide of state-by-state reporting requirements (see www.rainn.org/state-state-guide-statutes-limitations). Clinicians should become familiar with this information so they can reference it in their future work (RAINN, n.d.).

VOICES FROM THE FIELD: LONG HIN

Mr. Long Hin Siu shared his experiences working with BIPOC families and how to delicately balance the importance of being aware of cultural parenting practices and protecting children.

With all due sensitivity, the families' cultural background sometimes might have a factor that clinicians should give consideration to. BIPOC families that might have recently immigrated and might have a different perspective and standard around parenting compared with those that might be a third- or fourth-generation immigrants. While there are clear boundaries and distinction with physical abuse, sexual abuse, neglect, and in most psychological abuse, I often find psychological abuse challengingly blurry in BIPOC families. Perhaps it can be bias; however, it appears that emotional expression can be different in different cultures. For instance, the perception of anger expression in the "East," or collectivistic culture, and "West," or individualistic culture, is different. Giving additional consideration and seeking to understand the intention of their emotional expression can be helpful.

VOICES FROM THE FIELD: JIM

Mr. James Thomas shared his thoughts and experiences of the unfair treatment individuals from BIPOC families and those with poor socioeconomic status experienced with the U.S. child welfare system.

BIPOC families in my experience receive poorer treatment overall in the legal and child protective services world than White families. This is also impacted by socioeconomics. Families with more financial resources tend to receive better, fairer, and more useful support services when a child abuse allegation is substantiated. When writing court reports for adolescents in day treatment or our in-home therapy program, I tried to address or level some of this by writing reports collaboratively with parents/caretakers. As stated previously, our programs sought to send very clear signals that we welcomed the adolescents and families to our programs. We engaged them as people, not problems, and the family as a resource, not a deficit.

VOICES FROM THE FIELD: MICHAEL

Mr. Michael Lopez-Jensen provided his own question when asked the question about BIPOC families and child abuse and neglect.

How do we have open discussions about racist practices of the child welfare system?

HELPING GRANDPARENTS RAISE GRANDCHILDREN

Grandparents who raise grandchildren report an enormous sense of meaning and value in their work. This deep sense of meaning and value is often tethered by obstacles, including, but not limited to, (a) very little support from parents and others, (b) inability to monitor the well-being of their grandchildren, (c) difficulty safeguarding their own physical and mental health needs, (d) inability to maintain discipline in the home, (e) inability to meet grandchildren's ever-changing educational needs, (f) conforming to new discipline and limit-setting cultural norms for parents, and (g) managing the unexpected financial burdens that come with having a family later in life (Lent & Otto, 2018; Peterson, 2017; Yoo & Russell, 2020). Couple, marriage, and family practitioners are in an excellent position to assist grandparents with all of the aforementioned issues.

Support groups, psychoeducation, individual therapy, and family therapy are the most common therapeutic formats that have been recommended for helping grandfamilies (O'Hora & Dolbin-MacNab, 2015). Effective support groups help struggling grandparents with psychoeducation, advocacy, skill-building, communal problem-solving, and social support. Attending grandparents should be allowed to influence the topic and group interaction to a certain extent. Support groups often include the following: meals or snacks, attendance incentives, childcare, and transportation (Dannison & Smith, 2003). Common topics relevant to grandfamily support groups include social issues, financial support, grief and loss, stress management, and discipline strategies (O'Hora & Dolbin-MacNab, 2015). Support group effectiveness has been demonstrated empirically (e.g., Hayslip, 2003; Kelley et al., 2011); however, research conducted by Smith et al. (2003) indicated that support groups can produce poor results if they lack structure and goals, foster self-pity, lack effective leadership, and have poor cultural sensitivity. Storm and Storm (2011) suggest that support group facilitators emphasize optimism, clear parameters for group discussion, and require participants to set achievable short-term and long-term goals.

Individual therapy and family therapy are ideal formats for grandparents and grandchildren who are in need of a more intensive format and have issues that require a tailored approach to treatment. Individual therapy is recommended for grandchildren and grandparents who have mental health problems that are outside of familial relationships (e.g., oppositional defiant disorder, attention deficit hyperactivity disorder, anxiety, depression). Family therapy is recommended when there are relationship challenges that have a bidirectional emphasis, such as communication problems, issues around discipline, marital distress, financial hardships, trauma, and attachment difficulties (Strong et al., 2010). O'Hora and Dolbin-MacNab (2015) highlight the importance of family therapy modalities that emphasize the following: boundaries and hierarchy (e.g., structural and strategic family therapy), ability of grandparents to nurture grandchildren (e.g., human validation process, emotionally focused family therapy), and an action-oriented treatment centered on helping them achieve goals (e.g., solution-focused therapy, narrative therapy). Whatever modality is chosen, it is of utmost importance that clinicians create a session climate that encourages acceptance and humility, and ensures grandparents and grandchildren feel heard.

The following is a short series of interactions from a grandfamily therapy session. The clinician follows a general systems theory approach creating change and a positive therapeutic alliance:

Client A: This whole later-in-life parenting thing is a lot more work than I initially thought it would be. I'm taking several naps every day and all of my retirement is being gobbled up.

Client B: I just don't think we're doing a great job with parenting either. I feel completely out of the loop with Jason's schedule, and he is completely disorganized as well.

Clinician: The two of you sound extremely stressed and overwhelmed (*joining*).

Client A: We love the little guy, but we already raised our own kids.

Clinician: This is really more than you bargained for. It seems like you're trying to find a way for this new responsibility to work in your life (*reframing*).

Client B: We need to change something in our parenting style so Jason can do more around the house.

Clinician: I wonder if you have considered using a token economy or star chart to encourage responsible behavior.

Client B: No, but that sounds like something that might help.

Clinician: Okay, the first step is to create a list of behaviors you would like to see changed (*psychoeducation*).

Many custodial grandparents need services that are beyond the scope of therapeutic treatment. These families require an appropriate professional referral to community resources, such as churches, medical care, child day care, legal representation, community educational experiences, thrift shops, and food pantries. The referral process works best if all of the providers are on the same page (e.g., mental healthcare, medical care, school personnel, day care). Ensuring all stakeholders are clearly communicating information regarding the relevant resources to grandparents is key to a successful and holistic treatment (Dolbin-MacNab et al., 2009).

From a multicultural and diversity perspective, couple, marriage, and family practitioners look at the well-being of an individual within the larger context of their family history, past and present cultural dynamics of groups, and present contextual variables that could be making an impact on their well-being. For example, the values in the African American community around custodial grandparenting are shaped in part by historical and present-day oppression. Historically, African American children were banned from private children's aid programs, which became the foundation for the child welfare system in the United States. As a result, those within the African American community had very little resources and needed to create their own support networks and strong kinship care circles, which fostered the conceptualization that African American parenting was outside of Western ideals. According to McCarthy (2021), African American grandmothers may be influenced by the Strong Black Woman (SBW) schema.

The SBW schema is the racialized expectation that African American women self-sacrifice to care for those they love without the need of support and using incredible amounts of personal resilience and emotional strength. Although the SBW schema could potentially act as a protective factor and promote resilience, research has demonstrated that it increases stress and depressive symptoms, as well as creates low self-compassion and rejection of coping strategies, among African American women. Moreover, McCarthy advises that couple, marriage, and family practitioners working with African American custodial grandmothers are aware of the SBW schema and how it could influence family dynamics and grandmothers' willingness to employ coping strategies. As part of this conversation, the empowering nature of the SBW schema and its potential to cause stress, anxiety, and underutilization of support systems should be balanced (McCarthy, 2021).

VOICES FROM THE FIELD: JIM

Mr. James Thomas described his professional experience working with BIPOC grandfamilies and families.

In my experience, grandparents raising grandchildren for all families is a complex situation. Almost always, these family forms arise out of loss or conflict. Drug addiction, termination of parental rights, death, parental abandonment, these are adverse childhood experiences the ramifications of which grandparents deal with daily. Across cultures, these grandparents deserve our utmost respect, care, and support in their task. As Bowlby said, "[a]ny family that values its children must cherish their parents." And same if not more so with grandparents raising grandchildren. On the other hand, grandparent involvement, aunts and uncles, other kin helping to raise children is a great strength. In my time at Denver Children's Home in which I did the most work with BIPOC families and stepfamilies, I learned a great deal about the strength and power of kinship care and networks. Our family therapy team often sought to involve as many family members as possible in the support of an adolescent's work, not limiting it to those in the home or the biological parents wherever possible.

VOICES FROM THE FIELD: MICHAEL

Mr. Michael Lopez-Jensen provided a few interventions when describing tools for supporting BIPOC grandparents raising grandchildren.

Generational differences, support from multigenerational angles, the support of healthy faith communities or school networks.

HELPING PARENTS GRIEVE THE DEATH OF A CHILD

The death of a child is often considered the most difficult grief an individual can experience. This is due to a variety of factors, including the notion that a child is supposed to outlive their parents, the untimely loss of dear loved one, and how close children are to parents' hopes and dreams, as well as factors such as the nature of the child's death (e.g., fast and unexpected vs. slow and expected), the speed at which the parents form a bond with the deceased, the age of the child at the time of their death, and the type of death, including, but not limited to, miscarriage, stillbirth, sudden infant death syndrome, child illness, random acts of violence, and kidnapping. Please note that different ages often bring variability to the emotional experience; however, it is a mistake to think that the younger a child is the less attached a parent will be or the less painful it will be. Parents develop deep emotional bonds with children before they are born or conceived. Other grieving risk and protective factors are reviewed in Chapter 8 and are individual to the family and the griever (All Psychology Careers, 2021; Ayers et al., 2013).

While there is no "right" or "wrong" way to grieve the death of a child, families can suffer immeasurable emotional and psychological pain which, if processed incorrectly, can affect the parents, couple, siblings, and extended family in a variety of negative ways. Couple, marriage, and family practitioners work hard to bring awareness of the hurt and pain, allow for emotional expression, create a healthy grieving process, and minimize any subsequent familial damage (e.g., divorce, substance abuse, contempt). According to Bartel (2020), maintaining a connection with the deceased through family rituals is a common and accepted method for helping families work through the grieving process. Common examples include, but are not limited to, leaving an empty seat at the dinner table, observing a picture of the deceased child, daily prayer, telling familiar stories during family time, writing letters to the deceased child, and speaking directly to the deceased child within one's mind or imagination.

According to Weiss (1988), the process of grieving the death of a child can have a very negative effect on the parents/marital unit. This process typically entails parents/partners feeling a significant amount of depression, guilt, and physical symptomology. Spousal discord can emerge throughout any phase of the grieving process. These symptoms can be exaggerated versions of previously unresolved issues lying dormant within each partner. Unfortunately, grief causes these dormant symptoms to reemerge with a lot of intensity. The toxicity of the contempt and blaming that emerges can deeply fracture the relationship. The consequences of these interactions can range from hurt feelings to divorce. When clinicians work with couples who have just experienced the death of their child, it is imperative to provide space for each spouse to grieve in their own unique manner without fear, hostility, or retaliatory behavior from the other spouse. This can be as simple as gently guiding the partners back to a less blameful and critical stance. Clinicians should also attempt to help each partner acknowledge and recognize how their spouse copes with the enormity of this loss.

Couple, marriage, and family practitioners can help each spouse understand the unique nature of their partner's process by discussing different grieving styles. A large amount of discontent and anger can emerge within the spousal unit because each partner misunderstands the other person's manner of grieving. Differences can emerge due to gender, ethnicity, race, culture, and personal style. Table 9.4 breaks down common gender-based grieving behaviors, cognitions, emotions, and physical manifestations. The chart demonstrates both similarities and differences. Presenting information such as this can foster a deeper sense of understanding between spouses (Ayers et al., 2013; Woodgate, 2006).

In addition to acknowledging the grieving differences that might be present in the couple, it is important for each parent to understand that it is normal for many of these symptoms to be present for a short period or lengthy period of time, and that during the initial phases of grief they may need to relate to one another in a different manner (i.e., family flexibility; Klaassen, 2010). Once the initial traumatization and reaction slows

TABLE 9.4   GENDER-BASED GRIEVING BEHAVIORS, COGNITIONS, EMOTIONS, AND PHYSICAL MANIFESTATIONS

Grieving Construct	Maternal Grieving Behavior	Paternal Grieving Behavior
Nature of initial bond	Typically begins bonding before birth in a variety of ways, including physically, emotionally, and through hopes, dreams, and aspirations	Emotional and physical bonding typically begins after birth, and begins bonding through hopes, dreams, and aspirations prior to birth
Expression of emotion	Susceptible to depression, anxiety, traumatization, enormous amount of anger, and envy; it is more acceptable to express emotions in many cultures	Susceptible to a sense of resentment, disappointment, failure, and traumatization; it is unacceptable to express emotions in many cultures
Expression of cognition	Constant obsession about the loss of her child and a deep need for sensual reminders	Constant obsession about the loss of his child and becomes defensive and minimizes pain
Loneliness and isolation	Outwardly tries to act as if nothing happened, privately seeks out a few close friends to process emotions with, and is more likely to engage in therapy	Often tries not to grieve, feels ignored, abandoned, isolated, overwhelmed, and is less likely to engage in therapy
Negative coping	Feels unable to cope with daily life, obsessed over what happened to their child, feels irrational levels of responsibility and guilt for anything that happened to the deceased child, and difficulty with self-forgiveness	Substance use and abuse is common, can become angry at spouse for the untimely death, and closes off emotionally and cognitively about the topic
Existential suffering	Engages in the "why did this happen to my child" narrative, self-pity, feels a deep sense of injustice, and wonders where their dead child is now	Engages in the "why did this happen to my child" narrative, experiences numbness and existential vacuum, feels a deep sense of injustice, and wonders where their dead child is now
Physical symptoms of grief	Sleeping problems, mood swings, exhaustion, headaches, inability to concentrate, dry mouth, nightmares, shortness of breath, hallucinations, and repetitive motions	Sleeping problems, mood swings, exhaustion, headaches, inability to concentrate, dry mouth, nightmares, shortness of breath, hallucinations, and repetitive motions

Sources: Data from All Psychology Careers. (2021, July 12). *Loss of a child—Helping a grieving parent.* Retrieved May 4, 2022, from https://www.allpsychologycareers.com/mental-health/loss-of-a-child/; Woodgate, R. L. (2006). Living in a world without closure: Reality for parents who have experienced the death of a child. *Journal of Palliative Care, 22*(2), 75–82.

down, the family will have to cocreate a new normal and reality. Clinicians must work with families as roles shift and are replaced or reconstructed. Weiss (1988) suggested the use of the following tools to mitigate the grieving process: (a) assessment of each parent's family-of-origin bereavement history, (b) each parent's assumptions about gender expression of grief, (c) how to incorporate the dead child into the family in a different way, (d) family-of-origin myths regarding communication and feeling, and (e) a deeper shared understanding of each parent's unique grieving style. For example:

Clinician: Sheritta, it seems you are completely consumed with guilt over the miscarriage.

Client A: Yes, I am so mad at myself. I feel like God is punishing me. I am a complete failure.

Client B: It's obviously not her fault. I'm not sure how to convince her.

Clinician: Trevor, go ahead and face her and tell her what you just told me (*emphasizing individual boundaries*).

Client A: I know you're disappointed in me.

Client B: More like disappointed in the situation.

Clinician: I can tell you just want Sheritta to be happy again and to think about the miscarriage in a different way. Sheritta, could you please let Trevor know how you would like him to respond to you? (*restructuring dysfunctional subsystem boundaries*).

Client A: Sure, I want you to tell me you love me, hold my hand, or just tell me you understand. There is no way for you to fix this.

ASSESSING CONTEMPORARY FAMILY THERAPY ISSUES

Family therapy is an interactive, interdependent, and relational process that includes recursive feedback between all family members and the clinician. The therapist system includes all individuals engaging in the treatment of the family. The cybernetic perspective of double description is essentially the notion that change and stability are two sides of the same coin. In other words, families must change to maintain stability, or remain stable in order to change (Keeney & Ross, 1983). Given the iterative, recursive, and constantly changing structure of a family, assessment can be an interesting concept and process. Because the philosophy of family systems and the multitude of constantly moving parts, family assessment is a subjective and dialogic process used to gain information about the family and the therapist at a particular point in time during treatment. All family assessment experiences are heavily influenced by the therapist, and the scales are essentially working hypotheses that are meant to be reviewed, discussed, confirmed, or rejected. If confirmed, the clinician acknowledges that the assessment is simply a cross-sectional analysis of the developing therapist–family system (Cierpka et al., 2005; Keeney & Ross, 1983).

Table 9.5 provides a helpful breakdown of the chapter-based contemporary issues reviewed, two related empirical assessments, and a related reference for each assessment. Clinicians should consider incorporating these empirically validated assessments whenever relevant as they can be helpful in gathering a large amount of data in a short period of time. This information can bring a great deal of awareness to both the client(s) and the couple, marriage, and family practitioner and help guide treatment.

TABLE 9.5 CONTEMPORARY FAMILY THERAPY EMPIRICAL ASSESSMENTS AND RELATED REFERENCES

Contemporary Issue	Assessment Name	References
Cohesion and adaptability	Family Adaptability and Cohesion Evaluation Scale-IV (FACES-IV)	Olson, D. H. (2010). *FACES IV manual*. Life Innovations.
Cohesion and adaptability	Family System Test (FAST)	Gehring, T. M., Debry, M., & Smith, P. K. (2001). *The Family System Test (FAST). Theory and application.* Brunner-Routledge.
Stepfamilies	Questionnaire for Couples in Stepfamilies (QCS)	Beaudry, M., Parent, C., Saint-Jacques, M.-C., Guay, S., & Boisvert, J.-M. (2001). Validation of a questionnaire to assess the difficulties of couples in stepfamilies. *Journal of Divorce & Remarriage, 35*(1), 155–172. https://doi.org/10.1300/j087v35n01_10.
Stepfamilies	Remarriage Belief Inventory (RBI)	Garneau, C. L., Adler-Baeder, F., & Higginbotham, B. (2013). Validating the Remarriage Belief Inventory as a dyadic measure for step couples. *Journal of Family Issues, 37*(1), 132–150. https://doi.org/10.1177/0192513x13511954.
Multiracial families	Attitudes Toward Multiracial Children Scale (AMCS)	Jackman, C. F., Wagner, W. G., & Johnson, J. T. (2001). The Attitudes Toward Multiracial Children Scale. *Journal of Black Psychology, 27*(1), 86–99. https://doi.org/10.1177/0095798401027001005.
Multiracial families	Cross Ethnic-Racial Identity Scale-Adult (CERIS-A)	Worrell, F. C., Mendoza-Denton, R., & Wang, A. (2019). Introducing a new assessment tool for measuring ethnic-racial identity: The Cross Ethnic-Racial Identity Scale–Adult (CERIS-A). *Assessment, 26*(3), 404–418. https://doi.org/10.1177/1073191117698756.
Parenting	Parenting Satisfaction Scale (PSS)	Guidubaldi, J., & Cleminshaw, H. K. (1994). *Manual for the Parenting Satisfaction Scale*. Psychological Corporation.
Parenting	Parenting Alliance Measure (PAM)	Abidin, R. R., & Brunner, J. F. (1995). Development of a parenting alliance inventory. *Journal of Clinical Child Psychology, 24*(1), 3–40.
Obesity	Body mass index (BMI)	Nuttall, F. Q. (2015). Body mass index: Obesity, BMI, and health: A critical review. *Nutrition Today, 50*(3), 117–128. https://doi.org/10.1097/NT.0000000000000092.
Obesity	Pediatric Quality of Life Inventory (PedsQL)	Varni, J. W., Seid, M., & Kurtin, P. S. (2001). PedsQTM 4.0: Reliability and validity of the Pediatric Quality of Life Inventory™ version 4.0 generic core scales in healthy and patient populations. *Medical Care, 39*(8), 800–812.
The internet	Digital-Screen Exposure Questionnaire (DSEQ)	Kaur, N., Gupta, M., Kiran, T., Malhi, P., & Grover, S. (2021). Development and evaluation of the Digital-Screen Exposure Questionnaire (DSEQ) for young children. *PLoS One, 16*(6), e0253313. https://doi.org/10.1371/journal.pone.025331.
The internet	Parent–Child Internet Addiction Test (PCIAT)	Young, K. S. (1998). Internet addiction: The emergence of a new clinical disorder. *CyberPsychology and Behavior, 1*(3), 237–244.

(continued)

TABLE 9.5   CONTEMPORARY FAMILY THERAPY EMPIRICAL ASSESSMENTS AND RELATED REFERENCES (*CONTINUED*)

Contemporary Issue	Assessment Name	References
Child abuse and neglect	Checklist for Child Abuse Evaluation (CCAE)	Petty, J. (1990). *CCAE: Checklist for Child Abuse Evaluation*. Psychological Assessment Resources.
Child abuse and neglect	Child Abuse Potential Inventory (CAPI)	Milner J. (1986). *The Child Abuse Potential Inventory: Manual* (2nd ed.). Webster.
Grandparents raising grandchildren	Family Needs Scale (FNS)	Lee, E., Choi, M. J., & Clarkson-Henderix, M. (2016). Examining needs of informal kinship families: Validating the Family Needs Scale. *Children & Youth Services Review, 62*, 97–104. https://doi-org.libproxy.plymouth.edu/10.1016/j.childyouth.2016.01.021.
Grandparents raising grandchildren	Assessment Checklist for Children (ACC)	Tarren-Sweeney, M. (2007). The Assessment Checklist for Children—ACC: A behavioral rating scale for children in foster, kinship and residential care. *Children & Youth Services Review, 29*(5), 672–691. https://doi-org.libproxy.plymouth.edu/10.1016/j.childyouth.2007.01.008.
Grieving	Texas Revised Inventory of Grief (TRIG)	Nam, I., & Eack, S. M. (2012). Confirmatory factor analysis and cross-cultural examination of the Texas Revised Inventory of Grief (TRIG). *Families in Society: Journal of Contemporary Social Services, 93*(1), 65–73. https://doi-org.libproxy.plymouth.edu/10.1606/1044-3894.4177.
Grieving	Negative Life Events Scale (NLES)	Sandler, I. N., Wolchik, S. A., Braver, S. L., & Fogas, B. (1991). Stability and quality of life events and psychological symptomatology in children of divorce. *American Journal of Community Psychology, 19*(4), 501–520.

SUMMARY

In this chapter, readers were introduced to a variety of skills, conceptualization details, and techniques related to treating a variety of contemporary issues affecting today's families, including family cohesion and flexibility, blended and stepfamilies, multiracial families, contemporary parenting issues, obesity, the internet, child abuse and neglect, grandparents raising grandchildren, and parental grief after the death of a child. The main objective of this chapter was to describe the essence of the skills and assessments for conceptualizing and treating families suffering from these issues. Specifically, throughout the chapter, readers were provided with the essence of the contemporary issue, key skills and interventions, assessment measures, and in-depth conceptualizations that accentuate the powerful skills and techniques clinicians can utilize when treating families suffering from the explicated contemporary issues.

END-OF-CHAPTER RESOURCES

A robust set of instructor resources designed to supplement this text is located at http://connect.springerpub.com/content/book/978-0-8261-8775-8. Qualifying instructors may request access by emailing textbook@springerpub.com.

STUDENT ACTIVITIES

Exercise 1: Enhancing Family Cohesion and Flexibility

Directions: Review the following information and answer the prompts:

The circumplex model provides important information on assessing and treating family cohesion and flexibility (Olson et al., 1970, 1983). Review the examples provided in the cohesion and flexibility section of the chapter and answer the following prompts:

- Create two mock family therapy examples that accentuate the need for enhanced family flexibility and cohesion.

- Consider the interventions explicated in this chapter and in Chapter 4 and implement skills that you think could enhance family cohesion and flexibility in the examples you created.

- Next, write down two ways the families in your examples could become more dysfunctional in regard to family cohesion and flexibility and the skills you could use to enhance these aspects of the family.

Exercise 2: Article Review

Directions: Review the following instructions and answer the prompts:

Go to your university's online EBSCO Database and find Academic Search Premier. Search and find an article centered on therapeutically helping stepfamilies. Review the article in its entirety and answer the following questions related to the implications of this common family structure.

- What common challenges does this article showcase regarding helping stepfamilies?

- When working within this population, what specific techniques would work best to create a greater sense of harmony with children and stepparents?

- Search the internet and explore professional resources centered on helping stepfamilies. Create a list of five potential online resources you could offer stepfamilies.

Exercise 3: Working With Parents

Directions: Review the following instructions and answer the prompts:

This chapter explored a variety of information related to helping parents in a clinical setting. Take a few minutes to review the chart that describes common parenting dos and don'ts. As you consider this information, consider the notion that it is not helpful for clinicians to criticize parents. Answer the following prompts related to parent therapy:

- Create a clinical vignette that showcases your use of the skill in psychoeducation with two parents. Specifically, demonstrate how a clinician could teach their clients about three of the listed parenting dos and don'ts.

- Consider asking a parent to deliberately engage in a parenting practice in a session. What would you say to get the activity started? How would you stop the parent and provide corrective feedback without seeming too critical?

- At the end of this chapter, there were a few clinical assessments listed related to parenting. Take some time to look up a third scale that measures some aspect of parenting. Describe how clinicians deliver, score, and interpret the information derived from the assessment.

Exercise 4: Mandatory Reporting of Child Abuse and Neglect

Directions: Review the following instructions and answer the prompts:

The mandatory reporting of child abuse and neglect is an important skill for clinicians to understand and use effectively. Create two vignettes, one demonstrating child abuse and one demonstrating child neglect. Engage in the following instructions after you come up with the two scenarios:

- Review the following websites for general information on child abuse and neglect:
  - ☐ https://www.childwelfare.gov/
  - ☐ https://medlineplus.gov/childabuse.html

- Next, review your state's codified law regarding child abuse and neglect.

- Create your own informed consent/limits to confidentiality document. The following sample of New Hampshire limits to confidentiality can be used as an example:

  Everything that happens in counseling is, for the most part, confidential and protected under the law. I will not discuss anything about your counseling, or even identify that you are someone I'm working with, unless you give me written permission, your parent(s)/guardian(s) asks me for information from our sessions, or if one of the forthcoming instances are encountered. There are some instances when I will talk with someone about your case *without* obtaining your consent that is allowed under the New Hampshire state law. These include reviewing your case during supervision or peer consultation. Also, since confidentiality cannot be guaranteed in a group setting, informed consent and parent guardian permission for group participation is always required. There are other instances in which I am mandated under New Hampshire state law to break confidentiality. These include

  - ☐ if you make significant threats to self, others, or property;
  - ☐ if I witness or suspect the abuse and/or neglect of a child;
  - ☐ if I witness or suspect the abuse of an incapacitated adult;
  - ☐ if I am ordered by the courts to disclose information from our sessions;
  - ☐ if you are underage and your parent(s) or legal guardian(s) asks to review your case notes with me; and
  - ☐ finally, in the state of New Hampshire, it is considered sexual assault for an adult to engage in sexual activity with a person who is under the age of 16. If I determine that this is occurring, I am mandated by the state of New Hampshire to report.

Exercise 5: Grandparents Raising Grandchildren

Directions: Review the following instructions and answer the prompts:

There are a number of curricula that support grandparents raising grandchildren. Take some time to reflect on the relevant content from the chapter and review the following curricula:

- https://creatingafamily.org/foster-care/?gclid=Cj0KCQjwpcOTBhCZARIs AEAYLuWEnvh-BgyjQ_t7MO4pZx5IXPJQUoaqpb0duDj5Eu170czyjY4chX8a AqgjEALw_wcB

- https://pbfalv.org/second-time-around-grandparents-raising-grandchildren/

- https://aese.psu.edu/outreach/intergenerational/program-areas/kinship/ information-resources

Next, engage in the following instructions related to grandparents raising grandchildren:

- After reading all of the information that was presented, create a unique support group related to grandparents raising grandchildren.

- Identify topics for 10 support group sessions.

- How will you screen members? How many members would be appropriate for the group?

ADDITIONAL RESOURCES

HELPFUL LINKS

- "The Olson Circumplex Model: A Systemic Approach to Couple and Family Relationships": https://psychology.org.au/publications/inpsych/2011/february/sanders

- "Same Sex Parents and Their Children": https://aamft.org/Consumer_Updates/Same -sex_Parents_and_Their_Children.aspx

- "Grandparents Raising Grandchildren": https://www.aamft.org/Consumer_Updates/ grandparents.aspx

- "Grieving the Loss of a Child": https://aamft.org/Consumer_Updates/Grieving_the _Loss_of_A_Child.aspx

- "Multiracial Families": https://aamft.org/Consumer_Updates/Multiracial_Families.aspx

- "Stepfamilies": https://aamft.org/Consumer_Updates/Stepfamilies.aspx

- "Childhood Obesity": https://aamft.org/Consumer_Updates/Childhood_Obesity.aspx

- "Child Abuse and Neglect": https://www.aamft.org/Consumer_Updates/Child _Abuse_and_Neglect.aspx

- "Screening Screen Time: Evidence-Informed Guidelines for Parenting in the Digital Age": https://ftm.aamft.org/screening-screen-time-evidence-informed-guidelines-for-parenting -in-the-digital-age/

HELPFUL BOOKS

- Cohen, J., Mannarino, A., & Deblinger, E. (2006). *Treating trauma and traumatic grief in children and adolescents.* Guilford Press.

- Fung, J. (2016). *Obesity code.* Greystone Books.

Graber, D., & Borba, M. (2019). *Raising humans in a digital world: Helping kids build a healthy relationship with technology.* HarperCollins Leadership.

Hassink, S. (Ed.). (2007). *Pediatric obesity: Prevention, intervention, and treatment strategies for primary care.* American Academy of Pediatrics.

Hayslip, B., & Patrick, J. H. (2003). *Working with custodial grandparents.* Springer Publishing Company.

Helfer, M. E., Kempe, R. S., & Krugman, R. D. (1997). *The battered child.* University of Chicago Press.

Kamenetz, A. (2018). *The art of screen time: How your family can balance digital media and real life.* Public Affairs.

Kübler-Ross E., & Kessler, D. (2005). *On grief and grieving: Finding the meaning of grief through the five stages of loss.* Scribner.

Mitchell, E. (2004). *Beyond tears: Living after losing a child.* St. Martins.

Olson, D. H., Olson-Sigg, A., & Larson, P. J. (2008). *The couple checkup.* Thomas Nelson.

Olson, D. H., Russell, C. S., & Sprenkle, D. H. (1989). *Circumplex model: Systemic assessment and treatment of families.* Haworth Press.

Stillwell, E. E. (2004). *The death of a child: Reflections for grieving parents.* ACTA Publications.

HELPFUL VIDEOS

- Circumplex Model: https://www.youtube.com/watch?v=Kmcv5QAkFCE&t=7s
- Blended Families—AAMFT Podcast—Episode 32: https://www.youtube.com/watch?v=KGIxRvVsc3g&t=27s
- Interracial Families: The New Normal: https://www.youtube.com/watch?v=-ZKvfZZ3kUE&t=40s
- Interventions With Families in a Global Context—AAMFT Podcast—Episode 57: https://www.youtube.com/watch?v=BDW_raX4sCg
- Multicultural Therapy: https://www.youtube.com/watch?v=89ZwufIwKG4
- Parenting and Family Therapy: What Is Family Therapy With Stacie Marlow Badgett, LMFT: https://www.youtube.com/watch?v=MLsa2Y5mG-M
- Ask The Therapist: 5 Tips for Step-Parents: https://www.youtube.com/watch?v=ECMFyQ_xAwI
- Obesity: Causes, Signs and Symptoms, Diagnosis, and Treatment: https://www.youtube.com/watch?v=iQUJ1HV0PWc
- Screen Time: Is It Really All Bad?: https://www.youtube.com/watch?v=q3XLnHHPVI8
- AAMFT Videos on Child Abuse and Neglect: https://www.youtube.com/results?search_query=Child+abuse+and+neglect+AAMFT
- AAMFT Videos on Grandparents Raising Grandchildren: https://www.youtube.com/results?search_query=grandparents+raising+grandchildren+AAMFT
- AAMFT Videos on Parental Grief Over the Death of a Child: https://www.youtube.com/results?search_query=parental+grief+over+the+death+of+a+child+AAMFT

REFERENCES

All Psychology Careers. (2021, July 12). *Loss of a child*. Retrieved May 4, 2022, from https://www
.allpsychologycareers.com/mental-health/loss-of-a-child/

Atkin, A. L., & Jackson, K. F. (2021). "Mom, you don't get it": A critical examination of multiracial emerging adults' perceptions of parental support. *Emerging Adulthood, 9*(4), 305–319.
https://doi.org/10.1177/2167696820914091

Ayers, T. S., Wolchik, S. A., Sandler, I. N., Twohey, J. L., Weyer, J. L., Padgett-Jones, S., Weiss, L., Cole,
E., & Kriege, G. (2013). The Family Bereavement Program: Description of a theory-based prevention program for parentally-bereaved children and adolescents. *Omega, 68*(4), 293–314.
https://doi.org/10.2190/om.68.4.a

Bahadur, E. İ., Akkuş, P. Z., Yoldaş, T. Ç., & Özmert, E. N. (2021). How effective is family counselling on screen exposure of pre-school children? *The Turkish Journal of Pediatrics, 63*(2),
282–290. https://doi.org/10.24953/turkjped.2021.02.012.

Bandura, A. (1977). Self-efficacy: Toward a unifying theory of behavioral change. *Psychological
Review, 84*(2), 191. https://doi.org/10.1037//0033-295x.84.2.191

Bartel, B. T. (2020). Families grieving together: Integrating the loss of a child through ongoing
relational connections. *Death Studies, 44*(8), 498–509. https://doi.org/10.1080/07481187.2019
.1586794

Becvar, D., & Becvar, R. (2013). *Family therapy: A systemic integration*. Pearson Education.

Bennett, A. R., & Duchesne, M. M. (2020). *Social workers' knowledge and experience working with
mixed race youth and families* (Publication No. 1035) [Master's project, California State University - San Bernardino]. Electronic Theses, Projects, and Dissertations. https://scholarworks
.lib.csusb.edu/etd/1035

Bickel, G., Nord, M., Price, C., Hamilton, W., & Cook, J. (2000). *Measuring food security in the United
States: Guide to measuring household food security, revised 2000*. U.S. Department of Agriculture,
Food and Nutrition Service, Office of Analysis, Nutrition, and Evaluation. https://fns-prod
.azureedge.us/sites/default/files/FSGuide.pdf

Black, L. L., & Flynn, S. V. (2021). *Crisis, trauma, and disaster: A clinician's guide*. Sage.

Boyd-Franklin, N., & Bry, B. H. (2001). *Reaching out in family therapy: Home-based, school, and community interventions*. Guilford Press.

Bray, G. A. (1992). Pathophysiology of obesity. *The American Journal of Clinical Nutrition, 55*(2),
488S–494S. https://doi.org/10.1093/ajcn/55.2.488s

Brownell, K. D. (2000). *The Learn Program for weight management: Lifestyle, exercise, attitudes, relationships, nutrition*. American Health Publishing Company.

Brunsma, D. L., & Porow, M. (2017). Multiracial families: Issues for couples and children. In
S. Kelly (Ed.), *Diversity in couple and family therapy: Ethnicities, sexualities, and socioeconomics*
(pp. 289–308). Praeger/ABC-CLIO.

Centers for Disease Control and Prevention. (2009). *Parent training programs: Insight for practitioners*. U.S. Department of Health and Human Services: Centers for Disease Control and
Prevention. https://www.cdc.gov/violenceprevention/pdf/parent_training_brief-a.pdf

Centers for Disease Control and Prevention. (2017, September 30). *Adult obesity facts*. Retrieved
May 4, 2022, from https://www.cdc.gov/obesity/data/adult.html

Centers for Disease Control and Prevention. (2022, January 21). *QuickStats: Percentage of children aged 2–17 years with 2 hours of screen time per weekday, by sex and age group—National
health interview survey, United States, 2020*. https://www.cdc.gov/mmwr/volumes/71/wr/
mm7103a6.htm

Cierpka, M., Thomas, V., & Sprenkle, D. H. (Eds.). (2005). *Family assessment: Integrating multiple
perspectives*. Hogrefe & Huber Publishers.

Dannison, L. L., & Smith, A. B. (2003). Custodial grandparents community support program:
Lessons learned. *Children & Schools, 25*(2), 87–95. https://doi.org/10.1093/cs/25.2.87

De Jong, P., & Miller, S. D. (1995). How to interview for client strengths. *Social Work, 40*(6), 729–736.
https://eric.ed.gov/?id=EJ519504

Dhurandhar, E. J. (2016). The food-insecurity obesity paradox: A resource scarcity hypothesis.
Physiology & Behavior, 162, 88–92. https://doi.org/10.1016/j.physbeh.2016.04.025

Dolbin-MacNab, M. L., Rodgers, B. E., & Traylor, R. M. (2009). Bridging the generations: A retro-
spective examination of adults' relationships with their kinship caregivers. *Journal of Intergenerational Relationships, 7*(2-3), 159–176. https://doi.org/10.1080/15350770902851197

Durborow, N., Lizdas, K. C., O'Flaherty, A., & Marjavi, A. (2018). *Compendium of state statutes and
policies on domestic violence and health care*. Family Violence Prevention Fund. https://www
.futureswithoutviolence.org/userfiles/file/HealthCare/Compendium%20Final.pdf

Edwards, L. M., & Pedrotti, J. T. (2004). Utilizing the strengths of our cultures: Therapy with biracial women and girls. *Women & Therapy, 27*(1-2), 33–43. https://doi.org/10.1300/J015v27n01_03

Gehart, D. R. (2020). Screening screen time: Evidence-informed guidelines for parenting in the digital age. *Family Therapy Magazine, 19*(1). https://ftm.aamft.org/screening-screen-time -evidence-informed-guidelines-for-parenting-in-the-digital-age/

Gullotta, T. P., & Adams, G. R. (2005). *Handbook of adolescent behavioral problems: Evidence based approaches to prevention and treatment.* Springer.

Hager, E. R., Quigg, A. M., Black, M. M., Coleman, S. M., Heeren, T., Rose-Jacobs, R., Cook, J. T., Ettinger de Cuba, S. A., Casey, P. H., Chilton, M., Cutts, D. B., Meyers, A. F., & Frank, D. A. (2010). Development and validity of a 2-item screen to identify families at risk for food insecurity. *Pediatrics, 126*(1), e26–e32. https://doi.org/10.1542/peds.2009-3146

Hayslip, B. (2003). Death denial: Hiding and camouflaging death. In C. D. Bryant & D. L. Peck (Eds.), *Handbook of death & dying* (pp. 34–42). SAGE Publications, Inc. https://doi .org/10.4135/9781412914291.n4

Ivey, A. E., Ivey, M. B., & Zalaquett, C. P. (2017). *Intentional interviewing and counseling: Facilitating client development in a multicultural society.* Thomson/Brooks-Cole.

Jacob, J. J., & Isaac, R. (2012). Behavioral therapy for management of obesity. *Indian journal of endocrinology and metabolism, 16*(1), 28. https://doi.org/10.4103/2230-8210.91180

Jong-Un, K. (2007). A reality therapy group counseling program as an internet addiction recovery method for college students in Korea. *International Journal of Reality Therapy, 26*(2), 3–9. https://www.proquest.com/scholarly-journals/reality-therapy-group-counseling-program -as/docview/214442706/se-2

Kamenetz, A. (2018). *The art of screen time: How your family can balance digital media and real life.* Hachette UK.

Kaminski, J. W., Valle, L. A., Filene, J. H., & Boyle, C. L. (2008). A meta-analytic review of components associated with parent training program effectiveness. *Journal of Abnormal Child Psychology, 36*(4), 567–589. https://doi.org/10.1007/s10802-007-9201-9

Kazdin, A. E. (2005). *Parent management training: Treatment for oppositional, aggressive, and antisocial behavior in children and adolescents.* Oxford University Press.

Keeney, B., & Ross, J. (1983). Learning to learn systemic therapies. *Journal of Strategic and Systemic Therapies, 2*(2), 22–30. https://doi.org/10.1521jsst19832222

Kelley, S. J., Whitley, D. M., & Campos, P. E. (2011). Behavior problems in children raised by grandmothers: The role of caregiver distress, family resources, and the home environment. *Children and Youth Services Review, 33*(11), 2138–2145. https://doi.org/10.1016/j .childyouth.2011.06.021

Kenny, M. C., & McEachern, A. G. (2002). Reporting suspected child abuse: A pilot comparison of middle and high school counselors and principals. *Journal of Child Sexual Abuse, 11*(2), 59–75. https://doi.org/10.1300/J070v11n02_04

Klaassen, D. W. (2010). *Spiritual and relational dimensions of parental grieving* [Doctoral dissertation, University of British Columbia]. University of British Columbia Theses and Dissertations. https://open.library.ubc.ca/soa/cIRcle/collections/ubctheses/24/items/1.0053677

Knell, G., Durand, C. P., Kohl, H. W., Wu, I. H., & Gabriel, K. P. (2019). Prevalence and likelihood of meeting sleep, physical activity, and screen-time guidelines among US youth. *JAMA Pediatrics, 173*(4), 387–389. https://doi.org/10.1001/jamapediatrics.2018.4847

LaFromboise, T., Coleman, H. L., & Gerton, J. (1993). Psychological impact of biculturalism: Evidence and theory. *Psychological Bulletin, 114*(3), 395. https://doi.org/10.1037/0033-2909.114.3.395

Lent, J. P., & Otto, A. (2018). Grandparents, grandchildren, and caregiving: The impacts of America's substance use crisis. *Generations, 42*(3), 15–22.

Leppma, M., & Schimmel, C. J. (2019). Children and challenges: Counseling from a growth mind-set perspective. In A. Vernon & C. J. Schimmel (Eds.), *Counseling children & adolescents* (5th ed., 338–379). Cognella Academic Publishing.

Lillis, J., Hayes, S. C., Bunting, K., & Masuda, A. (2009). Teaching acceptance and mindfulness to improve the lives of the obese: A preliminary test of a theoretical model. *Annals of Behavioral Medicine, 37*(1), 58–69. https://doi.org/10.1007/s12160-009-9083-x

McCain, J. L., & Campbell, W. K. (2018). Narcissism and social media use: A meta-analytic review. *Psychology of Popular Media Culture, 7*(3), 308. https://doi.org/10.1037/ppm0000137

McCarthy, L. P. (2021). Attention to gender and race in interventions for custodial grandparents: A scoping review. *Journal of Feminist Family Therapy: An International Forum, 33*(4), 295–314. https://doi.org/10.1080/08952833.2021.1880186

Mellin, L. M., Slinkard, L. A., & Irwin, C. E., Jr. (1987). Adolescent obesity intervention: Validation of the SHAPEDOWN program. *Journal of the American Dietetic Association, 87*(3), 333–338. https://pubmed.ncbi.nlm.nih.gov/3819254/

Miller, W. R., & Rollnick, S. (2002). Motivational interviewing: Preparing people for change. Book Review [Review of the book Motivational interviewing: Preparing people for change, by W. R. Miller & S. Rollnick]. *Journal of Studies on Alcohol, 63*(6), 776–777. https://doi.org/10.15288/jsa.2002.63.776

Milner, J. S. (1986). *The child abuse potential inventory: Manual* (2nd ed.). Psytec.

Murphy, S. (2013). Are you what you eat? *Counseling Today*. http://ct.counseling.org/2013/02/are-you-what-you-eat/

O'Hora, K. A., & Dolbin-MacNab, M. L. (2015). Practice recommendations for mental health professionals: Perspectives from grandparents and their adolescent grandchildren. *GrandFamilies: The Contemporary Journal of Research, Practice and Policy, 2*(1), 5. https://scholarworks.wmich.edu/grandfamilies/vol2/iss1/5

Olson, D. H. (2000). Circumplex model of marital and family systems. *Journal of Family Therapy, 22*(2), 144–167. https://onlinelibrary.wiley.com/doi/pdf/10.1111/1467-6427.00144

Olson, D. H., Russell, C. S., & Sprenkle, D. H. (1983). Circumplex model of marital and family systems: VI. Theoretical update. *Family Process, 22*(1), 69–83. https://doi.org/10.1111/j.1545-5300.1983.00069.x

Olson, D. H., Sprenkle, D. H., & Russell, C. S. (1979). Circumplex model of marital and family systems: I. Cohesion and adaptability dimensions, family types, and clinical applications. *Family Process, 18*(1), 3–28. https://doi.org/10.1111/j.1545-5300.1979.00003.x

Papernow, P. L. (2016). Empathic joining. In G. R. Weeks, S. T. Fife, & C. M. Peterson (Eds.), *Techniques for the couple therapist: Essential interventions from the experts* (pp. 137–141). Routledge.

Papernow, P. L. (2018). Clinical guidelines for working with stepfamilies: What family, couple, individual, and child therapists need to know. *Family Process, 57*(1), 25–51. https://doi.org/10.1111/famp.12321

Patil, S. P., Craven, K., & Kolasa, K. M. (2017). Food insecurity: It is more common than you think, recognizing it can improve the care you give. *Nutrition Today, 52*(5), 248–257. https://doi.org/10.1097/NT.0000000000000232

Patil, S. P., Craven, K., & Kolasa, K. M. (2018). Food insecurity: How you can help your patients. *American Family Physician, 98*(3), 143–145. https://pubmed.ncbi.nlm.nih.gov/30215895/

Pearce, M. J., Boergers, J., & Prinstein, M. J. (2002). Adolescent obesity, overt and relational peer victimization, and romantic relationships. *Obesity Research, 10*(5), 386–393. https://doi.org/10.1038/oby.2002.53

Peterson, T. L. (2017). Changes in health perceptions among older grandparents raising adolescent grandchildren. *Social Work in Public Health, 32*(6), 394–406. https://doi.org/10.1080/19371918.2017.1327389

Polinko, N. K., & Popovich, P. M. (2001). Evil thoughts but angelic actions: Responses to overweight job applicants. *Journal of Applied Social Psychology, 31*(5), 905–924. https://doi.org/10.1111/j.1559-1816.2001.tb02655.x

Pratt, K. J., Lamson, A. L., Lazorick, S., White, C. P., Collier, D. N., White, M. B., & Swanson, M. S. (2011). Conceptualizing care for childhood obesity: A three-world view. *Journal of Children's Services, 6*(3), 156–171. https://doi.org/10.1108/17466661111176024

Prochaska, J. O., & DiClemente, C. C. (1983). Stages and processes of self-change of smoking: toward an integrative model of change. *Journal of Consulting and Clinical Psychology, 51*(3), 390. https://doi.org/10.1037//0022-006x.51.3.390

Puhl, R., & Brownell, K. D. (2001). Bias, discrimination, and obesity. *Obesity Research, 9*(12), 788–805. https://doi.org/10.1038/oby.2001.108

Rape, Abuse, and Incest National Network. (n.d.). State by state guide on *statutes of limitations*. Retrieved May 4, 2022, from https://www.rainn.org/state-state-guide-statutes-limitations

Robinson, S. (2006). Victimization of obese adolescents. *The Journal of School Nursing, 22*(4), 201–206. https://doi.org/10.1177/10598405050220040301

Robinson, T. N., Banda, J. A., Hale, L., Lu, A. S., Fleming-Milici, F., Calvert, S. L., & Wartella, E. (2017). Screen Media Exposure and obesity in children and adolescents. *Pediatrics, 140*(Supplement_2). https://doi.org/10.1542/peds.2016-1758k

Rockquemore, K. A., Laszloffy, T., & Noveske, J. (2006). It all starts at home: Racial socialization in multiracial families. In D. Brunsma (Ed.), *Mixed messages: Multiracial identities in the "Color-Blind" era* (pp. 203–216). Lynne Rienner Publishers, Inc.

Seto, A., Becker, K., & Lau, J. (2021). "When you take this jump and cross racial boundaries": Parents' experiences of raising multiracial children. *The Family Journal, 29*(1), 86–94. https://doi.org/10.1177/1066480720964713

Simon, G. E., Von Korff, M., Saunders, K., Miglioretti, D. L., Crane, P. K., Van Belle, G., & Kessler, R. C. (2006). Association between obesity and psychiatric disorders in the US adult population. *Archives of General Psychiatry, 63*(7), 824–830. https://doi.org/10.1001/archpsyc.63.7.824

Smith, P. K., Ananiadou, K., & Cowie, H. (2003). Interventions to reduce school bullying. *The Canadian Journal of Psychiatry, 48*(9), 591–599. https://doi.org/10.1177/070674370304800905

Sommers-Flanagan, R. (2012). Boundaries, multiple roles, and the professional relationship. In S. J. Knapp, M. C. Gottlieb, M. M. Handelsman, & L. D. VandeCreek (Eds.), *APA handbook of ethics in psychology, Vol. 1. Moral foundations and common themes* (pp. 241–277). American Psychological Association. https://doi.org/10.1037/13271-009

Storm, P., & Storm, R. (2011). Grandparent education: Raising grandchildren. *Educational Gerontology, 37*, 910–923. https://doi.org/10.1080/03601277.2011.595345

Strong, D. D., Bean, R. A., & Feinauer, L. L. (2010). Trauma, attachment, and family therapy with grandfamilies: A model for treatment. *Children and Youth Services Review, 32*(1), 44–50. https://doi.org/10.1016/j.childyouth.2009.06.015

Swing, E. L., Gentile, D. A., Anderson, C. A., & Walsh, D. A. (2010). Television and video game exposure and the development of attention problems. *Pediatrics, 126*(2), 214–221. https://doi.org/10.1542/peds.2009-1508

University of Texas at San Antonio. (2019, January 23). Those with inadequate access to food likely to suffer from obesity. *ScienceDaily*. https://www.sciencedaily.com/releases/2019/01/190123144522.htm

U.S. Department of Agriculture Economic Research Service. (n.d.). *Definitions of food security*. Retrieved March 10, 2022, from https://www.ers.usda.gov/topics/food-nutrition-assistance/food-security-in-the-u-s/definitions-of-food-security/

U.S. Department of Health and Human Services, Administration for Children and Families, Administration on Children, Youth, and Families, & Children's Bureau. (2018). *Child maltreatment 2016*. https://americanspcc.org/wp-content/uploads/2018/03/2016-Child-Maltreatment.pdf

U.S. Department of Health and Human Services. (2020, March 2). *How has Healthy People changed?* Healthy People 2030. https://health.gov/healthypeople/about/how-has-healthy-people-changed

Volpp, K. G., John, L. K., Troxel, A. B., Norton, L., Fassbender, J., & Loewenstein, G. (2008). Financial incentive-based approaches for weight loss. *JAMA, 300*(22), 2631. https://doi.org/10.1001/jama.2008.804

Wadden, T. A., Berkowitz, R. I., Womble, L. G., Sarwer, D. B., Phelan, S., Cato, R. K., Hesson, L. A., Osei, S. Y., Kaplan, R., & Stunkard, A. J. (2005). Randomized trial of lifestyle modification and pharmacotherapy for obesity. *New England Journal of Medicine, 353*(20), 2111–2120. https://doi.org/10.1056/NEJMoa050156

Warchal, J. R., & West, P. (2013). *Obesity is not new—Addressing it in counseling is.* ACA Professional Information/Library.

Weiss, R. S. (1988). Loss and recovery. *Journal of Social Issues, 44*(3), 37–52. https://doi.org/10.1111/j.1540-4560.1988.tb02075.x

Whitlock, E. P., O'Connor, E. A., Williams, S. B., Beil, T. L., & Lutz, K. W. (2010). Effectiveness of weight management interventions in children: A targeted systematic review for the USPSTF. *Pediatrics, 125*(2), e396-e418. https://doi.org/10.1542/peds.2009-1955

Wing, R. R. (2008). Behavioral approaches to the treatment of obesity. In G. A. Bray & C. Bouchard (Eds.), *Handbook of obesity: Clinical applications* (3rd ed., pp. 227–248). Informa Healthcare.

Woodgate, R. L. (2006). Living in a world without closure: Reality for parents who have experienced the death of a child. *Journal of Palliative Care, 22*(2), 75–82. https://pubmed.ncbi.nlm.nih.gov/17265659/

World Health Organization. (2021, June 9). *Obesity and overweight*. Author. https://www.who.int/news-room/fact-sheets/detail/obesity-and-overweight

Yoo, J., & Russell, D. W. (2020). Caring for grandchildren and grandparents' physical and mental health changes. *Journal of Child and Family Studies, 29*(3), 845–854. https://doi.org/10.1007/s10826-019-01618-y

Young, K. S. (1999). Internet addiction: Evaluation and treatment. *BMJ, 319*(Suppl S4). https://doi.org/10.1136/sbmj.9910351

Young, M. E. (2016). *Learning the art of helping: Building blocks and techniques* (6th ed.). Merrill.

CHAPTER 10

CONTEMPORARY ISSUES AND SKILLS IN YOUTH-BASED THERAPY

LEARNING OBJECTIVES

After reading this chapter, you will be able to:

- Identify youth resistance issues and skills for enhancing therapeutic connection.
- Identify youth attachment style, associated parenting behavior, and relevant skills.
- Describe trends, issues, and interventions to assist families experiencing sibling abuse.
- Recognize childhood bullying.
- Identify comprehensive antibullying programs and relevant skills.
- Recognize learning disabilities in youth.
- Demonstrate play therapy skills and interventions.
- Demonstrate filial therapy skills and interventions.
- Recognize theraplay skills and interventions.
- Identify the essence of sandtray and sandplay therapy.
- Recognize assessment measures used to analyze contemporary youth-based therapy issues.

INTRODUCTION TO WORKING WITH CHILDREN AND ADOLESCENTS

A large percentage of couple, marriage, and family practitioners want to specialize in working with children and adolescents. They are often motivated by their love and empathy for youth and because they want to make a difference in their lives. Many students that I have taught in master's- and doctoral-level counseling and marriage and family therapy programs over the years have written papers about their experiences with being supported by someone when they were younger, or a younger sibling, niece, or nephew that they supported and helped to feel special. There is no doubt that these experiences have fueled their fire to specialize in working with children and adolescence. While supporting healthy youth can be an enormous motivator, many emerging clinicians do not realize that children and adolescents often come to counseling against their will and due to adverse childhood experiences, including, but not limited to, sexual abuse, physical abuse, neglect, emotional abuse, divorce, family substance abuse, and intimate partner violence. The consequences of these adverse experiences often include a range of internalizing (e.g., anxiety, depression, isolation, somatic issues) and externalizing (e.g., aggression, bullying, oppositional and defiant issues, delinquent behavior, theft, vandalism) concerns demonstrated by the child or adolescent.

Adolescent clients can bring their own set of challenges to the unsuspecting clinician. Many of the students in the programs I have taught in are traditional bachelor- to graduate-age students (approximately 22–24 years of age). Many of them clearly remember what it was like to be a teenager and can recall a special community member, teacher, camp counselor, or therapist who helped them with their journey through the adolescent phase of life. A large number of adolescents come from abusive homes and impoverished living conditions, and have been dealing with adult-level contextual trauma (e.g., intimate partner violence, poverty, substance use, infidelity, rape). In addition to the normal resistance many adolescents feel around adults and a situation where they are likely being forced to attend therapy against their will, teenagers can be silent, indifferent, and manipulative to professional helpers. This is also the phase in life in which youth start to consider riskier behaviors with potential long-term consequences (e.g., relationships, sexual engagement, substance experimentation, ditching school, sharing intimate thoughts/images online, not trying school).

One additional area of competence that often intimidates early-career professionals is working with parents. Due to the multitude of parenting styles and practices, culturally bound traditions and expectations, and frequently changing societal norms around parenting practices, students can feel very unsure as to what constitutes appropriate parenting (e.g., spanking, time-out, hovering, intensity of parental supervision). Many trainees understand that helping parents is key to helping youth; however, they fear that they will not seem credible to parents unless they have their own families and life experiences with raising a family. Many early-career practitioners will comment that they look too young to provide parents with help. Students are also unaccustomed to working with caregivers who can seem fixated on the therapist fixing their child and uninterested in taking any responsibility for their own part in the issue or the more systemic occurrences that have contributed to the child's behavior. This, along with general parental defensiveness and hostility, can create a situation where trainees feel very defensive, scrutinized, and vulnerable. The unfortunate consequence of this is that emerging clinicians become less interested in directly supporting parents, providing parent education, engaging in family therapy, or having periodic consultations with parents about their child's progress in therapy. This is not only unhelpful for the parents' growth, but will also seriously limit the amount of healing and change clinicians can create in a child or adolescent's life.

Answering questions about competency, experience being a parent, age, religion, and other personal topics can be tricky for early-career professionals. The most popular inappropriate response to these inquiries is to ask the client why they are asking the question and for the practitioner to justify or prove their merit in this area of work. For example, "I wonder why you're asking this question" or "What would my answer do for you?" Whether deflecting or proving one's ability through presenting evidence of expertise, the outcome is the same; clients feel that their questions are unanswered or sense an underlying defensiveness and insecurity within the therapist. Clinicians need to own their experience or lack thereof directly and honestly. An example of how a clinician might appropriately respond to a question regarding their experience raising children could be the following: "It sounds like you are worried about whether or not I have children. No, I do not have children. Regardless of whether I have my own children, I want you to know that I am eager to work with you and help you achieve your goals." When the clinician answers the question directly and honestly, they will almost always alleviate the concerns raised by the client(s). If parents continue to take issue with lack of parenting experience, age, or any other factor, the best tactic may be to offer referrals.

Voices From the Field

This chapter features sections entitled Voices From the Field. These sections explore multicultural, social justice, equity, diversity, and intersectionality issues from the perspective of clinicians representing diverse ethnic, racial, and national backgrounds. This chapter will feature professional counselors who identify as Indian and Hispanic. The purpose of adding quotes from individuals representing minorities or who frequently serve diverse populations is to provide you, the reader, cutting-edge social justice and multiculturally oriented skills, interventions, and clinical conceptualization. The two individuals who took part in the Voices From the Field process came from different life contexts, different racial and ethnic backgrounds, and diverse intersections of cultural advantage and disadvantage. Participant information is provided in the following:

Dr. Jyotsana Sharma is a 41-year-old Indian cisgender woman. She is a licensed mental health counselor, approved clinical supervisor, nationally certified counselor, and serves as an assistant professor of counselor education at Oklahoma State University. In addition to her work as a faculty member, Dr. Sharma has worked with children and adolescents from a variety of life contexts and demonstrating a broad range of mental health issues.

Mr. Danny J. Shearer is a 60-year-old Hispanic cisgender man. He is a licensed marriage and family therapist and certified addictions counselor. Mr. Shearer serves his community in Colorado through addictions and family-based services. He has worked with children and adolescents from a variety of life contexts and demonstrating a broad range of mental health issues.

Participants were sent a questionnaire featuring five open-ended questions regarding their experiences practicing in the field. Participant quotes are placed throughout the chapter to enhance the content. Participant questions are as follows:

- Clinicians who work with children and adolescents frequently help youth who demonstrate insecure attachment patterns. Secure parental attachment greatly assists children in self-regulating their emotions and provides them with protection from mental illness. When providing therapy to ethnically/racially diverse youth who have suffered an attachment injury, what patterns have you noticed? What skills have you used to help them heal their attachment wounds?

- When resistance occurs in therapy, it can interfere with the therapeutic process. Resistance is something that most children use to ensure emotional and/or physical safety. Within your own work, how has your knowledge of child and adolescent resistance aided you as a clinician? Conversely, has your inexperience with certain styles of resistance ever come up during the therapeutic process? What, if any, patterns of resistance have you noticed when working with youth representing one or more communities of color?

- Sibling abuse has been defined as the physical, emotional, or sexual injury of one sibling by another. Sibling abuse and violence is centered on repeated patterns of escalating physical or sexual aggression that is primarily motivated by power and control. From your experience, what, if any, abuse patterns exist with ethnically/racially diverse siblings? What, if any, patterns have you noticed in stepfamilies? What skills have you used to help youth engaging in sibling abuse and violence?

- Bias-based bullying is a type of bullying that is directed at a marginalized community because of the individual's race, ethnicity, gender, religious belief, weight, sexual orientation, or ability. What has your clinical experience been with bias-based bullying? What skills or interventions have you utilized to help youth suffering from this hurtful behavior?

- Learning disabilities affect children's education, mental health, and socialization. Within your clinical practice, what unique experiences do you have with ethnically/racially diverse children who are diagnosed with a learning disability? Describe a few ways you have helped these children and their families.

CHILD AND ADOLESCENT RESISTANCE TO TREATMENT

The focus of this section will be on youth resistant to treatment. Counseling youth can be a significant challenge, especially when they are resistant, silent, and/or hostile/confrontational. There are a variety of resources available to help couple, marriage, and family practitioners work with resistant youth and their parents. For example, Sommers-Flanagan and Sommers-Flanagan (2011, 2014) offer an array of helpful techniques and interventions in two of their books: *Tough Kids, Cool Counseling: User-Friendly Approaches With Challenging Youth (Second Edition)* and *How to Listen So Parents Will Talk and Talk So Parents Will Listen*. These two textbooks are highly recommended comprehensive resources that go beyond the contemporary issues presented in this chapter. Backlund and Johnson (2018) described resistance as something that most humans use to ensure emotional and/or physical safety. They add that the world can create situations where people feel threatened and resistance is one tool that is commonly used to reduce the threat. When youth choose to attend counseling or are forced/required to engage in counseling, they naturally develop a sense of resistance to a potentially threatening situation.

Even when the change appears to be very positive, all of us can be resistant to it. This resistance is normal, and if our intention is to truly help someone heal their psychological wounds we should not be rushing them into an experience they do not fully trust and/or are not prepared to engage in. Two of the most bizarre aspects of any therapeutic relationship are the assumptions that clients should come in ready to disclose all relevant information from their past to a perfect stranger (i.e., the intake) and that they should be quickly ready to work toward changing salient aspects of their life (i.e., treatment plan goals). Unfortunately, children and adolescents are not behavioral software, and despite the clinical world's desire to produce fast and cost-efficient results with empirically based interventions, some clients resist cocreating immediate change with a practitioner and respond negatively to any clinical attempts. Unfortunately, when youth demonstrate this normal reaction to the unique dimensions of the therapeutic process, they are often referred to as resistant, oppositional, unmotivated, and noncompliant (Watson, 2006).

Relevant Skills and Interventions

Pope (1979) defined *client resistance* as "a process of avoiding or diminishing the self-disclosing communication requested by the interviewer because of its capacity to make the interviewee uncomfortable or anxious" (p. 74). Nystul (2001) suggested that client resistance can interfere with a practitioner's sense of self-efficacy and blocks the client's motivation to change. Most youth come into counseling with a personal background (e.g., abuse, neglect, bullying, adverse childhood experiences) that serves as further motivation to resist treatment and not trust the counselor. Resistance keeps them safe and in control. Sommers-Flanagan and Sommers-Flanagan (2014) created seven common resistance styles demonstrated in youth and the appropriate clinical response. These youth-based resistance styles are the following: (a) *the externalizer/blamer* (i.e., blames other people and things for personal problems), (b) *the silent youth* (i.e., refuses to speak or work with the practitioner), (c) the denier (i.e., denies having any issues to work on), (d) *the nonverbal provocateur* (i.e., uses irritating nonverbal behavior to avoid opening up), (e) *the absent youth* (i.e., refuses to enter the therapy room or misses appointments to avoid working on things), (f) *the attacker* (i.e., attacks a therapist's personhood to avoid any vulnerability), and (g) *the apathetic youth* (i.e., appears not to care about anything to avoid engaging in therapeutic work). These youth-based resistance styles, clinician response recommendations, and example responses are further elaborated in Table 10.1.

In families, children and adolescents may unconsciously resist positive change to protect other family members and ensure the homeostatic balance of the family system. For example, when parents scapegoat a child for their family's problems, the child may be motivated to emulate their concerns to ensure the consistency of the family structure. To avoid negatively affecting other family members, the youth might also avoid any positive change in their beliefs and behaviors. For example, April has been truant several times from school this month. Her unconscious motivation for skipping school is to keep her parents' attention focused on her behavior so they avoid arguing among each other about their failing marriage (Watson, 2006).

Clinicians work with resistance as a method for better understanding their clients. While client resistance and the accompanying anxiety and identity protection should be considered normative and part of the treatment process, couple, marriage, and family practitioners frequently use strategies to move therapy forward.

TABLE 10.1 COMMON YOUTH RESISTANCE STYLES, CLINICAL RESPONSES, AND EXAMPLES

Resistance Style	Recommended Response	Examples
The externalizer/ blamer	Clinicians are to empathize with the youth's affect and perspective, and not pass judgment.	"You really dislike your mom right now. Being forced to come to therapy really sucks."
The silent youth	Clinicians are to use reflection of feeling, paraphrasing, self-disclosure, and teaming up.	"I can tell you don't want to be in counseling, and you don't want me to know anything about you. Since your parents hired me, if I were you, I wouldn't trust me either. Instead of sitting here in silence, I suggest we team up so you can have more control over your life."
The denier	Clinicians are to either side with the youth after blaming others for mistakenly sending them to treatment, or initially confirming that the youth is fine and asking them to discuss their life anyway.	"Jeremy, it really doesn't seem like you need to be here. Why do you think your teachers requested it?"
The nonverbal provocateur	Clinicians allow disrespectful nonverbals to take place and ask the client how they are being treated; the clinician discloses their own thoughts about the negative nonverbals, why the clinician's thoughts/feeling arose, asks the youth if they have control over their nonverbals, and asks the youth to experiment with using/not using this with others.	"Amanda, I noticed that you rolled your eyes back and sighed. This felt hurtful to me and caused me to think that you don't find value in our time together. I challenge you to act like this once this week at school and let me know if anyone treated you differently."
The absent youth	Inform the youth that they can leave the session; however, the session will proceed without them. The practitioner will then serve food and drink during the parent/family session that is substituted. Partway through the session, a family member will be instructed to invite the youth back into session. If the youth is absent, the clinician should write a letter or engage in contingency management.	"You shouldn't feel like you have to come to therapy. If you truly don't want to be here, please feel free to step out and stay in the waiting room. Could you please ask your parents to come in while you're out there?"
The attacker	The clinician should remain calm and not respond in a hurtful or defensive manner; the clinician may describe the behavior as being more based on the youth's thoughts and feelings rather than the therapeutic relationship; the clinician should repeat as many times as necessary.	"Josh, I just met you and I don't believe we know each other well enough for you to call me a *jerk*. This appears to have more to do with your recent experience and less to do with the work we've done."
The apathetic youth	Clinicians empathize with youth apathy, worry out loud that there may be a real issue at play, and label the part that cares as the client's *real* self and the apathy as the client's fake self.	"There is a part of you that doesn't care, but I bet there is a part of yourself that does care. I would like you to label the real part of yourself that cares. Now label the fake part of yourself that doesn't care."

Sources: Data from Hanna, F. J., & Hunt, W. P. (1999). Techniques for psychotherapy with defiant, aggressive adolescents. *Psychotherapy: Theory, Research, Practice, Training, 36*(1), 56; Sommers-Flanagan, J., & Sommers-Flanagan, R. (2014). *Tough kids, cool counseling: User-friendly approaches with challenging youth.* John Wiley & Sons; Willock, B. (1986). Narcissistic vulnerability in the hyperaggressive child: The disregarded (unloved, uncared-for) self. *Psychoanalytic Psychology, 3*(1), 59–80. https://doi.org/10.1037/0736-9735.3.1.59.

Newman (1994) highlights 10 strategies proven to be effective in working with resistant clients: (a) educating the client about resistance, (b) using the Socratic method of questioning to bring out the client, (c) allowing the client to have choices and be an active director of the counseling process, (d) fostering collaboration between the counselor and the client, (e) brainstorming the pros and cons of continuing current behavior or changing, (f) empathizing with the client and their reason for feeling resistant, (g) discussing case conceptualization with the client, (h) using a language that mirrors that of the client, (i) maximizing the use of client self-direction, and (j) gently persisting when a client is either unable or unwilling to proceed.

VOICES FROM THE FIELD: JYOTSANA

Dr. Jyotsana Sharma shared her experiences and thoughts around working with youth who demonstrate resistance toward therapy.

Resistance is probably the most predictable pattern that emerges working in the field of counseling, especially with children and teens—who wants to change?! Even the most invested clients have a tough time realizing and/or accepting that change is needed. We have built-in biases that help us deflect and project onto others. With resistance, I try to use a psychodynamic approach integrated with motivational interviewing. It works with children and adolescents, especially when they feel disempowered in certain areas of their life—sometimes brainstorming choices that they might have, something that they never thought of works to dislodge some of the rusty parts of the brain we've stopped using or don't pay attention to when we are focusing on everything that is wrong in our lives. I worked with at-risk youth at one time and their avoidance and resistance gave me a chance to connect with them. I'd often find myself using humor and telling them "I know you don't hate me; you just want to talk to me from under the chair, or behind a closed door." Sometimes they'd answer back from under the chair, and sometimes I'd sit by their door and wait—either way, when they figured I wasn't going anywhere, the resistance softened, and we could actually have a conversation. Early on in my career as a counselor, when I did not realize how important the resistance was to establishing trust in the therapeutic relationship, to building rapport, to not only understand your client, but to let them understand you—I used to get frustrated. One of my supervisors (amazing person!) used to ask me "what does your client want from you?" and over the years that led me to think proactively about what a client wants or needs from me—validation, affirmation that life is tough, change is difficult, patterns are not easy to conquer—once I was able to answer these simple questions for each of my clients, I did better with resistance. In working with youth who were minoritized and marginalized, the common pattern I observed was they did not think that anyone would understand them or try to understand them, or even care about their perspective and how they viewed life. Till that point, often they had been told "you are the problem" and they had internalized "I am the problem," and as a result were unable to emerge from that vicious cycle or blame, shame, and internalization of others' opinions projected onto them.

VOICES FROM THE FIELD: DANNY

Mr. Danny J. Shearer shared his experiences and methods around working with youth who demonstrate resistance toward therapy.

I frequently use Stephen Porges's polyvagal theory to assist me when a client is resistant or guarded. Their security needs have been compromised, so coming into my office, they are extremely guarded, especially since I am not "familia." They are usually in the "sympathetic activation," the fight/flight mode (mobilized, activated, and agitated). I let them share their drug- and/or gang-related experiences and have them tell me how good it makes them feel, without me passing any judgment. This tends to elevate them to the ventral vagal activation (safe, engaged, social). It's imperative to find a way to connect and make the experience safe. If it's not safe and they can't run away, this would cause them to go into dorsal vagal activation (the shutdown mode). Personally, in my practice, I am mindful of utilizing more sensory activities such as doing our session at a basketball court and "shooting hoops." Their flight/fight mode is a sensory issue rather than a cognitive issue. Hence, sensory motor exercises are more ideal to help my clients feel safe or connected in the session.

CHILDHOOD ATTACHMENT ISSUES

The salience of youth having secure attachment bonds with caregivers has been brought up throughout this textbook. This chapter is no exception; however, the focus of this section will be on childhood attachment, the effect of childhood trauma on attachment, and effective treatment. Secure parental attachment greatly assists children in self-regulating their emotions. Attachment has been described as the enduring familial emotional bond that creates a secure connection within children to prepare them for independence and parenthood (Rees, 2005). The possible positive aspects to healthy early attachment include (a) adult ability to build safe and secure relationships, (b) ability to establish self-esteem, and (c) ability to create positive emotional connectedness with others (Sroufe et al., 1999). Healthy attachment can also provide protection from mental illness. For example, Crusto et al. (2010) discovered that caregiver support and positive parent–child interaction function as a shield to mental health disorders following childhood trauma.

The Phases of Attachment Development

The preattachment phase ranges from pregnancy to approximately 6 weeks of age (Bowlby, 1969, 1988). It is important to remember that attachment is a biologically driven strategy youth employ to create both physical and emotional protection and security. Prior to birth, both infants and mothers are being introduced to the attachment process and a foundation of security. During the second and third trimesters of pregnancy, the embryo and the mother have a nurturing attunement with each other that is heavily influenced by oxytocin (a hormone released by the pituitary gland). Neurobiologically speaking, oxytocin directs the social interaction, sense of security, closeness, and warmth between the embryo/infant and the mother (Lahousen et al., 2019; MacKinnon et al., 2014; McCall & Singer, 2012).

The birth process is a major attachment experience between the mother and the newborn baby. According to Lahousen et al. (2019),

> [a] major fall of progesterone right before birth continuously releases oxytocin and thereby triggers labor activity. Simultaneously, oxytocin relieves pain during labor. Following delivery, the new-born's suckling on the maternal breast promotes secretion of both prolactin and oxytocin. Breastfeeding provides a harmonious, highly satisfying, and stress-reducing communication between baby and mother (p. 2).

Following birth, oxytocin has also been associated with positive neurologic development in infants. Specifically, social learning and relational experiences are synchronized in the cortex and hippocampus because the GABAergic neurotransmission has been activated (Lahousen et al., 2019). In short, the oxytocin-fueled neurologic synchronization helps the infantile brain develop due to the critical influence of social experiences (i.e., infant and primary attachment figure interaction). As life begins, infants cannot effectively self-regulate their emotions. Attachment allows infants to emotionally self-regulate through involuntary stress regulation, which is adaptively directed by the hypothalamus–pituitary–adrenal (HPA) axis (Schore, 2005). This ability to self-sooth is helpful for independence, learning, exploring, and relationship-building. Bowlby (1988) described this as the preattachment phase of development. He described the child as desiring closeness and indicated that the infant is constantly in close contact with the mother and other family members. The baby uses verbal and nonverbal behavior to signal a need to the primary attachment figure (e.g., crying, grasping). At this stage, they are not fully attached to their caregiver and do not seem stressed when left with unfamiliar people.

During infancy, there is a connection between maltreatment and insecure attachment. Infant trauma usually has to do with the mother/caregiver–child relationship. Infants that have been abused tend to display an insecure type of attachment. While inadequately controlled infant stress can generate persistently inflated stress reactions, infant maltreatment or abuse can create a situation in which infants turn off their ability to regulate, altering the HPA axis function, which leads to a sense of fearlessness (i.e., relative bradycardia), anxiety, depression, and posttraumatic stress disorder (PTSD; Snoek et al., 2004).

According to Main and Hesse (1990), maltreated infants often have disorganized insecure attachment patterns. Specifically, the infant appears anxious and apprehensive due to not having an ability to self-soothe and handle stress. This inability to cope is fostered by a caregiver who creates a sense of disorganization by presenting themselves as the only source of comfort and nurturance for the infant and simultaneously frightening the infant through abusive and erratic behaviors (Van Ijzendoorn et al., 1999). When infant maltreatment takes place, the child often demonstrates a freezing behavior which represents fear of the abusive caregiver and a desire to seek proximity. The freezing response is a physical manifestation of the infant's inability to deal with the mixed messages from the primary caregiver. As infants demonstrating a disorganized attachment mature into children, they can also start dissociating to cope with the pain of parental maltreatment (Main & Hess, 1990).

Attachment in making (also known as the early arising attachment phase) starts around 6 weeks of age and ends between 6 and 8 months of age. During this stage of development, the infant has differential reactions toward people they know compared with those who are unknown. At this point, a basic sense of trust is starting to develop (Bowlby, 1969, 1988). Infants in the attachment in making phase are cocreating their internal working model (IWM) with caregivers and family members. An IWM is a template for how to engage in relationships and what to expect from relationships. This lifelong template guides youth around their values and responsibilities in relationships (Bowlby, 1969). For example, at this stage, infants begin to develop a sense of trust toward their caregivers and respond differently to familiar caregivers than they do to strangers. They also start to become aware that their actions (or lack thereof) affect everyone around them. These early life experiences begin to create the affective and cognitive matrices that affect the infant's future relationships and attachment style. Painful infant experiences, such as child abuse and/or neglect, can create negative IWMs of self and others. If not addressed in therapy, youth can develop higher attachment anxiety, insecurity, and needs.

Clear-cut attachment is a phase of infant/child development that occurs between 6 to 8 months of age and 18 months to 2 years of age. The reason it is likely entitled clear-cut is because the attachment bond between the primary caregiver and the infant is evident. For example, infants demonstrate stress and tearfulness when the attachment figure leaves them. The extent to which the child reacts to the caregiver's departure is dependent on their disposition, caregiver behavior, and environmental factors. In a child who demonstrates a secure attachment style, the caregiver's departure would bring about stress, but when the supportive caregiver returns and engages with the child in a supportive manner the anxiety would be reduced (Bowlby, 1969, 1988). While parents who consistently engage children in a nurturing and engaging manner in a structured environment produce a secure attachment style within their child, depending on the caregiver behavior and child response, additional internalized attachment bonds can emerge within children. Table 10.2 reviews common attachment styles, typical caregiver behaviors that correlate with the child's attachment, and predictable child responses.

TABLE 10.2 INFANT/CHILD ATTACHMENT STYLES: DESCRIPTIONS, CAREGIVER BEHAVIORS, AND INFANT/CHILD BEHAVIORS

Attachment Style	Description	Caregiver Behavior	Infant/Child Behavior
Secure	The child uses their primary attachment figure as a secure base; there is a balance between exploration, safety, and security.	The caregiver plays with their children, picks up the infant and reassures them, reacts quickly to their children's needs, and provides nurturance, structure, engagement, and appropriate challenge when needed.	The child protests when left alone, has discomfort with a stranger, seeks proximity, and cheers up when the primary attachment figure returns.
Anxious/ Avoidant	The child receives consistent rejecting/ignoring caregiving behavior, and in response they will avoid the parent during times of need and minimize displays of emotionality in their presence.	The caregiver consistently responds to the child's distress in rejecting ways, such as ignoring, ridiculing, or becoming annoyed, and does not show care and responsiveness beyond the child's basic needs.	The child does not protest when the parent leaves the room, continues playing and initiates contact with strangers, and turns away if the primary caregiver reapproaches. The child disregards personal needs to maintain proximity with the parent.
Anxious/ Ambivalent	The child receives inconsistent care from their parents. They are unsure if their parent will be there for them, and when in distress they will likely not have faith/trust in the parent; however, they will desperately seek their nurturance.	The caregiver responds to the child in an inconsistent and unpredictable manner, expecting the child to worry about the caregiver's needs, and amplifying infant distress and subsequent emotional reaction.	The child engages in extreme protest when left alone, and when the primary attachment figure returns they desire physical contact. Their behavior toward the attachment figure vacillates between clingy and avoidant, and they display negative, distressed, and angry emotions prior to receiving any parental attention.

(continued)

TABLE 10.2   INFANT/CHILD ATTACHMENT STYLES: DESCRIPTIONS, CAREGIVER BEHAVIORS, AND INFANT/CHILD BEHAVIORS (*CONTINUED*)

Attachment Style	Description	Caregiver Behavior	Infant/Child Behavior
Disorganized/ Disoriented	The child receives abusive and atypical care from their parents. They consequently rendered unable to find an appropriate solution to their distress, so they demonstrate odd, contradictory, and concerning behaviors.	The caregiver demonstrates abusive parenting and atypical behaviors that are sexualized, dissociated, and frightened. They consistently fail to attend to the child's needs and distress appropriately, and frequently provide inconsistent responses to their child.	The child is vulnerable to stress; has difficulty with self-regulation and control of emotions; reveals oppositional, hostile, and aggressive behaviors; engages in contradictory behaviors, stilling and freezing; and is afraid of their parent.
Reactive	The child does not receive connection, comfort, affection, nurturing, or proper engagement from their parents and others. When a child's basic emotional needs are unmet or ignored by their parents, they may develop callous, unemphatic, and unemotional traits that can conclude in behavioral problems, destruction of property, and curtness toward people and/or animals.	The caregiver responds to the child in an abusive or neglectful manner that deprives the child of their basic needs of comfort, affection, nurturing, engagement, and structure. The child may frequently relocate to different foster homes, residential treatment centers, or juvenile hall facilities, or have severely dysfunctional parents with severe mental health issues, criminal behavior problems, and/or substance abuse that severely impairs their ability to parent.	The child does not engage in proximity-seeking behavior; rarely shows signs of comfort; has trouble with emotional regulation; struggles to form emotional and meaningful bonds with anyone; and demonstrates reflexive, fearful, or anxious behaviors around any adult serving in the caregiver role.

Sources: Data from Ainsworth, M. D. S. (1978). The Bowlby-Ainsworth attachment theory. *Behavioral and Brain Sciences, 1*(3), 436–438. https://doi.org/10.1017/S0140525X00075828; American Academy of Child & Adolescent Psychiatry. (2014). *Attachment disorders.* aacap.org/AACAP/Families_and_Youth/Facts_for_Families/FFF-Guide/Attachment-Disorders-085.aspx; Rees, C. (2007). Childhood attachment. *British Journal of General Practice, 57*(544), 920–922. https://doi.org/10.3399/096016407782317955.

The differentiation and integration phase (also known as the formation of reciprocal relationship phase) of attachment ranges from 18 months to 2 years of life. This is a time of rapid growth and development. The toddler begins to understand language and develops a sense of reciprocity with their primary caregiver. The child will also inquire, negotiate, and start depending less on the caregiver. While Bowlby did not specify childhood stages, he did observe that 3-year-old children begin to understand that their parents have their own goals and plans. Consequently, children appear less concerned when their parent(s) leave them alone for a longer period (Bowlby, 1969, 1988).

Childhood Attachment and the Effects of Trauma

Trauma has been described as the most destructive factor in an attachment relationship (Fonagy, 2000). When children are traumatized, they deeply depend on primary attachment figures to help them soothe and cope with the resulting anxieties. Parental nurturing, engagement, and support following a traumatic experience greatly reduce the possibility of developing subsequent mental health issues in the affected youth (Crusto et al., 2010). Having a secure attachment with a caregiver provides a great deal of support and protection from the negative effects of trauma, PTSD symptomology, complex trauma, and the longer term effects of experiencing trauma (e.g., sleep disturbance, self-mutilation). Securely attached children are able to self-regulate their emotional arousal and have a secure base to turn to for safety when under threat. When traumatized children are unsupported by their attachment figures, they might develop a fearful and insecure space in their mind instead of a safe mental space (Courtois & Ford, 2009).

Children exposed to trauma, especially trauma perpetrated by a primary caregiver, can lead to negative consequences, including attachment insecurity, insecure disorganized attachment classification, and a decrease in the likelihood of having a positive IWM to guide future relationships (Bakermans-Kranenburg & Van Ijzendoorn, 2009). Additionally, a child's social and emotional development suffers due to traumatization. Developmentally speaking, traumatized children often are deficient in certain areas, including the ability to make and sustain social relationships; have attention-related and learning disabilities; have oppositional and/or detached affect toward parents; engage in substance abuse as adolescents and adults; and have major challenges in developing intimacy, trust, and interpersonal harmony with future partners (Cook & Kenny, 2005; Erozkan, 2016; Van der Kolk, 2005). Emotionally speaking, after experiencing trauma in the form of child maltreatment, it is often difficult for youth to express emotions like sympathy, empathy, and remorse. Lastly, research indicates that youth who have been traumatized via child maltreatment often have the same attachment style as their abusive caregiver, and when they become adults they often inflict the abusive behaviors they incurred with their own children (Erozkan, 2016; Van der Kolk, 2005).

Experiences alter and shape the brain's neural networks throughout the life span; however, children and adolescents absorb experiences at a much higher frequency when compared with adults (Black & Flynn, 2021). In fact, scholars indicate a 2-year-old has at least twice as many synapses as any adult, enabling faster learning than any other time in the child's life due to connections between brain cells (Sriram, 2020). Early life alterations in neural networks are often a reflection of the psychological impairments that are the cornerstone of complex traumatic stress disorder. Complex trauma often develops as a result of abuse and neglect and a parental disorganized/disoriented or reactive attachment style (Black & Flynn, 2021; Courtois & Ford, 2009). According to The National Child Traumatic Stress Network,

> [c]omplex trauma describes both children's exposure to multiple traumatic events—often of an invasive, interpersonal nature—and the wide-ranging, long-term effects of this exposure. These events are severe and pervasive, such as abuse or profound neglect. They usually occur early in life and can disrupt many aspects of the child's development and the formation of a sense of self. Since these events often occur with a caregiver, they interfere with the child's ability to form a secure attachment. Many aspects of a child's healthy physical and mental development rely on this primary source of safety and stability (n.d., para. 1).

The emergence of complex trauma and the shift in the neural networks are often the result of severe adverse child experiences. In other words, complex trauma often emerges as a result of the child experiencing multiple and/or repetitive bouts of abuse and neglect throughout their formative years. While neural pathways can change throughout the life span, it is very challenging to change one's personality, behavior, and emotional patterns following adolescents (Cicchetti et al., 1995; Courtois & Ford, 2009). The alterations in brain development, resulting from patterned abuse and neglect, unfortunately change the child's thought process and personality from a healthy and exploratory learning brain to a protective survival brain (Courtois & Ford, 2009).

Youth who develop a survival brain mentality try to foresee, stop, or defend against the harm caused by possible environmental dangers. The survival brain is reinforced and motivated to seek and detect any threats to the psyche or physical person and tries to organize and preserve bodily resources in the service of this alertness and protective adjustment (Courtois & Ford, 2009). In short, this preoccupation with survival stands in contrast to the dependable and exploratory bonds created with caregivers, and if it is not adjusted back to a more compatible learning style there could be long-term fundamental effects to the neural network and personality of the child (e.g., mental health disorders, personality disorders, suicidal ideation and suicide attempts, sleep disturbances; Courtois & Ford, 2009, 2013).

Lenore Terr (1991) took this a step further and differentiated type I and type II child trauma. Type I refers to youth who had a singular traumatic event. Symptoms of type I trauma are in the form of detailed memories and dreams of the experience. Because of the singular nature of the traumatic event, there is typically no memory loss or dissociation. Type II trauma includes children who have been victims of multiple traumatic experiences. These events could include, but are not limited to, incest, sexual abuse, physical abuse, severe emotional abuse, and neglect. Due to the frequency and extended period of abuse, most child survivors of type II child trauma have higher acuity symptomology, including dissociative states, recurring trance-like experiences, severe anxiety, depression, suicidal ideation and suicide attempts, sleep disturbances, self-mutilation, and PTSD (Courtois & Ford, 2009; Terr, 1991).

Relevant Skills and Interventions

Since attachment is centered on family relationships, systemic therapy is an optimal choice for treatment. Generally, attachment therapies involve both the child and the parent(s) meeting in a warm, nonjudgmental, culturally sensitive, and accepting therapeutic environment. Couple, marriage, and family practitioners work to understand, empower, and nurture children and adults suffering from attachment injuries. The cross-generational transmission of attachment styles often creates a need for all family members to receive treatment; otherwise, the parenting challenges and insecure attachment relational styles simply continue (Cohn et al., 1992; Cowen et al., 2009). Given the cross-generational transmission of attachment patterns, many clinicians will systematically trace parenting problems to their experiences as children. This creates awareness, sympathy, and tolerance for understanding the same issues their child is experiencing and, at times, motivation to change their parenting style (Bowlby, 1940). Systemically trained practitioners understand that attachment is contingent on culture. Given the contextual nature of attachment, clinicians adjust their therapeutic style accordingly.

According to Kobak et al. (2015), a key factor in attachment-based treatment is enhancing youth's IWM through implicit modeling of secure attachment, emotional processing of attachment narratives, reflective dialogue, and psychoeducation. According to Bowlby (1988), simply working with a clinician who models a secure IWM and treats the family in a manner that provides a healthy sense of nurturing, engagement, structure, and challenge can create a helpful model and inspire change. Youth will experience the validation and understanding they have been potentially missing at home, while parents will experience this and have a new frame of reference for how to create a secure attachment with their child or adolescent. In short, clients will feel understood, experience positive expectancies and increased confidence in the therapist, enjoy emotionally attuned communication, and experience a positive and supportive response to emotional distress stemming from attachment injuries (Bowlby, 1988; Kobak et al., 2015).

Greenberg et al. (2007) encourage the uncovering of caregiving narratives so youth can reexperience a sense of healing around their primary attachment needs and an understanding around their primary attachment emotions. Primary emotions such as shame, fear, and hurt need to be understood, potentially reframed, and managed. If the opportunity is possible and safe, the clinician will manage the child's or adolescent's primary attachment emotions to motivate contact-seeking behavior with their attachment figure. Secondary emotions (e.g., anger, jealousy, resentment, frustration) serve a protective function and tend to push attachment figures away. The clinician will work with any secondary emotions that are serving a defensive strategy so children/adolescents can feel safer about opening up and being vulnerable. As youth become more comfortable with engaging parents/caregivers with primary emotions, they are likely to see a reduction in conflict (Greenberg et al., 2007; Kobak et al., 2015).

Reflective dialogue is an additional way youth can enhance their IWM. According to Kobak et al. (2015), reflective dialogue encourages self-distancing by considering multiple perspectives and interpretations about a given situation. This is sometimes referred to as meta-cognitive thinking and generally involves creating a large-scale interpretation of oneself and others. Reflective dialogue is incredibly important to understand a child's or adolescent's attachment and/or autonomy needs. The therapeutic goal of these reflective dialogues is to create new interpretations and perspectives about the child's attachment and autonomy needs to preserve the unique nature of the IWM. To stimulate growth in these areas, sometimes therapists will replay a video of a child and caregiver behavior and ask the caregiver for their perception of the child's behavior. Once the interpretation is made, the therapist reframes it to be a relational problem and attempt to prevent further scapegoating, or provides psychoeducation around the youth's attachment and autonomy needs (Oppenheim & Koren-Karie, 2013). Psychoeducation can provide valuable understanding and insight into the attachment needs and responsibilities. Psychoeducation is used to provide family members with information on the attachment process, the secure cycle of attachment, how the expression of attachment needs changes as children age and develop, the importance of empathy, the freedom to negotiate different goals, and the child's needs for security and autonomy (Moretti & Obsuth, 2009).

Traumatized children often develop attachment issues, and if left untreated deep attachment injuries resulting from trauma can turn into an attachment-based disorder. Fortunately, there are many trauma/attachment-based treatments centered on helping children and adolescents recover, including, but not limited to, infant–parent psychotherapy (IPP; see Lieberman, 2004), childparent psychotherapy (CPP; see Lieberman et al., 2005), neurosequential model of therapeutics (NMT; see Perry & Hambrick, 2008), parent–child interaction therapy (PCIT; see Eyberg, 1988), play therapy (see Kottman, 2011), filial therapy (see Ginsberg, 1997), cognitive behavioral intervention for trauma in schools (CBITS; see Feldman, 2007), cognitive processing therapy (CPT; see Resick & Schnickle, 1993), and trauma-focused cognitive behavioral therapy (TF-CBT; see Cohen et al., 2000). For the purposes of this chapter, IPP and CPP will be reviewed.

As empirically based systemic treatments, IPP and CPP help to heal the wounds of traumatized, abused, and unattached infants and children. IPP and CPP are based on attachment, psychodynamic, developmental, trauma, social learning, and cognitive behavioral theories. These approaches are centered on the parent and infant/child working together to create a psychological partnership that is centered on (a) helping the infant/child self-regulate their emotions; (b) encouraging the parents to respond sensitively to the infant/child; (c) untangling the infant/child from the parents' own attachment-based early childhood issues; (d) training parents to become a calm, engaging, nurturing, and strong person to help the infant/child heal from the attachment-based injuries; (e) improving the childcaregiver relationship; (f) joint construction of trauma narrative; and (g) safely returning the infant/child to a normal developmental trajectory (Fraiberg et al., 1975; Lieberman et al., 2005). This evidence-based approach works best for children under 6 years of age.

The initial phase of IPP/CPP includes parent/caregiver meetings with the practitioner and the goal is to explore the nature and extent of the infant/child's traumatization. Subsequent sessions include the infant/child meeting together with the parent/caregiver. While various elements of the previously described psychological partnership are constantly being worked on, the main goal of the approach is to reinsert the parent/caregiver into the protective role supporting the traumatized infant/child (Lieberman et al., 2005). Simultaneously, the infant/child will be provided space to verbally and/or symbolically express the hurtful feelings and memories from the traumatization. Once the trauma experience is expressed and the caregiver/parent is in a supportive/protective position, the child's hyperarousal, numbing, and attachment-based reactions can come under conscious control (Twemlow et al., 2005).

VOICES FROM THE FIELD: JYOTSANA

Dr. Jyotsana Sharma shared her experiences and thoughts around working with youth who have attachment injuries.

In my experience, individuals who suffer attachment injury within non-Western sociocultural contexts show up differently than it is thought of or assessed within the Eurocentric perspective. First, how attachment forms within the sociocultural contexts of the individual child or teen is important to understand. This understanding cannot be surface level and must not be taken lightly. Stereotyping sociocultural norms within a particular ethnicity, race, culture, or community can be detrimental to the well-being of both the client, their contextual systems, as well as the therapeutic relationship. The best approach that I have found working with socioculturally diverse individuals is to listen from their point of view and their lens, really hear what they are trying to describe, believe what they say, and assess on a case-by-case basis by asking the client questions about what they want to see improve instead of forming my ideas of what is best for them.

The sideways approach, instead of the top-down approach, works best; this helps you journey alongside the client, resolve some of the power differential within the counseling relationship, and align with the client. I have experienced the same working with clients' parents—if you as a counselor are able to align with your client and make sure their parents know that your client is your priority, they will be able to accept your role and work with you. Over the years, I have noticed that lack of communication or discrepancy in the encoding and decoding of messages leads to patterns that continue to deepen the emotional distance between child or teen and adults in the family system. Depending on who I am working with and knowing where their unhappiness with their family or sociocultural system stems from, I have found success in asking clients to explore the family histories and systems—look for historical wounds or trauma within the family that can help them gain insight into where healing needs to start. Once that insight is gained, and along the way hopefully empathy and compassion for the family and sociocultural system, we can talk about what will help with wellness and quality of life for them and their family.

VOICES FROM THE FIELD: DANNY

Mr. Danny J. Shearer shared his experiences around working with youth from diverse cultures who demonstrate resistance toward therapy.

In my experience with diverse cultures, a lot of my clients are externally focused on outside validation: drug use, gang activity, stealing behavior, and the need to be cool (i.e., being noticed). The adverse childhood experiences a person has growing up can compromise their security needs. Thus, the looking for "something on the outside to fix me on the inside" increases.

SIBLING ABUSE AND VIOLENCE

Sibling abuse has been defined as the physical, emotional, or sexual injury of one sibling by another. *Sibling violence* has been described in a slightly different manner than sibling abuse due to its bidirectional nature and how it is centered on mutual aggression rather than unilateral nature of sibling abuse (Caspi, 2012). While the rationale for this distinction is understood, for the purposes of this section sibling abuse and violence have been combined. Sibling abuse and violence is one of the most common, least understood, and most underreported forms of family violence in the United States and perhaps the world (Kiselica & Morrill-Richards, 2007). In fact, historically speaking, prior to the 1970s child abuse and neglect was largely considered a family matter that was the responsibility of the parents to manage. When considering the different forms of child abuse, sibling abuse has been largely unacknowledged as abusive and was often framed as horseplay or a normal rite of passage that was related to sibling rivalry (Phillips et al., 2009). True sibling rivalry is when youth siblings compete for a variety of tangible and nontangible things (e.g., achievement, social relationships, attractiveness, toys). Sibling rivalry is mostly harmless and normal, and may even teach and shape youth in positive ways (e.g., understanding of what it means to compete for resources, lessons learned from experiences with winning and losing).

Sibling abuse and violence is centered on repeated patterns of escalating physical or sexual aggression that is primarily motivated by power and control. Behavioral examples of sibling abuse could be pushing, hitting, kicking, beating, using weapons, sexual assault, and humiliating. The negative consequences associated with sibling violence and abuse include psychological and physical harm, injury, traumatization, and death (Kiselica & Morrill-Richards, 2007). Survivors of sibling abuse have reported a myriad of negative consequences related to their history of abuse, including issues with alcohol and drugs, low self-esteem and depression, trauma, complex trauma and PTSD, criminal behavior, eating disorders, and the continuation of inflicting problematic violence and abuse into later years of life (Meyers, 2014; Stutey, 2017; Stutey et al., 2017). Despite its prevalence and being a source of an enormous emotional and physical pain and suffering for youth, prior to the 1970s these matters have a history of being kept private and dealt with by the family. In fact, Eriksen and Jensen (2006, 2009) discovered that sibling violence and abuse was the least researched and reported form of any family maltreatment. There is truly a culture of silence when it comes to sibling abuse and violence.

While research is thin regarding sibling abuse and violence, the information that has been uncovered paints a grim picture regarding the safety of children from their abusive siblings. Regarding prevalence, Kiselica and Morrill-Richards (2007) discovered that approximately 80% of children likely experience some form of sibling abuse and violence during their formative years. Researchers have suggested that sibling abuse and violence is the most common form of childhood victimization (Finkelhor et al., 2005), with 23% of familial incest victims indicating that they are survivors of sibling sexual assault (Rudd & Herzberger, 1999). Furthermore, Button and Gealt (2010) found that 30% to 80% of youth experience some form of sibling violence, and 3% to 6% of children have experienced sibling violence that involves weapons and objects that cause physical pain. In a research study surveying college students' perceptions of childhood abuse, Hoffman et al. (2005) discovered that over 60% of participants had experienced physical sibling violence. Similarly, Simonelli et al. (2002) discovered a large percentage of female (98%) and male (89%) participants describing an experience of emotional abuse from siblings. Lastly, research has indicated that sibling incest and sexual assault are a large-scale problem. For example, Caffaro and Conn-Caffaro (1998) determined that, although severely underreported, sibling sexual assault and incest take place much more frequently than parent-to-child sexual assault and incest. Similarly, classic research indicated that 60% of psychiatric outpatients had experienced some form of sibling sexual assault and incest (Bess & Janssen, 1982).

There are a variety of contextual factors to consider when discussing sibling abuse and violence. First, the age of the child can play a factor in the likelihood of abuse and violence. Young children who have fewer verbal skills use more violence. As children develop more effective verbal skills, their desire to use violence decreases. Siblings closer in age often experience a greater degree of violence than siblings further apart in age. Male to male siblings often demonstrate the most abuse and the most physical violence (Barnett et al., 2005; Noland et al., 2004). Regarding gender differences in sibling abuse, boys are more likely to engage in sibling abuse and violence and admit to being the perpetrators of sibling violence much more often than girls do (Caffaro & Conn-Caffaro, 1998; Kiselica & Morrill-Richards, 2007). Generally, boys are physically stronger, making abuse easier to employ. Furthermore, societal male gender role socialization encourages competitive and aggressive behaviors more intensively than female socialization messages, which can create gender-biased messages around permissiveness and acceptability of sibling abuse (Caffaro & Conn-Caffaro, 1998). Lastly, children exist in a comparative familial context (i.e., they frequently compare their experiences, goals, and possessions). Parents can unfortunately play into this by identifying siblings as good versus bad in some way. This role assignment can create a lot of unnecessary competition and rivalry, which can lead to future abuse and violence. For example, the parents described one sibling as athletic and the other as good at school, creating a situation that amplifies sibling insecurity with one another. They begin comparing each other in different ways (e.g., goals, achievements), leading to further aggression (Dunn & Plomin, 1991; Newman, 1994).

Following the Child Abuse Prevention and Treatment Act (CAPTA), originally enacted on January 31, 1974, clinicians became legally required to notify any suspicion of child abuse and neglect to statewide child protective services (CPS) agencies (Child Welfare Information Gateway, 2019). While CAPTA has been extremely helpful in protecting children from parent/adult-to-child abuse and neglect and sibling sexual abuse, there is currently no federal law and few state laws safeguarding youth from sibling abuse (Stutey, 2017; Stutey et al., 2017). The family culture of silence around familial abuse and violence typically starts with parents providing minimal consequences, boundaries, and education to their children regarding the harmful effects of siblings hurting each other. Parents may also inadvertently encourage further violence by describing it as a normal part of growing up, framing it as rivalry or horseplay, or informing their children to toughen up and/or fight back. This is precisely where the seeds of silence are planted, and underreporting comes into play. Specifically, because of the aforementioned family interactions, youth may feel that in speaking to others about their experiences they are betraying their family or being disloyal to the spoken/unspoken family vow of silence regarding sibling abuse and violence (Stutey, 2017; Stutey et al., 2017).

Relevant Skills and Interventions

As previously stated, there is a dearth of research examining the treatment of sibling abuse, and culturally it is a topic that is often inappropriately conceptualized as sibling rivalry or horseplay. Given the serious nature of sibling abuse and violence, it is important that clinicians avoid any intentional or unintentional minimizing of the abusive nature of these behaviors. According to Kiselica and Morrill-Richards (2007), due to the taboo and shame-inducing nature of sibling abuse, counseling can be especially difficult for youth and families. Additionally, many children and adolescents may be defensive, resistant, and uninterested in cooperating due to being forced by parents, courts, and/ or schools to participate in treatment. Given these factors, clinicians should be very thoughtful about establishing a safe therapeutic atmosphere, immediately engaging in the relationship-building process, and creating a nonthreatening atmosphere where children/adolescents can open up about the abuse. All of this becomes much harder if parents and/or children are mandated to participate in therapy.

If the siblings or the family is required to attend therapy involuntarily, clinicians are encouraged to go with the resistant energy and empathize with the discouraging nature of being required to do something they do not want to do. Clinicians could also offer to be an advocate for voluntary participation in treatment. Horne and Sayger (1990) described the notion of making a deal with the family in which the practitioner agrees to advocate with the court or school for voluntary participation in treatment in exchange for the family engaging in helpful strategies centered on reducing violence and abuse between siblings. Kiselica and Morrill Richards (2007) suggested approaching the family from a psychoeducational framework regarding helping them understand the nature of sibling abuse. During this psychoeducational experience, the clinician will teach the family about the nature of the problematic sibling behaviors and how the abuse is a learned response that is harmful and must be stopped. Regarding learned behavior, clinicians convey the idea that at some point the aggressive sibling discovered that they receive some sort of reinforcer if they abuse their sibling. The entire family is then invited to consider changing this problematic sibling behavior (Horne & Sayger, 1990).

During treatment, couple, marriage, and family practitioners must work hard to keep the focus on the entire system. The perpetrator of sibling violence may feel as if they are being scapegoated by the rest of the family. Additionally, the sibling victim may feel fearful that the process of therapy may cause the abusive sibling to engage in retaliatory behavior. If this is the case, the clinician must clearly communicate that this is a systemic problem that needs to be addressed by everyone in the family. This should reduce the shame and scapegoating the aggressive sibling may be experiencing. Simultaneously, the clinician must encourage the parents/caregivers to create space for the victim of the abuse to express their fears and pain. Following this disclosure, the parents must brainstorm ways to ensure there is appropriate supervision and boundaries at home.

As the family begins working through the issues related to sibling violence, clinicians frequently assure the parents/caregivers that the best progress is made when the entire family takes responsibility and works towards positive change (Horne & Sayger, 1990; Kiselica & Morrill-Richards, 2007). The American Association for Marriage and Family Therapy (AAMFT) encourages practitioners to be mindful of the following issues when conducting therapy around sibling abuse: (a) avoid minimizing rivalries between siblings by indicating similarities in their behavior; (b) avoid indicating differences in their behavior; (c) encourage positive and sensitive behaviors between siblings; (d) indicate ground rules upfront (e.g., no insults, physical aggression, belittling, taunting, coercive behavior); (e) set individual therapy experiences with each sibling; (f) encourage parents to monitor youth media choices and encourage healthy nonviolent choices;

TABLE 10.3 SAFE PROTOCOL

S	*Stop* any abusive, violent, or aggressive behavior immediately and work with family members to create a problem-solving culture.
A	*Assess* what has taken place and allow everyone a chance to share their thoughts and feelings about the situation.
F	*Find* out the best way to help siblings maintain a sense of peace and functional interactions (e.g., establish rules, responsibilities, method for handling disputes).
E	*Evaluate* new ways of handling business (rules, responsibilities, etc.) and determine if the change is reducing violence and abuse.

Source: Data from Wiehe, V. R. (2002). *What parents need to know about sibling abuse: Breaking the cycle of violence.* Bonneville Books.

(g) avoid solving sibling problems; (h) remind siblings the appropriate process for solving problems and disagreements; (i) hold each sibling equally responsible when agreed-upon rules are broken; (j) teach siblings to compromise; and (k) respect others and ensure the siblings have equal power within the sibling subsystem (Caffaro, n.d.).

While the focus is on the entire family system, throughout therapy, the couple, marriage, and family practitioner will change the therapeutic format to couple, parental, or individual as needed. As the family members make progress toward a safer nonviolent home environment, the clinician will inquire about family and sibling strengths. Families are encouraged to positively reinforce prosocial behaviors at home and in session. As various individual and family strengths are being emphasized, the clinician may provide psychoeducation on the harmful effects of abusive behaviors they notice (e.g., coercion). The tangible goals of treatment are to eventually cocreate healthy rules of conduct indicating the nature of appropriate and inappropriate sibling behaviors. Practitioners could enhance the agreed-upon list with reinforcers for appropriate behavior and punishment for inappropriate sibling behavior (e.g., contingency management, cost response). Siblings work in session on developing conflict resolution strategies for common issues that previously led to violence and/or abuse. Lastly, the family will consider additional external factors that add unnecessary pressure to the siblings and other family members (e.g., school, peer groups, contextual variables, racism), and potential solutions/coping skills (Hazler, 1996; Kiselica & Morrill-Richards, 2007; Wiehe, 2002). Table 10.3 describes the SAFE protocol developed by Wiehe (2002) to address sibling violence. This can be used as a guide for clinically addressing sibling abuse and violence.

VOICES FROM THE FIELD: DANNY

Mr. Danny J. Shearer shared his experiences around working with youth from diverse cultures who come from abusive homes.

In an abusive home, the eldest child usually gets the brunt of the abuse. Their empowerment needs can increase the frequency of abuse toward the younger siblings as a sense of empowerment or flexing one's muscle. In a Hispanic home, where the father is absent, the eldest boy becomes the "papasito" (i.e., little dad). Sometimes the family dynamic has bestowed the title onto him or even her, mostly covert and indirect. I tend to deal with this matter, when it is emotional and physical, with every mindfulness skill imaginable. I will tell a young client, "Let's work on being 15 years old versus being 45, like your dad." Working on not being parentified and being in the moment is essential.

According to the Centers for Disease Control and Prevention (CDC), bullying is a systemic experience deeply impacting victims of the bully, those who bully other people, and bystanders witnessing the bullying. According to Swearer and Hymel (2015), there is very little stability in the bullying role for youth. Many students experienced being in different bullying-oriented roles (e.g., bully, victim, bystander) across various times and contexts. While bullying can take place at any age, for the purposes of this chapter *bullying* is defined as a type of youth-based (i.e., child and adolescent) violence where unwanted aggressive behaviors are expressed by one youth or a group of youths toward another youth with the intent of deliberately causing harm.

Bullying is something that typically involves an imbalance of perceived power. It is usually a reoccurring form of violence involving one or more of the following: physical harm (e.g., punching, pushing), verbal insults or hurtful comments (e.g., name calling, derogatory statements), social and/or relational sabotaging (e.g., hurtful rumors, ostracizing from the group), or online defamation of character (e.g., social media comments). The negative consequences that often happen as a result of bullying include, but are not limited to, physical injury, trauma, stress, self-harming behaviors, academic problems, substance abuse, and death via suicide or homicide (CDC, 2019). Bullying frequently goes unreported. Children and adolescents often think (a) that nothing can be done to stop the bullying, (b) they will not be taken seriously, and/or (c) reaching out for help with the bullying issue will only increase the frequency of bullying behavior they have to endure.

Regarding the characteristics common to those who bully, scholars have found that perpetrators of bullying can be callous and unemotional, be higher in social intelligence, demonstrate psychopathic tendencies, be anxious, endorse masculine traits, have issues with problematic conduct, be victims to peer pressure, have antisocial personality traits, and be depressed (Fanti & Kimonis, 2012; Muñoz et al., 2011; Navarro et al., 2011). Regarding the traits of victims of bullying, scholars have found that they are likely to be rejected by peers, demonstrate symptoms related to hyperactivity, have physical health issues, have poor adjustment ability, have lower performance ability, be truant, and drop out of school (Gini & Pozzoli, 2013; Knack et al., 2011; Kumpulainen et al., 2001; Swearer & Hymel, 2015; Veenstra et al., 2007).

According to the National Center for Education Statistics (2019), 20.2% (one out of every five) of U.S. students report being bullied. According to student victims of bullying, the common motives behind being bullied include physical appearance, race/ethnicity, gender, disability, religion, and sexual orientation. A slightly higher percentage of female students reported being bullied at school (24% female vs. 17% male). Victims of bullying reported a few of the most common hurtful activities, including being made fun of, called names, or insulted (13%); a large percentage were victims of disparaging rumors (13%); a smaller percentage (5%) were pushed, shoved, tripped, or spit on; and 5% of victims were intentionally excluded and/or ostracized from groups/activities.

Regarding gender, males reported a larger percentage of physical bullying experiences (6% male vs. 4% female). Interestingly, a much higher percentage of female students experienced being bullied via rumor induction/slander (18% female vs. 9% male) and being intentionally ostracized and excluded from events (7% female vs. 4% male). Bullied students reported that bullying commonly occurred in the following places: the hallway or stairwell at school (43%), inside the classroom (42%), in the cafeteria (27%), outside on school grounds (22%), online or by text (15%), in the bathroom or locker room (12%), and on the school bus (8%). Lastly, while 46% of bullied students reported notifying an adult at school about the incident, a large percent (41%) of student victims reported that they believed the bullying would reoccur whether or not adults were informed (National Center for Education Statistics, 2019).

Online bullying (i.e., cyberbullying) is a hidden and extremely painful phenomenon, and is also a growing cultural concern. For example, an investigation by Patchin and Hinduja (2019) indicated that between the years 2007 and 2019 the percentage of individuals who suffered from online bullying more than doubled (18%–37%). According to the massive data set collected by the National Center for Education Statistics (2019), of the students (ages 12–18) who reported school-based bullying, 15% were bullied online or via text message. While this report indicated a unique population that experienced online bullying, Hamm et al. (2015) found that those who experienced physical bullying were also much more likely to be bullied online. Regarding prevalence, Modecki et al. (2014) conducted a meta-analysis of 80 bullying investigations and determined that 15% of all contemporary school-based bullying took place online. Online bullying has been found to peak in middle school (CDC, 2019). Additionally, Patchin and Hinduja (2020) discovered that 20.9% (one in every five) of youth aged 9 to 12 experienced online bullying. Patchin and Hinduja (2019) discovered that the top hurtful online bullying experiences included mean comments (25%) and disparaging rumors (22%). Lastly, regarding online gender differences, boys were found to have experienced a greater percentage of online physical threats, while girls were more likely to say someone spread rumors about them online.

According to Reed et al. (2015), there is a long-standing and strong correlation between youth experiencing bullying and suicidal-related behaviors, depression, violent activities, and substance use. Similarly, the CDC National Center for Injury Prevention and Control (2014) reported that youth who frequently describe being bullied are at an increased risk of suicide-related activities. While the CDC reports this powerful correlation, they also warn of the threat that normalizing the link between suicide and bullying could unintentionally cause the subsequent risk by creating suicide copycat behaviors among youth. A meta-analysis found that students who faced bullying were 2.2 times more likely to disclose the presence of suicidal ideation and 2.6 times more likely to engage in suicidal behavior when compared with nonvictimized peers (Gini & Espelage, 2014). Lastly, Espelage and Holt (2013) found that youth who both engage in bullying and are bullied are the highest risk group for suicide and serious mental health consequences.

Bias-Based Bullying

According to Walton (2018), bias-based bullying is a type of bullying that is directed at a marginalized community due to the individual's race, ethnicity, gender, religious belief, weight, sexual orientation, or ability. Phillips (2018) added that bias-based bullying is centered on youth bullying someone else because of who they are and/or some aspect of their identity. This bullying behavior includes things like hate crimes, offensive jokes, insensitive comments, and physically threatening and/or hurting someone based on their personhood. For example, an adolescent might start a rumor that assaults the character or slanders the reputation of a youth due to the color of their skin or sexual orientation. This bullying behavior can be engaged in a variety of formats (e.g., physical, verbal, social, or online) and is a systemic abuse of power that is intentional and engaged in frequently. Bias-based bullying brings a lot of negative consequences to targets representing one or more marginalized communities. In addition to the previously described negative youth outcomes that emerge as a result of bullying, a few of the health consequences found to be associated with bias-based bullying include (a) decrease in quality of life, (b) emergence of depressive symptomology, (c) decrease in self-esteem, (d) anxiety symptomology, and (e) negative behavioral patterns that are indicative of conduct disorder (Brody et al., 2006; Umana-Taylor & Updegraff, 2007; Walton, 2018).

Russell et al. (2012) found bias-based school bullying to affect more than one-third of all adolescents surveyed. Russell et al. also discovered that compared with general bullying, bias-based bullying was strongly linked to compromised health in youth. Contemporary research conducted by the National Center for Education Statistics (2019) took a closer look and indicated that in the United States, 23% of African American students, 23% of Caucasian students, 16% of Hispanic students, and 7% of Asian students indicated being bullied. Regarding bullying that is specifically centered on a youth's race, Rosenthal et al. (2015) discovered that bullying behavior and race-based bullying behavior were significantly correlated with negative physical health effects and emotions.

Kosciw et al. (2018) discovered that in a year time frame 70.1% of individuals who identified as LGBTQIA+ were verbally bullied due to bias against their sexual orientation, 59.1% were bullied due to their gender expression, and 53.2% were bias-bullied due to their gender. Additionally, regarding the style of bullying engaged in, Kosciw et al. (2018) found that 28.9% of their participants were physically bullied due to their sexual orientation and 48.7% experienced online bullying within the year. Additionally, Kosciw et al. (2018) discovered the school experience was very difficult for youth. Specifically, due to their sexual orientation, 59.5% of LGBTQIA+ students felt fearful and unsafe while attending school. Similarly, 44.6% of Kosciw et al.'s participants felt unsafe at school due to their gender expression and 35% due to their gender. Lastly, of the LGBTQIA+ students who reported they were considering dropping out of school, 42.2% indicated they were doing so due to the bias-based bullying they frequently faced at school.

Relevant Skills and Interventions

Bullying is a major public health problem that has sparked considerable research and scholarship. It is also a significant issue that preteens and teens face on a number of platforms (e.g., school, home, online). According to the AAMFT, the most effective bullying interventions involve multiple stakeholders (e.g., students [children], parents, teachers, members of the community). When adults from multiple areas of the child's life are involved, better results can be achieved due to everyone working together. Clinicians who hear about an instance of bullying should empathize and believe the victim. Additionally, helpers engage victims with listening and asking *who*, *when*, *how*, and *where* questions. The second step should include involving the bystanders in some way. Bystanders often do nothing about the bullying, or encourage it by witnessing it and socially reinforcing it. When bystanders witness the bullying and choose not to report it, they are creating a bigger problem for everyone involved (Pinjala & Pierce n.d.). Lastly, most schools have carefully created policies that outline an antibullying culture and what the consequences are if bullying occurs. Best practice suggests that these policies be applied equally to all students in the same manner. Table 10.4 provides a concise breakdown of major bullying prevention programs, program descriptions, and pertinent references.

According to O'Brien and Giordano (2017), when working with the victim of bullying, it is important for the clinician to listen, empathize, and serve as an advocate. While helping the victim is key, there should be a deliberate effort to encourage the victim to avoid being a passive participant, or from being completely dependent on adults to protect them from the bullying behavior. This inadvertently creates a sense of passiveness on the part of the victim, which essentially makes them targets. Regarding advocacy, a school counselor or a community-based practitioner could serve as a helpful aid in speaking with school administration, teachers, or the authorities. Lastly, while there

TABLE 10.4   BULLYING PREVENTION PROGRAM NAME, BRIEF DESCRIPTION, AND HELPFUL REFERENCES

Program Name	Brief Description	Helpful References
Comprehensive schoolwide bullying intervention programs	These programs have a standard set of materials used to create safe and supportive school environments that prevent bullying in multiple ways through antibullying campaigns, restorative justice, intervention programs focusing on individual counseling, groups, classrooms, and the entire school.	Farrington, D. P., & Ttofi, M. M. (2009). School-based programs to reduce bullying and victimization. *Campbell Systemic Reviews, 6,* 1–148.
STAC	STAC is a program that trains the bystanders to intervene and defend victims of bullying. STAC stands for *stealing* the show (i.e., using humor to distract students from the bullying behavior), *turning* it over (i.e., asking a safe adult for help), *accompanying* others (i.e., reaching out to the victim and saying this was inappropriate), and *coaching* compassion (i.e., encouraging a sense of understanding within the bully by encouraging empathy).	Moran, M., Midgett, A., & Doumas, D. M. (2019). Evaluation of a brief, bystander bullying intervention (STAC) for ethnically blended middle schools in low-income communities. *Professional School Counseling, 23*(1). https://doi.org/10.1177/2156759X20940641.
Bully Busters	Bully Busters is a research-based approach centered on using psychoeducation to control and prevent bullying. The content of the program includes information regarding bullying and victimization, interventions, prevention strategies, stress management techniques, and classroom activities. Modules include awareness of the bullying, recognizing the bully, recognizing the victim, teaching charge, assisting the victim, the role of prevention, and relaxation and coping.	Horne, A. M., Bartolomucci, C. L., & Newman-Carlson, D. (2003). *Bully busters: A teacher's manual for helping bullies, victims, and bystanders, grades K–5.* Research Press.
Bully-Proofing Your School	BPYS is intended to reduce bullying and increase knowledge about school safety for students, teachers, and parents. BPYS includes three major components: (a) heightening awareness of bullying; (b) teaching antibullying skills, avoiding victimization, and helping victims; and (c) building a positive school climate by involving the caring majority (i.e., bystanders). The caring majority is the most powerful group for creating a safe and compassionate school.	Garrity, C., Jens, K., Porter, W., Sager, N., & Short-Camilli, C. (1994). *Bully-proofing your school.* Sopris West.

(continued)

TABLE 10.4   BULLYING PREVENTION PROGRAM NAME, BRIEF DESCRIPTION, AND HELPFUL REFERENCES (*CONTINUED*)

Program Name	Brief Description	Helpful References
Steps to Respect	Steps to Respect was created to reduce school bullying problems by (a) enhancing staff understanding and responsiveness, (b) promoting socially responsible principles, and (c) educating others on the social-emotional skills used to counter bullying. Thus, the program also aims to promote skills (e.g., group joining, conflict resolution) associated with general social competence. There is a dual focus on bullying and friendship because friendship protects children from the negative effects of bullying. This comprehensive program includes a schoolwide program guide, training, and classroom modules for students in grades 3 through 6.	Committee for Children. (2001). *Steps to respect: A bullying prevention program.* Author.
Bully Prevention in Positive Behavior Support	BP-PBS is centered on removing antecedents and consequences that support bullying behaviors. The program is structured around a three-tier process. Tier 1 includes creating a positive and predictable environment for students at all times of the day. Tier 2 involves skills used with small groups of children who are struggling with the first tier. These groups receive more reinforcements, and professionals create individualized antecedents and consequences framework. Tier 3 includes support for students who do not respond to the first two tiers. It generally includes a very thorough analysis of the antecedents and consequences that maintain the bullying behavior.	Ross, S. W., & Horner, R. H. (2009). Bully prevention in positive behavior support. *Journal of applied behavior analysis, 42*(4), 747–759. https://doi.org/10.1901/jaba.2009.42-747.
Target Bullying Intervention Program	TBIP is an individualized cognitive behavioral program for students who have engaged in bullying behavior on multiple occasions. This program consists of one-on-one 3-hour cognitive behavioral interventions and instructions. Parents of student bullies are also included in the treatment. Parents of these students are part of treatment and are provided with surveys and feedback meetings, and counselors and teachers provide parents with specific feedback and practical recommendations.	Strawhun, J., Fluke, S., & Peterson, R. (2013, October). *The Target Bullying Intervention Program, program brief.* Student Engagement Project, University of Nebraska-Lincoln and the Nebraska Department of Education. http://k12engagement.unl.edu/target-bullying.

(continued)

TABLE 10.4   BULLYING PREVENTION PROGRAM NAME, BRIEF DESCRIPTION, AND HELPFUL REFERENCES (*CONTINUED*)

Program Name	Brief Description	Helpful References
Promoting Alternative Thinking Strategies	The PATHS program is a schoolwide initiative that was developed to reduce bullying, violence, aggression, and negative externalizing behaviors. While reducing these negative behaviors, students are encouraged to engage in healthy, peaceful, and adaptive styles of interacting. The PATHS modules are centered on helping youth in kindergarten through sixth grade.	Greenberg, M. T., Kusche, C. A., & Mihalic, S. (1998). *Promoting Alternative Thinking Strategies (PATHS; Book 10, Blueprints for Violence Prevention)*. Center for the Study and Prevention of Violence, Institute of Behavioral Science, University of Colorado at Boulder.

BP-PBS, Bully Prevention in Positive Behavior Support; BPYS, Bully-Proofing Your School; PATHS, Promoting Alternative Thinking Strategies; TBIP, Target Bullying Intervention Program.

is not any universal way to handle a bully, a few tips that may help youth include (a) never responding to online bullying attacks and always taking screenshots of the conversation; (b) always informing a trusted adult or stakeholder about what is happening; (c) immediately escaping situations in which the bully tries to be physical; (d) keeping trusted friends with them to avoid unwanted encounters; and (e) encouraging the youth to document repetitive patterns of bullying with the name of the bully, date, behavior, and location (GoodTherapy, n.d.).

Youth who bully others could also likely benefit from therapy. Unfortunately, these youth may be uninterested in acknowledging their bullying behavior. If they engage openly in treatment, they may gain insight into how their hurtful behaviors have negatively affected others, introspect on the reasons they engage in bullying behavior, and possibly learn new methods for communicating in a positive manner. People who engage in bullying behaviors often have an unresolved issue from childhood that possibly informs their bullying behaviors. Engaging with a clinician can be a helpful step toward addressing these issues from the past and stopping the bullying behavior (GoodTherapy, n.d.).

VOICES FROM THE FIELD: JYOTSANA

Dr. Jyotsana Sharma shared her experiences and thoughts around working with youth who have experienced bias-based bullying.

Bias-based bullying is an issue, and with the use of social media it has had a detrimental effect on the mental and emotional well-being of children and adolescents. Bias-based bullying has also taken a more subtle form with microaggressions, microinsults like "you speak great English compared to other Asians I've met," and microinvalidations like "being poor has nothing to do with making better choices." In my experience, this is a systemic issue and the major contributor to this issue is the sociopolitical climate that facilitates divisions and othering. Often, efforts to provide inclusive experiences can also lead to stereotyping and exclusion if the efforts are not well thought out. For example, if providing groups or interventions for youth who do not feel included, we offer a group on the third floor in a school without elevator access, we are automatically excluding individuals who are differently abled, or we offer cultural workshops that stay at a superficial level and paint marginalized communities single dimensionally. Bias-based bullying leads to disempowerment, and the way I have worked with disempowered youth is to try my best to provide them with choices they do have access to or create opportunities for those choices. It is extremely easy to state anecdotally that "we always have a choice," but do we really? For youth who have been historically and systemically marginalized and minoritized, it may not always be clear. My job then is to figure what that avenue might be through which my client feels empowered—and this is speaking on the individual counseling level.

VOICES FROM THE FIELD: DANNY

Mr. Danny J. Shearer shared his thoughts on the internal experiences youth have when they have experienced bias-based bullying.

Kids who are affected by bias-based bullying are constantly in the fight/flight mode (sympathetic activation). They have difficulty feeling safe or connected in order to function in school. One of my teen clients called it a "trifecta," being Latino, gay, and overweight. He is even shunned by his own culture.

LEARNING DISABILITIES

Every couple, marriage, and family practitioner should have a solid understanding of learning disabilities (LDs) due to the unique issues that emerge for youth and families affected. Sometimes LDs are referred to as learning disorders, and within the *Diagnostic and Statistical Manual of Mental Disorders*, Fifth Edition, Text Revision (*DSM-5-TR*; American Psychiatric Association, 2022), LDs are known as specific learning disorders. Regarding the organization of the *DSM-5-TR*, the specific learning disorder category includes the specifiers of impairment, including mathematics, reading, and written expression. The *DSM* defines *LDs* as neurodevelopmental disorders diagnosed in early childhood that are centered on persistent impairment in reading, written expression, and math. Specific learning disorders are further categorized as mild, moderate, and severe (American Psychiatric Association, 2022). Lastly, since there is a genetic predisposition associated with LDs, there are likely additional family members diagnosed with an LD in the family.

LDs affect education, mental health, and socialization. From an educational perspective, people with LDs are at risk of not attaining higher educational degrees, and if left untreated youth have a high probability of attaching a negative label to school and education (Hakkarainen et al., 2015). From a mental health perspective, youth with LDs are at higher risk of developing depression and anxiety (Maag & Reid, 2006; Nelson & Harwood, 2011), autism spectrum disorder (ASD), and attention deficit hyperactivity disorder (ADHD; Emerson & Hatton, 2007). Lastly, during the transitory and adjustment-oriented time of adolescence, youth diagnosed with an LD can experience a variety of challenging psychosocial outcomes, including loneliness, stress, and negative peer relationships (Locke et al., 2010; Whitehouse et al., 2009).

While LDs can create academic challenges, they are not related to how intelligent a child is, and although LDs cannot be cured they can be treated, managed, and minimized. According to Cortiella and Horowitz (2014), LDs are caused by neurobiological variations in brain composition and function. These variations can affect the way individuals communicate, store, process, receive, and retrieve information. Furthermore, LDs should not be confused with intellectual disabilities or developmental disabilities. Intellectual disabilities are based on an individual with a below-average intelligence quotient (IQ) and who often does not possess the skills needed for daily living (e.g., fetal alcohol syndrome, fragile X syndrome, genetic conditions, birth defects).

Developmental disabilities are very serious lifelong issues that affect people physically and/or cognitively (e.g., Down syndrome, cerebral palsy, blindness; CDC, 2022).

According to the American Psychiatric Association (2013), LDs affect approximately 5% to 15% of all people. Altarac and Saroha (2007) discovered the lifetime prevalence of LDs in U.S. youth was 9.7%. Although much attention is centered on childhood, LDs are known to often continue into adulthood. The most common type of LD is a reading disability (RD; Shaywitz et al., 2008). Approximately 80% of youth diagnosed with a specific learning disorder have a reading impairment specification. Dyslexia is the most common reading-oriented LD, affecting approximately 20% of the U.S. population (American Psychiatric Association, 2013; Shaywitz et al., 2021). Other LDs, such as in mathematics and written expression, are also quite prevalent (Moll et al., 2015). Prevalence rates indicate 7% of youth are affected by a mathematics-specific learning disorder and 3% to 5% of youth are affected by a disorder in written expression (American Psychiatric Association, 2013; Geary, 2012). While not recognized as an LD, ASD and ADHD often impact and/or are cooccurring neurodevelopmental disorders (American Psychiatric Association, 2013). Lastly, speech–language impairments (S/LI) are considered significant LD risk factors. S/LIs are very common in U.S. schools, and from a national perspective approximately 20% of all students with disabilities have an S/LI (U.S. Department of Education, 2018).

According to the CDC, when youth try hard to learn and still struggle with a specific set of skills over time, it could be a sign of an LD. Symptoms could include the following: difficulty telling right from left; reversing letters, words, or numbers after second grade; difficulty recognizing patterns or sorting by shape; difficulty understanding and following instructions or staying organized; difficulty remembering what was just said or read; lacking coordination; difficulty doing tasks with hands; and difficulty understanding the concept of time (CDC, n.d.). Clinicians should have a good understanding of the seven common LDs: dyslexia, dysgraphia, dyscalculia, auditory processing disorder, language processing disorder, nonverbal LDs, and visual perceptual/visual motor deficits. Table 10.5 depicts the common LDs, concise descriptions, and pertinent examples.

Students who qualify for an LD need supportive services to treat, manage, and minimize the effects. It is important for couple, marriage, and family practitioners to understand how families with children who have been diagnosed as having an LD afford expensive school-based services. In the United States, students with disabilities receive special education services under categories specified within the 2004 Individuals with Disabilities Education Act (IDEA). The specific learning disability (SLD) category of IDEA has certain requirements that qualify students for LD service. According to the IDEA (2004), to qualify for services, students must have difficulty with reading, writing, oral language, or math, in the absence of other cognitive, sensory, neurologic, or behavioral deficits (Weinstein et al., 2019). One of the best methods a parent can use to take control of their child's education is to advocate with their local school for the resources they need to succeed in the educational environment.

Since 2002, there has been a cultural push to support the mainstreaming, integration, and inclusion of students with LDs. Specifically, the No Child Left Behind Act (NCLB; 2002–2015) was the antecedent to the current Every Student Succeeds Act (ESSA), which supports the notion that all youth should receive a comparable education in the least restrictive environment regardless of intellectual, physical, or emotional ability. This sense of inclusion is experienced by families when they meet with school officials to develop individualized education programs (IEPs) for their child or adolescent that will be enacted upon within the school. The IEP is developed to provide youth diagnosed with LDs the necessary support to succeed in the academic environment and to receive important special education and related services (Weinstein et al., 2019).

TABLE 10.5 LEARNING DISABILITIES, DESCRIPTIONS, AND EXAMPLES

Learning Disability	Description	Examples
Dyslexia	Dyslexia is a language processing disorder that impacts reading, writing, and comprehension.	Difficulty decoding words or with phonemic awareness, identifying individual sounds within words
Dysgraphia	Dysgraphia is difficulty translating thoughts into writing (e.g., spelling, grammar, vocabulary, critical thinking, or memory).	Difficulty exhibiting letter spacing, poor motor planning and spatial awareness, trouble thinking and writing simultaneously
Dyscalculia	Dyscalculia is a learning disability centered on mathematical calculations. Individuals with dyscalculia struggle with math concepts, numbers, and reasoning.	Difficulty understanding clocks, counting money, recognizing patterns, recalling math facts, solving mental math
Auditory processing disorder	Auditory processing disorder is when people cognitively misunderstand information received and processed from the ear.	Difficulty processing sounds, confusing the order of sounds, being unable to filter different sounds (e.g., differentiating a voice from background noise)
Language processing disorder	Language processing disorder has to do with specific challenges in processing spoken language, impacting both listening and speaking skills.	Difficulty attaching meaning to sound groupings that create words, sentences, and stories
Nonverbal learning disabilities	Nonverbal learning disabilities are issues centered on decoding nonverbal behaviors and/or social signals.	Difficulty understanding body language, facial expressions and tone of voice, or the nonverbal aspects of communication
Visual perceptual/visual motor deficit	Visual perceptual/visual motor deficits include issues with the way the brain processes visual information and difficulty with fine motor activities.	Difficulty with hand–eye coordination; losing one's place when reading; difficulty using pencils, crayons, glue, and scissors; confusing similar-looking letters

Sources: Information derived from American Psychiatric Association. (2022). *Diagnostic and statistical manual of mental disorders* (5th edition, text revision). https://doi.org/10.1176/appi.books.9780890425787; and Centers for Disease Control and Prevention. (2021, February 22). *Learning disorders in children.* Retrieved April 4, 2022, from https://www.cdc.gov/ncbddd/childdevelopment/learning-disorder.html.

Youth who are diagnosed with an LD may have additional academic, relational, and family challenges. There is a tremendous amount of support in place centered on enhancing issues that are associated with most LDs. Strategies typically emerge as the result of numerous professionals (e.g., teachers, occupational therapists, school counselors) working together to create an IEP. These supportive services can also provide strategies that can assist youth in coping with the feelings that emerge from being diagnosed with an LD. Youth can feel a sense of stigma for a variety of reasons, including (a) being labeled with an LD, (b) being taken from their normal classroom for supportive education, and/or (c) finding it extremely challenging to cope with watching their peers move at a faster pace within the educational environment. Alternatively, if the child or adolescent receives much-needed educational services after a period of struggle, they may feel a great sense of relief and begin to realize future goals they could not have previously imagined. From a therapeutic perspective, family and/or individual therapy can be extremely helpful in assisting youth with LDs. Furthermore, modalities such as brief solution-focused therapy, support groups, family therapy, parent education, and play therapy can offer much-needed support and healing (Baum, 2007; Zieglar & Holden, 1988).

Couple, marriage, and family practitioners who assist youth by offering family-based services will likely work with parents who worry that their child will not succeed in school; however, given the number of accommodations in place, this is often not the case. Through providing parents with clear education on what their child's LD entails, how the professionals (within and outside of the school) will be assisting them, and how the parents can assist their child through adjusting the home environment to support areas of difficulty, parents can feel a great sense of support and relief. Parents should also be informed about the best parenting strategies to use when their child or adolescent is becoming angry and stressed because they feel they are working very hard and still receiving less than desirable results. Parents should work on supporting the child or adolescent, avoid minimizing the challenges, empathize with their pain, and help them understand that while LDs are lifelong challenges there are many methods and strategies available to help them achieve their dreams (Baum, 2007; Zieglar & Holden, 1988).

PLAY THERAPY

One long-standing approach to helping youth is play therapy. While the use of play in the treatment of youth was established by pioneers of child and adolescent counseling (e.g., Anna Freud, Melanie Klein, Margaret Lowenfeld), Virginia Axline (1911–1988) is the "Mother of Play Therapy" and the creator of nondirective (i.e., child-centered) play therapy (Pehrsson & Aguilera, 2007). While play therapy formally began with child-centered (i.e., nondirective) play therapy, there have been many theoretical variations, including, but not limited to, Adlerian play therapy, Jungian play therapy, cognitive behavioral play therapy, ecosystemic play therapy, gestalt play therapy, and psychodynamic play therapy (Kottman, 2011). The power of *play* is partly centered on helping children (a) heal psychological wounds and hurts; (b) express what is troubling them non verbally, verbally, behaviorally, and symbolically; (c) improve their understanding and awareness of important roles; (d) enhance their survival and adaptive behaviors; and (e) expand their emotional or social skills. Unfortunately, these incredible benefits can be missed by adults who may consider play as nothing more than something children do to pass time. Kottman (2011) defined *play therapy* as "an approach to counseling young children in which the clinician uses toys, art supplies, games, and other play media to communicate with clients using the 'language' of children—the 'language' of play" (p. 4). Play therapy is an evidence-based approach to helping children through a myriad of mental health issues; for a comprehensive review of the evidence base for play therapy skills and techniques, please see Phillips (2010) and Ray and McCullough (2015).

In a general sense, play therapy assists children suffering from a wide variety of social, emotional, behavioral, and learning problems by offering them a therapeutic process to symbolically play out their experiences; work through their emotional hurts; and cocreate a positive and enhanced understanding of self, others, and the world. Furthermore, play therapy has been found to access, influence, and rewire the sensory experiences stored in the brain (Green et al., 2010). The play therapist utilizes warm and empathic skills to encourage the child to feel a sense of safety and empowerment as they project their emotions, thoughts, and experiences on the various play mediums (toys, paint, sand art, dress-up). In addition, the play therapist intentionally utilizes play therapy skills to encourage children to express what is concerning them. At times, children will not have the vocabulary or awareness to express certain thoughts and feelings. The play therapist helps children express themselves in a developmentally appropriate manner that is a safe psychological distance from their problems (Kottman, 2011; Ray, 2011). Play therapy ranges in degree of structure, provides a collection of empirically based techniques, and is theoretically grounded in a variety of therapeutic traditions. While play therapy can and often is used with all ages (i.e., children, adolescent, and adults) and formats (e.g., family, individual, group), most play therapy clients are between the ages of 3 and 12 (Ray & McCullough, 2015).

Clinicians engaging children in the play therapy process develop a warm, supportive, and child-centered relationship as soon as the child walks through the door. There is an appropriate and healthy sense of permissiveness so the child can feel free to fully engage in the play and express their internal world in an external manner. Play therapy practitioners work hard to do the following: (a) reflect play experiences back to the child; (b) not label or identify objects played with; (c) allow children to make their own choices; (d) set limits and inform the child of responsibilities; (e) communicate congruence, unconditional positive regard, and empathy; (f) express interest, be engaged, and use open body posture; (g) have tolerance for noise and messiness in the playroom; and (h) encourage a sense of internal evaluation (Ray & Cheng, 2018). During the initial play therapy sessions, the clinician informs the child about the essence of the playroom. After the initial description and during subsequent sessions, the clinician will provide a quick reminder that the nature of the playroom is essentially a place where most things can happen. For example:

> *Clinician:* Javier, this is our playroom, and this is a place where you can play with toys in ways that you like. This is a place where most things can happen (Black & Flynn, 2021).

The following are concise descriptions and examples of common child-centered play therapy techniques promoted by noted authors (Black & Flynn, 2021; Kottman, 2011; Ray, 2011; Vernon & Schimmel, 2019).

Tracking

Concretely explain the actions of the child as they emerge. It is important not to put a label on or judge the child's experiences, as labeling creates a predetermined perspective on the play or toy. The goal of play therapy is to understand and strengthen the child's belief system. For example:

> *Clinician:* You wrapped the dinosaur with a blanket.

Restating Content

This technique uses developmentally normative language and avoids repeating back exactly what was said (i.e., parroting). Often, when engaging with small children, play therapists will sit directly next to them on the floor or in a chair. The communication provided will be direct or through the play taking place in the room. For example:

> *Client:* I'm putting these soldiers together on this side of the car. I'm sure they will win.

> *Clinician:* You are putting the soldiers there and they are likely to win.

Reflection of Feeling

Reflections of feelings state a feeling word and are provided in a tentative style. This is so the child knows the play therapist is paying attention to their experience and what they are communicating. When using any skill, it is important to ensure that the information is being provided in age, developmental, and intellectually appropriate manner. In this sense, it is also very important to avoid any psych jargon or words the child may not understand. Reflections of feeling are never stated as *how* or *why* questions as this may lead a child to a response or create a sense of defensiveness. For example:

> *Clinician:* You seem happy to move those back into the castle.

Providing Choices

It is important for youth to develop problem-solving and decision-making abilities. Providing age/developmental/intellectual-appropriate choices allows the child to feel the following: (a) a sense of empowerment and control, (b) the natural consequences of their choices, and (c) the ability to engage in limit testing. From the perspective of the play therapist and the child, a benefit to providing choices is the avoidance of a power struggle. For example:

> *Clinician:* You can throw that one or the one over there, which do you choose?

Setting Limits

This is not a form of discipline. It is a combination of reflection of feeling and providing choices delivered in the context of a therapeutic relationship with a neutral tone of voice. The basic structure includes providing a reflection of feeling, setting a limit regarding the inappropriate behavior, and offering different and more appropriate choices. For example:

> *Clinician:* You feel angry and want to tear apart all of the dress-ups. However, the dress-ups are not for tearing. You can tear the paper over the trashcan.

Returning Responsibility

Practitioners return responsibility in a variety of ways (e.g., metaphor, minimal encouragers, restating content, reflecting feeling, applying the whisper technique). For example:

> *Client:* Where should I put the food and the animals? The monster is coming.
>
> *Clinician:* (softly) You can decide on the safest place to put them.

Dealing With Questions

Questions are generally minimized in play therapy. Play therapists do not typically ask a lot of questions. If there is an occasion to use questioning, the therapist will carefully decide how and why to ask and/or respond to questions. For example:

> *Client:* What time does this clock say?
>
> *Clinician:* You are curious about the clock.

A second example could be the following:

> *Client:* When can I leave?
>
> *Clinician:* You're wondering about leaving.

Process Play

The play process becomes the focus of the session. The clinician provides information on what is happening in the room and what the child is behaviorally demonstrating. For example:

Client: (Draws the Pepsi symbol on easel and repeatedly points to it while staring at the play therapist).

Clinician: You are showing me that and seem to want me to do something.

Narration of the Therapist's Actions

During the play therapy process, the therapist will move around the room to ensure that there is a sense of connection and engagement with the child. For example:

Clinician: I am standing up and moving closer to you so I can see what you're doing.

FILIAL THERAPY

Filial therapy is known as a child-centered and relationship enhancement form of family therapy. It was created in the 1960s by Bernard and Louise Gurney (Guerney, 1964) and has a long history as an educational and skill training model that helps young children and their families. The essence of filial therapy is to help parents conduct play therapy with their own children. Parents are essentially trained to conduct child-centered play therapy by a filial therapist. The general family requirements include parents engaging in weekly 30-minute sessions for approximately 6 months to 1 year. During these highly structured sessions, parents learn to (a) allow their children to freely express themselves, (b) foster child self-regulation, (c) set effective limits for the child, (d) create a sense of openness and comfort between them and their child, and (e) acknowledge their child without judgment and with acceptance (Ginsberg, 2012).

Filial therapy requires parents to use play therapy as the primary method of achieving their goal of modeling healthy coping, expressive, and interpersonal skills to children. Furthermore, parents become more in tune, sensitive, empathic, and emotionally regulated when engaging with their children as a result of the intensive filial training (Ginsberg, 1997). When a parent and the child develop better interpersonal responses as a result of their filial training, they simultaneously develop enhanced *interpersonal reflexes* (Leary, 1957). These interpersonal reflexes trigger predictable responses in others, so positive parenting statements equate to positive child responses (Ginsberg, 1997). The key is changing the interpersonal habits that reside in the unconscious memory of the parent and the child. Filial therapists work hard to bring awareness to and change these negative internalized habits (Keisler, 1996; Sullivan, 1953).

Relevant Skills and Interventions

Regarding the role of the therapist, the filial therapist helps parents understand the family's presenting problem. While presenting problems may change, the ultimate therapeutic goal of the therapeutic work is centered on creating an environment where the child feels accepted, develops a nurturing bond with the parent, and can play freely. Next, the filial therapist guides and teaches the parents as they develop the play therapy skills that will help change the negative interpersonal reflexes. Third, the filial therapist works with parents to help use the play therapy skills intentionally and assist them in generalizing the skills to everyday life. As the filial therapy starts to wind down, the clinician will provide maintenance and eventually function as a consultant to help enhance specific concerns (Ginsberg, 1997, 2012). Table 10.6 provides the common phases of the filial therapy experience, descriptions of the phase, and examples to help actualize the process. Ginsberg (1997) has further refined the filial therapy experience by creating a 10-session program designed to provide greater structure around the ethos of each session.

TABLE 10.6 PHASES OF FILIAL THERAPY, DESCRIPTIONS, AND EXAMPLES

Name	Description	Examples
Presenting issue	Understand the presenting issue, child development, and family dynamics.	*Clinician:* It appears that the family is going through challenges with issues around flexibility and communication.
Informing the parents	The parents learn about filial therapy, the family connects the approach to their needs, and the therapist forms a relationship with the family.	*Clinician:* Filial therapy is essentially training you on how to be a quasi-therapist so you can form a healthy bond with your child.
Play therapy demonstration	The filial therapist/supervisor presents a play therapy demonstration with each child while the parents observe.	*Clinician:* Bobby, it's important for you to tell me that. You were disappointed that I didn't stand up and look. I'm standing up now and moving over to you. (*Clinician uses a combination of process play, reflection of feeling, and narration of their actions.*)
Training the parents	The filial therapist/supervisor trains the parents with mock play therapy sessions, shaping, feedback, and modeling.	*Clinician:* Okay, great job letting Beth know you understand her feelings. I want you to work hard to adjust your tone of voice to softer and at a slower, more nurturing pace.
Supervised play with children	The filial therapist/supervisor supervises play therapy sessions with children and provides frequent parental feedback.	*Clinician:* This week's session seemed much smoother. I noticed that you incorporated more tracking into your dialogue with Monique.
Discussion of observations	The filial therapist/supervisor discusses themes, patterns in parenting, and family issues, and engages in solution-finding discussions.	*Clinician:* When you arrived here 3 months ago, the family had just suffered a crisis, parenting appeared chaotic, and the emotional boundaries between family members appeared to be enmeshed. Recently, I noticed positive growth in the areas of child self-confidence, boundaries between parents and children, and while the family is still grieving the death of Grandma you appear to have started several traditions to honor her life.
Generalization	The filial therapist/supervisor guides the parents on how to generalize the play therapy skills to everyday life.	*Clinician:* Okay, great job using all the basic skills fluidly during session time. This week I want you to try to engage in three 15-minute play experiences in which you use the skills we've practiced outside of session. Report to me next week on how it goes.
Maintenance	The filial therapist/supervisor provides continual maintenance of adopted skills over time.	*Client:* Things are generally going well; however, I'm having a hard time remembering to offer options. *Clinician:* Okay, let me walk you through the process. . .
Consulting into the future	The filial therapist/supervisor switches their role to more of a consultant.	*Client:* There has been a tragedy in the family, and we are floundering. Could we please set up a consultation session? *Clinician:* Sure.

Sources: Data from Ginsberg, B. G. (1997). *Relationship enhancement family therapy.* John Wiley & Sons; Ginsberg, B. G. (2012). Filial therapy: An attachment based, emotion focused, and skill training approach. *American Counseling Association VISTAS Online 2012,* Article 73.

THERAPLAY

Theraplay was developed by Ann M. Jernberg (1928–1993). Among other career achievements, Jernberg created The Theraplay Institute in Chicago in 1972 and later authored the book *Theraplay: A New Treatment Using Structured Play for Problem Children and Their Families* (Jernberg, 1979). *Theraplay* has been defined as "an engaging, playful treatment method modeled on the health, attuned interaction between parents and their children: the kind of interaction that leads to secure attachment and high self-esteem" (Bundy-Myrow & Booth, 2009, p. 315). Further, theraplay is considered a short-term, strength-based, active approach that involves caregivers engaging in warm and nurturing playfulness to enhance the caregiver and child relationship and to model healthy attachment patterns (Dickinson & Kottman, 2019). While people of all ages may benefit from certain theraplay techniques, it is generally used in treatment of youth 12 years of age and under (California Evidence-Based Clearinghouse for Child Welfare, 2016). Theraplay has been approved by the U.S. Substance Abuse and Mental Health Services Administration (SAMHSA) as an evidence-based treatment on the National Registry of Evidence-Based Programs and Practices. Furthermore, theraplay has also been rated as promising by the California Evidence-Based Clearinghouse.

Theraplay is highly structured, integrating aspects of the theraplay tradition with child-centered play therapy. Theraplay includes interventions like affectionate touch between family members and directive modeling activities where the caregiver or the theraplay counselor demonstrates skills and appropriate behaviors for the child. According to The Theraplay Institute's website, "[t]heraplay uses practitioner guidance to create playful and caring child–adult interactions that foster joyful shared experiences. These activities build attunement and understanding of each other—replicating early relationship experiences that are proven to lead to secure attachment" (The Theraplay Institute, n.d., para. 1). The following procedures take place throughout the typical theraplay experience: (a) an initial meeting with the caregiver(s) to understand and conceptualize the caregiverchild relationship; (b) during the initial meeting, the clinician will have the family take the Marschak Interaction Method (MIM) to understand the nature of the relationship and child attachment; (c) the second meeting is centered on discussing the theraplay philosophy, reviewing the assessment findings, and developing a collaborative treatment plan; and (d) 8 to 12 30-minute theraplay sessions involving the parent(s), the child, and ideally two theraplay therapists.

During the first four of these 30 minute-sessions, one theraplay counselor will work with the child, while the other provides interpretive feedback to the caregivers for the entire session. The theraplay counselor who works with the child will frequently use intrusive interactions that mimic parent–child interactions to improve impaired parent–child relationships. This is usually done behind a one-way mirror, via digital technology feed in an observation room, or with parents sitting in the corner of the therapy room. After the fourth theraplay session, the caregivers will join the theraplay counselor working with the child for the final 15 minutes of each session. This is so the caregivers can practice theraplay techniques in vivo under the direct supervision of the theraplay counselor (Dickinson & Kottman, 2019). Following the 15-minute, in-session, caregiver-led session segments, clinicians encourage caregivers to use the newly acquired skills and processes at home.

Prosocial interactions that support a secure attachment pattern are at the core of theraplay sessions. Specifically, theraplay counselors model and encourage interactions that are centered on the following essential qualities: nurture (i.e., calming and soothing the child in a way that feels good to them), engagement (i.e., the child feels seen and heard by the adult), structure (i.e., the adult creates a predictable structure for the child), and challenge (i.e., the caregiver challenges the child in acquiring new skills and sense of competence; The Theraplay Institute, n.d.). The observational feedback and MIM assessment scores help indicate which of these essential qualities need enhancement. Once the areas are understood, the theraplay counselors work with the child around and various art and play mediums to enhance the essential quality. While there is not much actual talking going on during the sessions, theraplay counselors are directive, active, and flexible while working with children. The essence of this play is mentored to the caregivers, who begin engaging in theraplay work during the fifth session (Dickinson & Kottman, 2019).

SANDTRAY AND SANDPLAY THERAPY

The use of a sandtray is a common staple for any play therapy room or in the office of clinicians who specialize in working with youth. Sandtrays provide a therapeutic platform for use of multicolored sand, miniature toys, and water for children and adults to reflect, resolve inner conflict, and create their own symbolic microcosm that reflects their internal world. While there are a lot of variabilities regarding sandtray equipment, Margaret Lowenfeld developed a few standards for sandplay (i.e., the World Technique), including a metal tray (75 cm × 50 cm × 7 cm) filled about halfway with sand, a table that is approximately child waist in height, miniature objects (e.g., living objects, transport, scenery, equipment), and tools for moving the sand (e.g., shovel, sieve; Hutton, 2004). While sandtray work has been described as an approach for working with children, it is often applied to people of all ages. When practitioners use a sandtray with youth, they are observing behaviors, toys used, emotionality, and themes. For example, specific factors could include the miniatures used, how the child manipulates the sand, the intensity (or lack thereof) in the play, and relating sand-based experiences with experiences they have had in life (Sjolund & Schaefer, 1994).

Sandtray and sandplay therapies are two different models that involve the therapeutic use of sand. All sand work shares the philosophy that the use of sand is a concrete and physical demonstration of internal processes. Theoretically, sandplay therapy is grounded in Jungian psychology and sandtray can be flexibly used with many theoretical variations. Regarding professional organizations, the Association for Sandplay Therapy (https://sandplayassociation.com) is home to sandplay practitioners, while sandtray therapists can find a professional home with the International Association for Sandtray Therapy (https://sandtraytherapy.org). The Association for Sandplay Therapy also grants a number of certifications related to clinical work, consulting, and teaching sandplay. Given the shared interests within these organizations, many invested sand-based practitioners engage in both organizations. Additional unique factors associated with sandplay therapy include the noninterpretive nature of sandplay (i.e., the child describes the meaning), the noninterfering nature of sandplay (i.e., the clinician does not engage with the sand work), the nondirective approach to the work, and the lack of any expectation of the child to speak during session (Friedman & Mitchell, 1994; Hutton, 2004; Lowenfield, 1993). In comparison, sandtray therapy emphasizes the therapeutic relationship and the here and now, is highly interactive, expects clients to open up emotionally, and at times uses directives (DeDomenico, 2021).

Sandplay is theoretically grounded in Jungian psychology. The client's sand is applied to unconscious processes, archetypes, mandalas, and symbols (Friedman & Mitchell, 1994). The World Technique (Lowenfeld, 1993) is a key skill for sandplay therapists. This involves the client using miniatures, water, and other mediums within the sand to create a world. The world is essentially a physical expression of the client's internal world and symbolically and/or metaphorically represents their unconscious, subconscious, and imagination. During this work, the sandplay therapist does not speak and simply observes. Later, the clinician will analyze the content of the session. The sandtray therapist uses the sand and the associated props to engage the client, with the ultimate goal of unlocking and expressing information that would not be easily accessed in talk therapy. The sandtray is essentially a mirror of the client's emotional, cognitive, and behavioral world (DeDomenico, 2021).

ASSESSING CONTEMPORARY CHILD AND ADOLESCENT THERAPY ISSUES

The assessment of youth is often challenging, multidisciplinary, and taken from multiple sources (e.g., family, teachers). Toddlers (ages 12–36 months), children (ages 0–12), and adolescents (ages 13–18) all require special thought and accommodations when being considered for assessment (see Srinath et al., 2019, for a review). Assessing youth must incorporate their environment, and thus stakeholders like parents, extended family members, and teachers are often included. In addition to the challenge of including multiple people, the youth being assessed may demonstrate considerable resistance and may not think the issue being assessed is relevant to the problems in their life. Furthermore, these issues may be embarrassing to the child or adolescent, so their resistance may be centered on issues of social desirability. In addition to being resistant, due to their level of development, they may not be effective at reporting the duration or timing of the issues being assessed, hence the need for multiple stakeholders and settings in the assessment process. Unfortunately, clinicians who gather data from multiple child stakeholders run into a variety of issues, including inconsistency in reports, problems with attaining continuous reports, and corroborating findings that confirm a particular behavioral pattern or diagnosis (Srinath et al., 2019).

Due to the multidisciplinary and collaborative nature of child and adolescent assessment, it may be helpful to develop a staggered approach to care (Srinath et al., 2019). This could be as simple as spreading assessments across multiple weeks. Once the multisource assessment information has been collected and analyzed, it must be summarized and disseminated to important stakeholders so everybody stays on the same page in regard to the presenting issues and treatment plan. While there may be variability across assessment measures, gathering and analyzing multiple sources of information help with a variety of key clinical areas, including, but not limited to, family background and dynamics, parenting style and concerns, case conceptualization, treatment planning, assignment of roles and responsibilities, psychosocial background information, cooccurring medical and psychological issues, history of the presenting concern(s), diversity and social justice factors, and a full account of the client's treatment history, and provide the client and the family a clear understanding of what is going on in terms of presenting issues (Srinath et al., 2019).

Regarding the uncovering of important information, there is probably nothing more salient than the strength of the child/family and clinician therapeutic rapport. Once therapeutic rapport is developed, more authentic information is shared at a faster pace. A large hurdle that gets in the way of establishing the therapeutic relationship is when the child refuses to talk and share pertinent information. If this information cannot be sufficiently determined by other sources (e.g., family, educators), the clinician may have to do one or more of the following: wait until the child warms up, understand the reasons behind the youth's resistance to treatment, talk to the youth about nonclinical information (e.g., sports, games, school), and glean an understanding of any anxiety or trauma-related disorder that may be serving as a barrier to self-disclosure of any kind (Srinath et al., 2019). Table 10.7 reviews empirically validated assessments related to the topics and formats of counseling reviewed in this chapter.

TABLE 10.7   CONTEMPORARY YOUTH EMPIRICAL ASSESSMENTS AND RELATED REFERENCES

Contemporary Issue or Modality	Assessment Name	References
Resistance	Child and Adolescent Needs and Strengths (CANS)	Lyons, J. S., & Weiner, D. A. (Eds.). (2009). *Strategies in behavioral healthcare: Assessment, treatment planning, and total clinical outcomes management.* Civic Research Institute.
Resistance	Youth Outcome Questionnaire (Y-OQ)	Ridge, N. W., Warren, J. S., Burlingame, G. M., Wells, M. G., & Tumblin, K. M. (2009). Reliability and validity of the Youth Outcome Questionnaire self-report. *Journal of Clinical Psychology, 65*(10), 1115–1126.
Childhood attachment	Strange Situation Procedure	Ainsworth, M. D. S., & Wittig, B. A. (1969). Attachment and exploratory behavior of one-year-olds in a strange situation. In B. M. Foss (Ed.), *Determinants of infant behavior* (Vol. 5, pp. 113–136). Methuen.
Childhood attachment	Child Attachment Interview (CAI)	Shmueli-Goetz, Y., Target, M., Fonagy, P., & Datta, A. (2008). The Child Attachment Interview: A psychometric study of reliability and discriminant validity. *Developmental Psychology, 44*(4), 939–956. https://doi.org/10.1037/0012-1649.44.4.939.
Sibling abuse and violence	Sibling Abuse Interview (SAI)	Caffaro, J. V., & Conn-Caffaro, A. (1998). *Sibling abuse trauma: Assessment and intervention strategies for children, families, and adults.* Haworth Press.
Sibling abuse and violence	Juvenile Victimization Questionnaire (JVQ)	Finkelhor, D., Hamby, S. L., Ormrod, R., & Turner, H. (2005). The Juvenile Victimization Questionnaire: Reliability, validity, and national norms. *Child Abuse & Neglect, 29*(4), 383–412. https://doi.org/10.1016/j.chiabu.2004.11.001.
Bullying	Revised Olweus Bully/Victim Questionnaire (OBVQ)	Kyriakides, L., Kaloyirou, C., & Lindsay, G. (2006). An analysis of the Revised Olweus Bully/Victim Questionnaire using the Rasch measurement model. *The British Journal of Educational Psychology, 76*(Pt 4), 781–801. https://doi.org/10.1348/000709905X53499.
Bullying	Peer Relation Questionnaire (PRQ)	Panagiotou, M., Charalampopoulou, M., Bacopoulou, F., Velegraki, I. M., Kokka, I., Vlachakis, D., Chrousos, G. P., & Darviri, C. (2021). Reliability and validity of the Peer Relation Questionnaire in a sample of Greek school children and adolescents. *EMBnet.journal, 26*, e974. https://doi.org/10.14806/ej.26.1.974.
Learning disabilities	Assessing Linguistic Behaviors Communicative Intentions Scale (ALB)	Olswang, L., Stoel-Gammon, C., Coggins, T., & Carpenter, R. (1987). *Assessing linguistic behaviors.* University of Washington Press.
Learning disabilities	Developmental Indicators for the Assessment of Learning (DIAL-3)	Mardell-Czudnowski, C., & Goldenberg, D. S. (1998). *Developmental Indicators for the Assessment of Learning* (3rd ed.). American Guidance Services.
Play therapy	Children's Play Therapy Instrument (CPTI)	Kernberg, P. F., Chazan, S. E., & Normandin, L. (1998). The Children's Play Therapy Instrument (CPTI). Description, development, and reliability studies. *The Journal of Psychotherapy Practice and Research, 7*(3), 196–207.

(continued)

TABLE 10.7   CONTEMPORARY YOUTH EMPIRICAL ASSESSMENTS AND RELATED REFERENCES (*CONTINUED*)

Contemporary Issue or Modality	Assessment Name	References
Play therapy	Build-a-House Technique	Sharp, C. (2017). *The Build-a-House Technique.* CreateSpace Independent Publishing Platform.
Filial therapy	Extended Play-Based Developmental Assessment (EPBDA)	Gil, E. (2011). *Extended Play-Based Developmental Assessment.* Self Esteem Shop.
Theraplay	Marschak Interaction Method	Lindaman, S. L., Booth, P. B., & Chambers, C. L. (2000). Assessing parent–child interactions with the Marschak Interaction Method (MIM). In K. Gitlin-Weiner, A. Sandgrund, & C. Schaefer (Eds.), *Play diagnosis and assessment* (pp. 371–400). John Wiley & Sons.

SUMMARY

In this chapter, readers were introduced to a variety of key contemporary issues and relevant skills and interventions related to treating children, including child and adolescent resistance, childhood attachment issues, sibling abuse and violence, bullying, and learning disabilities in youth. In addition to youth-based contemporary issues and skills, there were four additional sections that highlighted important processes and skills related to play therapy, filial therapy, theraplay, sandplay therapy, and sandtray therapy. Lastly, the chapter ends with a concise breakdown of helpful youth-based assessments. The main objective of this chapter was to describe the nuances of the issues affecting today's youth and the pertinent clinical skills related to assessment and treatment. Specifically, throughout the chapter, readers were provided with contemporary examples, key information, in-depth conceptualizations, and clear clinical guidelines that accentuate the powerful effect the contemporary issue has on children and adolescents and pertinent skills and techniques for helping youth.

END-OF-CHAPTER RESOURCES

 A robust set of instructor resources designed to supplement this text is located at http://connect.springerpub.com/content/book/978-0-8261-8775-8. Qualifying instructors may request access by emailing textbook@springerpub.com.

STUDENT ACTIVITIES

Exercise 1: Attachment Styles and Phases

Directions: Review the following information and answer the prompt with the reflection questions:

Attachment styles developed during their childhood can influence the way people interact with others and the relationships they develop throughout their lifetime. Being knowledgeable on attachment styles and phases, particularly during childhood, can be of great help to a clinician who plans to work with children and families.

- Compare and contrast the phases of attachment development from the chapter.
- Consider how various attachment styles can influence children in different ways and how you would work with children from each attachment style.
- Consider the impact trauma would have on a child's sense of attachment.

Exercise 2: Sibling Abuse

Directions: Review the following instructions and answer the questions:

Go to your university's online EBSCO Database and find Academic Search Premier. Search and find an article focused on sibling abuse and/or sibling violence within the helping professions. Review the article in its entirety and answer the following questions related to the effects of child abuse and neglect on children and families:

- What are the factors that contribute to sibling abuse that are highlighted in the article as well as in the chapter?
- What are the long-term effects of sibling abuse both on the abused children and on the family system?
- What is a tentative plan you could create with the information in both this chapter and the article to ensure that you are able to work with families affected by sibling abuse/violence in an ethical and supportive way? Consider the relevant skills and interventions.

Exercise 3: Bullying

Directions: Review the following instructions and respond to the follow-up questions:

When working with children and family systems, bullying is a topic that can be expected to be brought up during counseling. Bullying has a deep impact on children, both as the victim and as the bully. The impact can reverberate into the family system and affect other members of the family. Bullying in childhood can have long-term effects on children; consequently, working with them around these experiences and creating a sense of healing are very important.

- Consider the common characteristics of a bully. How would you work with these children in a therapeutic context?

- Consider the characteristics of children who are victims of bullying. How would you work with these children in a therapeutic context?

- Bias-based bullying is an aspect of bullying to be aware of as a clinician. What unique skills and interventions would be useful when handling bias-based bullying in children?

Exercise 4: Learning Disabilities in Youth

Directions: Review the following information and come up with a mock plan that may be used when working with families:

Children who qualify for a learning disability generally need supportive services to treat, manage, and minimize the effects of their learning disability. It is important for a clinician working with children and/or families to understand how learning disabilities can affect children as well as their family system.

- Consider relevant therapeutic interventions and skills that you have learned about and/or utilized in your own work. How could these skills and interventions be used to best help future clients diagnosed with learning disabilities?

- Consider your ethical boundaries and clinical competencies related to working with youth who struggle with a common learning disability. When parents ask for assistance with their child's learning disability, what services would you feel comfortable offering?

- Consider being asked to conduct a learning disability assessment related to a child with possible dyslexia. What qualifications are needed to execute a learning disability assessment? Do some research and name two different empirically validated learning disability assessments and the training needed to conduct them.

Exercise 5: Article Review

Directions: Review the following instructions and answer the questions:

Go to your university's online EBSCO Database and find Academic Search Premier. Search and find an article focused on understanding filial therapy. Review the article in its entirety and answer the following questions related to the implications and possible effects of this phenomenon:

- How does filial therapy differ from play therapy? How are they similar?

- What are the important aspects of filial therapy that are necessary for it to be a useful intervention with families?

- Consider the filial therapy skills and interventions introduced in the chapter. Compare and contrast these with the skills and interventions you review in the article.

ADDITIONAL RESOURCES

HELPFUL LINKS

- "Engaging Avoidant Teens": https://ct.counseling.org/2020/05/engaging-avoidant -teens/

- "Managing Resistant Clients": https://ct.counseling.org/2010/02/managing-resistant -clients/

- "Interventions for Attachment and Traumatic Stress Issues in Young Children": https://ct.counseling.org/2019/04/interventions-for-attachment-and-traumatic-stress-issues-in-young-children/

- "Attachment Based Treatments for Adolescents: The Secure Cycle as a Framework for Assessment, Treatment, and Evaluation": https://www.ncbi.nlm.nih.gov/pmc/articles/PMC4872705/

- "Helping Children and Families Address and Prevent Sibling Abuse": https://ct.counseling.org/2017/02/helping-children-families-address-prevent-sibling-abuse/

- "Sibling Violence": https://aamft.org/Consumer_Updates/Sibling_Violence.aspx

- "Child Abuse and Neglect": https://www.aamft.org/Consumer_Updates/Child_Abuse_and_Neglect.aspx

- "Bullying for Mental Health Professionals": https://www.abct.org/fact-sheets/bullying-for-mental-health-professionals/

- "When Children Have Been Bullied: Healing Options": https://www.psychologytoday.com/us/blog/resolution-not-conflict/201110/when-children-have-been-bullied-healing-options

- "Bullying: How Counselors Can Intervene": https://ct.counseling.org/2016/06/bullying-counselors-can-intervene/

- "Bullying": https://aamft.org/Consumer_Updates/Bullying.aspx

- "Living With Learning Disabilities: Strategies for Family Support": https://www.counseling.org/resources/library/vistas/2009-V-Online/Dolan.pdf

- "Learning Disorders in Children": https://www.cdc.gov/ncbddd/developmentaldisabilities/learning-disorder.html

- "Play Therapy Makes a Difference": https://www.a4pt.org/page/ptmakesadifference

- "Filial Therapy": https://www.goodtherapy.org/learn-about-therapy/types/filial-therapy

- "Filial Therapy: An Attachment Based, Emotion Focused, and Skill Training Approach": https://www.counseling.org/docs/default-source/vistas/filial-therapy-an-attachment-based-emotion-focused-and-skill.pdf?sfvrsn=dedfaa57_12

HELPFUL BOOKS

- Barnett, O. W., Miller-Perrin, C. L., & Perrin, R. D. (2005). *Family violence across the lifespan: An introduction* (2nd ed.). Sage.

- Blaustein, M., & Kinniburgh, K. (2018). *Treating traumatic stress in children and adolescents: How to foster resilience through attachment, self-regulation, and competency* (2nd ed.). Guilford Press.

- Caffaro, J. V. (2014). *Sibling abuse trauma: Assessment and intervention strategies for children, families, and adults* (2nd ed.). Routledge/Taylor & Francis Group.

- Caspi, J., & Barrios, V. R. (2016). Destructive sibling aggression. In C. A. Cuevas & C. M. Rennison (Eds.), *The Wiley handbook on the psychology of violence* (pp. 297–323). Wiley Blackwell. https://doi.org/10.1002/9781118303092.ch16

- Colin, V. L. (1996). *Human attachment.* McGraw Hill.

- Crenshaw, D. A. (2017). Resistance in child psychotherapy: Playing hide-and-seek. In C. A. Malchiodi & D. A. Crenshaw (Eds.), *What to do when children clam up in psychotherapy: Interventions to facilitate communication* (pp. 18–37). Guilford Press.

- Kaduson, H. G., & Schaefer, C. E. (Eds.). (1997). *101 favorite play therapy techniques.* Jason Aronson.

- Lerner, J., & Kline, F. (2006). *Learning disabilities and related disorders: Characteristics and teaching strategies.* Houghton Mifflin Company.

- National Academies of Sciences, Engineering, and Medicine. (2016). *Preventing bullying through science, policy, and practice.* The National Academies Press. https://doi.org/10.17226/23482

- Swearer, S. M., Espelage, D. L., & Napolitano, S. A. (2009). *Bullying prevention and intervention: Realistic strategies for schools.* Guilford Press.

- VanFleet, R. (1994). *Filial therapy: Strengthening parent–child relationships through play.* Professional Resource Press/Professional Resource Exchange.

- Wiehe, V. R. (1997). *Sibling abuse: Hidden physical, emotional, and sexual trauma* (2nd ed.). Sage.

HELPFUL VIDEOS

- 6 Ideas for Working With Resistance: https://www.youtube.com/watch?v=3-NoofFldeM

- Attachment Theory, Attachment Style, and Developing Secure Attachment: https://www.youtube.com/watch?v=BRBTwWB9z9A

- Sibling Sexual Abuse: Working With Families: https://www.youtube.com/watch?v=cTjj21wOD7w

- Sibling Abuse: The Adult and the Inner Child: https://www.youtube.com/watch?v=CSy2mC0_QI8

- Learning Disabilities: What Are the Different Types?: https://www.youtube.com/watch?v=yG_xSBsFMPQ

- Play Therapy Works!: https://www.youtube.com/watch?v=_4ovwAdxCs0

- Special Playtime: Filial Therapy With Hany (Part 1): https://www.youtube.com/watch?v=uLTWr756p_Y

REFERENCES

Altarac, M., & Saroha, E. (2007). Lifetime prevalence of learning disability among US children. *Pediatrics, 119*(Supplement_1), S77–S83. https://doi.org/10.1542/peds.2006-2089L

American Psychiatric Association. (2013). *Diagnostic and statistical manual of mental disorders* (5th ed.). https://doi.org/10.1176/appi.books.9780890425596

American Psychiatric Association. (2022). *Diagnostic and statistical manual of mental disorders* (5th ed., text revision). https://doi.org/10.1176/appi.books.9780890425787

Backlund, M., & Johnson, V. (2018, August 8). The beauty of client and supervisee resistance. *Counseling Today, 61*(2), 46–51. https://ct.counseling.org/2018/08/the-beauty-of-client-and-supervisee-resistance/

Bakermans-Kranenburg, M. J., & van IJzendoorn, M. H. (2009). The first 10,000 adult attachment interviews: Distributions of adult attachment representations in clinical and non-clinical groups. *Attachment & Human Development, 11*(3), 223–263. https://doi.org/10.1080/14616730902814762

Barnett, O. W., Miller-Perrin, C. L., & Perrin, R. D. (2005). *Family violence across the lifespan: An introduction* (2nd ed.). Sage.

Baum, S. (2007). The use of family therapy for people with learning disabilities. *Advances in Mental Health and Learning Disabilities, 1*(2), 8–13. https://doi.org/10.1108/17530180200700014

Bess, B. E., & Janssen, Y. (1982). Incest: A pilot study. *Hillside Journal of Clinical Psychiatry, 6*(2), 171–187.

Black, L. L., & Flynn, S. V. (2021). *Crisis, trauma, and disaster: A clinician's guide*. Sage.

Bowlby, J. (1940). *Personality and mental illness*. Taylor & Frances/Routledge.

Bowlby, J. (1969). Attachment and loss: Volume I: Attachment. *In Attachment and loss: Volume I: Attachment* (pp. 1–401). The Hogarth Press and the Institute of Psycho-Analysis.

Bowlby, J. (1988). Developmental psychiatry comes of age. *The American Journal of Psychiatry, 145*(1), 1–10. https://doi.org/10.1176/ajp.145.1.1

Brody, T., Harnad, S., & Carr, L. (2006). Earlier web usage statistics as predictors of later citation impact. *Journal of the American Society for Information Science and Technology, 57*(8), 1060–1072. https://doi.org/10.1002/asi.20373

Button, D. M., & Gealt, R. (2010). High risk behaviors among victims of sibling violence. *Journal of Family Violence, 25*(2), 131–140. https://doi.org/10.1007/s10896-009-9276-x

Bundy-Myrow, S., & Booth, P. B. (2009). Theraplay: Supporting attachment relationships. In K. J. O'Connor & L. D. Braverman (Eds.), *Play therapy theory and practice: Comparing theories and techniques* (pp. 315–367). John Wiley & Sons.

Caffaro, J. (n.d.). *Sibling violence*. American Association for Marriage and Family Therapy. Retrieved April 4, 2022, from https://aamft.org/Consumer_Updates/Sibling_Violence.aspx

Caffaro, J. V., & Conn-Caffaro, A. (1998). *Sibling abuse trauma: Assessment and intervention strategies for children, families, and adults*. Haworth Press.

California Evidence-Based Clearinghouse for Child Welfare. (2016). *Theraplay*. http://www.cebc4cw.org/program/theraplay/detailed

Caspi, J. (2012). *Sibling aggression: Assessment and treatment*. Springer Publishing Company.

Centers for Disease Control and Prevention. (n.d.). *Learning disorders in children*. Retrieved April 4, 2022, from https://www.cdc.gov/ncbddd/developmentaldisabilities/learning-disorder.html

Centers for Disease Control and Prevention. (2019, October 3). *#StopBullying*. National Center for Injury Prevention and Control. Retrieved April 4, 2022, from https://www.cdc.gov/injury/features/stop-bullying/index.html

Center for Disease Control and Prevention (2022). *Developmental disabilities*. https://www.cdc.gov/ncbddd/developmentaldisabilities/index.html

Centers for Disease Control and Prevention, National Center for Injury Prevention and Control. (2014). *The relationship between bullying and suicide: What we know and what it means for schools*. National Center for Injury Prevention and Control, Division of Violence Prevention. Retrieved April 4, 2022 from https://stacks.cdc.gov/view/cdc/34163

Child Welfare Information Gateway. (2019). *About CAPTA: A legislative history*. U.S. Department of Health and Human Services, Children's Bureau.

Cicchetti, D., Ackerman, B. P., & Izard, C. E. (1995). Emotions and emotion regulation in developmental psychopathology. *Development and Psychopathology, 7*(1), 1–10. https://doi.org/10.1017/S0954579400006301

Cohen, J. A., Mannarino, A. P., Berliner, L., & Deblinger, E. (2000). Trauma-focused cognitive behavioral therapy for children and adolescents: An empirical update. *Journal of Interpersonal Violence, 15*(11), 1202–1223. https://doi.org/10.1177/088626000015011007

Cohn, D. A., Silver, D. H., Cowan, C. P., Cowan, P. A., & Pearson, J. (1992). Working models of childhood attachment and couple relationships. *Journal of Family Issues, 13*(4), 432–449. https://doi.org/10.1177/019251392013004003

Cook, W. L., & Kenny, D. A. (2005). The actor–partner interdependence model: A model of bidirectional effects in developmental studies. *International Journal of Behavioral Development, 29*(2), 101–109. https://doi.org/10.1080/01650250444000405

Cortiella, C., & Horowitz, S. H. (2014). *The state of learning disabilities: Facts, trends, and emerging issues* (3rd ed.). National Center for Learning Disabilities. https://www.ncld.org/wp-content/uploads/2014/11/2014-State-of-LD.pdf

Courtois, C. A., & Ford, J. D. (Eds.). (2009). *Treating complex traumatic stress disorders: An evidence-based guide*. Guilford Press.

Courtois, C. A., & Ford, J. D. (2013). *Treatment of complex trauma: A sequenced, relationship-based approach*. Guilford Press.

Cowan, P. A., Cowan, C. P., & Mehta, N. (2009). Adult attachment, couple attachment, and children's adaptation to school: An integrated attachment template and family risk model. *Attachment & Human Development, 11*(1), 29–46. https://doi.org/10.1080/14616730802500222

Crusto, C. A., Whitson, M. L., Walling, S. M., Feinn, R., Friedman, S. R., Reynolds, J., Amer, M., & Kaufman, J. S. (2010). Posttraumatic stress among young urban children exposed to family violence and other potentially traumatic events. *Journal of Traumatic Stress, 23*(6), 716–724. https://doi.org/10.1002/jts.20590

DeDomenico, G. S. (2021). *What is sandtray therapy?* Play. Build. Grow. PLC. https://www.playbuildgrow.com/more-information/detailed-description-sandtray-therapy

Dickinson, R., & Kottman, T. (2019). Play therapy. In A. Vernon & C. J. Schimmel (Eds.), *Counseling children & adolescents* (5th ed., pp. 111–146). Cognella Academic Publishing.

Dunn, J., & Plomin, R. (1991). Why are siblings so different? The significance of differences in sibling experiences within the family. *Family Process, 30*(3), 271–283. https://doi.org/10.1111/j.1545-5300.1991.00271.x

Emerson, E., & Hatton, C. (2007). Mental health of children and adolescents with intellectual disabilities in Britain. *The British Journal of Psychiatry, 191*(6), 493–499. https://doi.org/10.1192/bjp.bp.107.038729

Eriksen, S., & Jensen, V. (2006). All in the family? Family environment factors in sibling violence. *Journal of Family Violence, 21*(8), 497–507. https://doi.org/10.1007/s10896-006-9048-9

Eriksen, S., & Jensen, V. (2009). A push or a punch: Distinguishing the severity of sibling violence. *Journal of Interpersonal Violence, 24*(1), 183–208. https://doi.org/10.1177/0886260508316298

Erozkan, A. (2016). The link between types of attachment and childhood trauma. *Universal Journal of Educational Research, 4*(5), 1071–1079. https://doi.org/10.13189/ujer.2016.040517

Espelage, D. L., & Holt, M. K. (2013). Suicidal ideation and school bullying experiences after controlling for depression and delinquency. *Journal of Adolescent Health, 53*(1), S27–S31. https://doi.org/10.1016/j.jadohealth.2012.09.017

Eyberg, S. (1988). Parent–child interaction therapy: Integration of traditional and behavioral concerns. *Child & Family Behavior Therapy, 10*(1), 33–46. https://doi.org/10.1300/J019v10n01_04

Fanti, K. A., & Kimonis, E. R. (2012). Bullying and victimization: The role of conduct problems and psychopathic traits. *Journal of Research on Adolescence, 22*(4), 617–631. https://doi.org/10.1111/j.1532-7795.2012.00809.x

Feldman, R. (2007). Parent–infant synchrony: Biological foundations and developmental outcomes. *Current Directions in Psychological Science, 16*(6), 340–345. https://doi.org/10.1111/j.1467-8721.2007.00532.x

Finkelhor, D., Ormrod, R., Turner, H., & Hamby, S. L. (2005). The victimization of children and youth: A comprehensive, national survey. *Child Maltreatment, 10*(1), 5–25. https://doi.org/10.1177/1077559504271287

Fonagy, P. (2000). Attachment and borderline personality disorder. *Journal of the American Psychoanalytic Association, 48*(4), 1129–1146. https://doi.org/10.1177/00030651000480040701

Fraiberg, S., Adelson, E., & Shapiro, V. (1975). Ghosts in the nursery. A psychoanalytic approach to the problems of impaired infant–mother relationships. *Journal of the American Academy of Child Psychiatry, 14*(3), 387–421. https://doi.org/10.1016/s0002-7138(09)61442-4

Friedman, H. S., & Mitchell, R. R. (1994). *Sandplay: Past, present, and future.* Routledge.

Geary, D. C. (2012). Evolutionary educational psychology. In K. R. Harris, S. Graham, T. Urdan, C. B. McCormick, G. M. Sinatra, & J. Sweller (Eds.), *APA educational psychology handbook, Vol. 1. Theories, constructs, and critical issues* (pp. 597–621). American Psychological Association. https://doi.org/10.1037/13273-020

Gini, G., & Espelage, D. L. (2014). Peer victimization, cyberbullying, and suicide risk in children and adolescents. *JAMA, 312*(5), 545–546. https://doi.org/10.1001/jama.2014.3212

Gini, G., & Pozzoli, T. (2013). Bullied children and psychosomatic problems: A meta-analysis. *Pediatrics, 132*(4), 720–729. https://doi.org/10.1542/peds.2013-0614

Ginsberg, B. G. (1997). *Relationship enhancement family therapy.* John Wiley & Sons.

Ginsberg, B. G. (2012). Filial therapy: An attachment based, emotion focused, and skill training approach. *American Counseling Association VISTAS Online 2012*, Article 73. https://www.counseling.org/docs/default-source/vistas/filial-therapy-an-attachment-based-emotion-focused-and-skill.pdf?sfvrsn=dedfaa57_12

GoodTherapy. (n.d.). *Bullying support.* Retrieved April 4, 2022, from https://www.goodtherapy.org/learn-about-therapy/issues/bullying/bullying-support

Green, E. J., Crenshaw, D. A., & Kolos, A. C. (2010). Counseling children with preverbal trauma. *International Journal of Play Therapy, 19*(2), 95. https://doi.org/10.1037/a0017667

Greenberg, L. S., Auszra, L., & Herrmann, I. R. (2007). The relationship among emotional productivity, emotional arousal and outcome in experiential therapy of depression. *Psychotherapy Research, 17*(4), 482–493. https://doi.org/10.1080/10503300600977800

Guerney, B., Jr. (1964). Filial therapy: Description and rationale. *Journal of Consulting Psychology, 28*(4), 304–310. https://doi.org/10.1037/h0041340

Hakkarainen, A. M., Holopainen, L. K., & Savolainen, H. K. (2015). A five-year follow-up on the role of educational support in preventing dropout from upper secondary education in Finland. *Journal of Learning Disabilities, 48*(4), 408–421. https://doi.org/10.1177/0022219413507603

Hamm, M. P., Newton, A. S., Chisholm, A., Shulhan, J., Milne, A., Sundar, P., Ennis, H., Scott, S. D., & Hartling, L. (2015). Prevalence and effect of cyberbullying on children and young people: A scoping review of social media studies. *JAMA Pediatrics, 169*(8), 770–777. https://doi.org/10.1001/jamapediatrics.2015.0944

Hanna, F. J., & Hunt, W. P. (1999). Techniques for psychotherapy with defiant, aggressive adolescents. *Psychotherapy: Theory, Research, Practice, Training, 36*(1), 56–68. https://doi.org/10.1037/h0087842

Hazler, R. J. (1996). *Breaking the cycle of violence: Interventions for bullying and victimization.* Taylor & Francis.

Hinduja, S., & Patchin, J. W. (2019). Connecting adolescent suicide to the severity of bullying and cyberbullying. *Journal of School Violence, 18*(3), 333–346. https://doi.org/10.1080/15388220.2018.1492417

Hoffman, K. L., Kiecolt, K. J., & Edwards, J. N. (2005). Physical violence between siblings a theoretical and empirical analysis. *Journal of Family Issues, 26*(8), 1103–1130. https://doi.org/10.1177/0192513X05277809

Horne, A. M., & Sayger, T. V. (1990). *Treating conduct and oppositional defiant disorders in children.* Pergamon Press.

Hutton, D. (2004). Margaret Lowenfeld's 'world technique.' *Clinical Child Psychology and Psychiatry, 9*(4), 605–612. https://doi.org/10.1177/1359104504046164

Individuals with Disabilities Education Act. (2004). *Individuals with Disabilities Education Act 20 U.S.C. § 1400.* U.S. Department of Education.

Jernberg, A. M. (1979). *Theraplay: A new treatment using structured play for problem children and their families.* Jossey-Bass.

Keisler, D. J. (1996). *Contemporary interpersonal theory and research.* John Wiley & Sons.

Kiselica, M. S., & Morrill-Richards, M. (2007). Sibling maltreatment: The forgotten abuse. *Journal of Counseling & Development, 85*(2), 148–160. https://doi.org/10.1002/j.1556-6678.2007.tb00457.x

Knack, J. M., Jensen-Campbell, L. A., & Baum, A. (2011). Worse than sticks and stones? Bullying is associated with altered HPA axis functioning and poorer health. *Brain and Cognition, 77*(2), 183–190. https://doi.org/10.1016/j.bandc.2011.06.011

Kobak, R., Zajac, K., Herres, J., & Krauthamer Ewing, E. S. (2015). Attachment based treatments for adolescents: The secure cycle as a framework for assessment, treatment and evaluation. *Attachment & Human Development, 17*(2), 220–239. https://doi.org/10.1080/14616734.2015.1006388

Kosciw, J. G., Greytak, E. A., Zongrone, A. D., Clark, C. M., & Truong, N. L. (2018). *The 2017 national school climate survey: The experiences of lesbian, gay, bisexual, transgender, and queer youth in our nation's schools.* GLSEN. https://www.glsen.org/sites/default/files/2019-10/GLSEN-2017-National-School-Climate-Survey-NSCS-Full-Report.pdf

Kottman, T. (2011). *Play therapy: Basics and beyond* (2nd ed.). American Counseling Association.

Kumpulainen, K., Räsänen, E., & Puura, K. (2001). Psychiatric disorders and the use of mental health services among children involved in bullying. *Aggressive Behavior: Official Journal of the International Society for Research on Aggression, 27*(2), 102–110. https://doi.org/10.1002/ab.3

Lahousen, T., Unterrainer, H. F., & Kapfhammer, H. P. (2019). Psychobiology of attachment and trauma—Some general remarks from a clinical perspective. *Frontiers in Psychiatry*, 914. https://doi.org/10.3389/fpsyt.2019.00914

Leary, T. (1957). *Interpersonal diagnosis of personality.* Ronald Press.

Lieberman, A. F. (2004). Child–parent psychotherapy: A relationship-based approach to the treatment of mental health disorders in infancy and early childhood. In A. J. Sameroff, S. C. McDonough, & K. L. Rosenblum (Eds.), *Treating parent–infant relationship problems: Strategies for intervention* (pp. 97–122). Guilford Press.

Lieberman, A. F., Van Horn, P., & Ippen, C. G. (2005). Toward evidence-based treatment: Child–parent psychotherapy with preschoolers exposed to marital violence. *Journal of the American Academy of Child & Adolescent Psychiatry, 44*(12), 1241–1248. https://doi.org/10.1097/01.chi.0000181047.59702.58

Locke, J., Ishijima, E. H., Kasari, C., & London, N. (2010). Loneliness, friendship quality and the social networks of adolescents with high-functioning autism in an inclusive school setting. *Journal of Research in Special Educational Needs, 10*(2), 74–81. https://doi.org/10.1111/j.1471-3802.2010.01148.x

Lowenfeld, M. (1993). *Understanding children's sandplay: Lowenfeld's world technique*. Drake International Services.

Maag, J. W., & Reid, R. (2006). Depression among students with learning disabilities: Assessing the risk. *Journal of Learning Disabilities, 39*(1), 3–10. https://doi.org/10.1177/0022219406039 0010201

MacKinnon, A. L., Gold, I., Feeley, N., Hayton, B., Carter, C. S., & Zelkowitz, P. (2014). The role of oxytocin in mothers' theory of mind and interactive behavior during the perinatal period. *Psychoneuroendocrinology, 48*, 52–63. https://doi.org/10.1016/j.psyneuen.2014.06.003

Main, M., & Hesse, E. (1990). Parents' unresolved traumatic experiences are related to infant disorganized attachment status: Is frightened and/or frightening parental behavior the linking mechanism? In M. T. Greenberg, D. Cicchetti, & E. M. Cummings (Eds.), *Attachment in the preschool years: Theory, research, and intervention* (pp. 161–182). The University of Chicago Press.

McCall, C., & Singer, T. (2012). The animal and human neuroendocrinology of social cognition, motivation and behavior. *Nature Neuroscience, 15*(5), 681–688. https://doi.org/10.1038/nn .3084

Meyers, A. (2014). A call to child welfare: Protect children from sibling abuse. *Qualitative Social Work, 13*(5), 654–670. https://doi.org/10.1177/1473325014527332

Modecki, K. L., Minchin, J., Harbaugh, A. G., Guerra, N. G., & Runions, K. C. (2014). Bullying prevalence across contexts: A meta-analysis measuring cyber and traditional bullying. *The Journal of Adolescent Health, 55*(5), 602–611. https://doi.org/10.1016/j.jadohealth.2014.06.007

Moll, K., Göbel, S. M., & Snowling, M. J. (2015). Basic number processing in children with specific learning disorders: Comorbidity of reading and mathematics disorders. *Child neuropsychology, 21*(3), 399–417. https://doi.org/10.1080/09297049.2014.899570

Moretti, M., & Obsuth, I. (2009). Effectiveness of an attachment-focused manualized intervention for parents of teens at risk for aggressive behavior: The connect program. *Journal of Adolescence, 32*(6), 1347–1357. https://doi.org/10.1016/j.adolescence.2009.07.013

Muñoz, L. C., Qualter, P., & Padgett, G. (2011). Empathy and bullying: Exploring the influence of callous-unemotional traits. *Child Psychiatry & Human Development, 42*(2), 183–196. https://doi.org/10.1007/s10578-010-0206-1

National Center for Education Statistics. (2019). *Student reports of bullying: Results from the 2017 school crime supplement to the national victimization survey*. U.S. Department of Education. http://nces.ed.gov/pubsearch/pubsinfo.asp?pubid=2015056

The National Child Traumatic Stress Network. (n.d.). *Complex trauma*. Retrieved April 4, 2022, from https://www.nctsn.org/what-is-child-trauma/trauma-types/complex-trauma

Navarro, R., Larrañaga, E., & Yubero, S. (2011). Bullying-victimization problems and aggressive tendencies in Spanish secondary schools students: The role of gender stereotypical traits. *Social Psychology of Education, 14*(4), 457–473. https://doi.org/10.1007/s11218-011-9163-1

Nelson, J. M., & Harwood, H. (2011). Learning disabilities and anxiety: A meta-analysis. *Journal of Learning Disabilities, 44*(1), 3–17. https://doi.org/10.1177/0022219409359939

Newman, R. S. (1994). Adaptive help seeking: A strategy of self-regulated learning. In D. H. Schunk & B. J. Zimmerman (Eds.), *Self-regulation of learning and performance: Issues and educational applications* (pp. 283–301). Lawrence Erlbaum Associates.

Noland, V. J., Liller, K. D., McDermott, R. J., Coulter, M. L. & Seraphine, A. E. (2004). Is adolescent sibling violence a precursor to college dating violence? *American Journal of Health Behavior, 28*(1), S13–S23. https://doi.org/10.5993/AJHB.28.s1.3

Nystul, M. S. (2001). Overcoming resistance through individual psychology and problem solving. *Journal of Individual Psychology, 58*, 182–189.

O'Brien, E. R., & Giordano, L. A. (2017, June 5). Addressing religion and spirituality in counseling with bullying survivors. *Counseling Today, 59*, 40–45. https://ct.counseling.org/2017/06/addressing-religion-spirituality-counseling-bullying-survivors/

Oppenheim, D., & Koren-Karie, N. (2013). The insightfulness assessment: Measuring the internal processes underlying maternal sensitivity. *Attachment & Human Development, 15*(5-6), 545–561. https://doi.org/10.1080/14616734.2013.820901

Patchin, J. W., & Hinduja, S. (2020). Sextortion among adolescents: Results from a national survey of US youth. *Sexual Abuse, 32*(1), 30–54. https://doi.org/10.1177/1079063218800469

Pehrsson, D. E., & Aguilera, M. E. (2007). *Play therapy: Overview and implications for counselors (ACAPCD-12)*. American Counseling Association.

Perry, B. D., & Hambrick, E. P. (2008). The neurosequential model of therapeutics. *Reclaiming Children and Youth, 17*(3), 38–43. https://eric.ed.gov/?id=EJ869926

Phillips, D. A., Phillips, K. H., Grupp, K., & Trigg, L. J. (2009). Sibling violence silenced: Rivalry, competition, wrestling, playing, roughhousing, benign. *Advances in Nursing Science, 32*(2), E1–E16. https://doi.org/10.1097/ANS.0b013e3181a3b2cb

Phillips, R. D. (2010). How firm is our foundation? Current play therapy research. *International Journal of Play Therapy, 19*(1), 13–25. https://doi.org/10.1037/a0017340

Phillips, L. (2018, June 29). When bias turns to bullying. *Counseling Today.* https://ct.counseling.org/2018/06/when-bias-turns-into-bullying/

Pinjala, A., & Pierce, J. (n.d.). *Bullying.* American Association for Marriage and Family Therapy. Retrieved April 4, 2022, from https://aamft.org/Consumer_Updates/Bullying.aspx

Pope, B. (1979). *The mental health interview.* Pergamon.

Ray, D. C. (2011). *Advanced play therapy: Essential conditions, knowledge, and skills for child practice.* Routledge.

Ray, D. C., & McCullough, R. (2015). *Evidence-based practice statement: Play therapy.* Association for Play Therapy.

Ray, D., & Cheng, Y. (2018). *Child-centered group play therapy implementation guide.* University of North Texas Center for Play Therapy.

Reed, K. P., Nugent, W., & Cooper, R. L. (2015). Testing a path model of relationships between gender, age, and bullying victimization and violent behavior, substance abuse, depression, suicidal ideation, and suicide attempts in adolescents. *Children and Youth Services Review, 55,* 128–137. https://doi.org/10.1016/j.childyouth.2015.05.016

Rees, C. A. (2005). Thinking about children's attachments. *Archives of Disease in Childhood, 90*(10), 1058–1065. https://doi.org/10.1136/adc.2004.068650

Resick, P. A., & Schnicke, M. (1993). *Cognitive processing therapy for rape victims: A treatment manual* (Vol. 4). Sage.

Rosenthal, L., Earnshaw, V. A., Carroll-Scott, A., Henderson, K. E., Peters, S. M., McCaslin, C., & Ickovics, J. R. (2015). Weight- and race-based bullying: Health associations among urban adolescents. *The Journal of Health Psychology, 20*(4), 401–412. https://doi.org/10.1177/1359105313502567

Rudd, J. M., & Herzberger, S. D. (1999). Brother–sister incest—Father–daughter incest: A comparison of characteristics and consequences. *Child Abuse & Neglect, 23*(9), 915–928. https://doi.org/10.1016/S0145-2134(99)00058-7

Russell, S. T., Sinclair, K. O., Poteat, V. P., & Koenig, B. W. (2012). Adolescent health and harassment based on discriminatory bias. *American Journal of Public Health, 102*(3), 493–495. https://doi.org/10.2105/AJPH.2011.300430

Schore, A. N. (2005). A neuropsychoanalytic viewpoint: Commentary on paper by Steven H. Knoblauch. *Psychoanalytic Dialogues, 15*(6), 829–854. https://doi.org/10.2513/s10481885pd1506_3

Shaywitz, S. E., Morris, R., & Shaywitz, B. A. (2008). The education of dyslexic children from childhood to young adulthood. *Annual Review of Psychology, 59,* 451–475. https://doi.org/10.1146/annurev.psych.59.103006.093633

Shaywitz, S. E., Shaywitz, J. E., & Shaywitz, B. A. (2021). Dyslexia in the 21st century. *Current Opinion in Psychiatry, 34*(2), 80–86. https://doi.org/10.1097/YCO.0000000000000670

Sjolund, M., & Schaefer, C. E. (1994). The Erica method of sand play diagnosis and assessment. In K. J. O'Conner and C. E. Schaefer (Eds.), *Handbook of play therapy, advances and innovations* (Vol. 2, p. 231–252). John Wiley & Sons.

Simonelli, C. J., Mullis, T., Elliott, A. N., & Pierce, T. W. (2002). Abuse by siblings and subsequent experiences of violence within the dating relationship. *Journal of Interpersonal Violence, 17*(2), 103–121. https://doi.org/10.1177/0886260502017002001

Snoek, H., Van Goozen, S. H., Matthys, W., Buitelaar, J. K., & Van Engeland, H. (2004). Stress responsivity in children with externalizing behavior disorders. *Development and Psychopathology, 16*(2), 389–406. https://doi.org/10.1017/S0954579404044578

Sommers-Flanagan, J., & Sommers-Flanagan, R. (2011). *How to listen so parents will talk and talk so parents will listen.* John Wiley & Sons.

Sommers-Flanagan, J., & Sommers-Flanagan, R. (2014). *Tough kids, cool counseling: User-friendly approaches with challenging youth.* John Wiley & Sons.

Srinath, S., Jacob, P., Sharma, E., & Gautam, A. (2019). Clinical practice guidelines for assessment of children and adolescents. *Indian Journal of Psychiatry, 61*(Suppl 2), 158–175. https://doi.org/10.4103/psychiatry.IndianJPsychiatry_580_18

Sriram, R. (2020, June 24). *Why ages 2–7 matter so much for brain development.* Edutopia. https://www.edutopia.org/article/why-ages-2-7-matter-so-much-brain-development

Sroufe, L. A., Egeland, B., & Carlson, E. A. (1999). One social world: The integrated development of parent–child and peer relationships. In W. A. Collins & B. Laursen (Eds.), *Relationships as developmental contexts* (pp. 252–273). Psychology Press.

Stutey, D. M. (2017, February 28). Helping children and families address and prevent sibling abuse. *Counseling Today, 59*(8), 44–53. https://ct.counseling.org/2017/02/helping-children -families-address-prevent-sibling-abuse/

Stutey, D. M., Dunn, M., Shelnut, J., & Ryan, J. B. (2017). Impact of Adlerian play therapy on externalizing behaviors of at-risk preschoolers. *International Journal of Play Therapy, 26*(4), 196–206. https://doi.org/10.1037/pla0000055

Sullivan, H. S. (1953). *The interpersonal theory of psychiatry.* W. W. Norton and Company.

Swearer, S. M., & Hymel, S. (2015). Understanding the psychology of bullying: Moving toward a social-ecological diathesis–stress model. *American Psychologist, 70*(4), 344. https://doi.org/ 10.1037/a0038929

Terr, L. C. (1991). Acute responses to external events and posttraumatic stress disorders. In M. Lewis (Ed.), *Child and adolescent psychiatry: A comprehensive textbook* (pp. 755–763). Williams & Wilkins Co.

The Theraplay Institute. (n.d.). *Core concepts.* https://theraplay.org/what-is-theraplay/core -concepts/

Twemlow, S. W., Fonagy, P., & Sacco, F. (2005). A developmental approach to mentalizing communities: I. A model for social change. *Bulletin of the Menninger Clinic, 69*(4), 265–281. https:// doi.org/10.1521/bumc.2005.69.4.265

Umaña-Taylor, A. J., & Updegraff, K. A. (2007). Latino adolescents' mental health: Exploring the interrelations among discrimination, ethnic identity, cultural orientation, self-esteem, and depressive symptoms. *Journal of Adolescence, 30*(4), 549–567. https://doi.org/10.1016/j .adolescence.2006.08.002

United States Department of Education. (2018). *Thirty-ninth annual report to congress on the implementation of the Individuals with Disabilities Education Act 2007.* http://www2.ed.gov/about/ reports/annual/osep/2007/parts-b-c/index.html

Van der Kolk, B. A. (2005). Developmental. *Psychiatric Annals, 35*(5), 401. https://doi.org/10.3928/ 00485713-20050501-06

Van Ijzendoorn, M. H., Schuengel, C., & Bakermans–Kranenburg, M. J. (1999). Disorganized attachment in early childhood: Meta-analysis of precursors, concomitants, and sequelae. *Development and Psychopathology, 11*(2), 225–250. https://doi.org/10.1017/S0954579499002035

Veenstra, R., Lindenberg, S., Zijlstra, B. J., De Winter, A. F., Verhulst, F. C., & Ormel, J. (2007). The dyadic nature of bullying and victimization: Testing a dual-perspective theory. *Child Development, 78*(6), 1843–1854. https://doi.org/10.1111/j.1467-8624.2007.01102.x

Vernon, A., & Schimmel, C. J. (2019). *Counseling children & adolescents* (5th ed.). Cognella Academic Publishing

Walton, L. M. (2018). The effects of "Bias Based Bullying" (BBB) on health, education, and cognitive–social–emotional outcomes in children with minority backgrounds: Proposed comprehensive public health intervention solutions. *Journal of Immigrant and Minority Health, 20*(2), 492–496. https://doi.org/10.1007/s10903-017-0547-y

Watson, J. C. (2006). Addressing client resistance: Recognizing and processing in-session occurrences. *American Counseling Association VISTAS Online.* https://www.counseling.org/ resources/library/vistas/vistas06_online-only/Watson.pdf

Weinstein, Y., Sumeracki, M., & Caviglioli, O. (2019). *Understanding how we learn: A visual guide.* Routledge.

Whitehouse, A. J., Watt, H. J., Line, E. A., & Bishop, D. V. (2009). Adult psychosocial outcomes of children with specific language impairment, pragmatic language impairment and autism. *International Journal of Language & Communication Disorders, 44*(4), 511–528. https://doi.org/ 10.1080/13682820802708098

Wiehe, V. R. (2002). *What parents need to know about sibling abuse: Breaking the cycle of violence.* Bonneville Books

Ziegler, R., & Holden, L. (1988). Family therapy for learning disabled and attention-deficit disordered children. *The American Journal of Orthopsychiatry, 58*(2), 196–210. https://doi.org/ 10.1111/j.1939-0025.1988.tb01581.x

INDEX

AACD (American Association for Counseling and Development), 14

AAMC (American Association of Marriage Counselors), 12

AAMFT (American Association for Marriage and Family Therapy), 13, 217, 426

AAMFT (American Association for Marriage and Family Therapy) Consumer Report, 348

AAPI (Asian American and Pacific Islander) community, 189, 192–193

AASECT (American Association of Sexuality Educators, Counselors, and Therapists), 19–20

absent youth, youth-based resistance style, 413, 414

abuse and neglect, children, 341–343
  defined, 343
  emotional, 345
  mandatory reporting of, 389–392
  physical, 344
  sexual, 344–345
  skills for assisting with, 389–392
  types of, 343–345

ACA (American Counseling Association), 14

Academy of Professional Family Mediators (APFM), 21

accredited financial counselors (AFCs), 280–281

Ackerman, Nathan, 11

ACPA (American College Personnel Association), 14

ACR (Association for Conflict Resolution), 21

ACS (Approved Clinical Supervisor), 15

adaptability, family, 320
  skills for enhancing, 371–373

ADHD (attention deficit hyperactivity disorder), 106

Adler, Alfred, 36, 37

adolescents, 409–412

adult attachment, 223–224, 299

adult relationships, pornography use in, 239–240

adventure-based therapy, 18

advice giving, 127–128

AFCs (accredited financial counselors), 280–281

AFCPE (Association for Financial Counseling and Planning Education), 280

affair story, 284

affect, differentiation of, 267

African American/Black, 232

AFTA (American Family Therapy Academy), 17

Ainsworth, Mary, 223

allostasis, 199

allostatic load, 199, 318

American Association for Counseling and Development (AACD), 14

American Association for Marriage and Family Therapy (AAMFT), 13, 217, 426

American Association for Marriage and Family Therapy (AAMFT) Consumer Report, 348

American Association of Marriage Counselors (AAMC), 12

American Association of Sexuality Educators, Counselors, and Therapists (AASECT), 19–20

American College Personnel Association (ACPA), 14

American Counseling Association (ACA), 14

American Family Therapy Academy (AFTA), 17

American Medical Association, 231

American Personnel and Guidance Association (APGA), 14

American Psychological Association, 17

AMFTRB (Association of Marriage and Family Therapy Regulatory Board), 13

analytic neutrality, 39

anchoring, 160

Anderson, Harlene, 98

Andersen, Tom, 120

anti-Asian American and Pacific Islander sentiment, 192–193

anxiety, 3, 418

anxious/ambivalent, attachment style, 418

anxious/avoidant, attachment style, 418

apathetic youth, youth-based resistance style, 413, 414

APFM (Academy of Professional Family Mediators), 21

APGA (American Personnel and Guidance Association), 14

applied behavioral analysis, 18

Approved Clinical Supervisor (ACS), 15

armoring, 202

artificial insemination, 222

ARTs (assisted reproductive technologies), 221, 222

Asian American and Pacific Islander (AAPI) community, 189, 192–193
assessing contemporary child/adolescent therapy issues, 444–446
assessing contemporary couple therapy issues, 298–300
assimilative integration, 89
assisted reproductive technologies (ARTs), 221, 222
Association for Conflict Resolution (ACR), 21
Association for Financial Counseling and Planning Education (AFCPE), 280
Association for Humanistic Counseling, 52
Association for Specialists in Group Work, 9
Association of Marriage and Family Therapy Regulatory Board (AMFTRB), 13
attachment injuries, helping couples heal from, 265–267
attachment injury marker, 266
attachment process, 105
attachment styles, 105–106
attachment theory, 104–106
attacker, youth-based resistance style, 413, 414
attending skills, 130–134
    clarification, 132
    closed-ended questioning, 132
    goal setting, 131
    normalizing, 133
    open-ended questioning, 131
    paraphrasing, 132–133
    reflection of feeling, 134
    summarizing, 133
attention deficit hyperactivity disorder (ADHD), 106
attention problems, trauma symptom, 277
audience, 168
auditory (hearing) mode, verbal communication, 75
auditory processing disorder, 436
authoritarian parents, 329
authoritative parents, 329
autopoiesis, 96
avoidance of conflict, destructive couple communication style, 273

bad memories, Gottman predictor of breakup or divorce, 226
Balint, Michael, 36, 38
Bandura, Albert, 42, 43, 48–49, 58
Bateson, Gregory, 11
BCT-SUD (behavioral couples therapy for substance use disorders), 278–279
Beck, Aaron T., 58, 62, 141
behavioral couples therapy for substance use disorders (BCT-SUD), 278–279

behavioral therapy, 36
    applying, to systemic work, 49–50
    behavioral symbol, letter, and meaning key, 46
    classical conditioning, 43–44
    counterconditioning, 44
    operant conditioning, 44–47
    operant reinforcement and punishment, 45
    overview of, 41–42
    self-efficacy and modeling, 48–49
behaviorism, 41
Berg, Insoo Kim, 98, 140
bias, 195
bias-based bullying, 412, 429–430
Big Five Personality Index, 297
bigotry, 195
BIPOC (Black, Indigenous, and People of Color), 189
birth process, 416
Black, Indigenous, and People of Color (BIPOC), 189
Black Lives Matter (BLM), 23, 192–193
blended family, 322–325
    skills related to working with, 373–375
BLM (Black Lives Matter), 23, 192–193
Bobo doll study, 48
body language, Gottman predictor of breakup or divorce, 226
body posture, nonverbal communication, 76
bonds theory, 350
borderline personality disorder (BPD), 89
Bowen, Murray, 139
Bowlby, John, 223
BPD (borderline personality disorder), 89
Braverman, Lois, 91
Breuer, Josef, 36, 37
Brill, A. A., 36, 37
broadening and displacing symptom, systemic skill, 126
build love maps, Gottman's Sound Marital House level, 269
bulldozer parents, 330–331
Bully Busters, 431
Bully Prevention in Positive Behavior Support, 432
Bully-Proofing Your School, 431
bullying, 428–434, 445
    bias-based, 412, 429–430
burnout, 24

CACREP (Council for the Accreditation of Counseling and Related Educational Programs), 15
cancel culture, 91–92
CAPI (Child Abuse Potential Inventory), 391

CAPTA (Child Abuse Prevention and
    Treatment Act), 344, 425
cardiophysiology, trauma symptom, 277
care, defined, 328
Carkhuff, Robert R., 52
Carter, Betty, 139
cause-and-effect relationship, 5
CBFT (cognitive behavioral family therapy),
    138, 169–172
CBM (cognitive behavioral modification), 62
CBT (cognitive behavioral therapy), 89, 91,
    117, 288, 289, 294, 295, 386
CCE (Center for Credentialing and
    Education), 15
CDC (Centers for Disease Control and
    Prevention), 277, 428, 429, 435
Center for Credentialing and Education
    (CCE), 15
Centers for Disease Control and Prevention
    (CDC), 277, 428, 429, 435
Certified Family Life Educator (CFLE), 18
CFLE (Certified Family Life Educator), 18
change, sustaining, 285
change talk technique, 162
CHEA (Council for Higher Education
    Accreditation), 12
Child Abuse Potential Inventory (CAPI), 391
Child Abuse Prevention and Treatment Act
    (CAPTA), 344, 425
child custody, 67
Child Guidance Movement, 13
child maltreatment. *See also* abuse and neglect
    defined, 343
    risk factors for, 342–343
child mortality. *See also* death of child
    causes of, 349
    substantial global reductions in, 349
child protective services (CPS) agencies, 425
child-rearing adjustments, 8
childhood attachment issues, 416–424, 445
    attachment development, phases of, 416–419
    relevant skills and interventions, 421–424
    trauma, childhood attachment/effects of,
        419–421
children, 409–412
    attachment theory, 105
    and divorce, 64–65
    rights to confidentiality, 63–64
    therapeutic touch, use of, 65–66
    unique ethical issues, 63–66
choices, defined, 329
circular questioning, 124–125
circumplex model, 320, 371
clarification, counseling skill, 53, 132
clear-cut attachment, 418
client-centered therapy, 52–54

clarification, 53
concreteness, 54
confrontation and pointing out
    discrepancies, 53
genuineness, 54
immediacy, 53
nonverbal communication, 52
reflection of feelings, 53
self-disclosure, 54
silence, 53
client resistance, defined, 413
clinical world, 34–35
closed-ended questioning, 132
COAMFTE (Commission on Accreditation
    for Marriage and Family Therapy
    Education), 9
coercion/manipulation, destructive couple
    communication style, 272
cognitive behavioral family therapy (CBFT),
    138, 169–172
    cognitive restructuring, 171
    downward arrow technique, 170
    role-playing, 171–172
    theoretical tenets, 169–170
    validity testing, 170–171
cognitive behavioral modification (CBM), 62
cognitive behavioral therapy (CBT), 89, 91,
    117, 288, 289, 294, 295, 386
cognitive distortions, 57–59
cognitive restructuring, 61–62, 171
cognitive therapy, 36, 60–62
    cognitive distortions, 57–59
    irrational beliefs, 57–59
    overview of, 56–57
    rational emotive behavior therapy, 58–60
cohabitation contracts, 219
cohesion, family, 320–322
    skills for enhancing, 371–373
collaborative divorce, 292
collaborative therapy, 98
color-blindness, 375
Combs, Gene, 141
Commission on Accreditation for Marriage
    and Family Therapy Education
    (COAMFTE), 9
    foundational curriculum, 12–13
*The Common Sense Book of Baby and Child
    Care,* 7
communication, 73–74, 226, 321–322
communication and validation family therapy,
    157–160
    anchoring, 160
    family maps, 158
    humor, 159
    reconstruction, 159
    sculpting, 158

communication and validation family
therapy (*continued*)
theoretical tenets, 157
verbalizing presuppositions, 160
communication training, 125
comprehensive schoolwide bullying
intervention programs, 431
Computer and Internet Use in the United
States report, 237
concentration on negatives, destructive couple
communication style, 272
concreteness, counseling skill, 54
Conditioned Reflex Therapy, 43
conduct disorder, 106
confirming statements, 150
conflict, 122–123
defusing, 123
Conflict Resolution in Education
Network, 21
conflict, styles of couple, 8
consent, to treatment, 67–68
consequences, defined, 329
consistency, defined, 329
constructionism, 97–98
constructivism, 97–98
consultation, 63
contact-driven offenders, 340
contact, phases of, 101
contemporary issues/skills in youth-based
therapy
assessing contemporary child/adolescent
therapy issues, 444–446
bullying, 428–434
bias-based bullying, 429–430
relevant skills and interventions, 430–434
childhood attachment issues, 416–424
attachment development, phases of,
416–419
relevant skills and interventions, 421–424
trauma, childhood attachment/effects of,
419–421
children/adolescents, working with,
409–412
Voices From the Field, 411–412
filial therapy, 440–441
learning disabilities, 434–437
play therapy, 437–440
dealing with questions, 439
narration of the therapist's actions, 440
process play, 440
providing choices, 439
reflection of feeling, 438–439
restating content, 438
returning responsibility, 439
setting limits, 439
tracking, 438

sandtray and sandplay therapy, 443–444
sibling abuse and violence, 424–427
theraplay, 442–443
treatment, child/adolescent resistance to,
412–416
contemporary racism, 189–193
contempt, Gottman predictor of breakup or
divorce, 226
contingent relationship, 45
conversion therapy, 208
cooperative coparenting, 332–333
cotherapy, 118–120
Council for Higher Education Accreditation
(CHEA), 12
Council for the Accreditation of Counseling
and Related Educational Programs
(CACREP), 15
counseling skills, 115–116
Counselor, Social Worker, and Marriage and
Family Therapist Board (CSWMFT), 12
counselors. *See* professional counselors
couple and marriage therapy skills/
interventions
assessing contemporary couple therapy
issues, 298–300
attachment injuries, helping couples heal
from, 265–267
helping couples
crisis/disaster, 274–277
divorce/separation conflict, 290–293
financial stress, 280–282
infertility, struggling with, 262–265
internet addiction, struggling with, 293–296
intimate partner violence, 286–290
marital/relationship distress, 270–274
premarital therapy, 267–269
recover from infidelity, 282–286
sexual addiction/compulsivity, 296–298
substance abuse, 277–280
Voices From the Field, 261–262
couple, marriage, and family therapy
clinical world, 34–35
contemporary issues in
adult attachment, 223–224
delayed motherhood, 221–222
financial stress, 232–233
infertility, increased rates of, 220–221
infidelity, 233–234
internet, 237–241
intimate partner violence, 234–236
marital and relationship distress, 226–228
marriage, changing interest in, 218–220
premarital issues/warning signs, 224–226
reducing divorce conflict, 236–237
relationships, effects of crisis and disaster
on, 228–231

sex addiction/compulsivity, 241–242
substance abuse, 231–232
professional issues in, 33–35
systemic paradigm, 33–34
couples, 7–9
aging and retirement, 8–9
child-rearing adjustments, 8
classical conditioning, 44
commitment, 8
conflict, styles of, 8
ethical issues, 66–69
change of format and participation, 68–69
consent to treatment, 67–68
multiperson therapy, 66–67
interracial, 209
marriage issues, 8
racism effects, 196–197
Couples Coping Enhancement Training, couples psychoeducational program, 281
COVID-19 pandemic, 23, 69, 95, 192–193, 200, 227–232, 236, 280
CPS (child protective services) agencies, 425
create shared meaning, Gottman's Sound Marital House level, 269
Crenshaw, Kimberlé, 22
crisis and disaster, 299
crisis, trauma, and disaster (CTD), 23
criticism, Gottman predictor of breakup or divorce, 226
CSWMFT (Counselor, Social Worker, and Marriage and Family Therapist Board), 12
CTD (crisis, trauma, and disaster), 23
cultural attachment patterns, 224
cultural responsiveness, 71–73
culture
defined, 331
on parenting, 331–332
Current Population Survey (2020), 327
cybernetics, 34
first-order, 93–96
second-order, 96–97

Dattilio, Frank, 141
Davis, Dana-Ain, 317
Davis, Jesse B., 13
DBT (dialectical behavior therapy), 89, 91, 117
de Shazer, Steve, 98, 140
death of child, parental grief after, 348–350
skills for helping, 395–397
deconstruction, 161–162
defensiveness, Gottman predictor of breakup or divorce, 226
delayed motherhood, 221–222

denier, youth-based resistance style, 413, 414
depression, 3
devil's pact, 155
Diagnostic and Statistical Manual of Mental Disorders (DSM), 57, 294
Diagnostic and Statistical Manual of Mental Disorders, Second Edition (*DSM-II*), 208
Diagnostic and Statistical Manual of Mental Disorders, Fifth Edition, Text Revision (*DSM-5-TR*), 35, 97, 297
dialectical behavior therapy (DBT), 89, 91, 117
didactic teaching, 144–145
differential access to healthcare, 319
directives, 137–138
disaster, 23
discernment counseling, 18, 292
discrepancies, challenging and pointing out, 53, 135
discrimination, 189–195
disinhibition, 48
disorganized/disoriented, attachment style, 419
diversity, 71–73
Division 43, of the American Psychological Association, 17
divorce, children and, 64–65
divorce conflict, 300
divorce therapy, 18
Dolan, Yvonne, 140
dominating, interrupting/not listening, destructive couple communication style, 272
donor insemination, 221
downward arrow technique, 61, 170
Doxy.me, 24, 69
dreams, 40, 103–104
DSM (Diagnostic and Statistical Manual of Mental Disorders), 57, 294
DSM-II (Diagnostic and Statistical Manual of Mental Disorders, Second Edition), 208
DSM-5-TR (Diagnostic and Statistical Manual of Mental Disorders, Fifth Edition, Text Revision), 35, 97, 297
Duluth model, 288, 289
dyscalculia, 436
dysgraphia, 436
dyslexia, 436

eclecticism, 90
economic inequality, 318
educational disparities, 318
EFT (emotionally focused therapy), 91, 138, 172–176, 265, 266, 268, 279–280
Eitingon, Max, 36, 37
Ellis, Albert, 58

emotional abuse, 345
emotional neutrality, 143–144
emotionally focused therapy (EFT), 91, 138, 172–176, 265, 266, 268, 279–280
empathic conjecture/interpretation, 175
encounter, 172
evocative responding, 175
exploring and reformulating emotions, 172, 174
heightening, 175
personal/process disclosure, 175–176
softening, 174
theoretical tenets, 173
emotions, 172, 174
empathic conjecture/interpretation, 175
emphasizing individual boundaries, systemic skill, 126
empowerment, 155–156
empty chair technique, 102, 145–146
enactment, 148–149
encounter, the, 172
encouragers, 129–130
Enlightenment Era, 13
Epston, David, 98, 141
Erikson, Erik, 36, 37
ESSA (Every Student Succeeds Act), 435
ethical codes, 63
ethical decision-making, 63
ethical issues
children, working with, 63–66
couples and families, working with, 66–69
systemic work, 62–63
Every Student Succeeds Act (ESSA), 435
evocative responding, 175
exaggeration, 104
exceptions, 162
experiential family therapy, 138
externalization, 165–166
externalizer/blamer, youth-based resistance style, 413, 414

factual questioning, 144
failed repair attempts, Gottman predictor of breakup or divorce, 226
family, 6–7. *See also* family therapy
actualizing transactional patterns, 122
defined, 316
ethical issues, 66–69
change of format and participation, 68–69
consent to treatment, 67–68
multiperson therapy, 66–67
interactions, 6
interracial, 209
language, adopting, 166

modern, 7
racism effects, 196–197
underrepresented, 207–209
family maps, 158
Family Mediation Association, 21
family planning counseling, 18
Family Psychology, division of the American Psychological Association, 17
family rules, 56–57
family therapy, 315–316
assessing, 397–399
blended and stepfamilies, 322–325
child abuse and neglect, 341–343
defined, 343
emotional abuse, 345
physical abuse, 344
sexual abuse, 344–345
types of, 343–345
cohesion and flexibility, 320–322
death of child, parental grief after, 348–350
empirical assessments and related references, 398–399
grandparents raising grandchildren
opioid abuse and, 348
parenting concerns, 346–348
raising grandchildren, 345–346
internet use, issues related to, 335–337
increased screen time, outcomes associated with, 337–338
online predators, 339–341
pornography use, child and adolescent, 338–339
intersectionality affecting, 319
multiracial family, 325–327
obesity, 333–335
parenting, 327–329
impact of culture on, 331–332
metaphorical parenting styles, 330–331
postdivorce coparenting, 332–333
styles, 329–330
racism affecting, 317–319
skills and interventions, 367–368
blended and stepfamilies, 373–375
child abuse and neglect, 389–392
cohesion and adaptability, 371–373
death of child, parental grief after, 395–397
grandparents raising grandchildren, 392–395
issues with the internet, 387–389
multiracial families, 375–380
obesity, 385–387
parenting, 381–384
Voices From the Field, 368–370
fantasy-driven offenders, 340

fatigue, compassion, 24
fearful-disorganized strategy, 106
Federal Education Rights and Privacy
  Act (1994), 64
feedback, 135
  negative, 94–95
  positive, 94–95
feedback loops, 94
feeling. *See* kinesthetic (feeling) mode
feminism, 90–92
feminist family therapy (FFT), 91
Ferenczi, Sándor, 36, 37
fertility problems, discussions of, 263
FFT (feminist family therapy), 91
fight, trauma symptom, 277
filial therapy, 18, 440–441, 446
financial stress, 232–233, 300
Financial Therapy Association, 281
first-order cybernetics, 34, 93–96
Fisch, Richard, 140
Fishman, Charles, 139
Five Cs of Cotherapy Dilemmas, 119
flashbacks, trauma symptom, 277
flexibility, family, 320–322
flight, trauma symptom, 277
flooding, Gottman predictor of breakup or
  divorce, 226
Foa, Edna, 42, 43
forgiveness and reconciliation, 266, 267
foundational systemic skills, 121–128
  actualizing family's transactional
    patterns, 122
  advice giving, 127–128
  broadening and displacing symptom, 126
  circular questioning, 124–125
  communication training, 125
  defusing conflict, 123
  emphasizing individual
    boundaries, 126
  escalating conflict/stress, 122–123
  in-session behavior prescriptions, 128
  joining, 121
  modeling, 127
  out-of-session work, 128
  paradoxical injunction, 124
  reframing, 125–126
  restructuring dysfunctional subsystem
    boundaries, 126–127
Frederic, Burrhus, 44–45
Freedman, Jill, 141
freeze, trauma symptom, 277
Freud, Anna, 36, 38
Freud, Sigmund, 36, 37, 38–39, 104
Fromm-Reichmann, Frieda, 36, 37
frozen embryo transfer, 222

functional family therapy, 18
future, consulting into the, 441

GABAergic neurotransmission, 417
general systems theory, 34
generalization, 441
genogram, 143
genuineness, 54
gestalt techniques, 102–104
  dream work, 103
  empty chair, 102
  exaggeration, 104
  experiments, 103
  hot seat, 102–103
  making rounds, 104
gestalt theory and therapy, 100–102
  contact withdrawal, 101
  functioning of self, 101–102
  organism and environment field, 100
  self, 101
goal setting, 131
Goolishian, Harold A., 98
GoToMeeting, 24, 69
Gottman approach, 268, 270
Gottman, John M., 225
Gottman method, 88, 225, 293
Gottman-oriented practitioner, 268
grandparents
  difficulty areas, 347
  raising grandchildren, 345–346
    opioid abuse and, 348
    parenting concerns, 346–348
    skills for assisting, 392–395
Greenberg, Les, 141
grief, parental
  after death of child, 348–350
  gender-based, 396
  skills for helping, 395–397
group therapy, 9, 18
  cutting off, 10
  drawing out members, 10
  holding the focus, 9–10
  linking, 9
group work, 9–10
growth model, 54–56
  active engagement by therapist, 55
  family rules, 56–57
  humor, 56
  reframing, 56
  ropes, 55–56
Guerin, Philip, 139
Guerney, Bernard, Jr., 139
gunnysacking, destructive couple
  communication style, 272

Haley, Jay, 140
harsh startups, Gottman predictor of breakup or divorce, 226
hatred, 195
Health Information Technology for Economic and Clinical Health (HITECH) Act, 24, 69
Health Insurance Portability and Accountability Act (HIPAA), 18, 24, 69
Healthie, 24, 69
heightening, 175
helicopter parenting style, 330–331
HIPAA (Health Insurance Portability and Accountability Act), 18, 24, 69
HITECH (Health Information Technology for Economic and Clinical Health) Act, 24, 69
holistic healing, 202
homeostasis, 6
homophobia, 208
Horney, Karen, 36, 37
hot seat, 102–103
How to Listen So Parents Will Talk and Talk So Parents Will Listen, 412
HPA (hypothalamus–pituitary–adrenal) axis, 417
humanistic therapy, 36
    client-centered therapy, 52–54
    growth model, 54–56
    overview of, 50–52
humor, 56, 159
hypervigilance, trauma symptom, 277
hypothalamus–pituitary–adrenal (HPA) axis, 417

IAD (internet addiction disorder), 293–294
IAMFC (International Association of Marriage and Family Counselors), 14
ICD (International Statistical Classification of Diseases and Related Health Problems), 57
ICMA (International City/County Management Association), 194
ICSI (intracytoplasmic sperm injection), 222
identity confusion, 326
identity purgatory, 326–327
IEPs (individualized education programs), 435, 436
IFTA (International Family Therapy Association), 17
immediacy, 53, 134–135
in-session behavior prescriptions, 128
in vitro fertilization (IVF), 221, 222
individualized education programs (IEPs), 435, 436

indivisible self: an evidence-based model of wellness (IS-WEL model), 25
infertility, 299
    helping couples struggling with, 262–265
    increased rates of, 220–221
infertility counseling, 263
infidelity, 233–234, 300
influencing skills, 134–138
    challenging and pointing out discrepancies, 135
    directives, 137–138
    feedback, 135
    immediacy, 134–135
    interpretation, 136
    psychoeducation, 137
    reflection of meaning and values, 136
    self-disclosure, 136–137
informed consent, 68–69
informing the parents, 441
integration, 88–89
internal working model (IWM), 417, 420, 421
International Association of Marriage and Family Counselors (IAMFC), 14
International City/County Management Association (ICMA), 194
International Family Therapy Association (IFTA), 17
International Statistical Classification of Diseases and Related Health Problems (ICD), 57
internet, 237–241
    family issues related to, 335–337
        increased screen time, outcomes associated with, 337–338
        online predators, 339–341
        parents' best-practice standards for, 337
        pornography use, child and adolescent, 338–339
    helping families experiencing issues with, 387–389
    issue, description of problem, 388
internet addiction, 240–241
    helping couples who are struggling with, 293–296
internet addiction disorder (IAD), 293–294
interpersonal connection, stepfamilies and, 374
interpersonal reflexes, 440
interpretation, 136
The Interpretation of Dreams, 40
interracial couples, 209
intersectionality, 21–22, 71–73, 206
    affecting family, 319
intimate partner violence (IPV), 228, 229, 234–237, 286–290, 300
intracytoplasmic sperm injection (ICSI), 222

intrafallopian transfer, 222
intrapsychic family-of-origin work, 374
intrapsychic models, 5
intrapsychic versus systemic theories, 5
invitational skills, 128–130
    encouragers, 129–130
    nonverbal communication, 129
    observation, 129
    silence, 130
    vocal tone, 129
IPV (intimate partner violence), 228, 229,
    234–237, 286–290, 300
irrational beliefs, 57–59
issue
    addressing, 285
    clarification of, 285
IS-WEL model (indivisible self: an evidence-
    based model of wellness), 25
IVF (in vitro fertilization), 221, 222
IWM (internal working model), 417, 420, 421

Jackson, Don, 11, 36, 140
jamming technique, 156–157
Johnson, Susan, 141
joining, systemic skill, 121, 129
Jones, Alfred Ernest, 36, 37
Jones, Mary Cover, 41, 43
judgment, blame, attack/rejection, destructive
    couple communication style, 272
Jung, Carl Gustav, 36, 37

Kant, Immanuel, 87
Kelley, Harold H., 42, 43
Kelly, George, 58
Kerr, Michael, 139
kinesthetic (feeling) mode, verbal
    communication, 75
Klein, Melanie, 36, 37
Kohut, Heinz, 36, 38
Kübler-Ross's and similar phase/stage models
    for grief, 263

language processing disorder, 436
lawnmower parents, 330–331
Lazarus, Arnold, 58
LDs (learning disabilities), 434–437, 445
learning disabilities (LDs), 434–437, 445
lesbian, gay, bisexual, transgender, intersex,
    queer and/or questioning, asexual,
    and/or ally, plus (LGBTQIA+), 92, 194,
    200, 208, 221, 261, 262, 264–265, 273,
    274, 285, 286, 289, 290, 293, 295, 296,
    317, 328, 340, 430

Lewin, Kurt, 100
LGBTQIA+ (lesbian, gay, bisexual,
    transgender, intersex, queer and/or
    questioning, asexual, and/or ally, plus),
    92, 194, 200, 208, 221, 261, 262, 264–265,
    273, 274, 285, 286, 289, 290, 293, 295,
    296, 317, 328, 340, 430
liberation ideology, 375
licensed marriage and family therapists
    (LMFTs), 35
Lipchik, Eve, 141
LMFTs (licensed marriage and family
    therapists), 35
locating unique outcomes, 167

macroaggression, 194
Macy, Josiah, Jr., 11
Madanes, Cloe, 140
maintenance, 441
maintenance techniques, 147–148
maladaptive schemata, 61
manage conflict, Gottman's Sound Marital
    House level, 269
marginalization, 195
marital/relational distress, 299
marital/relationship distress, 226–228
marriage and family therapists (MFTs), 4, 9, 10
    definition of, 12
    professional identity, 12
    training of, 12–13
marriage and family therapy, 16
    roots of, 11–12
marriage and family therapy model-based
    techniques, 138–141
marriage, changing interest in, 218–220
*The Marriage Clinic: A Scientifically Based
    Marital Therapy*, 225, 268
marriage counseling, 11
Marschak Interaction Method (MIM), 442
Maslow, Abraham, 50, 51
McGoldrick, Monica, 139
MedFT (medical family therapy), 18–19
mediation, 18, 20–21, 291–292
medical family therapy (MedFT), 18–19
Meichenbaum, Donald, 58, 62
Melissa Institute, The, 62
memorandum of understanding (MOU), 291
memory limitations, trauma symptom, 277
mental health practitioners
    license, 35
Mental Research Institute (MRI), 11, 140
metaphorical parenting styles, 330–331
metaphorical tasks, 154–155
#MeToo movement, 91–92

MFTs (marriage and family therapists), 4, 9, 10
microaggressions, 375
  types of, 326, 327
microassaults, 326, 327
microinsults, 326, 327
microinvalidations, 326, 327
Milan Systemic Approach, 120
Milwaukee Brief Family Therapy Center, 98
MIM (Marschak Interaction Method), 442
mimesis, 148
minority stress model, 92
Minuchin, Salvador, 36, 115, 139
miracle question, 162–163
mixed messages, 74
modality, type of, 21
modeling-based learning, 48
modeling, systemic skill, 127
modern family, 7
modernism, 98–99
Montalvo, Braulio, 139
MOU (memorandum of understanding), 291
MRI (Mental Research Institute), 11, 140
multiculturalism, 21–22
multidisciplinary teams, use of, 18
multiperson therapy, 66–67
multiracial family, 325–327
  skills for engaging with, 375–380
multisystemic therapy, 18
Murdock, George P., 317

NAGCT (National Association of Guidance
    and Counselor Trainers), 14
narrative therapy, 98, 138, 163–168
  adopting family's language, 166
  audience/witnessing, 168
  externalization, 165–166
  locating unique outcomes, 167
  presupposition of change, 164–165
  restorying/reauthoring, 167–168
  theoretical tenets, 164
National Association for Community
    Education, 21
National Association for Mediation in
    Education, 21
National Association of Guidance and
    Counselor Trainers (NAGCT), 14
National Center for Education Statistics,
    428, 430
National Center for Health Statistics, 231
National Child Traumatic Stress Network, 420
National Council on Alcoholism and Drug
    Dependence, 231
National Council on Family Relations (NCFR),
    12, 17–18

National Defense Education Act (1958), 13
National Intimate Partner and Sexual Violence
    Survey (NISVS), 235
National Registry of Evidence-Based
    Programs and Practices, 442
National Survey on Drug Use and
    Health (2013), 232
National Vocational Guidance Association
    (NVGA), 14
NCFR (National Council on Family Relations),
    12, 17–18
NCLB (No Child Left Behind Act), 435
negative feedback, 94–95
negative sleep patterns, trauma symptom, 277
neglect, 345. *See also* child abuse and neglect
networks, 9–10
new relationship, creation of, 285
NISVS (National Intimate Partner and Sexual
    Violence Survey), 235
No Child Left Behind Act (NCLB), 435
nonverbal communication, 52, 75–76, 129
nonverbal learning disabilities, 436
nonverbal provocateur, youth-based resistance
    style, 413, 414
normalizing, 133
NVGA (National Vocational Guidance
    Association), 14

obesity, 333–335
  adolescent, 334
  behavioral techniques for treating, 387
  childhood, 333–334
  defined, 333
  issues contributing to, 334–335
  physical problems associated with, 335
  prevalence of, 334
  techniques for helping families struggling
    with, 385–387
observation, 129
observational learning, 48
observations, discussion of, 441
ODD (oppositional defiant disorder), 106
Olson, David H., 320
one-down stance, 152
one-pot method, 323
online addiction, 300
online bullying, 429
online dating, 238
online infidelity, 239
online predators, 339–341
open-ended questioning, 131
operant reinforcement, and punishment, 45
opioid abuse/grandparents raising
    grandchildren, 348

oppositional defiant disorder (ODD), 106
oppression, 71–73
ordeals, 154
out-of-session work, 128
overemotionality, destructive couple
    communication style, 273
overgeneralization/lack of specificity, destructive
    couple communication style, 272

panda parenting style, 331
Papernow's model, 373–374
paradoxical directives, 152–153
paradoxical injunction, 124
paraphrasing, 41, 132–133
parent management training (PMT), 18, 383
parental control, 328
parental grief, death of child, 348–350, 395–397
parental support, 328
parent–child interaction, 317
parenting
    contemporary, 327–329
        impact of culture on, 331–332
        metaphorical parenting styles, 330–331
        postdivorce coparenting, 332–333
        styles, 329–330
    dos and don'ts, 382–383
    skills for helping, 381–384
Parsons, Frank, 13–14
participants, 262
partner, mind reading/speaking for,
    destructive couple communication
    style, 272
Pavlov, Ivan, 41–44
people of color (POC), 93, 194, 199, 200
Perls, Fritz, 50, 51
permissive parents, 329–330
person-centered therapy, 50
personal disclosure, 175–176
PHI (protected health information), 69
physical abuse, child, 344
physical custody, 67
physical violence, 235
play therapy, 18, 437–440, 445, 446
    dealing with questions, 439
    narration of the therapist's actions, 440
    process play, 440
    providing choices, 439
    reflection of feeling, 438–439
    restating content, 438
    returning responsibility, 439
    setting limits, 439
    tracking, 438
play therapy demonstration, 441
pluralism, 90

PMT (parent management training), 18, 383
POC (people of color), 93, 194, 199, 200
political activism, 22
polyvagal theory, 415
pornography use, 338–339
positive feedback, 94–95
positive sentiment override, Gottman's Sound
    Marital House level, 269
postinfidelity stress disorder, 283
postdivorce coparenting, 332–333
postmodern therapy, solution-focused
    therapy, 160–163
postmodernism, 98–99
posttraumatic stress disorder (PTSD), 198, 274,
    275, 276, 283, 318, 417, 421, 424
Power and Control Wheel, 288, 289
*The Practice of Emotionally Focused Couple
    Therapy: Creating Connection*, 265
predators, online, 339–341
preimplantation genetic diagnosis, 222
preinfidelity, 285
prejudice, 195
premarital issues/warning signs, 224–226, 299
premarital therapy, 18, 20
    helping couples through, 267–269
PREP (Prevention and Relationship
    Enhancement Program), 271
presenting issue, 441
presupposition of change, 164–165
pretend technique, 153–154
Prevention and Relationship Enhancement
    Program (PREP), 271
privilege, 195
process disclosure, 175–176
professional counseling, 16
    roots of, 13–14
professional counselors
    professional identity of, 14
    training programs, 14–16
Promoting Alternative Thinking Strategies,
    bullying prevention program, 433
protected health information (PHI), 69
psychoanalysis, 36–38
psychoanalytic and psychodynamic theory
    applying, to systemic work, 41
    controversial aspects of, 38–39
    overview of, 36–38
    psychoanalytic family therapy, 39–41
psychoanalytic family therapy, 39–41
psychoeducation, 137, 422
    in stepfamily, 373–374
psychological/emotional violence, 235
psychotherapy, four waves of, 35–36
PTSD (posttraumatic stress disorder), 198, 274,
    275, 276, 283, 318, 417, 421, 424

racial battle fatigue, 93
racial macroaggressions, 195
racial microaggressions, 93, 195
racism, 4, 71–73, 193–195, 199–200
    affecting family, 317–319
RAD (reactive attachment disorder), 105–106
RAINN (Rape, Abuse, and Incest National
    Network), 391
Rank, Otto, 36, 37, 50, 51
Rape, Abuse, and Incest National Network
    (RAINN), 391
rational emotive behavior therapy, 58–60
Rayner, Rosalie, 41, 42
RC (recovery contract), 279
reactive, attachment style, 419
reactive attachment disorder (RAD), 105–106
reconstruction, 159
recovery contract (RC), 279
recursion, 94
reducing divorce conflict, 236–237
reenactment, 149–150
reengagement, 267
reflection of feelings, 41, 53, 134
reflection, of meaning and values, 136
reflection team (RT), 120–121
reflective dialogue, 422
reflective practice, 260
reflective thinking, 260
reframing, 56, 125–126
Reich, Wilhelm, 36, 38
rejecting parents, 330
relationships, effects of crisis and disaster
    on, 228–231
religion, 201
remarried family, 322
reparative therapy. *See* conversion therapy
replaying ancient history, destructive couple
    communication style, 273
resilience, defined, 24, 229
resistance, 40, 415, 445
restorying/reauthoring, 167–168
restraining technique, 152
restructuring dysfunctional subsystem
    boundaries, 126–127
rigid family, 320
Rogers, Carl, 13–14, 50, 51, 52
role-playing, 145, 171–172
ropes, 55–56
Rosman, Bernice, 139
RT (reflection team), 120–121

Salter, Andrew, 43
SAMHSA (Substance Abuse and Mental
    Health Services Administration), 442

sandplay therapy, 18, 443–444
sandtray therapy, 18, 443–444
SART (systematic affair recovery therapy), 284
SAST (Sexual Addiction Screening Test), 297
Satir, Virginia, 11, 34, 50, 51, 54–55, 140, 158
SBW (Strong Black Woman) schema, 394
scaling, 163
Schumer, Florence, 139
screen time
    defined, 338
    of internet, 337–338
    issues, 389
sculpting, 158
second-order cybernetics, 34, 96–97
secure, attachment style, 418
self-disclosure, 54, 136–137
self-efficacy, 48–49
Seligman, Martin, 58
session dynamics, 281–282
session management, 117–121
    cotherapy, 118–120
sex addiction, 300
sex addiction/compulsivity, 241–242
sex therapy, 18–20, 44
sexual abuse, child, 344–345
Sexual Addiction Screening Test (SAST), 297
sexual addiction/compulsivity, helping
    couples with, 296–298
sexual dysfunction, 19
sexual harassment, 92
sexual minorities, 323
sexual violence, 235
SFBT (solution-focused brief therapy), 98, 138,
    160–163
SFT (structural family therapy), 116, 138,
    146–150
share fondness/admiration, Gottman's Sound
    Marital House level, 269
shifting, 202
sibling abuse, 412, 424–427, 445
sibling violence, 424–427, 445
sideways approach, 423
silence, 53, 130
silent youth, youth-based resistance style,
    413, 414
SimplePractice, 24
Skinner, B. F., 41, 42, 45
SLD (specific learning disability), 435
S/LIs (speech–language impairments), 435
small t traumas, 265
SMH (Sound Marital House), 268–269
Smith, William, 93
snowplow parents, 330–331
social justice, 21–22
social networks, 10

social work, 11
socialization, racial and ethnic, 203–204
Society for Couple and Family Psychology, 17
Society for Humanistic Psychology, 52
Society of Professionals in Dispute
    Resolution, 21
socioeconomic deprivation, 318
Socratic questioning, 61
softening, 174
solution-focused brief therapy (SFBT), 98, 138,
    160–163
    change talk, 162
    deconstruction, 161–162
    exceptions, 162
    miracle question, 162–163
    scaling, 163
    theoretical tenets, 161
solution-focused techniques, 377
Sound Marital House (SMH), 268–269
sound relationship house, 225
SPATE (Student Personnel Association for
    Teacher Education), 14
speaker and listener technique, 271–274
specific learning disability (SLD), 435
speech–language impairments (S/LIs), 435
spirituality, 201
Spock, Benjamin, 7
STAC, bullying prevention program, 431
stalking, 235
Stampfl, Thomas G., 42, 43
statutory rape, 341, 344
Stekel, Wilhelm, 36, 37
stepfamilies, 322–325
    skills related to working with, 373–375
Stephen Porges's polyvagal theory, 415
Steps to Respect, bullying prevention
    program, 432
stonewalling, Gottman predictor of breakup
    or divorce, 226
straightforward directives, 150–151
strategic family therapy, 150–157
    devil's pact, 155
    empowerment, 155–156
    jamming, 156–157
    metaphorical tasks, 154–155
    one-down stance, 152
    ordeals, 154
    paradoxical directives, 152–153
    pretend technique, 153–154
    restraining technique, 152
    straightforward directives, 150–151
    theoretical tenets, 151
stress, 122–123
    body's response to, 199–200
    management, 199–200

armoring, 202
    religion and spirituality, 201
    shifting, 202
    support networks, 202
    therapy and holistic healing, 202
    racism-related, 204
Strong Black Woman (SBW) schema, 394
structural determinism, 96
structural family therapy (SFT), 116,
    138, 146–150
    confirming statements, 150
    enactment, 148–149
    maintenance techniques, 147–148
    mimesis, 148
    reenactment, 149–150
    theoretical tenets, 147
structural racism, 318
stuck insider, 324
stuck outsider, 324
Student Personnel Association for Teacher
    Education (SPATE), 14
substance abuse, 231–232, 299
Substance Abuse and Mental Health Services
    Administration (SAMHSA), 442
substance overdose, 231
summarizing, 133
supervised play with children, 441
support life dreams together, Gottman's
    Sound Marital House level, 269
surrogacy, 221
systematic affair recovery therapy (SART), 284
systemic counseling, 6
systemic paradigm, 33–34
    and clinical world, 34–35
    understanding and differentiating, 35–36
systemic practice, 115–116
    attending skills. *See* attending skills
    foundational skills. *See* foundational
        systemic skills
    influencing skills. *See* influencing skills
    invitational skills. *See* invitational skills
systemic racism, 71–73, 318
systemic work
    diversity and intersectionality, 71–73
    nonverbal communication, 75–76
    theoretical underpinnings, 87–88
    unique ethical issues, 62–63
    verbal communication, 74–75
systems, defined, 33
systems theory, 93

taken for granted, destructive couple
    communication style, 272
talk, the, Black families, 376

Target Bullying Intervention Program, 432
technology-assisted professional services, 70
telebehavioral health, 23–24, 69–70
TFT (transgenerational family therapy),
    142–146
theoretical model-based specialization, 18
theoretical tenets, 142, 147, 151, 173
therapeutic gossip, 119–120
therapeutic skills/interventions, 260
therapeutic touch, use of, 65–66
therapist, active engagement by, 55
theraplay, 442–443, 446
*Theraplay: A New Treatment Using Structured
    Play for Program Children and Their
    Families*, 442
Thibaut, John W., 42, 43
third-party reproductive technology, 222
Thompson, Clara, 36, 37
Thorndike, Edward L., 41, 43, 45
thought recording, 62
threats of physical or sexual violence, 235
tiger parent, 331
TOGETHER, couples psychoeducational
    program, 281
token economy, 46
    considerations and relevance, 47
top-down approach, 423
*Tough Kids, Cool Counseling: User-Friendly
    Approaches With Challenging Youth*, 412
training the parents, 441
traits, 5, 6
transference, 40
transgenerational family therapy (TFT),
    142–146
    didactic teaching, 144–145
    emotional neutrality, 143–144
    empty chair technique, 145–146
    factual questioning, 144
    genogram, 143
    role-playing, 145
    theoretical tenets, 142
transgenerational family therapy, 138
transphobia, 208
trauma, 3, 285
treating traumatized couples, 275–277
turn toward instead of away, Gottman's
    Sound Marital House level, 269
type I/type II child trauma, 420

underrepresented families, 193–194, 207–209
uninvolved parents, 330
unitary theory, 88–90

United Advocates for Children of
    California, 316
U.S. Census Bureau, 316
U.S. financial crisis (2008), 274
U.S. Hatch Act of 1887, 11

validity testing, 170–171
variable ratio reinforcement schedule
    (VRRS), 294
verbal communication, 74–75
    auditory (hearing) mode, 75
    kinesthetic (feeling) mode, 75
    visual (seeing) mode, 75
verbalizing presuppositions, 160
vicarious trauma, 24
violence, 92
visual (seeing) mode, verbal
    communication, 75
visual perceptual/visual motor deficit, 436
vocal tone, 129
Voices From the Field, 189–192, 261–262,
    368–370, 411–412
    Hughes, Sherritta, 190, 194–195, 197–198,
        200, 202–203, 205, 206, 209
    Kassing, Jennifer, 261, 264–265, 274, 286, 290,
        293, 296
    Lopez-Jensen, Michael, 369, 375, 379, 380,
        384, 391–392, 395
    Manigault, Alexandra, 190, 195–196, 198,
        200, 205, 207, 210
    Matthews, Tahira, 190, 196, 198, 200–201,
        203, 205, 207, 210
    Peters, Harvey, 261, 264, 273–274, 285–286,
        289, 293, 295–296
    Sharma, Jyotsana, 411, 415, 423, 433–434
    Shearer, Danny J., 411, 415–416, 424, 427, 434
    Siu, Long Hin, 369, 374–375, 377, 379, 380,
        384, 391–392, 394
    Thomas, James, 369, 375, 378–380, 384,
        389, 391–392
    Wang, Yu-Wei, 191, 196, 198–199, 201, 203,
        205, 207, 210
von Bertalanffy, Karl Ludwig, 34
VRRS (variable ratio reinforcement
    schedule), 294

Watson, John B., 41, 42
Watzlawick, Paul, 140
Weakland, John, 140
Webex, 24, 69
wellness, 24–25

Whitaker, Carl, 36, 50, 51, 140
White, Michael, 98, 141
Wiener, Norbert, 34
witnessing, 168
Wolpe, Joseph, 41, 43, 44
World Health Organization, 220
World War II, 11

xenophobia, 195

Young's strategy, 294–295

Zoom, 24, 69